MAHĀBHĀRATA
The End of an Era
(Yugānta)

MAHĀBHĀRATA
The End of an Era
(*Yugānta*)

Edited by

AJAY MITRA SHASTRI

INDIAN INSTITUTE OF ADVANCED STUDY
SHIMLA

ARYAN BOOKS INTERNATIONAL
NEW DELHI

Mahābhārata : The End of an Era

ISBN-81-7305-274-3

First published in **2004** by
INDIAN INSTITUTE OF ADVANCED STUDY
Rashtrapati Nivas, Shimla - 171005 (India)
and
ARYAN BOOKS INTERNATIONAL
Pooja Apartments, 4B, Ansari Road, New Delhi-110 002 (India)
Tel.: 23287589, 23255799; Fax: 91-11-23270385
E-mail: aryanbooks@vsnl.com

Computer Typeset at Sai Graphic Design, New Delhi
Printed in India at B.B.N. Printers, New Delhi

Prefatory Note

Winternitz describes the *Mahābhārata* as a 'literary monster'. Hopkins says it would be like combining fragments of Homer, Hesoid, Aristotle and the New Testament. Both agree that the *Mahābhārata* derives from popular heroic songs and ballads which have been conflated inartistically through the ages. This process is placed by both of them between the 4th century BC and the 4th century AD.

In contrast, the traditional Indian reader considers the *Mahābhārata* a unified work of supreme excellence which was originally composed by Kṛishṇadvaipāyana recited by Vaiśampāyana at the *Sarpa-sattra* of King Janamejaya and later recited by the Sūta Ugraśravas at the twelve-year *sattra* of the sage Śaunaka at Naimishāraṇya. The work had two versions. Without *upākhyānas* it consisted of twenty-four thousand verses, with the *upākhyānas,* one hundred thousand verses. This larger extent included the *Harivaṁśa* as *khila* or appendix. This process of elaboration *(samastavyāsa-kathana)* and *saṁvādas* has also occasionally updated some earlier description by adding a new and larger version. For example, *Śakuntalopākhyāna, Nalopākhyāna* and *Sāvitryupākhyāna* could have originally existed independently but are now woven into the texture of the principal work. Similarly in *Digvijaya* and *Tīrthayātrā* sections there are shorter and longer versions, the longer versions show a later geographical knowledge of places and peoples. In spite of its length, digressions, repetitions and occasionally plain additions of essentially independent works such as some of the texts in the Anuśāsanaparvan, the work can be and has been read as the single work of a genius which is at once *itihāsa, kāvya* and *smriti.*

The original work was presumably composed towards the end of the Vedic age as traditions asserts and as is suggested by the closeness of its language to that of the mertical *Upanishad*. It could be dated about *c.* 800 BC in its original form since Paṇini and Āśvalāyana refer to *Bhārata* and *Mahābhārata*, and Paṇini has to be placed prior to *c.* 500 BC. Some of the philosophical and didactic material was presumably added between *c.* 600 BC and *c.* 2nd century BC. After that sporadic interpolations occurred.

It is a mistake to think of the *Mahābhārata* as an epic in the Greek sense. Nor should one think of the *Mahābhārata* as a chaotic aggregation. It bears the stamp of a mighty creative genius, its unity is manifested by its story, characters, style, feelings and vision. Its strong intellectual temper of enquiry and independent criterion has been underlined by Aurobindo. Even the additions to the original poem have virtually been assimilated into the *Mahābhārata* and Indian reader reads the poem as it is, without seeking to dismember it. It may be recalled that at one time German scholarship took the Homeric epic to pieces but such criticism did not affect the literary students of Homer. It is a pity that the *Mahābhārata* has also been left largely to the historians.

The *Mahābhārata* is not a historical chronicle but to quote Tagore, 'perennial history'. It is not a poem of merely tragic or pathetic import though it has a good deal of tragedy and pathos. It is a vision of the victory of Right over Wrong and of Truth over Untruth, a vision of the moral man rising above merely instinctive conflicts and finding himself ultimately surrendering to God. The *Gītā* is its core and Kṛishṇa its moving spirit and its goal. The great battle begins with the moral and spiritual doubts of Arjuna which Kṛishṇa resolves by the teaching of *Karmayoga.* The battle ends in gory lament and an apparently pyrrhic victory. Yudhishṭhira now has doubts similar to those of Arjuna. Bhīshma instructs him in the duties of the kings but it is clear that beyond social ethics lies the goal of spiritual liberation and devotion to Kṛishṇa. Ancient masters like Madhva and commentators like Sadānanda have emphasized this. The greatest modern scholar of the *Mahābhārata,* Sukthankar has said the same thing in his posthumously published lectures on the meaning of the *Mahābhārata.*

The *Mahābhārata* is an *itihāsa* in the sense of archetypal or *sanātana* history, it is a poem which expresses a vision of the struggle and destiny of man in terms of a mythopoeic and demiurgic creativity. It is a work of authority that is a *śāstra* as embodying an ancient tradition of wisdom. The whole work is cast in the form of unforgettable images of scenes and persons.

G.C. Pande

Contents

Mahābhārata: Janapadas, Peoples and Cultural and Political Aspects

Mahābhārata and Epigraphy

Mahābhārata: Versions and Studies

Acknowledgements

It is my pleasant duty to acknowledge the valuable help I received from various quarters in convening the national seminar and bringing out this outcome in such a short time. It was in February 1999 that the then Director of the Indian Institute of Advanced Study, Prof. Mrinal Miri, requested me on behalf of the Governing Body to convene a national seminar on the *Mahābhārata* that year by way of heralding the twenty-first millennium. I accepted the invitation but pointed out that the time was too short and if the event was meant to presage the next millennium, it would be in the fitness of things to hold the seminar next year (2000), to which he readily agreed. But before the seminar was held, there was a change of guard and for some time Prof. Sibesh Bhattacharya acted as Director and later Prof. V.C. Srivastava took over and it was under his directorship that the seminar finally took place. I am highly thankful to all these for extending every possible help for conducting the seminar successfully. I have no words to thank adequately Prof. G.C. Pande, who as Chairman of the Governing Body of the IIAS, was always ready to extend to me the benefit of his valuable guidance and advice. After the seminar was over, Prof. Srivastava invited me to edit this anthology of valuable contributions and the outcome is now placed in the hands of interested readers.

I have received highly valuable assistance from several other quarters. I am beholden to the scholars who spared their valuable time in preparing the papers and participating in the deliberations of the seminar, but for them this endeavour would not have been possible. I am particularly thankful to Professors G.C. Pande, O.P. Bharadwaj, Sibesh Bhattacharya, A.A. Manavalan, B.B. Lal, V.D. Misra and Dr. N.R. Waradpande, who graciously accepted my request to chair the sessions of the seminar. One of the sessions was chaired by the undersigned also.

I cannot forget the valuable assistance rendered ungrudgingly by Dr. S.A. Jabbar, Academic Resource Officer, IIAS, regarding the administrative aspects of the seminar throughout, before, during and after, for which he deserves sincere thanks.

Last but not the least, I am very much beholden to my esteemed friend, Shri Devendra Handa, Fellow at the IIAS, for willingly undertaking the arduous task of going through the proofs with an exemplary care as a matter of love. Words fail to express my gratitude to him adequately.

'Prachi'
23 Vidya Vihar
Rana Pratap Nagar
Nagpur – 440022

AJAY MITRA SHASTRI

List of Abbreviations

ABORI	Annals of the Bhandarkar Oriental Research Institute
BMCAI	Catalogue of Indian Coins in the British Museum
BS	Bṛihat-saṁhitā
CAI	Coins of Ancient India by Alexander Cunningham
CII	Corpus Inscriptionum Indicarum
EC	Epigraphia Carnatica
EI	Epigraphia Indica
IA	Indian Antiquary
IAR	Indian Archaeology: A Review
JASB	Journal of the Asiatic Society of Bengal
JNSI	Journal of the Numismatic Society of India
JRAS	Journal of the Royal Asiatic Society of Great Britain and Ireland
JRASB	Journal of the Royal Asiatic Society of Bengal
Mbh.	Mahābhārata
ND	Numismatic Digest
OCP	Ochre-Coloured Pottery
PGW	Painted Grey Ware
SII	South Indian Inscriptions

List of Abbreviations

ABORI	Annals of the Bhandarkar Oriental Research Institute
BMCAI	Catalogue of Indian Coins in the British Museum
BS	Bṛihat-saṁhitā
CAI	Coins of Ancient India by Alexander Cunningham
CII	Corpus Inscriptionum Indicarum
EC	Epigraphia Carnatica
EI	Epigraphia Indica
IA	Indian Antiquary
IAR	Indian Archaeology: A Review
JASB	Journal of the Asiatic Society of Bengal
JNSI	Journal of the Numismatic Society of India
JRAS	Journal of the Royal Asiatic Society of Great Britain and Ireland
JRASB	Journal of the Royal Asiatic Society of Bengal
Mbh.	Mahābhārata
ND	Numismatic Digest
OCP	Ochre-Coloured Pottery
PGW	Painted Grey Ware
SII	South Indian Inscriptions

List of Contributors

Prof. K.D. Abhyankar
Dept. of Astronomy, Osmania University, Hyderabad - 500007

Dr. Ashvini Agrawal
Dept. of Ancient Indian History, Culture and Archaeology, Panjab University, Chandigarh - 160014

Prof. G.M. Ballabh
Dept. of Astronomy, Osmania University, Hyderabad - 500007

Prof. O.P. Bharadwaj
465, Sector 7, Panchakula - 134109

Dr. Bhagchandra Jain 'Bhaskar'
Parshvanath Vidyapeeth, Karaundi, Varanasi - 221005

Prof. Sibesh Bhattacharya
Fellow, Indian Institute of Advanced Study, Rashtrapati Nivas, Shimla - 171005

Dr. D.P. Dubey
Dept. of Ancient History and Archaeology, University of Allahabad, Allahabad - 211002

Prof. Chandrashekhar Gupta
Dept. of Ancient Indian History, Culture and Archaeology, Nagpur University, Nagpur - 440022

Dr. Mohan Gupta
B16/2, Mahananda Nagar, Ujjain - 456010

Shri Devendra Handa
1401, "PUSHPAC", Sector 49B, Chandigarh - 1600 47

Shri P.V. Holay
West Park Road, Dhantoli, Nagpur - 440012

Dr. M.R. Joshi
10, Narakersari Layout, Jairakash Nagar, Nagpur - 440025

Prof. B.B. Lal
F7, Hauz Khas Enclave, New Delhi - 110016

Prof. A. A. Manavalan
M3, Second Avenue, Indira Nagar, Chennai - 600020

Prof. V.D. Misra
Department of Ancient History, Culture and Archaeology, University of Allahabad, Allahabad - 211002

Dr. Susmita Pande
A-90, Alka Puri, P.O. BHEL Hospital, Bhopal- 462024

Dr. C.S. Radhakrishnan
Dept. of Sanskrit, Vivekananda College, Chennai - 600004

Dr. S. Ramaratnam
Principal, Vivekananda College, Chennai - 600004

Dr. K.V. Ramesh
Director, Oriental Research Institute, University of Mysore, Mysore - 570005

Prof. Shrinivas Ritti
Bharati, Navodaya Nagar, Dharwad- 580003

Dr. I.K. Sarma
Flat 4, 2nd Floor, Latha Apartment, Vidya Nagar, Hyderabad - 500044

Prof. Ajay Mitra Shastri
'Prachi', 23 Vidya Vihar, Rana Pratap Nagar, Nagpur - 440022

Dr. Yogeshwari Shastri
'Prachi', 23 Vidya Vihar, Rana Pratap Nagar, Nagpur - 440022

Prof. Bharati Shelat
Director, B.J. Institute of Learning and Research, Ashram Road, Ahmedabad - 380009

Prof. K.S. Singh
A40/3, SFS Flat, Saket, New Delhi - 110017

Shri K.M. Srivastava
142 Venus Apartments, Inder Enclave, Rohtak Road, New Delhi - 110089

Dr. N.R. Waradpande
38, Hindustan Colony, Amraoti Road, Nagpur - 440010

Introduction

It is now commonly, though not unanimously, believed that the Bhārata War was a historical event though fought on a much smaller scale than would appear from the *Mahābhārata* as it has come down to us.[1] Though essentially centring around a feud between two factions of a ruling family, it was joined by the ruling chiefs of a major portion of northern part of undivided India from Gandhāra in modern Pakistan in the north to Virāṭanagara (near Jaipur) in the south and from Gujarat in the west to Bihar in the east and thus involved a very large portion of what was then known as Bhārata. It is therefore rightly called Mahābhārata. It created a stupendous impact not only on the parts of the country that were directly involved in or concerned in any way with the war and places[2], monuments in far south and far east were also named after the Mahābhārata heroes, particularly the victorious Pāṇḍavas,[3] with several dynasties of these areas claiming descent from them.[4] We also have in some regions, shrines of some minor demoniac characters like Hiḍimbā.[5] It has also exerted an enormous influence on Indian thought, belief system and literary traditions. The *Bhagavadgītā*, which has moulded Indian devotional and philosophical thought, forms a part of the extant text of the Great Epic. Many Sanskrit and Prakrit literary compositions are based on the Mahābhārata War and role of its characters. Many of the plays of the celebrated Bhāsa have picked up some event or character of war for their themes. Some of the authors like Bhāsa and Kshemendra have attempted abridgement of the *Mahābhārata*. The followers of different sectarian denominations have developed their own versions which differ in many a case drastically from the popular version. Most of the modern Indian languages have not only a rich Mahābhārata-based literature but have developed their own renditions of *Mahābhārata*. The first poem of Kannada is the Bhārata of its first known poet, Pampa. There are folk and tribal versions of the *Mahābhārata* prevalent in different parts of the Indian subcontinent, and even some the so-called original tribes of India like the Muṇḍas and the Bodos, have their own accounts of stories, episodes, songs and dramatic performances based on it. What is most curious is that some of the tribes have developed myths and traced their descent to one or other of the characters of the Great Epic.[6] It is not only in India but wherever Indians went as in South-East Asia that the *Mahābhārata* is embedded in the life and culture of the people and there are different versions like Wayang in Java and folk performance based on it.[7] What is even more interesting, names of the Bhārata heroes enjoyed great popularity as shown by the fact that they are mentioned for the sake of comparison and people were named after the Mahābhārata characters even as early as the fourth century AD and the earliest citation of some *Mahābhārata* stanzas is met with in an inscription from Laos as early as the fifth century AD.[8] Thus our cultural traditions owe quite a lot to this great event.

There is, however, a sizable intellectual crème of indologists who do not share the view that the *Mahābhārata* has a historical core comparable to the Greek epic *Illiad* of Homer and strongly feel that it is a poetic-philosophical creation celebrating (and thereby stressing) the victory of good and justice over evil and injustice. They include such celebrities as Aurobindo Ghose, Rabindranath Tagore and the well-known *Mahābhārata* veteran, V.S. Sukthankar, and this view is now reiterated strongly by Prof. G.C. Pande in his inaugural speech of the seminar.[9]

Unfortunately, however, there prevails a complete uncertainty and indecision among those scholars favouring the historicity of the core of the Great Epic as regards the date of this epoch-making event. This is mainly due to differing statements of the astronomical facts in different parts of the text as well in some other works and their differing interpretations by different authorities. It is also not certain if the *Mahābhārata* stanzas containing these averments in their extant form found place in the original version of the *Mahābhārata*. We have explicit statements in the text itself that it had already passed through several recensions before receiving its present form. The original text comprised just a few thousand stanzas and was possibly the work of Kṛishṇadvaipāyana Vyāsa and probably known as *Jaya* as it concerned itself simply with the central theme, viz. the victory (*jaya*) of the Pāṇḍavas over the Kauravas. It was subsequently revised by Vaiśampāyana (and probably his school) with addition of some fresh material and it now turned into *Bhārata* containing about 24,000 stanzas. And finally with the accretion of considerable doses of fresh matter added deliberately from time to time with the explicit object of turning the work into an encyclopaedia of Indian culture[10] with all its components, it assumed the form of a compendium of all the existing knowledge called *Mahābhārata* with about 1,00,000 verses and was appropriately given the descriptive epithet *śata-sāhasrī saṁhitā*.[11]

These verses, however, do not find place in the critical edition of the Ādiparvan prepared by that greatest *Mahābhārata* savant, V.S. Sukthankar[12]. But even this edition admits that the text of the Great Epic went through several stages of growth. We are told that Kṛishṇadvaipāyana took three year of stringent continuous hard work to compose the *Mahābhārata* (Ādi, 56.32)[13] and transmitted it first to his five pupils – Sumantu, Jaimini, Paila, Śuka (his son)[14] and Vaiśampāyana – all of whom prepared their own *saṁhitas* or versions (Ādi, 57.74-75).[15] The last of these, Vaiśampāyana, recited it at the snake-sacrifice of King Janamejaya, the great-grandson of Arjuna (Ādi, 1.8-9)[16], where it was heard by the bard (*sūta*) named Ugraśvaas, son of Lomaharshaṇa, who narrated it afresh before the sages assembled at the twelve-year sacrifice of sage Śaunaka in the Naimisha forest (Ādi, 1. 1ff.). It had already become so popular that it was narrated by some poets and some were still narrating and, it was hoped, others would narrate this *itihāsa*. It became a subject of great knowledge 'in the whole world' and was being memorized in *extenso* and in brief by the brāhmaṇas (Ādi, 1. 24-26). Admittedly the text had already passed through several recensions which have taken a few centuries.

The most popular tradition dates the event a few years or just prior to 3102 BC which marks the beginning of the Kali age. The traditional date for the beginning of the Kali-yuga is found mentioned for the first time by the celebrated astronomer Āryabhaṭa (born AD 473)[17] and subsequently in the Aihoḷe inscription (dated AD 634) of the Chalukyan emperor Pulakeśi II of Badami (Bijapur district, Karnataka).[18] However, there also exist some other almost equally early traditions dating this event a few centuries subsequent to the start of the Kali age. According to a very persistent tradition, it occurred in 2449 (current) or 2448 (expired) BC. This notion is first referred to by Varāhamihira (mid-sixth century AD)[19] who in his *Bṛihat-saṁhitā* (XIII. 3) gives the interval between the period of the Mahābhārata hero Yudhishṭhira and the commencement of the Śaka era as 2526 years.[20] The celebrated Kashmiri poet-historian Kalhaṇa (twelfth century AD) in his *Rājataraṅgiṇī* (I. 56) cities this statement of Varāhamihira, dubs the notion that the Bhārata War took place at the end of Dvāpara as misleading (I. 49) and asserts that the Kurus and Pāṇḍavas flourished when 653 years of the Kali age had elapsed (I. 51).[21] Some modern Indian astronomers have tried to demonstrate that even some astronomical references in the *Mbh.* itself lend support to this date.[22] What is specially interesting in the present context is the fact that this tradition is also sought to be buttressed by some scholars on the basis of a certain assertion met with in one of the copperplate charters of the Prāgjyotisha monarch Bhāskaravarman (*c.* AD 600-650). It is averred in his Nidhānpur plates (verse 7) that Vajradatta, son of Bhagadatta, who had played an important role in the Bhārata War, was followed by his descendants who ruled for three thousand years after which Pushyavarman became the king.[23] And as Bhāskaravarman was a contemporary of Harshavardhana of Kanauj and Thānesar, who lived in the first half of the seventh century AD, and was twelfth in descent from Pushyavarman, the latter may be placed in the first half of the fourth century AD. And if we add 3000 years said to have elapsed between his accession and Bhagadatta's son Vajradatta, we reach about the middle (or first half) of the twenty-fifth century BC which tallies well with 2448 BC, the date of Yudhishṭhira according to Varāhamihira.[24] There is yet another tradition based on the varying statements in the Purāṇas about the interval betweeen Parīkshit, grandson of Arjuna and successor of Yudhishṭhira, and the coronation of Mahāpadma (Nanda) who flourished in the fourth century BC, just prior to the accession of Chandragupta Maurya. According to most of the scholars, it is given as 1050 or 1015 years, and accordingly the Bhārata War may have to be dated around the fifteenth century BC which is accepted by many. However, after carefully comparing the relevant Purāṇic passages on the question and the duration of the time allotted to various dynasties in different manuscripts, the indefatigable P.V. Kane has concluded that the correct reading most probably was *pañchaśatottaram*, and not *pañchāśad = uttaram* or *pañchadaś-ottaram* as found in the printed editions of the Purāṇas concerned.[25] And consequently the gap between Parīkshit and the coronation of Mahāpadma Nanda should be 1500 years and thus the Bhārata War, according to this tradition, will have to be dated in about 1900 BC. Thus far about literary and epigraphic evidence on the question.

However, archaeologists, who concede the historicity of the Bhārata War, are inclined to date the event somewhere between roughly 900 and 1500 BC, based on the time-bracket for the Painted Grey Ware (PGW) culture noticed at most of the sites in northern India associated with the activities of the Kauravas and the Pāṇḍavas and the Bhārata War as well as on some other considerations.[26] The find of some other materials including some seals in the underwater excavations at Bet Dwārakā in layers dating from about 1500 BC, has been taken by the excavator to confirm Kṛishṇa's association with the site during this period.[27] In short, there is a complete chaos both among ancient writers including astronomers-astrologers and historians and modern scholars about the chronological framework of this catastrophic happening, admitting though it was real. There are several scholars, especially of the traditional group, who uphold the general historicity of the tradition including the participation of all the powers, far and near, in the great war and circumstances and events leading to it, though they, too, agree that the descriptions are naturally magnified by the poets responsible for composing the text at various chronologically separated different stages.

Whether the Bhārata War was a historical event or not, there should be and is a complete unanimity about one point – the *Mahābhārata* as it has come down, is an encyclopaedia of multifaceted Indian life and culture down the ages. There is no aspect of life and culture left untouched by its authors whosoever they might have been. The *Bhagavadgītā*, which is pivotal to the understanding of Indian religion and philosophy through the stages and has naturally enjoyed great popularity and exerted unparalleled influence on leading ancient and modern Indian religio-philosophical luminaries as well as some modern foreign thinkers, forms part of this great work. What facet of Indian life is untouched by the *Mahābhārata*? Political life and thought, social institutions, occupations, classes, sports and pastimes, religious tourism or *tīrtha-yātrā* and geography, minerals and metallurgy, astrology and astronomy, military system and warfare including ethics of war, literary thought and practices, etc., are exhaustively dwelt upon in varying contexts. And in all these and other matters it is a veritable storehouse of information to any and every interested student of the past of India. And the authors of the work reveal their consciousness of this strange-looking fact when they aver that whatever in respect of Dharma (socio-religious duties), wealth, love-life (erotics) and final emancipation is here, is to be seen elsewhere, and what is missing in this work is not to be found anywhere else.

Dharme ch-ārthe cha kame cha mokshe cha Bhāratarshabha /
Yad = ih - āsti tad = anyatra yan = n-eh-āsti na tat kvachit //
(*Mbh.*, Ādi, 56/33).

In view of this phenomenal importance of the problems concerning the Great Epic and its all-pervasive character and national value, the Indian Institute of Advanced Study (IIAS), Shimla, wisely thought of organizing a national seminar on this great encyclopaedia of Indian life and culture, whose popularity continues unabated even after the passage of millennia and I was requested to act as its convenor. The idea was to focus pointed attention to varying facets concerning it and the colloquium actually evoked expectedly spontaneous enthusiastic interest and the response was simply encouraging.

The present anthology represents the papers presented at the seminar and naturally the topics are multidimensional like the Epic. Some of the papers presented could not be included for various reasons, while some other papers by scholars who could not participate in the seminar on some personal grounds have been included.

The papers are grouped into four broad sections. The first section concerns itself with the date and allied problems of the Mahābhārata War. The opening presentation by Prof. B.B. Lal dwells upon the evidence yielded by archaeological probings at the sites connected with the events of the war, situated in western Uttar Pradesh and concludes that the war took place somewhere around 900 BC. And an attempt to reconcile the archaeological evidence with the literary data concerning the number of generations elapsed between Nichakshu, who shifted the capital from Hastināpura to Kauśāmbi due to the former city being flooded by the Gaṅgā, to Udayana, a contemporary of the Buddha, leads him to date it slightly later in the ninth century BC. In the process he has arrived at an average of fourteen years per generation. His interpretation of the archaeological evidence is supported by Prof. V.D. Misra. Dr. I.K. Sarma, in the next paper, takes stock of all the popular theories about the date of the war based on archaeological data and makes a strong plea to relate it to the Harappan or Sarasvatī-Indus civilization and places it in the third millennium BC. So far the archaeological evidence.

The next three papers (4-6) dwell upon relevant literary data. After analysing the Purāṇic genealogies and astronomical evidences, Dr. Mohan Gupta concludes that the war took place around mid-twentieth century BC. Shri P.V. Holay analyses the various statements in the *Mbh.* and concludes that the tradition of the war taking place at the juncture of the Dvāpara and Kali resulting into placing it in the late thirty-first millennium BC is correct. He also gives what he calls the diary of the War. Profs. K.D. Abhyankar and G.M. Ballabh in their joint paper try to fix the epoch of what they term 'astronomical and historical of Kaliyuga' with a great bearing on the date of the war in 1500±300 BC which agrees fairly well with the dating by underwater archaeology around mid-second millennium BC. The absorbing question of the nature and types of weaponry described in the *Mbh.* is discussed by Dr. N.R. Waradpande who points out the imaginary character of the *astras* or missiles. Shri K.M. Srivastava dwells upon the problem of the location of the city of Kāmpilya, the capital of south Pāñchāla, the kingdom of Drupada, in the light of recent archaeological work by a team from the University of Venice (Italy) and Indian Archaeological Society represented by a team including the author, which points to the strong assumption that the ancient mound near the modern homonymous town represents the Kāmpilya of the Mahābhārata times.

The next section contains contributions on the *janapadas*, peoples and cultural and political aspects as found adumbrated in the *Mbh.* Shri Devendra Handa invites attention to the reference to some important *janapadas* of the Uttarāpatha which issued coins in their names, suggests their locations and on their antiquity, points to the chronological position of the relevant *Mbh.* passages. In the next paper the undersigned has taken stock of the *Mbh.*

allusions to the role of the Prāgjyotisha kings Bhagadatta and Vajradatta in the activities concerned with the war and observes that these were products of afterthoughts of some people with a view to impart antiquity and respectability to the ruling families of the North-East and that distances were too much for their participation in events taking place in the far off Uttarāpatha. Prof. K.S. Singh expatiates on the *Mbh.* ethnography of the North-East and shows that several of the peoples mentioned therein are identifiable with the present *janas* (tribes). The next two papers are devoted to the *tīrthas* (pilgrimage-centres) in the *Mbh.* The first paper by Prof. O.P. Bharadwaj dwells upon the Vedic *tīrthas* as described in the *Mbh.*, while the concept and practice of pilgrimage is the theme of the following paper by Dr. D.P. Dubey. Dr. Ashvini Agrawal in his article analyses the problem of *satī* in the context of Mādrī following her husband Pāṇḍu on his pyre and points out that the stanzas referring to this episode were added when the custom had become prevalent as in the days of the *Mahābhārata* it was not practiced. The *Mbh.* is an inexhaustible treasury of Indian thought and culture, and the last five articles of this part are devoted to a study of such matter. Drs. C.S. Radhakrishnan and Susmita Pande study the traces of Nyāya-Vaiśeshika and the data on the Pañcharātra cult in the work, the latter with reference to its Śāntiparvan. The Yaksha cult has enjoyed great popularity with people in general, irrespective of the sectarian affiliation and the information on it, as found in the text, is subjected to an analytical study by Prof. Chandrashekhar Gupta while the next article by Prof. Sibesh Bhattacharya is an attempt to find out the connection between the *Arthaśāstra* and *Dharmaśāstra* in the context of an important dialogue found in the Śāntiparvan. Dr. S. Ramaratnam studies the concept of communication as seen from some instances in the *Mbh.* in the concluding article of this section.

The sole article by Dr. K.V. Ramesh forming the next part, presents an almost exhaustive study of epigraphical allusions to the *Mahābhārata*, both war and work. It is pertinent to note in this context that as early as the fourth century AD, the *Mbh.* had become popular not just in the Indian subcontinent but even in South-East Asia where an inscription contains earliest citation from it. Its first datable description as a work containing a hundred thousand stanzas (*śata-sāhasrī saṁhitā*) is met with in a copperplate character dating from AD 534 in Central India, which is of immense value for the history of the growth of the work. These are only illustrative of the important epigraphic data on the *Mbh.* enshrined casually in inscriptions which form the theme of this paper.

The *Mahābhārata's* enormous popularity ever since the commencement of its composition is best revealed by its numerous versions by the votaries of different sects and in vernacular languages, and the closing section comprises scholarly contributions on this theme. Votaries of different sects moulded the *Mbh.* stories and characters to meet their sectarian requirements, and it is best exemplified by Jaina versions' studies, by Dr. Bhagchandra Jain 'Bhaskar'. The last articles by Profs. A.A. Manavalan, Shrinivas Ritti, M.R. Joshi and Bharati Shelat take stock of Tamil, Kannada, Marathi and Gujarati renditions and modern studies (in case of Tamil and Marathi) respectively. The Tamils show awareness of the *Mbh.* as early as the early centuries AD and there are Tamil versions of the work dating from around 5th-6th centuries AD. We also have modern writings based on the *Mbh.*, and research works in Tamil. The Kannada literature begins with the *Bhārata* or *Vikramārjuna-vijaya* of Pampa who lived in the tenth century and there were some other Kannada poems based on the *Mbh.* and moulded according to the individual needs of the authors. Marathi is blessed with several poetic writings based on the *Mbh.* right from the beginning of the thirteenth century AD when the famous saint-poet Jñāneśvara composed his well-known commentary on the *Bhagavadgītā.* Strangely enough, some Marathi writers regard the *Bhāgavata Purāṇa* as forming part of the *Mbh.* There has been a lot of modern research and study, sometimes motivated, in modern Marathi literature. Gujarati also has not lagged behind and there are several renderings of the text in full or of some *parvans* continuously from the fifteenth century.

The last paper (only one in Hindi) by Dr. Yogeshwari Shastri harnesses the references in the *Mbh.* with a view to fix the age of some prominent characters including Bhīshma, Droṇa, Abhimanyu, etc., at the time of the war and the reader is struck by the extraordinarily high age when one would find it very difficult, if not impossible, to fight. She gives the approximate age of other important participants like Yudhishṭhira, Bhīma, Arjuna, Kṛishṇa and others in a table appended at the end.

It will be seen from the above, naturally very brief reportage, that the present anthology comprises well-researched contributions and may be said to be *nakshatra-mālā* composed of twenty-six pearl-like papers which would make a highly absorbing reading for anyone interested in the epic studies. Naturally it does not touch upon all the aspects as no single work can; it would need Herculean effort of a dedicated team to study it exhaustively.

AJAY MITRA SHASTRI

NOTES AND REFERENCES

1. For different views on the historicity or otherwise of the Mahābhārata War, see S.P. Gupta and K.S. Ramachandran (eds.), *Mahābhārata: Myth and Reality-Differing Views*, Agam Kala Prakashan, Delhi, 1976.
2. Thus we have places named after Rukmiṇī and Bhīshma in the North-East.
3. It is best illustrated by the naming of the so-called *rathas* or chariots (actually shrines) after the five Pāṇḍavas and their wife Draupadī at Mahābalipuram (ancient Māmallapuram) on the shores of the southern ocean.
4. The Varman or Bhauma-Nāraka dynasty as well as many succeeding ones claimed to have descended from Bhagadatta and his son (or brother according to some divergent traditions) Vajradatta.
5. There is a mound at Mansar near Nagpur called Hiḍimbāchī Ṭekḍī ('Hiḍimbā's Mount'), and the late text *Sindūragiri-māhātmya* prescribes the worship of Hiḍimbā after bath in the local lake known as Mansar (Maṇisara which is an abbreviated form of ancient Maṇikālasara). In Himachal Pradesh also there is a shrine dedicated to her.
6. For an account of many of these versions, beliefs, and dramatic performances, see K.S. Singh (ed.), *The Mahābhārata: The Tribal and Folk Traditions of India*, Indian Institute of Advanced Study, Shimla & Anthropological Survey of India, New Delhi, 1993.
7. See for a detailed account, H.B. Sarkar, *Cultural Relations Between India and South-East Asian Countries*, Indian Council for Cultural Relations, New Delhi, and Motilal Banarsidass, Delhi, 1985, Ch. 14.
8. K.V. Ramesh, 'The Mahābhārata in Inscriptions', paper no. 20 in this volume.
9. The same line has been taken by several scholars including Rekha Jhanji in her *Human Condition in the Mahābhārata*, Indian Institute of Advanced Study, Shimla, 1995. See introduction.
10. अष्टौ श्लोकसहस्राणि अष्टौ श्लोकशतानि च।

अहं वेद्मि शुको वेत्ति संजयो वेत्ति वा न वा।।
चतुर्विंशतिसाहस्रीं चक्रे भारत संहिताम्।
उपाख्यानैर्विना तावद् भारतं प्रोच्यते बुधैः।।
इदं शतसहस्रं तु श्लोकानां पुण्यकर्मणाम्।
उपाख्यानैः सह ज्ञेयमाद्यं भारतमुत्तमम्।।

Mahābhārata (Gita Press edn.), Ādi, I.81, 102b-103a, 101b-102a.

However, traditionally the first statement is intended to refer to knotty stanzas in the work and not to actual extent of the text as commonly believed by historians and modern Sanskritists.

Thus came into existence the saying met with in the *Mbh.* (Ādi, 56. 33), itself *Dharme ch-ārthe cha kāme cha mokshe cha Bhāratarshabha/ yad = ih-āsti tad = anyatra yan = n-eh-āsti na tat kvachit.*

11. The expression first occurs in the Khoh copperplate charter of *Mahārāja* Śarvanātha dated AD 534. *Vide* J.F. Fleet, *Inscriptions of the Guptas and Their Successors, CII*, III, p. 137.
12. Bhandarkar Oriental Research Institute, Pune, 1933.
13. त्रिभिर्वर्षैः सदोत्थायी कृष्णद्वैपायनो मुनिः।
महाभारतमाख्यानं कृतवानिदमुत्तमम्।।
14. It appear from Ādi, I. 63 that he first taught it to his son and thereafter to other pupils:
इदं द्ववैपायनः पूर्वं पुत्रमध्यापयच्छुकम्।
ततोऽन्येभ्योऽनुरूपेभ्यः शिष्येभ्यः प्रददौ प्रभुः।।
15. वेदानध्यापयामास माहभारतपञ्चमान्।
सुमन्तुं जैमिनिं पैलं शुकं चैव स्वमात्मजम्।।
प्रभुर्वरिष्ठो वरदो वैशम्पायनमेव च।
संहितास्तैः पृथक्त्वेन भारतस्य प्रकाशिताः।।
16. जनमेजयस्य राजर्षेः सर्पसत्रे महात्मनः।
समीपे पार्थिवेन्द्रस्य सम्यक् पारिक्षितस्य च।।
कृष्णद्वैपायनप्रोक्ताः सुपुण्या विविधाः कथाः।
कथिताश्चापि विधिवद् या वैशम्पायनेन वै।।
17. षष्टयब्दानां षष्टिर्यदा व्यतीतास्त्रयश्च युगपादाः।
त्र्यधिका विंशतिरब्दास्तदेह मम जन्मनाऽतीताः।।
18. त्रिंशत्सु त्रिसहस्रेषु भारतादाहवादितः।
सप्ताब्दशतयुक्तेषु गतेष्वब्देषु पञ्चसु।
पञ्चाशत्सु कलौ काले षट्सु पञ्चशतासु च।
समासु समतीतसु शकानामपि भूभुजाम्।।

EI, VI, 1900-01, p. 7, verses 33-34
19. Though Varāhamihira started his writing activity in the beginning of the sixth century AD, the *Bṛihat-saṁhitā* containing the statement in question was composed about the middle of this century.
20. आसन् मघासु मुनयः शासति पृथिवीं युधिष्ठिरे नृपतौ।
षड्द्विकपञ्चद्वियुतः शककालस्तस्य राज्ञश्च।।
Despite varying interpretations of the expression *shaḍ-dvika-pañcha-yutaḥ* (for these interpretations, see Ajay Mitra Shastri, *Varāhamihira's*

India, I, Aryan Books International, New Delhi, 1996, p. 34, note 45), this happens to be the only correct interpretation and, as will be just seen, is backed by the Kashmiri chronicler Kalhaṇa.

It is held by some scholars that this stanza is of the sage Vṛiddha-Garga who is believed to have flourished in pre-Christian centuries when there could be no question of the knowledge of what is known as Śaka era commencing in AD 78 and therefore it is proposed to amend the reading *Śaka-kāla* to *Śakya-kāla* which again is regarded as meant for *Śakya-kāla* and intended to refer to the year of Buddha's *nirvāṇa*. However, the reading *Śakya-kāla* would violate the metre besides the fact that the early traditions of the prevalence of an era commencing from Śākyamuni Buddha's death does not exist. But there is no reason to hold that the stanza in question was extracted by Varāhamihira from Vṛiddha-Garga as supposed by these scholars. The previous stanza just avers that Varāhamihira 'would state the movement of the Saptaṛishis following Vṛiddha-Garga's opinion' (*kathayishyc Vṛiddha-Garga-matāt, Bṛihat-saṁhita,* XIII. 2). Obviously the wording is of Varāhamihira himself, and not of Vṛiddha-Garga. In fact, the relevant stanza of Vṛiddha-Garga as cited by Bhaṭṭotpala in his Vivṛiti commentary runs as follows and makes the point absolutely clear and certain:

तथा च वृद्धगर्गः

कलिद्वापरसन्धौ तु स्थितास्ते पितृदैवतम्।
मुनयो धर्मनिरताः प्रजानां पालने रताः।।

Bṛihat-saṁhitā with Bhaṭṭotpala's Vivṛiti commentary, ed. Sudhakara Dvivedi, I, in Ch. XIII.3.

Some scholars like Mohan Gupta ('The Date of Mahābhārata War: Purāṇic and Astronomical Data', included in this volume) believe that the stanza actually refers to the period elapsed from the time of the Mahābhārata hero Yudhishṭhira to the time of Varāhamihira though they actually refer to its citation by Kalhaṇa in his *Rāja-taraṅgiṇī* (1. 56). This is just impossible in view of his very explicit statement that the Kauravas and the Pāṇḍavas flourished 653 years after the beginning of the Kali age. See the following stanza.

21. शतेषु षट्सु सार्धेषु त्र्यधिकेषु च भूतले।
कलेर्गतेषु वर्षाणामभूवन् कुरुपाण्डवाः।।
22. See P.C. Sengupta, 'Astronomical References in the Mahābhārata and Their Implications', *JRASBL*, II, 1933, pp. 101-19; 'Bhārata Battle Traditions', *Ibid.*, IV, 1938, pp. 393-413.
23. वंश्येषु तस्य नृपतिषु वर्षसहस्रत्रयं पदमवाप्य।
यातेषु देवभूयं क्षितीश्वरः पुष्यवर्माऽभूत्।।

M.M. Sharma, *Inscriptions of Ancient Assam*, Guwahati University, Guwahati, 1978, p. 41, verse 7.
24. See P.V. Kane, *History of Dharmaśāstra*, III, Bhandarkar Oriental

Research Institute, Pune, 1946, pp. 898-99. However, Kane assigns an average of twenty years per reign and arrives at the beginning of the fifth century AD for Pushyavarman which would be too late a date for him. *Vide Pragjyotisha: A Pan-Indian Perspective*, Aryan Books International, New Delhi, 2001. Ch. II.

25. *History of Dharmaśāstra*, III, pp. 898-1000.
26. For a discussion of the evidence, see B.B. Lal, 'Excavations at Hastinapur and Other Explorations in the Upper Ganga-Sutlej Basin: 1950-52', *Ancient India*, Nos. 11-12, 1954-55, pp. 1-151. He found at Hastinapur a large part of the habitation of PGW culture washed away by a flood which, to him, corroborated the Purāṇic tradition that a serious flood in the Gaṅgā forced Nichakshu, son of Parīkshit, to shift his capital to Kauśāmbi. He dates this layer in about 800 BC shortly before which the Mahābhārata War must have taken place. His latest contribution on the theme is, 'This is How an Archaeologist Looks at the Historicity of Mahābhārata' in this volume. Vibha Tripathi (*The Painted Grey War and Iron Age Culture of Northern India*, Concept Publishing Company, Delhi, 1975, pp. 122-23) has summarized his main results. For a list of PGW sites known up to the 1970s, see *Ibid*., pp. 124-31.

    F.E. Pargiter (*Ancient Indian Historical Tradition*, London, 1922, pp. 175-82) after a careful analytical assessment of the total number of reigns between Parīkshit, who succeeded Yudhishṭhira, and Mahāpadma, who founded the Nanda dynasty that preceded the Mauryas, arrives at 950 BC for the time of the battle. However, though well-based on the Purāṇic data, his date suffers from the abnormally low averages assigned to individual reigns, viz. 18 years, and therefore stands in need of a review. S.B. Roy (*The Date of the Mahābhārata War*, Gurgaon, 1976, pp. 139-48) reviews the various current theories about the date of this event and himself argues in favour of a date about mid-fifteenth century BC (*Ibid*., pp. 116-48), his favoured date being around 1424 BC (*Ibid*., p. 148).
27. See his 'Marine Archaeological Investigation in Indian Waters and the Discovery of Submerged Dvārakā', *Mañjūshā: Dr. S.R. Rao 60th Brithday Felicitation Volume*, Bangalore, 1985, pp. 23-27; 'Excavations at the Submerged Ports: Dvārakā: A Case Study', *Marine Archaeology of the Indian Ocean Countries*, Goa, 1987, pp. 47-53.

    Some scholars are inclined to regard the Harappan remains as those of the Mahābhārata age and thereby push the date of the war back to around the third millennium BC. See I.K. Sarma, 'The Mahābhārata: A Critical Study of the Archaeological Data', included in this volume.

1

This is How an Archaeologist Looks at the Historicity of the *Mahābhārata*

B.B. Lal

THE PROBLEM AND AN ARCHAEOLOGIST'S APPROACH

No one need be surprised at the extremely divergent views that exist about the historicity of the *Mahābhārata*, as they do in the case of the other well-known Indian epic, the *Rāmāyaṇa*. To the faithful, every event, major or minor, and every description, howsoever unusual, is true to the very letter: be it the flight of Shri Rāma and his entourage back from Sri Lanka in an aeroplane (*pushpaka vimāna*), or the deployment of millions of soldiers in the battlefield at Kurukshetra at the time of the Mahābhārata War. The firm believer in absolute authenticity of these epics would care less if a modern technologist told him that the manufacturing of aeroplanes is a very recent phenomenon, or a demographer or military strategist doubted the deployment of a number of *akshauhiṇī* units in the Mahābhārata War, since each *akshauhiṇī* unit, according to the laid down norms, comprised 21,870 elephants, 21,870 chariots, 65,610 horses and 1,09,350 foot soldiers. On the other hand, to a complete non-believer in ancient Indian tradition these epics are nothing more than mere figments of imagination. For him, the *Rāmāyaṇa* was written just to portray the character of an ideal son and a God-fearing ruler. Likewise, he holds that the *Mahābhārata* is nothing more than a conglomeration of a series of tales written from time to time to suit certain situations.

The reason for such a confusion seems to be inherent in the very nature of these texts. Take, for example, the *Mahābhārata*. If Kṛiṣṇa was a historical figure, he is unlikely to have existed after Buddha since the history of India is fairly well documented after the latter, i.e. from the sixth-fifth century onwards. Thus Krịṣṇa must have been there prior to the sixth century BC. On the other hand, the *Mahābhārata* text includes references not only to the Yavanas, i.e. Ionian Greeks and the Romakas, i.e. the Romans but also to the Hūṇas (white Huns) who are well known to have appeared on the Indian horizon as late as the fourth century AD. There is thus a time gap of at least a thousand years between the Mahābhārata event and the *Mahābhārata* text, as available to us now.

Further, the *Mahābhārata* is famous, or infamous(?), for the interpolations that it has had. The present text comprises more than 100,000 verses. However, it is well known that at an earlier stage it had only 24,000 verses and was called the *Bhārata*. Still earlier, it was called the *Jaya* and had only 8,800 verses. One need not be surprised if there was yet another earlier version with a much smaller number of verses. Anyway, there is at least eleven times inflation from the earliest known text to the present one. All attempts to find out the original text on linguistic basis have failed so far and hence one does not know what the basic story must have been like.

Finally, one should not should lose sight of the fact that the *Mahābhārata* was not meant to be a history book (*itihāsa*). It was an epic (*prabandha-kāvya*) and the poet was at absolute liberty to let his imagination fly. Thus, fact and fiction, reality and imagination, had their own colourful blending; and it is now a challenge to everyone to separate the wheat from the chaff.

What does an archaeologist do to face such a challenge? His approach, as usual, is earthly, down to earth. Thus, as an archaeologist I thought that the best way, and evidently the only way open to an archaeologist, was to explore and excavate the various sites associated with the Mahābhārata story and to find out if these could throw any light on the issue. In this context, a very encouraging factor was that all the sites associated with the Mahābhārata story continue to bear the same name even to this day. For example, there is only one Hastināpura, one Mathurā, one Kurukshetra and so on. Thus, there is no confusion on that account and one can confidently treat the basic archaeological data recovered from these sites as authentic, irrespective of their subsequent interpretation by individuals.

THE KEY-SITES ASSOCIATED WITH THE MAHĀBHĀRATA STORY

Before taking up the archaeological evidence, it may be well worthwhile to narrate in a nutshell the main part of the Mahābhārata story in order to let the unfamiliar reader know which sites were associated with that story and in what manner. The key-site in the story is, of course, Hastināpura which was the capital of the Kauravas. Going by the same name even to this day, it is situated on the right bank of the Gaṅgā in Meerut District of Uttar Pradesh (cf. Fig. 1). As is well known, there was a dispute between the Kauravas and their cousins, the Pāṇḍavas, over the throne. The Kauravas held the reins, but the Pāṇḍavas contested the same. Driven by this enmity, the former thought of eliminating the latter by burning them alive in a lac-house (*lākshāgṛiha*) which they got specially built for the purpose at a place called Vāraṇāvata (modern Barnāwā), located at the junction of the Krishni and Hindon rivers, again in the same Meerut District. The Pāṇḍavas got a scent of the plot and managed to escape before its execution. They travelled westwards through the forest known as Khāṇḍavavana and reached a place called Virāṭanagara (modern Bairat) in Jaipur District, Rajasthan. The then local king, Virāṭa, after whom the place was named, welcomed the Pāṇḍavas and provided them all possible facilities. Having lived at Virāṭanagara for a pretty long time, the Pāṇḍavas sent a message to the Kauravas that they would not lay their claim to the throne if they were given just five villages. There is some discrepancy between the literary evidence and local tradition about the exact names of these five villages. However, these are generally believed to have been, from north to south, as follows: Pāṇiprastha (modern Pānīpat) and Soṇaprastha (modern Sonīpat), both in Haryana, Vṛikaprastha (modern Bāghapat in Uttar Pradesh), Indraprastha (Purānā Qilā area in Delhi) and Tilaprastha (modern Tilpat), again in Haryana. *Prima facie* this demand appears to be innocuous, but there was indeed more to it than meets the eye. Had the Kauravas agreed to surrender these five villages to the Pāṇḍavas, the latter would have got full control of the Yamunā system over a long stretch, from Pānīpat in the north to Tilpat in the south. On the east of the Gaṅgā, the Pāṇḍavas already had their allies, viz. the Pāñchālas, whose daughter Draupadī was married to them. (The Pāñchālas ruled from two places, namely, Ahichchhatrā in Bareilly District

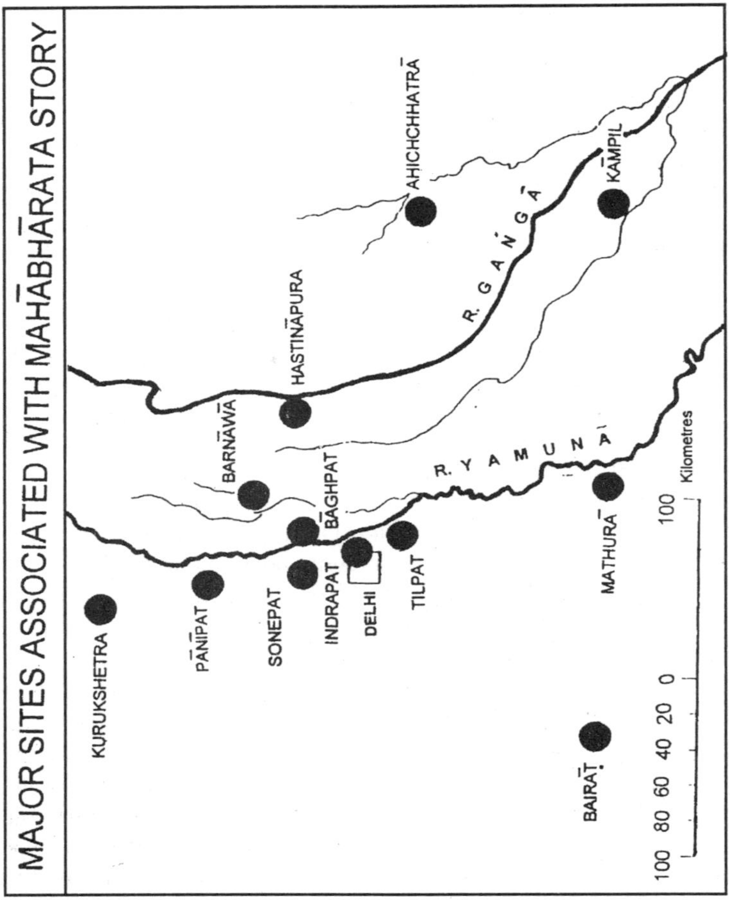

Fig. 1. Principal Sites Associated with the Mahābhārata Story

and Kāmpilya in Farukkhabad District, both in Uttar Pradesh.) Thus, had the Kauravas made over these five villages to the Pāṇḍavas, the former would have been completely sandwiched. Fully realizing the implications of the request of the Pāṇḍavas, the Kauravas turned it down. The ultimate result was the Mahābhārata War, which was fought at Kurukshetra, a place in Haryana, that continues to be called by the same name even today. Lord Kṛiṣṇa, who sided with the Pāṇḍavas, hailed from Mathurā, a place going by that very name in Uttar Pradesh.

EXCAVATIONS/EXPLORATIONS AT THE ABOVE-MENTIONED SITES

Of the sites mentioned above, Hastināpura, Indraprastha, Tilaprastha, Mathurā, Ahichchhatrā and Kāmpilya have been excavated and the rest subjected to thorough exploration. Since Hastināpura is the key-site in the story, the results of the excavations carried out there are given in some detail below.

The excavations at Hastināpura were carried out by the present writer way back in 1950-52 (Lal, 1954-55). As already mentioned, the site is located on the right bank of the Gaṅgā. Though the main stream now flows a few kilometres away, there does exist a minor channel not far from the site and is known as the Būḍhī Gaṅgā (i.e. Old Gaṅgā). The ancient mound stretches along the river for a little less than a kilometre and rises at places to a height of about 18 m above the surrounding ground level. Width-wise it measures only one-fourth of a kilometre, but this does not represent the original width of the settlement: as would be seen later, a good bit of the river-side part of the mound had been washed away by a mighty flood in the river in ancient times.

Though the site was not subjected to large-scale horizontal excavations, quite a few trenches were laid at different parts of the mound in order to ensure that a complete stratigraphic sequence was obtained. In fact, one of the trenches, named HST-1, was laid right across the mound to get a running story from one end to the other. Vertically, five periods of occupation were identified, with a break in between them all (Fig. 2). The characteristic features of these, from bottom upwards, were as follows.

Period I, the earliest, was distinguished by the occurrence of a pottery known to archaeologists as the Ochre Colour Ware. In the

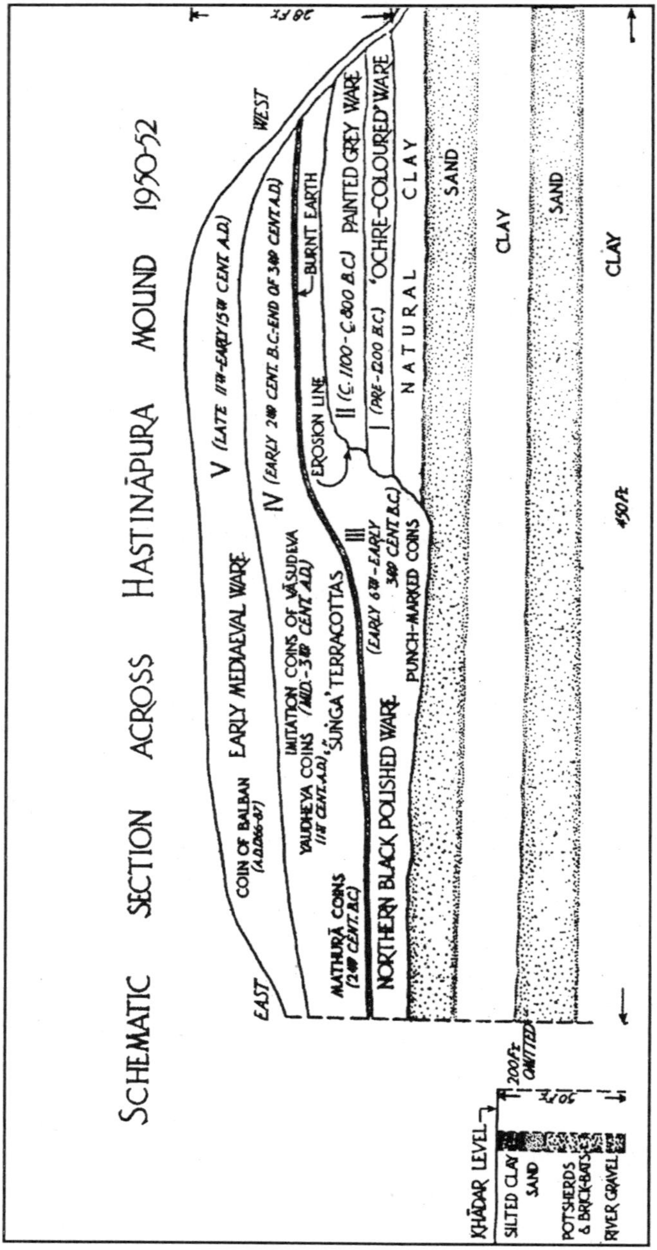

Fig. 2. Schematic Section Across Hastināpura Mound

Pl. I. Dish of Painted Grey Ware

absence of any better name, this was given to the pottery just because it left ochreous stains on the fingers when handled. No complete specimens were found and only small fragments lay embedded sporadically in a deposit of yellowish-brown clay which imperceptibly merged with the natural soil underneath. No other objects were met with. However, evidence from other Ochre Ware sites indicates that this ware often bore a red slip and was also sometimes painted with designs in black colour. The evidence from a site named Saipai, in Etawah District, Uttar Pradesh, conclusively shows that this ware was associated with what are known as the Copper Hoards. Besides other simpler types of tools, these hoards included harpoons, antennae swords, spearheads and anthropomorphic figures. However, as already stated, no such tool or, for that matter, any other antiquity was met with in the Ochre Colour Ware deposit at Hastināpura.

After an interval of time, the duration of which is difficult to determine but may have been anything up to half a millennium,

Pl. II. Bowl of Painted Grey Ware

the site was again occupied by people who used a very distinctive pottery called the Painted Grey Ware. As the name indicates, it was a ware with grey surface (and also a grey core), which was the result of its having been fired under reducing conditions in the kiln. On the surface, both inside and outside, there were designs painted in black colour, which included, besides simple horizontal or oblique lines, *svastikas*, sigmas, chains of short spirals, concentric circles, etc. The more noteworthy shapes in this ware were dishes, bowls (Pls. I & II) and globular drinking vessels. Though the associated culture-complex has since become known after this particular kind of pottery, as the Painted Grey Ware (PGW) Culture, the fact remains that this pottery was only the deluxe ware and accounted for just 10 to 15 per cent of the total pottery. There were also some specimens of a black-slipped ware, but the majority was that of a red ware, sometimes slipped.

Since, as already mentioned, the excavations were not horizontal in nature, no large-scale plans of houses were encountered.

However, walls of mud or mud-bricks were duly met with; so also a few examples of kiln-fired bricks. In order to give a better idea of the PGW Culture as a whole, we include here the data from other excavated sites of this culture-complex. Thus, the evidence from Bhagwanpura would indicate that some of the houses could have as many as thirteen rooms, besides a large open courtyard (Joshi, 1993). Bhagwanpura has also yielded evidence of substantial use of kiln-fired bricks.

In so far as the use of metal is concerned, it appears that there were two stages in the life of the Painted Grey Ware, in the earlier only copper/bronze was used, but later it was iron as well. Whereas some of the PGW sites in Punjab and Haryana belonged to the former stage, most of the sites in Uttar Pradesh have shown use of iron. The combined evidence from Hastināpura itself and from a site called Atranjikhera in Aligarh District, Uttar Pradesh (Gaur, 1983) indicates that the iron objects included tools for domestic use such as nails, hooks, axes and tongs and others that maybe used in warfare such as arrowheads, spearheads and daggers (Fig. 3). Jodhpura in Rajasthan has yielded a furnace with a side-hole into which the nozzle of the bellows could have been inserted to pump in air to raise the level of the heat as necessary. The use of iron by the PGW people is in marked contrast to its total absence during the Harappan times. Another noteworthy technological aspect of the PGW Culture was the manufacture of a variety of glass objects.

Agriculture and cattle-breeding seem to have been the mainstay of these people. The principal crops cultivated by them were wheat, barley and rice. The domesticated animals included the cattle, buffaloes, sheep, pigs and last but not the least, the horse. Wild animals were also hunted for meat and so also fishing was done.

The small finds associated with the PGW Culture included stone-moulds for jewellery, beads of semi-precious stones, antimony rods and nail-cutters of copper, ivory combs, etc. Amongst the terracotta figurines special mention maybe made of those having a fiddle-shaped body with pin-point decoration. This type continued well into the subsequent Northern Black Polished Ware Period and had a very wide distribution in terms of space. Of particular interest was a potsherd on which were engraved intersecting circles with centres duly marked. This not only shows the knowledge of

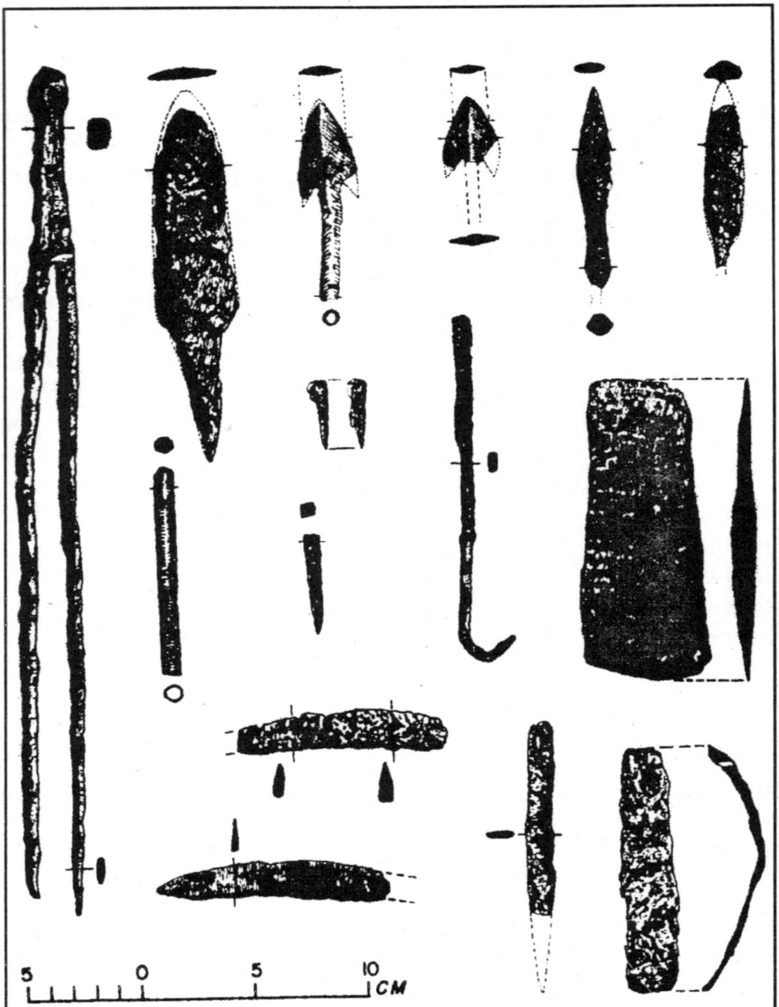

Fig. 3. Iron Objects Associated with Painted Grey Ware

geometry but also suggests the existence of a divider-like instrument.

Amongst the games played by the people, *chaupar* or *chausar* deserves special mention. The game continues even to this day. The board is usually made of cloth and has the form of a cross with all the four arms being of equal size. On each arm there are three rows of squares. The gamesmen, usually made of wood and coloured, are plano-convex in shape, while the dice are square-sectioned oblong pieces, generally of ivory and marked on respective sides with blind holes numbering 1, 2, 3 and 4. It is obvious that one cannot expect the survival of the cloth-made board of the PGW times, because of the hot and humid climate of India. However, excavations at various sites have duly yielded gamesmen of the aforesaid shape, though in terracotta (Pl. III), and the dice, usually made of bone and bearing the aforementioned kind of the numbering arrangement (Pl. IV). In this context, it must be mentioned that it was at this game that the Kauravas defeated the Pāṇḍavas.

The PGW occupation at Hastināpura continued for quite some time as indicated by several structural levels, accounting for a thickness of about 2.5 m. However, its end was sudden and sad. A huge flood in the Gaṅgā washed away a considerable portion of the settlement on the river-front, with the result that the site had to be abandoned. The evidence of this flood and of the severe damage inflicted was duly discovered in the excavation. A huge scar left by the erosion was noted on the eastern face of the mound (Pl. V). At the foot of this erosional scar there lay scattered a part of the washed-away material, overlain by layers of silt and sand. On finding this kind of evidence in the excavation, it just occurred to us that it was not unlikely that some of the washed-away material may still be lying buried deep in the river-bed, although most of it must have obviously been carried away by the floods. Accordingly, we bored four holes in the adjacent river-bed and to our pleasant surprise found in these bores at a depth of 15 m below the water-level (Pl. VI), potsherds characteristics of the PGW Period.

As a result of this massive destruction, the site had to be abandoned. However, it once again came under occupation after a couple of centuries. By now the painted designs on the PGW had disappeared and the fabric too became coarser. But some of the shapes, particularly the dish, continued. However, another deluxe ware emerged out of the black-slipped ware associated with the

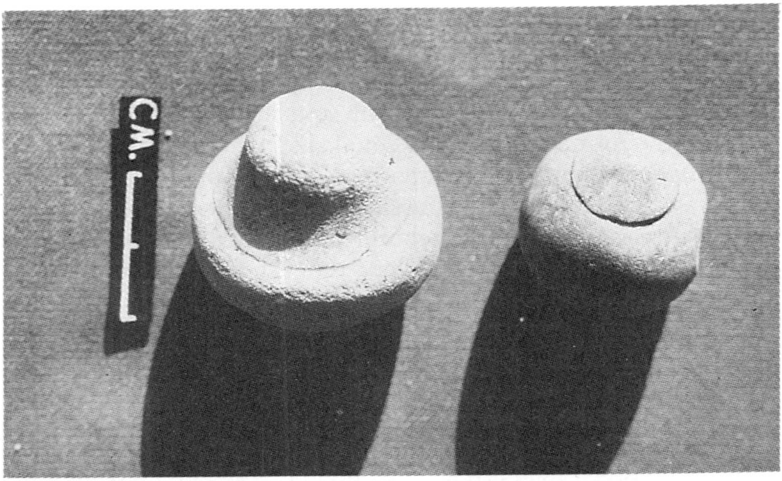

Pl. III. Gamesmen used in the game of *Chaupar*, associated with the Painted Grey Ware

Pl. IV. Die used in *Chaupar*, associated with the Painted Grey Ware

Pl. V. A heavy flood in the Gaṅgā washed away a major portion of the settlement at Hastināpura. The main points to the erosional scar left by the flood.

Pl. VI. With a view to finding out if any part of the washed-away material was left behind by the flood in the river-bed close to the mound, four holes were bored. In these were encountered potsherds associated with the Painted Grey Ware Culture, at a depth of 15 m below the water-level.

PGW. It is known to archaeologists as the Northern Black Polished Ware (NBPW). It had the same kind of fine grey core as that of the PGW. But the surface had a very fine lustrous slip in a variety of colours: black, indigo, silvery and golden. Shapes in the associated red ware also underwent some change. On the whole, the cultural component of Periods II and III, while showing a change, did reflect a generic relationship. This, it may be recalled, was quite in contrast to what happened between Periods I and II.

There are many other noticeable changes between Periods II and III. Thus, in the latter period there was profuse use of kiln-fired bricks, though no doubt mud bricks also continued to be used. With town planning, a system of public drainage also came into being for soakage of the sullage inside the houses, 'ring-wells' were used. That the economic level of the people had substantially risen is indicated by the introduction of systems of weights and coinage, both pointing to an augmentation in trade. Indeed, this was the time when the Sixteen States (*Ṣoḍaśa Mahājanapadas*) had come into being. It was also during this period that the two great religious figures, Buddha and Mahāvīra, were born. Nobody is sure about the time when the Brāhmī script originated, but it was during the NBPW times that we do have its clear evidence in the form of the inscriptions of the great emperor Aśoka.

The third occupation at Hastināpura too had a disastrous end. A large-scale fire engulfed the settlement, traces of which were noticed all over the area. As a result, the site was once more abandoned. However, this time also it was not long before the fourth occupation started. But there were some characteristics changes in the cultural equipment. For example, the Northern Black Polished Ware was completely given up and in the red ware, too, many new shapes made their appearance. There were new types of terracotta figurines, both male and female. The latter were distinguished by their round chubby faces, elaborate hairdo and ornaments, and are generally known as belonging to the 'Śuṅga' style. In the lower levels of this period were found the coins of the rulers of Mathurā (second century BC), followed by those of the Yaudheyas (datable to around the beginning of the Christian Era) in the middle levels, and imitation coins of the Kushāṇa king Vāsudeva (about the middle of the third century AD) in the upper levels. There is no evidence to indicate how this fourth occupation was abandoned.

However, there was a long gap between the fourth and the fifth (final) occupation of the site. This time the history was laid right in the medieval period. The ceramics were totally different and included two typically distinct glazed wares, one with a whitish sandy core and the other with a red and sturdy one. The former of these is known to have been introduced in India by the incoming Muslim rulers, while the latter seems to have been a local imitation of the former. That the scene was really set in the medieval times is established by the occurrence of a coin of Balban (AD 1266-87) in a middle level. With this period the settlement at the mound came to an end, though there do exist some later Jain temples in the neighbourhood. In fact, an altogether new settlement, planned by the Uttar Pradesh government has come up since we wound up our excavation in the middle of the last century.

THE CHRONOLOGY

We may now turn our attention to the chronological horizon of the various periods at Hastināpura. As per the details already given above, Period V is datable to ca. eleventh-fifteenth century AD and Period IV to ca. second century BC-third century AD. Since there was a gap between Periods III and IV, the end of the former may reasonably be ascribed to the third century BC. Up to this point the chronology is based entirely on the evidence of coins. Prior to this we have to fall back on a different kind of evidence.

When in 1951-52 Hastināpura was excavated, the Carbon-14 method of dating was not available in India and we had, therefore, to take recourse to what is called 'comparative stratigraphy'. Thus, for dating Period III the main basis was the occurrence, all through the strata, of the Northern Black Polished Ware. Excavations at Bhir Mound in Taxila (now in Pakistan), carried out much earlier, had given a very secure chronology of this ware. There eighteen specimens of the NBPW had been recovered, of which only one was found within the top 1.8 m, while the rest came from depths varying from 1.8 to 3.9 m below the surface. And here is the most significant point in the chronology of the NBPW. At a depth of 1.8 m below the surface were the coins of Alexander in a mint condition. It was therefore clear that at Bhir Mound the NBPW was essentially pre-Alexandrian in date. The 2.1 m thick regular occupational deposit (between 1.8 and 3.9 m) would show that at Bhir Mound the NBPW had made its appearance as early as the sixth century BC. Since the NBPW is essentially a product of the Gaṅgā valley, its emergence in the valley itself may well go back to the seventh century BC. With this kind of comparative data, the beginning of Period III at Hastināpura was dated to early sixth century BC.

Since there was a break of occupation between Periods II and III, and there were also some major elements of cultural evolution from the former to the latter period, as mentioned earlier, the end of Period II is unlikely to have been later than the eighth century BC. With this as the upper limit and with about 2.5 m thick regular occupation deposits, the site is likely to have been occupied by the PGW people around 1100 BC.

As already mentioned, there was not only a break of occupation between Periods I and II, but also a fundamental difference between their respective cultural assemblages. Thus, Period I must have well preceded 1200 BC.

The above chronological assessment of the various periods was made prior to the introduction of the Carbon-14 method of dating in India. It is, however, interesting to note that even after the application of the C-14 method, the position has remained by and large the same. In a paper of mine, published in 1980, I have given full details in this regard. Here, however, we give the gist of it.

There are five radiocarbon dates for Hastināpura, but all these pertain to the upper levels. Taking MASCA correction into account, these fall between 720-600+/-125 BC and 400+/-115 BC. This would indicate that the PGW settlement at Hastināpura may not have begun much before 800 BC. But here is a major snag in the application of these radiocarbon dates. The laboratory report clearly adds a rider that all these samples were mixed with rootlets and hence contaminated. One is thus left with no choice but to reject these Hastināpura dates, and turn round to the radiocarbon data from other PGW sites in the region. The middle PGW levels at Noh, District Bharatpur, Rajasthan, have yielded three C-14 dates. With the application of MASCA correction, these come to: 900+/-225 BC, 805+/-150 BC and 745+/-260 BC. This would mean that the beginning of the PGW settlement at Noh would go back to the eleventh-twelfth century BC. A similar evidence is provided by the site of Atranjikhera, already referred to earlier. Here, again from a mid-PGW level comes a C-14 date of 1025+/-110 BC, which on MASCA correction comes to 1155+/-110 BC. All the foregoing radiocarbon dates fully support the dating of the PGW settlement at Hastināpura, arrived at in 1952 by the comparative method, namely from *ca*. 1100 to 800 BC.

As regards the dating of Period I of Hastināpura, thermo-luminiscence dates from four other Ochre Colour Ware sites in the region, viz. Atranjikhera, Lal Qila, Nasirpur and Jhinjhana, provide collateral evidence (see Lal, 1972). Three of these dates range between 2650 and 2000 BC, another three between 2000 and 1500 BC and two in the neighbourhood of 1200 BC. Thus, the pre-1200 BC date suggested in 1952 for the OCW occupation at Hastināpura was fairly reasonable, if on the conservative side. Maybe, the settlement dated between 2000 and 1500 BC, but no one could be too sure of it.

THE HASTINĀPURA ARCHAEOLOGICAL EVIDENCE VIS-À-VIS THE *MAHĀBHĀRATA*

At Hastināpura, five periods of occupation have been found. Of these, the uppermost two (Periods V and IV) do not at all call for consideration in the context of the *Mahābhārata*, since these are far away from the likely date of that episode. Even Period III will have to be ruled out, since its dates range between 600 and 200 BC. Buddha and Mahāvīra lived in the earlier part of this period and as already stated at the beginning of this paper, if the Mahābhārata episode had any basis in history, it had to be pre-Buddha and pre-Mahāvīra.

We are now left with only Period I and II in the consideration zone. We would have opted in favour of Period I had there not been a very major snag. Of the large number of the Mahābhārata sites enumerated in the earlier part of this paper, only two, viz. Hastināpura and Ahichchhatrā, have yielded the Ochre Colour Ware. Thus, if the Mahābhārata scene is laid in the OCW period, sites like Mathurā, Indraprastha, Pāṇiprastha, Vṛikaprastha, Vāraṇāvata, Tilaprastha,Virāṭanagara, Kurukshetra, Kāmpilya, etc. were not at all in existence at that point of time. Could the Mahābhārata episode have been enacted without these sites? Obviously, not. Hence, the OCW occupation at Hastināpura could not claim its association with the Mahābhārata episode.

Thus, in final analysis of the archaeological evidence from Hastināpura, it is only the Painted Grey Ware Culture that qualifies for its association with the Mahābhārata period. In this context it must also be emphasized that all the sites associated with the

Mahābhārata, to which a reference was made in the earlier part of this paper, have invariably yielded the Painted Grey Ware – a fact which links them together.

And now we recall the most vital archaeological evidence ever recovered from Hastināpura. It is that the destruction of the PGW settlement at the site by a flood in the Gaṅgā. In this context, the texts aver:

> *Gaṅgayāpahṛite tasmin nagare Nāgasāhvaye*
> *Tyaktvā Nichakṣur nagaram Kauśāmbyām sa nivatsyati*

i.e. 'When the city of Nāgasāhvya (Hastināpura) is carried away by the Gaṅgā, Nichakṣu will abandon it and dwell in Kauśāmbī.'

While the aforementioned archaeological evidence duly confirms the destruction of Hastināpura by a flood in the Gaṅgā, we have to find out if there is any evidence about the shifting of the capital to Kauśāmbī. This could best come from a contemporary inscription mentioning that event. But, alas, there is no such inscription! As is well known, we do not yet have any inscription dating prior to the fourth century BC. Then is there any other kind of evidence which may throw light on the issue? The situation is not so bad as it would appear to be. Here again archaeology comes to our rescue. In the lowest levels of Kauśāmbī have been found sherds of the Painted Grey Ware. The Kauśāmbī PGW, however, does not present the ware at its peak, as it does in the middle levels of Hastināpura. The Kauśāmbī specimens bear only simple linear designs and are bereft of the more variegated ones like sigmas, *svastikas*, chain of spirals, etc. The texture is also slightly coarser. But these are the very features which have their own significance. They represent the decadent stage of the ware and thus provide a significant link between the fag-end of Hastināpura and the beginning of Kauśāmbī.

The Kauśāmbī PGW levels are bereft of any NBPW, which appeared only later. And since the emergence of the NBPW in the Gaṅgā valley is likely to go back to the seventh century BC, the PGW levels at Kauśāmbī may well be dated to ca. 800 BC. Thus, put together, the archaeological evidence from Hastināpura and Kauśāmbī would show that the flood at and the consequent desertion of the former site and the establishment of a settlement at the latter can safely be placed around 800 BC. It maybe recalled that the flood occurred during the reign of Nichakṣu who was the fifth ruler in succession from Parīkshit and the latter, in turn, ascended the throne of Hastināpura immediately after the Mahābhārata War. Thus, the War itself may be deemed to have taken place around 900 BC.

The above-mentioned date of the Mahābhārata War, arrived at on archaeological grounds, may now be cross-checked with the literary evidence. The texts say that after Nichakṣu there were nineteen rulers at the Kauśāmbī before Udayana came to the throne. While skeptics may doubt the historicity of the earlier kings of Kauśāmbī, even they would not deny that there existed a king called Udayana, since his contemporaneity with Buddha has never been questioned. It was he who invited Buddha to visit Kauśāmbī and the latter duly responded. Buddha passed away in 487 BC. Thus, Udayana can well be taken to have ruled around 500 BC.

Now comes the most baffling aspect of the issue: How many years did actually elapse between the time of Nichakṣu and that of Udayana? And the answer at once falls in the realm of subjectivity. There have been a number of estimates for the average reign per ruler. There are those who hold it to have been 33 years or even 37, but most sober scholars regard it to be an over-estimation. There are, however, other moderate estimates which deserve consideration. While A.L. Basham puts it at 19 years, Pargiter does it at 18. However, even while recommending the estimate of 18, Pargiter (1962: 181-82) inserts a caveat:

> I have examined 14 series of dynasties from 20 to 30 kings in various eastern and western countries; the longest average just exceeded 24 years in one case, the shortest was about 12 and the average of all was 19; but the average was higher in western countries and lower in the eastern countries. Hence the medium average for these contemporary eastern dynasties must be taken something less than 19 and 18 will be a fair, even liberal estimate.

Like Pargiter, I thought of doing my own exercise; and since the problem is related specifically to India, I thought of examining it in the light of Indian dynasties whose dates are already well known. Thus, to begin with, I took up the Muslim rulers of Delhi. Quṭbuddin Aibak was the first one to occupy the throne of Delhi after defeating Prithvi Raj Chauhan. The last Muslim ruler of Delhi was Bahadur Shah Ẓafar whom the British ousted. Altogether there were 47 rulers from the first to the last, and the total duration of their reigns was 652 years. This gives us an average of 13.9 years per ruler. When this average was presented to scholars, they were not happy with it, arguing that since there were many coups and killings in the various Muslim dynasties, the average is bound to be low. But they forgot that while some of the kings may have ruled for only a couple of years, there were others like Akbar and Aurangzeb each of whom ruled for nearly half-century. But this did not satisfy them. So I took up the ancient Hindu dynasties. Of these, the Guptas gave the highest average, which stood at 17.6 years. On the other hand, the Kaṇvas yielded an average of only 10.5 years and the Śuṅgas that of 11.2. The Mauryas stood in between. On piecing together the averages of all the Hindu dynasties whose reigns are well fixed, it was observed that their overall average was still a little less than 14 years per ruler. Thus, in the Indian context, whether medieval or ancient, the safe and reliable average would be around 14 years.

Taking this average of 14 years per ruler and multiplying it with the number of rulers that preceded Udayana back to the Mahābhārata War, viz. 24(19 from Udayana to Nichaksu and 5 further back to the War), the total period that elapsed would be 14 x 24 = 336 years. Since, as already stated, Udayana was ruling around 500 BC, the date of Mahābhārata War would work out to around 836 BC. It would, however, be too presumptuous to stick to a precise figure like this, and all that one can say is that even the literary-cum-historical analysis supports the date of ca. ninth century BC for the War, arrived at on the basis of the combined archaeological evidence from Hastināpura and Kauśāmbī.

OTHER DATES EXAMINED

But a doubt lurks in my mind if such a late date would please the orthodox school of scholars, for to them the Mahābhārata War is very 'hoary', going back to 3102 BC. The reason why they regard it to be so early is that an inscription at Aihcle, dated to Saka year 556, i.e. AD 634-35, mentions that 3735 years had elapsed since the Mahābhārata War. In this context, it must be emphasized that there is no mention of this kind in any other inscription, earlier or later, and thus one wonders where the author of the Aihole inscription got his information from – suddenly 3735 years after the event. Added to this is the fact that, as the archaeological data indicate, in 3102 BC the entire region where the Mahābhārata story was enacted was bereft of any habitational remains. However, there are a few other dates which do call for consideration: for example, 1424 BC (proposed by K.P. Jayaswal), 1400 BC (A.S. Altekar), 950 BC (F.E. Pargiter) and ninth century BC (H.C. Raychaudhury). As regards the first two dates, it may be recalled that this was the time up to which the Copper Hoard-cum-Ochre Colour Ware Culture may have persisted. But then, with the exception of Hastināpura and Ahichchhatrā, the remains of this Culture have not been found at any of the other sites figuring in the Mahābhārata story. Also conversely, no other Copper Hoard-cum-Ochre Colour Ware site, such as Nasirpur, Bahadarabad, Jhinjhana, Saipai, Bisauli, to name just a few, find any mention in the *Mahābhārata*. How can then one correlate the two?

We are now left with 950 BC (Pargiter) and ninth century BC (Raychaudhury). Pargiter's dating is based on the average of 18 years per reign. However, he himself thought this average of be "liberal", and, as shown earlier, a more reasonable average would be 14 years. Thus, even Pargiter's dating is a little off the mark. Raychaudhury's dating has an additional merit. He steers clear of the oft-debated Pauraṇic data and uses completely independent evidence, viz. that of the later Vedic texts. Thus, basing his arguments on the teacher-disciple sequence given in these texts, and working backwards from the known ones, he observes that the time of Parīkshit, who ascended the Hastināpura throne immediately on the conclusion of the Mahābhārata War, is likely to have been somewhere in the ninth century BC. And this is precisely what our archaeological evidence suggests.

Before we wind up this discussion on the date of the Mahābhārata War, one more aspect of the issue also needs to be examined. In recent years a late Harappan site, encroached upon by the sea, has been discovered at Dvārakā where Kṛiṣṇa lived in the later part of his life. Thus, according to this view, the Mahābhārata episode must have taken place some time at the beginning of the second millennium BC. However, there are two snags in this argument. In the first place, there were various settlements at Dvārakā, ranging from the late Harappan times all the way up to the medieval period, and there is no sound basis to identify any particular settlement, to the exclusion of the others, as having been associated with the time of Kṛiṣṇa. Secondly, and this is no less important a point to be considered, during the occupancy of this particular Dvārakā which is supposed to have been of the time of Kṛiṣṇa, namely at the beginning of the second millennium BC, none of the key-sites associated with the Mahābhārata story, even Mathurā from where Kṛiṣṇa himself hailed, was in existence. What then is the validity of this particular Dvārakā without there having been any contemporary Mathurā?

THE PICTURE AS IT FINALLY EMERGES

The foregoing archaeological evidence from Hastināpura and other sites related with the *Mahābhārata* indicates that it is the Painted Grey Ware Culture that was associated with it and that the event took place some time in the ninth century BC. But then a very vital question still remains unanswered. The *Mahābhārata* speaks of well-organized townships, palatial buildings and extraordinary weapons of warfare, whereas the Painted Grey Ware Culture cannot boast of any of these. A little pondering over the issue would, however, tell you that the answer lies in our proper understanding of the origin and growth of the *Mahābhārata* itself. As stated at the beginning of this paper, there were three factors that came into play. In the first place, even the earliest part of the text, which may not be earlier than the second century BC, is at least seven centuries later than the event itself. Secondly, the earliest version of the text, called the *Jaya* and having only 8,800 verses, suffered at least twice from major interpolations: first it rose to a 24,000-verse document and was known as the *Bhārata*, and now we have the *Mahābhārata* loaded with more than a 100,000 verses. Further, this inflation was not a one-day affair. The process was spread over a period of more than six centuries, right up to the Gupta times in the fourth century AD. And it is well known that the contemporary styles of living, art, architecture, etc., find their way most normally in a book. Thus, the inspiration for the town planning, high-rise buildings, etc., mentioned in the *Mahābhārata* may have come from the then prevailing conditions when the relevant parts were actually written. Finally, it must also be recognized that the *Mahābhārata* was definitely not meant to be a history book wherein facts and figures are expected to be accurately recorded. It was a *prabandha-kāvya*, an epic, in the writing of which the poet's imagination is completely unfettered.

APPENDIX

In the previous pages we referred to the various kinds of subsequent additions to the Mahābhārata story. How this process of interpolation and inflation takes place can be exemplified by something very recent, of which the present writer has had a personal experience.

It was January 1954. I was travelling from Calcutta to Delhi on an official visit. Piercing the mist of the morning, my train, Kalka Mail, steamed into Allahabad railway station. Suddenly I saw thousands and thousands of people jostling with one another on all the five-six platforms the station has. They were desperately trying to get out of Allahabad and never bothered about either buying a ticket or about the class of compartment they were getting into. About thirty people forced their way into my small compartment as well. In about ten minutes the train steamed off. I really could not make out what had happened and the incomers too were so horrified that except for occasional shrieks nothing came out from their mouths. They were completely exhausted and aghast and detrained in batches as their respective stations arrived.

By the evening I too reached my destination. After dinner, I switched on the radio. (There was no television – at least in India – at that time.) In came the news that scores of people had died and hundreds injured in the Kumbha Mela at Allahabad. Lakhs of them had gathered for a dip in the holy Gaṅgā on this occasion. Amongst the people who had assembled were Naga Sādhus (naked mendicants). The news had it that when these Sadhus were moving in, the elephants ran amuck and a few persons were run over. Out of fear, those nearby started running away. This set in a chain reaction and without even pausing to ascertain the extent of the problem, the entire crowd started running helter-skelter. In the great melee that followed, hundreds of men, women and children were trampled over. Many breathed their last on the spot, while hundreds got severely injured. Later, when the crowd somewhat thinned down, police vans took the injured to the hospitals and the dead to mortuaries for subsequent identification and cremation. During the pandemonium, the criminals had a field-day. They not only robbed the women folks of their jewellery, but even molested some of them. Most of these details came out in the newspapers the next morning. Later on the government, as usual, instituted an enquiry, and so on.

That was in 1954. Some thirty years later, we were excavating at Śṛiṅgaverapura, near Allahabad. We had the practice of sharing a week-end evening with the workmen, with a lot of dance and music. On one of the evenings I had a real surprise. One of the workers, playing on his *khartals*, sang to us a ballad which narrated in great detail the Kumbha Mela incident referred to above. Later on I learnt that, besides this Śṛiṅgaverapura version, there were two others, created by the ballad-singers respectively from Jhusi and Daraganj. While the basic fact, viz. that there occurred such and such incident at Allahabad on the occasion of the Kumbha Mela in 1954, constituted the core of all the three versions, each one had a lot of its own *mirch-masālā* (spicy additions and interpolations) so much so that one did not know which one to believe. When such deviations and distortions can take place in the narration of an event which took place before our very eyes and which was also immediately reported by electronic and print media, no wonder that the nucleus of the *Mahābhārata*, which must have been sung in the form a small ballad to begin with, swelled out of all proportions into perhaps one of the largest poetic narratives ever produced by mankind. The simple lesson is that we ought to be discerning enough to separate the wheat from the chaff.

NOTES AND REFERENCES

Gaur, R.C. 1983. *Excavation at Atranjikhera*. Delhi: Motilal Banarsidass.

Gupta, S.P. and K.S. Ramachandran (eds). 1976. *Mahābhārata: Myth and Reality, Differing Views*. Delhi: Agam Kala Prakashan.

Joshi, J.P. 1993. *Excavation at Bhagwanpura 1975-76*. Delhi: Archaeological Survey of India.

Lal, B.B. 1954-55. Excavations at Hastināpura and Other Explorations, 1950-52. *Ancient India*, 10 and 11: 4-151.

——— 1972. The Copper Hoard Culture of the Gaṅgā Valley. *Antiquity*, XLVI: 282-87.

——— 1980. Did the Painted Grey Ware Continue up to the Mauryan Times? *Puratattva*, 9: 64-80.

——— 1981. The Two Indian Epics vis-á-vis Archaeology. *Antiquity*, LV: 27-34.

Pargiter, F.E. 1962. *Ancient Indian Historical Tradition*. Delhi (reprint).

Raychaudhury, H.C. 1972. *Political History of Ancient India*. 7th edn. Calcutta: University of Calcutta.

Sahi, M.D.N. 1978. New Light on the Life of the Painted Grey Ware People as Revealed from the Excavation at Jakhera (Etah District). *Man and Environment*, II: 101-03.

Sharma, G.R. 1969. *Excavations at Kauśāmbī, 1949-50*. Delhi: Manager of Publications, Government of India.

Sharma, R.S. 1975-76. The Later Vedic Phase and the Painted Grey Ware Culture. *Puratattva*, 8: 63-67.

2

Mahābhārata and Archaeology

V.D. Misra

The two great Indian epics, the *Rāmāyaṇa* and the *Mahābhārata*, constitute the bedrock of Indian culture. They have sustained the Indian culture through the ages. However, the forms in which these two epics are available at present, were given to them across the centuries. The core of epics, particularly that of the *Mahābhārata*, would not have been so voluminous. The available *Mahābhārata* itself indicates at least three horizons. First it was known as *Jaya*. In that stage it contained only 8,800 *ślokas*. But with the passage of time this narrative got inflated in size and its name was also changed. Now it was known as *Bhārata* containing 24,000 *ślokas*. In the final form it became *Mahābhārata* with one lakh *ślokas*.[1] It is presumed that by 4th century AD, epic had acquired this form. Scholars like Winternitz pointed out that *Mahābhārata* as it stands, is a work of eight centuries ranging from 4th century BC to 4th century AD. But there is reason to believe that in the available *Mahābhārata* there might be passages antedating the 4th century BC.[2] Didactic portions of the epic, particularly the Śāntiparvan and Anuśāsanaparvan, appear to have been added to it later on, before or around 4th century AD.

There is a controversy about the historical contents of the *Mahābhārata*, as it was long back about the contents of the Homeric epics. One would appreciate that in an age when there was no printing press, the narrative contents of the epic were preserved in floating traditions and as such additions would have been made to the core of the story with the passage of time. In that process, myths and legends would have been created and the original character of the epic changed. But question is whether the epic, as it stands, has historical core at all or it is only a figment of imagination. Before addressing this question one has to carefully separate the wheat from the chaff. The narrative of the *Mahābhārata* centres around a conflict between two cousins – the Kauravas and the Pāṇḍavas. The original theme seems to be simple and the characters involved are associated with contiguous areas. If one has to construct the original story, the places like Hastināpura, Kurukshetra, Indraprastha, Mathurā, Kāmpilya, Bairāt, etc. would constitute an integral part of the story. The epic, as it is available, has acquired an all-India character but incorporation of various regions in the epic was a later phenomenon. But the question remains whether the epic contains historical core or not. In this connection the following points deserve attention[3]:

1. Dhṛitarāshṭra, a son of Vichitravīrya, is mentioned as a king of Kuru-Pañchāl region in the *Kāṭhaka Saṁhitā* (X.6).
2. Devāpi sacrificed for his brother Śāntanu as per the anecdote recorded in the *Ṛigveda* (X. 98).
3. Bharata, an ancestor of the Kauravas and the Pāṇḍavas, is reported to be son of Śakuntala and Dushyanta (*Śatapatha*, XIII. 5, 4, 11-12; *Aitareya Brāhmaṇa* VIII. 23).
4. Parikshit and his son Janamejaya are mentioned in the *Ṛigveda* (VII.18.12); *Aitareya Brāhmaṇa* (VIII. 21, IV. 27, V. 34, VII. 27), and *Śaṅkhāyana Śrauta Sūtra* (XVI. 8.27).
5. Purūrvas and Urvaśī, the originator of the Lunar dynasty, are mentioned in the *Ṛigveda* (X. 95.2-18) and *Śatapatha Brāhmaṇa* (XI. 5.1.1).
6. Devakīputra Kṛishṇa is mentioned in *Chhāndogya Upanishad* (III.17.6).
7. In the *Ashṭādhyayī* of Pāṇini (5th century BC) Krishṇa and Arjuna are deified.
8. Both *Bhārata* and *Mahābhārata* are mentioned in *Āśvalāyana Gṛihya Sūtra.*
9. 'Bhārata' War is mentioned in *Śānkhāyana Śrauta Sūtra* (6th century BC) (XV. 10-16).

Taking the above factors into consideration, it appears that some of the characters found associated with the story of the *Mahābhārata* are found mentioned right from the later Saṁhitas upto Pāṇini. This suggests some historical basis for the story of the *Mahābhārata*.

However, in this connection, the following observations of

Winternitz also deserve serious consideration[4]:

1. Individual sagas, legends and poems which were included in the *Mahābhārata* go back to the Vedic period.
2. The epic *Bhārata* or *Mahābhārata* did not, however, exist in the Vedic period.
3. Many moral stories and sayings which are contained in the *Mahābhārata* belong to the ascetic poetry, from which some Buddhists and Jainas have drawn from 6th century BC onwards.
4. If between the 6th and the 4th centuries BC the epic *Mahābhārata* had already existed, then it was not yet known in the motherland of Buddhism.
5. The existence of the epic called the *Mahābhārata* before the 4th century BC, has not been proved beyond doubt.
6. Between the 4th century BC and the 4th century AD the transformation of the epic *Mahābhārata* into its present form took place.
7. In the 4th century AD the work had on the whole already acquired its present volume, content and character.

Regarding the date of the battle there is considerable diversion of opinion and different dates have been suggested ranging from 3102 to 900 BC.[5] Now if we accept the historicity of the battle of the *Mahābhārata*, we have to accept that Hastināpura, Kurukshetra, Indraprastha, Mathurā, Ahichchhatrā, Kāmpilya, etc., as mentioned in the epic, are identical with their present namesakes, since no duplicate Hastināpura, Mathurā, Kāmpilya, etc., have been located so far. According to the testimony of the Purāṇas, Nichakshu was the fifth descendant of Parikshit.[6] During the reign period of Nichakshu the Gaṅgā washed away considerable portion of Hastināpura and consequently Nichakshu had to shift his capital to Kauśāmbī on the Yamunā.[7] King Udayana of Kauśāmbī, a contemporary of Buddha, stands 24th from Parikshit.[8] If we proceed from 500 BC as a central figure in the reign period of Udayana and tabulate the reign periods of his predecessors on the basis of average of the eighteen years per ruler on the basis of the known historical dynasties, we come to about 950 BC as the date of the battle of *Mahābhārata* as per Pargiter.[9] This date appears to be correct because around this period all the sites having relevance to the story of the *Mahābhārata* are found in occupation and from all these sites, an identical ceramic assemblage typified by the Painted Grey Ware has been obtained.[10]

In this connection, it maybe pointed out that if we accept other proposed dates, a lot of problems would arise. For example, if we accept 3102 BC as the date of the battle, then we have to obtain the archaeological relics pertaining to that age in the upper Gaṅgā Valley but such evidence has not been obtained so far. If we accept 1400 BC as the plausible date of the battle, that would also not solve the problem. Even though, from the upper Gaṅgā Valley, a pottery known as Ochre Coloured Pottery has been obtained from some of the sites related with the story of the *Mahābhārata*, i.e. Hastināpura,[11] Ahichchhatrā[12], etc., but this pottery is not reported from the other sites associated with the story of the *Mahābhārata*. Moreover, it appears that the people who participated in the battle had been using iron weapons[13] but in the present state of our knowledge the antiquity of iron in the upper Gaṅgā Valley cannot be pushed to 1400 BC. But it was definitely known to the PGW using people as is evident from the excavations from Alamgirapur,[14] Ahichchhatrā,[15] Atranjikhera,[16] Jakhera,[17] etc.

Some scholars have pointed out that the archaeological relics as obtained from the Painted Grey Ware sites in the upper Gaṅgā Valley do not match with the narrative of the *Mahābhārata*. But in this connection it maybe pointed out that the epic as it stands today contains horizons of different periods. The narrators went on adding the objects of their ages to the *Mahābhārata*. To understand the truth we have to sort it out from the myth. It is a fact that the bed of Bhīshma, the macehead of Bhīma, the bow and arrows of Karṇa and Arjuna and the glittering palace of Yudhishṭhira of Indraprastha have not been exposed at the relevant excavated sites. But these would never be exposed since these did not exist. On these issues we have to make a due allowance for poetic imagination. For understanding the narrative of the epic these details are not required. In the light of the available evidence, the thesis of Prof. B.B. Lal associating the Painted Grey Ware with the age of the battle of the *Mahābhārata*[18] has the unique merit of reconciling the archaeological evidence with the known literary data.

NOTES AND REFERENCES

1. A.A. Macdonell, *A History of Sanskrit Literature*, p. 239.
2. Maurice Winternitz, *A History of Indian Literature*, Vol. I, p. 44.
3. H.A. Phadake, in, *Mahābhārata: Myth and Reality, Differing Views* (ed. S.P. Gupta and K.S. Ramachandran), pp. 192-93, Agam Kala Prakashan, Delhi 1976.
4. Maurice Winternitz, *op. cit.*, pp. 453-54.
5. For details see B.B.Lal, *Ancient India*, Nos. 10-11, p. 149, S.P. Gupta and K.S. Ramachandran, ed., *op. cit.*, 1976.
6. F.E. Pargiter, *The Purana Text of the Dynasties of the Kali Age*, p. 65.
7. *Ibid.*
8. *Ibid.*
9. F.E. Pargiter, *Ancient Indian Historical Tradition*, 1922, p. 182.
10. B.B. Lal, *Ancient India*, Nos. 10-11, pp. 150-51.
11. *Ibid.*, pp. 10-11
12. *Indian Archaeology: A Review*, 1964-65.
13. S.P. Gupta and K.S. Ramachandran, ed., *op. cit.*, pp. 30-32.
14. *Indian Archaeology: A Review*, 1958-59, p. 50.
15. *Ibid.*, 1963-64, p. 43.
16. *Ibid.*, 1962-63, p. 34; 1963-64, pp. 47-48; 1965-66, p. 9.
17. M.D.N. Sahi, "Excavation at Jakhera (Dist. Etaha) 1986-93: A Brief Report", *Aspects of Indian Archaeology*, Jaipur, 1994, pp. 148-50.
18. B.B. Lal, "Excavations at Hastinapura and Other Explorations in the Upper Ganga and Sutlej Basins, 1950-52", *Ancient India*, Vols. 10-11, p. 151.

3

The *Mahābhārata*
A Critical Study of Archaeological Data

I.K. Sarma

The *Mahābhārata*, a *mahākāvya*, an epic poem, a great *itihāsa*, is regarded by all Indians as the *Pañchama Veda*. The thought contents of *Mahābhārata* belong to *philosophia perennes*. It is believed that places associated with it, the material culture, life patterns, the war weapons, transport of the times and the *Janapadas* (states) associated with the great battle might provide, if researched methodically, an archaeological identity to the culture as well as associated personalities. One should not assert that Mahābhārata War was a fiction or a simple family feud at the most. The wars were epoch-making and historical, the core of the story of wars maybe totally true and many *upākhyānas* have been added down the centuries to highlight and illustrate the *dharma*.

Yadihāsti tadanyatra, yannēhāsti na tatkrachit meaning, whatever has been stated here is found elsewhere, what is not found here is found nowhere.[1] Aśvalāyana refers to *Bhārata* and the *Mahā-Bhārata*.[2] Pāṇini (6th century BC) deals with the compound word *Mahā-Bhārata* thus – "*Mahān Vrīhi-bhāra-bhārata-pravṛiddheshu*". Vyāsa, the author of *Mahābhārata*, was also famous by the names Dvaipāyana and Bādarāyaṇa. Kātyāyana (4th century BC) cites the name of Vyāsa.[3]

As A. Ghosh held, "The result of Archaeology are viable and valuable in their own right, but tradition with all its versions and self-contradictions is immutable. Archaeology can confirm tradition, interpret it or reject it but cannot certainly alter it or create a new one".[4] As also pointed out by Sankaranarayanan, "Literature without Archaeology is lame and Archaeology without literature is blind".[5] Again A. Ghosh's pertinent remark way back in 1954 deserves to be recapitulated.

> It is indeed tempting to utilize archaeological evidence for substantiating tradition, but the pitfalls in the way should be guarded against, and caution is necessary that fancy does not fly ahead of facts.[6]

COMPOSITION AND DATING OF THE *MAHĀBHĀRATA*

The Kurukshetra war of the *Mahābhārata* has been the theme of several symposia and seminars for almost last fifty years. Conscious of the fact that though centuries of additions and alterations have crept in and made the epic, yet we cannot totally disbelieve its historicity at least the kernel of it, i.e. *Jayasaṁhitā*.[7] The *Mahābhārata* originally consisted of 8,800 verses under the title *Jayasaṁhitā*. It was enlarged to 24,000 verses and came to be known as *Bhārata*. Finally, it had one lakh verses and became *Mahābhārata*.[8]

We will examine here the various dates proposed for the events of the Mahābhārata War.

(1) A traditional group of scholars held that the Mahābhārata War was fought around 3102 BC. This is vouched for by the ancient Indian astronomers like Āryabhaṭṭa (5th century AD) and the Aihole *praśasti* (dated AD 634) of the Chālukyan king Pulakesi II.

(2) The second group of scholars date the event to 2600-2500 BC. Varāhamihara (AD 505) followed later by Albiruni (11th century AD), Kalhaṇa (AD 1150)[9] and Hisse-Borala inscription (AD 458) of the time of the Vākāṭaka ruler Devasena, are cited in support of this theory.

(3) The third group of scholars (K.P. Jayaswal and A.S. Altekar) favour a date range of 1400-1000 BC.[10] This is based on a Purāṇic passage which placed 1050 years as a period intervening Parīkshit's birth and accession of Mahāpadma Nanda (382 BC).

(4) The fourth group holds that the Mahābhārata War took place during 10th-9th century BC and that culture represented by the epic belonged to the iron-Painted Grey Ware Culture. War with iron weapons could not be earlier than 1200 BC as the earliest known date for iron implements indicates. The *Mahābhārata* mentions ample variety of swords, arrows, spears and other special weapons of war (*śataghṇī*). An interesting narration relates to the incident at the battlefield when the war part is over and

Kurus lost the battle and their lives. The old king Dhṛitarāshṭra and his queen, who were at the battlefield viewing the tragic losses, were approached by the Pāṇḍavas to pay obeisance to and express regrets at the great loss of their cousins in the war. While Bhīma who had killed Duryodhana approached closer to Dhṛitarāshṭra, Kṛishṇa placed an iron image of the size of Bhīma in between and the old king tightened his grip around this figure, instead of Bhīma, which was crushed to powder. That was the intensity of the feeling of Dhṛitarāshṭra who lost the entire family, more so, his pet son Duryodhana in the hands of Bhīma.[11]

Sankarnarayanan concludes that "in the 25th century BC, there had been one great war fought by the Bhāratas (Kurus). Of course it must have been fought not with iron weapons. Maybe this war had some connection with the Indus Culture and also with Ṛigvedic age."[12] Winternitz, who had studied the problem of the age of the *Ṛigveda* from almost all possible angles, fixed the date of the composition of the present *Ṛigveda* and the culture it represents at 2500 BC.[13] Again in 10th century BC, there was another great war fought by the Bhāratas themselves and this had connection with the advent of the Iron Age. Dvārakā, the headquarter of Kṛishṇa, according to the *Mahābhārata* and the Purāṇas was damaged and submerged in the sea in *c.* 1000-900 BC. This event is graphically described.[14]

ROLE OF KṚISHṆA IN *MAHĀBHĀRATA* AND ARCHAEOLOGICAL EVIDENCES FROM DVĀRAKĀ

The *Mahābhārata* cites Kṛishṇa as a king of Dvārakā attending the Draupadī-*svayaṁvara*. Kṛishṇa was born to Vāsudeva and Devakī who were kept as prisoners at Mathurā by Kaṁsa. Yādavas, tired of the onslaughts of Jarāsandha, moved from Mathurā to Kuśasthalī in Saurāshṭra under the leadership of Kṛishṇa. This was the ancestral motherland and Anārta (ancient name of Saurāshṭra), one among the provinces of the Yādava kingdom. Kṛishṇa founded a city near Kuśasthalī, which was in ruins and named it Dvārāvatī or Dvārakā. It was a highly prosperous city (*Suvraṇa-Dvārakā*). Sudden increase in sea level submerged this famed city and Mausalaparvan of the *Mahābhārata* (XVII, 8, 40-41) narrates how the city was deserted and the sea submerged it. Ancient texts refer to Dvārakā of Kṛishṇa as situated close to the sea, a *vāridurga* fort in water. A copperplate grant dated AD 574, issued by King Simhāditya refers to him as *Dvārakādhipati* cast in the mould of Śrī Kṛishṇa and formed the earliest epigraphic reference to the Kṛishṇa's Dvārakā.[15] The submerged structures discovered by S.R. Rao along with anchors, a seal of conch shell and the lustrous red ware pottery confirm that the Dvārakā of 1500 BC was raised at the confluence of the Gomatī river with the western sea.[16]

Kṛishṇa's effort to avoid Kurukshetra war is an exhibition of highest diplomacy of a king interested in the welfare of the country. The essence of his philosophy as contained in the *Mahābhārata* forms a separate entity – *Bhāgavadgītā*. That Kṛishṇa's life ends at the hand of a hunter called Jarāsandha clearly shows he was a human being. We would mention here an interesting identification of Kṛishṇa's depiction. E.J.H. Mackey discovered at Mohenjodaro a unique steatite tablet.[17] This depicts a young boy uprooting two trees from which emerge two human figures. Mackey compares the scene with uprooting of the trees Yamala and Arjun by the child Kṛishṇa as mentioned in the *Bhāgavata Purāṇa*.[18] V.S. Agarwala accepted this identification and held that Kṛishṇa's life story was known to the people of Indus 4000 years ago. The ancient Kurukshetra appears to be a vast territory encompassing not only the rivers Sarasvatī-Dṛiṣadvatī and Āpayā but also many lakes and hills.[19]

ARCHAEOLOGICAL SETTLEMENT AND THEIR ASSOCIATION WITH THE *MAHĀBHĀRATA*

An indologist of great repute, D.C. Sircar, who worked a great deal on the subject, declared that Mahābhārata War was a myth and not a historical event.[20] But *Devakīputra* Kṛishṇa, is a historical figure mentioned so in *Chhāndogya Upanishad*. We shall now consider the various proto-historic assemblages and find out their relationship and relevance to the great epic.

(1) Look at the extent of the Sarasvatī-Sindhū (Harappan) civilization. An area starting from Sutkagendor in Makran in the West, Alamgirpur (Meerut district in U.P.), Rakhigarhi (Haryana) and Hulas in the East, Manda (Jammu dist.), Rehmandheri (Pakistan) in the North to Daimabad in the South was regarded as the extent of this civilization. Its formative stage is now dated to 3500-3000 BC.[21] But this date is certainly not the earliest as we are yet to dig deep at several early Sarasvatī-Sindhū sites, more

specifically Mohenjodaro itself. The mature or urban phase is bracketed between 2700-2000 BC. J.P. Joshi observed: "To place the *Mahābhārata* prior to the rise of the Harappan culture is unfounded, nor can the culture depicted in the Mahābhārata be associated with the material remains of the Harappan culture or the Indus Civilization."[22] In 3000 BC, the Kuru-Pāñchāla region (Haryana) and U.P. were fully forested and no urban settlements are associated with Early Harappan or mature stages of this civilization. The real riddle of the Harappan Civilization's origin is the *raison d'etre* for its Indianness.[23] Therefore, H.D. Sankalia proclaimed that: "It now appears that the Indus Civilization had its roots in India–Sind, East Punjab, Haryana and Rajasthan".[24] To these we may now add Gujarat-Saurashṭra sites, and in the south right upto Aurangabad (Daimabad) district of Maharashtra. J.P. Joshi says that the Harappans entered Gujarat through the land routes passing through Rann and Kutch.[25] Several towns, rather urban cities of the Harappan Civilization like Lothal, Surkoṭaḍā and now Dholavira have provided enough relics that reflect the essence of urban cultural pattern as revealed in the nucleus of the *Mahābhārata*. In Gujarat, the Harappan towns are geographically closer to each other and to ancient Dvārakā, the city linked to Kṛishṇa-Vāsudeva. A new dimension to the magnificent Harappan urban architecture in stone comes from Dholavira, dist. Kutch, wherein exquisitely carved and polished pillars of hard stone were found in the forecourt and elaborate gateway entrances of the fortified city and the palatial halls within. It is, for the first time, that massive brick defences were bifacially veneered with cut stones.[26] Thus stone pillars of huge size with polished *kumbha* or drum bases, cylindrical tapering shafts and capital elements were known in Harappan cities of Gujarat. These recall the Kuru-Pāñchāla palaces described in the *Mahābhārata*.

(2) Again, the extension of late Harappan phase in western U.P. and Uttaranchal is attested to at Ambkheri (Dist. Saharanpur), Lal Qila and Saipai. The Copper Hoard-Ochre Coloured Pottery Culture of Gaṅgā-Yamunā doab has revealed an early beginning. The metal artefact evidences from Ganeswar region (Jodhpur, Sikar), dated to 2800-2200 BC clearly indicated not only a contemporaniety but a cultural linkage with the Harappans. B.K. Thapar, after a review of the latest evidences, held that the Copper Hoard Culture was in part contemporary with the Indus

Civilization.[27] Excavations at Dvārakā, followed by the recent underwater investigations established the flourishing nature of this city during late Harappan times.[28] A pre-Iron Painted Grey Ware preceded by a Late Harappan/OCP Ware Culture was encountered at Bhagawānpurā (Kurukshetra dist.), Dadheri and Sanghol (Ludhiana dist.), Katpalon and Nagar (Jalandhar dist.) and Manda (Jammu). A date range of 1500-1000 BC was given, but these dates are not absolute.

(3) A look at the distribution pattern of PGW sites reveals that portions of Punjab, north-eastern Rajasthan, northern and eastern Haryana, Western U.P. and old beds of Sarasvatī and Yamunā are integral with this ware. In the adjacent area of north Pakistan (Gandhāra), the Gandhāra-grave culture has a variety of PGW amongst its assemblage.[29] The PGW sites are known now from Tehri-Garhwal in Himalayan region as well.[30] The excavations at the type-sites like Hastināpura (1950-52) and Ahichchhatrā (1944) were small exercises and provided hardly any cultural details of their earliest inhabitants. In fact, the probes are smaller in scope and helped in no way to correlate the epic events of life as postulated and propagated by the excavators.[31] None of these Ochre Ware and PGW sites reflected any urbanized character known from the *Mahābhārata*. Therefore, Late H.D. Sankalia had commented,

> Popular mind, even of the educated Indian, cannot imagine that the authors of the Painted Grey Ware culture whom the archaeologist seem to associate with the Mahābhārata heroes, the Pāṇḍavas, Kauravas and Śrī Kṛishṇa, should have lived only 2700 years ago and not 5000 years ago? Disappointing in every way is the little knowledge that we have of this culture, whom one author dubs as the 'Ganges Civilization'. For except the wide distribution from Punjab in the north to Ujjain in the South and Bahāwalpur in the West on the North Rajasthan and Sind border to Bihar in the East, that is covering the Indo-Gangetic plains, the Vedic and Upanishadic Āryavarta and Brahmarshidēśa it has little to boast of by way of civilization.[32]

IDENTIFICATIONS AND PROBLEMS

En passant, should we not, for a moment, consider the hypothesis that the flourishing fortified towns of the Harappan Civilization such as Mohenjodāro, Harappā, Chānhudāro, Rehmāṇḍherī (all in the Punjab area of Pakistan), Rākhīgarhī (Haryana), Kālibangan (Rajasthan), Lothal, Surkoṭaḍā, Dholavīra and Dvārakā (Gujarat) represent the *Ur-Mahābhārata*? The solid bronze objects from Daimābād are examples of this impact. The portrait of a chariot on a terracotta seal apart, the bronze chariot yoked to a pair of prominently humped and horned bulls and driven by a robust nude male fronted by a dog kept on the tight rein in a commanding pose, are some unique evidences. Certainly such chariots are used in wars, though in this particular case, these appear to be of ritualistic importance and offered to appease a war god. So the several mature and later Harappan culture-sites may have formed the basis of the *Jayasaṁhitā Ur-Mahābhārata.*[33] The Harappan Civilization could not sustain long with its prosperous urbanity in several regions. It has lost its physical civilization, though we see its metaphysics enduring.[34] What were those compelling reasons for the fall and dissolution of such a vast empire? Probably several factors such as frequent floods, loss of the fertility of the soil, tectonic changes, general economic decline, loss of central authority and finally wars.[35]

The widespread Ochre Coloured Pottery (OCP) Culture, alongside the dispersal of copper hoards over the large territories stand witness to the panicky preparedness and the great impact of the Mahābhārata War involving the outlying *Janas* and *Janapadas,* nearly-30 according to an estimate.[36] As an aftermath of the great Kurukshetra war, the dismembered Harappans (Bharatas) reconciled to their fate, reverted to Gaṅgā-Yamunā doab and lingered for a few centuries till the Iron-PGW heralded a new era by 1000 BC. For that matter not a single OCP/PGW, iron using sites of this period provided any evidence of urban life patterns. But these early historical sites find mention frequently and the texts of the epic seem to have undergone several changes at the hands of the later compilers.

CONCLUSION

Notwithstanding what has been stated above, it must be admitted that so far the areas and sites associated with the Mahābhārata War have not yielded tangible data on the date and historicity of Kṛishṇa and Bhārata. Sanskrit scholars and linguists have not yet sifted and stratified the *Jaya, Bhārata* and *Mahābhārata* texts though we firmly believe that Bhārata War was a reality and not a myth. To recapitulate, the following principal sites are associated with the characters and events connected with the Mahābhārata War.

(1) Hastināpura (Dist. Meerut, U.P.), capital of Kauravas founded by Hastin and excavated by B.B.Lal on a meagre scale but lot of planned work at this site, as also at Ahichchhatra is necessary. (2) Barnāwā, ancient Vāraṇāvata, (Dist. Meerut, U.P.), where the Pāṇḍavas entered a lac house; (3) Bāghpat, ancient Vṛikaprastha (Dist. Meerut, U.P.). (4) Indrapat, ancient Indraprastha, (Purānā Qila, New Delhi), excavated by the Archaeological Survey of India; one of the five strategic villages on the Yamunā sought by the Pāṇḍavas to avert the war; (5) Panīpat, ancient Pāṇiprastha, (Haryana). (6) Bairāt, the ancient Virāṭanagar, (Dist. Jaipur, Rajasthan), excavated by K.N. Puri, Pāṇḍavas lived in exile here; (7) Mathurā, birthplace of Kṛishṇa; excavated severally but no pre-PGW levels have been met with; (8) Ancient Kuśasthali, Kṛishṇa came to Saurāshṭra via Sindh and Kutch; (9) Kurukshetra, plains where the present University of Kurukshetra is located. Thānesar (ancient Sthāṇiśvara) lies at the great divider lines between the traditional Madhyadeśa and Uttarāpatha, where excavations were undertaken to establish the antiquity and sequence of the site. Late Harappan or Bārā type material culture is seen at the Baharī and Madarsā mounds within Thānesar.[37]

None of the key-sites in the episode as detailed above have provided archaeological data datable earlier than 1500-1200 BC. No direct evidence was found so far from the excavated site of Hastināpura, Kauśāmbi, Mathurā, Kurukshetra bearing on either Kṛishṇa or *Mahābhārata*. Intensive explorations followed by multi-disciplinary problem-oriented excavation might give some clue on the epic events. As Lallanji Gopal cautioned, "Unless we are sure that we dug at the right spot we cannot overemphasize the negative argument of the absence of archaeological matter".[38]

NOTES AND REFERENCES

1. S.D. Kulkarni, *The Epics Rāmāyaṇa and Mahābhārata*, (Bhishma Series, Vol. III), Mumbai, 1992, p. 171.
2. *Āśvalāyana Gṛihya Sūtra*, III, iv, 4
3. See the *Vārttika* under Pāṇini's *Ashṭādhyāyi*, IV, 1, 97.
4. "Differing Views", in S.P. Gupta and K.S. Ramachandran (Ed.) *Mahabhārata: Myth and Reality, Differing Views*, New Delhi, 1976, pp. 148, 156.

5. "The Purāṇic Text on the Date of the Mahābhārata War: A Historical and Archaeological Approach", *Purāṇa* (Half Yearly Bulletin, All India Kashiraj Trust, Vyāsa Pūrṇima Number, Vol. XXVIII, No. 2, p. 148.
6. A. Ghosh (Ed.), *Ancient India*, Nos. 10 & 11, New Delhi, 1954-55, p. 3
7. P.L. Bhargava, "A Fresh Appraisal of the Historicity of Indian Epics", *Āchārya Udayavīra Shastri Felicitation Volume*, New Delhi, 1987, pp. 106-114.
8. Popular tradition recorded in the *Mahābhārata* itself.
9. S. Sankaranarayanan, *op. cit.*, 1986, pp. 165-66; *Rājataraṅgiṇī*, I, 49 & 51.
10. S.B. Roy, *Date of Mahābhārata Battle*, New Delhi, 1980. He takes into account the archaeological, astronomical and literary evidences and comes to the conclusion that this war took place in the later half of the 15th century BC. The generally accepted date is 1424 BC. Cf. N. Mahadevan, "The Date of Mahābhārata", *Vedāntakesarī*, March 1981.
11. S.D. Kulkarni, *op. cit.*, pp. 300-01.
12. Sankaranarayanan, *op. cit.*, p. 167.
13. M. Winternitz, *A History of Indian Literature*, Calcutta, 1927, pp. 290-310.
14. S.R. Rao, "Marine Archaeological Investigations in Indian Waters and Discovery of Submerged Dvārakā", *Mañjūshā, Dr. S.R. Rao 60th Birthday Felicitation Volume*, Bangalore, 1985, pp. 25-27.
15. *EI*, XI, 1911-12, p. 18, lines 11-12.
16. B.U. Nayak and S.R. Rao, "Existence and Location of Dvārakā City of Mahābhārata Era and its Subsequent Submergence: A Reality or a Myth", B.U. Nayak and N.C. Ghosh (Ed.), *New Trends in Indian Art and Archaeology, S.R. Rao's 70th Birthday Felicitation Volume*, New Delhi, 1992, Vol. II, pp. 479-90.
17. E.J.H. Mackey, *Further Excavations at Mohenjodaro*, Delhi, 1938, Vol. 2, p. 355, Fig. 90.
18. Cited in R.C. Sharma, "Archaeological Dimension of Śrī Krishṇa" in S.D. Trivedi (Ed.), *Essays on Indology, Polity and Administration; Shri R.K. Trivedi Volume*, Delhi, 1989, pp. 17 and 23, fn.1.
19. Yashpal, B. Sahani, R.K. Sood and D.P. Agrawal, "Remote Sensing of the Lost Sarasvatī River", *Proceedings of the Indian Academy of Science (Earth and Planetary Sciences)*, Vol. 89, 1984, pp. 23-24. Also *Purātattva*, No. 17, p. 3.
20. Jagatpati Joshi, "The Mahābhārata and Indian Archaeology", in B.M. Pande and B.D. Chattopadhyaya (Ed.), *Archaeology and History, Essays in Memory of Shri A. Ghosh*, Delhi, 1987, pp. 19-34.
21. B.B. Lal, *The Earliest Civilization of South Asia*, New Delhi, 1997, pp. 9, 246-53; also see for the latest dates on Sarasvatī-Sindhu Civilization, S.P. Gupta, "Revised Chronology of the Indus-Sarasvatī Civilization", T.P. Verma (Ed.), *Dating in Indian Archaeology: Problems and Perspectives*, Mysore, 1998, pp. 42-56. S.P. Gupta, "The Indus-

Sarasvatī Civilization: Some New Developments", in *The Lost Sarasvatī and the Indus Civilization*, Jodhpur, 1995, pp. 180-99.
22. J.P. Joshi, *op. cit.*, 1987, p. 20.
23. Walter Fairservis, Jr., *The Roots of Ancient India*, 1971, pp. 220, 228 and 239.
24. H.D. Sankalia in S.B. Deo and K. Paddayya (Ed.), *Recent Advances in Indian Archaeology*, Pune, 1985, p. 3.
25. J.P. Joshi, "Exploration in Kutch and Excavations at Surkotda and New Light on Harappan Migration", *Journal of Oriental Institute*, Vol. XXII, part 2, 1972, pp. 98-114; Also R.S. Bisht, "The Harappan Colonization of the Kutch, etc.", in Krishna Deva and Lallanji Gopal (Ed.), *History and Art*, Delhi, 1989, pp. 265-71.
26. R.S. Bisht, "A New Model of the Harappan Town Planning as Revealed at Dholavira in Kutch: A Surface Study of its Plan and Architecture" in *History and Archaeology, Prof. H.D. Sankalia Felicitation Volume*, 1989, pp. 397-402. Pls. 1-7. Figs. Also *Purātattva*, No. 20, 1991, pp. 70-81.
27. B.K. Thapar, *Recent Archaeological Discoveries in India*, Unesco, 1987, pp. 100-03.
28. S.R. Rao, "Excavation of Submerged Ports, Dwaraka: A Case Study", in *Marine Archaeology of the Indian Ocean Countries*, Goa, 1987, pp. 47-53.
29. *Purātattva*, No. 17, 1987, p. 3. A.H. Dani in *Mahābhārata: Myth and Reality*, 1976, pp. 61-67.
30. *Purātattva*, No. 17, 1987, pp. 12-13.
31. B.B. Lal, "Historicity of the Mahābhārata and the Rāmāyaṇa: What has Archaeology to Say in the Matter", in *International Seminar on New Archaeology and India*, ICHR, New Delhi, Oct. 15-17, 1988.
32. H.D. Sankalia, *Prehistory and Protohistory of India and Pakistan*, Pune, 1974, pp. 400-03.
33. It is Amarendranath who mooted the idea of linking Late Harappan OCP Ware sites with the Mahabhārata period. See *Mahābhārata: Myth and Reality, Differing Views*, 1976, pp. 19-20, 47-49, 160, 163 and 250.
34. R.E.M. Wheeler, *The Indus Civilization*, London, 1953, p. 95.
35. H.D. Sankalia, *op. cit.*, 1974, pp. 388-89; see also Gregory L. Poshell (Ed.), *Ancient Cities of the Indus, New Delhi*, 1979, Part-IX, pp. 289-323.
36. Niharranjan Ray, in *Mahābhārata: Myth and Reality, Differing Views*, p. ix.
37. Udayavir Singh, "Ancient Relics from Kurukshetra Region", *Kurukshetra*, 1987, pp. 35-40.
38. S.P. Gupta and K.S. Ramachandran, (Ed.), *op. cit.*, p. 13.

4

The Date of Mahābhārata War
Purāṇic and Astronomical Evidence

Mohan Gupta

PURĀṆIC EVIDENCE

According to the genealogy prepared and critically edited, the date of the Mahābhārata War can be arrived at with the help of certain references which occur in almost all Purāṇas. There are two such references – one indicating that at the time of Yudhishṭhira, the Pāṇḍava king, the constellation of the Great Bear (*Saptaṛishi*) were in Maghā (Regulus), the other indicating the time interval between King Parīkshit II and Mahāpadma Nanda, the first king of Nanda dynasty. The first reference is:

आसन् मघासु मुनयः शासति पृथिवीं युधिष्ठिरे नृपतौ।
षड्द्विकपंचद्वियुतः शककालस्तस्य राज्ञश्च।।*

(राजतरंगिणी, I.56)

The sages were in Maghā (α Leonis) constellation at the time when King Yudhishṭhira was ruling the earth: a period of 2526 years has elapsed since the time of the reign of that king.

The same reference in these very words finds place in the *Bṛihat-saṁhitā* of Varāhamihira. In the *Bhāgavata Purāṇa*, this position has been indicated in the following words:

---

*This stanza is actually a citation from the *Bṛihat-saṁhitā* (XIII. 2) of Varāhamihira which is generally and rightly taken to refer to the period that intervened between the Bhārata hero Yudhishṭhira and the commencement of the Śaka-Kāla or Śaka era. – Editor.

सप्तर्षीणां तु यौ पूर्वौ दृश्येते दिवि संस्थितौ।
तयोस्तु मध्ये नक्षत्रं दृश्यते यत् समं निशि।।

तेनैव ऋषयो युक्तास्तिष्ठन्त्यब्दशतं नृणाम्।
ते त्वदीये द्विजाः काले अधुना चाश्रिता मघाः।।

(Bhāgavata XII-2, 27-28)

Among the seven sages, the two sages (stars) are seen in the eastern direction in the sky and are in a straight line with a constellation in the zodiac. They remain with that constellation of the zodiac for 100 human years. They are now, in your period, (the period of Parīkshit II) situated in Maghā.

The second important reference which finds place in almost all the Purāṇas is as under :

यावत् परीक्षितो जन्म यावन्नन्दाभिषेचनम्।
एतद् वर्षसहसं तु ज्ञेयं पंचशतोत्तरम्।।

There are four variation of the last part of this verse in different Purāṇas :

1. ज्ञेयं पञ्चदशोत्तरम् : 1015 :
2. ज्ञेयं पञ्चाशदुत्तरम् : 1050 :
3. ज्ञेयं पञ्चशतोत्तरम् : 1500 :
4. शतं पञ्चदशोत्तरम् : 1115 : या : 1510 :

We know that there were nine Nandas who ruled for 100 years and then came Chandragupta Maurya. The time of Chandragupta Maurya is generally accepted as 324 BC by the historians. But if one computes the time of Chandragupta on the basis of Buddha's *nirvāṇa* in 544 BC, it comes to 354 BC because it is also accepted by historians that Mahāpadma came 90 years after Buddha's *nirvāṇa* which means that if we take the time of Nandas as 100 years, Chandragupta Maurya's time would be – 544 + 190 = 354 BC. Regarding the variations of the above references of Purāṇas, scholars like P.V. Kane and Śrīdharasvāmin, have almost finally settled the issue in as much as they have proved by various arguments that the correct version is ज्ञेयं पञ्चशतोत्तरम्: 1500 : which means that the time interval between Parīkshit and Mahāpadma Nanda is 1500 years. Śrīdharasvāmin, the great commentator of *Bhāgavata*, puts this interval as 1498 years. The arguments of these scholars find support from the fact that the period in which the intervening kings ruled totals up to 1498 or 1500. According to them 22, kings of Bārhadratha dynasty ruled for 1000 years, 5 Vītihotras for 138 years and Śiśunāgas for 362 years. This makes a total of 1500. Śrīdharasvāmin takes the reign of Śiśunāgas as 360 years instead of 362 and hence the time interval according to him between Parīkshit and Mahāpadma Nanda is 1498. The detailed time intervals of these kings have been given in various Purāṇas and they can also be seen in the genealogy of post-Bhārata Magadha kings prepared by me. Starting from Chandragupta Maurya if we add 100 years for Nanda and 1500 years for the period between Mahāpadma Nanda and Parīkshit; the time of Parīkshit comes at 324 + 100 + 1500 = 1924 BC. If we take the date of Chandragupta Maurya as 354 BC and accept the interval as 1498 instead of 1500, the period of Parīkshit comes as 354 + 100 + 1498 = 1952 BC. With the help of the list of generations, we find that there are 30 kings between Parīkshit and Kshemaka, the contemporary of Mahāpadma, in the Paurava dynasty; there are 35 or 36 kings between Mārjārī, the contemporary of Parīkshit and Mahāpadma in Magadha dynasty and there are 30 kings between Bṛihadbala, the contemporary of Parīkshit and Prasenajit, the contemporary of Mahāpadma in Ikshvāku dynasty. If we take an average of 50 years per generation, this also gives a time interval of 1500 years. Thus on the basis of genealogy of the kings, the date of the Mahābhārata War is in the 20th century BC.

ASTRONOMICAL EVIDENCE

We now turn to astronomical references in the *Mahābhārata*, which provide a clear interpretation regarding the date of the Bhārata War. I have for this purpose consulted the critical edition of *Mahābhārata* published by Bhandarkar Oriental Research Institute, Pune, to eliminate any uncertainty about the text. I may also mention some precautions to be taken while interpreting correctly an epic like the *Mahābhārata* for any specific purpose. The *Mahābhārata* being an epic, the great poetry, there are references about the facts and there are also the fictions. We have to carefully segregate the facts from the fictions. Then there maybe some descriptions which are used as rhetoric to heighten the eeriness of the atmosphere which the poet intends to create. The third precaution necessary in all interpretations, whether the interpretation of law, the constitution or a literary work, is that the interpretation should be according to the scheme and the basic theme, that maybe termed as the basic structure of the text. Any interpretation which is repugnant to the basic theme and the basic structure of the text cannot be accepted as correct.

The first important reference in this connection is colloquy of Kṛishṇa and Karṇa:

ब्रूयाः कर्ण इतो गत्वा द्रोणं शान्तनवं कृपम्।
सौम्योऽयं वर्तते मासः सुप्रापयवसेन्धनः।।

सर्वाषधिवनस्फीतः फलवानल्पमक्षिकः।
निष्पङ्को रसवत्तोयो नात्युष्णशिशिरः सुखः।।

सप्तमाच्चापि दिवसादमावस्या भविष्यति।
संग्रामो युज्यतां तस्यां तामाहुः शक्रदेवताम्।।

(*Mbh.*, V. 140.16-18)

According to this dialogue between Karṇa and Kṛishṇa, the latter tells former on way while returning from Hastināpura after the failure of peace-talks with Duryodhana – "Thou Karṇa! Returning from here (to Hastināpura) – tell Bhīshma Pitāmaha, Droṇa and Kṛipachārya – that this is a pleasant month when sufficient fodder for the animals and fuel for the people is available, the forests are full of herbs and fruits, there are no insects or flies, the mud has dried up: the rivers are full of sweet water, neither it is cold nor warm. (This is the best period for war). The Amāvasyā will fall on the 7th day from today and that Amāvasyā will be ruled by the start of Indra. War be begun on that day." The last words in this dialogue are very important. It mentions unmistakably that Amāvasyā falls on 7th day from that day and star ruling in that Amāvasyā is the star of Indra. The star of Indra is Jyeshṭhā and with the help of the description of time, we can safely conclude that this Amāvasyā is Amāvasyā of *Sarad ṛitu* when rivers are full of water, the mud has dried up and forests are full of green herbs and fruits and neither it is hot nor cold. Thus this Amāvasyā can only be the Mārgaśīrsha Amāvasyā according to the North Indian calendar and Kārttika Amāvasyā according to the South Indian calendar, i.e. the Amāvasyā which falls 15 days after the Kārttika Pūrṇimā. According to the scheme of the months and stars also, Amāvasyā with Jyeshṭhā as its star can fall only in Mārgaśīrsha because the star on the 15th day from Mārga Amāvasyā, i.e. of Mārga Pūrṇimā will be Mārgaśīrsha which tallies with Mārgaśīrsha as its month. This gives us a clear clue about the date of the beginning of the war.

The following verses gives a clear duration of the War as 18 days –

अहानि युयुधे भीष्मो दशैव परमास्त्रवित्।
अहानि पञ्च द्रोणस्तु ररक्ष कुरुवाहिनीम्।।

अहनी युयुधे द्वे तु कर्णः परबलार्दनः।
शल्योऽर्धदिवसं चैव गदायुद्धमतः परम्।।

तस्येव दिवसस्यान्ते द्रौणिहार्दिक्य गौतमाः।
प्रसुप्तं निशि विश्वस्तं जध्नुर्यौधिष्ठिरं बलम्।।

(Ādiparvan, I.2, 26-28)

The great warrior Bhīshma fought for 10 days; the general of Kuru army, Droṇa defended it for 5 days; Karṇa, known for his might to smash enemy forces, fought for 2 days; Śalya (the Army Chief of the last day of the Kaurava forces) for half a day and in the afternoon of the same day there was the mace duel between Bhīma and Duryodhana (in which Duryodhana was killed by Bhīma). At the close of that very day Aśvatthāman, Gautama and Hārdikya (Kṛitavarman) massacred the forces of Yudhishṭhira while they were sleeping during the night. This duration of 18 days is of great help to us for the purpose of our computation because this mentions that Bhīshma fell on the 10th day of the War. If we compute from Mārgaśīrsha Amāvasyā, the 10th day would fall on Mārgaśīrsha Śukla 9. This along with another most important reference in the *Mahābhārata*, i.e. the passing away of Bhīshma solves our problem. This reference is as follows:

परिवृत्तोहि भगवान् सहस्रांशुर्दिवाकरः।
अष्टपंचाशतं रात्र्यः शयानस्याथ मे गताः।
शरेषु निशिताग्रेषु यथा वर्षशतं तथा।।

माधोऽयं समनुप्राप्तो मासः सौम्यः युधिष्ठिर।
त्रिभागशेषः पक्षोऽयं शुक्लो भवितुमर्हति।।

(XIII.153. 26-28)

The thousand-rayed Lord Sun has turned (northward) now. Fifty-eight nights have passed while I have been lying on these sharp arrows and they looked like a hundred years. Yudhishṭhira, pleasant month of Māgha has come, only ¾th of it remains and this fortnight is the bright fortnight.

This description gives us the following details:

1. The sun turned northward on the day Bhīshma died. In fact, he was waiting for this Uttarāyaṇa to leave this world, as according to the scriptures, anybody dying during the Uttarāyaṇa goes to heaven.
2. 58 nights had elapsed from the day he fell in the battlefield.
3. The date on that day was Māgha Śukla 8, the word Māgha and Śukla have been mentioned in so many words while Tribhāgaśesha clearly indicates that it was half fortnight which means the 8th *tithi* (15/2 = 7.50). Incidentally, Māghaśukla Ashṭamī is celebrated as Bhīshma Ashṭamī traditionally and indicated as such in the *pañchāṅgas* of the country from times immemorial. This gives strength to our interpretation of the त्रिभागशेष: as Māghaśukla Ashṭamī.

Because the sun turned northward that day, we know from the primary astronomy that the sun entered *Sāyana* Makara on that day, i.e. 10th Rāśi of the zodiac. One Rāśi equals to 30°. The sun crossed 9 Rāśis on that day which means it was at 9 x 30 = 270° on that day. This gives the *Sāyana* position of the sun.

But nothing has been mentioned about the star on that day. The stars of the day, as we know, give us position of the moon on a particular day and these positions are *Nirayana*, i.e. Sidereal longitudes of the moon. Our object is to find out the star of the moon on the day of the passing away of Bhīshma. We know that the war began on Jyeshṭhā star. We also know that Bhīshma fought for 10 days and later on lay 58 nights on arrows which means that there was an interval of 68 days or 67 nights (9 + 58) between the beginning of the War and the passing away of Bhīshma. This shows that from Jyeshṭhā 68th star was ruling on that day. By straight computation it comes as Rohiṇī (2 rounds of zodiac 27 x 2 = 54 + 14 = 68 i.e. 14th star from Jyeshṭhā, i.e. Rohiṇī). Incidentally, there is a reference in the *Mahābhārata*, though interpolated, which mentions that it was the Rohiṇī star and Māghaśukla Ashṭamī on the day Bhīshma passed away. This occurs in Śāntiparvan, Chapter 87 of Gita Press (Gorakhpur) Edition of the *Mahābhārata* and as in the footnotes of Critical Edition.

शुक्लपक्षस्य चाष्टम्यां
माघमासस्य पार्थिव
प्राजापत्ये च नक्षत्रे
मध्यं प्राप्ते दिवाकरे

(Bhīshma passed away) on the 8th *tithi* of bright fortnight of Māgha ruled by the stars of Prajāpati (i.e. Rohiṇī) at the time when the Sun was in the mid-Heaven.

With these two basic and most important references, our search for the two string pillars on which the theory of the date of the Mahābhārata War can be constructed becomes complete. The rest is research, i.e. the interpretation and derivation from the above two important data and support from collateral references.

From the above discussion, we get the following data –

1. The War started on Mārga Amāvasyā, Jyeshṭhā star.
2. Bhīshma fell on 10th day, i.e. on Mārga Śukla 9.
3. Bhīshma passed away on Mārga Śukla 8. Rohiṇī star- 58 nights intervened between the fall of warrior Bhīshma and his passing away.
4. The sun turned northward on the day Bhīshma passed away which means the *Sāyana* (tropical) longitude of the sun on that day was 270° from the vernal equinox of that year.
5. The *Saptaṛishi* or the Great Bear were in Maghā (Regulus or α Leonis).

METHODOLOGY

In astronomy, there is an element known as *ayanāṁsa* or precision of equinoxes. There are two zodiacs or belt of stars and constellations in the sky – one in fixed zodiac or *Nirayana* zodiac followed in the Indian system of astronomy which starts from a fixed point in sky called Aśvinī (Mesha 0) and it has been identified as a point in sky which is 180° away from the bright star Chitrā (spica); the other is moving zodiac (*Sāyana*) which starts from the vernal equinox point of a year which is styled as Aries 0 and which shifts backwards every year at the rate of 0°-0'-50" (mean). This is followed by Western astrologers. It has got an accelerating motion and the current rate of precision is 50.3" per year. During the Mahābhārata times, it must have been less. The accumulated difference between the fixed (*Nirayana*) zodiac and the moving (*Sāyana*) zodiac of a year is called the amount of precision or *ayanāṁsa*. This means if the *ayanāṁsa* of a year can be found out, its time interval can be worked out from a given year on the basis of the rate of *ayanāṁsa*. In the present case, we have *Sāyana* longitude of the Sun and the *Nirayana* longitude of the Moon. Because the lunar day or *tithi* has also been given which is based on the *Nirayana* longitudinal difference of the Sun and the Moon, it is possible to work out the *Nirayana* longitude of the Sun. From both *Sāyana* and *Nirayana* longitudes of the Sun, the *ayanāṁsa* can be worked out by simple subtraction.

The *tithi*s or lunar days depend on elongation of Moon from the Sun, i.e. their difference in longitudes. When they are 12° apart, Pratipadā or the first *tithi* ends; when they are 24° apart, Dvitīyā or second lunar day or *tithi* ends. Thus every *tithi* is 12° extent in terms of angular difference between the Sun and the Moon and when they are 180° apart, it is Pūrṇimā. Similarly, a star (*nakshatra*) is 13°-20' extent from 0° of Aśvinī or Mesha 0° and they are 27 in number. Rohiṇī is the fourth star. The astronomical conversion of the date Māgha Śukla 8 Rohiṇī is –

a. The Moon is between 40° to 53°-20′.
b. The difference between Sun and Moon is between 84° (12° x 7) and 96° (12° x 8).
c. The *Saptaṛishi* in Maghā means that the solstitial collure is in Maghā or the *Nirayana* longitude of the Sun on the point of *Dakshiṇāyana* (summer solstice) in the Maghā star, i.e. between 120° and 133°-20' (Maghā is 10th star in Zodiac i.e. 13°-20' x 10).

Following equations can be formed-

Moon – Sun = 84° to 96°.
Moon = 40° to 53°-20′
Sun = (1) Moon–84° or (2) Moon–96°
Moon is between 40° and 53°-20′
Or (adding 360° for the sake of convenience)
Between 400° and 413°-20′

There are four options for the Sun –

Sun = 400° – 84° = 316° (1)
= 400° – 96° = 304° (2)
= (413°-20′) – 84° = 329°-20′ (3)

$$= (413^\circ\text{-}20') - 96^\circ = 317^\circ\text{-}20' \quad (4)$$

But from (c) above we know that the Sun is between 120° and 133°–20′ (Maghā) on the day of summer solstice (*Dakshiṇāyaṇa*) which means it will be between (120° + 180°) = 300° to 313°-20′ on the day of winter solstice (Uttarāyāṇa). Hence out of the above four equations, only (2) i.e. 304°. can be accepted, the others are out of the limits of 313°-20′. This gives us the *Nirayana* longitude of the Sun on that day as 304°.

The *nirayana* longitude of the Sun = 304°
The *sāyana* longitude of the Sun = 270°
Hence *ayanāṁsa* = 304°–270° = 34°
The time interval from the 0 *ayanāṁsa* year is

$$\frac{34}{0^\circ\text{-}0'\text{-}50''} = 2448 \text{ years}$$

The astronomical tradition gives us AD 499 as the year or 0° *ayanāṁsa*. Hence, 2448 – 499 = 1949 BC is tentatively the year of Bhīshma Nirvāṇa.

Having fixed this tentative date for the Bhārata War, the historians' task is almost over because precise date is not important for him. But the interpretation of the *Mahābhārata* for the date is not complete nor the task of an astro-scientist until other references regarding position of planets, comets and stars are also looked into and a consistent conclusion is drawn which fits all important references. Because the stars of the important days have been given along with position of planets, it should be possible to arrive at an exact date and day when the War began and also the succeeding events till the passing away of the great warrior Bhīshma.

We have known from above that the War began on Mārga Amāvasyā (as per Kṛishṇādi or North Indian *pañchāṅgas*) or Kārttika Amāvasyā (as per Shuklādi or South Indian *pañchāṅgas*), i.e. on the Amāvasyā which falls after Kārttika Pūrṇimā. In the following discussion, all references of lunar days and months will be with reference to North Indian *pañchāṅga*. The greatest confusion so far while fixing the position of planets, has been regarding the identity of these planets. In the *Mahābhārata*, the general allegation is that there are two or more contradictory or astronomically impossible references regarding the position of the planets; hence any consistent interpretation is impossible. But if we go through the text a little carefully, there is no such confusion nor contradiction. In fact, in the *Mahābhārata*, particularly in Bhīshmaparvan, there are references to comets and not to planets. If we compare these names of comets, which resemble the names of planets, with the great astronomical treatise of Varāhamihira, viz. *Bṛihat-saṁhitā*, there will be no difficulty in identifying them. Varāha in Ketuchāra Adhyāya of *Bṛihat-saṁhitā* has given a thousand types of comets. They are –

(a)	Sons of Sun	(रविजाः)	= 25 types of comets
(b)	Sons of Fire	(अग्निपुत्राः)	= 25 types of comets
(c)	Sons of Death	(यमपुत्राः)	= 25 types of comets
(d)	Sons of Earth	(धरातनयाः)	= 22 types of comets
(e)	Sons of Moon	(सोमपुत्राः)	= 3 types of comets
(f)	Brahmā's Son	(ब्रह्मसुत)	= 1 type of comet
(g)	Sons of Venus	(शुक्रपुत्राः)	= 84 types of comets
(h)	Sons of Saturn	(शनिपुत्राः)	= 60 types of comets
(i)	Sons of Jupiter	(गुरुपुत्राः)	= 65 types of comets
(j)	Sons of Mercury	(बुधपुत्राः)	= 50 types of comets
(k)	Sons of Mars	(भौमपुत्राः)	= 60 types of comets
(l)	Sons of Rāhu	(राहुपुत्राः)	= 33 etc.

The above list includes धरातनय, रविज and सोमपुत्र which also mean respectively the Mars, the Saturn and the Mercury in astrological parlour. Other terms like श्वेतो ग्रह (white planet) or अंगारक also create confusion being indicative of Venus or Mars whereas actually they are not, as per the context. But the basic characteristics of comets, which have also been styled as *grahas* or generally *mahāgrahas* is that they are all fiery – प्रज्वलितौ, ज्वलनार्कवर्णः पावकप्रभः, etc. are the epithets used for them and from them we can distinguish comets from planets in spite of similarity in names. Varāha has given this symptom of comet –

अहुताशाऽनलरूपं यस्मिंस्तत्केतुरूपमेवोक्तम्

(BS, Ketuchāra - verse 3)

Not being fire, if it looks like fire, it must be a Ketu or comet

Another caution while interpreting these references is that, at time these comets, sons of Saturn, Jupiter, or Venus have been referred to not as their sons but simply as बृहस्पतिः (Jupiter), शनैश्चरः (Saturn) or शुक्रः (Venus) which can be recognized by context and the meaning becomes clear by लक्षणा वृति (Indicative power) – one of the three powers of words – अभिधा, लक्षणा and व्यंजना (narrative, indicative and suggestive powers) when due to astronomical improbability, there is मुख्यार्थबाधा, obstruction to the principal meaning. Thus –

संवत्सरस्थायिनौ ग्रहौ प्रज्वलितावुभौ,
विशाखायाः समीपस्थौ बृहस्पतिशनैश्चरौ

(*Mbh.*, Bhīshma, 3.25)

Both the fiery comets – Bṛihaspati and Śanaishchara which stay in a star for a year, are now near the Viśākhā star.

Because Bṛihaspati, the planet, does not stay in a star for a year, the principal meaning (मुख्यार्थ) is obstructed and hence by लक्षणा, the indicative meaning has to be accepted which makes it a reference to a comet and not to a planet. Besides, these *grahas* have been qualified by the epithet प्रज्वलितौ (fiery, burning) which confirms the meaning. I have observed that all these references to comets occur in Bhīshmaparvan, Chapter III, the object of which is not so much to indicate the true sky position of these times as to heighten the eeriness of the atmosphere of war and destruction because these comets in the public perception are harbingers of death and destruction – the particular stars indicating particular warring country – as per astronomical Siddhānta. Thus (1) श्वेतो ग्रहः (*Mbh.*, 6.3.11) (BS, Ketuchāra, 4/39) destroys one fourth of population त्रिभागशेषाः प्रजाः कुरुते (2) Kapālaketu (*Mbh.*, 6.3.12) (BS, 11/55, 11/31) in Pushya destroys the king of Magadha; श्यामो ग्रहः (*Mbh.*, 6.3.15) (BS, 11/38.58) causes destruction of the sovereign in Jyeshṭhā, etc. Similarly, four other comets have been mentioned which can be identified easily and which justify the statement –

निःसरन्तो व्यदृश्यन्त सूर्यात् सप्त महाग्रहाः।

(8.26-24)

The seven great comets appeared as if coming out of the Sun.

With this background, we can easily determine the position of various planets at the time of Bhārata War.

POSITION OF VARIOUS PLANETS

Sun and Moon

As we already know, the War began on Mārga Amāvasyā, Jyeshṭhā star as anticipated and probably planned by Lord Kṛishṇa. Hence, the Moon is in Jyeshṭhā (226–40 to 240). The Sun being with Moon, is also in Jyeshṭhā or Vṛischika Rāśi.

Mars

There is a clear reference to Mars which is not comet –

कृत्वा चाङ्गरको वक्रं ज्येष्ठायां मधुसूदन
अनुराधां प्रार्थयते मैत्रं संगमयन्निव।

(Udyoga, 143.9)

The Mars transiting retrogade in Jyeshṭhā (Antares or α Scorpi) applies for Anurādhā, the star of Mitra (a form of Sun) as if providing a company for her. The other reference मघाष्वाङ्गारको वक्रः is in Bhīshmaparvan, Chap. III which, as I have said, is full of references to comets and not to planets and the context also makes it clear.

Mercury and Venus

Both are in Jyeshṭhā as per

भृगुसूनु र्धरासूनुः शशिजेन समन्वितौ

(Śalya, 11.18)

The son of Bhṛigu (Śukra or Venus).
The son of Earth (Maṅgala or Mars).
and the son of Moon (Budha or Mercury) were together.

शुक्रः प्रौष्ठपदे पूर्वे समारुह्य विरोचते
उत्तरे तु परिक्रम्य सहितः समदीक्षते।

(Bhīshma, 3.135)

This cannot be a reference to Venus but to a comet known as son of Śukra referred to as Śukra alone in this verse because Venus is maximum 60° apart from the Sun and because is in Vṛischika, Venus cannot go beyond Kanyā or Makara. Praushthapada or Uttarā and Pūrvā Bhadrapadā are in Mīna. This verse is also in Bhīshmaparvan, Chapter III, which I have mentioned, contains all references to comets.

Jupiter

Karṇaparvan (94, 51) gives clear indication –

बृहस्पतिः सम्परिवार्य रोहिणीम्
बभूव चन्द्रार्कसमो विशांपते।

O King ! Jupiter having accosted Rohiṇī (Aldebaran or α Tauri) has become like Sun and Moon (who have the prerogative of accosting Rohiṇī usually).

As discussed earlier, निशाखाया समीपस्थौ बृहस्पति शनैश्चरौ (Bhīshma, 3.27) is clearly a reference to comets, the epithets being ग्रहौ प्रज्वलिताबुभौ, both fiery *grahas*.

Saturn (Śani)

There are two clear references –

(i) प्राजापत्यं हि नक्षत्रं ग्रहस्तीक्ष्णो महाद्युतिः
शनैश्चरः पीडयति पीडयन् प्राणिनोऽधिकम्।

(Udyoga, 143.8)

The great bright and sharp planet Śanaiśchara (Saturn) is afflicting the Prajāpati – star (i.e. Rohiṇī), thus indicating great suffering to the people.

(ii) रोहिणीं पीडयत्येषः स्थितो राजन् शनैश्चरः।

(Bhīshma, 2.32)

O King! This Śanaishchara (Saturn) is afflicting Rohiṇī.

Thus the Saturn is clearly either in Rohiṇī star or near it, thereby afflicting the star by its aspect.

Rāhu

Rāhu and Ketu are north and south nodes of Moon. There is a clear reference in Bhīshmaparvan that there was eclipse on the day of War and also on the Pūrṇimā (Full moon day) preceding it –

चन्द्रसूर्यावुभौ ग्रस्तौ एकाह्ना हि त्रयोदशीम्
चन्द्रसूर्यावुभौग्रस्तौ एकमासीं त्रयोदशीम्
अपर्वणि ग्रहेणैतौ प्रजासंशयमिष्यतः।

(Bhīshma, 3.32)

अलक्ष्यः प्रभया हीनः पौर्णमासीं च कीर्तिकीम्
चन्द्रोभूदग्निवर्णश्च पद्मवर्णे नभस्तले।

(Bhīshma, 3.32)

The Sun and the Moon both have been eclipsed within a month on a Trayodaśī (13th lunar day). This unusual phenomenon of eclipses on a day other than the New Moon or Full Moon suggests destruction of the people... The Kārttika Pūrṇimā looked lustreless; the Moon became pale in the lotus-coloured sky.

Because of eclipses, the Rāhu or Ketu should be with the Sun and the Moon i.e. in Jyeshṭhā or nearby. With these derivations the map of heavens on the day of the beginning of the War is like this –

Mārga Amāvasyā
Kurukshetra
Sunset time

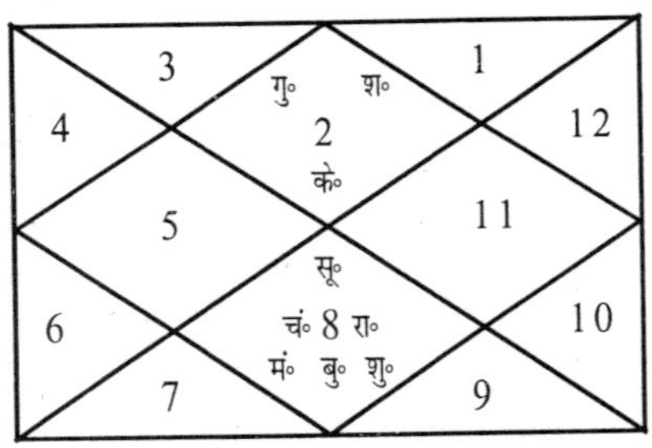

Astrologically, because all planets are divided in two houses, it indicates a clear war situation.

Our next task is to find out the precise year and precise day of the War so that when we make actual calculation of planets and stars for the day, we can compare how far the planetary position tallies with the position arrived at above. For that I had to wander with the help of calculator and computers a few years before and after 1949 BC – our tentative date arrived earlier. I struck at 1952 BC as the year when most of the conditions referred to in the *Mahābhārata* and discussed above satisfy. It was after months and months of constant thinking and calculations that I could fix up the precise date and calculate planetary positions and corresponding Julian year and dates. The results of my calculations are as follows:

		BC	Kali Year	Before Śaka	Julian Year
i	Beginning of Kali	3102(18/2) -(1150)	01 +(1150)	3179 -(1150)	1612 +(1150)
ii	The year of Mahābhārata War	1952	1151	2029	2762
iii	The date of Mahābhārata War	17th Oct. Thursday	Mārga 30 Guruvārā	Mārga Amā	17th Oct.
iv	Number of days from beginning of Kali (*ahargaṇa*)		420280 days		

I have expressed this date in the following words-

अमायां मार्गमासस्य एकपञ्चशिवे कलौ नक्षत्रे शक्रदैवत्ये आसीत् भारत भारतम् ।

v.	Julian days since the beginning, upto the date of Mahābhārata War		1008745		

vi. Planetary position : (as on 17th October, 1952 BC)

Graha	*Mean Position*	*True Position*	*Star*
Sun	235°-35′-18″	7^{s}-24°-37′-59″	Jyeshṭhā
Moon	240°-54′-02″	7^{s}-25°-57′-2″	Jyeshṭhā
Mars	262°-30′-30″	7^{s}-29°-57′-30″	Jyeshṭhā
Jupiter	42°-17′-37″	1^{s}-17°-35′-37″	Rohiṇī
Saturn	24°-11′-52″	0^{s}-13°-20′-52″	Bharanī
Rāhu	237°-28′-18″	7^{s}-27°-28′-18″	Jyeshṭhā
Ketu	57°-28′-18″	1^{s}-27°-28′-18″	Mṛigha

Sunset
Kurukshetra
17-10-1952 BC

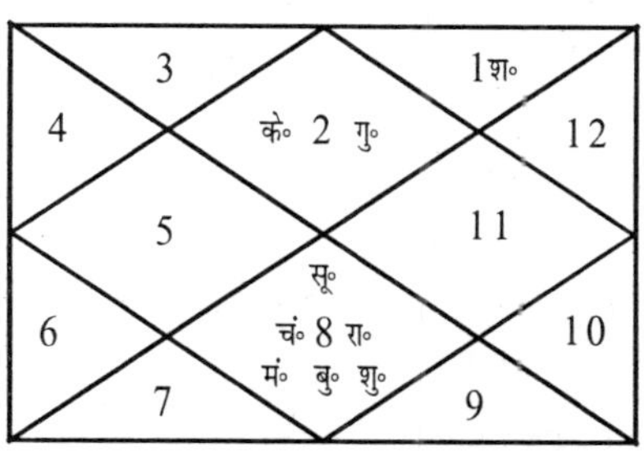

Ayanāṁsa = 30°-49′-45″(Lahiri)
Annual Rate of Precision 49.42″

vii.	The War ended	-	Pausha Kṛishṇa 2 Pushya star 3rd Nov., Sunday
viii.	Bhīshma died	-	Magha Śukla 8 Rohiṇī star 23rd December, Monday
	Ahargaṇa	=	420 347
	True Sun	=	300°-56′-23″ (*Nirayana*), 270° *Sāyana*
	The Moon	=	40°-54′-28″ (*Nirayana*) Rohiṇī Star

Eighth lunar day (Ashṭamī) in the morning.
It was ninth (Navami) at the time of Mid-day.

All coordinates precisely tally with the references in the Great Epic, as discussed earlier. Other important events:

1.	Birth of Lord Kṛishṇa	23rd June, 2045 BC, Wednesday Kali 1058, before Śaka 2122 Bhādra Kṛishṇa 8, Rohiṇī
2.	Birth of Yudhishṭhira	2nd August, 2045 BC 2122 before Śaka
3.	Beginning of Yudhishṭhira Era	2099 before Śaka (2526-427)
4.	Banishment of Pāṇḍavas	9th May, 1965 BC – Āshāḍha Kṛishṇa 8 Kali 1138
5.	Return of Pāṇḍavas from seclusion	16th May, 1952 BC – Āshāḍha Kṛishṇa 8 – Kali 1151 (Period of banishment 4755 days)
6.	Birth of Parīkshit	1951 BC
7.	Death of Dhṛitarāshṭra Maharshi Veda Vyāsa started writing *Mahābhārata*	1932 BC 1932 BC
8.	Passing away of Lord Kṛishṇa	1919 BC
9.	Pāṇḍavas left for forest Coronation of Parīkshit	1917 BC – Kali 1186 1917 BC – Kali 1186
10.	Passing away of Pāṇḍavas Death of Parīkshit and Coronation of Janamejaya	1916 BC 1857 BC – Kali 1246

To conclude, 17th of October 1952 BC, Thursday, Mārga Kṛishṇa Amāvasyā, Kali 1151 or Before Śaka 2029, Julian year 2762 is the date when Mahābhārata War began. In my detailed treatise on the subject, I have successfully refuted all theories which fix this date as 3138 BC, or 2448 BC, or 1400 BC, or 3102 BC. Neither the planetary position as mentioned in the *Mahābhārata* nor the phenomena of Uttarāyaṇa on the date of passing away of Bhīshma do obtain on respective days on these dates.

5

The Year of Kaurava-Pāṇḍava War

P.V. Holay

INTRODUCTION

The *Mahābhārata* is a religious poetry composed in three stages. Initially it consisted of only 8,800 verses composed by Kṛishṇa-dvaipāyana Vyāsa. The book was called as *Jaya*. Subsequently, in the second stage it was modified and enlarged with a total number of 24,000 verses by Vaiśampāyana. It was named as *Bhārata*. At the third stage, the book was modified and composed by Sauti, son of a charioteer Lomaharshana, with total number of about 1,00,000 verses. When a novel or poetry is written on historical events, its author does not change the particulars about their dates, though the events appear to be described in a fantastic manner. The particulars about the date of events are noted in *Mahābhārata* in *tithis* and *nakshatra* system prevalent in those days. However, we get three sets of planetary positions in the text; the earliest one describes the position of planets in the sky during the War period.

DIARY AND YEAR OF THE WAR

When we search the time of the Bhārata War[1], we have to find out (i) the diary of various important events before and during the War and (ii) the year of the Bhārata War. In the present paper, the aim is to fix the year of the Bhārata War. The diary of the Bhārata War is only an ancillary subject. I am therefore giving the diary of Bhārata War without going into the details of its proof. Such details are given by me in a Marathi book on the said subject.

SUMMARY OF THE DIARY

Kṛishṇa went to Hastināpura for peace talks in the month of

Kārttika. The peace talks failed. When Kṛishṇa was on his route to the town Upaplavya to visit Pāṇḍavas, Karṇa met him. Though Kṛishṇa told Karṇa that they should start the War on Kārttika Amāvasyā (new-moon day), the War did not start on that day. The Karttika month was followed by an *Adhikamāsa* (intercalary month). At the end of this month, on the day of *amāvasyā*, there was a solar eclipse at the dawn of the day. Thereafter the War began on the same day. On the tenth day after the commencement of the War, Bhīshmāchārya was fatally wounded. Due to compelling circumstances for both the sides, the War was stopped for 12 days. Thereafter the War resumed and continued for 8 days. It came to an end with the death of Duryodhana.

NAKSHATRA SYSTEM

For fixing the year of the Bhārata War, it is necessary to know the *nakshatra* system in the then prevalent calendar. There was no practice of naming the days as Sunday, Monday, Tuesday, etc. during the time of the Bhārata War. The days were named according to the position of the moon in the *nakshatras*. The path of the moon in the sky (ecliptic) was divided into 28 equal divisions (vide Annexure 2) marked by small group of stars or asterisms called *nakshatras*. At present, we count only 27 *nakshatras*. If we arrange these *nakshatras* according to their names in their respective divisions, one division between Dhanishthā and Śatabhishaj remains vacant. It was presumed that moon travels about one *nakshatra* division in a day. It takes 27 days to complete its journey in the *nakshatra* circle. It completed the journey of three circular rounds covering 81 *nakshatra* at the rate of one *nakshatra* per day and required additional day and *nakshatra* at the end of third round. This 28th *nakshatra* was called Abhijit. I have named it Purābhijit (please see Annex. 2). Positions of the planets were marked according to the name of the *nakshatra* divisions they occupied.

TITHIS

The *tithi* or the lunar day is a peculiarity of Hindu calendar. Moon takes about 29.5 days to cover a period from one new-moon to another, which is called a lunation (lunar-month). Hindus divide a lunation in 30 equal parts of about 23 hrs., 36 mins. each. For computing *tithis*, the angular distance between the sun and the moon is measured after the event of new-moon (अमावस्या). If the angle is between 0° to 12° the day is called 1st *tithi* and if the angle is 12° to 24°, it is called 2nd *tithi* and so on. This practice is followed after the introduction of Siddhānta system of astronomy probably by Āryabhaṭa I.

In all other countries as well as in the science of astronomy, lunar dates are computed as 'age of the moon' in number of days after the beginning of the lunation. Thirty days and 29 days are counted in alternate months as lunar dates, because its average length is 29.5 days. This calendar system was followed during the period of Bhārata War by the then Hindus.

NAMES OF THE LUNAR MONTHS

माघोयं समनुप्राप्तो मासः सौम्यो युधिष्ठिर।
त्रिभागशेषःपक्षोयं शुक्लो भवितुमर्हति।। Anu, 167,28।।
निवृत्तमात्रे त्वयने उत्तरे वै दिवाकरे।
समावेशयदात्मानमात्मन्येव समाहितः।। Śānti, 47,3।।

Many scholars search the year of Bhārata War on the basis of these verses. They give more importance to the word Māghamāsa. The lunar month in which full moon appears in the vicinity of the star Regulus (मघा) is called Māghamāsa. Other months are given their names in a similar way. In those days the practice of naming the months was different from that which exists today. The fact that two intercalary months occur in five years and five days, was given more importance while computing the years of sacrifices. An artificial year, with one day more in length, i.e. 366.25 days (instead of 365.25 days) was computed to adjust the intercalary months. As a result, if the first year in the set of fifteen years[2] was counted to start on the day of vernal equinox (वसंत संपात, i.e. 21st of March), the sixteenth year was expected to start on the 5th day of the next month, i.e. April. This period comprised six intercalary months. One fortnight (पक्ष) of the last lunar month was therefore dropped in every set of 15 years. It was therefore necessary to compute *Amānta māsa* (months ending in new-moon day) in the first set of fifteen years and *Paurṇimānta māsa* (months ending in full-moon day) in the second set of fifteen years. The calendar therefore included practice of omission of *paksha* (पक्षय).[3] The names of the lunar month therefore lost their relevance with the name of the *nakshatras*. The fifteen-year luni-solar *yuga* confused Duryodhana at the time of Gograhaṇa war. It also bewilders modern scholars. They think that the combination of the *tithi* S.8 with Rohiṇī *nakshatra* pertains only to Phālguna month. The author therefore gives separate annexure (No. 8) to show that once they also formed part of Māgha month as computed during the Bhārata War.

In this context the following verse assumes importance –

निवृत्तमात्रे त्वयने उत्तरे वै दिवाकरे।
समावेशयदात्मानमात्मन्येव समाहितः।
शुक्लपक्षस्य चाष्टम्यां माघमासस्य पार्थिव।
प्रजापत्ये च नक्षत्रे मध्यं प्राप्ते दिवाकरे।। Śānti, 47AA,3

Bhīshmācharyā died on (i) bright-eighth *tithi* (S.8) of the month of Māgha in the mid-noon of (ii) Rohiṇī (*Prajāpti*) day on the day of (iii) winter solstice. These three are sufficiently important particulars for our astronomical calculations. When the year of war was searched with this data by the method of precession of equinox, it is found as 3341 ± 240 years (see Annexure 3). This is the only verse in the *Mahābhārata*, which in clear words tells us the *tithi* and *nakshatra* of the day Bhīshmāchārya died. Other verses are ambiguous. As of rule we have to rely on unambiguous sentences and reject others.

SOME SPECIFIC INSTANCES SHOWING HOW SCHOLARS WERE MISLED

It is desirable to give here specific instances demonstrating how the name of the month Māgha has misled some scholars to come to wrong conclusions. Following are the names of the scholars with their respective findings about the year of the war –

(i) K.L. Daftari-1196 BC[4], (ii) V.G. Aiyer-1193 BC[5], (iii) D.N. Khedwal-1963 BC[6], (iv) R.P. Poddar-1500 BC.[7] All these scholars have based their findings on two events (a) Bhīshmāchārya died on the day of winter solstice and (b) on Māgha Śukla 8th. They presumed that the system of naming the lunar months was according to present *Siddhānata Jyotisha* system. (v) K.V. Abhyankar[8] presumed that Bhīshmāchārya died on Māgha Kṛishṇa 5th, where the month was named according to present system of *Siddhānata Jyotisha*. He further tried to find out the maximum difference in number of days between winter solstice and the aforesaid date of expiry of Bhīshmāchārya in last few years. The difference was found to be 69 days. He presumed that this is the period of precession of winter solstice from the date of the war. He therefore concluded that the year of the war was 3000 BC. His calculations were based on two wrong presumptions – (a) the date of death of Bhīshmāchārya was 12 days subsequent to the date mentioned in the *Mahābhārata*, i.e. Māgha K.5, (b) present *Siddhānata* system of naming the lunar months was followed in the relevant period. According to Abhyankar, the *nakshatra* of the day of the demise of Bhīshmāchārya was in Viśākhā *nakshatra* which is nowhere stated in the text. P.C. Sengupta (1947) finds that Bhīshmāchārya died on Māgha K. 7 of 2449 BC which means the *nakshatra* of that day was Ānurādhā, the *tithi* and *nakshatra* of the day of death of Bhīshmāchārya stated by K.D. Abhyankar and P.C. Sengupta are nowhere stated in *Mahābhārata*. They are hypothetical. This is contrary to the very premises on the basis of which we started our investigation. If a researcher is allowed to change the particulars of dates of important events, he will have a liberty to draw any conclusion of his choice.

P.C. SENGUPTA'S KALIYUGA

P.C. Sengupta searched the antiquity of the concept of Kaliyuga in Hindi calendar. He relied on the *Vedāṅga Jyotisha* and some Purāṇas to know the lunar day at the beginning of *Yugas*, and found that it was the full-moon day of Māgha month coinciding with winter solstice. The antiquity of such day as calculated by him is 2454 BC. Thereafter on the basis of some probabilities and surmises and without any verifiable material evidence, he came to the conclusion that Kaliyuga of the *Mahābhārata* was 2454 BC. In fact, he found the antiquity of *Ṛik*-text of *Vedāṅga Jyotisha*.[9] The *Yuga* he searched did not bear the adjacent *Kali* in the relevant texts. They are small luni-solar cycles comprising 5 years or 19 years. It appears that he was not aware that even before the *Vedāṅga Jyotisha*, during the

Śatapatha Brāhmaṇa (3000 ± 240 BC) Hindus used a luni-solar cycle of 5 years and 5 days for their calendars. Sengupta speculated that 5 years after his so called Kaliyuga, Bhārata War started in 2449 BC.[10]

Sengupta made wrong translation of, Bhīshmaparvan, ch. 2 verse 23 (अलक्ष्यः प्रभया हीनं ...) and concluded that the verse describes Mārgaśīrsha Paurṇimā. He further stated that the war began on that day. In fact, it is a description of Kārttika Paurṇimā which had occurred five days before the day of peace talks.

PLANETARY POSITIONS

The planetary positions given in chapter 3 of Bhīshmaparvan should be rejected. When we read chapter 3 of Bhīshmaparvan, we feel that Maharshi Vyāsa has given exaggerated and frightening description of the then atmosphere to the King Dhṛitarāshṭra to dissuade him from engaging in war with Pāṇḍavas. It appears that he has surpassed the well-known writer of science fiction, H.G. Wells, in this respect. A few years ago, comet Shoemaker exploded in the sky of the planet Jupiter. Several pieces of the said comet revolved around Jupiter forming a series of satellites. A similar description of the sky and atmosphere is given by Maharshi Vyāsa to Dhṛitarāshṭra. If we read the planetary positions given in the said chapter along with planetary positions given in other chapters we feel that 19 planets were simultaneously seen in the sky in those days (see Annex. 4). Venus was seen at a time at two places. Mercury and Saturn at three places each, Mars was seen at four places. In addition to these planets, 4 planets by name Śyāma, Śveta, Tivra and Tikshṇa were seen in the sky (Annex. 4). Heavy meteors showered the earth, cosmic dust was suspended everywhere in the earth's atmosphere creating darkness in daytime. Rivers started flowing in the opposite direction due to opposite gravitational pull from the satellites. It appears that genetic science had advanced so much in those days that mares gave birth to calves, and bitches gave birth to foxes (Annex. 5).

The particulars given by Sañjaya in respect of *tithis*, *nakshatras* and planetary positions in the sky are reliable. In the *Mahābhārata* it is mentioned that Sañjaya went from the battlefield of Kurukshetra to Hastināpura twice – (i) on the tenth day of the war when Bhīshmāchārya was fatally wounded, he reached

Hastināpura in short time and Dhṛitarāshṭra asked him eagerly the particulars of the event of the war (Droṇaparvan, Ch. 1, verse 7); (ii) After Śalya's death, the following events occurred – Sañjaya was arrested by the Pāṇḍavas at the battlefield. Dhṛishṭadyumna and Sātyaki decided to kill him. He was released at the intervention of Vyāsa. He removed his armour and started walking towards Hastināpura. After walking a distance of about one *krośa* (3 km), he saw Duryodhana completely covered with bloodstains. He gave a message through Sañjaya to his father Dhṛitarāshṭra that he was alive and was hiding in a tank (verses 37 to 39 in Śalya [Ch. 29]). I have therefore used his notes about the event marked by *tithis*, *nakshatras* and planetary positions.

MEANING OF THE WORDS पीडनं, संपरिवारणं

The words पीडनं and संपरिवारणं occur in the verses Udyoga 143.8; Bhīshma 32.2 and Karṇa 94.51 for example रोहिणी पीडयेन्नेष स्थितो राजन्शनैश्चरः. Here the author of the verses describes the position of the star रोहिणी (Aldebaran) in the sky in poetic manner stating that when Saturn rises in the eastern horizon (156°) day by day, it brings pressure on Aldebaran (रोहिणी 0°) to set in the west. Similar description about Jupiter with respect to Rohiṇī is given in Karṇa 94.51. This meaning is consistent with the Karṇa 37.4 निस्सरंतो व्यदृश्यंत सूर्यात् सप्त महाग्रहाः. P.C. Sengupta and K. Srinivasa Raghavan have wrongly interpreted these verses by holding that Jupiter and Saturn were close to Rohiṇī during the Bhārata War.

Two Rohiṇīs

Aldebaran i.e. alpha Tauri (in वृषभ) is called Kanishthā Rohiṇī or simply Rohiṇī while Antares, i.e. alpha scorpii (in वृश्चिक) is called Jyeshṭhā Rohiṇī or simply Jeshṭhā (Vana 230, 8-11).

ASSEMBLY OF EIGHT PLANETS AND URANUS

Though we have decided to make our calculations using planetary positions other than those given in chapter 3 Bhīshmaparvan, we have to face one more difficulty. The *Mahābhārata* gives close assembly of seven bright planets excluding the Sun. Such description is given at two places. In those assemblies, Rāhu (lunar ascending node) and Ketu (lunar descending node) are not included because they are not luminous.

दीप्यमानाश्च संपेतुः दिवि सप्त महाग्रहाः ।। Bhīshma, 17.2 ।।
निस्सरन्तो व्यदृश्यंत सूर्यात् सप्त महाग्रहाः ।। Karṇa, 37.4 ।।

The Sun and the Moon were considered as planets in the ancient astronomy. Even if we presume Moon as a planet, we have to search in all seven planets receding from the Sun (i.e. exclusive of the Sun). The eighth planet must be Uranus. It is visible to an observer with normal eyesight even without a telescope. Its magnitude is 5.6. The magnitudes of Aruṇdhatī (Alkor) and Revatī (Zeeta pisium) are 5.4 and 5.24 respectively. They were identified by sages during the Vedic period. Stars have practically no motion within themselves. Planets move on the background of the stars. Uranus moves very slowly on the background of the stars. It takes 84 years to complete its circular journey through stars. European astronomers could not therefore identify it separately as a planet till AD 1690. Vedic priests were required to observe the path of the planet, i.e. the chain of the *nakshatras* daily for the purpose of sacrifices. They must have therefore identified the planet Uranus. Its probable name might be Śuchi (Vana 3.17). Foreign invaders destroyed ancient Hindu literature. We could not even read our Brāhmī script nor have we deciphered Indus-Sarasvati (Harappan) script. We have retained only that part of our knowledge which we were required to use daily. Uranus was forgotten because of its faintness and slow motion. When it is shown that the civilization during the period of the Bhārata War saw eighth planet, it is for others to show that it was some other planet than Uranus.

THE STARTING POINT OF OUR SEARCH

The starting point of our search is the day of the beginning of Kaliyuga as found out by K.D. Abhyankar. In 1991, he found that on 7th Feb., 3104 BC seven planets including the Sun and the Moon had closely assembled in a very narrow range before the day-dawned. (Initial research was made by Sampat Ayangar. However, Abhyankar gave accurate position of the planets). The day they had found was 26 lunar months before the traditionally recognized day of beginning of Kaliyuga. The position of planets as found by Abhyankar are given in Annexure 6. (Abhyankar and Ballabh published their articles in this respect in 1996. Subsequently they have modified their views and provided additional probable date of the beginning of the planetary yugas. (See Abhyankar and Ballabh 2000). Those dates are discussed in this paper. This is the verifiable evidence comparable with the internal statement in text, i.e. *Mahābhārata.* As of rule it has to be given priority. Other evidence, *viz.* the Varāhmihira's *Bṛihat-saṁhitā* or the geneaological lists are external evidences and contradict each other. Therefore they are not discussed in this paper.

HISTORICAL CONCEPT OF THE BEGINNING OF YUGAS

KALIYUGA IN *MAHĀBHĀRATA*

The following verse in Ādiparvan is important for us when we think about the Kaliyuga. Sauti says:

> अंतरे चैव सम्प्राप्ते कलिद्वापारयोरभूत्।
> समंतपंचके युद्धं कुरूपाण्डवसेनयोः।। Ādi, 2.13।।

This verse gives the sequence of the events of war and popular concept of the beginning of Kaliyuga. War was fought at the end of Dvāpara, thereafter Kaliyuga began.

PLANETARY YUGAS

The concept of planetary yuga started not for astronomical calculations but for (i) the promulgation of calendars in the name of some king for yearly *yajñas* or for (ii) retaining good or bad omen in recollection of coincidence of a remarkable planetary position in the sky with some serious good or bad historical event. It is in the subsequent stage that such historical record of planetary assemblies was used for astronomical calculations. Now we have computer to trace the days of beginnings of such yugas. G.M. Ballabh prepared a computer programme to verify the positions of five visible planets, the Sun and the Moon in a period from 3500 BC to AD 3000 with an object to find out whether there was any ideal day of beginning of planetary yuga.[11] He found that there was none. However, he found four important days before 1000 BC on which there were close planetary assemblies (CPA) at four cardinal points of tropical years. For the convenience of narration, I have named them according to the English names of the months of their occurrence. Ballabh also gave the maximum angular span which they covered on these days. The dates of cardinal days are given in brackets.

	Name	*Date (BC)*	*Angle*	*Cardinal Point*
1.	April	16-4-3243	17°	Vernal equinox (16-4)
2.	Feb.	7-2-3104	25°	Winter solstice (15-1)
3.	June	16-6-1296	22°	Summer solstice (0-7)
4.	Oct.	12-10-1198	20°	Autumnal eq. (2-10)

(Please note that the interval between a cardinal day and the respective CPA is less than one lunar month).

Out of these four CPAs, first two pertain to the period of the *Śatapatha Brāhmaṇa*. S.B. Dikshit found its date as 3000 BC which is generally accepted. (S.B. Dikshit, Eng. edn., Vol. 1, p. 129). The *Śatapatha Brāhmaṇa* gives us the social and intellectual development of the then generation. The first (i.e. the April) CPA governed the then fifteen-year luni-solar calendar. Though it was the maximum ideal CPA as a base for planetary astronomy, it was not used for that purpose. We guess that it is the date of the end of Dvāpara Yuga. The second (i.e., the Feb.) CPA occurred at the time of Lord Kṛishṇa's death. It was therefore remembered as a sign of bad omen, i.e. the beginning of Kaliyuga. It is explained above that the war took place in a period 3341 ± 240 years BC. The third and the fourth CPAs are beyond the limits of this period (see Annexure 3). Secondly, they are not near the day of winter solstice, when Bhīshmāchārya as well as Kṛishṇa died. These dates cannot be considered as the beginning of the Mahābhārata Kaliyuga. Therefore we have to conclude, that 7-2-3104 BC is the date of the beginning of Mahābhārata Kaliyuga.

DEATH OF LORD KṚISHṆA

The relevant texts which give information about the death of Kṛishṇa are (i) Mausalaparvan of the *Mahābhārata* and (ii) the *Bhāgavata*.

Mausalaparvan

For the purpose of our search, the following verses from Mausalaparvan of the *Mahābhārata* are relevant. I am giving their translation by Manmath Dutt.

Vaiśampāyana addresses King Janamejaya –

Oh king! There was great unjust tumult between the descendants of Vṛishṇis (वृष्णि) after thirty-six years from the event of Bhārata War. They killed each other by the strokes of wooden pastles (Mausala, I.13).

When Lord Kṛishṇa saw this type of adverse effect of time and when he saw that new-moon (अमावस्या) occurred on 13th day from full-moon, he addressed all the citizens, "Bravo! Rāhu (राहु) has turned again the 14th *tithi* into new-moon day, the astronomical position (of planets) is the same as it was during the Great war. It is indicating destruction" || 19 ||.

When Kṛishṇa (केशिहन्ता) thought in this direction, he came to the conclusion, that, it is the thirty-sixth year from the end of the great war || 20 ||.

The rulers of Dvārakā city declared by the orders of Lord Kṛishṇa that "the best of the men Yādavas, should move for pilgrimage towards sea" (that is to Prabhāsa shrine प्रभासतीर्थ) || 24 ||.

Lord Kṛishṇa then went to Prabhāsa *tīrtha*. There also Yādavas fought amidst themselves. One day a tribal hunter shot an arrow which by mistake struck the heel of Kṛishṇa's leg.

Vaiśampāyana says:

Thereafter O king! The creator of the universe, dazzling bright, master of Yogīs, Lord of men went to his final dwelling by illuminating the earth and the heaven. (Mausala, Ch. 4.26.)

Shrīmad Bhāgavata

I could not find a clear statement about the beginning of Kaliyuga than the one given in *Shrīmad Bhāgavata*. (12.2.29)

विष्णोर्भगवतो भानुः कृष्णाख्योऽसौ दिवं गतः
तदाविशत् कलिर्लोकं पापे यद्रमते जनः ।।

When Bhagavān Vishṇu as bright as the Sun and well known by the name Kṛishṇa, went to luminous world (heaven) Kaliyuga began. People started indulging in sins.

FROM THE ASSEMBLY OF EIGHT PLANETS TO THE SEVEN PLANETS

Solar eclipse occurs in the same *nakshatra* only after a lapse of 18 years and 11 days. In the intervening period it occurs in different *nakshatras*. Therefore, the third occurrence of solar eclipse in a particular *nakshatra* should be expected at an interval of 36 years and 22 days from the first eclipse. If we read the aforementioned statement of Lord Kṛishṇa along with the natural rule, we have to conclude that he shifted from Dvārakā to Prabhāsa-shrine after a lapse of 36 years. The next question arises "for what period he lived in Prabhāsa-shrine?" I have proved hereinbefore that there was an assembly of eight planets in the sky during Bhārata War. This assembly included planets Saturn and Jupiter. The interval between two conseqútive conjunction of Saturn and Jupiter is 19.8 years. The day of the beginning of Kaliyuga, i.e. CPA Feb. 3104 BC is close to the day of winter solstice but the war started somewhere in the month of Kārttika and Mārgiśirsha, i.e. about 4 months earlier in the respective year. We must therefore say that Kaliyuga began 19 x 2 years plus 4 months, after the war. Nineteen solar years comprises 235 lunar months; therefore from the date of the war to the day of the beginning of Kaliyuga 235 x 2 + 4 = 474 lunar months must have passed. Every lunar month consists of 29.53088 days. With this data if we calculate and find out the date of the new-moon, after the failure of peace talks, we get it as 13th Oct. 3143 BC. Our conclusion would be supported by strong proof if we get an assembly of eight planets in the sky on this day. If we find assembly of eight planets on any new-moon day similar types of assemblies are expected to occur in next two new-moon days (see Annex. 7).

CONCLUSIVE PROOF ABOUT THE DATE OF THE WAR

I am giving six planetary positions in the sky at important events with sky maps in Annexure 7. The events are as follows:

(i) The new-moon day which followed the failure of the peace-talks:
सप्तमाच्चापि दिवसादमावास्या भविष्यति।
संग्रामं युज्यतां तस्यां तामाहुः शक्रदेवताम्।। Udyoga, Ch. 142.18।।

(ii) On Māgha day before the war:
मघाविषयगः सोमस्तद्दिनं प्रत्यपद्यत।
दीप्यमानाश्च संपेतुर्दिवि सप्त महाग्रहाः।। Bhīshma, Ch. 17. 2।।

(iii) The day of the beginning of the war, with eclipse at sunrise:
चंद्रसूर्यावुभौ ग्रस्तावेकमासीं त्रयोदशीम्
अपर्वणि ग्रहेणैतौ प्रजाः संक्षपयिष्यतः।। Bhīshma, Ch. 3.32 & 33।।

(iv) The planetary position at the dawn of the day of death of Karṇa:
निश्चरन्तो व्यदृश्यन्त सूर्यात्सप्त महाग्रहाः।। Karṇa, Ch. 37.94।।

(v) The western horizon at the dusk after the death of Karṇa:
सोमस्य पुत्रोऽभ्युदियाय तिर्यक्।। Karṇa, Ch. 94.49।।

(vi) On the day of the meeting of the Karṇa with Kṛishṇa after the failure of peace talks:
ततो निर्याय नगरात् प्रययौ पुरुषोत्तमः।
मंत्रयामास च तदा कर्णेन सुचिरं सह।। Udyoga, Ch. 137.29।।.

This is sufficient proof to conclude that the war began on 13th day of Nov. 3143 BC.

K. Srinivasa Raghavan made efforts to search the date of Bhārata War a few years near the beginning of the Kaliyuga. His colleague G.S. Sampath Iyengar found out the date of beginning of astronomical Kaliyuga. However, Raghavan did not take into consideration (i) the position of the eighth planet 'Uranus' and (ii) presumed that the planets Saturn and Jupiter were near Rohiṇī (Aldebaran). He, therefore wrongly concluded that the date of Bhārata War was 22 November 3067 BC.

JULIAN AND GREGORIAN CALENDARS

The dates of the six events given in Annexure 7 are according to Julian Calendar. J. Bently, Jas Burges, Srinivasa Raghavan and K.D. Abhyankar have in their books and papers used dates according to Julian calendar. The author of this paper has therefore used the said calendar. A common man is conversant with Gregorian calendar. Hence, it is necessary to write here about the development of European calendar.

In 46 BC, Julius Caesar on the advice of his astronomer Socigenus designed a calendar consisting of the solar year of 365.25 days. In the year AD 325, Counsel of Nicaea made efforts to link the calendar with tropical years, for example the day of vernal equinox should always be 21st of March. Even then, due to the absence of the knowledge about exact length of tropical year (365.242199 days) the dates in the calendar slipped. In 1582, Pope Gregory corrected the calendar by adding some days and by changing the rules of readjusting it at the end of centuries. As a result Europeans use Julian year of 365.25 days for events before 46 BC and the Gregorian year of 365.2422 days thereafter for fixing historical dates.

DEATH OF BHĪSHMĀCHĀRYA

The Bhārata War occurred a few days before 3142 BC. We therefore use (3142 – 45) = 3097 Julian year in our calculations. The tropical year is shorter than Julian year by (365.25 – 365.2422) = 0.0078 days. This difference totals to 24 days in 3097 years. Therefore, the date of winter-solstice at the death of Bhīshmāchārya was (22nd Dec. + 24 days i.e.) 15th January. Yudhishṭhira left Hastināpura on 15th Jan., 3142 BC to reach Bhīshmāchārya at Kurukshetra. He died on 18th Jan., 3142 BC. The crow-fly distance between Hastināpura to Kurukshetra is 140 km.

TRADITIONAL *YUGĀBDA*

According to Julian calendar, *Kali Yugābda* (युगाब्द) began at midnight on 17th Feb., 3102 BC. Therefore, the Bhārata War started 40 years and 98 days before the beginning of *Yugābda* and Bhīshmāchārya died 40 years and 30 days before *Yugābda*.

At present it is believed that Kaliyuga began on Chaitra Ś.1, 17th Feb., 3102 BC midnight in Julian calendar. The astronomical day of the beginning of Kaliyuga is 7th Feb., 3104 BC as found by K.D. Abhyankar. The question therefore arises that, why should there be a difference of 26 months in these two dates? As I think, the probable reason is that, after the departure of Lord Kṛishṇa to heaven, the Pāṇḍavas went forever to the Himalayas. Before proceeding to the Himalayas they performed the ceremony of coronation of Parīkshit, the grandson of Arjuna. His grandmother Subhadrā was instructed to supervise his administration.

अभिषिच्य स्वराज्ये च राजानं च परीक्षितम्।
दुःखार्तश्चाब्रवीद् राजा सुभद्रां पांडवाग्रजः।।
एष पुत्रस्य पुत्रस्ते कुरुराजो भविष्यति।
यदूनां परिशेषश्च वज्रो राजा कृतश्च ह।।महाप्रस्थानिक 1.7-8।।

NOTES AND REFERENCES

1. Nearly 125 dates ranging from 5561 to about 900 BC have been suggested by scholars for this important event. See Shriram Sathe, *Search for the year of the Bhārata War.*
2. For a detailed explanation, see P.V. Holay, *Vedic Astronomy*, 1994, pp. 107-08.
3. Śāntiparvan, 301, 46 & Dakshāyaṇīya Darśapaurṇima sacrifices in *Śatapatha Br.*, 1-2-10.
4. Daftari, Vol. 3, p. 50.
5. Shriram Sathe, p. 71.
6. Shriram Sathe, p. 72.
7. *Ibid.*
8. *ABORI*, XXV, p. 133.
9. Dr. P.C. Sengupta, "Bhārata Battle Tradition", Art 15, *JRABS*, 1938, pp. 397-402.
10. *Ibid.*, p. 339.
11. K.D. Abhyankar and G.M. Ballabh, "Astronomical and Historical Epoch of Kaliyuga", included in the present volume.

BIBLIOGRAPHY

1. *Mahābhārata*, Gita Press, Gorakhpur Edn.
2. *Mahābhārata*, critical edn., Bhandarkar Oriental Research Institute, Pune.
3. *Mahābhārata*, English translation by Manmath Nath Datta (1896), Rector-Keshub Academy, H.C. Das Elysium Press, 62/2 Bedon Street, Calcutta.
4. Shriram Sathe, *Search for the Year of Bhārata War*, Babasaheb Apte Smarak Samiti, Pune, 1983.
5. P.V. Holay, *Vedic Astronomy* (*Vedāṅga Jyotisha of Lagadhāchāraya*), Shri Babasaheb Apte Smarak Samiti, Nagpur, 1994.
6. K.D. Abhyankar and G.M. Ballabh, "Kaliyuga, Saptaṛishi, Yudhishṭhira and Laukika eras", *Indian Journal of History and Science*, Vol. 31(1), 1996, pp.19-33.
7. P.V.Holay, *Bhāratīya Yuddhāchī Dainandinī Vā Varsha* (Marathi), Bharatiya Itihas Sankalan Samiti, Mysore ,1999 Sali Agent.

8. K.L. Daftari, *Bhāratīya Yuddha Kālanirṇaya* (Marathi), in *Vidvatdatna Daftari Grantha Saṅgraha*, Vol. 3, Daftari Grantha Samiti, 1973.
9. K.V. Abhyankar, "Date and Time of the Bhārata War: A New Approach: Astronomical Considerations", *ABORI*, XXV, 1944, p. 133 ff.
10. Seminar Proceedings on "Astronomical Data as Aid to History", 1979, jointly arranged by Etharaj College for Women and Vaviatru Parvai, Shakti Sugars Ltd., Madras.
11. K.D. Abhyankar and G.M. Ballabh "Astronomical and Historical Kaliyuga" presented at the National Seminar on *Mahābhārata*, April 2000, by Indian Institute of Advanced Study, Shimla (included in the present volume).
12. P.C. Sengupta, *Ancient Indian Chronology*, Calcutta University, 1947.
13. P.C. Sengupta, *Journal of the Royal Asiatic Society of Bengal*, 1937, Art. 10.
14. P.C. Sengupta, "Bharata Battle Traditions", *Journal of the Royal Asiatic Society of Bengal*, 1938, Art.15.
15. S.B. Dikshit, *Bhāratīya Jyotisha Śāstra*. English edn., Government of India, Calcutta, 1968.

ANNEXURE 1
The Diary of the War Events

Order of events	*Tithi*	*Nakshatra*	Description of important events	Time interval between events
			Month of Kārttika	
a	Ś.12	Revatī	Kṛishṇa proceeds to Hastināpura	
b	K.5	Pushya	Peace talks (शांतिसभा) fails	
c	K.8	Pūr. Phalg	Meetings between Karṇa-Kṛishṇa	
d	29	Jyeshṭhā	Kārttika new-moon	
			Intercalary month (अधिकमास)	
e	Ś.6	Purābhijit	Extra *nakshatra*	
f	Ś.13	Kṛittikā	Lunar eclipse	
g	K.13	Pushya	Balarāma visits Pāṇḍavas and proceeds on pilgrimage. Rukmi visits Pāṇḍavas, then proceeds to Kurukshetra	
h	K.12	Anurādhā	Kṛitavarmān joins Kauravas with army	
i	K.13	Jyeshṭhā	Both sides performed lohābhihāra-ritual	
j	K.14	Mūla	Ulūka gives message of war to Pāṇḍavas	42 days
k	30	Pūr. Āshd.	Solar eclipse 1st Gītopadesha war begins	
			Month of Mārgiśirsha	
l	Ś.9	Bharaṇī	Bhīshma is fatally wounded war stops for 12 days	12 days
m	Ś.11	Rohiṇī	Kṛishṇa tells philosophical *Gītā*.	
n	K.7	Svāti	Droṇāchārya field marshal, war resumes	
o	K.9	Anurādhā	Death of Abhimanyu	
p	K.10	Jyeshṭhā	Death of Jayadratha and Ghaṭotkacha at night, war begins at lunar rise	
q	K.11	Mūla	Death of Droṇāchārya	58 days
r	K.13	Utt. Āsad.	Karṇa dies after two days	
s	29	Śravaṇa Amāvasyā	Śalya dies, Duryodhana dies in the presence of Balarāma	
			Month of Pausha	
t	30	Purābhijit	Extra *nakshatra*	
			Month of Māgha	
u	Ś.5	Aśvinī	Winter solstice (उत्तरायणारंभ) Yudhishṭhira proceeds to Kurukshetra	
v	Ś.8	Rohiṇī	Bhīshma breathes his last	

ANNEXURE 2

	Name of *Nakshatra*	28 Equal Divisions	Limits of *Nakshatra*	Place of Conjunction Division Star (180)
1	Aśvinī	321.429	(315 to 327.857)	324.20
2	Bharaṇī	334.286	(327.857 to 340.7143)	338.433
3	Kṛittikā	347.143	(340.7143 to 353.4286)	350.233
4	Rohiṇī	00.00	(353.4286 to 6.4286)	00.33
5	Mṛiga	12.857	(6.4286 to 19.2857)	13.95
6	Ārdrā	25.714	(19.2857 to 32.1428)	29.333
7	Punarvasu	38.571	(32.1428 to 45.00)	43.45
8	Pushya	51.429	(45.0 to 57.857)	54.214
9	Āśleshā	61.286	(57.857 to 70.7143)	64.45
10	Maghā	77.143	(70.7143 to 83.5714)	80.066
11	Pūrvā Phālgunī	90.00	(83.5714 to 96.4285)	91.006
12	Uttara Phālgunī	102.857	(96.4285 to 109.2857)	101.683
13	Hasta	115.714	(109.2857 to 122.1428)	120.0821
14	Chitrā	128.571	(122.1428 to 135)	134.066
15	Nishṭhya	141.429	Shifted to Svāti (Arcturus)	—
16	Viśākhā	154.286	(147.857 to 160.7143)	155.316
17	Anurādhā	167.147	(160.7143 to 173.5714)	172.80
18	Jyeshṭhā	180.00	(173.5714 to 186.4285)	180.00
19	Mūla	192.857	(186.4285 to 199.2857)	194.816
20	Pūrvā Āshāḍhā	205.714	(199.2857 to 212.1428)	206.533
21	Uttara Āshāḍha	218.571	(212.1428 to 225.0)	216.466
22	Śravaṇa	231.429	(225.0 to 237.857)	232.016
23	Dhanishṭhā	244.286	(237.857 to 250.7143)	247.516
24	Purābhjit Ep. Pegasus	257.143	(250.7143 to 263.5714)	216.31
25	Śatabhi Shaj	270.00	(263.5714 to 276.4286)	271.316
26	Pūrvā Bhadrapadā	282.857	(276.4286 to 289.2857)	283.716
27	Uttara Bhadrapadā	295.714	(289.2857 to 302.1428)	299.40
28	Revatī	308.571	(302.1428 to 315)	310.116

ANNEXURE 3

Year of Bhārata War by Precession of Solstices

For calculating the relative positions of planets one may use ephemeris of any year as a base. I have used the *Indian Ephemeris* of L.D.S. Pillai of the year 1995 as basis. Let us first find out the position of the Sun on the day of death of Bhīshma. The celestial longitudes of the Sun and the Moon were the same on the day of new-moon, that preceded the said day. Let us therefore find out the position of the moon seven days before the death of Bhīshma (because seven days had passed in between)

Rohiṇī (Aldebaran) = 69°4′335″ = 69.72689° ————St.(1)

Moon covers 12° in every *tithi* and 13.176° in a day. In seven days it would cover 13.176 x 7 = 92.235°. Let us find out where it was seven days before. (The answer maybe negative, hence we use 360° of the earlier round).

The position of the new-moon

= (360°+ 69.72689°– 92.235°) = 337.492°

This was also the position of the Sun on the new-moon day. Let us now find out the daily motion of the Sun. The direction of the major axis of the eliptical path of the earth has not changed much in last 5000 years. Therefore, the average relative angular velocity of the Sun between 332° to 340° is practically unchanged. It was 1.0045767° per day in AD 1995.

Let us find out what angular distance it travelled towards east in seven days.

1.0045767° x 7 = 7.0320°

Therefore, position of the Sun on the day of Bhīshma's death was

=337.491°+ 7.032° = 344.532 —— St (2)*

Precession: In the basic year (AD 1995) point of winter solstice was at 270°. Therefore, the total precession was 344.523°– 270°= 74.523°.

The time required for this precession:

=74.532 x 71.6 years = 5336 years.

Our basic year is AD 1995. Therefore the year of the war is 5336 -1995 = AD 3341. One division of *nakshatra* = 13.333. The point of winter solstice takes about 960 years to cover this distance. Our answer has therefore + or – limits.

* The year of the war is therefore 3341 ± 240 years. That is from 3101 BC to 3581 BC.**

*This *tithi* is Ashṭamī (8th) because:

Sun-Moon = St.(1) – St.(2)

= 360 – 344.523 + 69.7 = 85.177

Bhīshma, died at mid-moon, therefore we have to add quarter *tithi*
85.177° + 3° = 88.177° (limits of 8th *tithi* are 84° to 96°)

**In 3341 BC winter solstice used to occur on 18th Jan. In 3143 BC it was occuring on 15th of Jan. This difference occurred due to precession of solstice.

ANNEXURE 4

Planet	*Nakshatras*	Reference	Verses
Mercury	Viśākhā	(भीष्म 3.31)	बुधः संपतते़ऽभीक्ष्णं जनयन्सुमहद् भयं
	Viśākhā-Mūla	(शल्य 11.17)	भृगुसूनुधरापुत्रौं शशिजेन समन्वितौ
	Near the Sun	(कर्ण 94.49)	सोमस्य पुत्रोऽभ्युदियाय तिर्यक
Venus	Prashṭhupadā	(भीष्म 3.15)	शुक्रः प्रोष्ठपदे पूर्वे समारुह्य विरोचते
	Viśākhā-Mūla	(शल्य 11.17)	भृगुसूनुधरापुत्रौ शशिजेन समन्वितौ
Mars	Maghā	(भीष्म 3.14)	मघास्वंगारको वक्रः श्रवणेच बृहस्पितिः
	Abhijit to Śrav	(भीष्म 3.18)	ब्रह्मराशिं समावृत्य लोहितांगो व्यवस्थितः
	Anurādhā to Jyeshṭhā	(उद्योग 143.9)	कृत्वा चांगारको वक्रः ज्येष्ठायां मधुसूदन
	Viśākhā to Mūla	(शल्य 11.17)	भृगुसूनुधरापुत्रौ शशिजेन समन्वितौ
Jupiter	Viśākhā	(भीष्म 3.27)	विशाखायाः समीपस्थौ बृहस्पतिशनिश्चरौ
	Śravaṇā	(भीष्म 3.14)	मघास्वंगारको वक्रः श्रवणे च बृहस्पतिः
	Covering Rohiṇī	(कर्ण 94.51)	बृहस्पतिः संपरिवार्य रोहिणीम्
Saturn	Viśākhā	(भीष्म 3.27)	विशाखायाः समीपस्थौ ब्हस्पति शनिश्चरौ
	Pūrvā-Phālguṇī	(भीष्म 3.14)	भगं नक्षत्रमाक्रम्य सूर्यपुत्रेण पीड्यते
	Oppressing	(उद्योग 143.8)	प्राजापत्यं नक्षत्रं...शनैश्चरः पीडयति . . .
	Rohiṇī	(भीष्म 2.32)	रोहिणीं पीडयन्नेष स्थितो राजन्शनैचरः
All Planets	Maghā to Jyeshṭhā	(भीष्म 17.2)	मघाविषयगः सोमस्तद् दिनं प्रत्यपद्यत दीप्यमानश्च
	Near the Sun	(कर्ण 37.4)	निस्संरतो व्यदृश्यंत सूर्यात् सप्त महाग्रहाः

Besides these, four planets, viz. Śyāma, Śveta, Tīvra and Tikshṇa.

ANNEXURE 5
Fantastic and impossible events narrated in Chapter 3 of Bhīshmaparvan

(English translation of the verses is from Manmath Nath Datta (1896)-Recter-Keshub Academy; H.C. Dās, Elysium Press 65/2 Bendon Street, Calcutta)

गोवत्सं वडवां सूते श्वा सृगालं महीपते।
कुक्कुरान् करभाश्चैव शुकाश्चाशुभवादिनः।। 6।।

O king, the mare gives birth to calves, the bitch to jackals, the elephants to dogs, cocks, antelopes and parrots are all sending forth inauspicious notes. || 6 ||

विश्ववाताश्च वात्युग्रा रजो नाप्युपशाम्यति।
अभीक्ष्णं कम्पते भूमिरर्क राहुरूपैति च।। 11।।

Strong winds are fearfully blowing and the dust unceasingly flying. The earth is often quaking and Rāhu advances towards the Sun. || 11 ||

धूमकेतुर्महाघोरः पुष्यं चाक्रम्य तिष्ठति।
सेनयोरशिवं घोरं करिष्यति महाग्रहः।। 13।।

A fearful comet is rising, and is distressing the constellation Pushya. This great planet will cause terrible harm to both the armies || 13 ||

दिक्षु प्रज्वलितास्याश्च व्याहरन्ति मृगद्विजाः।।
अत्याहितं दर्शयन्तो वेदयन्ति महद् भयम्।। 24।।

Animals and birds on all sides utter harsh cries with their mouths burning like fire. This forebodes fearful events || 24 ||

प्रतिस्रोतो महानद्यः सरितः शोणितोदकाः।
फेनायमानाः कूपाश्च कूर्दन्ति वृषभा इव।। 34।।

The great rivers flow in opposite directions The waters of rivers have turned into blood. || 34 ||

पतन्त्युल्काः सनिर्घाताः शक्राशनिसमप्रभाः।
अद्य चैव निशां व्युष्ठामयनं समवाप्स्यथ।। 35।।

Meteors as effulgent as Indra's thunder fall on earth with loud sound. When this night passes away, a great danger will fall on you. || 35 ||

> विनिःसृत्य महोल्काभिस्तिमिरं सर्वतोदिशम्।
> अन्योन्यमुपतिष्ठद्भिस्तत्र चोक्तं महार्षिभिः || 36 ||

Sages with lighted torches in their hands will meet great difficulty to meet together, for thick gloom will cover the space || 36 ||

> महाभूता भूमिकम्पे चत्वारः सागराः पृथक्।
> वेलामुद्वर्तयन्तीव क्षोभयन्तो वसुन्धराम् || 38 ||

Earth trembles, and in consequence the four oceans, having exceedingly swelled, seem ready to overflow their banks in order to afflict the earth || 38 ||

> वृक्षानुन्मथ्य वान्त्युग्रा वाताः शर्करकर्षिणः।
> आभग्नाः सुमहावातैरशनीभिः समाहताः || 39 ||
> वृक्षाः पतन्ति चैत्याश्च ग्रामेषु नगरेषु च || 40 ||

Fearful winds with stones are blowing, crushing all the trees || 39 || Being crushed by the high wind and struck by lightening, sacred and common trees in villages and towns are falling down || 40 ||

> ध्यायन्तः प्रकिरन्तश्च व्याला वेपथुसंयुताः।
> दीनास्तुरंगमाः सर्वे वारणः सलिलाश्रयाः || 45 ||

Tiger appears to run hither and thither throwing off urine and excreta. The horses are all melancholy, the elephants are going into water. || 45 ||

ANNEXURE 6

The planetary position at the beginning of Kaliyuga by K.D. Abhyankar

Amānta Phālguna K. 14

J.D. 587724 = 7 Feb. 3104 B.C.J. 1-58 A.M.					
Planet	Sāyana β	Sāyana λ	Nirayana AD 285	Obs'ion Time	Sun-to Planet Dist.
Sun	0.0	294.5	342.5	Dawn	0.00
Moon	+5.0	273.5	321.5	Dawn	-21.0
Mercury	+2.0	278.3	326.3	Dawn	-16.2
Venus	-0.5	267.7	315.7	Dawn	-26.8
Mars	-1.1	277.8	325.8	Dawn	-16.7
Jupiter	-0.6	260.2	308.2	Dawn	-34.3
Saturn	-0.1	253.1	301.1	Dawn	-41.4

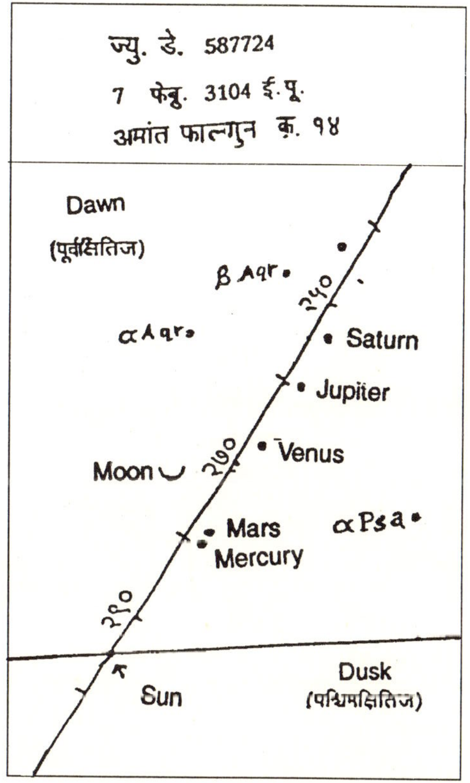

ANNEXURE 7A

Kārttika new-moon after failure of peace talks

सप्तमाच्चापि दिवसादमावास्या भविष्यति।
संग्रामं योजयेत्र तां ह्याहुः शक्रदेवताम्।। (उद्योग 142.18)

J.D. 573728 = 13 Oct. 3143 B.C.J.					
Planet	Sāyana	Nirayana Rohiṇī 0°	Nirayana AD 285	Obs'ion Time	Sun-to Planet Dist.
Sun	246.253	176.526	225.503	Dawn	0.00
Moon	243.993	174.266	220.243	Dawn	-2.26
Mercury	227.975	158.248	204.225	Dawn	-18.278
Venus	225.264	155.537	201.514	Dawn	-20.989
Mars	209.71	139.983	185.96	Dawn	-36.543
Jupiter	240.007	170.280	216.257	Dawn	-6.246
Saturn	226.392	156.665	202.642	Dawn	-19.86
Uranus	262.488	192.761	238.738	Dusk	+16.235
Rāhu	277.256	207.529	253.506	Dusk	+31.003

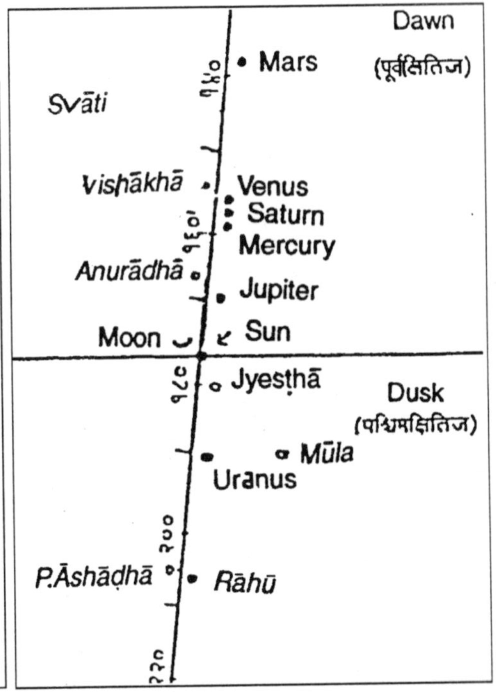

ANNEXURE 7B

Maghā-day before war

Intercalary Mārgaśirsha K. 5th

मघाविषयगः सोमस्तद्दिनं प्रत्यपद्यत।
दीप्यंमानाश्च संपेतुर्दिवि सप्त महाग्रहाः (भीष्म 17.2)

J.D. 573748 = 3 Nov. 3143 B.C.J.					
Planet	Sāyana	Nirayana Rohiṇī 0°	Nirayana AD 285	Obs'ion Time	Sun-to Planet Dist.
Sun	266.709	196.982	242.959	Dawn	0.00
Moon	151.524	81.797	127.774	Dawn	-115.185
Mercury	257.927	188.200	234.177	Dawn	-8.782
Venus	250.471	180.744	226.721	Dawn	-16.238
Mars	223.323	153.596	199.573	Dawn	-43.386
Jupiter	244.474	174.747	220.724	Dawn	-22.235
Saturn	228.508	158.781	204.758	Dawn	-38.201
Uranus	263.745	194.018	239.995	Dawn	- 2.964
Rāhu	276.196	206.469	252.446	Dusk	+ 9.487

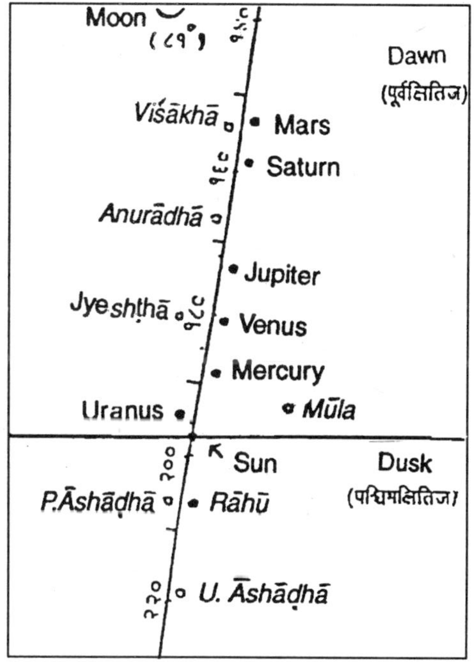

ANNEXURE 7C

Beginning of war solar eclipse at 6.51 a.m.

चन्द्रसूर्यावुभौ ग्रस्तावेकमासे त्रयोदशीम्।
अपर्वणि ग्रहावेतो प्रजाः संक्षपयिष्यतः।। (भीष्म 3.28)

J.D. 573758 = 13 Nov. 3143 B.C.J.					
Planet	Sāyana	Nirayana Rohiṇī 0°	Nirayana AD 285	Obs'ion Time	Sun-to Planet Dist.
Sun	276.977	207.25	253.227	Dawn	0.00
Moon	276.977	207.25	253.227	Dawn	0.00
Mercury	272.777	203.05	249.027	Dawn	-4.2
Venus	263.11	193.383	239.36	Dawn	-13.867
Mars	230.21	160.483	206.46	Dawn	-46.767
Jupiter	246.644	176.917	222.894	Dawn	-30.333
Saturn	229.46	159.733	205.71	Dawn	-47.517
Uranus	264.377	194.65	240.627	Dawn	-12.6
Rāhu	275.667	205.94	251.917	Dawn	-1.31

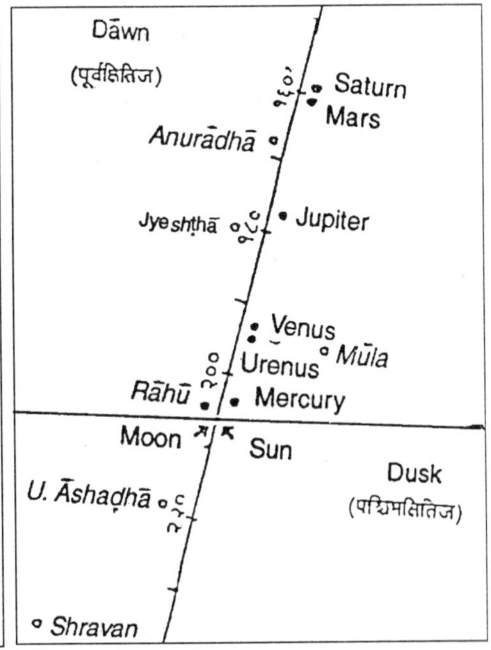

ANNEXURE 7D

Before dawn on the day of death of Karṇa, also after dusk Mārgaśirsha K. 14th

निश्चरन्तो व्यदृश्यन्त सूर्यात्सप्त महाग्रहाः। (कर्ण 37.4)
सोमस्य पुत्रोऽभ्युदिदाय तिर्यक् (कर्ण 94.49)

J.D. 573786 = 11 Dec. 3143 B.C.J.					
Planet	Sāyana	Nirāyana Rohiṇī 0°	Nirāyana AD 285	Obs'ion Time	Sun-to Planet Dist.
Sun	305.482	235.755	281.732	Dawn	0.00
Moon	285.20	215.473	261.45	Dawn	-20.282
Mercury	320.818	251.091	297.068	Dusk	+15.336
Venus	298.194	228.467	274.444	Dawn	-7.288
Mars	249.581	179.854	225.831	Dawn	-55.901
Jupiter	252.107	182.380	228.357	Dawn	-53.375
Saturn	231.521	161.794	207.771	Dawn	-73.961
Uranus	265.999	196.272	242.249	Dawn	-39.483
Rahu	274.184	204.457	250.434	Dawn	-31.294

निश्चरन्तोव्यदृश्यंत सूर्मात सप्त महाग्रहा (कर्ण ३७४)

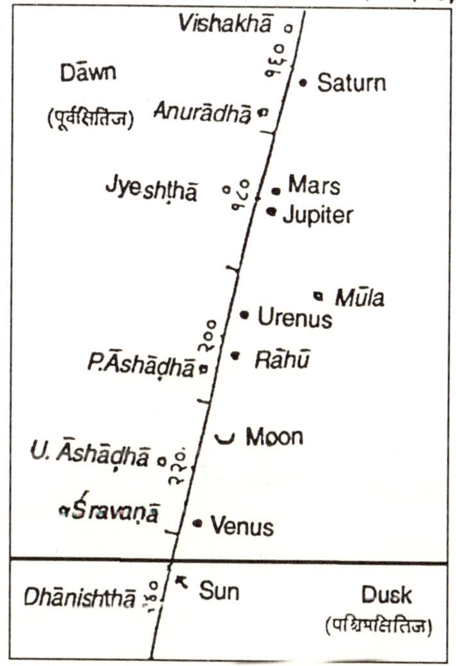

- सोमस्य पुत्रोऽभ्युदियाय तिर्यक् (कर्ण ९४४९)

ANNEXURE 7E

Meeting of Kṛishṇa and Karṇa after failure of peace talks

ततो निर्याय नगरात् प्रययौ पुरुषोत्तमः।
मंत्रयामास च तदा कर्णेन सुचिरं सह।। (उद्योग 137.29)

J.D. 573721 = 7 Oct. 3143 B.C.J.					
Planet	Sāyana	Nirayana Rohiṇī 0°	Nirayana AD 285	Obs'ion Time	Sun-to Planet Dist.
Sun	239.106	169.379	215.356	Dawn	0.00
Moon	155.569	85.842	131.819	Dawn	-83.537
Mercury	219.072	149.345	195.322	Dawn	-20.034
Venus	216.449	146.722	192.699	Dawn	-22.657
Mars	204.982	135.255	181.232	Dawn	-34.124
Jupiter	204.982	135.255	181.232	Dawn	-0.683
Saturn	225.604	155.877	201.854	Dawn	-13.502
Uranus	262.064	192.337	238.314	Dusk	+22.958
Rāhu	277.626	207.899	253.876	Dusk	+38.52

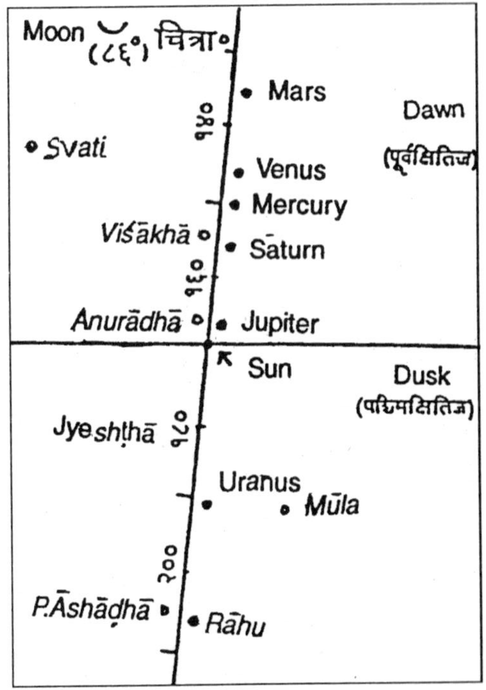

ANNEXURE 8

The name of the month in which Bhīshmāchārya expired

K. Srinivasa Raghavan, K.V. Abhyankar and I have, for the internal consistency of the text, found that one *Adhikamāsa* had followed the month in which the peace talks before the war failed. Some scholars have raised serious doubts about this proposition, hence this annexure. The following verse is always quoted about the practice of computation of *Adhikamāsa*. In this stanza from Virāṭaparvan, Bhīshmāchārya says:-

तेषां कालातिरेकेण ज्योतिषां च व्यतिक्रमात्।
पञ्चमे पञ्चमे वर्षे द्वौ मासावुपजायतः।। (विराट 52.3)

In the nature in five years and five days we have two *Adhikamāsas*, and in 15 years we have only 5½ *Adhikamāsas*. Therefore, the word कालातिरेकेण in the above verse means a few years before the end of 15 year cycle. Before we proceed with our subject it is necessary to know (1) at which of the four cardinal points of the solar year, the calendrical year used to begin and (2) which were the names of the six-monthly semesters of the year. The following passages in the *Śatapatha Brāhmaṇa* is important in this respect:-

वसंतो ग्रीष्मो वर्षा ते देवा ऋतवः।
शरद हेमन्ताः शिशिरास्ते पितरो य एषापूर्यतेऽर्धमासः
.........। यो यत्र उदगावर्तते देवेषु तर्हि भवति
देवास्तहर्य भिगोपायत्यथ दक्षिणावर्तते पितृषु तर्ही
भवति पितृस्तहर्यभिगोपायाति।।

Śatapatha Brāhmaṇa ii 1.3, 1-3

The year used to begin with spring season. The sun thereafter moved to the northern side of the ecliptic. Its path thereafter was called Devayāna and to the south of the ecliptic it was Pitṛiyāna. (To my mind they were so called because there was a traditional belief among Vedic bards that their ancestors came to Sarasvatī basin from southern India). Ballabh (2000) has found by computer programme that on 16-4-3243 BC, i.e. on the day of vernal equinox, there was a very close assembly of planets near the star Rohinī (Aldebaran). This must be a strong reason for the beginning of the year at the commencement of spring season. There was another pair of names indicating the two divisions of the tropical year. They were उत्तरायण and दक्षिणायन which began at winter solstice and summer solstice respectively.

Time for Inserting the Adhikamāsa

A question is raised as to how the five years were divided into two groups for inserting the Adhikamāsa, either in division of 3 + 2 years or 2½ +2½ years. If there was a practice to make two divisions of 2½ + 2½ years, the middle point of a year would also get importance. However, in verse of *Gītā* (Ch. 11.35) Kṛishṇa says मासानां मार्गशीर्षोऽहं, i.e. the month at the beginning of the second semester of the year before autumn. This shows that the two divisions for insertion of Adhikamāsa were of 2½ +2½ years.

A very important verse relevant to this point is kept on side-lines in the critical edition. It is in Devanāgarī manuscript dated AD 1494 collected by the then Govt. of Bombay. The verse reads as under:-

गते वर्षद्वये चैव पञ्चपक्षे दिनद्वये।
दिवसाष्टमे भागे पतत्येकोऽधिकमासः।। विराट 47.4।।

There is obvious error in the first line. The words पञ्चपक्षे deserve to be corrected as पञ्चमासे. The verse can be explained in mathematical equation about 12 x 2 + 5 solar months = 30 lunar months,

i.e. about 29 solar months = 30 lunar months.

When we add intercalary month to both sides we have about 30 solar months = 31 lunar months.

The words दिनद्वये appear in the first line of the verse because two intercalary months occur not only in five years but in five years and five days. Therefore, in half of the cycle we have to add 2½ days more. The author of the verse asks us to add $2^1/_8$ days instead of 2½ days. Considering the antiquity of the observer the difference deserves to be ignored.

Effect of Inserting Adhikamāsa at Wrong Point of Time

Our main object is to find out whether there could be a Māgha month in which, *tithi* Ś.8 would have Rohiṇī *nakshatra*. In fact, the addition of two Adhikamāsa in five years is not consistent with nature. The average interval for addition of an Adhikamasa is 32.57 solar months. The natural time for addition of 5th Adhikamasa should therefore be 13 years and 7 months after the beginning of the cycle, but the then civilization added it at the end of 12 years. That is a year and a month earlier. That changed the names of the months after 12 years in following manner.

Mahābhārata Month	*Natural Month*
Adhikamāsa	Mārgaśirsha
Mārgaśirsha	Pausha
Pausha	Māgha
Māgha	Phālguna
(and so for further 13 months)	

K.D. Abhyankar is of the opinion that the year of the relevant civilization began with winter solstice. Let us presume it to be so. In that case the summer solstice would start with Bhādrapada-māsa. Therefore, at the end of 12½ years the month Śravaṇa would be followed by the fifth Adhikamāsa which would unnecessarily shift the succeeding 13 months with following changes.

Mahābhārata Month	*Natural Month*
Adhikamāsa	Bhādrapada
Bhādrapada	Aśvina
Aśvina	Kārttika
Kārttika	Mārgaśirsha
Mārgaśirsha	Pausha
Pausha	Māgha
Māgha	Phālguna
(and so for further 13 months)	

It was therefore possible that the *tithi* Māgha Ś.3 could have Rohiṇī as its *nakshatra*.

6

Astronomical and Historical Epoch of Kaliyuga

K.D. Abhyankar and G.M. Ballabh

An attempt has been made to determine the epoch of Kaliyuga from astronomical and historical point of view. Ballabh's computations show that there was no superconjunction of planets as postulated by Āryabhaṭa during the long period from 3500 BC to AD 3000. However, taking simultaneous combustion (*asta*) of all planets on a new-moon day (*amāvasyā*), or their appearance together with the moon in the early morning before sunrise as near superconjunctions, we get 16-4-3243 BC and 7-2-3104 BC as the dates of the Kaliyuga close to the traditional date of 18-2-3102 BC.

Kaliyuga epoch can also be found by fixing the date of Mahābhārata War, which is supposed to have occurred around that time. The crucial event is Bhīshma's death, which is considered to have occurred at winter solstice. Taking the traditional *tithi* of Māgha Śukla 8 for this event, one finds a date of 1500 ± 300 BC which agrees well with the findings of undersea exploration of submerged Dvārakā near Beṭ Dvārakā by S. R. Rao. Pushing it to Māgha Kṛishṇa 8, as done by P.C. Sengupta (1947) one obtains 2449 BC which is Varāhamihira's estimate of Kali epoch. But one has to push it to Phālguna Śukla 8 if we want to go back to Āryabhaṭa's Kaliyuga as done by P.V. Holay (1999). However, he still calls it Māgha Śukla 8 by introducing an unnecessary intercalary month (*adhikamāsa*). The calendars of Mahābhārata War by Sengupta and Holay are juxtaposed.

ASTRONOMICAL CONSIDERATIONS

According to Āryabhaṭa (*Āryabhaṭīya*: Gītikā 3 & 4), the current Mahāyuga started when the sun, the moon and the five naked eye planets and the apogee as well as the ascending node of the moon's orbit (Rāhu) came together at Meshādi on Chaitra Śukla 1 at sunrise of Wednesday in Laṅkā. Further, according to him (*Āryabhaṭīya*: Gītikā 5), three-fourth of that Mahāyuga was over at the commencement of the present Kaliyuga. Consequently, at the beginning of Kali epoch, while the seven luminaries were at Meshādi, the apogee of moon was 90 degrees away and the ascending node (Rāhu) was 180 degrees away. *Pañchāṅga* makers take it to be the local sunrise at Ujjain on Julian date 18th February 3102 BC.

In order to test Āryabhaṭa's hypothesis, Ballabh has written a computer programme for finding close planetary grouping within a span of 30 and 10 degrees and has made computations from 3500 BC to AD 3000. It was found that there was no superconjunction of the Kaliyuga type during the entire period of 6500 years. The seven luminaries came closest together within a span of 11 degrees on the *amāvasyā* of 15-9-1186 AD when all the five planets were combust (*asta*). Similar situations occurred on three other times but with larger spans viz. on Julian dates 16-4-3243 BC, 26-6-1296 BC and 12-10-1198 BC within the span of 17, 22 and 20 degrees respectively. Out of these the one on 16-4-3243 BC is the closest to the traditional epoch of Kaliyuga. At that time the seven luminaries were together in Vṛishabha Rāśi along with Rāhu and the sun was at vernal equinox (*Vasanta Sampāta*) with tropical longitude equal to 359 degrees. So this superconjunction can be taken as an observed epoch of astronomical Kaliyuga in the sense that all the five planets and the moon were invisible due to their proximity to the sun. However, as the vernal equinox was near Rohiṇī at that time, it fits better with the Kṛittikādi list of *nakashatras* in *Yajurveda* instead of the Aświnyādi list of the Siddhānta period. Moreover, it does not include the beginning of the year in that epoch, because the year used to start at the winter solstice in those days (Abhyankar, 1988).

In an earlier paper (Abhyankar and Ballabh, 1996), we had identified the configuration of planets at sunrise at Ujjain on Julian date 7-2-3104 BC as representative of the Kaliyuga epoch, because that sight could be interpreted as the seven luminaries being together in the sky. It is now found by Ballabh that such configurations occur quite frequently: 26 times in the morning before sunrise and 19 times in the evening after sunset in the span of 6500 years for which computations were made. So apparently there is nothing special about such configurations. But the one on 7-2-3104 BC was unique in the sense that it occurred in the first month of the year which had begun on Phālguna Śukla 1 of 11-1-3104 BC with the sun at tropical longitude equal to 268 degrees near winter solstice. We have explained in that paper how the confusion between the year beginning at winter solstice of the earlier period and at vernal equinox in Siddhānta period gave rise to the erroneous theory of trepidation.

HISTORICAL CONSIDERATIONS

According to Āryabhaṭa, Kaliyuga started from the Mahābhārata War, but according to Mahābhārata tradition it started with the Mahānirvāṇa of Lord Kṛishṇa which took place 36 years after the war. Historians of Kashmir and Nepal used another marker for time measurement, viz. the Saptaṛishi or Loukika era which began with the ascension of Yudhishṭhira to the heavens 25 years after the beginning of Kaliyuga. According to these traditions, the Mahābhārata War occurred in 3138 BC, Kaliyuga started in 3102 BC and Saptaṛishi era commenced in 3077 BC. As Yudhishṭhira performed Rājasūya sacrifice 25 years before the Mahābhārata War, he ought to have ruled from 3163 BC to 3077 BC. But Varāhamihira says that Yudhishṭhira ruled some 2526 years before the beginning of Śaka era. This gives for him a date of 2449 BC, which would also then represent the era of the Mahābhārata War. Sengupta (1947) has drawn attention to a third alternative. In Purāṇas, it is stated that Mahāpadma Nanda came to power some 1015, 1050 or 1500 years after the Mahābhārata War according to three discordant recensions. As Chandragupta Maurya ascended the throne of Pātaliputra in 321 BC, fifty years after Mahāpadma Nanda, we get for the Mahābhārata War a date of 1386, 1421 or 1871 BC. The controversy between the three dates of 3138 BC, 2449 BC and 1650±200 BC might be resolved if we could determine the date of the Mahābhārata War from the astronomical references in *Mahābhārata*.

The most important astronomical reference pertains to the death of Bhīshmapitāmaha, which is said to have occurred on Bhīshmāshṭāmi, i.e. Māgha Śukla 8, one day after the winter solstice day of Rathasaptamī, i.e. Māgha Śukla 7. Now at present Māgha Śukla 8 occurs on February 5 on an average. As winter solstice occurs on December 22, there has been a shift of 45 days in the date of winter solstice due to the phenomenon of *ayanachalana*. At the rate of 71 years per day of *ayanachalana* we get a time lapse of 3200 years, which gives a date of about 1200 BC for the Mahābhārata War. As Māgha Śukla 8 shifts by ± 15 days around February 5 due to the mechanism of *adhikamāsas*, the date of the war could be put as 1200±1000 BC. These dates tally with the accounts of Purāṇas as well as with the *Vedāṅga Jyotisha* calendar. In *Vedāṅga Jyotisha,* winter solstice occurs when the sun arrives in Dhanishṭhā *nakshatra*, so its date depends upon the identification of that star. At present it is identified with the star β Delphini (*Nirayana* longitude =292 deg.) which gives a date of 1200 BC. But if we identify β Aquarii (*Nirayana* longitude = 300 deg.) with Dhanishṭha as suggested earlier (Abhyankar, 1991) the date can be pushed back to 1800 BC. It is likely that the above astronomical reference in the *Mahābhārata* and the statements in Purāṇas were incorporated in the *Mahābhārata* when *Vedāṅga Jyotisha* was in vogue. These dates also fit with recent undersea exploration at Beṭ Dvārakā by S.R. Rao which shows the evidence of submergence of Lord Kṛishṇa's Dvārakā below the sea around 1500 BC as reported in the *Bhāgavata Purāṇa.*

CALENDAR OF THE MAHĀBHĀRATA WAR

Now references to other *tithis* and/or *nakshatras* of the events before and during the war should also be considered for setting the date of the Mahābhārata War. Positions of planets are only of secondary importance because they are not unambiguously specified. These considerations might take us to earlier epochs, but sticking to Māgha Śukla 8 as marker of winter solstice will not help us as explained above. We shall consider two attempts: one made by P.C. Sengupta (1947) more than fifty years ago and the other recently by P.V. Holay (1999). Both assume that the war did not start on Śukla 1 immediately after the Kārttika *amāvasyā* with Jyeshṭhā *nakshatra*, because, as stated by Holay, time was required for the preparation between the breakdown of the peace parleys and the start of the war. But Sengupta, like the B group of Holay, starts the war 13 days later on the following Śukla 14, while Holay defers it by one lunar month. Consequently, Sengupta obtains 2449 BC as the year of the Mahābhārata War while Holay puts it in 3143 BC. Let us examine these two alternatives.

Holay has introduced an intercalary month (*adhikamāsa*) after Kārttika *amāvasyā* in order to start the war on Mārgaśīrsha Śukla 1 and to obtain Bhīshma's death at winter solstice on Māgha Śukla 8. Now Jyeshṭhā is the normal *nakshatra* for Kārttika *amāvasyā*, so there is no need to introduce an *adhikamāsa* at that time. Further, the winter solstice used to occur in Phālguna month and not in Māgha around 3143 BC (Abhyankar, 1998). However, Holay did not like to consider the *adhikamāsa* as normal Mārgaśīrsha, because it would have shifted the Mahābhārata War to the month of Pausha, which is not acceptable to many scholars. But the introduction of *adhikamāsa* has obscured the effect of pushing Bhishma's death of Phālguna Śukla 8. We have already remarked that the astronomical references in the *Mahābhārata* were probably inserted when *Vedāṅga Jyotisha* was in vogue.

Holay has further introduced a gap of 12 days in the war after Bhīshmapatana for which there is no evidence in the *Mahābhārata*. He has done this to achieve three things: (1) To push Jayadratha's death into the dark half of the month; (2) To have Gitajayanti on the traditional *tithi* of Mārgaśīrsha Śukla 11 and utilize the gap of 12 days for the exposition of adhyātmagītā; (3) To have 42 days gap between Balarāma's going on pilgrimage and his return at the end of the war to observe Duryodhana's death, for which he has also shifted Kṛishṇa-Balarāma meeting from Kārttika Kṛishṇa 5 to Adhika Mārgaśīrsha Kṛishṇa 3.

All these changes are not required in Sengupta's calendar of the Mahābhārata War, which is given in Table 1 as verified by us. All times are in IST for Kurukshetra (Lat. 30^0 00′ N, Long. 76^0 48′ E). The main features of Sengupta's calendar are:

1. Breakdown of peace parleys that took place on Kārttika Kṛishṇa 5. Balarāma leaves for pilgrimage after meeting Kṛishṇa on the same day having Pushya *nakshatra* on Julian date 11-10-2449 BC.
2. Kṛishṇa meets Karṇa on Kārttika Kṛishṇa 8 (14-10-2449 BC) which is followed 7 days later by Kārttika *amāvasyā* at Jyeshṭhā *nakshatra* on 21-10-2449 BC at 7:18 a.m. in Kurukshetra.

Table 1: P.C. Sengupta's Calendar of the Mahābhārata War

Tithi, Nakshatra	Event	Julian Date BC	Astronomical Phenomenon at Kurukshetra
Kārttika K 5, Pushya	Breakdown of peace parleys Kṛishṇa-Balarāma meeting Balarāma leaves on pilgrimage	11-10-2449	
K 8	Meeting of Kṛishṇa and Karṇa	14-10-2449	
K 30, Jyeshṭhā	Kārttika *amāvasyā*	21-10-2449	Jyeshṭhā (Antares) at 7:18 a.m.
Mārgaśīrsha Ś 12	Gītājayantī	1-11-249	
Ś 14, Kṛittikā	Anumati Paurṇimā	3-11-2449	Kṛittikā (Alcyone) at 2:28 a.m. and Rohiṇī (Aldebaran) at 10:17 p.m.
Ś 15, Rohiṇī	Beginning of Mahābhārata War	4-11-2449	
K 8	Bhīshmapatana	13-11-2449	
K 12	Death of Jayadratha	17-11-2449	
	Next morning	18-11-2449	Moonrise 5:03 a.m. Sunrise 6:46 a.m.
Pausha Ś 2, Śravaṇa	End of Mahābhārata War Return of Balarāma from pilgrimage and death of Duryodhana	21-11-2449	Śravaṇa (Altair) at 5:10 a.m.
Māgha K. 6, K 7	Uttarāyaṇa Bhishma's Death	9-1-2448 10-1-2448	0:40 a.m.

3. Mārgaśīrsha Śukla 14 was an *anumati* type *paurṇimā* with the moon conjuncting Kṛittikā on 3-11-2449 BC at 2:28 a.m. and Rohiṇī at 10:17 p.m. The war started on the next day, i.e. on 4-11-2449 BC, which was Śukla 15.
   (Here we would like to make the following suggestion. Since Mārgaśīrsha Śukla 11 is celebrated as Gītājayantī, we can take the 3 days from Śukla 11 to Śukla 13 as the period of *Gītā* discourse before the start of the war.)
4. Bhīshmapatana occurs on the 10th day of war, i.e. 13-11-2449 BC which was Kṛishṇa 8 of Mārgaśīrsha.
5. Jyadratha's death occurred on Kṛishṇa 12, i.e. 17-11-2449 BC. On the next morning, i.e. on 18-11-2449 BC, the moon rose with Jyeshṭhā *nakshatra* at 5:03 a.m. and the sunrise followed at 6:23 a.m.
6. The war ended with Duryodhana's death, which was observed by Balarāma after returning from pilgrimage on 21-11-2449 BC. It was Pausha Śukla 2 with the moon near Śravaṇa *nakshatra* at 5:10 a.m.
7. Winter solstice occurred on Māgha Kṛishṇa 6 at 0:40 a.m. on Julian date 9-1-2448 BC and Bhīsma expired on the next day on Māgha Kṛishṇa 7 on 10-1-2448 BC.

In this calendar, the interval between Balarāma's start and end of pilgrimage is 42 days and the interval between Bhīshmapatana and his expiry is 58 days, as required. The corresponding dates in Holay's calendar are: (1) 4-10-3143 BC and 1-11-3143 BC, (2) 7-10-3143 BC and 13-10-3143 BC, (3) 14-11-3143 BC, (4) 23-11-3143 BC, (5) 7-12-3143 BC, (6) 11-12-3143 BC and (7) 16-1-3142 BC.

We have already remarked that the position of planets given in the *Mahābhārata* are ambiguous and one can choose those which agree with one's point of view. Holay has laid stress on simultaneous appearance of all planets including Uranus. But his diagram for 3-11-3143 BC indicates that Uranus and Mercury were too close to the sun to be visible. Similarly on 11-12-3143 BC Mercury and Venus were combust (*asta*).

Sengupta has verified the following statements of the *Mahābhārata* in his work.

1. Saturn is only 10 deg. away and Jupiter is close to Rohiṇī (α Tauri) during 14-10-2449 to 21-11-2449 BC as stated in Bhīshma 2, 32/1: Udyoga 143, 8 and Karṇa 94, 51.

2. Mars moved from Chitrā to Viśākhā during the above period in the direct motion (*mārgī*) instead of it being in retrograde motion (*vakrī*) from Jyeshṭhā to Chitrā as stated in Udyoga 143, 9 & 10/1.
3. On 3-11-2449 BC the moon was near Rohiṇī and the sun was near Jyeshṭhā, the other (Jyeshṭhā) Rohiṇī, as stated in Bhīshma 3,17/1.
4. At sunset on the last day of the war Venus was combust (*asta*) and Mercury was seen before sunrise as stated in Karṇa 94, 49.

On the whole, Sengupta's calendar appears more cogent than that of Holay.

CONCLUSIONS

Accurate computations do not show any superconjunction of planets of the Kaliyuga type within the long period from 3500 BC to AD 3000. However, all the planets were combust (*asta*) on four *amāvasyā*s, out of which the one on 16-4-3243 BC is the closest to Āryabhaṭa's Kaliyuga epoch. But that close superconjunction occurred near the vernal equinox day of that period, i.e. at Rohiṇī instead of Aśvinī. Simultaneous appearance of all planets at the time of sunrise or sunset occurs quite often. But the one occurring on 7-2-3104 BC can also be taken as Kaliyuga epoch, because it could have been seen in the first month of the year, which used to start at winter solstice in those days.

As the beginning of Kaliyuga is associated with the Mahābhārata War, fixing its date can also determine the epoch of Kaliyuga. Taking Māgha Śukla 8, the traditional *tithi* of Bhīshma's death, as winter solstice day we get a date of about 1600±200 BC, which agrees with the undersea exploration near Beṭ Dvārakā. If one wants to go further back, the *tithi* of Bhishma's death has to be shifted in Indian *pañchāṅga*. Pushing it to Māgha Kṛishṇa 8 takes us back to 2449 BC, which agrees with Varāhamihira's estimate of Kali epoch.* But one has to push it to Phālguna Śukla 8 if one wants to go back to Āryabhaṭa's epoch of Kaliyuga.

* But Varāhamihira refers to the time of Yudhishṭhira, viz. Mahābhārata War, and not to the start of Kaliyuga. About the epoch of Kaliyuga almost all the Indian traditions are unanimous. In fact, the debate is about the date of the Mahābhārata War. — Ed.

NOTES AND REFERENCES

1. K.D. Abhyankar, 1991, *Indian Journal of History of Science*, Vol. 26, p. 1.
2. K.D. Abhyankar, and G.M. Ballabh, 1996, *Indian Journal of History of Science*, Vol. 31, p. 19.
3. K.D. Abhyankar, 1998, *Bulletin of the Astronomical Society of India*, Vol. 26, p. 61.
4. P.V. Holay, 1999, *Bhārtiyā Yuddhachī Dainandinī āni — Varsha*, Bhartiya Itihasa Sankalana Samiti, Mysore. (Vide also No. V in this Volume).
5. P.C. Sengupta, 1947, *Ancient Indian Chronology*, Calcutta University.
6. *Āryabhaṭīya* of Āryabhaṭa with the commentary of Bhāskara and Someśvara. Ed. K.S. Shukla, 1976, Pub. Indian National Science Academy, New Delhi.

7

The Weaponry in the Bhārata War

N.R. Waradpande

Our only source of information about the Bhārata War is the *Mahābhārata*. The epic now available, is not a unitary work composed by one author. This is clear from the fact that it contains astronomical, historical and archaeological data which point to different periods right from 3101 BC to the Christian era. The Northern course of the Sun when the moon was in the rohinī constellation in the bright half,[1] points to 3101 BC, Kārttika being the last month of autumn[2] could belong to the period after 2000 BC. The Northern course of the Sun in the Śravaṇa constellation,[3] the rapid spread of Buddhism,[4] the reference to Śakas, Hūnas and Yavanas (BVP 17/23) clearly refer to the first millennium before Christ.

The change in weapon-technology in these periods is also reflected in the descriptions in the *Mahābhārata*. The date 3101 BC belongs to the Chalcolithic Age when weapons were made of stone and copper; 2500 to 1500 BC was the Bronze Age when bronze replaced copper in a major way. The first millenium BC falls in the Iron Age when iron replaced bronze.

CHALCOLITHIC WEAPONS

Copper is soft and bends easily. So a full-length sword cannot be made out of copper. Such a sword would easily bend in mid-combat and render the warrior weaponless.

Mace

The close-combat weapon of the Kauravas and the Pāṇḍavas was the mace. The mace is a very unwieldy weapon. It is very heavy and the only effective blow possible with it is from above downwards. A blow from below upwards or even laterally would counteract its weight. Further, no thrusts with it are possible. The maces were made of stone (*adrisāramayī*). This shows that the mace would be useless against an opponent armed with a full-length sword. This is mentioned in the *Mahābhārata* itself.[5]

It is reasonable to infer that with the advent of the sword in the Bronze Age, the mace fell out of use. No maces were used in the Trojan war which was fought in 1200 BC when bronze swords were quite common and even iron swords were made by the Hittites. No war after 1200 BC is known to have employed maces.

The maces were made of stone (*adrisāramayī*).[6]

It should be noted that the Kauravas and the Pāṇḍavas were the leading powers of the day. So the arguments that, "even after the currency of fire-arms, tribes are using bows and arrows" is not relevant. If leading powers of the day use bows and arrows, the explanation lies in their backwardness.

There are three occasions on which the *Mahābhārata* speaks of the use of the "sword". (1) Bhūriśravas trying to behead Sātyaki.[7] (2) Dhṛishṭadyumna beheads Droṇa.[8] (3) Sātyaki beheads Kṛitavarman.[9]

Both Bhūriśravas and Dhṛishṭadyumna catch their victims by the hair in order to behead them. This clearly indicates that their "sword" was really a copper dagger and it was not possible for them to behead their victims with one blow, without catching them by the hair and operating their "sword" on their necks like a saw. Only a full-length sword can sever the neck with one blow without catching the victim by the neck.

The account in Mausalaparvan where Sātyaki draws his sword, advances and beheads Kṛitavarman must belong either to the Bronze or the Iron Age.

Long-Range Weapons

The long-range weapons were bows and arrows and the slings called *bhindipālas* (BVP 43/14). The *bhindipālas* are as effective as bows and arrows in what is called *saṅkulayuddha* or mass-warfare where accurate aiming is not very important. The bows and arrows are clearly superior in accurate aiming.

Different types of bows are mentioned. Those called *śārṅga* were made of horn. Horn is very difficult to bend though it is elastic. This means that one who can bend it, can send an arrow at a tremendous speed.

The bow of Arjuna was called *gāṇḍiva*. The word is derived from *gaṇḍa* meaning knot. 2/3 shafts of cane were tied to make the bow strong, so that it required great strength to string and stretch it. The arrow discharged by it had a great punch. Such bows were called *bhārasādhana* (BVP 74/53) or heavy performers. *Bhārasādhana* bows were *dvādaśaratnī* or twelve forearms in length (Droṇa 144/21), like the bows used by the warriors of Porus against Alexander. These were rested on the ground when they were used, not lifted like other light types of bows.

A light type of bow is reported to have been used by Droṇa to deal with attackers who came near his chariot. This bow did not have to be pulled much, thus saving the time for discharge of arrows and the number of arrows discharged per minute was much greater than that discharged by the heavy bow which had to be stretched right up to the ear with great exertion. When opponents are near, one cannot afford to spend so much time in striking.

Types of Arrows

The arrows discharged by this small bow were short and were called *vaitastika* or span-like (Droṇa 107/55). *Kshudraka* seems to be another type of short arrow (JVP 96/4).

An arrow called *vatsadanta* (BP 57/41) obviously had an arrowhead made of the tooth of young animals because a young tooth is stronger. The nails of a tortoise were also used as arrowheads (Droṇa 100/81).

The *nārācha* arrow (BVP 47/23) was wholly made of metal. (*sarvapārśive* or *sarvalohamaya*). *Nārācha* is also called *prakshveḍana* or a shrieker (*Amarakośa* II. 8.87). Shrieking bombs were used in the Second World War. They were not more destructive than ordinary bombs but the shrieking noise which they made, unnerved the enemy. *Nārācha* arrows must have similarly wrecked havoc. The word *nara* or *nala* stands for pipe. So the shaft of these arrows was made of a metal pipe. A pipe instead of a solid bar, besides making the arrow lighter, helps in increasing the noise. A few holes in suitable places will enhance the noise. The *Nārācha* arrows are mentioned also by the name *nalika* (BMP 90/32)

The arrow were generally made of cane-like shafts as is clear from the word *bāṇa* which stands for cane or bamboo. Such arrows had feathers stuck into holes made specially for this purpose at the rear end. This served to keep flight straight.

Some arrows are called by the name *viśikha*, i.e. without feathers (Śalya 15/72). These were most probably hollow metal shafts with metal fins in place of feathers.

The *bhalla* arrows obviously had spear-shaped heads. *Kshurapras* had razor-heads and were used for chopping off bowstrings or even limbs (Śalya 12/19). *Vikarṇa* or earless arrows (KP 84/8) were arrows which did not have ear-like protrusions behind the arrowhead. Such protrusions were intended to make it difficult for the arrows to be safely pulled out of the body of a soldier pierced by it. The *vikarṇa* or earless arrows were therefore recommended (Droṇa 157/11).

The types of arrows regarded as unfair were *nalika*, i.e. piped, poisoned or *lipta* and *bastaka*. The piped arrow was disapproved perhaps because frightening the enemy with its noise was regarded as unwarrior like. It is not clear why *bastaka* was disapproved. *Basta* means a goat and the *basta* arrow was perhaps made of the horn of a goat.

Other Weapons

Tomara (BVP 52/22) was a club studded with spikes. This weapon circumvents the main defect of copper, viz., bending, by using spikes. Spikes being short will not bend easily. Length is provided by the club.

Karpaṇa (BVP 52/22) was a weapon which was mainly used for cutting as against piercing as its name suggests. The word *karpaṇa* contains the root *kṛip* to cut. *Karpaṇas* are necessary when the opponent is to be hit on the leg or the arm, a man shot in the arm or the leg can still fight, but if his limbs are cut, he cannot do so.

Śaktis are mentioned as thrown. These are generally regarded as javelin. Ghaṭotkacha was killed by Karṇa by such a *śakti*.

Pāraśvadhas, i.e. battle-axes are frequently mentioned. Paraśurāma was famous for fighting with battle-axes. The battle-axes were more useful in the Chalcolithic Age because they circumvent the main defect of copper, viz. bending, if made too long. The length in the battle-axe is provided by the wooden shaft. Being lighter, battle-axes could have been more effective than the maces if the opponent was not heavily armoured.

Avaskanda (BVP 91/55) literally means pulling down. This was most probably a ring with a rope tied to it and thrown at the opponent. When the opponent was caught in it he was pulled down from his horse or elephant etc. Obviously this was done when the opponent was retreating so that his forward movement helped in pulling him down. This technique could not be used when the opponent was face to face; he would make short work of the *avaskanda*-holder by a thrust of his spear.

The *pāśa* (BVP 91/56) was a sort of noose by which the enemy was strangled. This was obviously used in body-contact combats like wresting. It would be suicidal if the enemy was at a sword's distance. The process of throwing the *pāśa* would be far more dilatory than the plunge of the dagger or the sword.

Shields of bullock-hide are mentioned by the word *ārshabha charma* (BVP 66/31). Clearly a shield of the hide of bullocks will not be a defence against a bronze or a steel sword. It could, however, be sufficient protection against the copper dagger or the sword of horn.

Not only the shields but also coats of mail were made of bullock-hide as is clear from the statement that Bhīshma's arrows did not stick in these coats (BVP 112/71). Coats of bullock-hide cushioned from inside would be a protection against copper arrowheads because when they did not strike exactly perpendicularly, they did not penetrate the coat but got stuck in it laterally. The length of a copper arrowhead is short because a long arrowhead can bend and become ineffective. Bhīshma's shots hit perfectly perpendicularly.

Bhīma is described as uprooting trees and fighting with them. These are clearly poetic exaggerations. Even an elephant cannot uproot trees like the palm which is said to have been used as a weapon. Fighting with the palm tree refers to fighting with the clubs made of the wood of palm trees.

A *śaikyāyasī gadā* (BVP 49/22) or a metal-sling-mace was thrown obviously like the hammer in the hammer-throws. Such hammers can be thrown to long distances. The *śaikyāyasī gadā* was thus a long-range weapon. Stone mace-heads being brittle were broken to pieces when they hit the copper coat of mail on the elephant's forehead, the front parapet of a chariot, the head of a horse and the body of a soldier. This coat of mail must have been well cushioned from inside and sufficiently thick to absorb the impact of the hitting mace-head. Being practically unbreakable, it is the stone mace-head that will break with the impact. If the mace-head is made of copper, it will not break and will be more effective against armour.

BRONZE AGE WEAPONS

Vipatha or *vipata* (BVP 55/27) literally means the "breaker". This is the name of an arrow. Arjuna used it to break the missiles of the enemy. These missiles which broke by striking another missile must have been made of stone or bronze, because neither copper nor iron will break with the impact of an arrow, a powerful shot will only make a hole in it.

There is an important description in the Abhimanyuvadha-parvan[10] – Jayadratha directs a blow to Abhimanyu with his sword. Abhimanyu parries it. So Jayadratha's sword gets stuck in his quiver which was made of leather (*charmaṇi*). When Jayadratha tried to pull it back, it was broken to pieces.

Obviously these swords were made of bronze. Only a bronze sword will break like this, not an iron one. It was not a copper sword because copper is less brittle even as compared to iron and it will never break with a mere pull. Moreover, the description shows that the sword was a full-length one (*mahānasiḥ*). Jayadratha must have aimed the blow somewhere under the neck below the armour-cover. Abhimanyu ducked ahead so that the blow fell on the quiver.

In another description Aśvatthāman's arrow breaks the sword of Śikhaṇḍin. Śikhaṇḍin then uses the piece left in his hand like a dagger and throws it on Aśvatthāman who then breaks this piece with another arrow.[11]

IRON AGE WEAPONS

Paṭṭīśa (BVP 91/56) is known as the *paṭṭa* or the rapier. This weapon belongs to the Iron Age since the very thing and elastic blade of the *paṭṭa* can be made only of steel.

Śataghnī (BVP 91/61) literally indicates that this weapon could kill a hundred in one round. This means that it could throw a stone so big that if it fell on a group of 100 soldiers, all of them would be killed.

The *śataghnīs* were most probably catapults like those of Archimedes with which he fought the Romans at Syracuse. The date of Archimedes is 287 to 212 BC. The bulk of the *Mahābhārata* was composed around this time.

ARCHAEOLOGY CORROBORATES LITERATURE[12]

The literary evidence is supported by archaeology. The discovery of copper weapons[13] in areas connected with the Bhārata War strengthens the traditional view that the Bhārata War was fought in the Chalcolithic Age. The copper objects recovered from the excavations are ascribed to a period near about 2800 BC by archaeologists. This is near about the traditional date of the Bhārata War.

The "swords" found, range from 42 to 75 cm. These are called antennae swords because of the antennae-like bifurcations of the hilt end. These swords are cast with antennae as one piece and have long blades with a short hilt. Even in a 75 cm sword, the blade and the tip would be 15 cm only. The thick median-ridged portion is designed to prevent the bending of the copper swords. Such a sword could not have been used in war like a regular sword.

They were perhaps used as the *hulas* in the Bhārata War which were buried in the ground so that the enemy trotting on it would be wounded enough to be unable to fight (Droṇa 166/20).

The advantage of the antennae is that the swords can be fixed securely in a narrow cleft made in heavy wooden logs. Such logs with antennae swords projecting out could be placed at the bottom of pits.

The second type of weapon is the harpoon. It is mid-ribbed, spear-headed with oblique or backward-curving barbs, quite often with a hole on a lug. It is clear that the spear-head was fastened to the shaft by strings passing through these barbs. The solitary hole was probably for the copper nail to be driven through it. The hole is solitary because driving a copper nail through hard wood is not easy. So nailing was very sparingly used for fastening. Arrowheads must have been similar to the harpoon.

I suggest that the *nataparva* arrows mentioned in the *Mahābhārata* are none other than these harpoons tied to a wooden-shaft. *Nataparva* literally means a bent joint. How the joint of an arrow can be bent was a puzzle to me until I saw this harpoon. The barbs in this harpoon are bent in the direction opposite to that of the line of its thrust and they were tied at these very places to the shaft. So they are really arrows whose joints are bent. These barbs were perhaps not bent in other types of arrows.

The third type of copper weapon is the anthropomorphic. This looks like a human figure with a hammered and blunted head, externally sharpened and incurved forearms and plain legs. The shape is cut from a plain copper sheet by beating from the top.

Though this looks like a human figure, it is really a weapon, its legs are exactly like a boomerang. When thrown, it goes whirling. Only a replica of this weapon was tested as a missile. The replica did not return like a boomerang, but experts believe that the original would. This, however, could not be verified since the museum does not lend its exhibits.

This then could be the prototype of Kṛishṇa's *sudarśana chakra*, its edges could serve to cut necks and hands. A bowstring caught inside the arms could also be easily cut.

One peculiarity of these copper weapons is that they are very often alloyed with arsenic, 50 per cent of the weapons have more than 1 per cent arsenic. Arsenic alloying makes copper harder and was a step towards bronze which is copper hardened by tin alloying.[14]

This arsenic alloying is referred to in the *Mahābhārata* by the word *śilāśita* (Śalya 24/39) which qualifies the word arrow. A *śilāśita* arrow is an arrow which is made thin-edged by the use of *śilā*, i.e arsenic. *Śilāśita* cannot be translated as thin-edged like a stone. The edges of copper can be made thinner than that of the stone because the stone will break if we try to give it a very thin edge. *Śilāśita* did not also mean "sharpened by a stone", because sharpening is done only on a stone and there is no point in saying that a particular arrow was sharpened by stone.

Arsenic alloying should not be confused with arsenic smearing. The smearing is referred to by the word *śitādhauta* (Śalya 25/5,55/27). The arrows were smeared with arsenic to make them poisonous. The word *śilā* in *śilādhauta* leaves no doubt that the word *śilā* in *śilaśita* refers to arsenic.

DATE OF THE BHĀRATA WAR

The find of the chalcolithic weapons can be regarded as archaeological evidence for the historicity of the Bhārata War. Those who oppose this view make much of the fact that these weapons have not been found at Kurukshetra. This objection sounds credible only on the view that the Bhārata War was fought within the municipal limits of the present-day Kurukshetra. Nothing could be farther from the truth. The *Mahābhārata* clearly states (JVP 98/12) that the place where Arjuna was pursuing Jayadratha was three *yojanas* from the place where Droṇāchārya was trying to capture Yudhishṭhira. Three *yojanas* come to about 24 to 27 miles. Thus, the front of the Bhārata War was at least 30 miles long.

It should be remembered that the front is not the base of operations. The rival armies do not put all the soldiers to the field at one go. The armies are encamped at some place from where they supply weapons and men to the front. These encampments are the bases from which the armies operate. The base of the Kauravas comprised the Punjab, Haryana, Rajasthan and Ahichchhatra, i.e. Rampur, (Senodyogaparvan 19). This is about 200 miles long. The Kauravas mobilized first, as clear from the statement that Duryodhana mobilized his army the very day peace-parleys broke down, while the Pāṇḍavas mobilized after Kṛishṇa returned to their camp. Since the Kauravas had already chosen a base to the west of Kurukshetra, the Pāṇḍavas chose base to the east. This base must have been facing the base of the Kauravas. Though the *Mahābhārata* does not give the geographical details of the Pāṇḍava encampment as it does in the case of the Kauravas, it clearly states that the Pāṇḍavas were facing the west (Udyoga 195/11) and the Kauravas the east. Agrawal gives a map of the chalcolithic sites. This map shows areas of Haryana, Rajasthan, Ahichchhatra, Hastinapura and the areas facing them in the east as chalcolithic. In other words, though the small area of Kurukshetra is not classified as chalcolithic, the areas where the armies were encamped were mostly chalcolithic.

LINGUISTIC EVIDENCE

That the period of the Bhārata War belongs to the earlier period of the *Ṛigveda* when swords were not invented, makes one expect that probably the Sanskrit language of this period did not have a word for the sword. It can be shown that this was in fact the case. The *Amarakośa* mentions the following words for the sword – *khaḍga, nistriṁśa, chandrahāsa, asi, ṛishṭi, kauksheyaka, maṇḍalāgra, karavāla* and *kṛipaṇa.*

All these words originally referred to the dagger. *Khaḍga* means the horn of a rhinoceros. This was used as a sword and is only 40 cm in length. *Nistriṁśa* means longer than thirty *aṅgulas.* An *aṅgula* is defined as equal to eight barley-grains placed with their middle portions touching each other. I have thus placed the said grains and found them to make half an inch. This is also the breadth of a finger (*aṅgula*). *Nistriṁśa* was therefore only about 15 inches. A 40 cm *nistriṁśa* made of copper has been found in Mohenjodaro.[14]

The Bhīshmavadhaparvan states that the *nistriṁśas* were thrown (82/30, 31, 67/17). This shows beyond doubt that they were not full-length swords because full-length swords are never thrown. Further, the statement must have been made in the pre-bronze-age when the word *nistriṁśa* had not acquired the meaning of a sword.

Another indication that the *nistriṁśa* was not a full-length sword is in the fight of Dhṛishṭaketu and Paurava (BVP 112/19, 20). They were both fighting with bullock-hide shields and *nistriṁśas*. If the *nistriṁśas* were full-length swords of bronze or steel, bullock-hide shields would be of no avail against them. So these *nistriṁśas* were clearly copper daggers or more likely the horns of the rhinoceros. The horns of the rhinoceros are on the average 40 cm or 30 *aṅgulas* in length. So the *nistriṁśa* longer than 30 *aṅgulas* was something outstanding.[15]

Chandrahāsa was the name of Rāvaṇa's sword. So it is a proper name. Proper names are not meant to designate the properties of the object named.

Asi is derived from the root as to throw and was thus a dagger which is very often used as a missile. *Ṛishṭi* is rendered by Sāyaṇa (*Ṛigveda-bhāshya* 9/112/1) as a tool for chiselling wood. So this was some sort of a carpenter's tool like the present *paṭāsī* which could not be longer than a dagger. *Kauksheyaka* was a weapon which could be kept in the cloth tied round the belly. So this could not be a full-length sword. *Maṇḍalāgra* was obviously a weapon with curved tip. No full-length swords are known to have curved tips. *Maṇḍalāgra* was therefore most probably a sickle-like weapon used for cutting throats.[16] *Karavāla* clearly refers to a *bala* or a puny weapon in the hand. *Kṛipaṇa* is derived from the root *kṛip* to cut and originally referred to a knife or a blade. A pair of scissors is called *kṛipaṇī*. This is the nominative singular of the word *kṛipaṇin*. There is tendency to drop the consonant 'n' at the end of word. So *Dharman* becomes *dharma*. When the word takes the form *kṛipaṇī*, it appears a dual of the word *kṛipaṇin*. The dual shows that the blade of a pair of scissors was called a *kṛipaṇī*. The root *kṛip* is not found in Pāṇini, but it is clearly seen in the word *kṛipaṇa* meaning miser, i.e. one who cuts expenditure.

It is thus clear that the older words for a knife were used for the sword when the sword was invented. This is usual in the history of a language.

The word *śilimukha* for the arrow also belongs to the Chalcolithic Age. *Śila* means a slab and the word *śili* is formed from it by adding the feminine suffix in the diminutive sense. *Śilimukha* thus means an arrow with stone head. This stone was granite. An *adrisāramaya* arrow or arrow having the strength of a stone is also mentioned (Droṇa 17/21). Bhīshma says that the sword was invented when meteors (*ulkā*) were studied.[17] This is likely because the meteors very often contain steel and sometimes an alloy of iron and nickel, i.e. stainless steel. By analyzing the meteor-metal, the method to make steel may have been invented.

It is generally supposed that the method of making steel was hit upon when it was noticed that in the process of purifying the copper iron ore mixed in it, which if mixed with carbon and was found to be very strong. Meteors are very rare to find and therefore the accidental discovery of steel while purifying copper is more likely. But better quality steel was perhaps discovered through the meteors.

Lay readers of the *Mahābhārata* at once think of the *astras* when one talk of the weaponry in the Bhārata War. Claims have also been made that these were like the modern inter-continental missiles and nuclear bombs. But the descriptions clearly show that they were not. They were not manufactured in factories and owned by the kings; they were taught to favourite disciples by the *gurus* and consisted of certain *mantras*. Modern weapons of mass destruction are not activated by *mantras*.

It is sometimes claimed that the science of *astras* was not the modern science of machines but a science based on the magical powers of the sounds used in the *mantras*. This is a mere assertion.

There is no evidence that *mantras* posses any such properties and nobody has ever demonstrated them. Those who make such claims should spend their energies in staging such a demonstration rather than challenging others to disprove their assertion. The *astras* are obviously the product of poetic imagination.

CONCLUSION

The oldest portions of the *Mahābhārata* indicate that the Bhārata War was fought with copper, stone, horn and nail weapons. This corroborates the astronomical evidence that the war was fought sometime around 3101 BC.

NOTES AND REFERENCES

The *Mahābhārata* quotations are from the southern recension. The weapons mentioned have been referred to in hundreds of places but only one or two references are regarded sufficient. Abbreviations: BVP = *Bhīshmavadhaparvan*, JVP = *Jayadrathavadhaparvan*, DVP = *Droṇavadhaparvan*, KVP = *Karṇavadhaparvan*, SVP = *Śalyavadhaparvan.*

1. P.V. Holay, The Year of the Kaurava-Pāṇḍava-War, See *Supra* No. 5 – Ed.
2. कौमुदे मासि रेवत्यां शरदन्ते हिमागमे। भगवद्यानपर्व
3. प्रतिश्रवणपूर्वाणि नक्षत्रणि चकार ह। अश्वमेधपर्व 44/2 आदिपर्व 71/34
4. एड्र्कचिह्ना पृथिवी न देवगृहभूषिता। वनपर्व 109/68
5. .... गदाशक्तिधरास्तदा।
   एकः खड्गधरो धीरः समर्थः प्रतियाधितुम्।। 145/41/44
6. आधूतां भीमसेनेन गदां दृष्ट्वा सुयोधनः।
   अद्रिसारमयीं गुर्वी आविध्यन्बह्वशोभत।। शल्यपर्व अ 51/75
7. अथ कोशाद्विनिष्कृष्य खड्गं भूरिश्रवाःशितम।
   मूर्धजेषु च जग्राह पदा चोरस्यताडयत्।। जयद्रथवधपर्व 121/44
8. विकृष्य पार्श्वतः खड्गं केशपक्षे परामशत्। द्रोणवधपर्व 160/39
9. इत्येवमुक्तवा खड्गेन केशवस्य समीपतः।
   आभिसृत्य शिरस्तस्य चिच्छेद कृतवर्मणः।। मौसलपर्व 3/29
10. ततो विक्षिपतः खड्गं सौभद्रस्य यशस्विनः।
    शरावरणपक्षान्ते प्रजहार जयद्रथः।।
    रुक्मपक्षान्तरे सक्तस्तस्मिंश्चर्मणि भास्वरे।
    सिन्धुराजकरोद्धूतः सोभज्यत महानसिः।।
11. शिखण्डी तु ततः खड्गं खण्डितं द्रौणिसायकैः।
    आविध्य व्यसृजत्तूर्ण द्रोणपुत्राय वेगतः।। भीष्मवधपर्व 77/37
    तमापतन्तं सहसा कालानलसमप्रभम्।
    शरैरचूर्णयद्द्रौणिर्दर्शयन् हस्तलाधवम्।। भीष्मवधपर्व 77/38

12. Researches into the much greater and persisting problem of Copper Hoards date back to 1822 when a harpoon was first discovered at Biṭhūr in Kanpur district of Uttar Pradesh. Since then there have been many finds, in groups as well as sporadically, of these objects, those in groups being rightly described as Hoards. They are made of almost 98% pure copper including some usual and other strange objects mostly found in the Gaṅgā valley in North India, the important regions being those covered by the present states of Uttar Pradesh, Bihar, Bengal, Orissa, Madhya Pradesh and Rajasthan. Kallūr in Karnataka has also yielded a solitary tool. As of now we have some ninety sites yielding nearly a thousand artifacts, Guṅgeriā (Madhya Pradesh) alone giving as many as 424 objects. The implements include celts – flat, shouldered and bar, rings, harpoons, anthropomorphic figures, *paraśu*-like double axes and antennae-hilted swords. The dates for these objects range between about 2800 BC [as at Gaṇeśvar in Rajasthan where a copper hoard was found in association with ochre-coloured ware (OCP)] and 1400 BC. Some scholars reject the association of the OCP as in its so-called original home it is dated in the time-bracket 1700-1400 BC.

    As regards the copper weapons supposedly used in the Mahābhārata war, some scholars are of the opinion that the antennae-hilted swords of the Copper Hoards were largely employed in this war. Some even suggested that the weapons, being of copper which is very soft metal, were very short and the antennae-hilted swords fit into that category. However, the fact is otherwise. The antennae-hilted swords are as long as 78 cm with 72 cm for short double-edged blade and 6 cm for the hilt (e.g. from Fatehgarh, Uttar Pradesh). It is wrong to say that the hilts of these swords are longer than the blade. The shortest of the antennae-swords measures 40 cm long with a 5 cm hilt. Even the hooked spearhead measures 32.5 cm with a 10 cm long hilt (Sarhauli, Uttar Pradesh) – Ed.
13. D.P. Agrawal, *Copper and Bronze Age of India*, p. 12.
14. D.P. Agrawal, *Indian Bronze Age Cultures and their Metal Technology*, p. 257.
15. A standard *Aṅgula* is commonly taken to denote ¾ of an inch – Ed.
16. According to ancient Indian writers, *Maṇḍalāgra* is a kind of sword with a rounded tip. It finds mention in the *Arthaśāstra* (II. 18) of Kauṭilya, Varāhamihīra's *Bṛihat-saṁhitā* (XLIX. 7) and the *Navasāhasāṅka-charita* (I. 74) of Padmagupta.
17. पेतुश्चोल्का महोत्पाताः शाखाश्च ममृदुर्द्रुमाः।
    ततस्तद्रूपमुपमुत्सृज्य बभौ निःस्त्रिंश एव सः।। शान्तिपर्व 145/41/44

8

Possible Location of Kāmpilya in the *Mahābhārata*

K.M. Srivastava

Kāmpilya is well known as one of the important capitals mentioned in the great epic *Mahābhārata*. The whereabouts of this capital according to certain scholars, were not identified for certainty in spite of the fact that there is an important brisk town called Kāmpilya in Farrukhābād district of Uttar Pradesh about sixteen kilometres north-west of the commercial centre of Kaimganj, a railway station on the Kasganj-Kanpur section of North-Eastern Railways.

Kāmpilya finds mentions in *Aitareya Brāhmaṇa*[1] with two kings of the state having universal fame, besides the *Mahābhārata*. In the *Mahābhārata*, in addition to other references, the place is known as the seat of King Drupada, father of Draupadī. The South Pāñchālas also had their capital at Kāmpilya.[2] The Pāñchālas occupied the country to the east of the Kurus between the mountains and the Ganges. Ahichchhatrā in Bareilly district of Uttar Pradesh happened to be the capital of North Pāñchālas.[3] River Ganges was the dividing line between the two territories. As at present, the ancient site of Kāmpilya was an important pilgrimage centre of the Jaina devotees, with Lord Mahāvīra having visited it. The place is also believed to be the birth and enlightenment place of the thirteenth Jaina *tīrthaṅkara*.[4]

In spite of the fact that the massive mound of Kāmpilya yielded the Painted Grey Ware (collected earlier also in 1961-62), said to be the *Mahābhārata* pottery, the small-scale excavations in 1975-76 conducted by K.K. Sinha could not finally identify its location. The location of the place was rendered doubtful by some of his specific statements. He said, "The Painted Grey Ware deposit above the natural soil exposed in a limited area, is 2.40 m in thickness. The debris overlying this deposit belongs to the late medieval period".[5] However, there are two very significant observations presented by him, on the basis of which far-reaching conclusions could be drawn. They are, "However, a drop of approximately 3 m from the centre of the mound was noticed between KPL 2 and KPL 4. An interesting feature of the ancient settlement was a mud embankment rising to a height of 1.70 m."[6] Both the statements are a clear-cut indication of heavy floods and destruction thereby in the area.

Certain scholars from Italy were attracted by the final solution of the problem of the location of Kāmpilya. As a sequel they accepted the invitation of the local Pāñchāla Research Institute. On the basis of the first field survey by them, one of the students of the University of Venice was asked to prepare a thesis on the problem of the discovery of Kāmpilya. The conclusions drawn by Sinha regarding late deposits were corroborated by the student. An expedition was thereafter organized by the above mentioned scholars in pursuance of the solution of the same problem in February 1996 with assistance of the photo prints prepared through remote sensing imagery of the Kāmpilya area. The expedition came across a vast site of ruins, about five kilometres westward from the town of Kāmpilya. The results of the discovery were published in the *Bulletin of the University of the Venice*[7] and in the *Journal of the Italian Embassy in India*.[8] Again, a subsequent expedition was undertaken in February 1997. During the course of this work, the team came across a big fortified town, with the walls measuring 780 m x 660 m orienting towards the points of the compass. On January 7, 1998, the discovery was officially presented in the Rashtrapati Bhavan in collaboration with the Director-General, Archaeological Survey of India, late Shri Ajay Shankar, and the Dean of the Faculty of Fine Arts, Banaras Hindu University, Prof. Srivastava, in the presence of the Italian Prime Minister, Prof. R. Prodi, and Indian Minister for Human Resources Development, Shri S.R. Bommai.[9]

With promising results of the first two expeditions, a third expedition by the Italian team was launched subsequently in January 1998. During the course of this campaign, the importance of the archaeological site, famous locally as Drupada Kilā, was confirmed. The antiquity of the site was evaluated in detail on the basis of the remains available there. According to the observations of the team, the bricks and terracotta fragments scattered on the surface could be assigned a date varying between the sixth century BC and the first century AD.

On the basis of the evidences collected by the Italian team during the course of the three expeditions, it was decided to launch a Kāmpilya Excavation Project with a view to ascertain the date of the locally famous Drupada Kilā and ultimately to determine the remains of Kāmpilya mentioned frequently in the *Mahābhārata*. The team requested various institutions in India for assistance in the work. The request was accepted by the Indian Archaeological Society, New Delhi, which entered into an agreement. The license to undertake excavation in the area was obtained by the society and the author, being the Vice Chairman of the Institution, had the privilege of participating in the work along with K.N. Dikshit, General Secretary, who happened to be the leader of the Project.

The Drupada Kilā site (lat. 27°36′ 13″ N – long. 79°12′30″ E) spreads over 9,00,000 m within a fortification wall visible on the surface from a long distance and made of brick bats. The sides of the fortification wall in a rectangular shape measure 780 m x 660 m with the longer axis oriented east-west. The average width of the wall in its visible parts is about 350 cm (with a maximum of about 500 cm) which stood upon an earlier mud structure. There are hardly any traces either of towers or ramparts at regular intervals. A wall head on the western side having some gaps in the structural activity with varied thickness of wall on the northern side lead to the presumption of entrance to the fortification. There are no walls at the north-eastern corner for about 100 m in both directions. This is probably due to erosion, collapse or removal caused by destructive floods and robbing activity of the local residents. The size of the bricks used in the wall was around 25 to 30″ x 40 to 45 x 55 cm.

A town with a surface of 50 hectares existing about the end of the first millennium BC in Doab, was no doubt an important settlement, though not so important as to become a capital under normal circumstances. The capital should have been at least ten times larger than most important towns, besides essential services. There was a great disparity between this and other capitals at the time, viz. Śrāvastī, Kauśāmbī, Mathurā, etc. Drupada Kilā could therefore be treated as a big town in Pāñchāla region, which was still unknown.

The cultural deposit within the Drupada Kilā happened to be about 5 m in the northern parts, while to the south the same is a little less. As it appeared on the surface, the inhabited area within the Kilā was built most probably of unbaked bricks. In some parts of the mound to the east, remains of a few burnt brick buildings were noticed.

During the course of the limited excavations it was very surprising to observe that the earliest occupation in the area could not be pushed back to times earlier than second century BC.

In view of the evidences of a later date along with no indications of the times of the *Mahābhārata*, it was decided to explore the surrounding areas of Kāmpilya town itself, where limited excavations were conducted in 1975-76. The busy town of Kāmpilya is situated along a massive mound with about 6 m cultural deposit over alluvial plain. This oval mound (700 m x 300 m long) is located along a scarp that dips suddenly to a plain. On the eastern side of the mound, under the steep slope lies the ancient course of the Ganges, (Būṛhī Gaṅgā, a channel of the Ganges), an abundant meandering course which is at present reduced to a small swamp, 140 m wide, along which there are bathing *ghāṭs* of the 16th century. The main river, that now flows 4 km farther to the north-east, must have changed its course. In addition, there are remains of a rectangular pond provided with steps for ablutions, which is called Draupadī Kuṇḍ. The north-eastern fringe of the mound is surmounted by two buildings of which the first is a little temple locally known as the place of *Ṛishi* Kapila. The second building has been recently restored and encloses the sanctum of a *Śivaliṅga*. The temple stands on a *dharmaśālā* and an annexe which is under the occupation of a *pujārī*. The local folks on the basis of tradition assert that Draupadī Kuṇḍ is the pond from which Draupadī emerged as a young girl seated on a lotus with a miraculous *liṅga* in her hand. This is an episode of the *Mahābhārata*, which occurred in Kāmpilya and is recognized by the local people. On the south-west extremity of the mound, walls of fortification of Kāmpilya, capital of South Pāñchāla appear. In addition, there are two temples of Jaina identity, one dedicated to Śvetāmbara and the other Digambara on the western end of the mound.

As already established by the excavators earlier, fragments of Painted Grey Ware and Nothern Black Polished Ware were scattered on the surface at Kāmpilya. A close study of the steep section near the channel of the river revealed that the successive occupations of the Painted Grey Ware and the Northern Black Polished Ware were subjected to heavy floods. As a sequel to the destruction by the devastating floods, the inhabitants resorted to safety measures. High mud platforms were raised to construct the dwellings and other structures over them. Sinha had come across such a platform during the course of his limited excavation, though he could not determine the purpose at that time. He, however, made an indirect reference to it in his sketchy report. He said, "An interesting feature of the ancient settlement was a mud-embankment rising to a height of 1.70 m." Similarly, there is a connected reference to floods as well. He said again, "However, a drop of approximately 3 m from the centre of the mound was noticed between KPL 2 and KPL 4." The conclusions drawn by Sinha regarding late deposits are also significant enough. When there will be recurrent floods there are bound to be a mixture of deposits in which the later ones will be more prominent.

In the sharp cutting of the section, mixture of washed flood deposits can be easily observed. Eroded material along with the occupational deposits are clearly visible in the steep cutting. They can be easily extracted by a soft scraping. Further, at the end of the mound, huge dressed stone boulders are found peeping out of the deep occupational deposit. They appear to be part of a fortification, though the exact time of its construction could not be assessed without proper excavation.

All the above mentioned indications lead to a strong assumption that the ancient mound near the modern town of Kāmpilya was the Kāmpilya of the *Mahābhārata* times. The fury of devastating recurrent floods led not only to its desertion in epic times but also rendered the establishment very poor. Thereafter the entire occupation was shifted to the present fortified area of Drupada Kilā. It was only on this account that the occupation at Drupada Kilā could not be pushed beyond second or third century BC. The antiquities from the excavation at Drupada Kilā, therefore, were also very poor. The present Kāmpilya has been identified by earlier archaeologists as well to be the original

Kāmpilya of the *Mahābhārata*. It is, however, established firmly by proper excavations.

Floods have been of quite a common occurrence in this part of the Gaṅgā valley. The area should be thoroughly explored in the light of the occupations during the time of Painted Grey Ware and subsequent times. A vast land of flooded area can be viewed from the top of the ancient mound at Kāmpilya. Beyond this land a very promising Painted Grey Ware site, viz. Bargain, is situated. With the aid of extensive explorations in the area and spotting of new sites, a very interesting story of the entire Kāmpilya land is likely to emerge. In the light of the supposed shifting of capital from Kāmpilya to Drupada Kilā, attention of the scholars maybe invited to the important ancient site of Hastināpura, another important *Mahābhārata* town in Uttar Pradesh.

Further, it maybe pointed out that the chemical analysis of the soils in the adjoining area by a geologist has indicated that all the Painted Grey Ware sites in the region are located in the older alluvium level whereas the later sites were all located in the younger alluvium level.

NOTES AND REFERENCES

1. *Aitareya Brāhmaṇa*, VIII, 23.
2. K.C. Jain, *Lord Mahāvīra and His Times*, New Delhi, 1974, p. 49.
3. *Ibid.*
4. *Ibid.*, pp. 51-52.
5. *IAR*, 1975-75, pp. 51-52.
6. *Ibid.*
7. "Cervanda Kāmpilya", *Asiatica Venetiana*, 1, 1996.
8. "Kāmpilya Rediscovered", *Journal of the Italian Embassy in India*, 5, Sept.-Oct., 1996.
9. *Kāmpilya: Quest for a Mahābhārata City*, Venetian Academy of Indian Studies, Series 2, New Delhi, 1999, p. 10.

9

Some Ancient *Janapadas* of Uttarāpatha vis-à-vis the *Mahābhārata*

Devendra Handa

The *Rāmāyaṇa* and the *Mahābhārata* may be regarded as the foundation supporting the edifice of the Hindu culture. To call them as mere epics or to compare them with the epics of the West is not justified because of their unique influence on the people through the ages.

The *Mbh*. dealing with the family feud resulting in the overthrow of the Kauravas by the Pāṇḍavas, forms the nucleus which assumed the present form by periodical additions of different kinds, making it a compendium of the fourfold aims of human existence and encyclopaedic in nature.

> *Dharme hyarthe cha kāme cha mokshe cha bharatarshabha /*
> *Yadihāsti tadanyatra yannehāsti na tat kvachit //*

Dharma, Artha, Kāma and *Moksha* are in fact the four crucial points round which revolves the Indian life. The *Mbh*. contains all that is worth knowing-

> *Sāṅgopanishadāṁśchaiva vedānāṁ vistara-kriyā*
> *Itihāsa-purāṇānāṁ unmesha-nimeshaṁ cha yatra /*
> *Chāturvarṇya-vidhānaṁ cha graha-nakshatra-tārāṇām*
> *Pramāṇaṁcha mayā atra sthāpitam //*

A study of the *Mbh*. is important from the point of view of history also. Since the nucleus of the family feud, with all its additions and interpolations, developed into an account of a great war in which practically all the peoples and potentates of the period took part, siding either with the Kauravas or the Pāṇḍavas, we get a lot of information regarding various *janapadas* which participated in the Mahābhārata War or have just incidentally been mentioned (see Appendix). The present paper deals with some tribes (*janapadas*) of the Uttarāpatha which find mention in the *Mbh.* and have also issued coins (for the location of these tribes see Maps 1&2). The name Uttarāpatha, literally meaning 'the northern route', i.e. the trade route which passed through northern India and connected it with the southern part (Dakshiṇāpatha) and the western world, later came to be applied to the region through which it passes, has been used in the different texts and at different times in different connotations.[1] We have, however, used it in the same sense in which it has been used in the great epic to denote northern India in a general way (*Mbh.*, Śāntiparvan 207/43).[2] Though much is now known about many of the tribes mentioned in the *Mbh.* from other sources also, yet we shall confine our discussion to some of the coin issuing tribes in the light of their description or mention in the great epic, in an alphabetical order.

ĀGREYAS

The *Mbh.* (Vanaparvan 254/20) mentions the Āgreyas as republican people, who were conquered by Karṇa during his western conquest-

> *Bhadrān Rohitakāṁśchaiva Āgreyān Mālavānapi /*
> *Gaṇān sarvān vinirjitya nītikṛit prahasanniva //*

P.L. Gupta thinks that the name 'Āgreya' is derived from 'Agra' and is corrupted into Prakrit 'Agācha' through Agajja (Sanskrit suffix *eya* changing into *jja*) and then 'Agachcha' or 'Agācha'. He has identified them with the people who issued square and round copper coins bearing the legends *Agodaka Agācha Janapadasa* and *Agāchamitapadabhish (ṭh) āyina[ḥ]**, found from Agrohā and the surrounding region.[3] M.J. Przyluski, however, equated Agrodaka with Aggaḷapura, a town of the Punjab region, mentioned in the *Vinayapiṭaka* as lying on the great trade-route which ran from the valley of the Gaṅgā to Taxila, and very ably and correctly identified Agrodaka with modern Agrohā near Hissar in 1926.[4] L.D. Barnett[5] identifies the Aggalas with the 'Agalasseis', who, according to the Greek historian Diodorus, were living in the neighbourhood of the Siboi (Śivas, Śibis) of the Jhang district (now in Pakistan), and who, according to Quintus Curtius, gave a very stiff resistance to Alexander. Bela Lahiri thinks that "since Agrohā

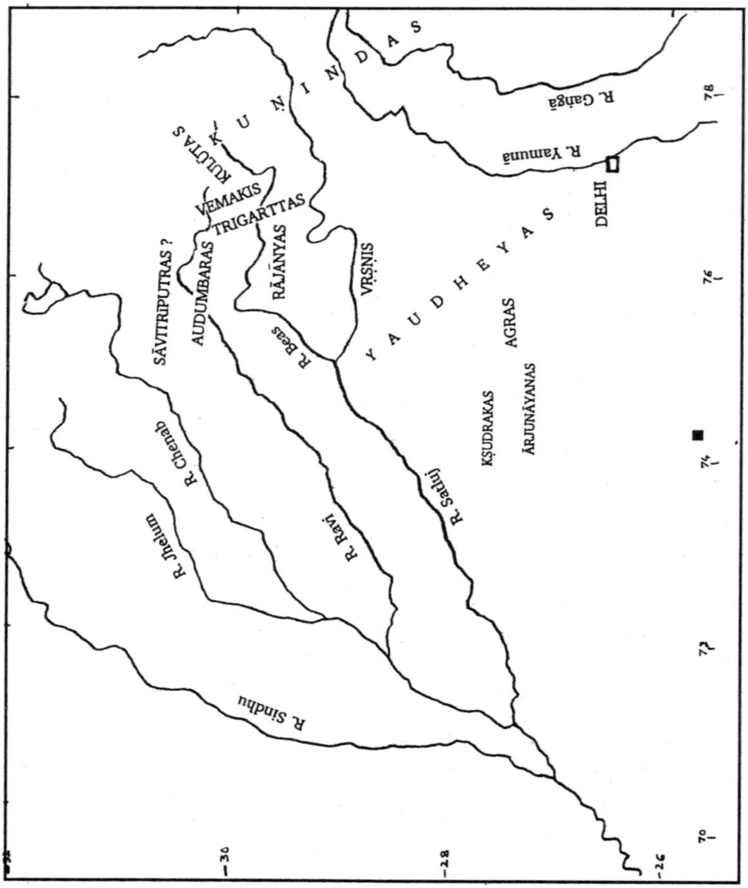

Map. 1 Location of Some North Indian *Janapadas*

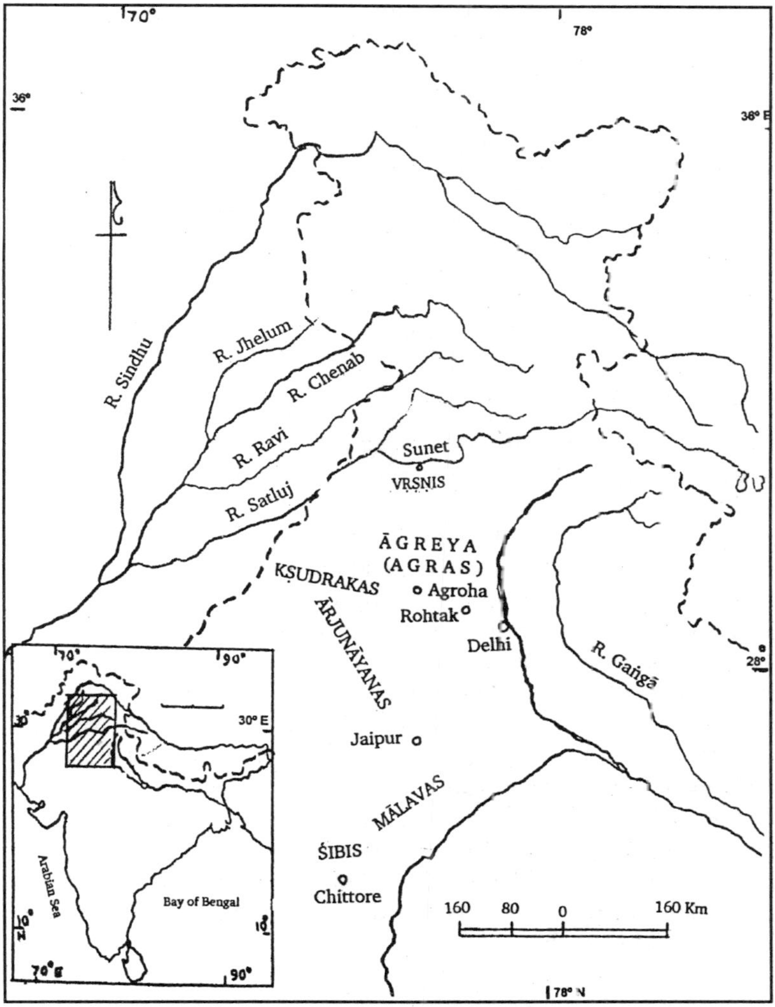

Map. 2 Location of Some Ancient Indian *Janapadas*

(in the Hissar District) is far separated from Jhang, the identification of the 'Agalasseis' with the legends seem to be doubtful".[6] P.L. Gupta, however, thinks that the legends among the Agrawal community of a struggle between Alexander and the Agrohā people support the identification of the 'Agalasseis' with the 'Agāchas' of coins.[7] It may be pointed out that like many other tribes who fought against Alexander (viz. the Siboi, Malloi, Oxydrakai, etc.) in the northwest but later shifted to Rajasthan, the Agalasseis too may have shifted from their original habitat and settled at and around Agrohā later. The name 'Agalasseis' as recorded by the Greek historian seems to be the exact transciption of the word *Agrāsaḥ*, an optional nominative plural form of Agra according to a grammatical rule of Vedic Sanskrit. The word Agacha, however, may better be derived from Agra-tya or its derivative form Āgrātya (*Cf. Pāśchātya, Dākshiṇātya*, etc.) rather than Āgreya. Dasgupta derives Agācha from Agratya thus: Agācha < Aggacha <Aggachcha < Agratya.[8]

The passage of the *Mbh.* gives us some idea of the location of the tribe also as it mentions the Āgreyas along with the Bhadras, Rohītakas and Mālavas. The Bhadras seem to have been the people residing at and around the modern town of Bhadra (Bhādarā), located at a distance of about 65 km west of Hissar on the old bed of the Vedic river Dṛishadvatī, identified with modern Chiṭāng or Chauṭāng.[9] A part of the town is located on a huge ancient mound which yields, amongst others, early historic remains also. The Rohītakas may be well imagined to have been the people of the modern town of Rohtak which is referred to at another place also in the *Mbh.* in the context of the Yaudheyas. The Mālavas were located around Nagarī near Chittorgarh in Rajasthan. The reference to the Āgreyas in the *Mbh.* thus seems to indicate the period when they were located at and around Agrohā and not in northwest Punjab of Pakistan. The relevant text of the *Mbh.* may not, therefore, have been finalized before the second-first century BC which approximately is the date of their coins found from Agrohā and elsewhere.

ĀRJUNĀYANAS

The Ārjunāyanas have been mentioned in Pāṇini's *Gaṇapāṭha* and then in Samudragupta's Prayāga *praśasti* along with the

Yaudheyas, Mālavas, Prārjunas etc.[10] J.F. Fleet held that the Ārjunāyanas may have been connected with the Pandoouoi or Pāṇḍava tribe of Punjab mentioned by Ptolemy.[11] Some other scholars also believe that, as their name indicates, they may have descended from the third Pāṇḍava Arjuna, just as the Yaudheyas are believed to have descended from the eldest Pāṇḍava brother Yudhishṭhira.[12] The Ārjunāyanas issued some copper and base silver coins which have come down to us.[13] On the basis of the distribution of their coins it is surmised that they may have occupied some part of Rajasthan near Mathurā[14] [J. Allan placed them 'within the triangle Delhi-Jaipur-Agra' and mostly scholars have accepted this view] or most probably an area near Mathurā to the Nohar-Bhadra region of district Ganganagar of Rajasthan.[15] Some of their coins contain legends which have been deciphered as '*Ārjunāyanānāṁ jaya Bhadrarāmasa*'.[16] We feel that the intended legend was *Bhadrārāmasa Ārjunāyanānāṁ jaya* and the first word of the legend here indicated the name of the capital city of the Ārjunāyanas just as in the case of Agra and Śibi coins which contain the legends *Agodaka Agācha janapadasa* and *Majhimikāya Śibi-janapadasa* respectively, and thus refer to their metropolises Agrodaka and Majhamikā (modern Nagarī near Chittor in Rajasthan).

It is, however, strange that a tribe which finds mention in Pāṇini's *Gaṇapāṭha* and Prayāga *praśasti* and whose name seems to be connected with Arjuna, has neither been mentioned in the *Mbh.* nor in any of the Purāṇas. Is it not possible then that they were better known after their chief city and were called Bhadras? The verse from the *Mbh.* quoted above in connection with the Agras and their contemporaneity with them seems to point in the same direction.[17] They are also identified with the Bhadrakāras which have sometimes been mentioned as Madrakāras. The Madras were divided into various branches.[18]

AUDUMBARAS

The Audumbaras or Udumbaras are mentioned in the *Mbh.* (Sabhāparvan 52/13) as bringing presents for Yudhishṭhira. They are known to us from some other literary works and a number of their copper and very few silver coins issued by their kings Śivadāsa, Rudradāsa and Dharaghosha.[19] The silver coins belong only to the last mentioned ruler. They may be described as follows:

Obverse : Sage Viśvāmitra standing, facing with right hand raised, traces of skin over left arm. Kharoshṭī legend in front *Viśpa/mitra;* around *Mahadevasa raña Dharaghoshasa;* below, Odubarisa.

Reverse : Trident with axe on right; tree in an enclosure on left; Brāhmī legend around *Mahādevasa raña Dharaghoshasa,* below *Odubarisa.*

The portraiture of the sage betrays Greek impact but the label inscription helps us identify the figure satisfactorily. The relationship between the Audumbaras and sage Viśvāmitra was first brought to light by K.K. Dasgupta[20] on the basis of the *Kālikā Purāṇa*, generally believed to have been written between seventh and tenth centuries AD. Ajay Mitra Shastri, however, traced the antiquity to a much earlier period by pointing out three different passages in the *Mbh.* according to which Gādhi's wife had to embrace the *udumbara* (fig) tree before giving birth to Viśvāmitra. The antiquity of the myth, as pointed out by Shastri, can be traced back to a considerably earlier period, though in somewhat different forms. Viśvāmitra belonged to Kuśika *gotra* which was also the *gotra* of the Audumbaras. This *gotra* finds mention in the Vedic texts.[21] Pliny (VI.75) also refers to the Audumbaras as Odombeores on the mouth of the Indus and the Gujarati brāhmaṇas of Kachchh of the Audumbara caste are believed to be their descendants.[22] Probably like many other tribes of the north, the Audumbaras, or probably one of their section, migrated to western India in ancient times.

The tree depicted on the Audumbara coins was conjecturally though correctly identified as fig tree (*ficus glomerata)* by Cunningham,[23] but the story of Viśvāmitra's birth provides certainty to this identification.

The reverse of the square copper coins of the Audumbaras shows a storeyed temple with trident-axe on right. It was referred to as a pointed-roofed temple of two or three storeys with pillars by Cunningham.[24] John Allan took it to be a Buddhist structure – 'two-storeyed domed stūpa'.[25] K.P. Jayaswal described it as a secular structure which represented either the mote-hall of the Audumbaras or some other public building.[26] It was, however, S.V. Sohoni who correctly identified it as a Śaiva temple citing the evidence of Bhāsa's *Pratimā-nāṭaka* and pointed out that the temples of this type were still popular in the Kullu and Beas valleys.[27] A complete absence of such structural temples, belonging to the early historic period, however, indicates that these temples must have been of perishable materials like wood. Since the sacred, thorny, fruit-giving, milky and fragrant trees were not recommended for construction in ancient times, fig wood may not have been used in such temples. It is quite likely that the word *udumbara*, which later became conventional for the door-sill in the construction of temples, was introduced by the Audumbaras.

In a *vṛitti* on Pāṇini's *Ashṭādhyāyī*, Chandragomin gives an important piece of information in a verse in his *Vyākaraṇa* (II. 4, 103) which says :

> *Udumbarās-tilakhalā-madrakārā yugandharāḥ /*
> *Bhuliṅgāḥ śaradaṇḍāś-cha śālvā'vayava-saṁjñitāḥ / /*

i.e. the Udumbara, Tilakhala, Madrakāra, Yugandhara, Bhuliṅga and Śaradaṇḍa are the sections of the Śālvas. A passage of the *Mbh.* (II, 48/12) refers to the Audumbaras as *durvibhāgāh*-

> *Kāyavyā daradā dārvāḥ śūrā vaiyāmakāstathā /*
> *Audumbarā durvibhāgāh pāradā bāhlikaiḥ saha / /*

Moti Chandra took the word *durvibhāga* in the sense of 'disunited' and as qualifying the preceding word *Audumbarāḥ*. He thus held that the epic passage "may point to the Audumbara connections with the Sālva federation of which the Udumbaras with the Tilakhalas, Madrakāras, Yugandharas, Bhuliṅgas and Śaradaṇḍas were a member."[28] Dasgupta, however, takes the word *durvibhāga* in the sense of 'difficult to be disunited', i.e. strong.[29] The distribution of the Audumbara coins which have all been found from Paṭhānkoṭ, Kāngrā, Jwālāmukhī and Irripal in the present Hamīrpur (old Kāngrā) district indicate that they were a well-knit people living in the neighbourhood of the Vaiyāmakas (Vemakas) whose coins, too, have sometimes been found from that region.

KULŪTAS

The *Mbh.*, the *Rāmāyaṇa* and the Purāṇas mention the Kulūtas under various phonetically similar names like the Ulūtas, Ulūkas, Kolūkas, Kaulutas, Kulatthas, etc. In the Bhīshmaparvan (8/58) they are mentioned as Ulūta and associated with Kashmir,

Gandhāra, Abhisāra, etc., whereas at another place in the same parvan (8/64) they are referred to as Kulattha and classed with the Yavanas, Chīnas, Kambojas, Hūṇas and Pārasīkas. Their country has been mentioned in the Karṇaparvan (12/475 & 485). Sabhāparvan (27/5 & 11) refers to the Kulūtas and their king Bṛihanta who was vanquished by Arjuna during his conquest of the quarters –

Tairavi sahitaḥ sarvairanurajya cha tān nṛipān /
Kulūta-vāsinaṁ rājan Bṛihantam-upajagmivān //
and
Kulūtānuttarāṁśchaiva tāṁścha rājñaḥ samānayat

In the *Vishṇudharmottara Purāṇa*,[30] Bharata is said to have met Kulūtādhipati Jaya between the Vipāśā and the Irāvatī while going to Kekaya from Ayodhyā. The *Rāmāyaṇa* refers to the Kaulūta or Kaulūtaka amongst the western tribes, but the *Bṛihat-saṁhitā* places them in the northeastern division at one place (14/29/30) and in the northwest division at another (24/22). They are mentioned along with the Trigarttas and Chīnas in one place (10/11) and with the Madras in two places (4/22 & 17/18)[31] P.L. Gupta concludes on the basis of these references that, "the people called Kulūta were divided into two distinct groups: one existed in the Himalayan region close to Trigarta and the other in the Punjab in the neighbourhood of Madra."[32] It may be pointed out that the Trigarttas and the Madras were probably neighbours in ancient times and the references to the Kulūtas living in the neighbourhood of Trigarttas and the Madras should not be interpreted in terms of two different people bearing the same name.

Coins and literary works like the *Bṛihat-saṁhitā, Kādambarī, Bālabhārata,* etc., leave little doubt to their exact name having been Kulūta. About a dozen copper coins of the Kulūtas are known to us. The first one, a round copper coin of Vīrayaśas (now in the British Museum, London), was published by Cunningham, but unfortunately he did not record the provenance of his coin.[33] Later, eleven square copper coins were obtained by Marshall[34] in his excavations at Sirkap (Taxila). They belong to Vīrayaśas, Vijayamitra, Satyamitra and Āryamitra. It was, however, Bergny who read the name of the tribe as Kulūta correctly on these coins.[35] P.L. Gupta thinks, "Since these coins were found in archaeological excavations and their provenance is beyond doubt Taxila, it can be said that these Kulūta rulers existed in the Gandhāra region. They were, most likely, the ones who are mentioned in the *Mahābhārata* and the Purāṇas. They had perhaps little to do with the normal type Himalayan region".[36] But since the name of Vīrayaśas is found on the British Museum as well as the Taxila coins, P.L. Gupta states further that, "we are inclined to surmise that the Kulūtas originally inhabited the Gandhāra region, probably not far from Madra. Later when the local tribes of the Punjab were hard pressed by the foreign invaders – Indo-Greeks or Śaka-Pahlavas – the Kulūta people, in all likelihood, moved to the Himalayas and established a new kingdom in the area which is now called Kūlū (sic). This perhaps took place in the time of Vīrayaśas".[37] If it is to be believed we would have to establish the precedence of the coins of the Taxila type over the British Museum type. This has not been done by anyone yet. We have already seen above that the Kulūtas mentioned along with the Trigarttas and the Madras at two different places may have actually been the same people. The great scholar seems to have very conveniently forgotten that Taxila was a great centre of art, culture, trade, education, etc. and coins from one region or place could go to such centres with traders or travellers. In literature we find enough of evidence to take them as mountainous people rather than belonging to a place like Taxila. If the similarity of name of Kṛishṇayaśas of the Kanhiara biscriptual (Brāhmī and Kharoshṭī) inscription,[38] only about 20 kilometres east of Kāngrā, holds any validity in this connection, it, too, points to the mountainous region being the original habitat of these rulers. Both, the coins and the *Mbh.*, indicate the Kulūta to have been a monarchical state.

Kulūta may not have been a very big and/or powerful state in ancient times and may have been forgotten soon. This may be the reason that when the epic and Paurāṇic accounts of their existence were added to them, not much was known about them, not perhaps even about their exact name. This would indicate that the passages of the *Mbh.* referring to them were interpolated much after their coin issuing stage, i.e. *circa* second century AD.

KUṆINDAS

The Kuṇindas have been mentioned in the *Mbh.* at several places, sometimes under phonetically variant names. At one place they are mentioned along with the Paiśāchas, Ambashthas and Barbaras, all described as mountainous people (VII. 119, 14) while at another place (*Mbh.*, II. 48, 3-4) they are referred to as cattle rearing and extracting *paipīlika* gold, which they sent to Yudhishṭhira at the time of his *rājasūya* along with other people –

Khaśa ekāśanā jyohāḥ pradarā dīrgha-veṇavaḥ /
Paśupāścha kuṇindāścha taṅgaṇāḥ parataṇgaṇāḥ //
Te vai pipīlikaṁ nāma varadattaṁ pipīlikaiḥ /
Jātarūpaṁ droṇameyamahārshuḥ puñjaśo nṛipāḥ //

Arjuna is stated to have conquered the Kuṇinda country and rendered the Kuṇindas as soldier-less (*ibid.*, II. 23, 13-14) –

Pūrvaṁ Kuṇinda-viashaye vaśe chakre mahīpatīn /
Dhanañjayo mahābāhurnātitīvreṇa karmaṇā //
Ānartān-kālakūṭāṁścha Kuṇindāṁścha vijitya saḥ /
Sumaṇḍalaṁ pāpajitaṁ kṛitavānanusainikam //

Hundreds of their groups in the Himalayas and their king have also been mentioned in the *Mbh.* (II.141, 25-26) –

Kirāta-taṅgaṇākīrṇaṁ kuṇinda-śata-saṅkulam /
Himavatymarairjushṭaṁ bahvāścharyasamākulam //
Subāhuśchāpi tān dṛishṭvā pūjayā pratyagiṛhṇata /
Vishayānte kuṇindānāmīśvaraḥ prīti-pūrvakam //

Their mountainous habitat and their riches are attested to by other literary works also. The distribution of their coins from Kāngrā in Himachal Pradesh to Kāshīpur in Uttaranchal (Map 3) pinpoints their territory in the Siwāliks and corroborates the evidence furnished by the *Mbh.* that they were '*Parvata-vāsa-nitya*'.

The Lord of the Kuṇindas mentioned in the *Mbh.* (III.141,26) has not been referred to by his personal name though we get the name of Amoghabhūti on their coins. There has been some controversy whether Amoghabhūti is a personal name or a title. Rajendralal Mitra interpreted *Amoghabhūtisa* as a title meaning 'of unflinching faith'[39] and K.P. Jayaswal took it as an official title meaning 'of unfailing prosperity'.[40] P.L. Gupta holds that :

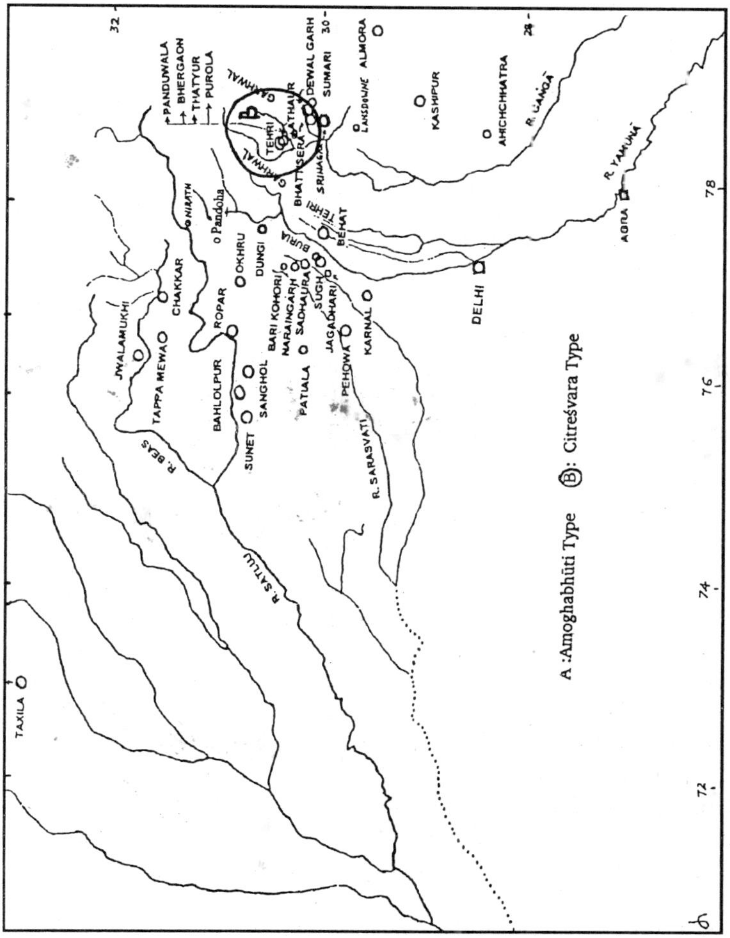

Map. 3 The Kuṇindas: The Distribution of their Coins

The term Amoghabhūti stands for Śiva. It needs (sic) not be said that Amogha and Bhūti, are the two names of Śiva. The two names are put together to highlight his two aspects. The entire legend on the coins may well be compared with the legend *Bhagavata Mahādevasa* on the Vemaki coins. The legend here conveys 'the god Śiva, the king of the Kuṇinda people'.[41]

But some coins of a hoard found from village Chakkar near Mandi and published by Gupta himself bear the legend *Maha(ā)ra(ā)jasa Ama(o)ghabhu(ū)tis [y*]a* leave little doubt to their having been issued by a king of the name of Amoghabhūti.[42] Gupta's view that, "Most likely, the Kuṇinda people lived first in the western part of Himachal Pradesh and at some time later they migrated to the east and settled in the region covered by Garhwal, Saharanpur and Ambala"[43] is also based on a wrong assumption that only silver and neat fabric coins have been found in western Himachal Pradesh and that those found from Garhwāl, etc., are of coarse fabric.[44] I also don't subscribe to the general belief that the Chitreśvarna type copper coins showing unicephalous and tricephalous Śiva which have been found only from Garhwal and are more than two centuries later than the Kuṇinda coins belong to the Kuṇindas.[45]

KSHUDRAKAS

The Kshudrakas have been mentioned in the *Mbh.* at various places. In the great war they had sided with the Kauravas (Bhīshmaparvan 51/16; 59/76; 87/7). Paraśurāma had annihilated the Kshudrakas earlier (Droṇaparvan 70/11). They were killed by Arjuna (Karṇaparvan 5/47). Like many other tribes, they had brought presents for Yudhishṭhira at the time of his *rājasūya* sacrifice (Sabhāparvan 52/15).

The Kshudrakas find their first mention in the *Gaṇapāṭha* of Pāṇini (IV.2, 45).[46] R.G. Bhandarkar[47] identified the Kshudrakas with the Oxydrakai of the Greek historians.[48] Megasthenes tells us that the Persians in the sixth century BC had 'hired mercenary troops from India, namely, the Hydrakes (Oxydrakai = Kshudrakas)'.[49] This statement is repeated by Arrian also.[50] Evidently, the Kshudrakas had achieved rather an international reputation as extraordinarily brave people in the sixth century BC, so that even an alien ruler was tempted to hire them to accomplish his military designs. The *Mbh.* also depicts them as brave warriors. Even in the fourth century BC, they were one of the most powerful republican states whom Alexander met during his retreat down the Indus. They lived to the northeast of the Mālavas, the Malloi of the Greek historians, who dwelt on the Hydaspes, i.e. on the Jhelum below its confluence with the Chenāb.[51] The *Mbh.* (Vanaparvan 52/15) also refers to them along with the Mālavas. They had formed a league with the Mālavas and gave a very stiff resistance to Alexander.[52] Patañjali (I.32; I.83; II.412) seems to give the Indian version of their fight when he says that they alone came out victorious – *Ekākibhiḥ Kshudrakairjitaṁ*, while the Greek historians talk of a treaty between them and Alexander. Since the Kshudrakas are not traceable in the subsequent centuries, it is believed that they were amalgamated with the Mālavas, probably during their migration from the Punjab to eastern Rajasthan[53] which had begun during the Indo-Greek occupation of the Punjab and probably continued down to the Scythian conquest.[54] The discovery of their copper coins bearing the Brāhmī legend *Kshudrakānāṁ Jaya* from Pāṇḍusar in the Nohar tahsil of district Gangānagar in Rajasthan, however, proves beyond doubt that they had moved to that region from their original home and set up an independent republican state in northern Rajasthan during the second century BC.[55] Their mention along with the Yaudheyas, Lalitthās (Kuṇindas ?) and the Uśīnaras in the Karṇaparvan (*Mbh.* VIII. 4,46) indicates that the relevant verse of the *Mbh.* was composed before they settled in Rajasthan.

MĀLAVAS

The *Mbh.* tells us of a hundred sons of King Aśvapati of Madra begotten from his queen Mālavī as a result of the boon obtained by Sāvitrī from Yama (Vanaparvan 297/59-60). They were all destined to rule for a very long time. The Mālavas are referred to as an important *janapada* of India (Bhīshmaparvan 9/60, 62). The Mālavas are said to have been vanquished by Nakula (Sabhāparvan 32/7), Karṇa (Vanaparvan 254/20), Kṛishṇa (Droṇaparvan 11/17), Arjuna (*ibid.* 19/16) and Yudhishṭhira (*ibid.* 157/28). Earlier, Paraśurāma, too, had annihilated these kshatriyas (*ibid.* 70/11-13). The Mālavas are said to have attended the *rājasūya* sacrifice of Yudhishṭhira and paid him a rich tribute (Sabhāparvan

34/11 and 52/15). Their mention along with the Lalitthās (Kuṇindas ?), Trigartas, etc., in the Droṇaparvan [*Atha prahasya bībhatsur lalitthānmālavānapi / Māchellakāṁ-strigartāṁścha yaudheyāṁśchārdayachchharaiḥ* / /18,16], with the Madrakas in the Karṇaparvan [*Mālavā madrakāśchaiva*. (4,46)] and with Śibis and Trigartas (II.32,7) indicates that these verses were composed when the Mālavas were still in the vicinity of the said tribes and had not moved to Rajasthan from where most of their coins have been obtained.

As noted above, the Mālavas had confederated with the Kshudrakas to meet the challenge of Alexander (*Mbh.* II.50, 15; V.57,18; VI.59,13 etc.). During their movement from northwest Punjab to Rajasthan, they seem to have settled in the present day Indian Punjab – in the Ferozepur, Bhaṭiṇḍā, Sangrūr, Ludhiānā region to be more precise – to which they gave their name.[56] Recently, some small and light weight square/rectangular copper coins which remind us of the Mālava coins have been found from Sunām in district Sangrūr, which forms part of the Mālwā region of Punjab. They share the characteristics of Mālava coins but seem to be anterior to them as is indicated by small hitherto unnoticed punch-marks. These coins may tentatively be associated with the Mālavas when they were living in the Mālwa region of Punjab. Their passage from Punjab to Rajasthan may be traced through the ancient site of Malab in the Farīdābād district of Haryana which still bears their name and also yields early historic remains.

RĀJANYAS

The Rājanyas were mentioned by Pāṇini in his *Gaṇapāṭha* first. They have been grouped with the Śibis, Trigartas, Madras, Kekayas, Yaudheyas, etc. in the *Mbh.* (II.50,14). They were put to death by Yudhishṭhira along with the Yaudheyas, Āraṭṭas and Madrakas (*Mbh.* VII.132,25) –

> *Yaudheyāraṭṭarājanyamadrakāṇaṁ gaṇānyudhi /*
> *Prāhiṇonmṛityulokāya śūrān bāṇairyudhishṭhiraḥ //*

A similar reference occurs elsewhere also (*Mbh.* VII.136, 5).

Rājanya copper coins bearing biscriptual legends have been found from the Mānaswāl plateau of district Hoshiārpur[57] but their coins bearing only the Brāhmī legend come from Mathurā or nearby area of Rajasthan. The references in the *Mbh.* clearly indicate the period when they were living in the Punjab. We may mention here that an archaeological site yielding grey ware, early historic and medieval remains bearing the name Rājinī Devī, after the goddess whose temple exists there, may have been connected with the Rājanyas. The female deity depicted on Rājanya coins may have been this Rājinī (<Rājanyā) Devī. They may have migrated from here like many other tribes under the alien pressure.

SĀVITRĪPUTRAS

Pāṇini has referred to about thirty *āyudha-jīvi saṁghas*, i.e. tribes living by the profession of arms, under the three groups of *Dāmnyādi, Pārśvādi* and *Yaudheyādi* and the *Sāvitrīputrakas* figure in the first group.[58] In Sanskrit suffix *ka* is added to a word in the sense of 'born amongst or in the family of'. So the word Sāvitrīputrakas means 'born amongst or in the family of Sāvitrīputras'. The Sāvitrīputrakas thus trace their origin from the hundred sons of Sāvitrī and Satyavān. The story of Sāvitrī and Satyavān is given in details in the *Mbh.* and some other texts.[59]

Sāvitriputrakas have been mentioned in the *Mbh.* amongst the Kuru warriors killed by Arjuna :

Rādheyāḥ sūtaputrāścha bhrātrāścha mahārathāḥ /
Kekayāḥ sarvāśchāpi nihatāḥ Savyasāchinā //
Mālavā Madrakāśchaiva Draviḍāśchograkarmiṇaḥ /
Yaudheyāścha Lalitthāścha Kshudrakāśchāpyuśīnarāḥ //
Māvellakāstuṇḍikerāḥ Sāvitrīputrakāścha ye /
Prāchyodīchyāḥ pratīchyāścha dākshiṇātyāścha mārisha //

It is for the first time that I have identified two of their square copper coins in the British Museum, London. One of these was included by Allan in his Catalogue in 1936 but remained unidentified[60] or wrongly identified[61] all these years. The second coin was a later acquisition and remained undeciphered and unidentified. I visited the British Museum to see these coins in 1991 and later acquired their photographs and published them.[62] These coins show a stylized tree (?) and the Kharoshṭī legend *Sāvitripura janapadasa* on the obverse and a horse on the reverse. The use of Kharoshṭī indicates that the coins were in use somewhere to the north of the river Sarasvatī as we have no coins from the south of this river with Kharoshṭī legends. The Sāvitrīputras were closely associated with the Madras and the Sālvas and may have thus been ruling somewhere in their vicinity, probably between the Satluj and Rāvī but only future discoveries will enable us to pinpoint their territory. The coins belong to the later part of the second century BC. The scarcity of these coins indicates that the Sāvitrīputras did not rule for a long period. The relevant portion of the *Mbh.* may not have therefore been written long after the second century BC.

ŚIBIS

Like most other tribes, the Śibis, too, were located in the Punjab in district Jhang (now in Pakistan). They are a people of great antiquity as this name occurs in the *Aitareya Brāhmaṇa* and a Ṛigvedic hymn (X. 179) is ascribed to Śibi Auśīnara in the *Anukramaṇī*. The Greek historians refer to them as Siboi or Sibae and locate them at the confluence of the Hydaspes (*Vipāśā=Beās*) and Akesines (*Chandrabhāgā=Chenāb*).

All their coins, however, have come from Rajasthan, mostly from Nagarī near Chittor and some other places around. They bear the legend *Majhamikāya Śibi janapadasa* reminding us of some other tribes who have issued coins mentioning their metropolises. Majhamikā (Mādhyamikā) is generally identified with Nagarī. Since most of the passages of the *Mbh.* [*Kāśmīrāḥ Kundamānāścha Paurakā Haṁsakāyanāḥ/Śibi-trigarta-yaudheyā rājanyā Madra-Kekayāḥ//* (Vanaparvan 52/14); *Śibīnikshvākumukhyāṁścha Trigartān Saindhavānapi* (*Ibid.*, 267/28); *Tān Daśārṇān sa jitvā cha pratasthe Pāṇḍunandanaḥ/Śibīṃstrigartānambahsṭhān Mālavān Pañchakarpaṭān//* (Sabhāparvan, 32/7); *Ambashṭhān Mālavāñchhūrāṁstrigartān sa Śibīnapi/Prāhiṇonmṛtyulokāya kruddho yuddhe Yudhisṭhiraḥ//* (Droṇaparvan, 157/28)] mention them along with the Trigartas, probably they are represented as located in the Punjab before their movement to Rajasthan.

TRIGARTAS

The *Mbh.* contains innumerable references to the Trigartas whose king Suśarman, too, is referred to quite often.[63] They are described as wonderful charioteers (*rathodārāḥ, mahārathāḥ*), knowing the 'science of bow' (*dhanurvedavida*), invincible by the enemies (*ajeyāḥ śatrubhiḥ*) and prominent fighters (*dhurandhara-kshatriyas*). Literally, Trigarta means 'three pits' and the term represents the three valleys of the rivers Satluj, Beās and Rāvī. They are equated with the Jālandharas (*Jālandharās-trigartāḥ syuḥ*). Literary references point to Kāngrā-Jalandhar region as their habitat. There is no evidence of their movement anywhere from this region. Allan had published a square copper coin of the Trigartas bearing the four-tiered 'stūpa' and traces of Kharoshṭī legend on the obverse and three symbols with Brāhmī legend *Trakata janapadasa* on the reverse. Incidentally, this remains the only known coin of the tribe yet. P.L. Gupta has described the so-called 'stūpa' as 'a four-storeyed pillar structure with a dome at the top and a curvilinear eave around the roof above the ground floor. The structure is supported by a high railing and probably also a gate or pillared-post in the front'.[64] I feel that the structure depicted on this unique Trigarta coins is only three-tiered and the pillared-post in front has a bird perched on it. It is my hunch that the bird depicted is a cock. As such, it is probably a *Kukkuṭa-dhvaja*. Such *dhvajas* carrying a weapon or the vehicle of the deity was a usual thing in ancient times. We know of some other *Garuḍa-* and *Kukkuṭa-dhvajas* also. This hunch of mine goes well with the description of the Trigartas in the *Mbh.* as wonderful warriors. It is well known that *Kukkuṭa* is the emblem of the war-god Kārttikeya. The Trigartas, like the Yaudheyas, may have been the worshippers of Kārttikeya.

VEMAKIS

The *Mbh.* (II.48,12) refers to the Vaiyāmakas –

> *Kāyavyā Daradā Dārvāḥ śūrā Vaiyāmakāstathā/*
> *Audumbarā durvibhāgāḥ Pāradā Bāhlikaiḥ saha//*

They are generally identified with the Vemakis who issued silver and copper coins. The known silver coins are of the following description.

Obverse : Elephant to right with trunk upraised, a line below and a trident-axe in front under the head of the animal; Brāhmī legend around from XI o'clock *Rājño Vemakisa Rudravarmasa Vijayaka.*

Reverse : Bull standing to right, a wavy line below; lotus in front under the head of the animal; Kharoshṭī legend from IV o'clock *Raña Vemakisa Rudravarmasa* with *Vijayaya* below.

Similar silver coins but bearing the legend *Bhagavata Mahadevasa Rajaraja* in Brāhmī and *Bhagavata Mahadevasa Rajaraña* in Kharoshṭī are also attributed to these people by some scholars. I have, however, shown the untenability of this view. Some scholars attributed those coins to the Audumbaras which, too, is a false notion.[65] A new king bearing the name of Bhavavarman has also been brought to light by me recently.[66] A hoard of silver coins which included the Vemaki, Audumbara, Bhagavata Mahadevasa type and Kuṇinda coins was found in the early 1980s from Pālampur but was smuggled to London from where it dispersed to various places.[67]

The legend on the singular copper coin of the Vemakis was very controversial. It has recently been deciphered correctly by me as *Rājñ(o) Vemakisa Śivapālasa,* the correctness of which is vouched for by two other coins in private collections which I have seen. The reference to the Vemakis in the *Mbh.* seems to have been put in *circa* first century BC or so.

VṚISHṆIS

The Vṛishṇis were a well-known people of ancient India from the later Vedic period onwards. They have been mentioned by Pāṇini and Kauṭilya's *Arthaśāstra* describes them as a republican corporation. The *Mbh.* refers to Vṛishṇi, a kshatriya of the Yadu race, whose descendants came to be known as the Vṛishṇi. Kṛishṇa also belonged to the Vṛishṇi clan.[68]

In spite of copious literary references, a silver coin discovered by Cunningham and subsequently placed in the British Museum, has remained for long the sole evidence of their political existence. The coin bears a sort of *nandipada* standard in railing with a composite animal, half-lion and half-elephant, in front and circular Brāhmī legend *Vṛishṇi-rājajña-gaṇasya tratarasya* on the obverse and an elaborate twelve-spoked wheel with Kharoshṭī legend *Vṛishṇi-rājañña-ga...* within a pellet border on the reverse. The coin is generally assigned to *circa* first century BC. Cunningham did not record the provenance of this coin and published it under Audumbara coins.[69]

The *Mbh.* (XVI.7, 70), the *Bhāgavata* (X.60, 37-38; XI.31, 25 etc.) and the *Vishṇu Purāṇa* (V.38, 19) indicate that the Vṛishṇis were settled by Arjuna in the Pañchanada region after the calamity that befell on them at Dvārakā where they had established themselves when Mathura, their original home, was invaded by the demons.[70] Numerous seals and sealing founds from Sunet, now in the municipal limits of Ludhiana in Punjab, furnish evidence of its being the Vṛishṇi stronghold. About two and a half dozen small round copper coins published earlier by Rodgers have been attributed to ten Vṛishṇi rulers who ruled here probably after the fall of the Kushāṇas and before the rise of the Yaudheyas during the third century AD.[71] The relevant portion of the *Mbh.* referring to their settlement in the Pañchanada, thus, seems to have been added sometime during the third-fourth century AD.

YAUDHEYAS

The Yaudheyas were an *āyudhajīvi-saṁgha* who have been documented in our literature and inscriptions from about 5th century BC to *circa* twelfth century AD and were at the height of their power from the middle of the second century BC to the fourth century AD (but for an interregnum of alien ascendancy) during which period they issued their coins also.[72] So much has been written about this celebrated republic that it is difficult to say something new. They have been mentioned at various places in the *Mbh.* Cunningham[73] traced their descent from Yudhishṭhira who had a son named Yaudheya begotten from his wife Devikā, daughter of Govāsana of the Śaibya tribe, as mentioned in the *Mbh.* (I.90,83) –

> *Yudhishṭhirastu Govāsanasya Śaibyasya Devikāṁ nāma kanyāṁ svayaṁvarāṁ lebhe/Tasyāṁ putraṁ janayāmāsa Yaudheya-nāma//*

The Yaudheyas have been described in the *Mbh.* to have suffered defeats at the hands of Arjuna, Bhīma and Yudhishṭhira (Droṇaparvan, 19/16; 161/5;157/30 etc.) and even before the war, they are described to have been amongst the subordinate people who brought presents to Yudhishṭhira when he performed the *Rājasūya* sacrifice (Sabhāparvan, 52/14). Jagannath Agrawal had thus shown the untenability of this view long back[74] but some scholars go on following and supporting the view of Cunningham still.[75]

They have been described to have been conquered even by Nakula during his conquest of the western quarter –

Tato bahudhanaṁ ramyaṁ gavāśvadhanadhānyavat /
Kārttikeyasya dayitaṁ Rohitakamupādravat //
Tatra yuddhaṁ mahad vṛttaṁ śūrair-Mattamayūrakaiḥ /
Marubhūmiṁ sa kārtsnyena tathaiva Bahudhānyakam //

The association of Kārttikeya and his dear city Rohītaka (modern Rohtak) with the Yaudheyas is referred to here. That the Yaudheyas occupied the Bahudhānyaka region is evident from their earliest coins bearing the legend *Yaudheyānāṁ Bahudhāñake* (Map 4). But the Yaudheyas have not been mentioned by their name directly. They have been called Matta-mayūrakas. Peacock is the vehicle of Kārttikeya, shown with him in the *Yaudheyagaṇasya Jaya* type coins also. I think that the Yaudheyas were the earliest people to depict peacock with Kārttikeya though it became a significant feature of the images of the god during the Gupta period. Even the earliest depiction of cock with Kārttikeya occurs on a Yaudheya coin.[76]

A unique silver coin of the tribe, now preserved in the British Museum, shows six-headed Kārttikeya and six-headed Shashṭhī on the obverse and the reverse carries the Brāhmī legend *Bhagavata Svāmino Brahmaṇyadevasya Yaudheya*.[77] On the copper coins of this class, however, the last word is missing and is sometimes replaced by the word *Kumārasya*. Nisar Ahmad thought that since the word Yaudheya is substituted by Kumāra, this later word also stands for the name of a tribe like the word Yaudheya. He found some references in the *Mbh.* and the Purāṇas regarding the existence of a tribe bearing this name and came forward with the theory that these coins belong not to the Yaudheyas but to the Kumāras.[78] P.L. Gupta commended this theory.[79] Ajay Mitra Shastri rejected this attribution on grammatical ground as the name of the tribe in the legend occurs with the genetive singular suffix *sa*.[80] Gupta treated Shastri's objection as 'grammatical jugglery' and not only vehemently upheld but even 'usurped' it later.[81] I have, however, demonstrated that the Critical Edition of the *Mbh.* does not contain the name of the Kumāra tribe and even if we accept it for the sake of argument, the tribe existed in the Dakshiṇāpatha and not in the

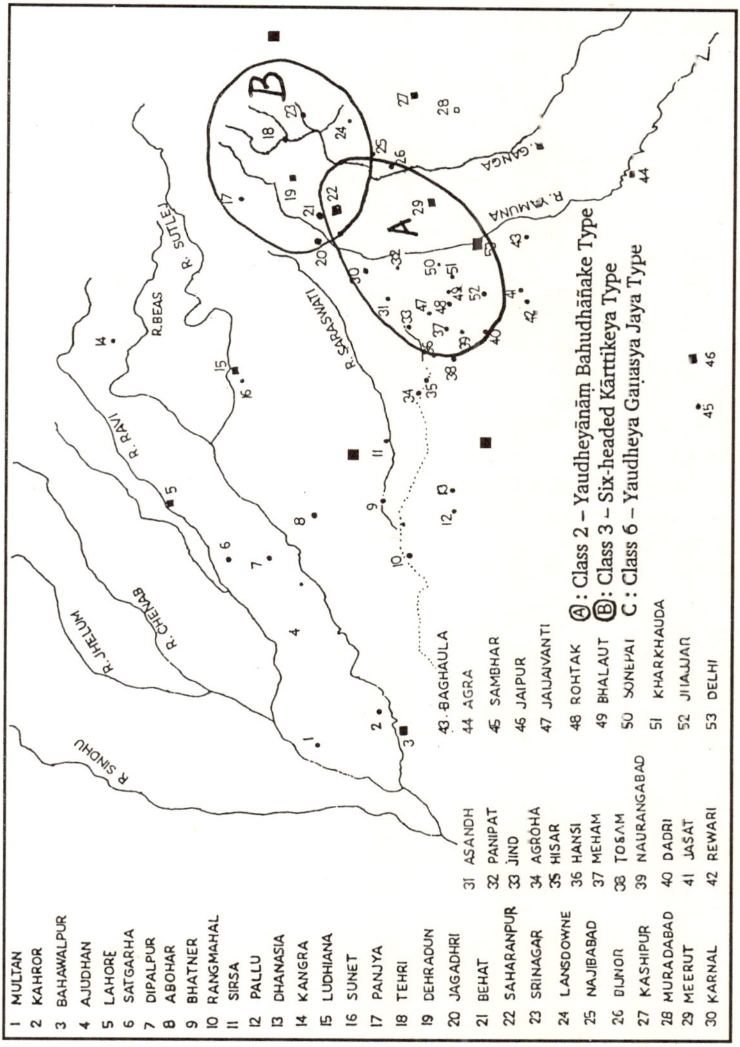

Map. 4 The Yaudheyas: The Distribution of their Coins

region where these coins are found. There are many specimens on which the word Kumārasya, too, is missing but otherwise they are the same. The internal evidence of the coins themselves clearly indicates that the word Kumāra stands for Kārttikeya and not for any tribe.[82]

We thus see that the *Mbh.* not only throws light on various tribes but also helps us to locate them and even trace their movements. With the help of the textual, archaeological and numismatic date at our disposal, we can in certain cases determine even the date of certain passages of the *Mbh.* wherein we find references to these tribal republics.

NOTES AND REFERENCES

1. See for details B.C. Law (1972), *Historical Geography of Ancient India* (Hindi), Lucknow: Uttar Pradesh Hindi Granth Academy, pp. 17, 20, 23, 70 etc.
2. I have utilized both the Critical Edition and the Gītā Press Edition. When the Parvan name is given, the references should be understood to have been taken from the latter and when the roman number has been used for the Parvan, the reference is taken from the former.
3. *JNSI*, IV; See also John Allan (1936), *BMCAI*, London : British Museum, pp. cliii, clvii, 279, pl. xlv.9 and pp. 282-83, pl. xlv.21-24.
4. J. Przyluski, (1962), *Ancient Peoples of the Punjab – The Udumbaras and Salvas*, Eng. tr. by Chitrabhanu Sen from the original French articles published in *Journal Asiatique*, 1926 and 1929, Reprint, Calcutta.
5. *Bulletin of the School of Oriental and African Studies*, X, pp. 237 ff.
6. Bela Lahiri, (1974), *Indigenous States of Northern India* (*Circa 200 B.C. to 320 A.D.*), Calcutta, p. 248 (henceforth *ISNI*).
7. *JNSI*, IV.
8. K.K Dasgupta, (1974), *Tribal History of Ancient India – A Numismatic Approach*, Calcutta (henceforth *THAI*), p. 9, fn. 45.
9. E.J. Rapson (ed.) (1968), *Cambridge History of Ancient India*, Vol. I, 3rd Reprint, Delhi, p. 72; B.C. Law, (1937), *Geographical Essays*, Vol. I, London, p. 91.
10. See for details *THAI*, pp.17ff.
11. *IA*, XIII, pp. 331, 349.
12. Alexander Cunningham (1882), *Archaeological Survey Report: Report for the Year 1878-79 (CASR)*, XIV, p. 140.
13. P.L. Gupta (1977), "Coins of the Arjunayanas," *ND*, I (1977), pp. 14-18, Pl. II.1-3.

14. *BMCAI*, p. lxxxiii.
15. Devendra Handa, (1985), *Studies in Indian Coins and Seals*. Delhi, p. 42.
16. Nisar Ahmad, (1993), "Coins of the Ārjunāyanas," *ND*, 17, p. 18.
17. The Uttama-bhadras have been mentioned in the Nāsik Cave Inscription of the time of Nahapāna as having been defeated by his son-in-law Ushavadāta near Pushkar [D.C. Sircar, (1965), *Select Inscriptions*, Vol. I, 2nd ed., Calcutta, p. 169].
18. For details see, M.R. Singh, (1972), *Geographical Data in the Early Purāṇas – A Critical Study*, Calcutta: Punthi Pustak, pp. 153ff.
19. For details see, *BMCAI*, pp. ixxxiii ff, 122 ff; *THAI*, pp. 38-70; *ISNI*, pp. 216-25.
20. *THAI*, pp. 43-44.
21. Ajay Mitra Shastri, (1965), "*Mahābhārata* on the Relations Between Viśvāmitra and the Audumbaras," *Purāṇa*, Varanasi, Vol. VII, Part I, pp. 362-66.
22. K.P. Jayaswal, (1955), *Hindu Polity*, 3rd ed., Bangalore (henceforth *HP*), p. 161.
23. Alexander Cunningham, (1891), *Coins of Ancient India*, London (Reprint, Varanasi, (1963) (henceforth *CAI*), p. 66.
24. *CASR*, XIV, p. 136; *CAI*, p. 68.
25. *BMCAI*, pp. 122f.
26. *HP*, p. 154.
27. S.V. Sohoni, (1942), "A Note on Audumbara Temple Coins", *JNSI*, IV, pp. 55-57.
28. Moti Chandra, (1945), *Geographical and Economic Studies in the Mahābhārata*, Lucknow, p. 90.
29. *THAI*, p. 39, fn. 7.
30. Śrī Veṅkaṭeśvara Press, Bombay, Ch. 207, vv. 22-23.
31. For *Bṛihat-saṁhitā* references, see Ajay Mitra Shastri, *Varāhmihira's India*, Aryan Books International, New Delhi: 1996, pp. 80-81.
32. Parmeshwari Lal Gupta, (1988), *Numismatic History of Himachal Pradesh*, Delhi : B.R. Publishing Corporation (henceforth *NHHP*), p. 10.
33. *CAI*, p. 66.
34. J. Marshall, (1975), *Taxila*, Reprint, Delhi, Vol. III, Pl. 252-57.
35. E.J. Rapson, (1900), "Notes on Indian Coins and Seals I", *JRAS*, p. 125.
36. *NHHP*, p. 11.
37. *Ibid*.
38. *CASR*, IV, pp. 175-76.
39. *JASB*, 1875, p. 89.
40. *HP*, p. 70, fn. 1.
41. *NHHP*, p. 26.

42. Devendra Handa, (1993), "Some Interesting Kuṇinda Coins", *Oriental Numismatic Society Newsletter*, No. 137.
43. *NHHP*, p. 26.
44. Devendra Handa, (1991), "A Note on the Kuṇinda Coins from Sumari and Some Other Sites," *ND*, 15, pp. 18-22.
45. Devendra Handa, (1999), "The Attribution of the Chitreśvara Type Coins," *Oriental Numismatic Studies*, New Delhi, Vol. 2, pp. 33-43, Pls. II-II.
46. V.S. Agrawala, (1963), *India as Known to Pāṇini*, 2nd edn., Varanasi, pp. 455, 471-74.
47. *IA*, 1873, p. 200 ff.
48. J.W. Mc Crindle, (1896), *The Invasion of India by Alexander the Great as Described by Arrian, Q. Curtius, Diodoros, Plutarch and Justin*, Westminster, p. 238. Curtius, however, refers to them as Sudracae.
49. R.C. Majumdar, (ed.) (1968), *The Age of Imperial Unity*, 4th ed., Bombay, p. 40.
50. *Indica*, X.10.
51. V.A. Smith, (1903), *JRAS*, pp. 655 ff.
52. For details of their fight, see Handa (1985), pp. 30 ff.
53. Jayaswal, *HP*, p. 146; A.S. Altekar, (1958), *State and Government in Ancient India*, 3rd ed., Delhi, p. 120.
54. D.C. Sircar, (1968), *The Age of Imperial Unity*, p. 163.
55. See for details Handa, (1985), pp. 30-35, Pl. XIII. 9-10.
56. The whole of this region is still known as Mālwā and its language is called Malwai. Places like Maler-Kotla and Malot in this region seem to contain the remnants of their name. Maler-Kotla was originally the twin village, Mālera being the old habitation and Kotla belonging to the Muslim period. Maler may have been derived from Mālavā-nagara (*Cf. Bikaner* <*Bīkā-nagara*). It has yielded three-dotted diminutive 8-*ratti* Indo-Sasanian silver coins which indicate its habitation in the early historic period. Malot seems to have derived from Mālavā-koṭṭa.
57. *BMCAI*, p. cxxiii.
58. V.S. Agrawala, *India as Known to Pāṇini*, p. 448.
59. *Mbh.*, Vanaparvan, chs. 293-99; *Devī Bhāgavata* IX.26-28; *Matsya Purāṇa*, chs. 207-213; *Vishṇudharmottara Purāṇa*, II. 36-41; *Brahmavaivarta Purāṇa*, II.23-24 etc.
60. *BMCAI*, p. 213, no. 20, Pl. XLIV. 13.
61. Michael Mitchiner, (1976), *Indo-Greek and Indo-Scythian Coinage*, Vol. 7, London, p. 628, attributed the coin to Sivachatrapura *Janapada*.
62. Devendra Handa (1998), "Coins of the Sāvitrīputras," *The Numismatic Chronicle*, Cambridge, No. 158, pp. 243-248, Pl. 55.4-5.

63. Udyogaparvan, 164/8; 166/9-13; Bhīshmaparvan 56/4; 61/12-13; 72/7; 102/9-23; Droṇaparvan, 4/8; 11/17; 17/16-17; 19/16; 70/12; 141/2-8; 157/28; Karṇaparvan 4/18; Śalyaparvan 27/31-48; etc. See also B.C. Law, (1973), *Tribes in Ancient India,* 2nd ed., Poona.
64. P.L. Gupta (1985), "Bearing of Numismatics on Early Indian Art History in the Background of Epigraphy," *Indian Epigraphy: Its Bearing on the History of Art*, Ed. Asher and Gai, New Delhi, pp. 10-11, fig. 15; *NHHP*, pp. 13-14.
65. Ajay Mitra Shastri (1964), "Was Mahadeva an Audumbara King?", *JNSI*, XXVI, pp. 157-61; Devendra Handa (1995), "The Riddle of King Mahadeva", *ND*, 19, pp. 1-12.
66. Devendra Handa (1993), "New Vemaki Silver Coins", *Numismatic Circular*, London, Vol. CI, No. 6, p. 187.
67. A friend had passed on the photographs of this hoard taken in Delhi to me. I tried to trace its whereabouts and learnt that it had ultimately reached London from where it dispersed to various places. P.L. Gupta has also referred to it in his *NHHP*, p. 50, fn. 59. I have published some papers on the coins of this hoard from the photographs I had obtained.
68. For references see Handa (1985), pp. 66 f.
69. *CAI*, p. 70, Pl. IV.15; also *BMCAI*, p. 281, Pl. XVI.5.
70. *Kānaneshu cha ramyeshu parvatehsu nadīshu cha /*
Nivasannānayāmāsa Vṛishṇi- dārān Dhanaṁjayah //
Sa pañchanadamāsādya dhīmānatisamṛiddhimat/
Deśe go-paśu-dhānyāḍhye nivāsamakarot prabhuḥ //
(Mausalaparvan, 7/44-45). See also *Harivaṁśa*, Gita Press, ed., I. 35, 19-22.
71. Handa (1985), pp. 66-74, Pl. XV. 1-3.
72. Devendra Handa (1991), "The Yaudheyas and Their Coins", *Numismatic Studies*, New Delhi, Vol. 1, pp. 64-77.
73. *CASR*, XIV, p.140.
74. Jagannath Agrawal (1970), "An Ancient Republic of the Punjab – The Yaudheya-Gana", in *Essays on History, Literature, Art and Culture (Presented to Dr. M.S. Randhawa on his sixtieth birthday by his friends and admirers)*, eds. K.S. Bedi and S.S. Bal, New Delhi, pp. 49 ff.
75. M.K. Sharan, (1972), *Tribal Coins – A Study*, Delhi, pp. 64 ff.
76. For details see Devendra Handa (1993), "A Unique Yaudheya Copper Coins", *Numismatic Circular*, London, Vol. CI, No. 6, pp. 193-94.
77. *BMCAI*, Pl. XXXIX.21.
78. Nisar Ahmad, (1977), "The Kumaras—A Forgotten Ancient Indian Tribe", in *Seminar Papers on The Tribal Coins of Ancient India*, edited by J.P. Singh and Nisar Ahmad, Varanasi, pp. 184-85.
79. P.L. Gupta (1978), Editorial Note to K.K. Maheshwari's article, "New Tribal and Monarchical Coins", *ND*, II, p. 23.

80. Ajay Mitra Shastri (1984), "Interesting Kuṇinda and Yaudheya Coins," *ND*, VIII, pp. 35-36.
81. P.L. Gupta (1987), "The Brahmanya Coins," *ND*, XI, pp. 130 ff; *NHHP*, pp. 27-29.
82. Devendra Handa (1993), "The Attribution of the Brahmaṇyadeva Type Coins," *Proceedings of the XIth International Numismatic Congress*, Vol. III, Louvain-la-Neuve, pp. 227-31.

APPENDIX

Janapadas (Tribes) Mentioned in the *Mahābhārata**

Āgreya**	Aṭavīśikhara	Aṭhida
Adhirājya	Anupāvṛitta	Anūpa
Antachāra	Andhakāraka	Andhra/Āndhra
Aparakāśī	Aparākunti	Aparamlechccha
Aparavallava	Aparaseka	Aparānta
Abhīshāha	Abhīsāra	Ambashṭha
Ayavāha	Araṭṭa	Ātreya
Ānarta	Ābhīra	Āmaratha
Ārochaka	Audumbara/Udumbara**	Utkala
Uttamāśva	Uttara Kosala	Uttara Pāñchāla
Upagiri	Upatyaka	Uraga
Ulūta/Ulūka/Kulūta**	Ekapāda	Karaka
Karaṭa	Karabhañjaka	Karīti
Karīshaka	Karūsha	Karkakhaṇḍa
Karṇāṭaka	Kaliṅga	Kāka
Kaksha	Kachchha	Kātāraka
Kānti	Kanyakāguṇa	Kāmboja
Kālatoyaka	Kālada	Kāśi
Kāśmīra(/ka)	Kirāta	Kuk(k)ura
Kuṇḍala	Kuṇḍīvisha	Kuṇḍīvṛisha
Kuntala	Kunti	Kuṇḍāparānta
Kumāra	Kuru (Jāṅgala)	Kuru-Pāñchāla
Kuruvarṇaka	Kuruvinda	Kulattha
Kulinda/Kuṇinda**	Kuśādya (Kulūta**)	Kuśalya
Kuśavindu	Kekaya	Kaitava
Koṅkaṇa	Kokavaka	Kosala
Krūra	Kshudraka**	Gandhāra
Gārgya	Girigahvara	Guha
Guhyaka	Godhā	Goparāshṭra
Gomanta	Ghaṭa	Ghoraka
Chakrāti	Charmamaṇḍala	Chibuka
Chīraka	Chūchuka	Chūchupa
Chedi	Chola	Chaura
Jaṭhara	Jāṅgala	Jhillika
Taṅgaṇa	Tanaya	Tarala
Tāmradvīpa	Tāmraliptaka	Tālachara
Tālavana	Tālākaṭa	Tittira
Tilabhāra	Tīragraha	Tuṇḍikera
Tushāra	Tomara (Trigarta**)	Tripurā
Tripurī	Tryaksha	Darada/Dārada
Darva	Daśamālika	Daśārṇa

Dānabhāri
Dārvī
Durgāla
Draviḍa/Drāviḍa
Dvyaksha
Dhurandhara
Dhenuka
Dhvajini
Nabhakānana
Nara
Nākula
Nishāda
Nīpa
Nepāla
Naikapṛishṭha
Nairṛita
Pañchakarpaṭa
Pañchagaṇa
Pañchāla
Paṭachchara
Parataṅgaṇa
Parakāmboja
Paśu
Pahlava
Pākhaṇḍa
Pāṇḍurāshṭra
Pāṇḍya
Pārada
Pārasika
Pa[ā]rvatīya
Pārśvaroma
Pāśivāṭa
Pulinda
Pauṇḍra
Pratimatsya
Prasthala
Prāchya
Prāvṛisheya
Proshaka
Proshṭha
Ballava
Bahirgiri
Bahuvādya
Bāhli[ī]ka
Bodha
Bhadra
Bhadrakāra
Bhārata
Bharadvāja
Bharukaksha
Bharga
Bhallāṭa
Bhārgava
Bhūliṅga
Bhūshika
Maṅga
Maṇḍaka
(Mattamayūra)
Matsya
Madra/Madraka
Madrakaliṅga
Madhumān
Maṇḍaga
Malaja
Malada
Maśaka
Masīra
Mahottha
Mādreyajāṅgala
Mānavarjaka
Mārisha
Māruta
Māla
Mālava**
Māvellaka
Māhika
Māhishaka
Māheya
Mithilā
Mūshaka
Mṛittikāvatī
Mekala
Merubhūta
Mohana
Yamaka
Yakṛillomā
Yadu
Yāmuna
Yugandhara
Yaudheya**
Ra[ā]maṭha
Ramaṇachīna
Rājanya**
Rūpavāhika
Romaka
(Lalittha)
(=Kuṇinda)**
Vaṅga
Vatsa
Vadhra
Vanavāsika
Vanāyu
Valkala
Vasāti
Vāṭadhāna
Vātaja
Vānava
Vāravāsya
Vikarṇa
Vikalpa
Vikuñja
Vijaya
Vidabha
Vi[/ai]deha
Vindhyachulika
Vṛishṇi**
Veṇupa
Vetrika/Vaiyāmaka**
Vyūka
Sālveya
Śaka
Śarmaka
Śaśika
Śālva
Śālvaseni
Śālveya
Śibi**
Śuṇḍika
Śūrasena
Śūrpāraka

Śaivāla	Sakṛidgraha	Sanīya
Saṇu	Samaṅga	Samantara
Samavegavaśa	Sāmudraniṅkuṭa	Sāvitrīputraka**
Siddha	Sindhu	Sindhupulinda
Sindhusauvīra	Sukandaka	Sukuṭa
Sudāmā	Sudṛishṭa	Sudeshṇā
Sunaya	Sunītha	Sumallika
Surabhīpattana	Surāshṭra	Susaṁkula
Susthala	Suhma	Sairindhra
Somadheya	Sauśalya	Sauhṛida
Stanaposhaka	Stanavāla	Svaksha
Svarāshṭra	Huṇḍa	

*The list of these *janapadas* has been compiled from *Mahābhārata kī Nāmānukramaṇikā,* Gītā Press, Gorakhpur, VS 2016 and follows Sanskrit alphabetical system.

** The *janapadas* marked by double star have issued coins also.

10

Prāgjyotisha in the *Mahābhārata*
A Study

Ajay Mitra Shastri

PRĀGJYOTISHA AND PRĀGJYOTISHAPURA

The Bhārata War was an epoch-making event or so made out to be by the authors of the *Mahābhārata* wherein ruling powers of most of the prominent regions, even far-flung ones, of what was known in the past as Bhāratavarsha took an active part. Of them, Prāgjyotisha and its rulers were one of the most important.[1] This geographical unit is also mentioned in the Kūrmavibhāga (Ch. LVIII) section of the *Mārkaṇḍeya Purāṇa* and Varāhamihira's *Bṛihat-saṁhita* (XIV. 23, 31)[2] which locate it in the eastern division of what they call Bhāratavarsha. It continued to be in vogue even after the other name Kāmarūpa came into existence[3] and became more popular in the rest of India,[4] and the local rulers continued to pride in the assumption of the title *Prāgjyotish-eśvara* or *Prāgjyotish-ādhipati*, 'lord of Prāgjyotisha'. It appears to have comprehended a very extensive area and included not only Assam and perhaps the some of the adjoining hilly regions of the North-East but also a considerable portion of West Bengal and Bangladesh. F.E. Pargiter had rather an inflated notion about its extent. He opined that it comprised not only a major portion of Assam but also the Jalpaiguri, Coochbihar, Bogra, Mymensingh, Dhaka and Tippera districts and some parts of the Pabna district (most of which now forms part of Bangladesh) of Bengal as well as probably eastern part of Nepal.[5] In his opinion, generally speaking, Prāgjyotisha 'comprised the whole of North Bengal proper'.[6] Some historians are not satisfied with this extent and go even beyond it. They hold that its western boundary was formed by the river Kosī and that the

Purnea district of Bihar formed a part of this kingdom.[7] But the untenability of these theories is demonstrated by the fact that North Bengal was actually called Puṇḍra or Puṇḍravardhana-*bhukti* which was quite distinct from Prāgjyotisha and bordered it on the west.[8]

The name Prāgjyotisha, as understood by the authors of the *Mahābhārata*, appears to have connoted almost the whole region, plains and mountains, which during the British period formed the state of Assam, Manipur and Tripura. It follows from the statement that the army of Bhagadatta, king of Prāgjyotisha who is represented to have played a leading role in the Bhārata War, comprised the Chīnas, Kirātas and the residents of the mountainous and marshy regions.[9] In fact, it is one of the earliest texts containing references to Prāgjyotisha, the other earlier text referring to it is the *Vālmīkīya Rāmāyaṇa*.[10]

Its capital was Prāgjyotishapura which was situated close to the city of modern Guwahati and is believed to be represented by the modern village of Dispur, about two miles south of Guwahati.[11] The *Mbh.* just mentions the city without saying anything about its foundation. But some later works refer to a myth regarding its origin. Thus, the *Kālikā Purāṇa* (XXXIX.126), dating from about the tenth century AD, avers that in former times lord Brahmā while staying here created stars in consequence of which the city came to be designated as Prāgjyotishapura. This tradition is sought to be supported by some scholars, but without any convincing evidence.[12] Others are opposed to this tradition and trace its origin to some Austric formations like Pagar-juh (o)-tich (cha-chh) referring to the region of extensive high hills which mark the topographical features of the region and regard Prāgjyotisha as its Sanskritized form.[13] Still others are inclined to connect it with the Chinese immigrants and feel that the Chao Zuthis migrating to India were also called Zuthis and those coming to Assam came to be known as Prāg Zuthis who provided the basis for the Sanskrit name Prāgjyotisha.[14] A review of these theories is enough to show that wild imagination has played quite an important role in their make-up. We, however, feel strongly that the name is Sanskrit in its origin and has absolutely nothing to do with any other linguistic formation. It has two components, viz. *prāk* and *jyotisha*, both of which must be accounted for while formulating a theory. The prefix *prāk* denotes in Sanskrit 'east' or 'before' or 'earlier'. To us, the full name may refer to the region as one where 'sun rises before (or earlier than) the other regions' or the 'eastern land of sunrise'. The *uttarapada* (second part) *jyotisha* refers to the most obvious astronomical phenomenon as sun undoubtedly is.[15]

PERSONAGES

The *Mbh.* refers to the personages connected with Prāgjyotisha very frequently and supplies many a detail about them. This is as it ought to be, for its rulers were supposed to have played a vital role in the Bhārata War. It refers not just to Prāgjyotisha but also to Naraka, the supposed progenitor of all the major ruling families of the region, and his birth from lord Vishṇu in his boar (Varāha) manifestation and the earth, his being killed by Kṛishṇa and to his son and successor Bhagadatta and the latter's son and successor Vajradatta who are repeatedly mentioned in the Assamese chronicles as well as copperplate charters in connection with the origin and early history of the local dynasties. Let us see what the extant text of the *Mbh.* has to say about them.

First as to Naraka. We find him associated with the city and fort of Prāgjyotisha and styled Bhauma ('son of Bhūmi,' viz. earth) and said to have stolen the bejewelled earrings of the divine mother Aditi. The gods led by Śakra could not defeat him in war due to Vishṇu's weapon (*Vaishṇavāstra*) received by him from Vishṇu. At their entreaty Kṛishṇa invaded his city which had six thousand nooses with knives at their ends on its borders. He first destroyed the demon Mura, who was in charge of the fort and killed Naraka together with his retinue numbering six thousand at Nirmochana and recovered the earrings.[16] Elsewhere, in an account of Kṛishṇa's valorous feats, we are told that Kṛishṇa killed Naraka, who had lived for several aeons, at Nirmochana near Prāgjyotisha, tied with nooses six thousand great demons who were protecting the fort and rescued thousands of girls from his captivity whom he later married.[17] At another place he is spoken of as the 'son of earth' (*jagatyās=tanaya*).[18] At yet another place, we come across his being killed by lord Vishṇu, the heap of his bones looking like a mountain and Vishṇu's act of rescuing the earth in his Varāha (boar) manifestation and the commotion (*kshobha*) resulting from this act[19] in such a manner as to approximate the tradition of Naraka's birth from this act, albeit it is not stated explicitly.

Many more details are found about Bhagadatta, mainly because of and in connection with his participation in the Bhārata War which bear a much greater historical look as compared to those about his father Naraka. In Droṇaparvan (XXIX. 1-36), Kṛishṇa is reported to have told Arjuna how Vishṇu[20] gave Naraka his weapon and how after his demise it came to Prāgjyotisha and Bhagadatta who is described as a Prāgjyotisha king. Being intimately associated with the Mahābhārata heroes and Bhārata War, he naturally claims much greater attention. In Ādiparvan (LXVII. 9) he is styled as an *asura* together with Bāshkala.[21] He is reported to have participated in Draupadī's *svayaṁvara* together with other monarchs (Ādi, CLXXXV. 12). Albeit an ally of the Magadhan king Jarāsandha, he was Pāṇḍu's friend and loved Yudhishṭhira like his own son (Sabhā, XIV. 14-16). In the context of the *digvijaya* (conquest of quarters) preceding Yudhishṭhira's *Rājasūya* sacrifice, he at the head of an army comprising primarily of Chīna and Kirāta soldiers as well as those inhabiting the oceanic as well as marshy areas (*sāgar-ānūpa-vāsibhiḥ*)[22] had to fight a sanguinary war lasting full eight days with Arjuna in course of the latter's northern campaign, but was deeply impressed by his valour and agreed to act as per his wishes and pay taxes to Yudhishṭhira. It was as much due to his avowed friendship with Arjuna's real father Indra and with Pāṇḍu (Sabhā, XXVI. 7-16). We are also told that Bhīma during his eastern expedition reached the Lauhitya (Brahmaputra) region and compelled the Mlechchha kings to present jewels, sandalwood, aloe wood, clothes, pearls, precious stones, blankets, gold, silver and coral in large quantities (*ibid.*, XXX. 26-29).[23] The non-mention of Bhagadatta, the most prominent of the kings of the Lauhitya region, appears queer, as the Lauhitya formed the western boundary of Prāgjyotisha. It may perhaps indicate that Prāgjyotisha was not included among the Mlechchha kings reportedly humbled by Bhīma. He again finds mention in the context of the *Rājasūya* of Yudhishṭhira. He is in that context referred to as the lord of Prāgjyotisha (*Prāgjyotish-ādhipa*) and the Mlechchhas (*Mlechchhānām=adhipa*) and represented as accompanied by the Yavanas at the Pāṇḍava monarch's court with costly presents including fast-moving horses of excellent breed, swords with pure ivory handles and ornaments studded with precious stones.[24] Karṇa is also reported to have won a victory over him and thereafter proceeded to the Himavat mountain and Nepāla (Vana, CCLIV. 5-7).[25]

We get numerous allusions to his role in the Bhārata War. Drupada wanted to invite him to fight on the side of the Pāṇḍavas, and, what is interesting to note in this connection, he is said to have inhabited the (region of the) eastern ocean (*pūrva-sāgara-vāsin*, Udyoga, IV.11). We are not told if the invitation was really sent, but he together with his army consisting of the Chīnas and Kirātas went to fight to aid Duryodhana (*ibid.*, XIX. 15). He fought in the war right from the first day with several heroes including Virāṭ (Bhīshma, XLV. 49-51), Ghaṭotkacha (*ibid.*, LXIV. 59-62; LXXXIII. 32-38), Sātyaki (*ibid.*, CXI. 7-13), Bhīmasena (*ibid.*, LXIV. 47-54; XCV. 76; CXIII-CXIV), the Daśārṇa king (*ibid.*, XCV. 46-49; Droṇa, XXVI. 37-39), Kshatradeva (*ibid.*, XCV. 73), Drupada (*ibid.*, XIV. 40-42) and Ruchiparvan (*ibid.*, XXVI. 52-53) with varying results. He also fought several times with Arjuna at whose hands he finally met his death (*ibid.*, CXIII-CXIV; CXVI. 56-60; Droṇa, XIV-XXIX). Bhagadatta was succeeded after his death in the Bhārata War by his son Vajradatta who, too, fought with Arjuna taking it as an opportunity to avenge his father's death but was destined to taste a discomfiture at the hands of his father's killer (Āśvamedhika, LXXVI. 1-26).

From these accounts of Bhagadatta two things stand out prominently. They concern the nature of population of his kingdom and the extent of Prāgjyotisha. First, his army and apparently his subjects included the Chīnas and the Kirātas[26] which would show the mixed character of the population of the North-East where he ruled. And secondly, during his supposed reign Prāgjyotisha was very extensive; and the inclusion of the area from the Bay of Bengal in the south to the Himalayas in the north is most probably suggested by the descriptive epithets *Pūrva-sāgara-vāsin* and *parvata-pati* for him at several places, as we have seen. Almost the whole area presently covered by the states carved out of Assam appears to have formed the sphere of its influence, if not, conceptually at least, its integral part.

Another significant fallout of this descriptions of wars in which Bhagadatta was reportedly involved is the vastly important role played by the elephants. The excellent qualities of his elephant named Supratīka are highlighted as well as his supremely heroic deeds (Bhīshma, LIX and Droṇa, XXVI. 5ff.) in connection with his fatal war with Arjuna. He is eulogized as 'not inferior to Indra in battle and expert in driving elephants'. Even his dreaded enemy Arjuna, who would hardly be expected to indulge in hyperbole about him, highly praises him for his elephant forces and his skill in managing them, especially his own elephant (*ibid.*, XXVI. 5ff). It is thus clear that elephantry had a highly important place in the forces of Bhagadatta, and this leads us to the inference that, as at present, elephants were available in profusion in ancient Prāgjyotisha also.

The short list of items presented by Bhagadatta to Yudhishṭhira is also very significant for the economic history of Prāgjyotisha whose economic products they must have been.

And lastly what is particularly noticeable in the present context is the fact that the name Kāmarūpa, which had come into being by the first century BC at the latest,[27] is conspicuous by its absence in the relevant passages of the *Mbh*. It should suffice to show that the portions of the text concerning Prāgjyotisha belong to the earlier stratum of the text that had already been composed prior to the first century BC at the latest.

As we have seen, Vajradatta, who fought with Arjuna valiantly in course of latter's campaign of protecting the sacrificial horse of his elder brother Yudhishṭhira, was son and successor of Bhagadatta.

Another son of Bhagadatta was Kṛitaprajña who reportedly met his end at the hands of Nakula in the Bhārata War (Karṇa, V. 28).[28] Evidently, he was the elder of the two. There is no doubt that Kṛitaprajña is here a proper name of one of the sons of Bhagadatta and not an adjective of his son as thought by some,[29] for that would leave us with only an adjective for his son whose name would be missing. Likewise, it is difficult to identify him with Pushpadanta spoken of by Bāṇabhaṭṭa in his *Harshacharita* (uchchhvāsa VII) in between Bhagadatta and Vajradatta,[30] for what would involve difference of names. A better way to account for the non-mention of any son of Bhagadatta other than Vajradatta in the epigraphic records of Assam would be to postulate that the two other sons being younger or dead earlier could not come to power and are in consequence ignored in them as was the normal practice while giving the genealogy and order of succession in the royal families. It is equally possible that Bāṇabhaṭṭa did not get correct information on this point or that the latter had no son to succeed him or if there was any he might have predeceased him and both were followed by Vajradatta's line which would easily account for their non-mention in later inscriptions.

The legend regarding the demon king Bāṇa also figures in the *Mbh*. In its southern recension we are told that his capital was at Śoṇitapura[31] which has generally been identified by historians with modern Tezpur in Assam.[32] He was an ardent devotee of lord Śiva whose favour he enjoyed. Kṛishṇa's son Aniruddha is reported to have fallen in love with his daughter and to have been put behind the bars by Bāṇa and in the battle that ensued Kṛishṇa killed Bāṇa by his Sudarśana chakra.[33]

THE DATE OF THE BHĀRATA WAR: EPIGRAPHIC EVIDENCE FROM PRĀGJYOTISHA

The historians now generally agree that the Bhārata War was a historical event though fought on a very modest scale between two factions of a fairly powerful ruling family with several other powers fighting on one or other side. There is, however, wide divergence on the question of its date, both in ancient traditions and among modern historians. And as would be shown presently, an inscription from Prāgjyotisha is supposed to have an important bearing on this problem. The most popular tradition dates the event a few years or just prior to 3102 BC which marks the beginning of the Kali age. The Kaliyuga is found mentioned for the first time by the celebrated astronomer Āryabhaṭa (born AD 473)[34] and reiterated in the Aihoḷe inscription (dated AD 634) of the Chālukya emperor Pulakeśi II of Badami (Bijapur district, Karnataka).[35] However, there also exist some other early traditions dating this event a few centuries later. According to a very persistent tradition, it occurred in 2449 (current) or 2448 (expired) BC. This notion is first referred to by Varāhamihira (mid-sixth century AD) who in his *Bṛihat-saṁhitā* (XIII. 3) gives the interval between the period of the Mahābhārata hero Yudhishṭhira and the commencement of the Śaka era as 2526 years.[36] Kalhaṇa (twelfth century AD) in his *Rājataraṅgiṇī* (I.56) cites this statement of Varāhamihira, dubs the notion that the Bhārata War took place at the end of Dvāpara as misleading (I.49) and asserts that the Kurus and Pāṇḍavas flourished when 653 years of the Kali age had elapsed (I.51).[37] Some modern Indian astronomers have tried to demonstrate that even some astronomical references in the *Mbh.* itself lend support to this date.[38] What is of special interest in the present context is the fact that this tradition is also buttressed by some scholars on the basis of a certain assertion met within one of the copperplate charters of the Prāgjyotisha monarch Bāskaravarman (*c.* AD 600-650). It is averred in his Nichānpur plates (verse 7) that Vajradatta, son of Bhagadatta, who had played an important role in the Bhārata War, was followed by his descendants who ruled for three thousand years after which Pushyavaman became king.[39] And as Bhāskaravarman, who was a contemporary of Harshavardhana of Kanauj and Thanesar and flourished in the first half of the seventh century AD, was twelfth in descent from Pushyavarman, the latter may be placed in the first half of the fourth century AD. And if we add 3000 years reportedly elapsed between his accession and Bhagadatta's son Vajradatta, we reach about the first half of the twenty-fifth century BC which tallies well with 2448 BC, the date of Yudhishṭhira according to Varāhamihira.[40] There is yet another tradition based on the varying statements in the Purāṇas about the interval between Parīkshit, grandson of Arjuna and successor of Yudhishṭhira, and the coronation of Mahāpadma (Nanda) who flourished in the fourth century BC prior to the accession of Chandragupta Maurya. According to most of the scholars, it is given as 1050 or 1015 years, and accordingly the Bhārata War may have to be dated around the fifteenth century BC. However, after carefully comparing the relevant Purāṇic passages on the question and the duration of the time allotted to various dynasties, P.V. Kane has concluded that the correct reading most probably was *pañchaśatottaram*, and not *pañchāśd=uttaram* or *pañchadaś-ottaram* as found in the printed editions of the Purāṇas concerned.[41] And consequently the gap between Parīkshit and Mahāpadma Nanda's coronation should be 1500 years and thus the Bhārata War, according to this tradition, will have to be dated in about 1900 BC. However, archaeologists, who concede the historicity of the Bhārata War, are inclined to date the event somewhere between roughly 900 and 1500 BC based on the time-bracket for the Painted Grey Ware (PGW) culture noticed at most of the sites in northern India associated with the activities of the Kauravas and the Pāṇḍavas and the Bhārata War as well as on some other considerations.[42] The find of some other material including some seals in the underwater excavations at Bet Dvārakā in layers dating from about fifteenth century BC has been taken by the excavator to confirm Kṛishṇa's association with the site during this period.[43]

PRĀGJYOTISHA RULING FAMILIES CLAIMING DESCENT FROM NARAKA AND BHAGADATTA

And what is most pertinent to note in the present context, practically all the ruling families of Prāgjyotisha during historical period supplanting one after the other claimed from these personages. The earliest records laying such a claim date from early seventh century AD. The copperplate charters of the Prāgjyotisha king Bhāskaravarman *alias* Kumāra of the first half of the seventh century AD, who played a significant role in pan-Indian politics like his traditional ancestor Bhagadatta, and brought the North-East on the national politico-cultural map of India, trace the origin of the line from the earth and lord Vishṇu's Varāha (Boar) manifestation and from Bhagadatta whom they describe as Naraka's son and successor. It is also averred that Bhagadatta participated in the Bhārata War wherein he lost his life and was followed on the throne by Vajradatta who was his son according to most of the sources while a few later records regard him as his brother.[44] As we have seen, we even come across a statement in the Nidhānpur plates of Bhāskaravarman that has an important bearing on the date of the Bhārata War since when his family is reported to have ruled.

DID THE FAMILIES REALLY DESCEND FROM MAHĀBHĀRATA HEROES?

Despite the persistence of these traditions, it may be regarded as almost certain that a family (as of Naraka and Bhagadatta) ruling over so far off a region as Prāgjyotisha could not have participated in a rather not so large, though highly important, war between the two factions of a family (Pāṇḍavas and Kauravas) as Bhārata War undoubtedly was. Distances covering a few thousand kilometres were too great a hurdle for that.

Actually the *Mbh.*, as admitted by the text itself, underwent at least three stages of growth, which must have taken quite a few centuries. The original text comprising just a few thousand stanzas was possibly composed by Kṛishṇadvaipāyana Vyāsa and was probably known as *Jaya* because it simply concerned itself with the central theme, viz. the victory (*jaya*) of the Pāṇḍavas over the Kauravas. It was later revised by Vaiśampāyana (and probably his school) with addition of fresh material and now it turned into *Bhārata* containing some 24,000 stanzas. And finally with the accretion of some other considerable doses of matter added from time to time with the object of turning the text into an encyclopaedia of Indian culture[45] with all its components, it assumed the form of a compendium of all the existing knowledge called *Mahābhārata* with nearly 100,000 verses and was appropriately called *śata-sāhasrī saṁhitā*.[46]

However, these verses are not included in the critical edition of the Ādiparvan prepared by that great *Mahābhārata* authority, V.S. Sukthankar.[47] But even this edition also admits that the text of the Great Epic went through several stages of growth. We are told that Vyāsa took three years of stringent constant labour to compose the *Mahābhārata* (Ādi, 56.32)[48] and transmitted it first to his five pupils Sumantu, Jaimini, Paila, Śuka (his son) and Vaiśampāyana all of whom published their own *saṁhitās* or versions (Ādi, 57.74-75).[49] The last of these, Vaiśampāyana, recited it at snake-sacrifice of Janamejaya, the great-grandson of Arjuna (Ādi, 1.8-9)[50] where it was heard by the bard (*sūta*) Lomaharshaṇa named Ugraśvaas who narrated it afresh before the sages assembled at the twelve-year sacrifice of sage Śaunaka in the Naimisha forest (Ādi, 1. 1ff.). It had already become so popular that it was narrated by some poets and some were still narrating and, it was hoped, others would narrate this *itihāsa*. It had become a subject of great knowledge in the whole world and was being memorized *in extenso* and in brief by the brāhmaṇas (Ādi, 1. 24-26). Admittedly the text had already passed through several recensions which must have taken a few centuries.

Obviously the whole episode of Bhagadatta was concocted in later times with the object of securing a high antiquity and legitimacy for the rule of the most prominent local line and later it was inherited by others. Another object of tracing the origin from Vishṇu (Varāha) and earth was to impart a hallowed lineage and the Naraka episode were meant to satisfy the aspirations of the mixed local population, more especially the aboriginals. Such practices are not restricted to Prāgjyotisha alone; they are found in almost all the regions of Bhāratavarsha. If so, when was this legend concocted and attained popularity? As we have seen, the *Mbh.* mentions only the name Prāgjyotisha, while the other name, viz. Kāmarūpa, which had come into existence by the first century BC, is conspicuously absent. We may thus conclude that the entire Bhagadatta legend had already become popular sometime prior to this date.

NOTES AND REFERENCES

1. Here we have utilized the Gita Press edition of the text. Most of the references to Prāgjyotisha and its rulers are, however, met with in the critical edition as well.
2. For a discussion of the *Bṛihat-saṁhitā* evidence, *vide* Ajay Mitra Shastri, *Varāhamihira's India*, Vol. I, Aryan Books International, New Delhi, 1996, p. 89.
3. It is first mentioned in so far as definitely datable sources are concerned in the *Prayāga praśasti* (line 22) of the Gupta emperor Samudragupta where its ruler is included among the bordering kings (*pratyanta-nṛipatis*) who surrendered to the mighty Gupta invader. Kālidāsa also refers to Kāmarūpa and Prāgjyotisha as alternative territorial names in connection with the description of his hero Raghu's *digvijaya* (*Raghuvaṁśa*, IV. 81-84). In case we place him in the first century BC following the unanimous Indian tradition, the antiquity of the name may go back by a few centuries.
4. In North Indian inscriptions, this name is employed more commonly.
5. 'Ancient Countries of Eastern India', *JASB*, 1897, p. 106.
6. *The Mārkaṇḍeya Purāṇa* , English translation, p. 328, fn.
7. For instance, see K.L. Barua, *Early History of Kāmarūpa*, Shillong, 1933, pp. 2, 5-6, etc.
8. For an elaboration of the exact position, see D.C. Sircar, *Studies in the Geography of Ancient and Medieval India*, 2nd Edn., Motilal Banarsidass, Delhi, 1972, pp. 159-65.
9. See references cited later in this paper.
10. Some scholars are of the view that allusions to it are met with in the *Śatapatha-brāhmaṇa* and the *Śāṅkhāyana-śrautasūtra* also. But these beliefs are based on erroneous interpretations of the passages and there is in reality no mention of it in any part of the Vedic literature as shown by M.M. Sharma. See his *Inscriptions of Ancient Assam*, Guwahati, 1978, Introduction, pp. 1-3.

11. K.L. Barua, *op. cit.*, pp. 12-13.
12. Our attention is invited to the presence of a Navagraha temple on a hill called Chitrāchala near Guwahati which may have been responsible for the name Prāgjyotishapura (E.A. Gait, *History of Assam*, p. 15). They also find support for it in the presence of numerous Assamese manuscripts dealing with astronomy and astrology, the prevalence of solar and fire worship in early Assam and the association of the popular Bihu festival with fire-worship and fertility rites as well as the supposed astronomical significance of the region. For these and a few other points, see D.B. Spooner, 'The Zoroastrian Background of Indian History', *JRAS*, 1915, pp. 433-36; K.L. Barua, *op. cit.*, 13; *Studies in the Early History of Assam*. Jorhat-Guwahati, 1973, pp. 12-13; B.K. Barua, *Cultural History of Assam*, p.11; P.C. Choudhury, *History and Culture of the People of Assam up to the Thirteenth Century A.D.*, Guwahati, 1959, p. 29.
13. B. K. Kakati, *The Mother Goddess Kāmākhyā*, Guwahati, 1943, p. 6.
14. R.M. Nath, *The Background of Assamese Culture*, Shillong, 1948, pp. 5-6.
15. See Ajay Mitra Shastri, *Prāgjyotisha: A Pan-Indian Perspective*, Aryan Books International, New Delhi, 2001.
16. Udyogaparvan, XLVIII. 80-85. *Vide* also the southern recension quoted after Sabhāparvan, XXXVIII. 29 at pp. 337ff., which supplies the same description with added details.
17. *Ibid.*, CXXX. 43-45.
18. Droṇaparvan, XXIX. 32.
19. Vanaparvan, Ch. XLII.
20. We are told that Kṛishṇa himself in one of his four manifestations (*mūrtis*) at the behest of the earth goddess gave her son Naraka the Vaishṇavāstra and after his death at the hands of Kṛishṇa it came to Prāgjyotisha. See *Mbh.* Droṇa, XXIXX. 25-36.
21. Bāshkala is named in the same stanza just before Bhagadatta, but there is absolutely nothing to warrant the suggestion that the latter was born, even partially, from the former (*Mahābhārata ki Nāmānukramaṇikā*, Gita Press, Gorakhpur, Vikrama Saṁvat 2016, under 'Bhagadatta')
22. स किरातैश्च चीनैश्च वृतः प्राग्ज्योतिषोऽभवत्।
अन्यैश्च बहुभिर्योधैः सागरानूपवासिभिः।।

Sabhāparvan, XXVI.9

23. एवं बहुविधान् देशान् विजित्य पवनात्मजः।
वसु तेभ्य उपादाय लौहित्यमगमद् बली।
स सर्वान् म्लेच्छनृपतीन् सागरानूपवासिनः।
करमाहारयामास रत्नानि विविधानि च।
चन्दनागुरुवस्त्राणि मणिमौक्तिककम्बलम्।
काञ्चनं रजतं चैव विद्रुमं च महाधनम्।।

ते कोटिशतसंख्येन कौन्तेयं महता तदा।
अभ्यवर्षन् महात्मानं धनवर्षेण पाण्डवम्।।

24. प्राग्ज्योतिषाधिपः शूरो म्लेच्छानामधिपो बली।
यवनैः सहितो राजा भगदत्तो महारथः।।
आजानेयान् हयाञ्छीघ्रानादायानिलरंहसः।
बलिं च कृत्स्नमादाय द्वारि तिष्ठति वातिः।।
अश्मसारमयं भाण्डं शुद्धदन्तत्सरूनसीन्।
प्राग्ज्योतिषाधिपो दत्त्वा भगदत्तोऽव्रजत् तदा।।
Sabhāparvan, XXXI.14-16

25. It was reportedly his first success in his northern expedition after which he ascended the Himavat mountain and having reduced the Haimavatika (Himalayan) chiefs he proceeded to Nepal whereafter he descended to the plains and going to the east he vanquished the rulers of Aṅga, Vaṅga, Kaliṅga, Śuṇḍika, Mithilā, Magadha, etc.
26. These are Kirrhadae of the classical writers.
27. As we have seen above, the Kāmarūpa is mentioned as an alternative name of Prāgjyotisha by Kālidāsa who flourished in the first century BC following ancient Indian tradition supported by archaeological evidence.
28. भगदत्तसुतो राजन् कृतप्रज्ञो महाबलः।
श्येनवच्चरता संख्ये नकुलेन निपातितः।।
29. *Vide* for this suggestion, M.M. Sharma, *Inscriptions of Ancient Assam*, Introduction, p. 8.
30. *Ibid.*
31. Southern recension following Sabhāparvan, XXXVIII. 29, pp. 337ff.
32. In the local dialect *tez* = *śoṇita* = 'blood'. Thus, Tezpur = Śoṇitapura.
33. We have confined ourselves to only the legend met with in the southern recension as that alone has some bearing on the history of Prāgjyotisha.
34. षष्ट्यब्दानां षष्टिर्यदा व्यतीतास्त्रयश्च युगपादाः।
त्र्यधिका विंशतिरब्दास्तदेह मम रन्मनोऽतीताः।।
35. त्रिंशत्सु त्रिसहस्रेषु भारतादाहवादितः।
सप्ताब्दशतयुक्तेषु गतेष्वब्देषु पञ्चसु।।
पञ्चाशत्सु कलौ काले षट्सु पञ्चशतासु च।
समासु समतीतसु शकानामपि भूभुजाम्।।
EI, VI, 1900-01, p. 7, verses 33-34.
36. आसन् मघासु मुनयः शासति पृथिवीं युधिष्ठिरे नृपतौ।
षड्द्विकपञ्चद्वियुतः शककालस्तस्य राज्ञश्च।।
Despite varying interpretations of the expression *shaḍ-dvika-pañcha-yutaḥ* (for these interpretations, see Ajay Mitra Shastri, *Varāhamihira's India*, I, p. 34, note 45), this happens to be the only correct interpretation and, as will be just seen, is backed by the Kashmiri chronicler Kalhaṇa.
It is held by some scholars that this stanza is of the sage Vṛiddha-

Garga who is believed to have flourished in pre-Christian centuries when there could be no question of the knowledge of what is known as Śaka era commencing AD 78 and therefore it is proposed to amend the reading *Śaka-kāla* to *Śakya-kāla* which again is regarded as meant for *Śākya-kāla* and intended to refer to the era of Buddha's *nirvāṇa*. However, the reading Śakya-kāla would violate the metre besides the fact that there does not exist early traditions of the prevalence of an era commencing from Śākyamuni Buddha's death. But there is no reason to hold that the stanza in question was extracted by Varāhamihira from Vṛiddha-Garga as supposed by these scholars. The previous stanza just avers that Varāhamihira 'would state the movement of the Saptarishis following Vṛiddha-Garga's opinion' (*kathayishye Vṛiddha-Garga-matāt, ibid.*, XIII.2). Obviously, the wording is of Varāhamihira himself, and not of Vṛiddha-Garga. In fact, the relevant stanza of Vṛiddha-Garga as cited by Bhaṭṭotpala in his Vivṛiti commentary runs as follows and makes the point absolutely clear and certain:-
तथा च वृद्धगर्गः–
कलिद्वापरसन्धौ तु स्थितास्ते पितृदैवतम्।
मुनयो धर्मनिरताः प्रजानां पालने रताः।।
Bṛihat-saṁhitā with Bhaṭṭotpala's Vivṛiti commentary, Ed. Sudhakara Dvivedi, I, on Ch. XIII. 3. Some scholars like Mohan Gupta ('The Date of Mahābhārata War: Purāṇic and Astronomical Data', included in this volume) believe that the stanza actually refers to the period elapsed from the time of the Mahābhārata hero Yudhishṭhira to the time of Varāhamihira though they actually refer to its citation by Kalhaṇa in his *Rājataraṅgiṇī* (I. 56). This is just impossible in view of the explicit statement that the Kauravas and the Pāṇḍavas flourished 653 years after the beginning of the Kali age. See the following stanza.

37. शतेषु षट्सु सार्धेषु त्र्यधिकेषु च भूतले।
कलेर्गतेषु वर्षाणामभूवन् कुरुपाण्डवाः।।
38. See P.C. Sengupta, 'Astronomical References in the Mahābhārata and their Implications', *JRASBL*, II, 1933, pp. 101-19; 'Bhārata Battle Traditions', *Ibid.*, IV, 1938, pp. 393-413.
39. वंश्येषु तस्य नृपतिषु वर्षसहस्रत्रयं पदमवाप्य।
यातेषु देवभूयं क्षितीश्वरः पुष्यवर्माऽभूत्।।
M.M. Sharma, *op. cit.*, p. 41, verse 7.
40. See P.V. Kane, *History of Dharmaśāstra*, III, Bhandarkar Oriental Research Institute, Pune, 1946, p. 898-99. However, Kane assigns an average of twenty years per reign and arrives at the beginning of the fifth century AD for Pushyavarman which would be too late a date for him. *Vide Prāgjyotisha*: *A Pan-Indian Perspective*, Aryan Books International, New Delhi, 2001.

41. *History of Dharmaśāstra*, III, pp. 898-1000.
42. For a discussion of the evidence, see B.B. Lal, 'Excavations at Hastinapur and Other Explorations in the Upper Ganga Sutlej Basin: 1950-52', *Ancient India*, Nos. 11-12, 1954-55, pp. 1-151. He found at Hastinapur a large part of the habitation of PGW culture washed away by a flood which, to him, corroborated the Purāṇic tradition that serious flood forced Nichakshu, son of Parikshit, to shift his capital to Kauśāmbī. He dates this layer in about 800 BC shortly before which the Mahābhārata War must have taken place. His latest contribution on the theme is 'This is How an Archaeologist Looks at the Historicity of Mahābhārata' in this volume. Vibha Tripathi (*The Painted Grey Ware and Iron Age Culture of Northern India*, pp. 122-23) has summarized his main results. For a list of PGW sites known up to the 1970s, *Ibid.*, pp. 124-31.

    F.E. Pargiter (*Ancient Indian Historical Tradition*, pp. 175-82) after a careful analytical assessment of the total number of reigns between Parikshit, who succeeded Yudhishṭhira, and Mahāpadma, who founded the Nanda dynasty that preceded the Mauryas, arrives at 950 BC for the time of the battle. However, though well-based on the Purāṇic data, his date suffers from the abnormally low averages assigned to individual reigns, viz. 18 years, and therefore stands in need of a review. S.B. Roy (*The Date of the Mahābhārata War*, pp. 139-48) reviews the various current theories about the date of this event and himself argues in favour of a date about mid-fifteenth century BC (*Ibid.*, pp. 116-48), his favoured date being around 1424 BC (*Ibid.*, p. 148).
43. See his 'Marine Archaeological Investigation in Indian Waters and the Discovery of Submerged Dvārakā', *Mañjūshā: Dr. S.R. Rao 60th Birthday Felicitation Volume*, Bangalore, 1985, pp. 23-27; 'Excavations at the Submerged Ports: Dvāraka: A Case Study', *Marine Archaeology of the Indian Ocean Countries*, Goa, 1987, pp. 47-53.

    Some scholars are inclined to regard the Harappan remains as those of the Mahābhārata age and thereby push the date of the war to around the third millennium BC. See I.K. Sarma. 'The Mahābhārata: A Critical Study of the Archaeological Data', included in this volume.
44. But in the Tezpur and Parbatiyā charters (verse 4) of Vanamāladevavarman (M.M. Sharma, *op. cit.*, pp. 97 and 116) of the ninth century AD, Vajradatta is described as one of the two sons of Naraka, the other being Bhagadatta.
45. अष्टौ श्लोकसहस्राणि अष्टौ श्लोकशतानि च।
    अहं वेद्मि शुको वेत्ति संजयो वेत्ति वा न वा।।
    चतुर्विंशतिसाहस्रीं चक्रे भारतसंहिताम्।
    उपाख्यानैर्विना तावद् भारतं प्रोच्यते बुधैः।।

इदं शतसहस्रं तु श्लोकानां पुण्यकर्मणाम्।
उपाख्यानैः सह ज्ञेयमाद्यं भारतमुत्तमम्।।

Mahābhārata, Ādi, I. 81, 102b-103a, 101b-102a.

However, traditionally the first statement is intended to refer to knotty stanzas in the work and not to actual extent of the text.

Thus came into existence the saying met with in the *Mbh.* (Ādi, 56.33), itself *Dharme ch-ārthe cha kāme cha mokshe cha Bharatarshabha/ yad=ih-āsti tad=anyatra yan=n-eh-āsti na tat kvachit.*

46. The expression first occurs in the Khoh copperplate charter of *Mahārāja* Śarvanātha dated AD 534. *Vide* J.F. Fleet, "Inscriptions of the Guptas and their Successors", *CII*, III, p. 137.
47. Bhandarkar Oriental Research Institute, Pune, 1933.
48. त्रिभिर्वर्षैः सदोत्थायी कृष्णद्वैपायनो मुनिः।
हाभारताख्यानं कृतवानिदमुत्तमम्।।
49. वेदानध्यापयामास महाभारतञ्चमान्।
सुमन्तुं जैमिनिं पैलं शुकं चैव स्वमात्मजम्।।
प्रभुर्वरिष्ठो वरदो वैशम्पायनमेव च।
संहितास्तैः पृथक्त्वेन भारतस्य प्रकाशिताः।।
50. जनमेजयस्य राजर्षेः सर्पसत्रे महात्मनः।
समीपे पार्थिवेन्द्रस्य सम्यक् पारिक्षितस्य च।।
कृष्णद्वैपायनप्रोक्ताः सुपुण्या विविधाः कथाः।
कथिताश्चापि विधिवद् या वैशम्पायनेन वै।।

11

Ethnography of the *Mahābhārata* and the North-East*

K.S. Singh

This paper seeks to explore the ethnographic dimensions of the *Mahābhārata* in terms of the parameters of a contemporary ethnographic project (1985-2000) on the People of India (POI). The dimensions include (i) a notion of space, (ii) the emergence of territorial and ethnic identities, (iii) identification, listing and distribution of peoples, (iv) the linkages and affinities among the peoples and (v) the diffusion of the Mahābhārata traditions.

The *Mahābhārata* corpus, as it has come down to us, has evolved, absorbed and incorporated many traditions over centuries, particularly during the period from 2nd century BC to 2nd century AD when it was mainly compiled. As it developed from *Jayā* to *Bhārata* to *Mahābhārata*, it became the story of all peoples of India. Indeed the *Mahābhārata* is a great assemblage of peoples, 363 of them, which is the largest number in the ancient texts. They meet on the battlefield as equals – an enemy is not to be underrated – and are generally mentioned in respectful terms and outside of it. They are also bound by many ties of affinities and have many linkages, which speak of the vitality, maturity and understanding of a civilizational process, reflecting the consciousness of a vibrant civilization.

* The material for this paper was originally collected for a paper on Ethnography of Ancient India to be published in a volume edited by Prof. G.C. Pande for the Project of History of Indian Science, Philosophy and Culture. However, as the paper could not be completed, the material on the *Mahābhārata* was taken out and developed and fresh material was added for the North-East in this paper.

The second part of this paper deals with the north-east including the hills, which like other parts of India has its linkages with the epic, its heroes, its episodes through an ongoing process of creative adaptation. There are four aspects to it. First, the participation of Bhagadatta with his army of Chīnas and Kirātas in Kurukshetra War; second, Sanskritization of tribes and reconstruction of genealogies linking them to the Mahābhārata characters like Bhīma, Hiḍimbā, Ghaṭotkacha and Arjuna; third, their legends and folklores about the visit of the Mahābhārata heroes and matrimonial alliances and Mahābhārata themes that figure prominently in literature and performing arts leading some communities to call themselves a Mahābhārata people; fourth, some of these reconstructions are being critically reexamined today as the north-eastern communities are engaged in search for identity.

The *Mahābhārata*, probably the first comprehensive ethnography of India, has been explored as such by scholars, particularly historians, who have generally applied the colonial concept of tribe to describe the people (*jana*). While it is not the purpose of this paper to present an overview of the literature in this field, one may briefly mention the leads thrown up by three important pieces of writing. The first is the *Ethnography of Ancient India* by Robert Shafer (1954), which, despite the title, concentrates on the ethnography of the *Mahābhārata* rather than the whole of ancient India. What impresses this author is the "great number of ethnic names" of "nations, tribes or regions", about three hundred of them – in fact, it is three hundred and sixty-three, which is much more than the geographical names given in the Purāṇas, which he finds "much more limited and much more corrupt" than the list given in the *Mahābhārata*. He also describes the *Mahābhārata* as an original "Kuru epic", developed later with the compilation and interpolations over several hundred years. He further describes the epic as essentially the story of a native rebellion, led by Kauravas against the Āryan exploitation symbolized by the Pāṇḍavas, who forced "tribes and nations", particularly the non-Āryans, to pay exorbitant tribute and acknowledge the overlordship of Yudhishṭhira. The epic, according to him, thus is an apologia about the Pāṇḍavas, their eulogy, in fact an apologia for extermination of the kshatriyas resulting from the Mahābhārata War. Such views are not entirely supported by the reading of the *Mahābhārata* as it exists today. While Āryanization in terms of the spread of the Indo-Āryan language, Sanskrit, was underway, a synthesis of various cultures was emerging, a mixture of morphological types was going on. The native non-Āryan groups fought on both sides, the larger number, no doubt, on the side of Kauvaras because they were in power and had a larger army. The *Mahābhārata* did establish the primacy of the Pāṇḍavas and their mentor Lord Kṛishṇa for forty years till it was challenged by peoples on the periphery, but such things were going on all the time in Indian history. Robert Shafer has, however, a point when he says that the people speaking Tibeto-Burman languages, once occupied the Gaṅgā valley or parts of it, and gave us probably such names as Gaṅgā, Aṅga, Vaṅga and, Kaliṅga though today they are confined to the Himalayas and the north-east. It is difficult to agree with the view that at the time of the Mahābhārata, the Āryans were the invaders and the land was dominated by non-Āryans or that the waves of Indo-Āryans moved from Kailāsh-Mānasarovar region along with the Sutlej into the north-western parts of the subcontinent and from there towards the Gaṅgā-Yamunā valley. Although Āryanization had been going on at "geometric rather than arithmetic rate" for the last 2000 years, the process was not so complete at the time of the Mahābhārata, nor is it so even today. There is a shade of racism in Shafer's analysis when he talks of gradation of colours for the four varṇas too literally. It is wrong to say that the Vaiśyas were Tibeto-Burmans. The identification of "races" with cultures and languages is not generally accepted today. Shafer quotes Patañjali to describe the brāhmaṇas as having a white complexion and yellow and red hair; there are also references to Kṛishṇa or dark-skinned brāhmaṇas of which Veda Vyāsa was an example. The POI study of brāhmaṇa groups shows that they are heterogeneous in terms of biological, cultural and linguistic traits. The Bhīls were not Nahals. In fact, the Nahali language is neither Muṇḍāri nor Draviḍian. Bhīlī is now accepted as a member of the Indo-Āryan language family. Certainly the *Mahābhārata* presents a picture of a mixed society, with people particularly rulers, marrying across groups of people, speaking different languages and practising different cultures and of an emerging synthesis which has been the hallmark of Indian civilization from the beginning.

K.C. Mishra's *Tribes in Mahābhārata* is a major work which describes many dimensions of the *Mahābhārata* including its ethnography both at territorial and ethnic levels. Like Shafer, he deals with the various lists of the tribes, compiled in the *Mahābhārata* but persists, like other historians, with the colonial notion of tribe. This work is followed by Mamata Choudhury's *Tribes in Ancient India* (1977) in which she puts the number of the tribes mentioned in the ancient texts at about 700, almost half of which is mentioned in the *Mahābhārata*. Although she valiantly tries to define the tribe in the traditional anthropological sense, as an "aggregate of stocks of kindred persons forming a community, claiming descent from a common ancestor", her use of the word 'tribe' as by other historians using this notion of 19th century Indian ethnography, is not free from difficulties. In fact, the right course for the historians would have been to use the native Sanskrit term, *jana*, mentioned in the *Mahābhārata* and other texts.

This is an issue taken up by the distinguished historian Niharranjan Ray (Introductory Address 1977, pp. 6-15). He uses the native terms *jana* and *jāti*, which he rightly says belong to the same roots, that is *jan*, that is to be born into or give birth to. Thus Nihar Babu makes a distinction between *jana*, which he identifies with the communities, peoples, and present-day tribes and *jāti* which he describes as a complex production organization. Both have

> something to do with birth and biological heredity and hence with familial and social relationships. But behaviourally, as seen through history, it had also a social and economic purpose and function, regulated by birth and heredity. Here was thus a system which was directed not towards mobility but towards stability and security.

[He mentions] a whole lot of *janas* like:

> . . . the Savaras, the Kulūtas, the Kollas, the Bhillas, the Khaśas, the Kinnaras and a countless number of many others whom today we know as 'tribes', bearing almost the same recognizable names. . . . It is significant that in this huge body of literature whenever such and other communities of people find mention, they are always referred to in the plural number, collectively as a people or *janāḥ, Andhrāḥ, Śavarāḥ, Kinnarāḥ*, etc., just as we have *Vaṅgāḥ, Māgadhāḥ, Pāñchālāḥ, Aṅgāḥ, Cherāḥ, Pāṇḍyāḥ*, etc. An analysis of such names and the context in which they are referred to shows very clearly and unmistakably that all such communities had each a territorial habitat of their own which can still be identified.

With the passage of time, each of these communities lent their names to the territory inhabited by them, and the territories came to be known as *padas*. Most of the local names of districts, divisions and states that we know of today, have come down to us from the *padas* of old; but quite a number of them have also lost their name and identity in their larger and more powerful neighbours. . . .

A careful analysis of the long list of *janas* in epic, Buddhist, Purāṇic, and secular literature of early and medieval times and the context in which they are mentioned, makes it very clear that hardly any distinction was made, until very late in history, between what we know today as 'tribes' and such communities of people who were known as the Gandhāras and Kambojas, Kāsīs and Kośalas, Aṅgas and Magadhas, Kurus and Pāñchālas, for instances. At any rate, in the whole body of historical data at our disposal there is hardly anything to suggest that these communities of people belonged to two different social and ethnic categories altogether. In fact, in the literary sources I have referred to, the communities of people whom today we refer to as 'tribe' and those that we know from history as belonging to more advanced stages of socio-economic and cultural growth there is hardly any evidence to show that in the collective mind of India's communities of people there was any consciousness of a difference between the two sets of *janas*.

According to Ray there are three types of *janas* – first, there were *janas* of foreign origin who were absorbed into brāhmaṇical religion and socio-economic production system of *jāti*.

One has only to remember what happened to the Śakas, the Kushāṇas, the Ābhīras, the Jñātrikas or Jāṭs, the Gurjaras or Gujars, the Hūns or Hūṇas and other allied peoples, many of whom are mentioned as *janas* in the list of people as given in the epics and the Purāṇas, in the Buddhist and secular literature and in land grants and other historical documents. The Islamized Turks, Afghans, Iranians and Mongols were certainly able to maintain their religious and cultural identity, even to extend the frontiers of Muslim society within India, but let it be noted that they too had to succumb to the socio-economic organization of Brāhmaṇical Hinduism, to the same production system as that of the *jāti*. Indeed, once they had fallen into the production system of the *jāti* it was no longer possible for them to resist its social implications. The same thing happened to the communities of people of the Tibeto-Burman stock who trudged into Assam and our north-eastern regions in the thirteenth century. Those of the *janas* of foreign origin that came to exercise political authority as kings and as members of royalty, nobility and the court, were given the *jāti* status of Kshatriyas; those that eventually took to agriculture came to be self-styled as Vaiśyas; but the large majority had to be content with very low jāti status in Hindu socio-economic hierarchy, including those like the Hūṇas who allowed themselves to be recruited as mercenary soldiers by regional rulers. . . .

Secondly, there were *janas* of the indigenous (this term has become controversial) origin who were absorbed into Hindu-Brāhmaṇical social organization. Those "*janas* who were defeated in war and taken prisoners, were immediately made economically and socially subservient altogether, being reduced to slaves, labourers and servants. Eventually, they came to be incorporated in the Hindu social organization, but seem to have been given a place at the lowest bottom, not very different from that of the *Chaṇḍālas*."

Thirdly, there were *janas* who were in the periphery of the Āryāvarta.

These were *janas* that today lie all along our eastern and north-eastern frontiers and along the central and western Himālayas up to a height of 13,000 feet, *janas* that are predominantly of the Tibeto-Burman stock, except perhaps the Nāgas and one or two other less known *janas*. This entire Himalayan area from our eastern frontiers to Ladakh is naturally a very sensitive one, and for more than one reason, a very significant one as well from the political and economic points of view. Many of these *janas* do not, for obvious reasons, make their appearance in history or in our historical geography before the nineteenth century, but many others do, for instance, the Nāgas who are mentioned by Ptolemy in the second century A.D., the Khaśas, the Kirātas which seem to be almost a blanket name for all the Tibeto-Burman peoples in our eastern and north-eastern frontiers, the Kinnaras of the Kinnaur district of Himachal, the Kullūtas of the Kullu valley, the Bhoṭas of the Bhutan-Sikkim area, and a few others whose names appear in the traditional Purāṇic list of *janas*. Our medieval Assamese, Bengali, Maithili and Hindi literature, too, gives us a few names of such peoples.

Then there is a belt of *jana* territory in middle India and the Islands. Then there is the whole belt along the old Pāryiyātra, Vindhya and Śuktimat hills which are collectively known to us as the Vindhyan ranges, stretching from almost the borders of Rajasthan to what are called the Chhotanagpur and Orissa hills which are but extensions of the Vindhyan ranges. All along these ranges and their slopes and feet and in the forests and valleys nursed by them live and have been living for centuries some of the oldest *janas* known to our history and culture: the Nishādas and the Śavaras, the Kollas and Bhillas, for instance, and many other cognate and semi-cognate *janas* of whom history and historical geography have not kept any record. But we know from one of our epics, the *Rāmāyaṇa*, that part at any rate of this area was the region that was called *janasthāna*, the land *par excellence* of the *janas*. Ethnically the majority of the *janas* seem to be of proto-Austroloid origin though a few of them speak language of Draviḍian affiliation.

Besides these two geographical areas of non-*jāti janas* there is also a good number of them in smaller aggregates and dispersed in relatively smaller areas in almost all the southern States, especially in Andhra Pradesh and Kerala, and in Maharashtra. But these *janas* are all more or less in close contact and communication with socially and culturally, politically and economically more powerful communities belonging to the *jāti* complex. And finally there are the isolated aggregates of relatively much less developed *janas* in the Andaman and Nicobar Islands.

The People of India project based on an ethnographic survey of all people of India reinforced the view that India is a land of many communities. These communities called *jana* in the ancient texts are the original formation, the basic units of our civilization, rooted in ecology, in the resource endowments of various regions and in their social and cultural organizations, their languages and dialects. Even though they have evolved from the simple to the complex social organization or complex systems of production as Nihar Babu puts it, they share many traits of a community, such as endogamy, resource-based occupations, notions of purity and pollution, order of hierarchy in incipient or developed forms. From this point of view the tribes are at the one end of the pole and the present-day caste at the other end, but both are people, the *jana*, the inhabitants of the land. The tribes are the relatively isolated *janas*, distant and backward. The distinction made by Ray between *jana* and *jati* is not supported by the ancient texts (the *Mahābhārata* as will be described later, treats *janas* as people, neither tribe nor caste) which generally treat them interchangeably, and later mention *jatis* more than *janas* which in fact fades away.

II

We now turn to the salient features of the ethnography of the *Mahābhārata*.

The first is the *notion of space*, which is crucial to ethnography as people at one level of their multi-level identity generally derive their identity from space. In the ancient period there was the notion of *bhūmi, vasudhā* and *chakravarti-kshetra*, which was the political space to be conquered and ruled. Jambūdvīpa was the name given to this space. This name, for the first time, occurs in the Aśokan inscriptions. The *Mahābhārata* has a chapter entitled "Jambūdvīpa-nirmāṇa-khaṇḍa", section V of Bhīshmaparvan. Jambūdvīpa derives its identity from a tree *jambū* (rosewood) which is both mythical as it is said to stand near Mount Meru and real because the land abounds in *jambū* trees, rapturously described by ancient environmentalists as a wonder tree gifted with many attributes and properties. However, the notion of Jambūdvīpa gradually expanded from its first description which applied to the Aśokan empire to mind-boggling proportions as this was gradually extended to greater India or even beyond that, to all continents (except the Americas and Australia). It is said in the *Mahābhārata* and its later versions that there were seven divisions (*varshas*) of Jambūkhaṇḍa (Section XI of Bhīshmaparvan) including Bhārata. Bhāratvarsha, located in Jambūdvīpa gradually became a part of it (*Jambūdvīpe Bharatkhaṇḍe*).

The *Mahābhārata* speaks of the love of the land, and states that the tract of land known by Bhārata's name is the beloved land of Manu and of Indra. The *Mahābhārata* also has the notion of Bhārata derived from Bharata, the founder of Bhārata lineage, which is gradually widened to cover the entire country lying south of the Himalayas and bounded by the oceans. This notion of Bhāratavarsha crystallizes in the *Vishṇu Purāṇa* and is celebrated in literary works composed by Kālidāsa, Rabindranath Tagore and Subramania Bharati.

This Jambūdvīpa is intersected by mountains, rivers, forests, deserts, pasture lands, sea coasts, etc. The name of these mountains and rivers also occurs in many lexicographic works. The six mountains extend from the eastern to the western boundaries including Himavatta and there are hundreds of rivers with beautiful names of which many can be identified in different parts of the country today.

The land was divided into *janapadas*, peopled by specific groups. The relationship of *jana* and *janapada* was intimate. Both were interchangeable concepts. The *Mahābhārata* describes in mythical terms, the Jambūkhaṇḍa as a great seat of humanity where men are all of golden complexion and women are like apsarases and all are without sickness, without sorrow and always cheerful. The *Mahābhārata* notes the bio-ethnic diversities of India where reside people of diverse *jatis* (*vasanti teshu sattvāni nānājātīni sarvashaḥ, idam tu Bhāratam varshaṁ tato haimavataṁ param). Rashṭra* is a territorial unit occupied by people, like Ādirāshṭra, Goparāshṭra etc. The space was also traditionally divided into countries *(varshas* or *rāshṭras).*

There is also a notion of the sacred land. The core of the culture and religion of the Indo-Āryans is formed by Kuru-Pāñchāla and Matsya land. There are lands which are degraded such as the Sindhu land or Vāhlīka where foreigners live.

The *Mahābhārata* mentions *jāti* occasionally as segments of *jana*, for example, various *jatis* of Kirātas are mentioned (*Kirātānāṁ cha jātayaḥ*), or *jāti* and *jana* seem to be interchangeable. There is also a mention of *kula* (*vaiśya-śūdra kulāni cha*). However, most of the names are in terms of *jana* and *janapada*. But later texts mention as many as 65 *jatis* and 71 occupation groups. The historians are more concerned with *jāti* than *jana*, with the transition from *varṇa* to *jāti*, proliferation of *jāti*, etc.

As mentioned earlier, the *Mahābhārata* is the most comprehensive ethnography of ancient India in terms of the identification and listing of communities called *janas* and their territories called *janapada*. There were 363 of them.

The listing of communities in the *Mahābhārata* is based on a number of inventories including 'geography' (231 entries), the *digvijaya* list (212), the *dyūta* or tribute to the Pāṇḍavas (296), army formation (158), the additional data (108) as Shafer puts it. There are a number of repetitions in the list. The *digvijaya* campaigns were led by the four Pāṇḍava brothers – Bhīma in the east, Arjuna in the north, Nakula in the west and Sahadeva in the south. Karṇa also was on his *digvijaya* trail, mostly in the east and also in the north. The lists contain mostly the names of the people (*jana*). [The author has avoided the use of the word tribe and mentioned people]. A few places are also mentioned in the list such as Avanti, Kuntī,

Kuru, Kāśī, etc.

Some of the communities maybe mentioned as illustration. The north-west (Central Asia, Persia and Afghanistan) was dominated by "foreigners", namely, the Pahlavas, Sakas, Hūṇas, Yavanas, Kambojas and Bahlikas. The west roughly comprising Kashmir, Punjab, Rajasthan and Gujarat had communities such as Daradas (the Darads of today), the Piśāchas, Vahlīkas, Yādavas of various segments, Surashaṭras, etc., the central region called Madhyadeśa later had many dominant groups such as Kurus, Pāñchālas, Sālvas, Vatsas, Sūrasenas, etc. The northern Himalayan region had Trigartas, Khaśas, etc. who were also spread in the plains. The east had Aṅgas, Vaṅgas, Kirātas, Chīnas, Puṇḍras, etc. The south had Cholas, Pāṇḍyas, Keralas, Andhras, Draviḍas, Karṇātas, Mūshakas, etc.

Apart from these ethnic categories, there were also communities who derived their identity from ecology. The mountain dwellers included Arbuadas (Mount Abu), Haimvatas, Vindhyamūlakas; from deserts Marudha; from rivers and waterfronts Kauśijakas (Kosī), Saindhavras (Sindhu), Sindhu-Sauviras; from pastures Paśupas, Govindas; from frontier Aparānt. However, the large number of people belonged to forests, jāṅgalas, daṇḍakas, etc., because these were abundant in those days. These should be seen together with the forest dwelling communities such as Ādirāshṭra, Vānarāsyas (there is a community called Vanva-mānush), Nishāda.

Some contemporary tribes can be identified like Muṇḍas, Śavaras, Kokuratas or Korku, Kārusha or Kurukh, Kollagir or Kolī, Nishāda or Bhīl.

An analysis of this list of communities shows that they are mostly concentrated in the north-western and western parts of the subcontinent and central region later known as Madhyadeśa. The communities from south of India, the east and the north-east are only a few.

When the first encounter of peoples took place in the court of Yudhishṭhira or on the battlefield, some people looked different, even strange, and were noted for their style of living or dressing or plainly mythologized as in the Greek accounts. These were 'Ekapāda', that is the people who ran so fast that it appeared as if they had only one leg – the author was told about a community among the denotified groups in western India which fitted this description. The Lambakarṇa, i.e. the people with long ears were obviously people who wore turbans with their tail hanging on both sides. The Trinetra, three-eyed people, were probably those who put on prominently a tattoo mark or a tattoo *tilaka* shaped like an eye in the middle of their forehead.

The *Mahābhārata* describes some people as low, barbarous, sinful, born of the mythical cow of Vaśishṭha. But on the whole the *Mahābhārata* also mentions the positive qualities of the people described as mlechchhas such as their martial prowess; their resources including chariots of good quality or horses of good breed, their fertile country and sometimes their dress and language which is not intelligible. The Mahābhārata story also shows how various communities, who met on the battlefield or outside, had generally developed a mature, healthy and respectful relationship, which derived from sharing of values becoming increasingly common. There were all kinds of affinities based on sharing, experiences of living together including studying together – Bhagadatta and Pāṇḍu studied together – friendships, etc. There were also animosities, members of one lineage fighting another, members of the same lineage fighting one another. There were also attempts made by some communities to avoid the war. Thus the Cholas and Pāṇḍyas, according to the local version of the *Mahābhārata*, tried to mediate, threw a feast to which they invited both Kauravas and Pāṇḍavas, though eventually, they sided with the Pāṇḍavas.

People are described in clusters such as Kuru-Pāñchāla, Kāśī-Kosala-Karusha, etc. Migrations of peoples are indicated generally not only from the west to the east or from the north to the south (Malwa) but also from the east to the west particularly of those who were driven out by Jarāsandha.

The power equation among communities was in a state of flux. The Kurus were the dominant group with Yādavas as a close second. Some communities were in a state of decline such as Haihaya, Videha, the *gaṇas* in the north-west, etc. The sheer range of ethnic diversities is fascinating.

The Kirātas or the Indo-Mongoloids need to be specially mentioned because in recent years there is an effort to distinguish the East Asians from the Central Asians. In the *Mahābhārata*, we can identify the East Asians in terms of Chinese or Tibetan-Mongoloids, and Kirātas. The Nāgas of the north-east are mentioned by Ptolemy. The Central Asian Mongoloid groups including the Śakas, Hūṇas, etc., were also known. The *Mahābhārata* gives a graphic description of the Kirātas.

They were golden coloured (yellow) tribes whose army looked as if a forest of yellow *karṇikāra* flowers had descended and they lived on tubers and fruits. They were clad in skin, were strongly built and wore steel coat of mails. They came from Himavat and seemed at a distance to be of a smoky colour. They had well-trained elephants.

The Nāgas elsewhere in the country are not included in the list of *janas* and *janapadas* but some of the branches are mentioned like Kokara (identified by the author with Kokrah, i.e. modern Chhotanagpur). However, recent researches in history and anthropology of the Nāgas persuaded us to look afresh at the Nāga material in the *Mahābhārata*. Nāga derives from the word *nog* or *lok* which has a much wider range than the Nāga for hills. The Nāgas in the *Mahābhārata* occupied *patāla* which was near Hastināpura. But the Nāgas as a folk community occupied a much larger and more diversified space including hills, plains, sea-coast, etc., having only the Nāga cult or Nāga totem as their marker. According to the *Mahābhārata,* one branch of Nāgas, Takshaka, occupied the territory from Takshaśilā upto Hastināpura and the other branch Karkoṭakas was distributed from Vindhya to Khukhra which was later the name of medieval Chhotanagpur. The Pāṇḍavas had incurred the wrath of Takshaka by burning down the forest for their capital. The Nāgas seem to have supported the Kauravas in the battle even though Kuntī was a Nāga-*kanyā*. In fact, both Yādavas and Nāgas closely interacted as they settled down as agriculturists. Balarāma, who was an incarnation of Śeshanāga, had plough as his weapon. After the Mahābhārata War, Arjuna went out on a mission to placate the Nāgas, married Ulūpī and begot a son, Yeravan. But Takshaka never forgave the Pāṇḍavas. They killed Parīkshit whose son Janamejaya took a terrible revenge by massacring the Nāgas and scattering them far and wide. Many Nāga families in middle India trace their origin to this episode. Janamejaya later married Takshaka's daughter and peace was restored between the Nāgas and the Pāṇḍavas.

III

The Mahābhārata traditions have diffused widely. Like all regions of India and many parts of Southeast Asia, the north-eastern region perceives its linkages with the Mahābhārata tradition in a number of ways. The Mahābhārata heroes including Lord Kṛishṇa is believed to have visited some places in this region, and the episodes of the epic are associated with the literature, folk tradition and performing arts. The Mahābhārata heroes were married locally (Singh, 1993b).

The most explicit reference to the north-east, including the hills, occurs in the Mahābhārata War with reference to the heroic deeds performed by and powerful support given to the Kauravas by Bhagadatta, the ruler of Prāgjyotisha (the land of the early sun). He was the son of Naraka, the founder of the dynasty bearing the same name, who was born of the union of Bhūmi (Mother Earth) and wild boar. There is a profound symbolism in the original myth bereft of brāhmaṇical embellishments that occurred later. Boar was the most powerful creature of the period, which could move with the speed of wind and gore to death an elephant and tiger. It could lift the earth and was apotheosized into an incarnation of Vishṇu. The Earth was mother to many tribes including Muṇḍās (*enga* is the word for mother). This Naraka was the founder of first and the longest surviving dynasty before the Ahoms appeared on the scene. According to another tradition, Naraka was born at the foot of hills. He was the lord of the Kirātas, the Himalayan mountain people, and the Chīnas (the Tibetan-Mongoloids) representing the East Asians, and the kingdom included the north-eastern hills and the low-lying marshy land of south Assam. Naraka, who had become irreligious and presumptuous and possessed of demoniac ideas, was killed by Kṛishṇa. He was succeeded by his son Bhagadatta. Kṛishṇa is also said to have rescued 16,100 women from the custody of Naraka and married them. Barua describes Bhagadatta as follows:

> Bhagadatta is frequently mentioned in the *Mahābhārata* as a powerful warrior. He is celebrated as a 'warrior king' and 'the mighty king of the *mlecchas*', and is described as 'the best wielder of the elephant-goad', among the kings assembled on the Kaurava side in the Great War and as 'skillful with the chariot'. Bhagadatta alone of the northern kings is famed for his long and equal contest with Arjuna. He is dignified with

the title 'Śiva's friend' and esteemed as being not inferior to Śakra in battle. He is also specially named 'the friend of Pāṇḍu', and is referred to in terms of respect and kindliness by Kṛishṇa when addressing Yudhishṭhira: 'Bhagadatta is thy father's aged friend; he was noted for his deference to thy father in word and deed, and he is mentally bound by affection and devoted to thee like a father'. Bhagadatta was killed in the Mahābhārata war and was succeeded by his son Vajradatta (B.K. Barua 1951, pp. 18-19).

Kṛishṇa is said to have again intervened in the affairs in Assam. The Bodos told the author that they had given Kṛishṇa his spouse Rukmiṇi who was a Kirāta woman of immense beauty. Kṛishṇa fell in love with her and she taught him the art of dancing known as Garbā which is performed during Navarātras (Narzary 1991). While the author is not sure of the authority that the Bodos cited for it, this version figures prominently in local literature. In fact it is celebrated in a work called *Rukmiṇī Haraṇa*. Rukmiṇi's father Bhīshmaka had his capital at Kuṇḍina, a name which survives in the Kundil river at Sadiyā.

A somewhat controversial connection with the Mahābhārata tradition relates to Manipur. According to an 18th century account, a Manipur ruler Garīb Nawāz (1707-48) publicly embraced Brāhmaṇism and is said to have replaced the original name of Kanglei (pak), i.e. the dry land, with Mekhalā (female wrapper worn by Pārvatī which fell on the land) and Manipur. Śiva drained away the water in the valley through a tunnel which was made by his trident (*triśūla*). The serpent god Ananta was so overjoyed that he sprinkled the land with sparkling gems (*maṇi*). Arjuna is said to have visited Manipur twice. On the first occasion he married the princess Chitrāṅgadā and begot a son named Babhruvāhana. All historians are unanimous in rejecting the identification of Manipur with the Mahābhārata which in fact lay in Kaliṅga along Mahendra mountains, i.e. Eastern Ghats. However, the Brahmakhaṇḍa of the *Bhavishya Purāṇa*, a work of the 14th century, mentions a cluster of kingdoms in the east including Barendra, Tāmralipta, Hiḍimbā, Maṇipurakam, Tripuram, etc. But this evidence is of doubtful value.

The resurgent Meiteis in their search for identity repudiate the Mahābhārata connections (Kabui). However, the Purāṇic version continues to be peddled. For instance, in the serial titled 'The Story After the Mahābhārata' (Mahābhārata ke Bād kī Kathā) there is a new spin on the Mahābhārata connection of Manipur. The mother of Bhīshma, Gaṅgā, through her sister Kāmākhyā, the presiding deity of Assam, conspires to get Arjuna killed by his Kirāta son Babhruvāhana to avenge Bhīshma's death in the hands of the Pāṇḍava hero! But Kṛishṇa's intervention restores the life of Arjuna.

The third intervention by Kṛishṇa occurred when he rescued his grandson Aniruddha from the custody of Bāṇa and got him and Bāṇa's daughter Ushā married formally. Tejpur has now been renamed Śoṇitapur, the capital of Bāṇa where his fort and the place where Ushā and Aniruddha met and secretly married according to Gāndharva rites, are still identified.

The Sanskritization of the tribal chiefs in the 17th-18th centuries witnessed linking of these rulers with the Mahābhārata heroes. Bhīma was the favourite link through his wife Hiḍimbā, who is still a Himalayan spirit (Aryan, 1992) and their son Ghaṭotkacha with the Kachhāri rulers. The capital of Kachhāri kingdom Dimāpur is a corruption of Hiḍimbapur. In fact, Hiḍimba was the old name of Kachhar. According to Endle, the Kachhāri ruler Kṛishṇa Chandra and his brother Govinda Chandra were both placed for the first time inside the body of a large copper image of a cow, reminiscent of *hiraṇyagarbha* ritual for purification, and accept Bhīma as their mythological ancestor. The Darsang Kachhāris speak of themselves as Bhīm-Ni-Fsa, i.e. children of Bhīma, though according to Endle, they seem to attach little value to this highly imaginative ancestry (Endle, pp. 6-7).

In fact, there seems to be an attempt made systematically to subvert or explain away the linkages of the Mahābhārata with some people in the north-east as perceived by them from an earlier period. As the Manipur story shows, the break with the Mahābhārata relations seems to be complete. A historian has no doubt to be rigorous in pursuit of his craft, his methodology based on facts and his broad understanding of societal processes. However, one cannot ignore anthropological dimension, particularly of archaeology, linguistics and oral traditions being used slowly now to reconstruct the scientific history of the pre-literate people, as is being attempted in the north-east. Perceptions of linkages among peoples and with regional and pan-Indian traditions have been documented by anthropologists, and this is a resource that cannot be ignored; in fact such anthropological inputs are required to reconstruct the people's view of the larger society, no matter how weak the historical foundation might be. If the Bodos have a view of the relationship with pan-Indian traditions, this cannot be described as something imaginary but has to be seen as people's efforts to link with historical traditions.

IV

The *Mahābhārata* describes Jambūdvīpa as a cluster of communities which are homogeneous occupying specific territories (*janapadas*). Later these communities broke up into segments. For example, the Ābhīras were stratified into the four varṇa categories of Ābhīra Brāhmaṇa, Ābhīra Kshatriya, Ābhīra Vaiśya and Ābhīra Śūdra. The Gaddis and Pangawals of Himachal Pradesh still have today the Brāhmaṇa and Rājput segments which can intermarry. The POI shows how all regions of India, big and small, are in a microcosm, multi-ethnic, multilingual and multi-religious. And yet there is a good deal of sharing of traits of biological and cultural, within a region. In other words, the Mahābhārata notion of *jana* or people of a territory still endures.

To conclude, the *Mahābhārata* is an impressive piece of ethnography. It is not comprehensive in the sense in which modern ethnography is. But it is vibrant. It covers the human surface of India in terms of descriptions which are no doubt scanty, and relationship with communities which is interesting both on the battlefield and outside of it. Above all, it explores the ethnic diversity of the land.

There is a continuity in ethnographic traditions which links up the *Mahābhārata* with the present-day endeavours to understand the extraordinary range of diversities – biological, linguistic and cultural – and also the dynamic process of interaction among the people of India. The *Mahābhārata* material, therefore, is an integral part of the evolving traditions of Indian ethnography and will always remain relevant to its understanding.

BIBLIOGRAPHY

Aryan, Subhashini, "The Hiḍimbā Devi Temple in Mandi", *Swagat,* Indian Airlines, February 1992.

Barpujari, H.K., *The Comprehensive History of Assam,* Vol. I, Publication Board, Assam, Guwahati, 1990.

Barua, B.K., *A Cultural History of Assam* (*Early Period*), Vol. I, 1951, Guwahati.

Bharucha, Rustom, 'Peter Brook's Mahābhārata: A View from India', *Economic and Political Weekly,* Vol. XXIII, No. 32, 1988.

Chatterjee, Suniti Kumar, *Kirātajana-Kṛiti, The Indo-Mongoloids: Their Contributions to the History and Culture of India,* The Asiatic Society, Calcutta, 1951.

Choudhury, Mamata, *Tribes of Ancient India,* Indian Museum, Calcutta, 1977.

Deshpande, C.R., *Transmission of the Mahābhārata Tradition,* Indian Institute of Advanced Study, Shimla, 1978.

Endle, Sidney, *The Kacharis,* Macmillan & Co., London, 1911.

Gerald, D. Berreman, *Hindus of Himalaya,* University of California Press, Berkeley, 1963, pp. 381-85.

Hershman, Paul, *Punjabi Kinship and Marriage,* Hilary Standing (ed.), Hindustan Publishing Corporation (India), Delhi, 1981.

Kabui, Gangumai, "Glimpses of Land and People of Ancient Manipur" in Naoram, Sanjaola (ed.), *Manipur Past and Present,* Vol. I, Mittal Publisher, 1988.

Kantawala, S.G., "Marriage and Family in the *Mahābhārata*: Some Aspects" in B.K. Maitilal (ed.), *Moral Dilemmas in the Mahābhārata,* Indian Institute of Advanced Study, Shimla, 1989.

Karve, Irawati, *Yugānta: End of an Epoch,* Sangam Book, 1974.

Kulkarni, S.M., "An Unresolved Dilemma in Dyūtapavan: A Question Raised by Draupadī" in B.K. Maitilal (ed.), *Moral Dilemmas in the Mahābhārata,* Indian Institute of Advanced Study, Shimla, 1989.

Leuva, K.K., *The Asur: A Study of Primitive Iron-smelters,* Bharatiya Adimjati Sevak Sangh, New Delhi, 1963.

Mishra, K.C., *Tribes in the Mahābhārata: A Socio-Cultural Study,* National Publishing House, New Delhi, 1987.

Narzary, D.D. (compiler), *Some Important Quotations Regarding the Historical Background of the Bodos,* September 20, 1991, Pioneer Printer, Kokrajhar.

Parasher, Aloka, *Mlecchas in Early India,* Munshiram Manoharlal Publishers, 1991.

Phukhan, K.T., *Assam Buranji,* Majumdar Press, Calcutta, 1906.

Ray, Niharranjan, "Introductory Address", *The Tribal Situation in India* edited by K. Suresh Singh, Indian Institute of Advanced Study, 1972, pp. 3-33.

Roy, Pratap Chandra, *The Mahābhārata* (edited by Hirala Hadhar, Vol. V, Bhishmaparvan), Oriental Publishing Company, Calcutta, 1955.

Roy, S.C., *The Mundas and Their Country*, The Kuntaline Press, Calcutta, 1912.

Saletore, B.A., *The Wild Tribes in Indian History*, Motilal Banarasidass, Lahore, 1935.

Sarma, E.R., "Sree Kṛishṇa, Arjunavishādayoga", in B.K. Maitilal (ed.) *Moral Dilemmas in the Mahābhārata*, Indian Institute of Advanced Study, Shimla, 1989.

Shastri, Ajay Mitra, "Āryāvarta and Jambūdvīpa" in S.B. Dev and S.V. Kamath (eds.), *The Aryan Problem*, Bharatiya Itihasa Sankalan Samiti; Pune, 1993.

———, *Ancient North-East India (Prāgjyotisha): A Pan-Indian Perspective*, Aryan Books International, New Delhi, 2001.

Shafer, Robert, *Ethnography of Ancient India*, Otto Harrassowitz, Wiesbaden, 1954.

Shastri, Pandit Ram Chandra, *Śrīmad Mahābhāratam*, Part-III, 'Bhārata Bhāvadīpa' (edited by Nilkantha), Chitrashala Press, Pune, 1931.

Singh, K.S., *Tribal Movements in India*, Vol. I, Manohar Publishers and Distributors, New Delhi, 1982.

———, *People of India, An Introduction*, Anthropological Survey of India/ Seagull Books, Calcutta, 1993.

———, *People of India, National Series*, Vols. IV, V and VI: India's Communities, Anthropological Survey of India/Oxford University Press, 1998.

———, (ed.), *The Mahābhārata in the Tribal and Folk Traditions of India*, Indian Institute of Advanced Study and Anthropological Survey of India, Shimla, 1993b.

Singh, K.S. and Birendranath Datta (eds.), *Rāma-Kathā in Tribal and Folk Traditions of India*, Anthropological Survey of India, Calcutta, 1993a.

Singh, K.S., and S. Manoharan, *Languages and Scripts, People of India, National Series*, Vol. III, Anthropological Survey of India/Oxford University Press, 1993.

Sircar, D.C., *The Geography of Ancient and Medieval India*, Delhi, 1960.

Sorensen, S., *An Index to the Proper Names in the Mahābhārata*. Motilal Banarasidass, Delhi, 1978

Subha Rao, T.V., "Telugu Folk Additions to Mahābhārata", *Folklore*, June, Vol. 17, No. 6, 1976.

Sukthankar, V.S., S.K. Belvakar and P.L. Vaidya (eds.), *Critical Edition of Mahābhārata*, 18 volumes, Bhandarkar Oriental Research Institute, Poona, 1967.

12

Vedic *Tīrthas* in the *Mahābhārata*

O.P. Bharadwaj

The word *tīrtha* is derived from the root √*tṛī* (to swim, to cross waters), and from very early times, assigned meanings like 'watering place', 'path to a watering place', 'ford of a river', 'piece of water', 'bathing place', or 'place of pilgrimage on the banks of sacred stream'.[1] At least at one place in the *ṚV*[2] its occurrence can be best explained in the sense of 'a holy place' or 'place of pilgrimage', in which it is now popularly used.

Using the root √*tṛī* in its figurative sense, lexicons explain the word *tīrtha* as तरत्यनेन तीर्थम् or तरति पापादिकं यस्मात्, with which one is cleared of sins; तीर्थतोयस्य स्नाने पुण्यत्वम्,[3] merit lies in a bath in the waters of the *tīrtha*. In other words, it is the waters that are purifying.

This idea goes back to the Vedic age when waters were already considered pure and divine (शुचयः, देवीः)[4] and purifying (पुनानाः).[5] "Whatever sin is found in me, whatever evil I wrought; if I have lied or falsely sworn, Waters! Remove it from me", prays the Ṛigvedic seer.[6] Water held in them the first germ of creation[7] and in waters were available all sorts of medicinal ingredients.[8] The divine character of water is celebrated in four entire hymns[9] and many stray *ṛiks* of the *ṚV*. In another hymn,[10] rightly called *Nadī-stuti*, the seer addresses three times seven rivers and invites them to receive his praise. The major rivers Gaṅgā, Yamunā, Sarasvatī, Śutudrī (Satluj), Parushṇī (Ravi), Asiknī (Chenab), Vitastā (Jhelum) and Sindhu are here addressed along with minor rivers including several from Afghanistan and Baluchistan. The seer of the *AV*[11] also prays to the *ghee*-dripping, clean and purifying waters to behold him with auspicious eye, to touch his skin with their auspicious body and to grant him felicity and their blessings.

According to the *ŚB*[12] it is the union of Prajāpati with waters, earth etc., which brought about creation. The Waters are also *śuddhāyuvaḥ*[13] and thus source of life as well as cleanliness. Waters are abode of all gods.[14] Hence they have been equated with all the gods.[15]

As we shall see, this sentiment for waters runs through the *Mbh.* with equal force, as is the case with two other elements of nature, which may also be considered here.

In the *ṚV*[16] large trees called *vanaspati* 'lord of forests' are addressed as deities. *Araṇyānī*, the whole forest, has been invoked as a deity, in the form of the jungle-goddess.[17] She is the mother of beasts and abounds in food without tillage. Plants (*oshadhi*) are also personified as divine. An entire hymn of the *ṚV*[18] is devoted to the praise of their healing power. In the *AV*[19] a medicinal herb is called "a goddess born on the goddess earth". In the *AV*[20] and later Saṃhitās,[21] the Gandharvas and Apsarās are spoken of as inhabiting trees like the banyan (*nyagrodha*), sacred fig (*aśvattha*) and its other varieties like *udumbara* and *plaksha*. The banyan was first born in Kurukshetra out of Soma spilt from the tilted cups of gods and was called *nyubja* from which were born the other *nyagrodha* trees.[22] The *ŚB*[23] associates the origin of *aśvattha*, *udumbara*, and *nyagrodha* with god Indra. The *aśvattha* was born from the honour flowing from his skin, *udumbara* from the force flowing from his flesh and *nyagrodha* out of sweet drink flowing from his bones.

Mountains, conceived in the *ṚV* as divinely animate, have been invoked as deities nearly twenty times in the plural and four times in the singular,[24] frequently with other natural objects[25] or with gods.[26] They are manly, firmly fixed and rejoicing in plenty. *Parvata* sometimes also appears to be a mountain god, conceived anthropomorphically as a companion of Indra.

If the waters, forests and mountains are holy, purifying, bounteous and divine, it is but natural that the earth, which they join with other elements, should also be praised likewise. This is done in *AV* XII.I, a remarkable hymn, running into sixty-three verses dripping with affection, reverence and gratitude, where sentiment turns into emotion as the seer, declaring himself to be the son of Mother Earth,[27] presents a picture the like of which is not met in any other literature of the ancient world.[28] It repeatedly speaks of the sacred forests,[29] waters[30] and hills[31] adorning Mother Earth who is herself purifying.

"In the valley of the mountains and at the confluence of rivers the learned were blessed with wisdom", says the Veda.[32] And according to the *Mbh.*[33] holiness of the *tīrthas* is known from some extraordinary effect of the soil, beauty of the waters and acceptance of the sages. On this yardstick, the waters, forests, mountains and the earth themselves can be called *tīrthas*. The Vedic tradition in this respect did not die out. It is, in fact, alive even now and was particularly noticed in the medieval period. Taking only the case of water, for instance, Alberuni[34] says that,

> ... in every place to which holiness is ascribed the Hindus construct ponds intended for ablutions. In this way they have attained a very high degree of art, so that our people (the Muslims), when they see them, wonder at them and are unable to describe them, much less to construct anything like them.... The ponds become particularly famous for holiness either because some important event has happened at them or because there is some passage in holy text or tradition which refers to them.

In the *Mbh.*[35] all the rivers are regarded as mothers of the whole world and givers of great merit. They are also known as mothers of sacrificial altars.[36] They have the power to wash away ill luck and sin and to bestow upon the bather beauty and fortune. Waters have healing, hence supernatural or divine powers.[37] They are divine witness against wrong, for which reason, one who pronounces a curse or takes an oath, touches water, as one does while accepting a gift.[38] The major rivers invoked in the *Nadī-stuti* hymn of the *ṚV*, noted above, are described in the *Mbh.* for the merit that their waters grant. To mention only a few, Gaṅgā's holiness is noted and the merits of various kinds accruing from performance of sacrifices are attributed to a bath in it.[39] The holy Yamunā is said to be frequented by *brahmarshis* and it destroys sins. Māndhātri, Sahadeva Somaka, Droṇa, Bharata and other important personalities performed sacrifices at its banks.[40] The Śatadru is to be remembered every morning and evening.[41] The Asiknī or Chandrabhāgā makes one sinless like a *muni* if one takes bath in it for seven days.[42] A bath in the Vitastā should be taken for the *tarpaṇa* of gods and manes. It grants the merit of performing a *Vājapeya* sacrifice.[43] The Sindhu should be remembered every morning and a bath in it leads one to heaven.[44] Sarayu also should be remembered morning and evening and drinking its water instantly destroys sins.[45]

The *Mbh.* speaks of divine trees and groves. The *aśvattha* is the chief of trees and typifies that tree of life which is rooted in god above.[46] *Nyagrodha, udumbara* and *aśvattha* are Vishṇu's forms.[47] Trees are not lifeless. They experience pain and pleasure and are able to hear, move and feel.[48] In a village the one tree which is conspicuous is called a *chaitya* and is worshipped.[49] The *Mbh.* describes several holy forests like the Kāmyaka,[50] Dvaita,[51] Phalakī,[52] Madhu,[53] Vyāsa,[54] Sīta,[55] Khāṇḍava[56] and Saugandhika.[57]

In case of mountains too, the *Mbh.* echoes the Vedic sentiments. They are intimately associated with gods.[58] Kailāśa is the home of Śiva and Kubera. The gods are said to have their playgrounds and palaces generally on the summit of mountains like Meru, Kailāśa and Maināka.[59] Some of these earthly resorts are said to carry their footprints even now.[60] All this reminds us of Kālidāsa's description of Himālaya as *devatātmā* and of its region as *devabhūmi*.[61]

As to Mother Earth, she is included in the *Mbh.* among the divinities to be worshipped.[62] She is the goddess being 'Lord as to sowing seeds'.[63] What is most interesting, however, is that the *Mbh.* gives us a *tīrtha*-name Pṛithivī between the *tīrthas* Pāriplava and Śālūkinī.[64]

Vedic *tīrthas* are first mentioned in connection with the performance of sacrifice, a ritualistic practice going back to hoary antiquity. According to Maurice Philips,[65] "it is older than the hymns for they were composed for its celebration". "With the sacrifice the gods sacrificed to the sacrifice. These were the first ritual laws," says the *ṚV*.[66] By sacrifice gods created all things.[67] And Vishṇu and Indra made the world spacious for the sake of sacrifice.[68] The *Mbh.* also refers to the creation of sacrifice along with man by the Lord of Creatures and ascribes the birth of water to sacrifice.[69]

The *ṚV*[70] refers to Bharata princes kindling sacrificial fires on the sacred rivers Sarasvatī, Dṛishadvatī and Āpayā, as well as the lake Mānusha. The number of such venues of sacrifice will increase as we proceed. It would therefore be better to deal with them one by one.

1. SARASVATĪ

Sarasvatī is the river *par excellence* of the *ṚV* which describes it as rushing down right from the mountains to the ocean[71] with a tempestuous roar,[72] *asuryā*[73] or divine mightiest of her class,[74] best of rivers,[75] best of mothers[76] and best of goddesses.[77] It is lauded in three hymns of the *ṚV* and numerous detached verses. It is often invoked with other deities and several times associated with the sacrificial goddesses Iḍā and Bhāratī.[78] In the Brāhmaṇas it is identified with *vāch*, speech.[79] It is a purifier[80] and stimulates, directs and prospers the devotion of her worshippers. The *ṚV* and *SV* are the springs of its waters.[81] At some point of time between the composition of the nucleus of the *ṚV* and the age of the *AV* and the Brāhmaṇas, a seismic – tectonic – volcanic upheaval took place in its upper reaches which led to the reduction in the flow and partial diversion of the waters of the Sarasvatī resulting in its disappearance at Vinaśana, identified with Kālībangan,[82] and shifting of its source from Himalayan glaciers to Lavasa in Pachchad subdivision of district Nahan in Himachal Pradesh.[83] Its identification with Ghaggar is now generally accepted.[84] In the Brāhmaṇa-Sūtra period, Sārasvata sacrifices were performed beginning at Vinaśana and proceeding upstream along the river to its source and then turning to the Yamunā for *avabhṛitha*. If the later Vedic age is assigned to the period from the mature Harappan phase to its end,[85] we could visualize the performers of Sārasvata *sattras* stopping on their upstream trek, from Kalibangan to Lavasa, at sites like Sirsa, Banawali, Kunal, Tohana, Patran, Banur, Chhatbir, Chandigarh and Nada.

In the *Mbh.* the name Sarasvatī has been appropriated by a small stream rising near Adbadri in the lower Siwaliks and running by Thanesar to meet the Aruṇā-Mārkaṇḍā river at Arnai near Pehowā before joining the Ghaggar-Sarasvatī near Akalgarh. This stream which has now virtually ceased to exist, has been called Prācī Sarasvatī at several places.[86]

The *Mbh.* also describes the Sarasvatī as sacred, the best and foremost of the rivers, flowing to the ocean.[87] It is the daughter of Brahmā, born of the Plaksha tree and remover of sins.[88] By the time of the composition of the Great Epic numerous *tīrthas* had come up along its banks which gave it the epithets *tīrthamālini*[89] and *tīrthaśatopetā*.[90] On account of the swelling numbers of sages along its banks, the *tīrthas* developed into towns,[91] which resounded with the sound of *svādhyāya* and shone with the *agnishṭoma* fires.[92] Names of personages like Vasishṭha,[93] Viśvāmitra,[94] Matināra,[95]

Dadhīchi,[96] Yayāti,[97] and many others were associated with it. Its confluences with the Aruṇā[98] and the ocean[99] were considered particularly holy. The final tribute is paid to the river in these words:

There is no pleasure like living on the Sarasvatī, no merits like those accruing from staying on the Sarasvatī, people attain heaven on reaching the Sarasvatī and they always remember it. The Sarasvatī is the holiest of rivers and brings prosperity to people. On reaching the Sarasvatī people never worry about sins, here in this life or heareafter.[100]

In short the great esteem accorded to this river in the Vedic literature is further enhanced in the *Mbh.*

2. DṚISHADVATĪ

Apart from the mention in *ṚV* III 23. 4 already noticed, the Dṛishadvatī finds mention under the name of Aśmanvatī in connection with a purifying bath after the performance of a funeral ceremony.[101] The Brāhmaṇas and the Śrautasūtras[102] describe the Dārshadvata sacrificial sessions, which began with *dīkshā* at Vinaśana and after a trek upstream along its course ended at Triplaksha on the Yamunā. It has been identified with the bed in which now the Hansi-Hissar branch of the western Yamunā Canal flows.[103] Sothi, Karoti, Siswal, Rakhigarhi, Hansi, Jind, Asandh and Srughna could be the stopovers for the performers of Dārshadvata *sattras* starting at Kalibangan. According to the *Mbh.*, the country lying between the Dṛishadvatī on the south and Sarasvatī in the north is as holy as the heaven itself.[104] At its bank Śiva gave instruction to Yudhishṭhira.[105] Anyone offering *tarpaṇa* to gods and manes after a bath in this river earns the merit of performing Atirātra and Agnishṭoma sacrifices.[106]

3. ĀPAYĀ

The name of river Āpayā occurs only once in the *ṚV* in the hymn already noted.[107] The *Mbh.*[108] spells the name as Āpagā and places it one *krosha* to the east of Mānusha. *Siddhas* lived at its banks and anyone offering meals of *śyāmāka* rice in the name of gods and manes to one brāhmaṇa earns the merit of feeding ten million of them.[109] Worship of manes and gods after a bath in this river and a night's stay brings the merit of performing an Agnishṭoma.[110] It probably flowed in the bed of Chautang nala with Balu, Bhagwanpura and Daulatpur as the venues for kindling the sacrificial fire on its banks.

4. MĀNUSHA

As already seen, Mānusha is noted in the *ṚV* along with the Sarasvatī, Dṛishadvatī and Āpayā as the scene of kindling sacrificial fires by the Bharatas. The *AB*[111] records a story to explain the name Mānusha. The seed of Prajāpati fell and gathered into a lake. The gods ordained that it must not go waste: मा इदं दुषद्. Since they said मा इदं दुषद् so it came to be called मादुष which in course of time became Mānusha. In the *JB*[112] Kshatra son of Pratardana is said to have been attacked by ten kings at Mānusha during the *Dāśarājña* war. In another passage of the *JB*[113] Mānusha is placed on the Himalayas, which is obviously wrong. Being the name of a town and tank in the *ṚV*, it has been identified with the village now called Manas located about 5 km to the west of Kaithal on a large reservoir of water.[114]

The *Mbh.*[115] regards it a world famous *tīrtha* where black antelopes, afflicted by the hunter's arrows, submerged and acquired human forms. Anyone taking a bath in this *tīrtha,* while practicing *brahmacharya,* is purified of all sins and honoured in heaven.

5. VINAŚANA

The name Vinaśana appears first in the Brāhmaṇas[116] for the place where the Sarasvatī loses itself in the desert. *Dīkshā* was taken at this place for the performance of the Sārasvata and Dārshadvata sacrificial sessions. These *sattras* were performed upstream along the two rivers and ended at their sources followed by *avabhṛitha* or the lustral bath in the Yamunā. The place has been identified with Kālībangan.[117]

According to the *Mbh.*[118] here, at the upper end of the desert, the Sarasvatī went underground. A visit to this *tīrtha* brings one emancipation from all sins and the merit of the performance of a *Vājapeya* sacrifice and the world of Soma.[119] The river is said to have vanished here on account of hostility towards the Śūdras and Ābhīras.[120] The name Vinaśana is sometimes equated with

Kurukshetra.[121] According to the *Bhāgavata Purāṇa*, Devavrata Bhīshma fell fighting here.[122]

6. PLAKSHA-PRĀSRAVAṆA

It was the source of the Sarasvatī, so named as the river was born here from the plaksha tree.[123] Names like plakshajā,[124] plakshajātā and plakshavatī[125] have also been given to the river on the basis of this myth. The place was forty-four days' journey from Vinaśana on horseback. Here the Sārasvata *sattras* ended followed by a lustral bath in the Yamunā.[126]

The *PB*[127] appears to place Plaksha-prāsravaṇa in the region of *svarga*. In a similar passage the *JB*[128] equates Sarasvatī with speech and Plaksha-prāsravaṇa with heaven itself.

The *Mbh.*[129] also describes it as the source of Sarasvatī and locates it in the Saugandhikavana. A bath taken in its waters flowing out of an anthill is said to earn a man the merit of performing an Aśvamedha after worshipping manes and gods.[130]

7. ŚARYAṆĀVAT

Śaryaṇāvat occurs in several passages of the *ṚV*[131] as the name of a lake in connection with the production of superior quality of Soma and recovery of the horse's head of Dadhyañch by Indra.[132] The *JB*[133] places it in the lower or western part of Kurukshetra which was called Śaryaṇā.

The *Mbh.*[134] describes a *tīrtha* called Śaśayāna on the Sarasvatī where ponds in the form of a rabbit existed, with a bath in which one always shines like the moon and earns the merit of gifting a thousand cows. The *tīrtha* is located a couple of stages above Vinaśana and considering its very odd and unlikely name, we are inclined to take it as a scribal error for Śaryaṇā or Śaryāṇā which is given in the *Gaṇapāṭha* to Pāṇini's *Ashṭādhyāyī* as a variant reading.[135]

8. NĀVAPRABHRAṂŚANA

It is mentioned in the *AV*[136] apparently as the name of the place where Manu Vaivasvata is believed to have left the boat that saved him during the Great Flood. The *ŚB*[137] in its account of the Deluge, where Manu is forewarned and his boat steered to safety by a fish, names the place as Manoravasarpaṇa or 'Manu's descent'. Situated on a peak of the Himalayas, the place must have been considered holy, being associated not only with the medicinal plant of *kushṭha* known as 'universal remedy' and the 'visible manifestation of ambrosia' but also with *aśvattha* called 'the seat of gods in the third heaven'[138] as well as with Manu, the progenitor[139] and the first ruler of the post-Deluvian human race.[140]

In the *Mbh.*[141] the place is given the name of Naubandhana or '(the site of) the tying of the boat' by Manu when the flood subsided. According to this verse, the peak of the Himalayas on which Manu fastened his boat is still known by the name of Naubandhana.[142] The name has been identified with Nahan a district headquarters in Himachal Pradesh and old capital of the Sirmur State, situated at an altitude of 932 metres.[143]

9. ŚAKAMBHARA

The name first occurs in the *AV* (V.22.4). This hymn is addressed to *takman* or malarial fever which is called the 'boxer *(mushṭihā*— who kills with a fist blow) of Śakaṁbhara'. This description is justified from the fact that the area between Jaipur and Jodhpur, where the town and lake of Śakaṁbhara or Sambhar lie, was subject to outbreaks of malaria. There is no laudatory reference to Śakaṁbhara in the Vedic literature.[144]

The *Mbh.*[145] describes it as the seat of goddess Śakaṁbharī, so named as she lived on *śaka* once a month for a thousand divine years. *Ṛishis* devoted to her visited the place and they were also treated to *śaka*. Anyone passing three nights here in strict *brahmacharya* and subsisting on *śāka* alone earns the merit of eating *śāka* for twelve years.

10. KAPISHṬHALA

The name of this *tīrtha*, now called Kaithal, reminds one of sage Kapishṭhala known to Pāṇini (VIII. 3.91). A *saṁhitā* of the Kapishṭhala branch of the Kaṭhas is available in a fragmentary manuscript.[146] There is nothing else in the Vedic literature regarding the sanctity of this place.

The *Mbh.*[147]mentions a *kedāra*, a big reservoir which spreads over fields of Kapishṭhala. One practising austerities here burns one's sins and acquires the power of becoming invisible. As a result of a personal visit to the site we are inclined to believe that the Mānusha lake of the *ṚV* is identical with this Kedāra and both refer to one and the same reservoir of water which at one time probably covered many miles of land including the distance of about 5 km separating the town of Manas from Kaithal. The two towns apparently shared the sanctity attached to Mānusha lake.

11. PARISĀRAKA

According to a story in the *AB*,[148] the seers while performing a *sattra* on the Sarasvatī expelled Kavasha Ailūsha from Soma as he was the child of a slave woman and left him in the desert to die of thirst. He addressed the *Aponaptṛīya* hymn to the Sarasvatī who hastened to flow all around him as a result of which the place was named Parisāraka. The story suggests its location somewhere below Vinaśana. The *Mbh.*[149] appears to have changed the name to Saraka and shifted it in the region of Kapishṭhala or Kaithal. It is mentioned with Rudrakoṭi. By worshipping Śiva here on *chaturdaśī* all one's desires are fulfilled.

12. NAIMIŚA

From early Vedic times Naimiśa finds mention as the name of a region and its dwellers called Naimiśiyas or Naimiśeyas.[150] They are known as performers of *sattras* or long sacrificial sessions which often continued for as long as twelve years at a stretch and sometimes even longer.[151] Names like Pratardana Daivodāsi,[152] Baka Dālbhya[153] and Śitibāhu Aishakṛita[154] are associated with it and it was considered a place of special sanctity.

The *Mbh.*[155] mentions the people of Naimiśa as Naimiśas along with the Kurus, Pañchālas and Matsyas as people who understand *dharma*. Sauti related the story of the *Mbh.*[156] here and a number of Purāṇas were composed in this very region.[157] Gods performed sacrifice here.[158] Brahmā resides in this holy *tīrtha* of *siddhas* along with gods. It is the best of the *tīrthas* on the earth[159] and the number of *tīrthas* in Naimiśa is said to equal the number of *tīrthas* in the whole world.[160] It is holy and always fit for sacrifice and brings the merit of performing *Gomedha* sacrifice.[161]

The original Naimiśāraṇya, Naimiśakuñja of the *Mbh.* (Vana, 83, 108), was located below Pṛithūdaka along the bank of the

Dṛishadvatī and extended towards the Sarasvatī so as to comprise the lower part of the Sarasvatī-Dṛishadvatī *doab* called Brahmavārta.

13. KĀRAPACAVA

It was the place on the Yamunā where the performers of Sarāsvata *sattras* went for the lustral bath after completing the *sattra* at Plaksha-prāsravaṇa.[162]

The *Mbh.*[163] describes it as Kārapavana in the same situation. Balarāma took a bath here, distributed gifts and offered *tarpaṇa* to manes and deities and then left for the holy hermitage of Mitrāvaruṇa.

14. KHĀṆḌAVA

PB[164] mentions a sacrifice performed by the two sages Dṛiti, son of Indrota and Vātavat in the Khāṇḍava forest. In the *BŚS*[165] Khāṇḍavaprastha is named as a town in this forest. The *TA*[166] mentions Khāṇḍava as the southern half of Kurukshetra.

The *Mbh.*[167] describes the burning of the Khāṇḍava forest, located on the Yamunā, by Agni with the help of Kṛishṇa and Arjuna. Khāṇḍavaprastha, later named Indraprastha, was a very old town later associated with personages like Purūravā, Nahusha and Yayāti. It was built by Viśvakarman after the site was purified by Vyāsa. Brāhmaṇas well versed in Vedas came here.

15. PRABHAVYAMARMA

In the description of Sārasvata *sattras*, the *LŚS*[168] locates this place at the confluence of the Dṛishadvatī and Sarasvatī. In the *PB*[169] it is called the site of Dṛishadvatī's *apyaya* or merger with the Sarasvatī.

The *Mbh.*[170] calls it 'holy saṅgama' and adds that gods led by Brahmā and sages rich in austerities collect here on *śukla-chaturdaśi* of Chaitra. A bath taken here brings one lot of gold and purification from all sins and leads to Brahmaloka.

16-17. NAITANDHAVA AND PARIṆAH

Describing the Dārshadvata *sattra*, the *KŚS*[171] states that in the second year the sacrificial fire should be kindled at Naitandhava which, according to the commentator, lay near the Sarasvatī. In the third year it was required to be kindled at Pariṇah which was the name of a lake according to the *JB.*[172] The *LŚS*[173] takes it to represent 'risen ground' which appears to find support in the *TA*[174] and the *KŚS.*[175] While Naitandhava was a few stages above Vinaśana, Pariṇah lay near the confluence of the Dṛishadvatī and Sarasvatī. These places are not noted in the *Mbh.*

18. TRIPLAKSHA

In the *PB*[176] and the Srautasūtras,[177] Triplaksha appears to denote the region near the Yamunā where lustral bath was performed by people undertaking the Dārshadvata *sattra.*

It maybe identified with the *tīrtha* named Plakshāvataraṇa in the *Mbh.*[178] where the performers of Sārasvata *sattras* took the lustral bath. Here Sahadeva is said to have kindled sacrificial fire and distributed a hundred thousand *dakshiṇās*; Bhārata performed thirty-five Aśvamedha sacrifices and Marutta performed a *sattra* under the protection of sage Saṁvarta. From the description of the rivers Sarasvatī and Dṛishadvatī in this region it appears to represent the country extending from the source of the Sarasvatī to the Yamunā in the Sivaliks.

19. KURUKSHETRA

The name Kurukshetra signifying the 'land of the Kurus' first occurs in the later saṁhitās and Brāhmaṇas where it is always regarded as a particularly sacred country.[179] Gods like Indra, Agni, Soma, Vayu and Vishṇu are said to have performed sacrifices here. Hence it was called the place of divine worship.[180] Kurukshetra is the altar of Prajapati and it is equal to the whole earth.[181] The *PB* relates a story in which Indra and Ruśaman make a wager to run around the earth. While Indra runs around the earth, Ruśaman equals his feat by running around Kurukshetra.[182] "The gods performed a sacrifice with Kurukshetra as their altar of which Khāṇḍava was the southern half; Tūrghna or Srughna (modern Sugh near Jagadhari) the northern half and Pariṇah the lower half and the desert or Marus the rubbish heap," says the *TA.*[183] It is the land of the holy rivers Sarasvatī, Dṛishadvatī and Āpayā and the lakes Mānusha and Śaryaṇāvat and other *tīrthas*. In fact, the whole land, being devayajana is a *tīrtha.*

The same is the case in the *Mbh*. It is Prajāpati's Uttaravedī and the gods, in earlier times, performed *sattras* here.[184] The sages and gods undertook Sārasvata sacrificial sessions here.[185] The number of *tīrthas* has now multiplied into hundreds and many of them are associated with the names of gods and sages. In the Sannihatī *sarovara* the waters of all the rivers, tanks, wells and other reservoirs come together on every *amāvasyā* or the fifteenth day of the dark half of every lunar month.[186] Prajāpati himself first erected the sacrificial post at Brahmasara and performed here the *ishṭikṛita* sacrificial session which lasted for a thousand years.[187] Those who reside in Kurukshetra, in reality, live in heaven[188] because, favoured by the gods, sages, brāhmaṇas and pious men it was extremely sacred and sanctifying and leading to heaven.[189] Even the wind-blown dust of Kurukshetra leads the sinner to *moksha*.[190] In this land was fought the war between the gods and demons and here the sage Sārasvata taught the Vedas.[191] It was the land of dharma.[192] As ordained by Indra and gods like Brahmā, no other place on earth would be holier than Kurukshetra.[193] The Great Epic,[194] therefore, declares that, "Naimisha is the holiest *tīrtha* on the earth and Pushkara in the intermediate region; Kurukshetra, however, is the best of *tīrthas* in all the three worlds". Even if one simply expresses one's desire to go and live in Kurukshetra, one is freed from all sins.[195] The sanctity enjoyed by Kurukshetra in Vedic age is thus further enhanced in the *Mbh*.

20. UDAPĀNA

The existence of this *tīrtha* is related to *ṚV* i.105, 17 which has been translated by Griffith[196] as follows: "Trita, when buried in the well, calls on the gods to succour him. Bṛihaspati heard his call and released him from distress. Mark this may woe, ye Earth and Heaven!" Sāyaṇa[197] introduces the hymn with the following story based on the version of the *Sāṭyāyana Brāhmaṇa*: "In olden days there were three seers, Ekata, Dvita and Trita. Once while tormented by thirst in a desert forest they came upon a well. There the one named Trita entered the well for drinking water. He took it himself and offered it to the two others from the well. Those two having drunk the water threw Trita in the well, took away all his wealth and after covering the well with the wheel of the chariot, went away. Then, fallen in the well and unable to come out of it,

Trita remembered all the gods, in his mind, to save him. So he saw this hymn as a prayer to them...." The *Sāṭyāyana Brāhmaṇa* is now available only in fragments and its version is identical with the one given in the *JB* (i. 184).[198] The story occurs in the *Bṛihad-devatā*[199] also where a wolf is introduced out of fear of whom Trita fell in the well. There is no mention of Sarasvatī in all these versions. Even the word used for well is *kūpa*, not *udapāna*.

The *Mbh.*,[200] however, calls it the *udapāna* of Trita and locates it in the bed of Sarasvatī or near it and goes on to add that the Sarasvatī shot forth to save Trita who further won a boon from the gods that whoever took a bath in that well would earn the position of one who is entitled to Soma. At this *tīrtha* Balarāma worshipped the brāhmaṇas, gave them much wealth and took bath. His next stop upstream along the Sarasvatī was Vinaśana which suggests that the Udapana *tīrtha* was below Vinaśana.

21-22-23. SUDINA-AHAN-IIĀSPADA

Although these three names find mention among *tīrthas* in the *Mbh.* and thence in the *Vāmana Purāṇa*, they have been undoubtedly fabricated out of expressions occurring in *ṚV* 3.23,4[201] which is reproduced below in *pada-pāṭha* along with corresponding translation in English:

> नि त्वा दधे। वर आ पृथिव्याः। इलायाः पदे। सुदिनत्वे अह्माम्।
>
> I place thee, in the best spot of earth, the seat of Iḷā, on the best day of all days.
>
> दूषद्वत्याम् मानुषे आपयायाम् सरस्वत्यां। रेवत्। अग्ने। दिदीहि।।
>
> On the Dṛishadvatī, Mānusha, Āpayā, Sarasvatī, richly Agni shine.

The second half of the *mantra* contains four names; one of a lake-town and three of rivers which had all acquired a sacred character by the time this hymn was composed. In the first half Iḷāyāspada is explained by Sāyaṇā and Veṅkaṭamādhava to mean 'in the Uttaravedī' denoting Kurukshetra and by modern scholars to mean 'in the seat of Iḷā'. *Sudinatve* (loc. sing. of *Sudinatva*) means 'the best day'. And *ahnāṃ* (the gen. pl. of *ahan*) means 'of days'. Evidently it is impossible to visualize the use of these three expressions as names of places. Someone out of ignorance or mischief placed the three expressions Iḷāyāspada, *Sudina* and *ahan* in the same category as the four *tīrtha* names in the second line and, taking the form Iḷāspada of the first expression, converted them into *tīrtha* names. It was not difficult to interpolate them in the *Mbh*. Vanaparvan *tīrtha-yātrā* account[202] which is in any case disorderly and disorganized. These *tīrtha*-names of the *Mbh*. are undoubtedly apocryphal.

This brief survey of the Vedic *tīrthas* in the light of the *Mbh*. leads to some interesting conclusions.

As already noted, the concept of *tīrtha* was known to the *ṚV*. Out of the twenty-three *tīrthas* considered here, ten names are common to both, Vedic literature and the *Mbh*. These are nos. 1, 2, 4, 5, 6, 9, 10, 12, 14 and 19; eight, viz., nos. 3, 7, 8, 11, 13, 15, 18 and 20 have received new names; and in case of three, viz., 1, 11 and 12, their location has been shifted. Only two, viz., 16 and 17 fail to find mention in the Great Epic while three names in it, viz., 21, 22 and 23, are apocryphal. The remark that except Vinaśana and Parisāraka no other *tīrthas* in the *Mbh*. tally with those named in the Brāhmaṇas and Śrautasūtra is, therefore, not justified.[203]

The *Mbh*. is described as a veritable repository of ancient Indian lore and many of its legends, ideas and geographical names can be traced to their Vedic sources.[204] Take for instance, the Āpayā, Dṛishadvatī and Sarasvatī. The first was probably a small tributary of the second and the combined stream joined the Sarasvatī even in the Ṛigvedic period. The two are not mentioned in the *nadī-stuti* hymn and by the time of the *Mbh*., had been reduced to rainy season rivulets as they have been described along with many other streams. The Sarasvatī alone is said to be perennial.[205] However, as we have noted above, the *Mbh*. Sarasvatī is not the Vedic river but only a small stream joining the Ghaggar-Sarasvatī whose name it has appropriated. The great importance and sanctity attached to it in the *Mbh*. only reflects its Vedic image. It is still the river *par excellence*, flowing right to the ocean[206] and more sacred than even the hallowed land of Kurukshetra.

While the Vedic *tīrthas* are venues of sacrifices in the *Mbh*., it is a bath in the *tīrthas* that is said to bring the merit of performing one or more sacrifices. To add to the importance of *tīrthas* they are now often described as proper places for performing *śrāddha* and offering *tarpaṇa* to the manes and gods. The idea was to link the institution of *śrāddha* with that of *tīrtha-yātrā* and in this way to inculcate the spirit that the entire land is holy where one's ancestors lived for countless generations, as stated in the *AV* (12.1,5).[207]

The institution of *tīrtha-yātrā* originated in Kurukshetra in the later Vedic age of the Brāhmaṇas and Sūtras which describe the *sattras* or long sacrificial sessions spreading over many days and involving traversing of long distances with stopovers at regular stages on the route. In course of time the number of these stops increased and spread over the land. However, the performance of sacrifice was a costly affair and difficult to undertake for a man of ordinary means. A visit to *tīrthas* was naturally considered much less expensive and equally satisfying. Efforts made by the rulers to make the journey safe and comfortable, as much for the common travellers as for the pilgrims who were advised to travel light,[208] further popularized *tīrtha-yātrās*. Says Aśoka in his Pillar Edict VII "On the roads, too, banyan trees have been planted by me to give shade to man and beast; mango-gardens have been planted and wells dug at every half-*kos*; rest-houses too, have been erected and numerous watering places were made here and there for the comfort of man and beast".[209]

The *Mbh.* mentions many *tīrthas* outside Kurukshetra. Within this land their number multiplied faster. *Tīrthas* like the sacred lake of Mānusha and the holy well of Udapāna provided inspiration for conversion of every big pond or well into a *tīrtha.*[210] The Sarasvatī became *tīrthamālinī* and Kurukshetra came to be regarded as the foremost of the *tīrthas.* But so did the number of priests with their increasing appetite for more income from *dakshiṇās*. So, more *tīrthas* would be welcome, even if they had to be created. We have already noted five such cases in the *tīrtha*-names Ahan, Sudina, Iḷāspada, Saraka and Pṛithivī. Many more names appear to be fictitious, some duplicated from old names and some coined unintelligently. Pañchanada,[211] Koṭitīrtha,[212] Brahmāvarta,[213] Rudrakoṭi,[214] Trivishṭapa,[215] Sutīrtha,[216] Kiṁdāna,[217] Kiṁjapya,[218] Kiṁdatta[219] are only a few examples.

While the priests were avaricious, some of the pilgrims were also no less so. They made it their business to move from one *tīrtha* to the other staying for long spells to enjoy free boarding and lodging. This was bound to invite a reaction. And it did. So we find in the *Mbh.*[220] Tulādhāra advising Jājali not to be a guest of the country wandering about *tīrthas* because all rivers are as holy as Sarasvatī, all hills sacred (like the Himalayas) and one's own soul is a *tīrtha.*

Such aberrations not withstanding, the institution of *tīrtha-yātrā*, rising in the Brāhmaṇa-Sūtra age and gathering momentum fast to reach its peak of popularity in the *Mbh.* and the Purāṇas, is still flourishing. The reason, in the words of Mookerji, is that "the institution of pilgrimage is entirely an expression of love for the motherland, one of the modes of worship of the country which strengthens the religious sentiment and expands the geographical consciousness. . ., it enables people to think and feel that India is not a mere congeries of geographical fragments, but a single though immense organism, filled with the tide of one strong pulsating life from end to end".[221] It has, therefore, been rightly described as a regional and national identification process having a basis in Hindu cosmography, mythology and ascetic lifestyle and provided the motivation for late Śankarāchārya's foundation of the four *maṭhas* at border points of the subcontinent.[222]

NOTES AND REFERENCES

1. See *Śabdakalpadruma*, Delhi, 1961, Vol. ii, p. 625; Kshīrasvamī's Commentary on *Amarakośa*, iii 3, 86; Herman Grassmann, *Worterbuch Zum Rigveda*, Indian ed., Delhi, 1999, p. 537; and Monier Williams, *Sanskrit English Dictionary*, Delhi, p. 449.
2. *ṚV*, X.31, 3 तीर्थेन दस्ममुपयन्त्यूमाः (tr. Portions of oblation reach deities like *tarpaṇa* offered at a *tīrtha*). Cf. P. V. Kane, *History of Dharmaśāstra*, (Hindi tr.), Lucknow, 1980, iii. 1300.
3. *Śabdakalpadruma* ii. p. 625
4. *ṚV*, 7.49, 1-4; also 7.49, 2 where they are called शुचयः
5. *ṚV*, 7.49.1; also *AV*, 1.33, 1.
6. *ṚV*, 10.9, 8.
7. *ṚV*, 10.82, 6.
8. *ṚV*, 1.23, 20.
9. *ṚV*, 7.47 & 49 and *ṚV*, X.9 & 30.
10. *ṚV*, 10.75.
11. 1.33, 4.
12. vi.1,1-2.
13. *TS* 1.3.82, *Vide* also *BSS*, vii. 12, 18.
14. *ŚB*, xiv. 2, 3-13.
15. *VGS*, ii. 17.
16. 1.90, 8; 7.34, 23 & 10.64, 8.
17. *ṚV*, 10.146.
18. 10.97.

19. 6.136.1.
20. 4.37, 4.
21. *TS*, 3.4, 8, 4.
22. *AB*, 7.30-31; *ŚB*, xiii. 2, 7, 3 etc.
23. xii. 7, 1, 1 & 9.
24. *VM*, 154.
25. 7.34, 23.
26. 6.49, 14.
27. *AV*, 12.1, 12 :. . . . . . .माता भूमिः पुत्रो अहं पृथिव्याः।
28. V.S. Agrawala *Bharat ki Maulik Ekta* (Hindi), Allahabad *Vikrama* 2011, pp. 58-80.
29. Verses (vv), 2,11,17,19,23,56.
30. vv., 3,9,19,23.
31. vv., 11,19.
32. *ṚV*, 8.6, 28; and *YV*, 5.26, 15: उपह्वरे गिरीणाम् संगथे च नदीनाम् धिया विप्रो अजायत। *YV* has संगमे.
33. Anuśāsana (Anu), 108, 19.
34. Edward C. Sachau, *Alberuni's India*, Reprint, Delhi, 1964, ii, 144-145.
35. Bhīshma, 9, 37.
36. Vana, 212, 24.
37. *EM*, p.3.
38. *Ibid.*
39. Anu, 25, 68; also Vana, 85, 88-99 as a *tīrtha*; and Anu, 26, 26-96 for greatness and holiness.
40. Droṇa, 68, 8; and Vana, 125, 21-26.
41. Anu, 165, 18.
42. Sabhā, 9, 19; also Bhīshma, 9, 23 and Anu, 25, 7.
43. Sabhā, 9,19; and Bhīshma, 9, 16.
44. Anu, 146, 18; and Bhīshma, 9, 21.
45. Anu, 165, 21; and 169, 20-21.
46. *EM*, p. 7; *Mbh.*, Bhīshma, 34, 26.
47. Anu, 126, 5; and 148, 101.
48. Śānti, 184, 107.
49. Ādi, 138, 25.
50. Vana, 5, 258.
51. Vana, 24, 13 & 20; and Śalya, 37, 27.
52. Vana, 83, 86-87.
53. *Ibid.*, 282, 27-28.
54. *Ibid.*, 83, 93.
55. *Ibid.*, 83, 59-60.
56. Ādi., 221-226; and 61, 35; 61, 45 etc.
57. Vana, 84, 4; *Vamana Purāṇa* (Gita Press ed.), 34, 4-5 mentions seven forests together. In place of Dvatta, Khāṇḍava and Saugandhika we have here Aditivana and Sūryavana.

58. *EM*, p. 59.
59. Ādi, 119, 11.
60. Vana, 139, 4ff.
61. *Kumārasambhava*, 1, 1 (1) : अस्त्युत्तरस्यां दिशि देवतात्मा हिमालयो नाम नगाधिराजः। ....
and 5.45 : दिवं यदि प्रार्थयसे वृथाश्रमः पितुः प्रदेशास्तव देवभूमयः।
62. *EM*, p. 55; Anu, 31, 7.
63. *EM*, p. 56; Ādi, 88, 13.
64. Vana, 83, 13.
65. *The Teaching of the Vedas*, Reprint, Delhi, 1976, p. 190.
66. 10.90, 16. Tr. by Wendy Doniger O'Flaherty, *The Rigveda: An Anthology*, Penguin, 1981, pp. 29-32.
67. *ṚV*, 10. 90, 8-10.
68. *ṚV*, 7. 99,4.
69. *Bhagavadgītā*, 3, 10: सह यज्ञाः प्रजाः सृष्ट्वा. . . . .
and 14 (c) यज्ञाद् भवति पर्जन्यः . . . . .
70. 3. 23, 4. For text see *infra.*
71. 7.95, 2.
72. 6. 61, 8.
73. 7. 96, 1.
74. 7. 95, 1.
75. 2. 41, 16.
76. *Ibid.*
77. *Ibid.*
78. *VM*, p. 87.
79. *ŚB*, 3, 9. 1, 7; Also *AB* 3.1; 10
80. *ṚV*, 1. 3, 10.
81. *TB*, 1. 4. 4, 9.
82. O.P. Bharadwaj, *Studies in the Historical Geography of Ancient India*, Delhi, 1986, pp. 20-43.
83. *Ibid.*, pp. 8-19.
84. O.P. Bharadwaj, *Ancient Kurukshetra*, New Delhi, 1991, pp. 22-44.
85. Bharadwaj, 1986, pp. 20-43.
86. Bharadwaj, 1991, "Pehowa Inscription of King Bhoja of the Imperial Pratihāra Dynasty", *EI*, 1, p. 187, 11. 14-15; *Vāmana Purāṇa*, 21, 19; *Bhāgavata Purāṇa,* Gita Press, 4. 19. 1; *IA*, VI, p. 192; and *Padma Purāṇa, Sṛishti*, 18, 220-221.
87. Anu, 134,15.
88. *Vāmana Purāṇa*, 23, 13.
89. Vana, 19, 3; and 90, 31.
90. Śalya, 39, 31.
91. *Ibid.*, 37, 44.
92. *Ibid.*, 37, 46-47.
93. *Ibid.*, pp. 43, 4.

94. *Ibid.*
95. Ādi, 95, 26-27.
96. Vana, 100, 13.
97. Śalya, 41, 32-34.
98. Vana, 83, 151-153; and Śalya, 43, 30-43.
99. Śalya, 35, 77.
100. *Ibid.*, 38-39.
101. 10.53, 8.
102. V. 1, I., p. 374, e.g. see *ŚŚS*. xiii, 29, 1-29.
103. Bharadwaj, 1991, pp. 45-59.
104. Vana, 83, 4; 204.
105. Sabhā, 78, 15.
106. Vana, 87-88.
107. 3, 23, 4.
108. Vana, 83, 67 (ii).
109. *Ibid.*, 83, 68-69.
110. *Ibid.*, 83, 70.
111. 3. 33; also of. *ŚB*. iii. 5.3,21.
112. iii, 245.
113. iii, 263.
114. M.L. Bhargava, *The Geography of Ṛigvedic India*, Lucknow, 1964, p. 30-33; and Ram Gopal, "A New Interpretation of the Vedic Word Mānusha", *Journal of the Gaṅgānath Jha Research Institute*, XVII, May-August 1961(Plt. 3-4), pp. 193-202.
115. Vana, 83, 65-66.
116. *PB*, 25. 10, 6; see V. 1 ii, p. 300 for more references.
117. See Bharadwaj, 1986; pp. 20-43.
118. Vana, 82, 111.
119. *Ibid.*, 84, 112.
120. Śalya, 37, 1; In Vana, 129, 4, it is said to have vanished at the gate of Nishādas.
121. *Trikāṇḍaśesha*, ii. 1, 14: कुरूक्षेत्रं विनशनं कौशाम्बी वत्सपत्तनम्।
122. I. 9.1: इति भीतः प्रजाद्रोहात् सर्वधर्म विवित्सया।
ततो विनशनं प्रागाद् यत्र देव व्रतोऽपतत्।।
123. *Mbh.*, Ādi, 169, 20-21, where it is called Plakshajātā
124. *Vamana Purāṇa*, 42, 7.
125. *Mbh.*, Anu, 165, 25.
126. *PB*, 25. 10, 1-23.
127. *Ibid.*
128. ii, 297-298.
129. Śalya, 54, 9-11.
130. Vana, 84, 4-8.
131. V.I. ii. 364.
132. I. 84, 14; and 8. 6, 39 etc.

133. iii. 64.
134. Vana, 82, 114-116.
135. K.D. Shastri, *The Gaṇapāṭha Ascribed to Pāṇini*, Kurukshetra, 1967, p. 149; and V.S. Agrawala, *India as Known to Pāṇini*, 2nd ed., Varanasi, 1963, p. 510.
136. 19.39.8: यत्र नाव प्रभ्रंशनं यत्र हिमवतः शिरः।
तत्रामृतस्य चक्षणं तत्र कुष्ठोऽजायत।।
स कुष्ठो विश्वभेषजः साकं सोमेन तिष्ठति।।
137. 1.8,1.
138. *AV*, 19.39, 6; and 5. 4, 3.
139. *AV*, 3.24, 2: इमा याः पञ्च प्रदिशो मानवीः पञ्चकृष्टयः।
and the *Mbh.*, Vana, 185, 49.
140. All the post-Deluvian ruling dynasties originate from him. *Mbh.* Vana, 187, 53.
141. *Ibid.*, 187, 47-51.
142. *Ibid.*, 50 (ii) तच्च नौबन्धनं नाम शृङ्गं हिमवतः परम्।
50 (i) ख्यातमद्यापि कौन्तेय तद्विद्धि भरतर्षभ।।
143. Bharadwaj, 1986, pp. 1-7.
144. *Ibid.*, p. 205 and passim.
145. Vana, 84, 13-18.
146. Ed. Raghu Vira, Lahore, 1932, Intro. pp. 1-2.
147. Vana, 83, 72-74.
148. 2, 19; and 8, 1; also *ŚB* 12.3.
149. Vana, 83, 75-76 & 77(i) - 81. It is said to contain the sanctity of three crores of *tīrthas.*
150. V. 1, i, 460.
151. *PB*, 25. 6, 4.
152. *KB*, 26.5.
153. *Kāṭhaka Saṁhitā*, 10, 6.
154. *TB*, i, 364.
155. Karṇa, 45. 30.
156. Ādi, 1, 9-25.
157. Bharadwaj, 1986, pp. 129-137 for details and location.
158. Ādi, 196, 1.
159. Vana, 83, 202-203.
160. Vana, 84, 61.
161. Vana, 84, 62 & 64.
162. *PB*, 25. 10, 23; also see V. 1. 1. 149.
163. Śalya, 54, 12-15.
164. 25.3, 6.
165. 17, 18.
166. 5, 1, 1: तेषां कुरूक्षेत्रं वेदिरासीत्, तस्यै रवाण्डवो दक्षिणार्ध आसीत्,
तूर्ध्न मुत्तरार्धः, परिणज्जघनार्थः मरवः उत्करः . . . .
167. Ādi, 206, Southern recension reading after verse 25 and verses 28-

29 and 38; (ii) also Ādi, 223-225 for description of burning of Khāṇḍava forest by Agni.
168. Ram Gopal, *India of Vedic Kalpasūtras*, Delhi, 1959, p. 101. *ŚŚS*. XIII. 29. 29; *LSS*, 10. 19, 1, etc.
169. 25.10.15.
170. Vana, 82, 125-127.
171. 24.6, 30-32; also Ram Gopal, 1959, p. 101.
172. ii. 300.
173. 24. 6. 32.
174. 5. 1, 1.
175. 24. 6, 32.
176. 25. 13, 4.
177. *LŚS*, 10. 19, 9 etc.
178. Vana, 90, 4-8.
179. V. 1. i, 169.
180. *ŚB*, 14. 1, 1, 2; also *MS*, 2. 1. & 4.5, 9 etc.
181. *PB*, 25. 13, 3.
182. *Ibid*.
183. See n. 166 *supra*.
184. Śalya, 53, 24; 53, 1.
185. Vana, 129, 21.
186. *Ibid*., 83, 193-194.
187. *Ibid*., 129, 1.
188. *Ibid*., 83, 4; and 204, 205.
189. Śalya, 55, 7.
190. *Ibid*., 53, 22.
191. *Ibid*., 51, 1, 3.
192. *Bhagavadgītā*, 1, 1.
193. Śalya, 53, 16-17.
194. Vana, 83, 202, 203.
195. *Ibid*., 205, 206.
196. *The Hymns of the Rigveda*, tr. & com., 2 vols., Benaras, 1920. Vol. I, pp. 136-138.
197. *Ṛigveda Saṁhitā*, Vaidic Samshodhan Mandal ed., 5 vols., Vol. 1, pp. 639-640; also Sāyaṇa on *AV* 18.4.89.
198. B.K. Ghosh, *Collection of the Fragments of Lost Brāhmaṇas*, Reprint, Delhi, 1982, pp. 19-21.
199. Ed. Macdonell with tr. & notes etc., 2 vols., Reprint, Delhi, 1965, iii. pp. 132-136.
200. Śalya, 35, 89-90; and 36, 1; 29-33; 47; and 54 (ii) - 55.
201. For detailed discussion see Bharadwaj, 1991, pp. 115-120.
202. Ilāspada; *Vana*, 83, 77; Ahan: *Ibid*., 83; and Sudina: 83, 100.
203. P.V. Kane, *History of the Dharmaśāstra*, iv, p. 681.
204. Ram Gopal, 1959, p. 109.

205. This is the condition reflected in the *Vāmana Purāṇa* (34, 8) where much material has been borrowed from the *Mbh.*
वर्षा कालवहाः सर्वा वर्जयित्वा सरस्वतीम्।।
206. Anu, 134, 15; एषा सरस्वती पुण्या नदीनामुत्तमा नदी।
प्रथमा सर्वसरितां नदी सागर गामिनी।।
207. V.S. Agrawala, *Matsya Purāṇa: A Study*, Varanasi, 1963, p. 113; *AV*, 12. 1, 5: यस्यां पूर्वे पूर्वजना विचक्रिरे।
208. *Mbh*. Vana, 90, 18; Lomaśa to Yudhishṭhira:
गमने कृतबुद्धिं तं पाण्डवं लोमशोऽब्रवीत्।
लघुभर्व महाराज लघुः स्वैरं गमिष्यसि।।
209. R.K. Mookerji, *Aśoka*, Reprint, Delhi, 1972, p. 22.
210. *Cf. Gautama Dharma Sūtra*, 19, 14:
सर्वे शिलोच्चयाः सर्वाः स्रवन्त्यः पुण्याः ह्रदाः
तीर्थानि ऋषिनिवासाः गोष्ठ परिस्कन्दाः इति देशाः।
211. *Mbh.,* Vana, 83, 16.
212. *Ibid.*, 83, 17.
213. *Ibid.*, 83, 53.
214. *Ibid.*, 83, 77.
215. *Ibid.*, 83, 84.
216. *Ibid.*, 83, 54.
217. *Ibid.*, 83, 89.
218. *Ibid.*
219. *Ibid.*, 83, 98.
220. Śānti, 263, 40 (ii): सर्वा नद्यः सरस्वत्यः सर्वे पुण्याः शिलोच्चयाः।
41 (i): जाजले ! तीर्थमात्मैव मास्म देशातिथिर्भव।।
221. R.K. Mookerji, *Fundamental Unity of India*, Bharatiya Vidya Bhavan, 1970, p. 47.
222. D.G. Mandelbaum, *Society in India*, Berkeley, 1984, pp. 401ff.

ABBREVIATIONS USED

AB	*Aitareya Brāhmaṇa*
AV	*Atharvaveda*
EM	*Epic Mythology*, E.W. Hopkins, reprint, Delhi, 1968
JB	*Jaiminīya Brāhmaṇa*
KB	*Kauśītiakī Brāhmaṇa*
LŚS	*Lātyāyana Śrauta Sūtra*
Mbh.	*Mahābhārata*, Gita Press ed.
MS	*Maitrāyāṇī Saṁhitā*
PB	*Pañcaviṁśa Brāhmaṇa*
ṚV	*Ṛigveda*
ŚB	*Śatapatha Brāhmaṇa*
ŚŚS	*Śāṅkhāyana Śrauta Sūtra*
SV	*Sāmaveda*
TA	*Taittirīya Araṇyaka*
TB	*Taittirīya Brāhmaṇa*
TS	*Taittrīya Saṁhitā*
VGS	*Vaikhānasa Gṛihya Sūtra*
VI	*Vedic Index*, Keith and Macdonell, 2 vols., reprint, Delhi, 1967.
VM	*Vedic Mythology*, A.A. Macdonell, reprint, Delhi, 1971.
YV	*Yajurveda*

13

The Concept and Practice of Pilgrimage in the *Mahābhārata*

D.P. Dubey

Pilgrimage to sacred places occupies an important place in the list of duties presented for their followers by various religions. It is an extremely interesting religious phenomenon of Indian cultural tradition. Kane[1] has controverted the suggestion[2] that institution of pilgrimage began with the Buddhists and the Jainas. The word *tīrtha* occurs 8 times in the *Ṛigveda*, twice as *tīrtham* in the accusative singular form and 6 times as *tīrthe* in the locative singular form. It is used in the sense of a watering or a bathing place or in the sense of a passage leading to or a ford through water.[3] He points out that the importance of holy places, visiting them and performing religious rites were known in the Brāhmaṇa period, and the word *tīrtha* came to denote "a locality or spot or expanse of water which gives rise to the accumulation of righteousness (merit) owing to its own peculiar nature without any adventitious circumstance".[4] Though we do not refute the facts pointed out by Kane, we would like to point out that pilgrimage finds a regular provision in the *Mahābhārata* which provides an early account of the introduction of *tīrthayātrā* as a religious practice. The focus of this study is the concept and practice of pilgrimage to holy places as reflected in the *Mahābhārata*.

The *Mahābhārata* is the oldest and the most important source of information about the places of pilgrimage in ancient period. The epic assumes an already well-established practice, closely conforming to the literal meaning of *tīrtha* (sacred ford) *yātrā* (journey). The *Mahābhārata* attaches great importance to *tīrthayātrā* and suggests that it is a rather lonely quest for religious merit, particularly suited for those who cannot afford expensive religious sacrifices. The seer Pulastya says:

> In this world the seers in the Vedas have taught the sacrifices in due order and what exactly will be the result of each of them, here as well as hereafter. But those sacrifices are out of reach of the poor man, sacrifices require many utensils and large variety of materials. Kings or wealthy men may sometimes have no company, are isolated and do not operate jointly. Here is the rite, which is within the reach even of the poor and in merit equals the result of sacrifices. This is the most secret teaching of the seers: the meritorious visit to holy places even surpasses sacrifices. He who has never kept a fast for three days and nights, has not visited holy places and has not given gold nor coins, is indeed reborn a poor man. He who has performed the *agnishṭoma* and similar such sacrifices with liberal gifts does not reap such fruit as from the visit of holy places.[5]

This is indeed a simple and clear formula: pilgrimage is equivalent to the Vedic sacrifices; it surpasses them in merit, and is much less costly. The *Mahābhārata* preferably expresses *tīrthaphala* in terms of merit and the standard it uses as a rule is the merit accruing from different Vedic sacrifices:

> When a man has taken a bath in that excellent holy place (Prabhāsa) and has become pure, of pure mind, he reaps the fruit of an *agnishṭoma* and an *atirātra*.[6]
>
> When a man has taken a bath in Kanakhala and fasted for three days and nights, he acquires the merit of an *aśvamedha* and attains heaven.[7]
>
> He who bathes in the confluence of the Gaṅgā and the Yamunā at Prayāga acquires all the merits of *rājasūya* and *aśvamedha* sacrifices.[8]

The *Mahābhārata* thus harmonized pilgrimage with the Vedic religion. Also, pilgrimage and sacrifice are put on par by equating the merit gained by a pilgrim with that derived from one or more great Vedic sacrifices, irrespective of what religious act is prescribed in the holy place concerned. Sometimes the epic exactly specifies the result the pilgrim will reap by a given act in a given place. This may be *moksha*, rebirth in heaven, purification from sin, fulfilment of wishes, beauty, etc. However, the practice of pilgrimage was mainly introduced to simplify the otherwise complicated sacrificial routine. And the *Mahābhārata* brought pilgrimage into harmony with the Vedic-Brāhmaṇic tradition.

Ritual accompanies pilgrimage from the outset. A simple visit to holy places is not enough. A person should perform some religious act fetching merit at the particular holy place. These acts mostly consist of giving gifts, or taking a bath, or fasting, or oblations to *pitṛis*, or simple night stay, or even the performance of *yajña*. Thus the *Mahābhārata* says:

Bathing in Rāmahrada and offering oblations of water to the *pitṛis* in the river Vipāśā, and observing a fast for 12 days, one becomes cleansed of all sins.[9]

Balarāma touched the waters of Udapāna on the Sarasvatī, and gave away diverse kinds of wealth there, and worshipped many brāhmaṇas.[10]

Giving away many costly gifts at Chamasodbheda-tīrtha, Balarāma passed one night there and performed his ablutions duly.[11]

The religious merit acquired by the visit to various holy places and the performance of various meritorious rites differed according to the importance attached to the place and the action performed therein. Thus, if a bath would obtain heaven in one place, in another place it would fetch a celestial plane, or a company of *apsarās* or simply a merit equal to the performance of an *aśvamedha*. Again, if it was especially meritorious to take bath in one place, in the other fasting would be more important and oblations to ancestors in the third, though most frequently we meet with the prescription of ablutions (*abhisheka*) or a bath (*snāna*). The different *tīrthas* had varying importance. So also, the motives that impel individuals to undertake pilgrimages are diverse and have been thoroughly investigated by Diehl.[12] But in the *Mahābhārata* the event of pilgrimage is more significant, motives consisting of earning religious merit by performing prescribed rituals at the *tīrtha* and the deity are not the focus of pilgrimage.

Along with the sanctity attached to the visits to holy places, an equal importance is attached to the ethical standard achieved by the person who visits them. Thus, in the beginning of his discourse on pilgrimage, Pulastya makes it very clear that a visit to a holy place is of any value, only if a person is pure in heart and full of faith. In a discussion about the merit obtained through a visit to these places, he declares:

. . . only that person can enjoy the merit acquired through pilgrimage whose hands, feet, mind, knowledge, *tapas* and fame, all these are well controlled. One who does not ask, but accepts only that which is given to him, obtains the religious merit by visiting various places of pilgrimage. Again, one who avoids hypocrisy, is non-indulgent in worldly affairs while on a pilgrimage, eats less and is of controlled senses, acquires the merit of visiting a *tīrtha*. Again, one who entertains no anger, who is always truthful and who is tolerant towards all the creatures, obtains the fruit of pilgrimage.[13]

Medieval digests on *tīrthas* reproduce all these four verses as *mahābhārate pulastya uvāca*. In the *Padma Purāṇa*, the third verse is missing, possibly because the compiler of the *Padma Purāṇa* chose to borrow only three verses from the *Mahābhārata*. Richard Salomon[14] has not noted these verses, in question, appearing in the *Mahābhārata*, though in the *Tristhalīsetu Sāmānya-praghaṭṭaka* of Nārāyaṇa Bhaṭṭa they occur in the same order in which they are noticed in the epic.

In the *Mahābhārata*, there are long passages devoted to the visiting of holy places: the Tīrthayātrā (sub-) parvan in the Āraṇyakaparvan,[15] another Tīrthayātrā (sub-) parvan in the Śalyaparvan[16] which describes Balarāma's pilgrimage to the holy places on the Sarasvatī, to begin with Prabhāsa and ending at Kārapachana, and a shorter one in the Dānadharma (sub-) parvan in the Anuśāsanaparvan.[17] Of these Āraṇyakaparvan section is the most important. The narration of *tīrthas* is occasioned by the advisability for the four Pāṇḍava brothers to go on a pilgrimage to different *tīrthas* after the departure of Arjuna to the Indraloka for acquiring the lore of *astra* (weapon). There was a great need of recreation for them to overcome the despondency caused by the separation of their dear brother. The epic reads:

> *dhanañjayo tsukāste tu vane tasmin mahārathāḥ/*
> *nyavasanta mahābhāgā draupadyā saha pāṇḍavāḥ//*[18]

After this comes the Pulastya-*tīrthayātrā* which contains the discourse of the sage Pulastya to answer Bhīshma's question, what result will be reaped by the man who makes a clockwise circumambulation of the world.[19] After some introductory remarks, he gives in fact a pilgrim's itinerary, which spans the whole subcontinent.[20] The pilgrim is first supposed to visit Pushkara and to go from there via Ujjayinī to the Narmadā. From there, he has to turn to the north-west to Arbuda (Mount Abu) and again southward to Prabhāsa. Here the *pradakshiṇā* actually begins. He should visit the Indus, the Punjab, Vinaśana (the site of disappearance of the Sarasvatī) and reach Kurukshetra. On his eastward way, he is to proceed as far as the Karatoyā river in the present-day Bangladesh. Then after having visited Gaṅgāsāgarasaṅgama, he should continue southward, bathe in the Kāverī and in the sea at Kanyātīrtha (Kanyākumārī). On his way back, he should follow the west coast as far as Gokarṇa and after having visited several holy places in the Deccan, complete his long pilgrimage by bathing at Prayāga. Bhardwaj has demonstrated this from scrambled account of *tīrthas* in the itinerary presented by Pulastya.[21]

The thread of narration is again taken up after a lapse of 5 chapters by Dhaumya who goes on describing various *tīrthas* that are situated in the four quarters.[22] Then in the subsequent chapters Lomaśa has escorted the four Pāṇḍava brothers to different *tīrthas* and explained their merits in the capacity of a guide and a mentor.[23] It may be noted that the Dhaumya and Lomaśa accounts of *tīrthas* begin with Naimishāraṇya and end at Ārshṭisheṇa-āśrama/Viśālā- Badarī. The description of one *tīrtha* after the other is made more or less on geographical line. But it may be noted that almost all the *tīrthas* are either of legendary or of historical importance and perhaps it is for this reason that it is considered a place worth visiting. If we analyse the accounts minutely, we can discuss several stages in the growth of pilgrimage as a religious practice.

The *tīrtha* sections in the *Mahābhārata* describe a few out of the numerous holy places on the earth, with the result that the disagreement about their numbers in the texts is bewildering. Sixty lakh and ten thousand are located in Prayāga alone:

daśatīrthasahasrāṇi shashṭikoṭyas tathāparāḥ/
yeshām sānnidhayam atraiva kīrtitam kurunandana//[24]

While the Anuśāsanaparvan supplies a list of 81 *tīrthas*, the Śalyaparvan refers to the sanctity of 43. The Āraṇyakaparvan contains the names of about 350 *tīrthas*. About 235 holy places and rivers are mentioned in the Pulastya dialogue, and about 53 are enumerated in the Dhaumya dialogue, while 60 are referred in the Lomaśa itinerary. More than 3,300 verses are devoted to the description of *tīrthas* in the Āraṇyakaparvan (verses 2,400), Śalyaparvan (verses 77) and Anuśāsanaparvan (verses 66). However, no details are given in the *Mahābhārata* about the physical setting of these places, their population or relative distances in any form. In this respect, these descriptions are indeed disappointing. The *tīrthas* enumerated in the *Mahābhārata* cover a very wide area, rather the whole country and embrace the boundaries of this land.

The *Mahābhārata* is supposed to have assumed its present form between the 4th century BC and the 4th century CE, but there is no unanimity on the date of composition of the Tīrthayātrā (sub-)parvan. Bhardwaj assigns the Tīrthayātrā section of the Āraṇyakaparvan to *circa* 3rd century BC.[25] According to D.C. Sircar, it was composed earlier than the Gupta period.[26] Bulcke places the composition of the Āraṇyakaparvan in the 2nd century CE.[27] Jacob Ensink considers the *tīrtha* passages late addition to the epic and assigns the *tīrtha* sections to the first centuries of the current era.[28] On the basis of "the frequent descriptions of the various *tīrthas* and the frequency with which the personalities in the epic are made to visit them", Dhairyabala Vora suggests that "by the time of the final edition of the epic, *tīrthayātrā* must have been a very popular practice". She considers the Tīrthayātrāparvan to be a later interpolation added sometime after the beginning of the current era.[29] Vora thus seems to be inclined to place the Tīrthayātrā section in the range of 100-300 CE. The Berlin collections of Sanskrit palm leaf MSS from Qizil (Chinese Turkistan) comprise, among other numerous fragments, a list of the 100 sub and 18 major parvans of the *Mahābhārata* in Kushāṇa characters,[30] and Tīrthayātrā (sub-) parvan in the Āraṇyakaparvan figures in the list at serial no. 33. This is the oldest record of the extant parvan-list of the *Mahābhārata* and may obviously be assigned to the first two centuries of the current era. Given that there are errors, omissions and interpolations, and considering that the compiler was relying on a tradition of respected antiquity, we may safely place the composition of the Tīrthayātrā (sub-) parvan between the 1st century BC and the 1st century CE. The list of Dhaumya is ancient and shorter. The list of Pulastya is longer and comparatively of later date. The list of Lomaśa may figure in between the two.

The Anuśāsanaparvan does not belong to the original *Mahābhārata* but is arguably a later addition to the epic and the single chapter on *tīrthas* may have been appended to it sometime during the 4th-5th century CE. The section of Balarāma's *yātrā* in the Śalyaparvan may have been the oldest of all, stylistically and meticulously. But the frequent occurrences of *kathās* in the itinerary compel us to think otherwise. However, it has a striking similarity to the performance of *Sārasvatasattras* known from the Brāhmaṇas and the Śrautasūtras.

The ritual of *yātsattras* (itinerant sacrificial sessions) begins at Vinaśana, the place where the Sarasvatī river disappears in the sands of the Indian desert. It naturally comes to an end at the source of the Sarasvatī, the place called Plaksha Prasravaṇa. The sacrificial bath (*avabhṛitha snāna*) is then taken at Kārapacana on the Yamunā. The result of the duly completed *Sārasvatasattra* is the attainment of heaven. The *Jaiminīya Brāhmaṇa* says:

> They proceed along the Sarasvatī. Sarasvatī is the Word. The Word is the way of the gods. So they proceed by the way of the gods. They go upstream. Heaven, one might say, is upstream. So they go to heaven. They go to the north-east. Heaven is in the north-east. So they mount to heaven. They go as far as Plaksha Prasravaṇa. Plaksha Prasravaṇa is the completion of the Word. That is heaven. So they go to heaven.[31]

Thus, Balarāma's *yātrā* was the journey to heaven for heavenly bliss, it was not an ordinary journey. As compared to the Pulastya-*yātrā*, it is not loosely knit in the texture of the epic.

The chapters on places of pilgrimage in the Purāṇas have some similarities with the description in the *Mahābhārata*, but there are also differences. The portion of the Pulastya-*tīrthayātrā* episode is common to the epic and the *Padma Purāṇa*. In both the texts the interlocution is between Bhīshma and Pulastya. But the verses have a natural and logical position in the *Mahābhārata*. M.V. Vaidya, after analysing the issue, has remarked that "the *Mahābhārata* version of the Pulastya-*yātrā* is the basis of and therefore prior to the *Padma Purāṇa* section of *tīrthayātrā*."[32] There cannot be any doubt about the original and the borrower in this case.

To sum up, the Tīrthayātrā sections in the *Mahābhārata* portray a picture of Indian quasi-spiritual geography, which ultimately became the basis of the development of the norms of Indian culture down to the ages. The *Mahābhārata* has, in fact, interpreted the Indian cultural geography which aimed at knowing the country and meeting her people in ancient period. The Tīrthayātrāparvan gives us a vivid picture of India, which was dotted with numerous places of pilgrimage throughout her length and breadth. The idea was that people from different parts of India should visit them and admire their sanctity. This practice was introduced to encourage unity among the people and free mixing with each other. It was so nicely propagated that the *tīrthayātrā* became an essential part of life. History knows that many personalities journeyed to all these places in India in the past. The *Mahābhārata* gives the first systematic treatment of the institution of pilgrimage which was dealt with added importance and popularity in the Purāṇas and digests on *tīrthas*.

NOTES AND REFERENCES

1. P.V. Kane, *History of Dharmaśāstra*, Vol. IV (Poona: Bhandarkar Oriental Research Institute, 1953/1973, second edn.), pp. 554-55.
2. D.R. Patil, *Cultural History from the Vāyu Purāṇa* (Delhi: Motilal Banarsidass, 1946/1973, reprint), p. 334.
3. Kane, *op.cit.*, pp. 554-55; C.S. Venkateswaran, "The Vedic Conception of Tīrtha", *Proceedings and Transactions of the All India Oriental Conference*, 21st session, Srinagar (Ed. V. Raghavan, Poona: Bhandarkar Oriental Research Institute, 1966), Vol. II(i), pp. 14-18.
4. Kane, *op. cit.*, p. 555.
5. *Mahābhārata* (Eds. V.S. Sukthankar *et al.*, Poona : Bhandarkar Oriental Research Institute, 19 vols., 1933-59), III. 80.34-40.
6. *Ibid.*, III. 80.77.
7. *Ibid.*, III. 82.28.
8. *Ibid.*, III. 83.76.
9. *Ibid.*, XIII. 26.44.
10. *Ibid.*, IX. 35.52.
11. *Ibid.*, IX. 34.79.
12. Carl G. Diehl, *Instrument and Purpose: Studies on Rites and Rituals in South India* (Lund, 1956).
13. *Mahābhārata*, III. 80.30-33.
14. R. Salomon, *The Bridge to the Three Holy Cities* (The Sāmānya-praghaṭṭaka of Nārāyaṇa Bhaṭṭa's *Tristhalīsetu*, Delhi : Motilal Banarsidass, 1985), p.173.
15. *Mahābhārata*, III, 80-153.
16. *Ibid.*, IX. 34-53.
17. *Ibid.*, XIII. 26.
18. *Ibid.*, III. 80.1.
19. *Ibid.*, III. 80. 10, 28.
20. *Ibid.*, III. 80.84.
21. S.M. Bhardwaj, *Hindu Places of Pilgrimage in India* (Burkeley: University of California Press, 1973), pp. 45-52.
22. *Mahābhārata*, III. 85-90.
23. *Ibid.*, III. 91-153.
24. *Ibid.*, III. 83.79.
25. Bhardwaj, *op.cit.*, p. 15.

26. D.C. Sircar, *Studies in the Geography of Ancient and Medieval India* (Delhi: Motilal Banarsidass, 1960), p. 178.
27. C. Bulcke, *Rāmakathā: Utpatti aur Vikāsa* (Prayaga: Hindi Parishad Prakashan, University of Allahabad, 1962), p. 33.
28. J. Ensink, "Hindu Pilgrimage and Vedic Sacrifice", in *Ludwick Sternback Felicitation Volume* (Ed. J.P. Sinha, Lucknow: Akhila Bharatiya Sanskrit Parishad, 1979), Pt. I, p. 114.
29. Dhairyabala, P. Vora, *Evolution of Morals in the Epics* (Bombay : Popular Book Depot, 1959), p. 244.
30. Dieter Schlingloff, "The Oldest Extant Parvan-list of the Mahābhārata", *Journal of the American Oriental Society*, Vol. 89, 1969, pp. 334-38.
31. *Jaiminīya Brāhmaṇa* (Eds. Raghuvira and L. Chandra, Sarasvati Vihar series no. 31, Nagpur, 1954), 2. 299.
32. M.V. Vaidya., "Tīrthayātrā in the Āraṇyakaparvan and the Padma Purāṇa", in *A Volume of Studies in Indology Presented to Prof. P.V. Kane* (Eds. S.M. Katre and P.K. Gode, Poona : Oriental Book Agency, 1941), pp. 530-37.

14

Widow Burning and the Mādrī Episode

An Analysis of the Evidence of the *Mahābhārata*

Ashvini Agrawal

The origin and antiquity of the custom of burning the widow along with the body of the dead husband, popularly known as *satī* and referred to in the literature and inscriptions as *anugamana, sahagamana, sahamaraṇa,* etc., is a subject of controversy amongst the modern scholars. The general impression is that the custom of *satī* originated in India and its antiquity goes back to hoary past.[1] However, there is hardly any evidence to support such a view. A single hymn in the *Ṛigveda,*[2] often quoted as evidence of the existence of the custom of *satī,* is not only of doubtful nature and controversial, but it does not even refer to the actual burning of the widow. Except for this verse, which is repeated in the *Atharvaveda*[3] and refers to the burning of the widow as a custom of bygone times[4], there is not a single reference to this custom in the vast ocean of Indian literature up to the beginning of the Christian era.

However, a few instances of widow burning in the two great epics of India – the *Rāmāyaṇa* and the *Mahābhārata* – are stressed upon time and again as a proof of the existence of the custom and require a close examination. The *Rāmāyaṇa* contains a solitary reference to the burning of Vedavatī's mother.[5] The story here is legendary and can in no way be connected with the custom of *satī.*[6] There is no other reference to widow burning in the entire epic. On the contrary, we have all the three wives of Daśaratha alive after his death and none of the ladies in Rāvaṇa's camp died with her husband.

Coming to the evidence of the *Mahābhārata* on the subject, there are a few instances where the widows ended their lives with their husbands. But each of these cases appears to have special reasons and they cannot be grouped together to be termed as evidence of the prevalence of the custom of *satī*. We shall have to examine them individually to see if they are fit to be designated as the instances of *satī* and that too at a time when the great epic had not taken its final form as yet. In the *Mahābhārata*, Draupadī as Sairandhrī was ordered to be burnt on the pyre of Kīchaka after the latter's death at the hands of Bhīma.[7] Not only that Sairandhrī was not actually burnt but also the cause of such an order was said to be an ancient custom of burning slave or slaves with the ruler and not wives. There is no question of *satī* in this case as the persons involved were not husband and wife and as the story indicates, it may have been purely an act of vengeance.

The Mausalaparvan contains two instances: First where four wives of Vasudeva, viz., Devakī, Bhadrā, Rohiṇī and Madirā, burnt themselves with him[8] and the second where Rukmiṇī, Gandhārī, Śaibyā, Haimavatī and Jāmbavatī amongst the consorts of Kṛishṇa ascended the funeral pyre with him.[9] All other wives of Kṛishṇa survived him and those like Satyabhāmā retired to forest for penance. This passage of the Mausalaparvan appears to be a later interpolation and may have been added to remove the discrepancy between the Purāṇic accounts given in the *Bhāgavata Purāṇa*, *Vishṇu Purāṇa*, etc., that were composed in the Gupta period or even later and those of the *Mahābhārata*. It is quite probable in the light of the fact that none of the ladies in the Pāṇḍava or Kaurava camps is shown to have burnt herself with her husband in the great epic.

The most well-known instance contained in the *Mahābhārata* is that of Mādrī ascending the funeral pyre of her husband Pāṇḍu, after the latter's death in the forest as a result of copulating with Mādrī in spite of the curse forbidding him to do so.[10] This episode is always construed as a direct instance of *satī* in the great epic and the prevalence of the custom during this period is stressed on its basis. However, such a conclusion is unwarranted in the light of the circumstances under which the incident took place. The reasoning given for it is quite different from that of the custom of *satī*. It is therefore worthwhile to discuss it in some detail in the context of socio-cultural ethos of the epic period.

As the story goes, Pāṇḍu once killed a sage and his wife in the form of deer when they were copulating and was cursed by the sage that he would die as a result of a similar action. Aware of the curse and full of remorse, Pāṇḍu led the life of an ascetic with his wives Kuntī and Mādrī and their sons. One day while Kuntī was busy looking after the brāhmaṇas invited for sacrifice on Arjuna's completion of fourteenth year, Pāṇḍu began to rove in the woods with his favourite wife Mādrī. Soon the sweetness of surroundings aroused desire in him and he copulated with Mādrī and died. Full of remorse, Mādrī plunged into grief that was accentuated by the words of Kuntī who blamed her for not protecting their husband from his lustful behaviour.[11] It was at this moment that Mādrī decided to end her life along with her husband Pāṇḍu. Kuntī also expressed a similar desire but neither so emphatically nor did she talk of it as the 'only *dharma*' for her, which is the basic reason given for the custom of *satī* when it became popular at later times. Mādrī gave two reasons for her resolve. Firstly, she said that since she was the cause of her husband's death, she must die with him. Secondly, she told Kuntī that she herself was not capable of treating all their sons alike and shall incur the sin of ill-treating her stepsons, which she did not want. On the other hand, Kuntī was capable of looking after all the five sons like her own, was wise and well protected by her paternal family; so she alone should live.[12] Nowhere does she talk of any religious merit of the act or following any such tradition where a wife's *dharma* was to die on the funeral pyre of her husband. She does not even talk of any past or prevalent custom of this type that clearly establishes that the whole episode was a result of a peculiar situation and Mādrī's personal resolve to end her life along with her husband due to her attachment to him.

On the other hand, the prevalent cultural ethos of the time are reflected in the words of the sages assembled by the side of the body of Pāṇḍu, who tried their best to dissuade Mādrī from her resolve.[13] They told her in no uncertain words that her resolve shall not only endanger the welfare of her sons that was insecure under the rule of Dhṛitarāshṭra and his sons but also that a pious woman is she who leads the life of brahmacharya after her husband's death. Following the rigid rules of discipline, controlling her desires of heart and body and restraining her speech, she bears suffering. Performing the vows and fasts like Chāndrāyaṇa, etc., she sleeps on the ground, gives up salt and pungent foods and takes her meals only once a day. Therefore, it is proper for a noble woman to destroy her sensual and worldly feelings by observing these penances after the death of her husband. Such a lady who devotes herself to the memory of her dead husband causes the deliverance of her husband, her sons and herself.[14] "Therefore, it is proper and behoves both of you to live."[15]

Herein lies the essence of the prevalent tradition of the time. It did not permit the immolation of the widow, a practice that came into vogue at a much later date, but expected her to live a pure and simple life after the death of her husband. The absence of the practice of *satī* during the epic period is also attested by numerous references to living widows contained therein. We have already referred to the survival of Kauśalyā, Sumitrā and Kaiykeyī, the wives of Daśaratha after the latter's death as mentioned in the *Rāmāyaṇa*. In the Mahābhārata War, numerous heroes died in both the Pāṇḍava and Kaurava camps. None of their wives became *satī*. On the other hand, we are told that they performed the last rites of their husbands after the war and offered the oblations of water on the banks of the Gaṇgā.[16] This sets the stamp of certainty on the issue that the Mādrī episode can neither be cited as an example of the custom of widow burning in ancient India nor of its prevalence during the epic period.

NOTES AND REFERENCES

1. For detailed discussion on the subject see the author's paper—"*Satī* – How Old? How Indian?", *Haryana Sahitya Akademi Journal of Indological Studies*, III, pp. 91-98. Also see P.V. Kane, *History of Dharmaśastra*, Vol. II, Pt. I, pp. 618-19; and A.S. Altekar, *The Position of Women in Hindu Civilization*, pp. 137-38.
2. *Ṛigveda*. X. 18. 7-8.
   इमा नारीरविधवाः सुपत्नोराञ्जनेन सर्पिषा सं विशन्तु।
   अनश्रवोऽनमीवाः सुरत्ना आरोहन्तु जनथो योनिमग्रे।।
   उदीर्ष्व नार्यभि जीवलोकं गतासुमेतमुप शेष एहि।
   हस्तग्राभस्य दिधिषोस्तवेंद पत्युर्जंनित्वमभि संबभूथ।।
3. *Atharvaveda*, XVIII. 3.1.
   इंच नारी पतिलोकं वृणाना निपद्यत उपत्वा मर्त्य प्रेतम्।
   विश्वं पुराणमनुपालयन्ती तस्य प्रजां द्रविण चेह धेहि।।
4. Recently archaeological evidence from Ināmgāon and some other sites such as Mahādah, where instances of joint burial have come to

light, have been cited as examples of the prevalence of the custom of *satī* in the prehistoric times. In this connection it may be noted that not only such instances are very few, it is by no means certain that the couples so buried were husband and wife and further that if they were husband and wife, the latter did not die a natural death. The whole theory becomes questionable and highly speculative in the light of the fact that joint burials of two males have also come to light. *Cf.* H.D. Sankalia, M.K. Dhavalikar *et al.*, *Excavations at Inamgaon*.

5. *Rāmāyaṇa*, Uttarakāṇḍa, 17.15, Pune, 1988, pp. 263 ff.
6. Some scholars have referred to Meghanāda's wife becoming *satī*. However, there is no such reference in the *Rāmāyaṇa* of Vālmīki.
7. *Mbh.*, Virāṭaparvan, IV. 23.
8. *Ibid.*, Mausalaparvan, VII. 18.
9. *Ibid.*, VII. 73-74.
10. Ādiparvan, 124.
11. *Ibid.*, 124. 18-20.
12. *Ibid.*, 124. 26-28.
13. *Ibid*. This portion is missing from certain versions of the *Mahābhārata* including the critical edition prepared by the Bhandarkar Oriental Research Institute, Pune. But it is contained in the southern version. It is also included in the Gita Press Gorakhpur edition, V.S. 2013. We find no reason to omit it. It is possible that the verses were removed from the northern recension of the epic at a later date when *satī* had become popular in Northern India.
14. *Ibid*.
    मृते भर्तरि या साध्वी ब्रह्मचर्यव्रते स्थिता।
    यमैश्च नियमैः भ्रान्ता मनोवाक्कायजैः शुभैः।।
    व्रतोपवासनियमैः कृच्छ्रैश्चान्द्रायणादिभिः।
    भूशय्यां क्षारलवणवर्जनं चैकभोजनम्।।
    येन केनापि विधिना देहशोषणतत्परा।
    देहपोषणसंयुक्ता विषयैर्हृतचेतना।।
    देहव्ययेन नरकं महदाप्रोत्यसंशय।
    तस्मात्संशोषयेद् देहं विषया नाशमाप्नुयुः।।
    भर्तारं चिन्तयन्ती सा भर्तारं निस्तरेच्छुभा।
    तारितश्चापि भर्ता स्यादात्मा पुत्रस्तथैव च।।
15. *Ibid*.
    तस्माज्जीवितमेवैतद् युवयोर्विद्म शोभनम्।।
16. *Cf.* Strīparvan.

15

The Early Traces of Nyāya-Vaiśeshika in the *Mahābhārata*

C.S. Radhakrishnan

The *Mahābhārata* enjoys a very unique place as the largest literary work in the world. Consisting of one lakh verses, as available now, it is truly encyclopaedic in character. The epic itself declares that whatever is found in it can be seen elsewhere and whatever is not in it, cannot be found elsewhere:

Yadihāsti tadanyatra yannehāsti na tat kvachit

Whether it is poetry or philosophy, love or warfare, relaxation through sports or adherence to righteousness, narration of tales or never-exhaustible discussions on the concept of Dharma, the *Mahābhārata* provides a vast substratum. The epic contains the *Bhagavadgītā*, the Song Divine, which is a quintessence of the vast Upanishadic teaching and has been translated into a maximum number of languages in the world. Yet another piece, the *Vishṇusahasranāma* is a popular devotional literature in itself.

It will not be an exaggeration to say that India's contribution to philosophy is immense and immeasurable. The inquiry of the mankind into a wonderful, sometimes baffling and mysterious nature of the Universe and its relationship with him, developed into a mass of literature on philosophy. Apart from the Vedic literature, consisting of its Karmakāṇḍa and Jñānakāṇḍa, there came into being, the Darśanas, or systems of philosophy. The very etymology of the Darśana is that through which as a means one is able to arrive at the truth: *dṛisyate anena tattvam*. That the derivative sense of this word is based purely on grammar and has nothing to do with any religious or philosophical implication is clear from the fact that even the materialistic or the atheistic philosophy is called by the same term like the *Chārvāka darśana*, etc. So much so that there are works like *Avaidikadarśanasaṅgraha* giving an account of Lokāyata or materialism, Buddhism and Jainism.

Though in the day-to-day parlance, the words *āstika* and *nāstika* are used to denote the theists and atheists, the division of the Darśanas basically into two has a different criterion altogether. The division into Āstikadarśana (or Vaidikadarśana) and Nāstikadarśana (Avaidikadarśana) is not based on the existence or otherwise of God but on the acceptance or otherwise of Veda as an authority. The orthodoxy of the Darśana is purely based on its subservience to the Vedas. It is for this reason that the Mīmāṁsā school, which is silent on God, is classified under the Vaidikadarśana.

Freedom of thought and inquiry resulted in the six systems of philosophy, collectively called the Shaḍ-Darśanas, taking shape. They are the Nyāya and Vaiśeshika, the Sāṁkhya and Yoga and the Pūrva-Mīmāṁsā and the Uttara-Mīmāṁsā. The enumeration is normally in this order, in pairs. The pairing is supposed to be due to the similarity of the two systems involved. But between the Pūrva-Mīmāṁsā and the Uttara-Mīmāṁsā, there is a world of difference in approach and content. The former is ritualistic whereas the latter is philosophic. But there has been so much of harmony between Nyāya and Vaiśeshika that their pairing is always justified. Their approach, logical by all means, and the facts arrived at are very similar though not the same. They further have the pride of place for systematizing the Epistemology and Ontology respectively.

Mention is made in the *Mahābhārata* of these systems. For instance, in the *Vishṇusahasranāma*, we read:

Yogo jñānaṁ tathā sāṁkhyam
vidyāḥ śilpādi karma cha
Vedāḥ śāśtrāṇi vijñānam
etat sarvaṁ janārdanāt

Though Nyāya, Vaiśeshika or even Mīmāṁsā, for that matter, are not explicitly mentioned in the above list, it has to be understood that the term vidyāḥ includes them:

aṅgāni vedāś chatvār
mīmāṁsā nyāyavistaraḥ

purāṇaṁ dharmaśāstraṁ cha
vidyāḥ hyetāś chaturdaśa

The Nyāya system is variously known as Ānvīkshikī, Pramāṇa-śāstra, Hetu-śāstra and Tarka-vidyā. The logical acumen with which it analyses everything can be analysed in words, has won for it a lofty place among the systems. Even Kauṭilya pays rich tributes to it in his *Arthaśāstra* (Ch.II):

pradīpaḥ sarva-śāstrāṇāṁ
upāyaḥ sarvakarmaṇāṁ
āśrayaḥ sarva-dharmāṇāṁ
śaśvat ānvīkshikī matā

The Ānvīkshikī had been used as synonymous with Ātmavidyā, both constituting 'the science of inquiry'. The *Mahābhārata* uses it in this sense:

Trayī chānvīkshikī chaiva vārtā cha Bharatarshabha
Daṇḍanītiś cha vipulā vidyāḥ tatra nidarśitāḥ
(Śāntiparvan, ch. 56)

Manu also uses it in this sense only:

त्रैविद्येभ्यःत्रयीं विद्याद् दण्डनीतिश्च शाश्वतीं।
आन्वीक्षिकीं चात्मविघां वार्तारम्भांश्च लोकतः।।

Gradually, the term bifurcated itself into philosophy and logic. ईक्षा means 'to see' like 'darśana'. But अन्वीक्षा is 'what follows the perception, viz., the inference' which is the backbone of logic. This is how Nīlakaṇṭha, a commentator on the epic, derives the term while explaining a verse in the Śāntiparvan (Mokshadharma, ch. 180 v. 47):

ईक्षा प्रत्यक्षं तामनुप्रवृत्ता ईक्षा अन्वीक्षा धूमादिदर्शनेन वह्न्याद्यनुमानं तत्प्रधानां आन्वीक्षिकीं तर्कविद्यां कणभक्षाक्षचणादिप्रणीतंशास्त्रम्।

His interpretation, of course, is not without reason. The episode is of Indra in the form of a jackal saying to sage Kāśyapa that he has been reduced to this plight due to a curse for over-indulgence in arguments just for the sake of argument and not with any sincere motive to arrive at the truth:

अहं आसं पण्डितको हैतुको वेदनिन्दकः।
आन्वीक्षिकीं तर्कविद्यां अनुरक्तो निरर्थिकाम्।।
हेतुवादान् प्रवदिता वक्ता संसत्सु हेतुमत्।
आक्रोष्टा चाभिवक्ता च ब्रह्मवाक्येषु च द्विजान्।।
नास्तिकः सर्वशंकी च मूर्खः पण्डितमानिकः।
तस्येयं फलनिर्वृत्तिः सृगालत्वं मम द्विज।।

(Śāntiparvan, 180. 47-49)

It is evident that Ānvīkshikī here refers to Nyāya and Vaiśeshika as propounded by Akshacharaṇa or Akshapāda, i.e. Gautama and Kaṇabhakshaṇa or Kaṇabhuj, i.e. Kaṇāda respectively. These two sages wrote the sūtras or aphorisms which became the source-book for the respective systems. Gautama is variously known as Gotama, Medhātithi, Dīrghatapas or Dīrghatamas and Akshapāda. Apart from being a generic name, Gotama is a Vedic *ṛishi*, son of Rahūgaṇa and a composer of a few Ṛigvedic hymns. Dīrghatamas appears as a Vedic sage (*ṚV.*, 1. 158, 4-5), a son of Uchathya and Mamatā. Due to Bṛihaspati's curse, he was born blind and much later the vision was restored by the gods. The *Mahābhārata* which has a flair for etymology, explains the word Gotama as one whose effulgence removes the darkness:

गोभिः तमो मम ध्वस्तं जातमात्ररय देहतः।

(Anuśāsanaparvan, 62)

There are verses in *Mahābhārata* identifying Gautama with Medhātithi:

मेधातिथिः महाप्राज्ञः गौतमः तपसि स्थितः।

(Śāntiparvan, 266.11)

Bhāsa, a pre-Kālidāsa dramatist refers to the Nyāyaśāstra of Medhātithi:

भोः साङ्गोपांङ्ग वेदम धीये मानवीयं धर्मशास्त्रं,
माहेश्वरं योगशास्त्र . . . मेधातिथेः न्यायशास्त्रम्

(*Pratimānāṭaka*, V, p. 79)

The *Mahābhārata* states that one should not discuss Vedānta with such a person who is bent upon mere arguments, the *Tārkika*:

स्नातकानामिदं शास्त्रं वाच्यं पुत्रानुशासनं।
न तर्कशास्त्रदग्धाय तथैव पिशुनाय च।।

(Śāntiparvan, 246. 18)

The Upanishads, which stress upon reaching the Ultimate Truth by resorting consistently to one means, abhor over-indulgence in arguments where one may miss the end for the means: नैषा तर्केण मतिरापनेया says the *Kaṭhopanishad*.

Vyāsa is identified with Bādarāyaṇa, the author of the *Brahmasūtra* which enshrines the Vedānta.

Such verses are said to be veiled sarcastic remarks about Nyāya. Such remarks are found in the *Rāmāyaṇa*:

धर्मशास्त्रेषु मुख्येषु विद्यमानेषु दुर्बुधाः।
बुद्धिमान्वीक्षिकीं प्राप्य निरर्थं प्रवदन्ति ते।।

(*Rāmāyaṇa*, Ayodhyā, 100.39)

There is a legendary story of a counter vilification of Vyāsa who prostrated before Gautama and would not get up unless he is looked at by the latter not with his natural eyes but with a new pair of eyes in the feet. Another story is that Gautama, who was so much absorbed in philosophical contemplation that he fell into a well. God provided him with another pair of eyes in his feet to prevent such mishaps. These stories are just attempts at explaining the name 'Akshapāda'. But notwithstanding this, Ākshapādī refers to the Nyāya system.

The very first mention of the Nyāya is found in the Ādiparvan (I.67) of the epic:

न्यायशिक्षा चिकित्सा च दानं पाशुपतं तथा।
हेतुनैव समं जन्म दिव्यामानुषसंज्ञितम्।।

Though the word Nyāya is understood elsewhere as referring to "right", "method", "analogy" or "maxim", the epic uses it here only in the sense of Logic. There are many verses in the epic to prove it. For instance:

न्यायतन्त्राण्यनेकानि तैस्तैरुक्तानि वादिभिः।
हेत्वागमसदाचारैः यदुक्तं तदुपास्यताम्।।

(Śāntiparvan, 210. 22)

Even the Lord is referred to as Nyāya in the *Vishṇusahasranāma*:

अग्रणीः ग्रामणीः श्रीमान् न्यायो नेता समीरणः।

Explaining this, Ānandagiri, the commentator, says that the Lord can be understood through the means of Nyāya and hence is himself called Nyāya.

प्रमाणानुग्राहकस्तर्को न्यायः। तदनुगृहीतप्रमाणगम्यो भगवानपि न्यायशब्दने . . . प्रतिपाद्यते। निश्चितं ईयते निर्णीयतेऽनेन करणे घञ्च् इति न्यायः।

It is not just the occurrence in the epic of a few words of the names of the system and of its author that makes the systems' link with the epic pronounced. Many concepts had found their way into the descriptions inadvertently. For instance, when king Dushyanta entered into the hermitage of sage Kaṇva on the banks of river Mālinī, he could hear the chanting of the four Vedas in the different rendition of Saṁhitā, Pada and Krama. Mention is made in this context of the grammarians, the astrologers, the materialists, the philosophers, the experts who could understand the language of birds, and the Vaiśeshikas. The adjectives used to refer to the logicians are indeed significant.

न्यायतत्त्वात्मविज्ञानसम्पन्नैः वेदपारगैः।
नानावाक्यसमाहारसमवायविशारदैः।।
विशेषकार्यविदिभ्श्च, मोक्षधर्मपरायणैः।
स्थापनाक्षेपसिद्धान्तपरमार्थज्ञतां गतैः।
द्रव्यकर्मगुणज्ञैश्च कार्यकारणवेदिभिः।।

(Ādi., 79. 37-41)

The terms स्थापना, आक्षेप and सिद्धान्त are pointers to the very methodology adopted in every Nyāya-Vaiśeshika text, viz., the proposition of the theory, the objections raised or the *prima facie* views, पूर्वपक्षः and the establishment of the theory by disproving the objection raised by the opponent. Further, many technical terms of this canon, like Samavāya, Viśesha, Dravya, Karma, Guṇa, Kārya, Kāraṇa, etc. are also met with.

In the Sabhāparvan (V. 3-5), there is a description of sage Nārada who is well-versed in many systems of philosophy:

न्यायवित धर्मतत्त्वज्ञः षडंङ्ग विदनुत्तमः।
ऐक्यसंयोगनानात्वसमवायविशारदः।।
पञ्चावयवयुक्तस्य वाक्यस्य गुणदोषवित्।
उत्तरोत्तरवक्ता च वदतोऽपि बृहस्पतेः।।
धर्मार्थकाममोक्षेषु यथावत् कृतनिश्चयः।।

Among the many significant terms, here is the word पञ्चावयववाक्य. It is an obvious reference to, nay, even a prerogative of the Nyāya system which is popularly known as the five-member syllogism. It consists of Pratijñā (Proposition), Hetu (Reason), Udāharaṇa

(Example), Upanaya (Application) and the Nigamana (Deduction or Conclusion).

Regarding the Vaiśeshika elements in the epic, it has to be said that there is no mention of the name of Kaṇāda. But the concept of atom whence the name Kaṇāda for the system, is referred to in the epic:

Aṇumātreṇa Vapushā (Mahābhārata, V. 16. 12)
Aṇu vā yadi vā sthūlam (Ibid., XII. 8. 16)

The word 'Nihśreyasa' is used in many places in the epic to mean Moksha. For e.g. *Ihanihśreyasam prāhuch vṛddhāḥ niśchitadarśanāḥ* (*Mbh.* V. 63.9)

The word, in fact, is frequently used in the Nyāya-Vaiśeshika system. In the latter it appears in the very second Sūtra:

Yato 'bhyudaya-nihśreyasa-siddhiḥ sa dharmaḥ

The word Vaiśeshika itself is found in a few verses of the epic:

Vishaye vartamānānāṁ yaṁ te Vaiśeshikaiḥ guṇaiḥ
Prāhur vishayagoptāraṁ tasmai goptrātmane namaḥ
(*Mbh.,* XII. 47. 71)

Further, the striking similarity of ideas in the epic and the Vaiśeshika draws our attention as in the following:

Hīnādādeyamādau syād samānāt tadanantaram
Asambhave vādadīta viśishṭādapi dhārmikāt
(*Mbh.,* XII. 141. 39-40)

Etena hīna-sama-viśishṭa-dhārmikebhyaḥ parasvādānam vyākhyātam

(*Vaiśeshika-sutra,* VI. 1. 15)

It is said that Kaṇāda got his name because of his theory that the gross matter originated from the atom, *aṇu* or *kaṇa*. There is also a traditional story that the sage lived a very austere life, eating the grains fallen of their own accord on the ground, just like a pigeon. Another verse tells us that one should not find fault with what others eat, but should imbibe the best in their words:

Kaṇān vā bhakshayatvānyaḥ māhishāni dadhīni vā
Yuktiyuktaṁ vacho grāhyaṁ

The *Mahābhārata* advocates simplicity of life, even eating the grains like a pigeon:

Asvastano' tha kāpotīmāśrito vṛittimāharet

The *Bhagavadgītā* statement that *jñāna* leads to the cessation of action is in agreement with the Nyāya-Vaiśeshika view:

Jñānāgniḥ sarva-karmāṇi bhasmasāt kurute yathā

(*Gītā*, IV. 37)

Padārtha-tattva-jñānād eva nihśreyasābhigamah, jñānādeva tu kaivalyam iti uktatvāt

Tarkasaṅgrahadīpikā, p. 67 (Bombay Sanskrit and Prakrit Series, 1963)

It is, hence, beyond doubt that many concepts of the twin-system in their earlier stages can be discerned in the *Mahābhārata*.

NOTES AND REFERENCES

S.C. Vidyabhusana, *History of Indian Logic*, Motilal Banarsidass, Delhi, 1978.

Mahābhārata, Oriental Books Reprinting Corporation, Delhi, 1979.

S.C. Vidyabhusana, *Nyāyaśāstra* of Gotama, Calcutta.

Vaiśeshikasūtram, Ed. Muni Sri Jambuvijayagi, Gaekward Oriental Series, No. 136, Baroda, 1961.

Rāmāyaṇa, Nirnaya Sagar Press, Mumbai, 1888.

Tarkasangrahadīpikā, Bombay Sanskrit and Prakrit Series, No. LV, 1963.

16

The Pañcharātra Cult in the Śāntiparvan of the *Mahābhārata*

Susmita Pande

The Pañcharātra cult in the Nārāyaṇīya section of the Śāntiparvan emerges as a great universal religion of love with deep spiritual humanism and an enlightened monotheism which had the Upanishadic monism in its background. Its concepts of *bhakti*, *avatāravāda* and *vyūhas* incorporated the different levels of spiritual experience and helped the devotee in his cognitive intention of spiritual reality on the one hand and in the self-expression of the divine since he is regarded as immanent in the individual.

But the above views could not be accepted by the pre-independence historians of India whose views were blindly repeated by the post-independence historians. The views which have shaped the historiography of Indian religions rest on the belief that religions in India in the pre-Christian ages consisted of only mythological stories, poetic fancies and ritualistic superstitions as in the Vedic religion, or of atheistic system of morality as in Buddhism. The principal virtue of early Indian religions has been seen in its exemplification of historical evolution.

Some of the post-independence historians like D.D. Kosambi and S.A. Dange have seen the growth of different religious sects in India more in the light of social theories than in the light of social history. Vaishṇavism has suffered most in the light of the above views. Kosambi had concluded that the *Gītā* is a mass of confusion and that the Kṛishṇa saga is a conglomeration of several heterogeneous elements mingled together into a harmonious whole.[1] Hence the history of Vaishṇavism was always regarded as a patchwork of different isolated myths and rituals and different types of gods, Vedic and tribal, who by some quirk of fate were fused into one. The element of myth, ritual, and belief were seen to arise out of given social or environmental conditions in accordance with certain primitive modes of thought.

Hopkins had turned the Śāntiparvan and Anuśāsanaparvan as pseudo-epic without any genuine logic or historical facts. Sudhakar Chattopadhyaya had assigned the Nārāyaṇīya section of the Śāntiparvan to the earlier centuries of the Christian era. This view has been examined further below and it seems to be based totally on imaginative reconstruction rather than proven historical data. But since most of the scholars have repeated this point of view, it has seriously affected the historiography of Vaishṇavism and the history of religious facts. What is more, Winternitz opined that Kṛishṇa did not figure in the original epic.[2] Oldenberg, Jacobi, Eliot and others regarded Kṛishṇa as an intrusion in the original story. Hopkins had called the *Bhagavadgītā* also an interpolation which he felt, was unnecessary to prove.

It is pity that the views of Hopkins which regard Śāntiparvan as a later addition, have been repeated blindly by scholars without examining the logic of his arguments. The greatest scholar on the *Mahābhārata*, V.S. Sukthankar, opposed this view, saying that it is no more interpolation than the epic nucleus. The nuclear epic theme and the intrusive didactive interlude are just two aspects in different mediums of one and the same central idea, quite consciously and deliberately expressed in two different ways. He opines that the interpolation of Āraṇyaka, Śānti and the Anuśāsana Parvans will be seen to have a vital function to perform and must be regarded as performing an integral part of the original poem in its received form which in fact is the only form known to us and of which we can be sure. It will thus be realized that not a single line of the didactic matter is lacking in purpose and in organic connection with the whole.[3]

Most of the scholars opine that the *Mahābhārata* has a composite texture formed by strands belonging to several different historical ages. Scholars have dispensed with lines, passages, chapters and even whole books of the *Mahābhārata* in order to get the epic nucleus. But Sukthankar has taken a very rational view that the mere process of stripping off what we regard as spurious, will not automatically leave us with the unalloyed original. Our hypothetical nucleus maybe just a projection of our own subjective feelings. Hence he suggests that it is much better if we concentrate on the inner meaning of the epic that is available in its present form.[4]

The other problem which faces us in writing an account of religion in the *Mahābhārata* is that some of its passages believed to be genuine by tradition have been omitted in the critical edition, e.g. the celebrated prayer of Draupadī to Kṛishṇa when Duḥśāsana tries to strip off her garments, is a notable omission but it has been traditionally accepted through the ages. This parvan was edited by F. Edgerton. It should be noted that Sukthankar in his lectures which formed the text of *On the Meaning of the Mahābhārata* has also given readings which are not incorporated in the text of the critical edition and has used and relied on the vulgate for the purpose of his lectures.[5]

The danger with the modern tendency for the search of the epic nucleus by our analytic adventures is that what we get may not be the original we are looking for but merely a projection of our own feelings. In a recent book on Vaishṇavism (ed. by Steven J. Rosen), Alf Hilitebeitel of the George Washington University has also supported the views of Sukthankar and concludes that to try and read beyond the text to prior stages is risky and speculative.[5a] Instead of discovering the inner and the deep cultural values reflected in the epic, the historians look for 'the lost paradise of the primitive kshatriya tale of love and war for which most of the western savants had been mainly searching and which the Indian people had long outgrown and discarded'. Even if the nucleus was the heroic poem only, why should it be presumed that it was totally divorced from the ethical and religious elements. The *pāriplava ākhyānas* formed an intrinsic part of the Aśvamedha sacrifice. Hence the secular and religious were not segregated. The attainments of the worldly assets, spiritual knowledge and communion with the gods, all went together. Hence to assume that a purely secular epic was brāhmaṇized later with brāhmaṇical philosophy, ethics and brāhmaṇical law, is arbitrary.[6]

The age of the *Mahābhārata* was an age of transition when the old aristocratic and ritual order yielded place to a new order in which lawless tyranny, social miscegenations, religious scepticism and heterodoxy were emerging as significant features, people were confused about the perennial law and the law of the age, between *pravṛitti* and *nivṛitti*, between *karma* and *naishkarmya*. These concepts are reconciled in the Pañcharātra doctrine of the

Mahābhārata by the doctrine of *bhakti* which was emerging as the highest religio-philosophical ideal and which synthesized ultimately the diverse traditions of the age. Similarly the myths in the *Mahābhārata* should not be regarded as purely fanciful or representing mere contemporary social or historical background, but they represent the perennial truth and the true ethos of Indian culture. Hence there is a logic of their being interwoven into the main story. This brings to mind the opinion of A.N. Jani that some passages were contributed by local temple priests who inculcated the local myths connected with particular holy places dedicated to Śiva and Vishṇu into the text. Here we must remember that it is modern thought which suffers from ethnocentric tendency that makes distinctions between tribal or higher religions, not the traditional history. It is true that the *Mahābhārata* amalgamates the Vedic, Āgamic and tribal traditions but this amalgamation is of common ideals permeating all the different levels of civilization and culture and not the inculcation of primitive norms into the sophisticated spheres. If the second alternative is believed, it should be remembered that ideas get transformed in different cultural contexts. This is especially true when Sudhakar Chattopadhyaya and other scholars say that the worship of Vāsudeva and other Vṛishṇi chiefs was the result of the hero worship of these tribal chiefs. This phase led to the emergence of the non-Vedic or non-brāhmaṇic Pañcharātra sect. These heroes were apotheosized and identified with the Vedic god Vishṇu. Now this is a very strange hypothesis, because there are no other historically parallel instances of such a phenomenon anywhere else. Ancient thought clearly distinguishes between gods and heroes. Heroes maybe godlike and semi-divine in origin. Respect and homage maybe paid to them, they maybe eulogized and glorified, but they are always different from the unborn and immortal gods who have no individual personality but are omnipresent. Besides, there is no proof that *vyūhavāda* is a late doctrine. *Vyūhavāda* is an emanatory doctrine which formed the crux of the Āgamic systems. According to it, the supreme reality is a projectional modification from the subtle to the gross. The same idea is reflected in the *Gītā* when Kṛishṇa says *Vṛishṇinām̐ Vāsudevo'smi* and identifies the *saṅkhyānatattvas* as his *Prakṛiti*.[7] Since the *Gītā* was mostly concerned with establishing the theory of *avatāravāda*, *vyūhavāda* could only find a stray reference here. But in the Śāntiparvan, ch. 326, the identification of the *vyūhas* with the *saṅkhyānatattvas* is very explicit.[8] But yet it is said that those who go beyond the worship of Aniruddha, Saṅkarshaṇa and Pradyumna and worship only Vāsudeva with *ananyā bhakti* acquire *paramapada*.[9] It is a repetition of the idea of the *Gītā* where the lord says that the devotee can worship him in any form but the highest level of spiritual experience is attained by the worship of Vāsudeva.[10] I have argued in many papers that *vyūhavāda* was of a very early date.[11]

Recently I came across the views of Dennis Hudson of Smith College who is also of the same opinion. In his article "Vraja Among Tamils" he has said that rather than assuming that the five Vṛishṇi heroes had been fused with a four *vyūha* doctrine from another tradition (that of Nārāyaṇa), the evidence suggests instead that the story of the Vṛishṇi heroes was intended to illustrate the *vyūha* doctrine. Their stories depict narratively the operation of *vyūhas* in the lines of Bhāgavata Sādhakas.[11a]

Another argument of Sudhakar Chattopadhyaya for regarding Śāntiparvan as late is that Pañcharātra sub-sect developed out of inspiration from the Mahāyāna Buddhism of Central Asia and hence the Nārāyaṇīya section of the *Mahābhārata* is of the early centuries of the Christian era. He identifies Meru with Pāmīr where the Pañcharātra code was formulated. This, he says, is possible only in the Kushaṇa age when Central Asia was in the empire of Kanishka. But as we all know and V.S. Agrawala has rightly pointed out that the concept of Meru was a complex idea involving not only geographical but religious and cultural connotations. According to the Bhuvanakosa, Mount Meru is the centre of the Earth forming the pericarp of the four-petalled lotus – Bhadrāśva, Jambūdvīpa, Ketumāla and Uttarakuru which are not only geographic divisions but are also cultural territories with religious significance. Meru is similar to Prajāpati having four faces, viz., eastern which is white having brāhmaṇical virtues, southern being yellow indicating vaiśyas, western being black of śūdras and northern being red of kshatriyas.[12]

The origin and development of the Pañcharātra is shrouded in mystery. Here Pañcharātra is connected with Nārāyaṇa who is said to have performed a Pañcharātra *sattra*. Later on the Pañcharātra texts like the *Īśvarasaṁhitā* connect themselves with the Ekāyana branch of the Vedas.[13] The *Chhāndogya Upanishad* also mentions this *vidyā* though does not specify it. But this *vidyā* is connected with Nārada and in the *Mahābhārata,* Nārada is considered as the worshipper and propounder of the Pañcharātra doctrine. An ancient writer Nāgeśa says that the Kāṇva branch of the *Yajurveda* was known as *Ekāyana* branch. The *ṛishis* connected with the Pañcharātra are said to belong to the Kāṇva branch.[14] It has also been pointed out that Utpalācharya of Kashmir (10th century AD) mentions the *Pañcharātra Śruti* and *Pañcharātra Upanishad* and that it is possible that the *Pañcharātra Śruti* existed till this time and it might have been that of the Ekāyana branch,[15] which would give a Vedic orthodoxy to the Pañcharātra. Tarapada Bhattacharya has opined that the *Mahābhārata* in the original form was perhaps a Saptarātra cult of Brahmā. According to him, *rātra* means *tanu* or body of Brahmā after he gave up his life after creation. The *rātra* cult was pre-Vedic and it was the worship of the elements (five, seven, or nine).[15a]

Here it can be said that though various cults were developing from the Vedic age, there was still a transparency about the concept of Gods and the Upanishadic idea of Gods as the powers of Brahman prevailed largely (*Kena Upanishad,* IV. 205).

In fact all the personalities of the Vedic religion manifest as the characters of *Mahābhārata* and the whole Vedic pantheon is reactivated in the story. So the *Mahābhārata* is tied into the Vedic tradition.

Sudhakar Chattopadhyaya opines that the Nārāyaṇīya section of the *Mahābhārata* is in agreement with the Vedas and was composed in Kushaṇa times. It also shows Mahāyāna influence. The non-Vedic Pañcharātra was composed after the days of the Kushaṇas and Śāṇḍilya was its founder.[16] Śaṅkarāchārya had specially condemned the anti-Vedicism of Śāṇḍilya.[17]

The Purāṇas are also divided in their opinion regarding the acceptability of the Pañcharātra cult. The *Vishṇu, Nārada, Bhāgavata, Garuḍa, Padma* and *Varāha* which are called *Sāttvika Purāṇas* and are purely Vaishṇava in character, accept it while the *Kūrma, Skanda, Sāmba, Bṛihannaradīya, Liṅga* and *Agni Purāṇas* and *Sūta Saṁhitā* criticize this doctrine.

A glimpse of the later sectarian position of Vaishnavism could help in determining the earlier simplicity of the Pañcharātra cult of the *Mahābhārata.* Describing the detailed structure of the later sectarianism is not within the purview of the present paper.

The specific branches of Vaishṇavism are described in *Vishṇu*

Saṁhitā as Vaikhānasa, Sāttvata, Ekāntika, Śikhin and Mūla. Scholars believe that Ekāntika and Śikhin were branches of the Sāttvata doctrine. Those who worshipped only Vāsudeva were Ekāntins and those who worshipped other members of the *vyūha* were Śikhins. The Śāntiparvan (336.3) also explains the Ekāntikas as those who worship only Vāsudeva and not the *vyūhas*. The Mūlas, i.e. Pañcharātrikas worshipped Nārāyaṇa with his three associates – Nṛisimha,Varāha and Kapila. Vishṇu was worshipped according to the Vaikhānasa Agamas along with Purusha, Satya, Achyuta and Aniruddha. Later on Vāsudeva with his *vyūhas* became a prominent deity of the Pañcharātrikas and the associates of Nārāyaṇa assumed on the basis of Jayākhya Saṁhitā—Nṛisimha, Varāha and Kapila must have been amalgamated as the *vibhava* form of the Lord.[18]

A detailed analysis of the Vaikhānasa and Pañcharātra sects of the later age shows that while the Vaikhānasa Āgamas were more in keeping with the Vedic views, the Pañcharātrikas were more flexible in their outlook. It seems that the Vaikhānasa tradition arose with tradition of retiring to the forests to meditate on the inner and esoteric meaning of sacrifices rather than mere complicated ritual. *Bhakti* was a natural outcome of this tendency as they saw a continuation in the different levels of reality *ādhiyajña, ādhidaivata* and *adhyātma,* which resulted in a rich emotional experience of *bhakti*. This tradition lays importance on the various penances for the worship of Vishṇu.

The Pañcharātrikas tradition had seven sects according to the *Brahmāṇḍa Purāṇa*, viz. Brāhmā, Śaiva, Kaumāra, Vāśishṭha, Kāpila, Śaunakeya and Nārada.[19] The *Kūrma Purāṇa* also says that the Pañcharātra tantra was made to project the people regarded as Vedabāhya. This was done by taking the inspiration from the Śaivas.[20]

The *Kūrma Purāṇa* also says that this tradition was for the illegitimate children and like कुंडगोलादिभिः श्रुतः, i.e. it was liberal in its attitude and everybody had access to it. The Pañcharātra-rakshā of Vedantadeśika distinguishes Pañcharātra into Mantra, Āgama, Tantra and Tantrāntara branches and it has been suggested that Tantrāntara was the original Pañcharātra and that it was difficult to define distinction among all the Vaishṇava sects.

The fully developed Pañcharātra system believed in the six supernatural qualities of the Lord (*jñāna, bala, aiśvarya, vīrya, śakti* and *tejas*), fivefold manifestations of the Lord (*Para, Vyūha, Vibhava, Antaryāmin* and *Arcan*), sixfold functions of the Lord (*Tirodhāna, Śṛishṭi, Sthiti, Vināśa, Nigraha* and *Anugraha*), the six stages of the doctrines of grace (*anukūlāsya saṁkalpa, pratikūlasya varjanaṁ, rakshishyati viśvasya, goptṛitva-vāraṇaṁ, ātma-nikshepa* and *kārpaṇya*).

Although the *Jayākhya Saṁhitā* has divided the Pañcharātra Vaishṇavas into three groups, it is not very clear about the nature of their differences, the various methods of worshipping Vishṇu, the extent of their renunciation, etc. The meaning of the name Vaikhānasa pertains to *ṛishi* and to the third *āśrama*. Vikhanasa was one of the *āchāryas* and his name is also another name of Brahmā and in the Nārāyaṇīya section it is Brahmā who emerges out of Nārāyaṇa first and preaches this doctrine to various *ṛishis*.

But if we read the Nārāyaṇīya section carefully it would be obvious that it shows the early stage of the religion of *bhakti* where there were no sectarian differences. It really was a generic term for all the Vaishṇava tendencies. The section expounds the doctrine of the *vyūhas* as well as speaks of the Vaikhānasa *ṛishis* as belonging to the same tradition. In the Vaikhānasa tradition after Nārāyaṇa comes Vikhanasa, then Kāśyapa then Marīchi. In the Pañcharātra tradition also, Marīchi is one of the seven *chitra śikhaṇḍi ṛishis* who spread this Śāstra.

It is mentioned clearly in ch. 336 of Śāntiparvan that the religion of *ekāntika bhakti* was followed by phenapa *ṛishis* who transmitted this to the Vaikhānasa *munis*. Still later on Valakhilya *ṛishis* obtained this. In a verse[21] of the same chapter it is also stated to have been related to the Barhishad *munis*. In the *Vaikhānasa Dharmasūtras*, the Vaikhānasa are divided into Audumbara, Vairiñcha, Vālakhilya and Phenapa. All these can go to the forest, with their wives. The *Bṛihatparāśara* (ch. 11) also mentions these. Although in the beginning of the chapter it is said that the Ekāntikas are better than mere followers of *yatidharma*, i.e. *vānaprasthins* who recite the Vedas and Upanishads meticulously. Hence it seems that the cult already incorporated diverse tendencies within it. The elements of the later Smārta Vaishṇavas can also be seen here as it is said that Brahmā passed this *dharma* to Rudra (336-15) and Rudra and Nārāyaṇa are one:

रूद्रो नारायणश्चैव सत्वमेकं द्विधाकृतम् ।
लोके चरति कौन्तेव व्यक्तिरथं सर्वकर्मस ॥

Śānti, 328.24.

Another important feature of the cult was that it claims to comprise of the issue of four Vedas, Sāṅkhya, Yoga and Āraṇyakas.

एवमेकं सांख्ययोगं वेदारण्यकमेव च ।
परस्परायान्येतानि पाञ्चरात्र च कथ्यते
एष एकान्तिनां धर्मो नाराणपरात्मकः । 336.76

The *dharma* is propounded in each *yuga* by Nārāyaṇa to Brahmā, Sanatkumāra is also associated with it. The chapter further connects the cult with the *Sāmaveda* as the Brāhmaṇa Jyeshṭhā of this lineage acquired it from *Bārhishada munis*.

The Śāntiparvan mentions the Sāṅkhyan *tattvas* as various levels of reality, the highest being Vāsudeva. The classical Sāṅkhyan duality is not accepted. Vāsudeva is regarded as the highest twenty-fifth *tattva*; the Purusha who is *nirguṇa, nishkala* and *nishparigraha* and pervades the entire world.[22] He is also the *guru* of the world.[23] Vāsudeva is *kshetrajña* or *ātman*, Saṅkarshaṇa is *jīvā*, Pradyumna is *manas* and Aniruddha is *ahaṁkāra*. Brahmā emerges from him and then the entire creation. Hence two levels of creation are visualized here as in all the Āgamic systems – pure and impure. The acceptance of Sāṇkhyanā *tattvas* as the various levels of reality with the highest being God was seen in the various Upanishads, e.g. *Śvetaśvatara* and *Kaṭhā*. The Yoga was utilized in transcending these levels of existences. It is said in the Śāntiparvan that all moving and stationary objects in the world '*sadasat*', *jīvā* and *prakṛiti* are really created by Vāsudeva.[24]

It is said that the earth is absorbed in water, water in fire, fire in air, air in *ākāśa, ākāśa* in *manas, manas* in *avyakta* and *avyakta* in *nishkriya purusha*.[25] This reminds us of the similar passage in the *Kaṭhopanishad*. Hence the theory of emanation is combined with the Sāṅkhya principles which are used to secure the end of such a monothesim as has in its background the Upanishadic monism. All the gods are treated as aspects of Nārāyaṇa. The *virāṭa rūpa* shown by the Lord in the Śāntiparvan also illustrates the same idea.

The most important aspect of the Pañcharātra is its philosophy of *bhakti* which is propounded in the Śāntiparvan. In fact some of the modern scholars[25a] have begun to believe that the central teaching of the *Mahābhārata* is *bhakti*. As a means it is regarded as serving or worshipping the divine with the help of names and forms. As an end it is a loving communion with the divine person. The first has the sense of serving the Lord in the sense of the root *bhaj* and the second of sharing the root *bhaj*. Both the senses are illustrated here. *Bhakti* is of the nature of *ekantika* or *ananya*. The *mokshadharmaparvan* of Śāntiparvan illustrates this idea by the story of Vasu Uparichara. Vasu Uparichara was a friend of Indra and a devotee of Nārāyaṇa, who had taken birth on the earth due to the curse of the gods as he had interpreted "बीजैर्यज्ञेषु यष्टव्यमिति" as the performance of Yajñas by herbs and not by goat and he had thus supported the *ṛishis*. He worshipped Nārāyaṇa according to the Sāttvata *vidhi*.[26] And the Pañcharātrikas received food and offering first in his court.[27] The *Pañcharātra śāstra* was created by seven chitraśikhaṇḍin *ṛishis* – Marichi, Atri, Aṅgiras, Pulastya, Pulaha, Kratu and Vasishṭha. The śāstra was unique as it was both for *pravṛitti* and *nivṛitti* for the sake of mankind.

इदं शतसहस्त्रं हि लोकानामिदमुत्तमम् ।
लोकतंत्रस्य कृंत्सनस्य यस्माद्धर्मः प्रवर्तते ॥
प्रवृतौ निवृत्तों च योनिरेतद् भविष्यति ।
ऋृग्यजुःसामभिर्जुष्टमथर्वाङ्गिः रसैस्तथा ॥

Śānti, 322.36

Reconciliation between the Vedic ideas of *pravṛitti* and Śramaṇa ideas of *nivṛitti* was the problem of the age and the two have been reconciled by saying that neither was this world shuning *nivṛitti* nor *pravṛitti* in the sense of running after the worldly goods. It is distinguished from *pravṛitti-lakshaṇa* and has a new concept of *nivṛitti*. It is said to be the basis of both *pravṛitti* and *nivṛitti dharma*.

The myth of saving the Vedas has this significance, i.e. rescuing the Vedic religion from deteriorating into pure ritualism and pursuit of worldly ends which is illustrated by the Hayagrīva-*avatāra* episode.[28] This *ekantika bhakti* of the sāttvata tradition was prevalent in all *kalpas* and reverted back to Nārāyaṇa at the end of each *kalpa*. Its origin is connected with the *Samaveda*, *Ṛigveda* and *Araṇyaka-Rahasya* and *Saṅgraha*. It was devoted to *ahiṁsā* and egalitarianism.

Uparichara is said to have performed a sacrifice for which his guru was Bṛihaspati and Ekata, Dvita and Trita were the chief *śadasyas*. Bṛihaspati could not get a vision of Nārāyaṇa as he got violent. Ekata, Dvita and Trita could not get his vision as they had performed very difficult penances. Only Vasu Uparichara could get his *darśana* as he was devoted to *ahiṁsā* and *nishkāma karma.*[29]

Ekata, Dvita and Trita went to Śvetadvīpa where they saw many people engaged in *mānasajapa* who saw Nārāyaṇa but Ekata, Dvita and Trita blinded by his light could not see him properly. They were told that he reveals his form to only those who worship him with *ananya bhakti*[30] and he reveals his form to those for whom he shows his grace[31]. Nārada could get his *darśana* in Śvetadvīpa because of his *ekāntika bhakti.*[32] He could see his *Viśvarūpa* too. Constant remembrance of Nārāyaṇa is also prescribed.

तांस्त्वं भजस्व सततं साधयस्व यथागतम्।

The Śāntiparvan enumerates various *avatāras* as Varāha, Nṛisiṁha, Vāmana, Paraśurāma, Dāśarathi Rāma, Kṛishṇa, Nara, Nārāyaṇa, Haṁsa and Hayashirsha. All these perform deeds for the welfare of the people लोकार्याणि कृत्वा च पुनः स्वां प्रकृतिं गतां। (326-94). Varāha synthesizes the idea of *yajña, avatāra* and worship[33]. Hayagrīva reformed the Vedic rituals.

Kṛishṇa is the highest *avatāra* who is beyond *Kshara* and *Akshara* and the recepient of all sacrifices. He is a multi-dimensional character who transforms the epic to transcendental heights. It was natural for Him to be identified with Vāsudeva, Vishṇu and Nārāyaṇa in the *Mahābhārata* as we shall see below. The *ṛiks* of Vishṇu has the elements of *bhakti* in the *Ṛigveda.* D.C. Sircar had seen non-Āryan elements of *bhakti* in them but it should be remembered that *bhakti* is a universal emotion which can sprout at anytime and place. Vishṇu was the god of righteousness who helped men in times of adversity and was identified with sacrifice. He was also connected with the dwarf and boar. All these elements connect him with the Vaishṇavas in the *Mahābhārata*. The essential bond between Vedic Vishṇu and cult god was constituted by the triple thread of righteousness, sacrifice and acting as saviour.

The views of R.P. Chandra and Suvira Jayaswal that Kṛishṇa of *Ṛigveda* was a non-Āryan chief does not hold ground. Griffith has rightly pointed out that the verse seems to refer to the aid which Indra renders his friend Soma pictured as dark moon against hostile forces.[34] Hence neither is he a non-Āryan chief nor a demon as Sāyaṇa has interpreted it. H.C. Raichaudhuri's view that Kṛishṇa of *Chhāndogya Upanishad* can be identified with the historical Kṛishṇa is tenable even though Kṛishṇa of the *Chhāndogya* was instructed by Ghora Aṅgirasa and of the *Mahābhārata* by Sāndipani. There have been innumerable examples in the Vedic age of people learning from many gurus like Janaka from Yājñavalkya and *vice versa*. Secondly, Ghora Aṅgirasa is not called Kṛishṇa's guru as such; he only instructed Kṛishṇa.

The name Pañcharātra occurs first in the *Śatapatha Brāhmaṇa* in connection with five great sacrifices. Suvira Jayaswal's[35] contention that Nārāyaṇa was a tribal deity who demanded human sacrifice flies in the face of the *Śatapatha Brāhmaṇa* which speaks of Nārāyaṇa as a seer. In the *Ṛigveda* also he is a seer. As to the Purushamedha, it was essentially a symbolic idea since the actual immolation and sacrifice of the victims was not required. Its root is to be found in the Purusha sūkta of the *Yajurveda*. The idea of sacrifice ultimately symbolized the idea of self-sacrifice. That any real human sacrifice was contemplated in the *Śatapatha Brāhmaṇa* is out of question as it is clear from the *Mahābhārata* that the essential feature of Bhāgavatism was non-violence.

Similarly the view of Farquhar regarding Saṅkarshaṇa, Pradyumna and Aniruddha as three different local divinities[36] who were brought together with Kṛishṇa to form a combined sect is conjectural. Saṅkarashaṇa is connected with snakes but snake-worship was a popular feature of Indian religious life. Many deities were associated with it. It did not mean that Saṅkarashaṇa was a totally separate deity. Similarly not regarding Pradyumna and Aniruddha as connected with Kṛishṇa would be disregarding traditional history.

Hence Kṛishṇa Vāsudeva or Nārāyana or Vishṇu of the *Mahābhārata* is not a fusion of different gods into one by some quirk of fate. In the Yānasandhiparvan (67) Dhṛitarāshṭra asks Sañjaya how he is able to see Kṛishṇa as supreme lord of the universe. Sañjaya answers that it was possible due to pure emotion which is achieved by *bhakti* and *śāstra* injunctions:[37]

शुद्धभावं गतो मक्त्या शास्त्राद्वेदि जनार्दनम्

Some other recent scholars now believe that there is no reason for believing that Kṛishṇa was gradually appointed by the late phase of Pañcharātra. If we look at the text objectively, it is obvious that he is not anything other than divinity. Kṛishṇa can be seen at a number of levels in the *Mahābhārata* but these levels are not historically emergent. They are levels in which the text is reflecting theology which is quite comprehensive. Kṛishṇa was known for his superhuman wisdom as a supreme Yogin who had reviewed the teaching of Yoga coming down from Vivasvat to Ikshvāku who had also realized his own identity with the supreme Godhead (Nārāyaṇa or Vishṇu) and who also realized that, being given a historical role, he was also an incarnation, and the extention of the Vedic notion of manifestation. This identification with *vyūha*s was in keeping with the Āgamic theory of emanation according to which the ultimate reality is more than the Quiscence of the absolute. He is a creative power who expressed himself in the universe.

Hence the Pañcharātra cult of the *Mahābhārata* shows a high watermark of monotheism with monoism in its background which regarded the ultimate reality as more than the numerical concept of one or many. It was the development of the quest of ethico-soteriological values of the age and also of an inner reformation of the Vedic ritualism which began in the middle Vedic period. This resulted in the compromise between *Pravṛitti* and *Nivṛitti*, *karma* and *naishkarmya*, sacrificial ritual and *bhakti* by developing *bhakti* and grace as the highest value.

Hence against the prevailing modern hypothesis of the *Mahābhāraṭa* being a haphazard patchwork spread over centuries is the traditional opinion which perceives the work as a unity though it admits that it was elaborated (*upabṛiṁh*) more than once. Ānandavaran and Shri Aurobindo had recognized the basic unity of the work even though *upabṛiṁhaṇa* superposed historical layers over the original poem. This basic unity is also reflected in the Pañcharātra cult of the Śāntiparvan.

Hence the Śāntiparvan of the *Mahābhārata* which has the Pañcharātra cult as a theme can be summarized as reflecting the amalgamation or rather the natural growth of the *advaitic* and monotheistic ideas of later Vedic age and Upanishads providing a metaphysical background to *bhakti*; secondly, it shows an essential unity of various visions of Vedic, Āgamic and tribal traditions; thirdly, the synthesis of Vedic tradition of *Pravṛitti* with Śramaṇic *Nivṛitti*. Fourthly, it provides the background of the metaphysical ideas of evolution, Upanishadic monotheism and monism and stereological ideas and the highest ethical social values of *Dharma*.

NOTES AND REFERENCES

In this paper the *Mahābhārata*, ed. Śūpārda Dāmodara Sātavalekar, Svādhāya Maṇḍal, Paradi (Gujarat), 1979, has been used.

1. Suvira Jayaswal, *The Origin and Development of Vaiṣṇavism*, p. 65. She has quoted Kosambi in support of this view.
2. M. Winternitz, *History of Indian Literature*, I, p. 457, Oldenberg, *Das Mahābhārata*, pp. 37, 43.
3. V.S. Sukthankar, *On the Meaning of the Mahābhārata*, pp. 85, 86.
4. *Ibid.*, p. 31.
5. G.C. Jhala, Introductory Note in the *On the Meaning of Mahābhārata*.

5a. Alf Hiltebeital, *Mahābhārata in Vaishṇavism: Contemporary Scholars Discuss the Gauḍīya Tradition*, p. 52. Also Susmita Pande, "Religious Movements in the *Mahābhārata*", *History of Indian Science, Philosophy and Culture*, Vol. 1. Part-II, Ed. G.C. Pande.

6. A.N. Jani, "The *Mahābhārata* as an Organic Growth of the Oral Literary Tradition in Ancient India", in *The Mahābhārata Revisited*, ed. R.N. Dandekar, p. 81.
7. Kṛishṇa identifies his *apara prakṛiti* with the five elements, *manas, buddhi* and *ahaṅkāra*.
   भूमिरापो ऽनलो वायु रवं मनो बुद्धिरेव च अहंकार इतीयं में भिन्ना प्रकृतिरष्टधा
8. In ch. 326 it is said that Vāsudeva is the *ātman* of all, Saṅkarashaṇa is his manifestation as *jīva*, Pradyumna *manas* and Aniruddha as *ahaṅkāra*.
9. Śānti, 336.3: चतुर्थ्यां चैव ते गत्यां गच्छन्ति पुरुषेत्तमम्
   एकान्तिनस्तु पुरुषा गच्छन्ति परमं पदम्
10. Gītā, VII-24.
11. I have argued that the *vyūha* doctrine was early in many papers as-
    (1) "Religious Movements in the *Mahābhārata*", *op. cit.*
    (2) "Kṛishṇa Kathā in the Vaishṇava Purāṇas" (Seminar on Purāṇas conducted by Vidya Niwas Misra in December 1998 at Varanasi).
    (3) "Historiography of Vaishṇavism" (Seminar on Historiography, Allahabad Museum).

11a. Dennis Hudson, "Vraja Among Tamils – A Study in the Bhāgavata Diaspora to *c.* 950 C.E.", p. 9 for "The continuing tradition of Vraja", Jan. 4-10, 1944 at the Seminar organized by Sri Chaitanya Prema Sansthan, Vrindavana.

12. V.S. Agrawala, *Matsya Purāṇa: A Study*, p. 185.
13. एष एकायनो वेदः प्रख्यातः सर्वतो भुवि
14. *Jayākhya Saṁhitā*, 6-109; also 6.116
15. Baladeva Upadhyaya, *Bhāgavata Sampradāya* (Hindi), pp. 115-22. He has quoted *Spanda Pradīpikā*, p. 99.

15a. Tarapada Bhattacharya, *The Cult of Brahmā*, Varanasi, 1969, p. 65.

16. Sudhakar Chattopadhyaya, *Evolution of Theistic Sects in Ancient India*, pp. 158-59.
17. According to Śaṅkara, only some portions of the Pañcharātra are in accordance with the Vedas, not all. He specially criticizes its views and says that *Jīva* cannot be created by *Paramātman* and believes that in the *Vyūha* doctrine Vāsudeva is *paramātman* and Saṅkarshaṇa *jīvātman*. For details, see Susmita Pande, *Birth of Bhakti in Indian Religions and Art*, p. 104.
18. V.S. Pathak, "The Early Vaishṇava Pantheon", *JUPHS*, 1951-52.
19. पञ्यरात्रं सण्तविधं ज्ञानिनां ज्ञानंदं परम् ।
    ब्राह्मं शैव्र च कौमारं वासिष्ठं कापिल परम् ।
    श्रैनकीयं नारदीयमिदं सण्तविधं स्मृतम् ॥
20. *Kūrma Purāṇa*, 16. 118-119:
    एवं सम्बोधितों रूद्रो माधवेन मुरारिणा ।
    चकार मोहशास्त्राणि केशवोऽपि शिवेरितः ॥
    कापालं नाकुलं वामं भैरवं पूर्वपश्चिमम् ।
    पञ्चरात्रं पाशुपतं तथान्यानि सहस्त्रशः ॥
    Vide also 16.117.
21. सहोपनिषदान्वेदान्ये विप्राः सम्यगास्थिताः ।
    पठन्ति विधिमास्याय ये चापि यतिधर्मिणः ॥ Śānti, 336.5

    तेम्यो विशिष्टां जानामि गतिमेकान्तिनां नृणाम् ।
    केनैष धर्मः कथितो देनेन ऋृषिणापि वा ॥ Śānti, 336.6
22. Śānti, 326.41-42.
23. *Ibid*. According to Sri Aurobindo, the real purpose of the *avatāra* is to act as the spiritual precepter.
24. Śānti, 326.40.
25. *Ibid.*, 326.29-30.

25a. Alf Hitebeital, *op.cit*.

26. Śānti, 322.19.
27. *Ibid.*, 322.24.
28. *Ibid.*, 335.
29. *Ibid.*, 323.
30. *Ibid.*, 336.66.
31. *Ibid.*, 336.70.
32. *Ibid.*, 326.70.
33. *Ibid.*, 333.11-12.
34. *Ṛigveda*, VIII 96.13.
    अव द्रत्सो अंशुमतीर्मति ठदियानः कृष्णों दशमिः सहस्त्रेः ।
    आवत्रमिन्द्रः शच्या धमन्तमप स्नेहितीर्नृमणा अधत्त ॥
35. Suvira Jayaswal, *op.cit.*, p. 35.
36. Alf Hitebetal, *op.cit.*
37. Susmita Pande, "Religious Movements in the Mahābhārata", in *History of Indian Science, Philosophy and Culture*, Vol. I, Pt. II, Ed. by Dr. G.C. Pande.

17

Yaksha Cult in the *Mahābhārata*

Chandrashekhar Gupta

Yakshas are described in the *Mahābhārata* as demi-gods (*upadevatā*) or a special type of god genius (*deva-yonī-viśesha*). They are supposed to have been born out of the huge cosmic egg (*virāṭa-aṇḍa*) soon after the birth of Brahmarshis, etc.[1] Along with the Yakshas, Piśāchas and Guhyakas are also described in this context and are called Yaksha in some places. It is said that Śukadeva had narrated the story of the epic to the Yakshas.[2]

Generally, Yaksha and Yakshī (Yakshiṇī) were of fair features and good complexion and a handsome man or a beautiful maiden at the first encounter was welcomed with an enquiry whether he/she was a Yaksha/Yakshiṇī.[3] The female associates of Damayantī, having sight of Nala, thought him to be either a god, Yaksha or Gandharva. Similarly, Damayantī was considered as a Yakshī or Rākshasī by the traders when she was left by Nala in the woods and was wandering in dirty appearance covered with half *sārī*.[4] Again, when the encamping caravan was attacked by the wild elephants in the night, the traders blamed her for the calamity calling her Rākshasī, Yakshī, Piśāchī and Bhayaṅkarī.[5] In another instance, Draupadī was questioned by Jayadratha through king Koṭika when he was seen in Kāmyaka vana. Astonished by her extreme beauty he asked her, whether she was a goddess, or Yakshī, or Dānavī or a demon maiden (*Daitya-varāṅganā*).[6] Thus, it is clear from these references that Yaksha-Yakshī had a beautiful as well as ferocious appearance like that of a demon.

Alternately, it may be suggested that Yakshas, etc., were well-versed in facelifting. Some also had ugly or strange-limbed bodies as some of their names suggest, e.g., Gaṇḍakaṇḍu, Gajakarṇa,

Varāhakarṇa, Śaṅkukarṇa.[7] Besides, a Yaksha is named Piśācha in the same list.[8] Some names illustrate their typical physical features, viz. Viśālaka (of huge appearance), Tāmroshṭha (whose lips are of copperish tinge), Hemanetra (of golden-hued eyes), Pushpānana (whose face resembles a flower), Piṅgalaka (of reddish complexion), etc.[9]

Yakshas were ruled by Kubera who was also known by various synonyms, viz. Vaiśravaṇa, Dhanada, Yaksharāṭ, Naravāhana, Dhanādhyaksha, Rājarāja, etc.[10] Kubera is also lord of the Rākshasas and the Guhyakas. Guhyaka is also a proper name of a Yaksha described in the list of the Yakshas attending Kubera-*sabhā*.[11] It is also used as a synonym of Yaksha in general. They are said to be carrying the Kubera-*sabhā* (*Guhyakairuhyamāna*).[12] Devas and Gandharvas are playing music[13] and the Apsarās are performing dances[14] in the Kubera-*sabhā*. Kinnara named Nara, is also present in the *sabhā*.[15] It is said that lakhs (*Śata-sahasra*) of Yakshas are attending the *sabhā* of Kubera, while actually only twenty-six are named.[16]

Maṇibhadro' tha Dhanadaḥ Śvetabhadraścha Guhyakaḥ /
Kaśerako Gaṇḍakaṇḍuḥ Pradyotaścha Mahābala // 15
Kustumbaruḥ Piśāchaścha Gajakarṇo Viśālakaḥ /
Varāhakarṇa Tāmroshṭhaḥ Phalakakshaḥ Phalodakaḥ // 16
Haṁsachūḍaḥ Śikhāvarto Hemanetro Vibhīshaṇaḥ /
Pushpānanaḥ Piṅgalakaḥ Śoṇitodaḥ Pravālakaḥ // 17
Vṛikshavāsyaniketaścha Chīravāsaścha Bhārata /
Ete Chānye Cha Bahavo Yakshāḥ Śatasahasraśaḥ // 18

Here, Maṇibhadra, Dhanada, Śvetabhadra, Guhyaka, Kośeraka, Gaṇḍakaṇḍu, Pradyota, Kustumbaru, Piśācha, Gajakarṇa, Viśālaka, Varāhākarṇa, Tāmroshṭha, Phalakaksha, Phalodaka, Haṁsachūḍa, Śikhāvarta, Hemanetra, Vibhīshaṇa, Pushpānana, Piṅgalaka, Śoṇitoda, Pravālaka, Vṛikshavāsin, Aniketa and Chīravāsa are mentioned by name and others by proxy.

Interestingly, here Maṇibhadra is mentioned first. He is an important Yaksha next only to Kubera and at places he is described as at par with him. Dhanada, often a title of Kubera, is here a proper name. Guhyaka and Piśācha are here again proper nouns, but they are often employed for a category of demigods like the Yakshas.[17] Guhyaka and Yaksha are also considered as synonyms.[18]

Yakshas also attend the *sabhā* of Brahmā, along with the Suparṇa, Koleya, Gandharvas and Apsarās[19] though in the same context Yakshas are omitted earlier.[20]

Kubera is said to have his abode on Mandarāchala in Śvetagiri, identified with Kailāśa. This place is guarded by 88,000 Gandharvas and four times that number by Kinnaras and the Yakshas.[21] It was a majestic structure. The stepped well of Kubera is called Mandākinī (Anuśāsana, 19/32).[22]

Kubera is not only the master of the Yakshas but he is also the lord of the Rākshasās (*Yaksharākshasādhīpa*, Vana, 159/27) and the Guhyakas are said to have borne him (*Guhyakairuhyamāna*, Sabhā, 10/3). One of his names, Naravāhana, simply describes him as having man/men as his mount. A sculptural representation found on the *stūpa* of Bhārhut in Satanā district of Madhya Pradesh, now housed in the Bhārhut Gallery of the Indian Museum, Kolkata, depicts him as standing with folded hands on a couchant dwarf human figure. It has a label *Kupiro yakho* in Brāhmī script of *c.* second century BC. This leaves no doubt about his identification as Naravāhana Kubera.[23] Kubera has been credited with a special weapon called *Antardhyāna*, but its details are not given.[24] The literary meaning of *Antardhyāna* would be 'disappearing or vanishing'. In sculpture depictions, Kubera is shown normally as seated holding a goblet or a typical money purse in the form of *mungoose* (*nakulaka* = *nyaulī* in Hindi) and rarely holding a snake. He is portrayed as a pot-bellied dwarfish man, modelled after a rich man living with all luxuries. The earliest representation may be in the form of Yaksha statues belonging to *c.* fourth–third centuries BC onwards. In early Yaksha figures, the sturdy standing figure is shown either holding a simple money purse in his left hand with the other in *abhaya-mudrā* or carrying a *chāmara* (fly-wisk) in one hand while the other is akimbo (*kaṭi-hasta-mudrā*). Some figures bear labels giving the names of the Yaksha as Nandī and Maṇibhadra; hence, it cannot be said definitely that early Yaksha statues represent Kubera. Sculptures representing Kubera, i.e. those holding attributes like goblet, *nakulaka*, *nāga*, etc., started later from *c.* second century AD.

Gandhamādana mountain also was the abode of the Yakshas, Gandharvas, Devas, etc.[25] Once, when Bhīma visited this place, Yaksha women – sitting by the side of their beloveds – started casting covetous glances at him.[26] On this Gandhamādana mountain, Arishṭisheṇa had his *āśrama* where the Pāṇḍavas stayed and had a conflict with the natives. Significantly, though this war was between the Pāṇḍavas (excluding Arjuna, who had gone to Indrakīla mountain to placate Śiva and obtain from him the Pāśupatāstra) and the Yakshas, Gandharvas and Devas residing there, this episode is called Yakshayuddhaparvan.[27] This simply indicates that, though there were various groups of Vyantara Devatās under Kubera, in general, they were called Yakshas. Here, their physical features are described as Śaṅkukarṇa (conical ears), Mahākāya (huge bodies), Mahājava (swift in movements), etc.[28] Māṇivāra (same as Maṇibhadra) Yaksha and Kubera, the lord of the Yakshas (*Yaksharāṭ*)[29] who had their abode on Mandara mountain in Śvetagirī (Kailāśa) were heavily guarded by the armed Gandharvas, Kinnaras and Yakshas.[30]

Some of the Yakshas were of helpful nature. One Brāhmin worshipped a ghost named Kundadhara Megha who was pleased with him and presented him before the gods. There, Yaksha Maṇibhadra was enquiring about the wishes of the persons and according to their merits, recommending them to the gods for boons.[31]

Yaksha-chief Kubera (*Dhanādhyaksha*) and treasures (*nidhis*) were worshipped with salute and offering of variegated flowers (*sumanobhirvichitraiḥ*), fried sweet dish preparation (अपूप equivalent to *mālapūā* in Hindi and *ghāraga* in Marathi) and a mixed cereal boiled rice cuisine (*khichaḍī*) by the Pāṇḍavas before digging out a buried treasure.[32] According to Ananda K. Coomaraswamy, the offerings were of meat, sesamum seeds and flowers.[33]

Against several references to the Yakshas either in a general way or by proper names, there are only a few allusions to Yakshīs but no proper name is given. While describing the *tīrthas* at Kurukshetra, a well-known (*lokaviśruta*) Yakshiṇī shrine is mentioned.[34] Again, a Yakshiṇī shrine at Rājagṛiha is described and we are told that one who bathes in this *tīrtha* and eats the *prasāda* gets rid of the sin of brahmanicide (*brahmahatyā*).[35] It is astonishing that at both these places the proper names of the Yakshiṇīs are not mentioned.

Maṇibhadra Yaksha is the most important and significant one in the list of the Yakshas. As stated above, his name appears first in the list of Yakshas attending the Kubera-*sabhā*. He is also named as Māṇivara.[36] Like Kubera, he resides on Mandarāchala, which is guarded by numerous Gandharvas, Kinnaras and Yakshas. In this context he is called Yakshendra, Manujaśreshṭha and Maṇibhadra.[37] There are some interesting references in the *Mahābhārata* which reveal important facets of this cult.

In the Nalopākhyāna, Maṇibhadra is the tutelary deity of the merchants and is equivalent to Kubera. Seeing Damayantī in the forest, the merchants welcomed her and evoked Maṇibhadra calling him the lord of the Yakshas (*Yakshāraṭ*) which is Kubera's title.[38] When the caravan, encamped near a pond in the forest was destroyed by elephants, the surviving traders repented for not having worshipped Maṇibhadra[39] and Kubera.[40]

From this episode it is clear that though Kubera was the supreme lord of the Yakshas, etc., Maṇibhadra also was considered equivalent to him. He might have been first worshipped by the traders as their community deity for simple protection from various calamities and gradually raised to the status of Kubera, the lord of the Yakshas. In this context, we have to consider archaeological data also. Some colossal and majestic stone sculptures carved in the round have been found from Mathura (Parkham, Baroda, Jhing-ka-nagala), Bharatpur (Noh), Vidisha, Gwalior (Pawaya), Bharhut, Sanchi, Varanasi (Rajghat), Orissa (Udaygiri and Sisupalgarh), Maharashtra (Ajanta, Pitalkhora, Karad, etc.) and Bihar (Patna, Didarganj, etc.). They represent both male and female. Some images are inscribed.[41] On the basis of palaeography, iconography, sculptural style and evidence of polishing (which was a watermark of the Mauryan workmanship), they are placed between *c.* fourth century BC and early centuries of the Christian era.

In the present context two Yaksha images – one from Parkham (Mathura Museum no. C1)[42] and the other from Pawāyā (Gwalior Museum)[43] deserve special attention. Both bear inscriptions on their pedestal which identify them as Maṇibhadra. Unfortunately, both the hands of Parkham Yaksha are broken.[44] The Pawāyā image is holding a purse in his left hand while the right one is bent and raised up, but the portion above the wrist is lost.[45]

The Pawāyā Yaksha statue inscription is specially important as it gives clue not only for the identity of the image as Maṇibhadra but also gives the iconography of this Yaksha. From the position of his right hand, we may suggest that it was in *abhaya-mudrā* and the left hand carried the money purse. Maṇibhadra, being associated with the treasures (*nidhis*)[46] and being the presiding deity of the traders, money purse was his logical attribute. The cult of Maṇibhadra was so much popularised due to the support of the rich that he rose to the high status at par with Kubera, the lord of the Yakshas, and they are seen closely associated.[47]

Here, it may be suggested that all these early Yaksha images were of Maṇibhadra and established by the traders at their camping and trading places along the ancient trade routes. In this early period we have no iconic representation of Kubera. His earliest sculptural representation is found on Bhārhut railing where he is shown standing on the shoulders of a couchant Yaksha (or Guhyaka) with folded hands.[48] In Kushāṇa period Kubera is shown holding goblet and purse.[49] So, in all probability, the earlier Yaksha images depicted Maṇibhadra Yaksha and served as a model for the later Kubera images.

In another episode, nine more Yakshas are mentioned. Garuḍa had to fight with them while bringing the nectar (अमृत) from Indra to get his mother freed from Kadrū, the mother of the Nāgas. These Yakshas are named as Aśvakranda, Reṇuka, Krathena, Tapana, Ulūka, Śvasana, Nimeśa, Praruja and Pulina.[50] But except their names nothing is known.[51]

Amongst other Yakshas described in the Great Epic, Machakruka, Arantuka, Tarantuka and Piṅgala may be mentioned. Machakruka, Arantuka and Tarantuka were the *dvārapāla* (door-keeper) Yakshas in the Kurukshetra region. While describing Kurukshetra, it is said that it was a great meritorious Brahmakshetra on the banks of river Sarasvatī and Brahmā, Deva, Ṛishis, Siddhas, Charaṇas, Gandharvas, Apsarās, Yakshas, Nāgas, all were attending it. Here, Machakruka Yaksha was the *dvārapāla* of great strength.[52]

On the outskirts of Kurukshetra, fixing its limits, there was another *dvārapāla* Yaksha. His name was Arantuka and he is called Yakshendra, i.e. the lord of the Yakshas, an epithet of Kubera.[53] Tarantuka and Arantuka are also mentioned along with Machakruka in another context.[54]

There is an interesting reference of Yaksha Sthūlakarṇa, who exchanged his own manhood with Śikhaṇḍin in lieu of her woman-hood for a short period but was forced to continue the status as he was found in female form by his lord Kubera who cursed him to continue it (Udyoga, 192/45-50). It appears that the Yakshas had the capacity of changing sex as revealed in this episode. This is also echoed in the *Kathāsaritsāgara*.[55]

In the Buddhist text *Mahāmāyurī*, Tararka and Kutararka, Yaksha-chiefs (*Yakshendra*) are mentioned as related to Kurukshetra. Sylvan Levi has suggested their equation with Tarantu and Karantaka of the *Mahābhārata*. (Vanaparvan, 83.15, 52,208).[56]

Piṅgala Yaksha is also styled as Yakshendra residing in crematorium (*śmaśāna*) and said to be a friend of the Rudra.[57] He is probably the same as Piṅgalaka enlisted with the Yakshas attending the Kubera-*sabhā*.[58]

Yakshagraha is said to be a state of mental disorder due to the possession by a Yaksha. This can be equated with Skandāpasmāra who was born from the body of Skanda and had turned ferocious by his order. A problematic image from Tālā[59] (dist. Bilaspur, Chhattisgarh) with depiction of various animals and human faces, attached to various parts of his body can be considered as the therio-anthropomorphic representation of Skandāpasmāra.[60]

The *Yakshapraśṇa* episode describes an incident where a Yaksha (later said to be Dharma himself) prohibits the Pāṇḍavas from drinking water from his pond before answering his questions. The Yaksha appears in the form of a *baka* (crane) and asks more than a hundred questions to Yudhishṭhira, who answers them satisfactorily.[61] These questions are of high philosophical standard and difficult for a common man to answer. Therefore, *Yakshapraśṇa* has become a proverb in vernacular languages to indicate a difficult situation.

The tradition of putting questions is quite old and is also practised in some other civilisations. In the *Mahābhārata*, there is one more instance which narrates a similar tradition. In Dvaitavana, Bhīma is caught by an *ajagara* (python) who was actually king Nahusha, who had become Indra, but due to his misbehaviour with the Saptarishis, was turned into a python.[62] Here, questions are put by both and with the answers given by Yudhishṭhira, Nahusha is liberated from the curse. This folk tradition of questioning and answering is still practised in Rajasthan and Maharashtra in the form of singing competition between the two groups, namely, the Kalagī and Turā.

Besides these Yakshas found mentioned in the *Mahābhārata*, there are a few more who, though not called Yaksha categorically, may belong to this category. For example, Naigameya, the third brother of Kumāra-Kārttikeya (Ādi, 66/24; Śalya, 44/37), is the well-known Vyantara-deva with antelope/goat/ram head. He is the commander-in-chief of Indra and also the protector of children. His images are found from Mathura and Vidarbha regions. In the *Mahāmāyurī*, he is spoken of as the Yaksha of Pāñchālī.[63]

Similarly, Jarā, the demoness of Rājagṛiha, who joined the two halves of Jarāsandha's body, is Hāriti Yakshī described in the Buddhist texts.[64] Ghaṇṭākarṇa (Śalya, 45/23),[65] Bhāṇḍira,[66] etc., are said to be the Yakshas in other sources. According to the *Mahāmāyurī*, there are several places associated with their presiding Yakshas. Some of these places are also referred to in the *Mahābhārata*, but due to reasons not known to us, the concerned Yakshas are not mentioned.

Thus, it is quite clear from the above discussion that the cult of the Yakshas was quite popular during the period when the *Mahābhārata* was composed.

NOTES AND REFERENCES

1. *Yakshāḥ sādhyaḥ piśāchās cha guhyakāḥ pitaras tathā /*
tataḥ prasūtā vidvāṁsaḥ śishṭā brahmarshisattamāḥ //
— Ādi, 1/35 (Gita Press Edn.)
var. – *brahmarshayomalāḥ* 1/1/33 (Cri. Edn.)
2. *Yadāśraushaṁ yaksharūpeṇa dharmaṁ samāgataṁ dharmarājeṇa sūta /*
Praśnanuktān vibruvantaṁ cha samyak tadānaśaṁse vijayāya sañjaya //
— *Ibid.*, 1/1/113
3. *Ko'yaṁ devo' thavā yaksho gandharvo vā bhavishyati /* — Vana, 155/17
It is interesting to note in this context that Buddha also is called a Yaksha – Rama Nath Misra, *Yaksha Cult and Iconography*, Munshiram Manoharlal, Delhi, 1981, pp. 16, 36, etc.
4. *Yakshī vā rākshasī vā tvamutāho'si varāṅganā /* — Vana, 64/120
5. *Rākshasī vā dhruvaṁ yakshī piśāchī vā bhayaṅkarī /*
Tasyā sarvaṁ idaṁ pāpaṁ nātra kāryā vichāraṇā // — *Ibid.*, 27
6. *Atīva rūpeṇa samanvitā tvaṁ na chāpy araṇyeshu vibheshi kiṁ nu /*
Devī nu yakshī yadi dānavī vā varāpsarā daityavarāṅganā vā //
— *Ibid.*, 265/2
7. *Ibid.*, Sabhā, 10/15–16; Vana, 161/38.
8. *Ibid.*, Sabhā, 10/16.
9. *Ibid.*, 15–17.
10. Vana, 111/10–11.
11. Sabhā, 10/15.

12. *Ibid.*, 10/3
13. *Ibid.*, 10/9.
14. *Ibid.*, 10/10–13.
15. *Ibid.*, 10/14. *Kinnarā nāma gandharvā narā nāmo tathāpare /*
16. *Ibid.*, 10/15–18.
17. *Yakshāḥ sādhyāḥ piśāchaś cha guhyakāḥ pitaras tathā /* — Ādi 1/35
18. In Sabhā 11/49–50 while describing the courtiers attending the *Sabhā* of Brahmā, Rākshasa, Piśācha, Dānava, Guhyaka and noble animals, etc., are mentioned but Yakshas are omitted. This may be a mistake or suggestion to identify them with the Guhyakas. Also, see Ananda K. Coomarswamy, *Yaksas*, Pt. I, pp. 7ff.
19. *Yakshān Suparṇān Kāleyān Gandharvāpsarasastathā /*
 — 2/11/36 (Cri. Edn.); Sabhā, 11/56.
20. *Ibid.*, 11/49–50.
21. Vana, 139/5–7.
22. *Ibid.*, 141/23–24; Udyoga, 191/11.
23. *Apsarobhiḥ parivṛitaḥ samriddhyā Naravāhanaḥ /*
 Iha Vaiśravaṇas tāta parvasandhishu dṛiśyate // — Vana, 159/26
 Kubera is described as having a human being for his mount in the iconographic texts like the *Bṛihat-saṁhitā* of Varāhamihira. See Ajay Mitra Shastri, *Varāhamihira's India, I,* Aryan Books International, New Delhi, 1996, pp. 145–46, fig. 13–Ed.
24. Vana, 41/38. Yakshas have the normal arms and weapons like *gadā* (mace), *parigha* (a curved dagger), *nistriṁśa* (sword), *śūla* (long pointed spear), *śakti* (spear), *paraśvadhā* (battle-axes), etc.
 Gadā-parigha-nistriṁśa-śūla-śakti-paraśvadhāḥ /
 Pragṛihīta vyarochanta yaksha-rakshasa-bāhubhiḥ — *Ibid.*, 160/48
 At one place, they are said to have holding different types of weapons (*nānāpraharaṇa*) — *Ibid.*, 139/7
25. *Sa yaksha-gandharva-sura-brahmarshigaṇa-sevitam /* — *Ibid.*, 146/21
26. *Yaksha-gandharva-yoshābhir adṛiśyābhir nirīshitaḥ /*
 Navāvatāra-rūpasya vikrīḍānniva Pāṇḍavaḥ // — *Ibid.*, 30
27. *Ibid.*, Chapters 158–164.
28. *Tamāsīnaṁ mahākāyāḥ śankukarṇā mahājavāḥ /*
 Upopaviviśur yakshā rākshasāś cha sahasrasaḥ //
 —*Ibid.*, Yakshayuddha, 161/138
29. *Śvetaṁ giriṁ pravekhsyāmo Mandaraṁ chaiva parvataṁ /*
 Yatra Māṇivaro yakshaḥ Kuberaś chaiva yaksharāṭ // — *Ibid.*, 139/5
30. *Ibid.*, 139/6–7.
31. Mokshadharmaparvan, Kuṇḍadhāropakhyāna — Shānti, 271/1–30
32. *Pūjayitvā dhanādhyakshaṁ praṇipatyābhivādya cha //*
 Sumanobhir vichitrābhir apūpaiḥ kṛiśareṇa cha /
 Śankhādīṁś cha nidhīn sarvān nidhipālāṁś cha sarvaśaḥ //
 — Aśvamedhika, 66/11–12

33. *Yaksas*, Pt. I, p. 25.
34. *Tatraiva cha mahārāja yakshiṇīṁ lokaviśrutām /* — Vana, 83/23
A.K. Coomaraswamy mentions this in the context of Rājagṛiha, which was different.
35. *Tato Rājagṛihaṁ gachchhet tīrthasevī narādhipa //* 104
Upaspṛiśya tatas tatra kakshīvāniva modate /
Yakshiṇyā naityakaṁ tatra prāśnīta-purushaḥ śuchiḥ // 105
Yakshiṇyāstu prasādena muchyate brahmahatyayā / — Vana, 84
36. *Supra*, note 29. According to A.K. Coomaraswamy, other names of Maṇibhadra are Maṇichara and Maṇimat. He is a Yaksharāja and Kubera's chief attendant (5, 192, 44f) – *Yaksas*, Pt. I, p. 7.
37. *Yakshendra manujaśreshṭha Māṇibhadramupāsate //* — Vana, 139/7
38. *Tataḥ no Yaksharāḍ adya Maṇibhadraḥ prasīdatu //* — *Ibid.*, 64/130
Kuberaśchaiva yaksharāṭ / — *Ibid.*, 139/5
39. *Te'bruvan sahitāḥ sarve kasyedaṁ karmaṇaḥ phalam /*
Nūnaṁna pūjitosmābhir Maṇibhadro mahāyaśāḥ // — *Ibid.*, 65/22
40. *Tathā yakshādhipaḥ śrīmān na vai Vaiśravaṇaḥ prabhuḥ /*
Na pūjā vighnakartṛīṇām athavā prathamaṁ kṛitā // — *Ibid.*, 23
41. V.S. Agrawala, *Studies in Indian Art*, p. 116ff.
42. *Ibid.*, pp. 116–118.
43. *Ibid.*, pp. 118–119.
44. *Ibid.*, Fig. 37.
45. *Ibid.*, Figs. 36, 38. It may have been in *abhaya* posture.
46. Cf. Aśvamedhika, 66/11; *Yaksas*, Pt.I, p. 25.
47. Maṇibhadra is found mentioned in a number of other texts. His worship continued till *c.* 11th–12th century AD in the form of Maṇiyā/ Māṇika bīra/devī. A separate article is being prepared by the author on the cult of Maṇibhadra.
48. V.S. Agrawala, *op. cit.*, p. 89, fig. 50; A.K. Coomaraswamy, *Yakshas*, Pt.I, p. 39, Pl. 3.1.
49. *Ibid.*, p. 40, Pl. 14.1; Pt.II, p. 72, Pl. 4.2; N.P. Joshi, *Bhāratīya Mūrtiśāstra* (Marathi), Mahārāshṭra Vidyāpiṭha Grantha Nirmiti Maṇḍala, Pune – Nagpur, 1979, pp. 312ff.
50. *Aśvakrandena vīreṇa reṇukena cha pakshirāṭ /*
Krathanena cha śūreṇa tapanena cha khecharaḥ //
Ulūkaśvasanābhyāṁ cha nimesheṇa cha pakshirāṭ /
Prarujena cha saṁgrāmaṁ chakāra Pulikena cha // — Ādi, 32/18–19
51. A sculpture depicting Garuḍa on one side and a corpulent Yaksha on the other, has been found in excavation at Paunī, district Bhaṇḍārā, Vidarbha (see Amarendra Nath, *Further Excavations at Pauni*, 1994, Archaeological Survey of India, New Delhi, 1998, p. 88, Pl. XXV). According to us, it depicts fight between Garuḍa and the Yakshas described in the Epic.

52. Vana, 83/9. Brahmakshetra and Brahmapura are places of the Yakshas.
53. *Tato gachchheta rājendra dvārapālamarantukam /*
Taśmcha tīrtham Sarasvatyāṁ yakshendrasya mahātmanaḥ //
— Vana, 83/52
Abhivādya tato yakshaṁ dvārapālamārantukam /
Koṭirūpam upaspṛiśya labhed bahu suvarṇakam //
— 3/81/171 (Cri. Edn.); Vana, 83/200
54. *Tarantukārantukayoryadantaraṁ rāmahradānāṁ cha machakrukasya /*
Etat Kurukshetrasamantapañchakam pitāmahasyottaravediruchyate //
— 3/81.178 (Cri. Edn.); Vana, 83/208
55. Rama Nath Misra, *op. cit.*, p. 158.
56. *Kurukshetre cha yakshendrau tarārkakutarārkakau /* — 57
V.S. Agrawala, "The Geographical Contents of the Mahāmāyūrī, *JUPHS*, Vol. XV, Pt. II, pp. 28, 44.
57. *Vyāpṛitastu śmaśāne yo nityaṁ rudrasya vai sakhā /*
Pingalo nāma Yakshendro lokasyānandadāyakah // — Vana, 231/51
58. Sabhā, 10/17.
59. Vana, 230/23–26, 53. Also see Rama Nath Misra, *op.cit.*, pp. 152–53.
60. Chandrashekhar Gupta, "Identity of Unique Sculpture from Tālā", in L.S. Nigam (Ed.), *Riddle of Indian Iconography* (*Zetetic on Rare Icon from Tālā*), Sharada Publishing House, Delhi, 2000, pp. 117–20.
61. Vana, 313/28–133.
62. *Ibid.*, 179–81.
63. *Yaksas*, Pt. I, pp. 12–13, 25.
64. Sabhā, 17/35–41; 18/1–10. For details see Rama Nath Misra, *op.cit.*, pp. 73ff.
65. Śalya, 45/23–24 where he is a *pārshada* of Skanda.
66. Sabhā, 38/29ff, The wood and tree in Vraja region are known as Bhāṇḍīra.

18

Arjuna's View of State

A Link Between *Arthaśāstra* and *Dharmaśāstra* (Based on Śāntiparvan)

Sibesh Bhattacharya

I

State in early India continues to get substantial scholarly attention. Although the way state functioned and the distribution of power over and between various limbs and segments of state have been an area of interest for a number of scholars,[1] the question that seems to have been pivotal in recent discussions regarding the character of state in early India has centred around the problem of ascertaining the extent to which the state had been 'religious' in character. The basic premise of the debate had been spelt out by Coomaraswamy.[2] The relationship between the priest and the king or between brāhmaṇas and kshatriyas was demarcated as the crucial area for an understanding of the religiosity of state. Coomaraswamy asserted that in early Indian state the temporal authority held a subordinate position to the spiritual authority. Heesterman, on the basis of his analysis of coronation rites described in the ritual literature, concluded that kingship had its own religious loci and did not depend on priesthood to sanction its authority.[3] Gonda in his extensively documented work on the religious nature of early Indian kingship fortified and also amplified the argument of Heesterman.[4] Gonda's thesis was that the office of king in ancient India was a repository not only of majesty and power but also of religious sanctity. More importantly, this religious sanctity was not a secondary sanctity derived from an outside source. Gonda argued that religiosity was an inherent characteristic of the office of king. The works of

Gonda and Heesterman have provided the ground for the view that seems to dominate the opinion of contemporary Western scholars interested in the question of kingship in ancient India.[5] Some scholars have also drawn attention to the fact that Indian kings often attempted to validate their authority by claiming that they were administering the kingdom on behalf of the guardian deity of the kingdom, who was the real ruler.[6] This theory of the duality of sources of religious sanctions operating in the state and society is very interesting and deserves thorough and detailed examination, for it challenges some of the basic notions associated with the understanding of the social and political organizations in early India. It is generally believed that one of the fundamental principles on which Indian social organization was based, was the principle of the separation of the 'religious', 'political' and 'economic'. We would consider the validity and implications of this theory elsewhere. Dumont, however, takes a somewhat different position. He maintained that the core function of king and state in ancient India was essentially secular, which was to provide protection to the subjects.[7] We are inclined to agree with this position.

It is not necessary for us to review or to critique all these theories in detail here. Here we would only limit ourselves to a partial development of one of our arguments. The fact that a discipline (*śāstra*) dedicated exclusively to the study of state/ politics developed, and that this discipline was able to achieve a degree of autonomy from the pervasive presence of religious and ritual literature is an indication that the necessity of viewing state from secular perspective was recognized. Fortunately, it is possible to locate the period when this development had taken place with some amount of certainty. It appears that towards the end of Vedic period, or to be more precise, when the period of the composition of the sacrificial literature called the Brāhmaṇas came to an end, the discipline devoted to the study of politics began to develop. Here we will also not go into the question why this development took place at that time. It may, however, be mentioned that the later and post-Vedic period was marked by the growth of relatively larger states.[8] The administration and organization of these states were becoming relatively more complex and cumbersome and demanded greater expertise. These experts were both theoreticians as well as practitioners. Kauṭilya in his

Arthaśāstra refers to Arthaśāstrins of yore who belonged either to the category of *vaktṛin* or to *prayoktṛin*.[9] It may also be pointed out that during the post-Vedic period a number of basically secular disciplines in order to act as aids to the study of the Vedas covering restricted areas had also developed.

However, it would be wrong to lose sight of the fact that all these disciplines despite their secular subject matter and secular perspectives never claimed full autonomy from the Vedas and thus their relation with the religious aspects was never completely severed. These 'secular' disciplines should therefore not be placed in the same category as the anti-Vedic philosophies of Chārvākas or Buddhists. The discipline devoted to the study of state, government and politics was known by different names like Arthaśāstra, Daṇḍanīti, Rājanīti, Rajaśāstra, Nītiśāstra, etc. It is not clear whether these terms were used synonymously or they denoted distinctiveness of character. It appears that three classes of works acquired a special prominence in the field of state and politics: Dharmaśāstra, Arthaśāstra and Nītiśāstra. While Arthaśāstra and Nītiśāstra were concerned exclusively with polity and politics, the concern of Dharmaśāstra covered a much wider area. Politics, which was called by the name of Rājadharma (can be translated roughly as conduct proper for kings) in the Dharmaśāstra literature, constituted only a part of its theme. And because Dharmaśāstra itself constitutes a part of a larger collection of ritual literature, Rājadharma discussed in Dharmaśāstra does not have the same degree of secularity as the theme of politics dealt within the Arthaśāstra. It is apparent from Kauṭilya's *Arthaśāstra*, the only text belonging to the Arthaśāstra school yet discovered, that within the boundaries of politics and the problems of governance, religion was generally kept at bay. Arthaśāstra thus should generally be described as predominantly secular in its attitude.

II

Although other than Kauṭilya's work no text belonging to the Arthaśāstra school has yet been discovered, there is ample evidence to indicate that the school was an extensive one. Kauṭilya mentions a large number of his predecessors.[10] It is interesting that some of the teachers mentioned by Kauṭilya are also referred to in the *Mahābhārata*.[11] The *Mahābhārata* also gives us a significant bit of additional information, which we do not find in Kauṭilya. It tells us that the great warrior Arjuna was an expert in Arthaśāstra.[12] This information assumes special significance when put against the backdrop of the long peroration of Arjuna in the beginning of Śāntiparvan to dissuade Yudhishṭhira from renouncing the world at the end of the Kurukshetra war.[13]

The situation is interesting. When the war was over, Kuntī revealed to her sons that Karṇa actually was their eldest brother. On hearing this Yudhishṭhira was seized by a terrible sense of remorse and an overpowering sense of futility of worldly possessions and he started wondering if it would not make more sense to renounce the world. Arjuna made three speeches to the effect that for a kshatriya king to take recourse to such a step was untenable and undesirable. The situation is interesting because it so closely parallels the situation in the Bhīshmaparvan immediately before the war began when Arjuna himself had been overpowered by a spell of asceticism and which led Kṛishṇa to deliver the message of the *Bhagavadgītā*. Then Arjuna was the target of the teaching; he now along with his other brothers and Draupadī assumed the role of persuader. Our interest in the episode, however, extends beyond the reversal of role of Arjuna; we find this episode interesting because the arguments advanced by Arjuna extend and deepen our insight into the attitude of Arthaśāstra thinkers on the roles of state and kingship.

III

The way Arjuna began his argument is again strongly reminiscent of the *Bhagavadgītā*. In the same vein as Kṛishṇa had rebuked him (Arjuna) in the *Bhagavadgītā*, Arjuna, too, began by rebuking Yudhishṭhira for misapprehending completely the course of proper conduct for a prince belonging to a ruling kshatriya family.[14] Renunciation was a path to be adopted by the *ṛishis* (*aśvastanamṛishiṇāṁ hi*), the path of a king followed a different direction.[15] The extermination of one's enemies in order to 'conquer the world' was a course of conduct entirely in keeping with kshatriya duty and ethics.[16]

If, O king, abandoning this swelling kingdom, you live in the observance of the wretched mode of life led by a mendicant, what will the world say of you? Why do you say that abandoning all the good things of the earth, divested of prosperity, and bereft of resources, you will lead a life of mendicancy like a vulgar person? You have taken birth in a royal lineage. Having conquered this whole earth, out of folly you want to live in the woods abandoning everything that is virtuous and desirable (*dharamārtha*).[17]

To rule over the kingdom, which meant the same thing as the protection (*rakshaṇa, pālana*) of people, was not just the right but also the duty of a ruler. Running away from this responsibility was not only imprudent, it was also sinful.

Giving up the kingdom if you retire to forest, in the absence of a ruler wicked men will destroy sacrifices. And that sin will certainly taint you.[18]

And ruling over and administering a state would automatically demand readiness to fight. According to the Arthaśāstra school of thought, the readiness to fight was not merely a necessity imposed by the requirements of self-defence; the role of the king included both the acquisition (*lābha*) of new territory as well as the nurturing (*pālana*) of the old.[19] In fact, the entire text of the *Arthaśāstra* is devoted to the elaboration of the 'means of the acquisition and protection of the earth'[20]. The purpose of *Daṇḍanīti* has been explained as the acquisition of things not possessed, the preservation of things possessed and augmentation of things preserved and finally to bestow the things preserved and increased to people who are worthy to receive them.[21] It maybe noted here in passing that the Arthaśāstra point of view did not approve of acquisitiveness on the part of the ruler for its own sake; the king ought to endeavour to acquire more and more in order to serve the ends of welfare. Anyway, to revert back to the earlier point, the Arthaśāstra tirelessly emphasizes that the ruler should always try to extend his territory by conquest. Kauṭilya devoted two books of his treatise on discussing how a king should go about executing the plans of conquest and extending his dominion.[22]

Conquest and aggrandizement, especially for those who were capable, were counted as acts of merits and virtue; it was not kshatriya-like to look upon victory in war as cause of regret or of feelings of shame or guilt. This was a major burden of the arguments advanced by Arjuna to dissuade Yudhishṭhira from renouncing the world. And we find his arguments are in keeping with the Arthaśāstra precepts. The enjoyment of earth through conquest was regarded as a legitimate kshatriya ambition; it was even painted as a noble ideal that a kshatriya warrior should strive for. It is interesting that in the second chapter of the *Bhagavadgītā*, Kṛishṇa too, takes up this line of argument. In course of seven verses, from thirty-one to thirty-seven, Kṛishṇa gives a succinct exposition of the kshatriya duty to fight a righteous war and not to flinch from it.[23] There is no higher virtue for a kshatriya than to fight a *Dharmayuddha*. Such righteous wars, in fact, open the very doors of heaven for the kshatriya warrior; it is a privilege granted only to kshatriyas. If a kshatriya refuses to fight a *Dharmayuddha*, he not only forfeits his reputation but also runs away from his 'duty' (*dharma*) and thus becomes guilty of sin (*pāpa*).

> If you are slain (in battle) you will attain the heavens, if you win you will enjoy the earth. Therefore, O son of Kuntī, rise up determined to fight.[24]

In the *Gītā* this line of argument was not pursued fully; it was given up in favour of the deeper metaphysical discourse on the meaning and end of human life. Although the central philosophy of the *Gītā* does not directly concern us here, it maybe mentioned in passing that it does provide the wider perspective for the kshatriya duty 'to fight'. Otherwise the kshatriya ideal could be misconceived as an advocacy for dehumanized bloodthirsty trade in war.

Even the gods, argues Arjuna, have been continuously fighting and killing the asuras, even though the asuras were gods' own kinsmen.[25]

> Without piercing the heart of others, without doing the most frightful acts and without killing ... no one can achieve great fortune ... Indra became Mahendra only after killing Vṛitra.[26]

It is impossible even to keep alive without doing violence to others, says Arjuna. Creatures feed on creatures, the stronger live upon the weaker.

> The mongoose devours the mice; the cat devours the mongoose; the dog devours the cat; the dog in its turn is devoured by the leopard. . . . This entire world, both that moves and that moves not (*jaṅgama, sthāvara*), is the food for living creatures. This is a law ordained by gods. . . . Therefore, O king, you ought to become what you are by birth.[27]

Even gods themselves obtained heaven through fighting wars.

Kingdoms can be built only by taking others' possessions; there is nothing wrong in conquests. If conquest and appropriation of others' property were forbidden to rulers, how would they be able to meet their obligations to people?[28]

This part of Arjuna's argument has crucial significance; war and aggrandizement are parts of royal obligations and not of royal sports. It is an obligation owed to a concept of larger social good and an appreciation of the core of this concept of larger social good is central to an understanding of the view of state and kingship being enunciated here by Arjuna. The office of king is a demanding one; it is not a position suitable for the faint-hearted. It demands hard decisions and 'frightful acts' (*karmadāruṇam*).[29] But all these are to be undertaken by the king for the good of people (*prajā*) and for the well-being of everybody (*sarva*).[30] Like water flowing in every direction from the great ocean, the activities and the wealth of king ought to enrich the whole world.[31] The king has to conquer and accumulate wealth as a means for the performance of his duties.

The renouncing of the world and adopting the ascetic mode of living is not a conduct prescribed for the kshatriyas. True renunciation is a very difficult pursuit; in fact, one may fall a victim to the seduction of ascetic life. There is a certain amount of external charm, even glamour, in the ascetic mode of living. One may without achieving a genuine inner detachment, repair to the forest. Such renunciation is actually false and may only serve as a cloak to cover up the inability or unwillingness to face one's family and social obligations. This falsity may take on two different appearances. And Arjuna draws attention to both of them.

One of these modes of false asceticism amounts merely to the transference of domesticity from the bosom of the society to that of the forest. The limitations of the domestic life that cause the basic impulse for repairing to the forest life practically remain unaltered. "The very ascetics (*tāpasa*) cannot support their lives without killing creatures. Living beings abound in water, on earth, in fruits. How one can keep alive without killing them?"[32] There are living beings so numerous and so minute that their existence can only be inferred, but cannot be seen; and they are killed with the batting of an eyelid. So it is idle to pretend that one can live without destroying life.[33] There are people who leave behind the feelings of anger and vanity and their homes in their villages, renounce the world and repair to the forest, but they end up by setting up family life (*kuṭumbadharma*) anew in the forest by gathering fruits and herbs, tilling land, cutting wood and trees, building houses and performing rituals and sacrifices just like householders.[34] Retiring to the forest in these cases was unnecessary.

Asceticism could thus only be superficial, external and formal. This actually amounts to running away from one's duties.[35] Leading a normal householder's life and discharging the duties of the *gṛihastha* were worthier than taking to renunciation. This is the message that Arjuna conveyed in his narration of the encounter between Indra and a few adolescent brāhmaṇa ascetics.[36] Indra, as can be guessed, completely succeeded in convincing the young lads how wrong they were in renouncing the world and the young ascetics promptly agreed to retrace their steps and return to their families. But the really substantial part of this narrative for us is the contention that the institution of family and domesticity (*kuṭumbavidhāna)* are the very basis of all virtuous acts.

> I, therefore, tell you to bear the very difficult burden of domesticity. Without doubt, penance is the foremost of everything and is the root of all creatures. Asceticism, however, is to be obtained by leading a life of domesticity, upon which depends everything.[37]

Gṛihasthāśrama was often regarded as the most important and basic *āśrama* on which every other *āśrama* depended.[38] This claim bears an obvious kinship with the assertion in the *Arthaśāstra* that among the *chaturvarga*, *artha* is the principal and central one on which depended all the others.[39]

The centrality of *artha* in the scheme of human life, both at individual as well as social planes, was strongly emphasized by Arjuna. In his agruments Arjuna used the expressions *artha* and *dhana* both, and often synonymously. But it is also clear that the expression *artha* was used in a wider sense to signify one of the *purushārthas*. Arjuna in course of his arguments underlined the importance of both wealth in the ordinary sense as well as the crucial role of *artha* as one of the *chaturvargas*. *Artha*, Arjuna argued, was the necessary base for all other desirable human pursuits. *Artha* was compared to the high mountain from which spring all the streams of life-sustaining activities. It was the very basic condition not only for good and meaningful life but for the continuance of life itself (*prāṇayātrā*). *Dharma, kāma,* even *svarga,* all emerge from *artha.*[40] *Artha* thus had a foundational role in the society.[41]

Just as *artha* is for the society, so is wealth (*dhana*) for an individual, argued Arjuna. Without wealth one could not even properly meet one's religious obligations; wealth (*dhana*) procreates *dharma* just as mountains give birth to rivers (*dhanād dhi dharmaḥ sravati śailādgiṛinadī yathā*).[42] Poverty is a curse for a poor man, for even when he is standing at a safe distance, he is falsely accused of offence committed by others. But poverty is more than a curse; it is also a sin.[43] Wealth increases the prestige of the family; wealth leads to *dharma* (*dhanād dharmaḥ pravartate*). On the other hand, the poor gain neither this world, nor the next.[44] A man of wealth is considered a real man (*pumān*), a wealthy man is considered a truly learned person (*paṇḍita*), and only a wealthy man really has friends and relatives.[45] Therefore, acquisition of wealth is a virtue. It is especially so for a king.[46]

These arguments of Arjuna appear somewhat tedious and banal. These also have a ring of blatant acceptance of the hegemony of Mammon. However, the context in which these arguments were advanced should not be lost sight of. And considering the demands of the occasion, a bit of overkill on the part of Arjuna can perhaps be forgiven. When read against the perspective of the overall tenor of the totality of Arjuna's arguments, these statements about the curse of poverty and the contrasting advantages of wealth lose some of their offensive edges. We have already noted above that Arjuna was actually not arguing for self-aggrandizement and acquisition and accumulation of poverty for their own sake.[47] A metaphor of mountain sending down bountiful rivers in all directions seems to represent Arjuna's point of view. The king with his conquests and acquistions ought to act as such a mountain or an ocean full to the brim sending out streams of rewards in all directions.[48]

IV

In the course of his efforts at persuading Yudhishṭhira not to give up his throne, Arjuna discusses over a full chapter in the Śāntiparvan the importance of *daṇḍa* for the maintenance of law and order in the society.[49] This chapter also reflects Arjuna's point of view in a much more cohesive and concentrated manner than the two other chapters; the enunciation is sober and disciplined; the marshalling of arguments has an attractive linearity about it with very little digressions. It appears that by the time Arjuna reaches this chapter, he has come to terms with himself and has been able to leave behind the feelings of anger and annoyance at Yudhishṭhira's stand, which he showed often in the earlier chapters. There are no overstatements and exaggerations, which could possibly distort his intentions or the burden of his statements. This chapter, therefore, maybe taken as the reflection not only of the kernel of Arjuna's thesis, but also as the most authentic reflection of Arjuna's attitude.

In the present chapter, Arjuna actually pursues the development of one single point: the absolute necessity of political authority for an orderly and secure society. This political authority he defines as *daṇḍa*. The necessity of political authority arises from the 'nature of this world'. 'Look at the nature of this world', says Arjuna to Yudhishṭhira (*svabhāvaṁ paśya laukikam*).[50] An appreciation of the proper import of this statement is crucial to an understanding of the core of Arjuna's thesis. He is emphasizing two things, 'this world' and 'its nature'. The *laukika* world has to be distinguished from the *pāramārthika,* and the *svabhāva* or the innate nature has to be understood as pertaining to this *laukika* world. This is the temporal world, the world of our everyday experience; the world where the social life and social existence have their beings. It is important to remember that society has to operate within the bounds of this *laukika* order of things. This *laukika* world is the same as the visible *dṛishṭārthaka* or the *pratyaksha* world and it obeys its own laws.[51] Arjuna is emphasizing the reality (*svabhāva*) of this temporal social world and not the 'reality' (*svabhāva*) from the ultimate ontological point of view. It is the political order that he is drawing our attention to.[52]

Svabhāva also means the natural state; thus the *svabhāva* of the *laukika* world might be interpreted as the 'natural state' or the state of nature. Elsewhere in the Śāntiparvan, we do find the description of a state of nature, which bears certain external similarity with the state of nature of Rousseau.[53] But by the *svabhāva* of the *laukika* world Arjuna does not mean this pristine state of happiness and perfection; for Arjuna the innate nature of social world means more forces of greed, selfishness, violence, etc., which had led to the decline from the original pristine state.

Arjuna, in fact, does not refer to any pristine golden past to derive the ground for political authority and state; he keeps himself confined to the existent situation, the moral and the psychological makeup of men and society. As a matter of fact, the general tone of his argument has a ring of universality about it; nowhere he betrays the impression that he thought that it was a special condition characterizing only his own time. His view of men and society, and we hasten to add that Arjuna speaks only about the 'nature' and the conduct of the 'social man' within the framework of the *dṛishṭārthaka* visible world and does not consider the question of the ultimate spiritual essence of man, is almost reminiscent of Hobbes. In Arjuna's formulation, selfishness, greed, covetousness and the resultant violence seem to rule the social world. The natural propensity of this world is towards chaos, insecurity and violence (*mātsya-nyāya*), where the weak are preyed upon by the strong.[54] If not restrained, *pāpa* would overwhelm *dharma* and drown the world in bottomless darkness. There is another element that very powerfully conditions the conduct of men in society; it is fear (*bhaya*). Arjuna argues that fear can, in fact it does, act as an important instrument of social control. However, different people respond to different kinds of fear.

> Some people desist from sinful acts because of the fear of punishment by the king (*rājadaṇḍabhayāt*); some people desist out of fear of the punishment by Yama (*yamadaṇḍabhāyat*) or also because of the fear of next world (*paralokabhaya*). And some people desist from sinful acts because of the fear of each other.[55]

Therefore, *daṇḍa* is the real protector of the society; it forms the very basis on which the social life is founded.

> Thus, O king, the course of this world is so fixed that everything is dependent on the rod that chastises. It is because of the fear of the rod of chastisement (*daṇḍa*) that people do not devour each other. Had *daṇḍa* been not nurturing, the world would have sunk into blind darkness.[56]

It is rare to find a person who is naturally endowed with virtue and righteousness. The entire world responds to the coercion of *daṇḍa* alone (*sarvo daṇḍajito loko*),[57] it is out of the fear of *daṇḍa* that people become disposed towards the obedience of rules and regulations. The wise regard *daṇḍa* as the embodiment of fear (*daṇḍaṁ bhayaṁ vidurbudhāḥ*) itself.[58] But *daṇḍa* is not just coercive power; it does not just represent fear alone, *daṇḍa* is also the embodiment of *dharma*.[59] *Daṇḍa* punishes the people, but *daṇḍa* also protects them (*daṇḍaḥ śasti prajāḥ sarvā daṇḍa evabhirakshati*); the world can sleep peacefully because *daṇḍa* keeps awake without sleep.[60] The place and the role of *dharma* in the making of *daṇḍa* give the latter its real meaning and significance.

Why is it that people should submit to the coercive authority of *daṇḍa*? Arjuna seems to be positing a pair of mutually opposing fears: the fear of chaos, the dark abyss of bottomless insecurity, a kind of cannibalistic existence on the one hand, and the fear of the red-eyed, ever-wakeful and ever-ready-to-strike authority of state (*daṇḍa*) on the other.[61] People naturally prefer to submit to the 'regular' and 'regulated' coercive authority of state than to continue to live in the perpetual fear of uncertainty and insecurity where life can be 'nasty, brutish and short' (*mātsyanyāya, arājaka*). It must be noted, however, that Arjuna unlike Bhīshma,[62] does not think it necessary to derive the authority of king or state from any popular covenant. He derives the authority from the security and fulfilment that the state symbolizes. The state brings order in the disorder of *mātsyanyāya*.

> In order to liberate human beings from greed and delusion (*asaṁmohāya martyānām*), and to protect the welfare of people (*arthasaṁrakshaṇāya cha*) rules have been established in this world (*maryādā sthāpitā loke*) called by the name of *daṇḍa*.[63]

Wherever *daṇḍa* rules in accordance with the 'natural' principle of justice (*sunṛitaḥ*), the people there do not look withered (*prajastatra na muhyanti*) and the ruler there is endowed with right vision (*netā chet sadhu paśyati*). In such a country the society runs orderly and on even keel.[64] The obedience to state springs from the order and regularity that the state ensures; all the ends of life, the *purushārthas* and the *chaturvargas* can flourish when protected by *daṇḍa*. In short, the authority accrues to *daṇḍa* because *daṇḍa* represents the antithesis of *mātsyanyāya*. The Creator (*vidhātā*) himself for the protection of *dharma* created *daṇḍa*,[65] and *dharma* in its turn was enunciated for the maintenance of society (*lokayatrartham*).[66]

Daṇḍa thus represents order. And, although political authority represents the core and the foundation of this order, the scope of this order extends much beyond the mere political domain in its conception. This order penetrates into and permeates areas that are now sometimes distinguished as political, economic, social, moral, etc. *Daṇḍa*, in fact, carries on its back the entire social existence of man. In the absence of *daṇḍa* the very structure of society would fall to pieces. The entire social spectrum, including the order of students (*brahmachārin*), the householder (*gṛihastha*), the one who has repaired to forest (*vānaprasthin*), or the wandering friar (*bhikshuka*), all obey the obligations of their stations on account of *daṇḍa*; 'they stay on to their paths' (*manuhsya vartmani sthitāḥ*).[67]

> If *daṇḍa* had not been distinguishing the good from the bad, the whole world would have been enveloped in utter darkness and all things would have been confounded.[68]

But for it, the economic, moral and religious cohesion of the society would disappear, reducing it into chaos.[69] This holistic view of 'order' which does not readily agree to separate the political from the social, economic and the ethical, was a characteristic feature of ancient Indian political thinking.[70] In the accounts of genesis or of the origin of state and kingship in early India, whether in Vedas, Epics, Purāṇas, Smṛitis, or in Buddhist or in Jaina works, the social and political organizations and authorities are described as arising together and in unison. The social and political domains were not regarded as distinct entities; and the concept of 'interdependence' would not be able to adequately and exhaustively express in the nature of their mutual relationship. In the Indian concept, and more so in the arguments of Arjuna, this relationship is not of the same nature as that of between two links in a chain. This relation is viewed as much more intimate and organic in nature.[71] The relationship can perhaps be described as similar to the one that exists between the tree and the fruits. And in Arjuna's formulation it is *daṇḍa* that can be likened to tree and the nature of the society can be compared to the fruit; the social domain depends on the political domain. If we distinguish the two domains in the same way as the tree and fruits are distinguished in Arjuna's formulation, political domain definitely has primacy over the socio-economic domain.

Although Arjuna has painted the evils that characterize the state of *mātsyanyāya*, which is the same thing as the absence of political authority (*daṇḍa*) and order (*dharma*), in bold strokes, he has not dealt with the issue of the origin of *mātsyanyāya* and that of the state. It is interesting that Kauṭilya too, does not show much interest in these questions. From the attitude of Kauṭilya it appears that the Arthaśāstra school took these questions as settled and assumed that the issues and implications associated with them were too well known to require fresh consideration. However, we feel that it may not be out of place to underline some of the central implications of the accounts of the origin of *mātsyanyāya* in early Indian literature, for they have important bearing upon the concept of political authority propounded by Arjuna.

One of the chief constituents of *mātsyanyāya* is obviously the lack of security. It has been emphasized time and again in early Indian tradition that the main function of the state is to provide protection *(rakshaṇa)* to people and to look after (*pālana*) them. *Rakshaṇa* and *pālana* are allied concepts and they supplemented each other. Protection mainly implied defence against external aggression and maintenance of internal security and order. *Pālana* implied the ruler's responsibility to promote people's welfare and to give succour to the poor, weak, destitute and defenceless. The king was expected to make the people happy (*prajārañjana*). The term *rājan* was often derived from *rañjana*, the king is one who keeps the people happy. Similarly, kshatriya was described as one who heals the wound (*kshata*) of people. The lack of these features produces *mātsyanyāya*. Apparently, the factors that were regarded as responsible for *mātsyanyāya* were greed and covetousness. But these were apparent factors. The greed and covetousness themselves were contingent upon the moral and spiritual decline of the mankind; and the rate and proportion of this decline differentiated one *yuga* from another. It is not the defect in the moral constitution of an individual or a few individuals that brings about this 'fall' from a state of perfection to that of depravity, aggression and violence creating the need for civil society and state.[72] In Indian concept it is the decline in *dharma* that in real terms produces the *mātsyanyāya* and the legitimacy of the state and political authority derives from the fact that they represent the instruments for the recovery of the eternal innate universal principle (*dharma*) back to society. Thus the *daṇḍa* proper is the same thing as *dharma*.[73]

V

Arjuna's views are interesting from several angles. One of these angles has already been hinted above. We have noted above that Arjuna is described in the *Mahābhārata* as an expert in the Arthaśāstra. Arjuna's interventions in the interesting debate on the propriety of a victorious kshatriya prince taking recourse to *vānaprastha* mode of life may afford us a peep into one of the variants of Arthaśāstra point of view. Even a glance at the very surface would at once bring out striking similarities between the attitudes of Arjuna and Kauṭilya.

In their 'political' concerns both appear out and out 'worldly' in their outlook; they do not seek validation of the authority and power of state from any notion of original bestowal, either through divine intervention or any form of covenant. Kauṭilya, of course, does refer to the well-known account of the acceptance of Manu Vivasat as the first king by people in order to escape 'the law of fishes' and compares the king's power with that of Indra and Yama, but the context in which he does so seems to indicate that he does not set much store by it. This reference at the most has only a peripheral significance in Kauṭilya's scheme of the validity of royal authority.[74] The mystique of political authority in the formulation by the Arthaśāstra thinkers is located within the rational ground that it is only the political authority, which provides the lone feasible alternative to the horrors of *mātsyanyāya*. Arjuna in his arguments makes no attempt whatsoever to invest the office of the ruler with any kind of divine or extraterrestial coating of authority. The state and kingship in Arjuna's formulation derive their *raison d'être* and sanction from the fact that without the protective umbrella of political authority, civil life cannot exist. It is the *rakshaṇa* and *pālana* of the subjects that is the supreme function and duty of the ruler. The king is thus a father figure as he protects (*rakshaṇa*), and he is also like a mother because he tends and nurtures (*pālana*).[75] The state derives its sanction because it is a social need and not because it reflects the will of god or partakes of divine character. This generally is the point of view of the Arthaśāstra thinkers.[76] Kauṭilya, as a matter of fact, does not seem to be overly concerned with the issue of the origin of state; his attitude seems to indicate that he considers the state as an existing reality, its necessity is taken for granted by people so absolutely that it requires no elaboration. Arjuna in his entire discourse does not even remotely refer to the question of the origin of state or kingship, though the core of his argument is directed to the elucidation of the absolute necessity of political authority for the existence of the civil society.

Arjuna's discourse thus can be placed midway between the Dharmaśāstra and Arthaśāstra. The acquisition and protection of territory are the coping stones of Kauṭilyan structure, the concept of *dharma* and its place in the functional horizon of state and royal policies are conspicuous by their absence. It is the strengthening and deepening of the interests of the ruler which is the prime concern of Kauṭilya.[77] It must, however, be added that Kauṭilya is never tired of repeating that righteousness of personal conduct on the part of the ruler and conscientious commitment to people's welfare are the very foundations on which all the interests of king rest. 'Happiness of the king issues out of the happiness of people' is the foundational maxim of Kauṭilya.[78] It is not the nature of the advocated state policies that distinguished the attitude of Arthaśāstra from that of Dharmaśāstra; both agreed broadly that the protection of the interests of people constituted the ground for the growth and continuation of the interest of the state. The real difference lay in the identification of the foundation and legitimacy of the authority of the state. In the Dharmaśāstra school, the state derives its validity, according to Arthaśāstra, from the fact that it embodies the principles of *dharma* within the political domain. The political domain in this formulation is made overtly dependent on the universal principle of *dharma*, which was regarded as the very basis that holds the world. The political domain thus does not have any autonomy of its own in this view. The Arthaśāstra attributes much more autonomy and centrality to the political domain. The state draws its validity, according to Arthaśāstra, from within the political domain itself; the legitimacy of the state arises from its ability to protect the society from the evils of *mātsyanyāya*. In the Dharmaśāstra 'politics' (*rājadharma*) is only a part of a larger scheme in which *dharma* holds the pivotal position, in the Arthaśāstra the 'gaining and the nurturing of the earth' is the axis round which revolve all the earthly activities. Arjuna also identifies the political authority with *daṇḍa*, which separates order from chaos. His views and approach have a distinct similarity with those of Kauṭilya. Yet, like the Dharmaśāstra, he identifies *daṇḍa* with *dharma*. Although he generally avoids referring to any universal moral principle beyond the political domain as a source of legitimacy of state and kingship, he veers round to the Dharmaśāstra standpoint that political authority finally merges into the larger notion of *dharma*.

In Arjuna's formulation, no space has been provided for the conflict between the 'ṣacerdotal' and the 'political'. It is a non-issue and does not figure at all in the political universe drawn by Arjuna. The primacy of political order is asserted in strong and unambiguous terms. It is the state and kingship that lends security and order preparing the ground for the growth and existence of a fulsome social life which included both *Varṇa* and *Āśrama* orders. It is the state and kingship which make it possible for people to discharge their religious and ritual duties; even the lives of the mendicants and friars in their forest abodes or in their attachment-free wanderings are made possible because of the security provided by political authority. Arjuna's views do not in any way support the contentions of Gonda and Heesterman.[79]

NOTES AND REFERENCES

1. For a recent example see Kumkum Roy, *The Emergence of Monarchy in North India*, Delhi, 1994.
2. A.K. Coomaraswamy, *Spiritual Authority and Temporal Power in the Indian Theory of Government*, Delhi, reprint, 1978.
3. J.C. Heesterman, *The Ancient Indian Royal Consecration*, The Hague, 1957. In his more recent publications on the same theme, Heesterman takes a more and more pronounced anthropological view of the real meaning of early Indian rites in the coronation ceremonies and states that these ritual practices in reality represent political contests, often fought on physical level of a bygone era, *vide, The Inner Conflict of Tradition*, Delhi, 1985.
4. J. Gonda, *Ancient Indian Kingship from Religious Point of View*, Leiden, 1969.
5. For an example see S.N. Eisenstadt and Harriet Hariman 'State Formation and Political Dynamics in India and Europe' in *Dynamics of State Formation*, ed. Martin Doornbos and Sudipta Kaviraj, New Delhi, 1997.
6. Herman Kulke, *Kings and Cults*, Delhi, 1993.
7. Louis Dumont, 'The Conception of Kingship in Ancient India', *Religion/Politics and History in India*, The Hague, 1970, pp. 62-88.
8. Whether state existed in Vedic society and when the tribal

organizations transformed themselves into states are still being debated upon. G.H. Ghurye, *Vedic India*, Bombay, 1979: R.S. Sharma *Material Culture and Social Formations in Ancient India*, Delhi, 1983: Romila Thapar, *From Lineage to State*, Delhi, 1984 give an idea about the contour of the debate. Earlier works are still relevant. See A.A. Macdonell and A.B. Keith, *Vedic Index*, Vol. II. Delhi, 1968 sv. *Rājan Rājya*, etc. pp. 210-21; U.N. Ghoshal, *A History of Hindu Public Life*, Calcutta, 1945.

9. *Arthaśāstra*, 1.5.8.
10. R.P. Kangle, *Kauṭiliya Arthaśāstra*, Part III, Bombay, 1965, pp. 42ff.
11. *Ibid.*
12. *Mahābhārata*, Śānti, 161.9.
13. *Ibid.*, 12.8; 12.11 & 12.15.
14. *Ibid.*, 12.8.2-9.
15. *Ibid.*, 12.8.12.
16. *Ibid.*, 12.8.4.
17. *Ibid.*, 12.8.7-9.
18. *Ibid.*, 12.8.10.
19. *Arthaśāstra*, see note 20.
20. The opening *sūtra* of Kauṭilya's work reads "This single (treatise on the) Science of Politics has been prepared mostly by bringing together (the teachings of) as many treatises on the Science of Politics as have been composed by ancient teachers for the acquisition and protection of the earth (*pṛithivyā lābhe pālane cha*), *ibid.*, 1.1.1; *pṛithivyā lābhapālanopāyāḥ śāstramartha śāstramti, ibid.*, 15.1.1-2.
21. *Ibid.*, 1.4.3.
22. *Ibid.*, books 6 & 7.
23. *Bhagavadgītā*, 2.31-37.
24. *Ibid.*, 2.37: *Hato vā prāpsyasi svargṁ jitvā vā bhokshyase mahiṁ/ Tasmād utthishṭha Kaunteya yuddhāya kṛitaniśchayaḥ.*
25. *Mahābhārata*, 12.8.25.
26. *Ibid.*, 12.15.14-15.
27. *Ibid.*, 12.15.20-23: 'become what you are by birth' means 'act and behave like a kshatriya king'.
28. *Ibid.*, 12.825-30.
29. *Ibid.*, 12.15.14.
30. *Ibid.*, 12.8.34-35.
31. *Ibid.*, 12.8.32.
32. *Ibid.*, 12.15.24-25.
33. *Ibid.*, 12.15.26.
34. *Ibid.*, 12.15.27-28. It is not that Arjuna is here saying that the life of hermits in forest is sham. He is only trying to underscore that it is not easy to escape the bonds of domesticity and the mere change of locale from village to forest is not enough.

35. The anti-ascetic sentiment expressed here by Arjuna is not really directed against the philosophy of detachment or even against asceticism *per se*; it is more of an expression of opposition to some of the anti-Vedic doctrines which were called *nāstika* way, see, for example *Ibid.*, 12.11. The *Mahābhārata* attitude towards the philosophy of detachment, or even towards asceticism, cannot be properly understood from the negative sentiments against the *nāstika* doctrine alone. The *Bhagavadgītā* and the Mokshadharma section of Śāntiparvan should also be taken into account. It may also be mentioned that some of the non-Vedic ascetic orders were sensitive to the fact that all those who joined their orders were not always motivated by the noblest urges. In the *Milindapañha*, the *thera* Nāgasena admits that there were a large number of hangers on in the Buddhist monasteries; there were people who wanted to escape the arms of law or people who thought joining the monastery was an easy way of earning livelihood, *Milindapañha*, II 1.5, Eng. tr by T.A. Rhys Davids, *The Questions of King Milinda*, Sacred Books of the East, pp. 49-50.
36. *Mahābhārata*, 12.11.
37. *Ibid.*, 12.11.20-25.
38. P.V. Kane, *History of Dharmaśāstra*, Vol. II. pt. I. pp. 424-25.
39. *Arthaśāstra*, 1.7.6-7. These *sutras*, however, refer only to *trivarga*, *artha*, *dharma* and *kāma*; *moksha* is omitted.
40. Here *svarga* obviously stands for *moksha*; and the reference is clearly to the four *purushārthas*, *Mahābhārata*, 12.8.17.
41. *Ibid.*, 12.8.16-17. Arthaśāstra can be described as 'social science'. *Artha* is territory populated by men and Arthaśāstra is the science that deals with the means to acquire and protect such territory. This is how Kauṭilya defines the nature and scope of Arthaśāstra, *Arthaśāstra*, 15.1.1-2. The way *artha* has been identified as constituting the basis of social life by Arjuna is akin to Kauṭilya's position.
42. *Ibid.*, 12.8.23.
43. *Ibid.*, 12.8.14; cf. *Mrichchhakaṭika*, Act I, Henry W. Wells, ed. *Six Sanskrit Plays*, London, 1964, pp. 50-51.
44. *Ibid.*, 12.8.22.
45. *Ibid.*, 12.8.19.
46. *Ibid.*, 12.8.12.
47. See p. 268 and notes 29-31.
48. *Mahābhārata*, 12.8.16, 23, 32.
49. *Ibid.*, 12.15. The whole chapter is devoted to the exposition of the significance of the political authority for an ordered and civilized society. Compared to the other two earlier chapters, viz. *Ibid.*, 12.8 and 12.11 this chapter is marked by a stronger texture of logic and form and there is a greater degree of tightness of arguments in the manner in which the arguments are developed.

50. *Ibid.*, 12.15.4.
51. For the ramifications of the distinction between the *dṛishṭārthaka* and the *adṛishṭārthaka* in the context of state and political authority in early India, see Sibesh Bhattcharya, 'Pluralism and Visible Path (*Pratyaksha Mārga*) and Early Indian Idea of Polity', Section V, *Proceedings of Indian History Congress*, Session 54.
52. It is not being contended that political order can exist autonomously and in conflict to the ultimate nature of reality; political order, in fact has to have coherence with the fundamental order of the universe. On the relation between the idea of political order and the concept of ultimate order in the universe in reference to early India, see Ramashray Roy, *Beyond Ego's Domain*, Delhi, 1999, especially chapter 10 'Kshatrasya Kshatram'.
53. *Mahābhārata*, 12.59.14, there was no state, no ruler, no law, no agency to enforce law; the people protected each other with the help of *dharma.* Similar accounts of perfectly harmonious living are also found in Buddhist and Purāṇic texts. Although the origin of state and kingship had been derived from the decline from this pristine state caused by greed and covetousness through a mechanism of covenant, there are some fundamental differences between these Indian accounts and the scheme of Rousseau. In Rousseau's account the degeneration began on account of the degeneration on the part of a few covetous individuals, in Indian accounts generally the decline has been presented as not due to the depravity of a few individuals, but as wholesale decline in the very stature, both moral as well as biological, of the entire mankind. It is more of a consequence of the spiritual decline of the age. See Ramashray Roy, *Vedic Vision and Political Order* (the work is in progress, the author kindly showed me some parts of the manuscript).
54. Although the expression *mātsyanyāya* has not been used, the reference to it is very clear; 'like fishes in water, the stronger will prey on the weaker', thus goes the description in *Mahābhārata*, 12.15.30. It is interesting that at one place Arjuna likens the ruler with 'fisherman' (*matsyaghāta*), *Ibid.*, 12.15.14. At first sight this simile looks a little odd; in order to see its significance it has to be placed in the context of *matsyanyāya.*
55. *Ibid.*, 12.15.5-6.
56. *Ibid.*, 12.15.7.
57. *Sarva loka* here obviously refers to the social world and not to such worlds as *pitṛiloka*, *devaloka*, etc.; the reference is obviously only to the *laukika* world.
58. *Ibid.*, 12.15.43 .
59. *Ibid.*, 12.15.2, *daṇḍaṁ dharmaṁ vidurbudhāḥ.*
60. *Ibid.*

61. *Ibid.*, 12.15.2-8, 10-13, 30, 34, 36-42, etc.
62. *Ibid.*, 12.59.
63. *Ibid.*, 12.15.10.
64. *Ibid.*, 12.15.11-12. *Ṛita*, and later *dharma*, were regarded as the innate ethical principle that governed the universe, see Sibesh Bhattacharya, note 51.
65. *Ibid.*, 12.15.35.
66. *Ibid.*, 12.15.49.
67. *Ibid.*, 12.15.12.
68. *Ibid.*, 12.15.32.
69. The entire chapter *Ibid.*, 12.15, is filled with examples of undesirable consequences of the absence of *daṇḍa*: people would not honour 'contracts' (*samaya*), the girls (*kalyāṇī*) would not milk cows and would refuse to respect the vows of fidelity and marriage, rites would not be performed and the ritual failures would spell disaster.
70. My friend Ramashray Roy is engaged in considering and unravelling the details and the nuances of this vision of order in his current project at the Indian Institute of Advanced Study, Shimla, on *Vedic Vision of Political Order*.
71. In the archetypal statement about the origin of the social organization in the Purushasūkta in the *Ṛigveda* (XII.19) the organic character of the society found expression. Unfortunately this aspect got pushed to the background under the weight of separation and hierarchy which tended to be overemphasized in later literature.
72. The early Indian traditions about the origin of kingship thus differ from the Western Contractualists. The Śāntiparvan account, (*Mahābhārata*, 12.59) of the kingless perfect state, despite its apparent similarity with Rousseau. The state of nature, in its core concept is different from that of Rousseau. In Rousseau's account, the founder of the civil society was the one who put a fence around a piece of land and claimed that it was 'his' and found the people simple enough to believe him. In the Indian account, it is the reduction of the spiritual and ethical content of the age, and not defects of individual characters, that ushered in the decline. I am grateful to my friend Ramashray Roy for drawing my attention to this difference.
73. *Mahābhārata*,12.15.2,35.
74. *Arthaśāstra*,1.13.1-14. In these *sūtras,* Kauṭilya explains how secret agents of the state should keep watch over people and control seditious activities. Kauṭilya uses the account of the 'origin of kingship' and the god-like majesty of the station of king as a strategy and an instrument of control to prevent sedition. It forms no part of the formulation of the source or the basis of the authority of the state. Moreover, even in these *sūtras,* it is the notion of *mātsyanyāya*

which holds the central position of driving home the fact among people that it is always an advantage to give obedience to king.

75. Arjuna and Kauṭilya do not actually use any such direct expression as father or mother for the king, but this idea seems to have been embedded in Indian consciousness from very early time. In the *Ṛigveda*, gods were often compared to affectionate father and sometimes to mother. Indra, for example is frequently compared to the protective and indulgent father and in one verse at least is compared to the affectionate and kind mother. See Macdonell and Keith, *Vedic Index*, Vol. I, Delhi, 1968, p. 256; *Ṛgveda*,VII.1.6 Eng.tr. R.T. Griffith, *The Hymns of the Rigveda*, Delhi, 1986. In one of his inscriptions, the Mauryan king Aśoka asks his officers to handle the people in their charge in the way conscientious nurses handle little babies, Pillar Edict IV, D.C. Sircar, *Inscriptions of Aśoka*, Delhi, 1957, p. 70. The expression *māi-bāp* seems to have been part of Indian vocabulary since much longer times than the linguistic features of the expression would suggest.

76. It probably needs to be underscored that the attitude of the Dharmaśāstra school on these points was quite different from that of Arthaśāstra school. Dharmaśāstra embellish state and kingship with a good deal of divine and other worldly mystique.

77. We have elaborated this point in an article, 'State in the Arthaśāstra Tradition' in Vol. 1, Pt. 2, ed. by G.C. Pande in the series on the *History of Science and Culture in Indian Civilization.*

78. *Arthaśāstra*, 1.19.34.

79. See Section I above.

19

The Concept of Communication as Developed in the *Mahābhārata*

S. Ramaratnam

Communication is an important aspect of human life. As a study, it has gained prominence in recent times with the development of Management Science. According to one estimate, about 75% of human activity is spent in communication, speaking or writing. Most of the problems of the world can be traced to misunderstanding and misunderstanding arises due to lack of communication, improper communication or wrong communication.[1] Effective communication can bring about better interpersonal relationship. It can improve the industrial relations and pave the way for optimum use of human resources. It can even bring about better international understanding and mutual faith.

What is communication? According to the American Society of Training Directors, communication is the interchange of thoughts and information that brings about mutual understanding and confidence on good human relations. According to Newman, communication is an exchange of facts, ideas, opinions or emotions by two or many persons.

Communication is made through symbols like facial expression, hand and body gestures, groaning, screaming, etc. But, by far, the most important and effective means of communication is through words.

According to Indian tradition, there exists a permanent relationship between word and its sense.

नित्यः शब्दार्थसंबन्धः

(*Vākyapadīya*, I. 23)

Just as the sense organs of perception have a natural power to perceive what comes into their purview, so also words have a natural capacity to convey ideas:

इन्द्रियाणां स्वविषयेष्वनादिर्योग्यता यथा।
अनादिरर्थैः शब्दानां संबन्धो योग्यता यथा।।

(*Ibid.*, III. 29.)

According to the Nyāya and Vaiśeshika system, the words have a peculiar power called *śakti* which is responsible for conveying the fixed sense. In later Nyāya-Vaiśeshika texts, this *śakti* is attributed to God:

अस्मात् पदात् अयमर्थो बोद्धव्यः इति ईश्वरसंकेतः शक्तिः।

(*Tarkasaṁgraha*)

Kālidāsa says that the word and sense are united together like Śiva and Pārvatī:

वागर्थाविव संपृक्तौ वागर्थप्रतिपत्तये।
जगतः पितरौ वन्दे पार्वतीपरमेश्वरौ।।

(*Raghuvaṁśa*, I.1)

Communication is not just passing on information to somebody. Unless the information is well understood by the receiver, in the same sense as intended by the sender, the process of communication is not complete. The process of communication can be represented thus:

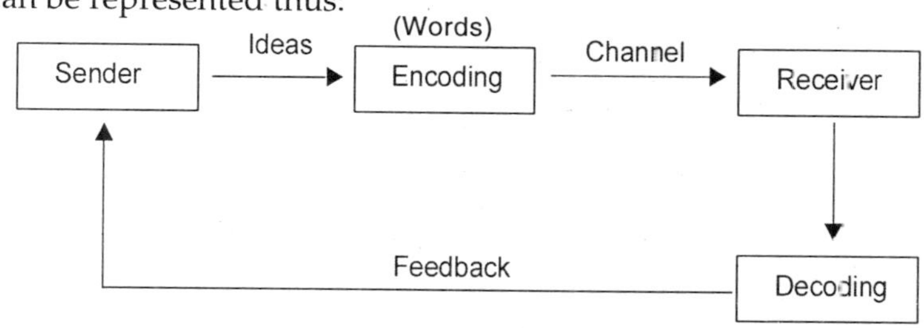

The sender decides the subject matter of communication and sets about the task of encoding his ideas, generally in the form of words. Then a channel is selected. It reaches the receiver, who decodes it and understands the message.[2] The instruction is carried out and that is how the sender gets the feedback.

What are the features of a good communication?[3] The *Arthaśāstra* gives the following list: अर्थक्रमः (arrangement of subject matter), संबन्धः (connection between the words), परिपूर्णता (completeness), माधुर्यं (sweetness), औदार्यं (exaltedness) and स्पष्टत्वं (clarity). All these tally with the principles of communication as dealt within Management Studies as well. For example, with respect to clarity, one is expected to avoid unfamiliar words and use familiar words instead. An illustration drawn from the Industry maybe given. "The machine has a tendency to develop excessive and unpleasant audial symptoms when operating at elevated temperatures" may very well be rendered crisply as "The machine tends to get noisy when it runs hot".

Illustrations of a good communication can be drawn from the *Mahābhārata*.

(i) *Arthakrama* refers to the arrangement of subject matter. In a communication, attention should be paid to what should come first and what should follow and in what order. There should be a cogency with respect to the order of the informations that are conveyed. A mission should set forth its objectives and necessity, the possibility of a solution, the deciding authority with respect to the decision to be taken, the conditions for carrying out the objectives and the pros and cons of the mission. For instance, during his peace mission, Kṛishṇa presents in his communication,

(a) the purpose of his visit
(b) the cause of the war
(c) why peace is advocated
(d) the possibility of peace
(e) who should take a decision on peace
(f) conditions for peace
(g) his own role as a peace-maker
(h) how the peace is made
(i) what will happen if peace is rejected

As for the purpose of his visit, Kṛishṇa says,

कुरूणां पाण्डवानां च शमस्स्यादिति भारत।
अप्रणाशेन वीराणां एतत् याचितुं उपागतः।।

(Udyoga, p. 259)

Oh, Bhārata, I have come here to beg for peace between the Pāṇḍavas and the Kauravas so that destruction of warriors on either side could be prevented.

Any communication, especially a peace mission, should begin

with a touch of humility. We may see that Kṛishṇa, for all his position and power, does not fight shy of begging for peace. At the same time he is very firm in pointing out that the war has been forced on the Pāṇḍavas on account of the adamant attitude of Duryodhana.

ते पुत्रास्तव (कौरव्य) दुर्योधन पुरोगमाः।
धर्मार्थौ पृष्ठतः कृत्वा प्रचरन्ति नृशंसवत्।।

(*Ibid.*)

These sons of yours, headed by Duryodhana, are behaving like wicked men pushing behind nobility and material good.

In a bilateral agreement, both the parties should be equally benefited. Offer and acceptance are the two sides of a contract. The offer should be made in such a way that the other party is convinced about the possibility of gains for himself and accepts it. After indicating the advantages of peace for both the parties, Kṛishṇa sets forth what would be the loss for the Kauravas if they do not agree for peace.

कुरूणां पाण्डवानां च शमस्यादिति भारत।
अप्रणाशेन वीराणां एतत् याचितुं उपागतः।।
सेयमापन्मद्दाघोरा कुरुष्वेव समुत्थिता।
उपेक्ष्यमाणा (कौरव्य) पृथिवीं घातयिष्यति।।

(*Ibid.*, p. 259)

The Kauravas will be facing a dreadful calamity if they do not opt for peace. The entire kingdom would be destroyed.

Then Kṛishṇa points out that peace is not impossible even at this stage.

शक्या चेयं शमयितुं त्वं चेदिच्छसि (भारत)।
न दुष्करो ह्यत्र शमो मतो मे भरतर्षभ।।

(*Ibid.*, p. 260)

Kṛishṇa states categorically that peace is dependent on Dhṛitarāshṭra. As for the Pāṇḍavas, Kṛishṇa takes personal responsibility of convincing them.

त्वय्यधीनश्शमो राजन् मयि चैव विशांपते।
पुत्रान् स्थापय कौरव्य स्थापयिष्याम्यहं परान्।। (*Ibid.*)

The condition for peace is that the Pāṇḍavas should be given their due share of the kingdom.

पित्र्यं तेभ्यः प्रदायाशं पाण्डवेभ्यो यथोचितम्।
ततस्सपुत्रस्सिद्धार्थो भुङ्क्ष्व भोगान् परन्तप।।

(*Ibid.*)

Now Kṛishṇa has to establish that he is impartial to both the parties so as to provide credibility to his role as a peace-maker. He also strikes a note of caution.

अहं तु तव तेषां च श्रेय इच्छगमि भारत।
लोभे अतिप्रसृतान् पुत्रान् निगृहीष्व विशांपते।।

(*Ibid.*)

I wish good luck to you as well as to the Pāṇḍavas. Restrain your sons, that have gone berserk out of greed.

Kṛishṇa, out of humility, began by saying that peace is begged. But his humility should not be mistaken as a sign of weakness. He, therefore, points out that the Pāṇḍavas are quite prepared for the war if it is inevitable. Now the ball is in the court of Dhṛitarāshṭra who will be held responsible for the outbreak of war.

स्थिताश्शुश्रूषितुं पार्थाः स्थिता योद्धुं अरिन्दमाः।
यते पथ्यतमं राजन् तस्मिंस्तिष्ठ परन्तप।।

(*Ibid.*)

Sambandha is the statement of subject matter with complete compatibility between the parts of the statement. In a sentence like *kuntīputro vināyakaḥ,* this is absent. On the other hand, in the speech of Vidura there is very good *sambandha.*

त्यजेत् कुलार्थे पुरुषं ग्रामस्यार्थे कुलं त्यजेत्।
ग्रामं जनपदस्यार्थे आत्मार्थे पृथिवी त्यजेत्।।

(Udyoga, 37.15)

An individual should be abandoned for the sake of a family, a family for the sake of a village, a village for the sake of a country and the whole earth for the sake of one's soul.

कृत्यानि पूर्वं परिसंख्याय सर्वा
ण्यायव्यये चानुरूपां च वृत्तिम्।

संगृह्णीयादनुरूपान् सहायान्
सहायसाध्यानि हि दुष्कराणि।।

(*Ibid.*, p. 22)

After consideration of all the duties to be discharged, the income and expenditure and due remuneration, one should take suitable assistants. Even the most difficult things are indeed accomplished with the help of others.

अस्तब्धमक्लीबमदीर्घसूत्रं सानुक्रोशंश्लक्ष्णमहार्यमन्यैः।
अरोगजातीयमुदारवाक्यं दूतं वदन्ति अष्टगुणोपपन्नम्।।

(*Ibid.*)

A messenger should possess these eight qualities, viz., presence of mind, boldness, readiness in action, tenderness, refinement in manners, incorruptibility, sound health and dignified speech. *Paripurṇatā* or completeness results when a statement is self explanatory with reason, illustration and the like.

भवितव्यं सदा राज्ञा गर्भिणीसहधर्मिणा।
कारणं च महाराज शृणु येनदेमिष्यते।।
यथा हि गर्भिणी हित्वा स्वयं प्रियं मनसोऽनुगम्।
गर्भस्य हितमादत्ते तथा राज्ञाऽप्यसंशयम्।।
वर्तितव्यं कुरुश्रेष्ट नित्यं धर्मानुवर्तिना।
स्वं प्रियं समभित्यज्य यद् यल्लोकहितं भवेत्।।

(Śānti, 56. 44-46)

Here, the view expressed is that a ruler should give up his own personal comforts and pleasures. The reason given is that the interest of the people must be uppermost in his mind. If he indulges in pleasures, his interest in the welfare of the people will be pushed to the background. An illustration is set forth in this context. A ruler should be like a mother bearing a child in her womb. The expectant mother always desires the welfare of the child and sacrifices her own pleasures and comforts.

Mādhurya is the use of words that have a pleasing sense which is easily conveyed by the speaker and easily understood by the listener[4] as well. An illustration for this can be found in the speech of Nārada.

काच्चिदर्याश्च कल्पन्ते धर्मे च रमते मनः।
कुलीनाश्च अनुरक्ताश्च कृतास्ते वीर मन्त्रिणः।। (Sabhā, p. 97)

Are you getting the desired benefits? Is your mind attached to virtue? Are your ministers devoted and sincere?

Audārya is exaltedness. It is the representation of noble ideas through decent expressions. For example:

नास्ति विद्यासमं चक्षुः नास्ति सत्यसमं तपः।
नास्ति रागसमं दुःखं नास्ति त्यागसमं सुखम्।।

(Śānti, p. 407)

There is no eye equal to the learning, no penance equal to the observance of truth, no misery equal to the desire and no happiness equal to renunciation. *Spashtatva* is clarity of expression or the absence of obsolete words and bombastic expressions. In sentences like *rāmalakshmaṇau bharataśatrughnau ahvayataḥ*, there is lack of *spashtatva*. On the other hand, in the below mentioned verse there is clarity of thought and expression.

सत्यं ब्रह्म सत्यं तपः
सत्यं सृजति च प्रजाः।।
सत्येन धार्यते लोकः
स्वर्गं सत्येन गच्छति।।

(Śānti, 183.1-2)

The sentences in the verse have not more than two or three words and are simple enough to be understood even by common men.

As to what can be communicated through official document, the *Arthaśāstra* (II.10.23-24) says,

निन्दा प्रशंसा पृच्छा च तथाख्यान भथार्थना।
प्रत्याख्यान भुपालम्भः प्रतिषेधोऽय चोदना।।
सान्त्वमभ्युपपतिश्च भर्त्सनाःनुययौ तथा।
एतेष्वर्थाः प्रवर्तन्ते त्रयोदशसु लेखजाः।।

Censure, praise, query, statement of facts, request, refusal, blaming, prohibition, injunction, appeasement, help, threatening and prohibition are the thirteen elements that can be communicated in a document. While these can be expressed rather plainly in day-to-day talk, the same have to be conveyed in a different tone in an official communique. For example, Kṛishṇa censures Arjuna when the latter gets confused on the battle-front and refuses to fight.[5] But the censure is done in a dignified way without causing any damage to Arjuna's reputation as a great warrior.

कुतस्त्वा कश्मलमिदं विषमे समुपस्थितम्।
अनार्यजुष्टमस्वर्ग्यम्कीर्तिकरमर्जुन।।

(*Gītā*. II.2.)

How has this confusion overtaken you at this critical juncture? It is unbecoming of a noble soul, it will not lead to heaven and it will not contribute to your fame.

नूनं च तव नैवास्ति मन्युर्भरतसत्तम।
तते भ्रातृंश्च मां चैव दृष्ट्वा न व्ययते मनः।।

(Vana, p. 168)

Draupadī addresses Yudhishṭhira thus: "You, best of the Bhāratas, there seems to be no anger (for the just cause) in you. Your mind is not pained on seeing your brothers and me. The anger is indeed a quality that should be shunned by all men. Anger is the root cause of all troubles. But anger should be shown against injustice; otherwise it will be misunderstood as a sign of weakness." Hence Draupadī arouses the anger of the Pāṇḍavas. Her intention is that the silent suffering in the forest should not lead to complacency and inaction.[6]

The praise of a deserving person or an action should be spontaneous. It should come from the heart and should not simply be an outward expression of words alone. Praise showered on an undeserving person will only amount to flattery. In Arjuna's praise of Kṛishṇa there is sincerity and devotion.

पितासि लोकस्य चराचरस्य
त्वमस्य पूज्यश्य गुरुर्गरीयान्।
न त्वत्समौऽस्तयभ्यधिकः कुतोऽन्यो
लोकत्रयेऽप्यप्रतिमप्रभावः।।
तस्मात्प्रणम्य प्रणिधाय कायं
प्रसादयै त्वामहमीशमीडचम्।
पितेव पुत्रस्य सखेव सख्युः
प्रियः प्रियायार्हसि देव सोदुम्।।

(*Gītā*, XI. 43-44)

You are the father of the world and all its creatures, the movable and the immovable. You are the greatest and the most respected preceptor. Oh, the Lord of incomparable power, there is none equal to you in all the three worlds. Where is one better than you?

As for query, the entire *kachchit sarga* in the Sabhāparvan is significant wherein Nārada enquires of Yudhishṭhira about his administration. One example may be cited here:

कच्चित्कृतं विजानीषे कर्तारं च प्रशंससि।
सतां मध्ये महाराज सत्करोषि च पूजयन्।।

(Sabhā, p.100)

Great king, do you recognize a work done, acclaim the doer and honour him with rewards in the midst of good people.

Whatever is said about motivation in the Management Science is given in a nutshell in this verse. Recognition of merit is one of the important motivating factors. According to Maslow's theory of organizational behaviour, human needs are classified into five levels, in a hierarchical fashion thus:

1. Physiological needs
2. Safety and security
3. Belongingness
4. Self-esteem
5. Self-actualization

The physiological needs can be satisfied through economic factors and that is why the adequate reward for the work done is recommended. The safety and security needs arise from the instincts of self-preservation and a concern for the future. A sense of belongingness can be infused into the minds of subordinates by establishing a warm, harmonious inter-personal relationship. Everybody feels that his worth, capability and strength must be recognized and appreciated. Frustration leads to inferiority complex, weakness and helplessness. In order to avoid such feelings among the subordinates, an administrator has to acclaim the merits of the good workers in public and acknowledge their contribution. Self-actualization is the desire to become what one is capable of becoming. This can be done by enthusing the subordinates to set higher goals for themselves and to achieve them. All these ideas are briefly indicated in the *Mahābhārata* verse cited. Humility is the hallmark of a request. An expression of humility in a request may generally ensure its acceptance. We make a request only when we find that it is impossible to achieve a target all by ourselves. All individuals are dependent on one another. In an establishment, the employer and the employees are inter-dependent. An employer can get the work done more easily through a request than by a command or an order. Likewise, the employees can get their problems settled through requests and peaceful negotiations. In the quest for knowledge, a humble request alone can bring about the desired result. This is how a request can be communicated.

कार्पण्यदोषोपहतस्वभावः
पृच्छामि त्वां धर्मसंमूढचेताः।
यच्छ्रेयः स्यान्निश्चितं ब्रूहि तन्मे
शिष्यस्तेऽहं शाधि मां त्वां प्रपन्नम्।।

(*Gītā*, II.7)

With my normal nature being spoiled by weakness and with my mind confused with regard to duty, I am asking you. Please tell me what is proper for me. I am your disciple. Please save me. I have surrendered unto you.

A statement of facts has to be straight and to the point. For example:

सर्वाभिशङ्की नृपतिर्यश्च सर्वहरो भवेत्।
स क्षिप्रं अनृजुः लुब्धः स्वजनेनैव बध्यते।।

(Śānti, 57.27)

A king who suspects everything, who allows himself to be deprived of his wealth, who is crooked and who is greedy, is killed by his own people.

A refusal can be blunt or polite depending upon the situation. Duryodhana refuses bluntly to part with even an inch of space when a peace proposal is put forth by Krishṇa.

यावद्धि तीक्ष्णया सूच्या विद्धयेदग्रेण केशव।
तावदप्यपरित्याज्यं भूमेर्नः पाण्डवान्प्रति।।

(Udyoga, p. 267)

In Arjuna's refusal to fight, on the other hand, there is politeness.

न हि प्रपश्यामि ममापनुद्यान्
यच्छ्गेकमुच्छोषणमिन्द्रियाणाम्।
अवाप्य भूमावसपत्नमृद्धं
राज्यं सुराणामपि चाधिपत्यम्।।
एवमुक्त्वा हृषीकेशं गुडाकेशः परन्तप।।
न योत्स्य इति गोविन्दमुक्त्वा तूष्णीं वभूव ह।।

(*Gītā,* II.8.9)

As in the case of *nindā,* there has to be a touch of decency in *upālambha* or blaming also. There cannot be any justification in the act of Bhīshma and Droṇa when they kept quiet while Draupadī was molested in the open court. Draupadī takes them to task summarily but without insulting them.

द्रोणस्य भीष्मस्य च नास्ति सत्त्वं
क्षतुस्टथैवास्य महात्मनोऽपि।
राज्ञस्तया हीनमधर्ममुग्रं
न लक्षयन्ते कुरुवृद्धमुख्याः।।

(Sabhā, p. 132)

Is there no good sense in Bhīshma, Droṇa, Vidura and Dhṛitarāshṭra? Do not these Kuru elders notice this terrible unrighteous act?

In the prohibition of a certain act, the reasoning has to be powerful and the logic has to be unassailable. This is what we find in Gāndhārī's words when she exhorts her husband to abandon Duryodhana.

मा कुलस्य क्षये घोरे कारणं त्वं भविष्यसि।
वद्धं सेतुं को नु भिन्द्याद् धर्मच्धगन्तं च पावकम्।।
शमे स्थितान्को नु पार्थान्कोपयेद्भरतर्षभ।
राजन्नयं मद्वचनात् त्यज्यतां कुलपांसनः।।

(Sabhā, p. 153)

Do not become the cause of the terrible destruction of our family; who will break the dam that has been built? Who will blow up the extinguished fire? Who will infuriate the Pāṇḍavas who have settled for peace? Oh, king, on my word, let this disgrace of the family, Duryodhana, be abandoned.

It is a pity that Gāndhārī's words were not heeded to, which resulted in the destruction of the Kauravas.

An injunction has to be firm and authoritative. For example:

वत्सलास्सर्वभूतानां वाच्याः श्रोत्रसुखा गिरः।
परिवादापवादौ च पारुष्यं चात्र गर्हितम्।।
अवज्ञानमंहकारो दम्भश्चैव विगर्हितः।।

(Śānti, p. 410)

Affectionate words, pleasing to the ears of all beings, must be spoken; reviling, scandal and violence in speech are forbidden; insulting others, egotism and hypocrisy are condemned.

Difference of opinion and misunderstanding are bound to appear between individuals. But an administrator must try to appease the affected party through a proper communication. During their forest life, Draupadī becomes impatient and blames the creator of partiality, citing their own calamity and the prosperity of the Kauravas. For this, Yudhishṭhira says:

नाहं धर्मफलोकाङ्क्षी राजपुत्रि चराम्युत।
धर्म एव मनः कृष्णे स्वभावाच्चैत मे घृतम्।
न धर्मफलमाप्नोति यो धर्मं दोग्धुमिच्छति।।

(Vana, p. 169)

Princess, I do not observe Dharma expecting fruit out of it. But my very nature and mind are set on Dharma only. He who exploits Dharma misses its true purpose.

धर्म एव पल्वो नान्यत्स्वर्गं द्रौपदि गच्छताम्।
ईश्वरं चापि भूतानां धातारं मा च वै क्षिप।।

(Vana, p. 169)

Dharma alone is the boat for those who want to go to heaven. Do not blame the Lord who is the creator of all beings.

Help can be procured even from unfriendly camps through communicating skills. Thus Duryodhana secures the services of Kṛishṇa's army through his clever words.

A certain amount of threat maybe needed for a leader to bring about discipline. This is what Kṛishṇa adopts when he senses that his peace mission may fail. He threatens Duryodhana of grave consequences:

यच्चेभ्यो याचमानेभ्यः पित्र्यंशं न दित्ससि।
तच्च पाप प्रदाताऽसि भ्रष्टैश्वर्यो निपातितः।।

(Udyoga, p. 268)

That which you do not like to give to the Pāṇḍavas who beg for their rightful paternal share, will be taken away forcefully from you and you will fall from your grace and power.

In propitiation, there should be an expression of sincerity and devotion. When Draupadī's appeal to the elders of the court and to her own husbands failed to save her, she propitiated Lord Kṛishṇa and appealed to him fervently. Then came the help from the Lord.

शङ्खचक्रगदापाणे द्वारकानिलयाच्युत।
गोविन्द पुण्डरीकाक्ष रक्ष मां शरणागताम्।।
हा कृष्ण द्वारकावासिन् क्वासि यादवनन्दन।
इमामवस्थां संप्राप्तां अनाथां किमुपेक्षसे।।
कृष्ण कृष्ण महायोगिन् विश्वात्मन् विश्वभावन।
प्रपन्नां पाहि गोविन्द कुरूमध्येऽवसीदतीम्।।

(Sabhā, p. 138)

Oh lord, armed with conch, discus and mace. Oh, the lotus-eyed Govinda, protect me who has sought refuge in you. Oh, Kṛishṇa, where are you? Why do you neglect the helpless being who has come to this critical state? Kṛishṇa, the great Yogin, the Soul of the Universe, the creator of the Universe, Govinda, save the suppliant creature perishing in the midst of the Kurus.

If the propitiation is sincere enough, the appeal connected with it will definitely be answered and so is the case with respect to Draupadī also. She is saved by the Lord at the right moment.

Communication will be effective if it is made spicy with humour. This verse from the *Mahābhārata* has a tinge of subtle humour in it.

अनर्थे चैव निरतं अर्थे चैव पराङ्मुखम्।
न ते भर्तारमिच्छन्ति षण्डं पतिमिव स्त्रियः।।

People do not like to have him as their ruler who is ever intent on useless pursuits and averse to the useful one, like women who would not like to have eunuchs as their husbands.

Truth is the very essence of communication, but raw truth may sometimes do more harm than good. So the *Mahābhārata* says:

सत्यं ब्रूयात् प्रियं ब्रूयात् न ब्रूयात् सत्यमप्रियम्।
प्रियं च नानृतं ब्रूयात् एष धर्मः सनातनः।।

(II.5)

Truth is to be uttered but it has to be pleasant. Do not speak the truth that is not liked. A falsehood, though pleasant, should not be spoken. If the communication is in the form of an advice, the *Mahābhārata* gives the following guidelines:

शुभं वा यदि वा पापं द्वेष्यं वा यदि वा प्रियम्।
नापृष्टः कस्यचिद् ब्रूयात् यइन नेच्छेत् पराभवम्।।

(II.4)

One who does not want to be humiliated should not advice, whether good or bad, agreeable or not without being asked.

An administrator should be careful about his communication. He should not blame others unnecessarily. The *Mahābhārata* says:

परं क्षिपति दोषेण वर्तमानः स्वयं तथा।
यश्च क्रुध्यत्यनीशानः स य मूदतमो नरः।।

(I.45)

A good administrator should be aware of his own limitations and mistakes. That man who is himself blameful, yet casts blame on others, becomes angry with those over whom he has no mastery, is the greatest fool.

There should be an element of suspense in the communication. It will create an interest in the minds of the listeners and arouse their curiosity. A verse from the *Mahābhārata* can be cited in this context:

एकया द्वे विनिश्चित्य
त्रीं चतुर्भिः वशे कुरु।
पञ्च जित्वा विदित्वा षट्
सप्त हित्वा सुखी भव।।

(I.51)

By one, discriminate two, control three by four. Conquering five, knowing six and giving up seven, be happy. (One – intellect. Two – the right and the wrong. Three – friend, foe, neutral. Four – conciliation, use of money, divisive tactics, punishment. Five – the five senses. Six – the six measures of foreign policy. Seven – the seven vices, namely, women, wine, gambling, hunting, harsh words, severity of punishment and waste of wealth).

In communication, harshness should be avoided.

द्वे कर्मणी नरः कुर्वन् अस्मिन् लोके विरोचते।
अब्रुवन् परुषं कचित् असतो नार्चयन् तथा।।

(I.61)

By not speaking harsh words and by not worshipping the wicked, a man becomes famous.

A proper control is necessary in the use of words.

वाक्संयमो हि नृपते सुदुष्करतमो मतः।
अर्थवच्च विचित्रं च न शक्यं बहु भाषितुम्।।

(II.77)

Control of speech is said to be most difficult and to hold on a long discourse with variety and substance is not easy too.

Communication is a two-way process. The receiver will have to respond effectively for the communication process to be completed. His response should be positive. Evasive answers or a zig zag reply will lead nowhere. The *Mahābhārata* says:

पृष्टों धर्मं निर्व्रूयात् गोकर्णशिथिलं चरन्।
धर्मात् भ्रश्यति राजेस्तु नास्य लोकोऽस्ति न प्रजाः।।

(III.38)

One who is asked about virtue should not reply in a zig zag manner like a mule wandering about. A king who gives such a reply (while occupying the seat of a judge) loses both the kingdom and the subjects.)

He should not be afraid of censuring the wicked whoever it be. He gets half the sin, the sinner a quarter of it and audience, the other quarter.

त्रेष्टेऽर्धं तु हरेत्तत्र भवेत् पादश्च कर्तरि।
पादस्तेषु सभासत्सु यत्र निन्द्यो न निन्द्यते।।

(III.40)

Harsh words must be avoided in a communication. The *Mahābhārata* says:

मर्माण्यस्थीनि हृदयं तथाऽसून् रूक्षावाचो निर्दहन्तीह पुंसाम्।।

(IV.7)

Harsh words consume the vital parts of the body, the bones, the heart and vital breaths. Therefore, a virtuous man should always avoid harsh words.

रूक्षां वाचं रुशतीं वर्जयेत्।

(IV.6)

A man uttering harsh words, being acrimonious in disposition, hard-hearted, piercing men with wordy thorns, carries the goddess of death in his tongue.

अरुन्तदुं परुषं रूक्षवाचं वाक्कण्टकैः वितुदन्तं मनुष्यान्।
विद्यात् अलक्ष्मीकतमं जनानां मुखे निबद्धां निर्ऋतिं वै वहन्तम्।।

(IV.8)

On many occasions, silence is a better way of communication rather than words. The *Mahābhārata* says:

अव्याहतं व्याहतात् श्रेय आहुः
सत्यं वदेत् व्याहृतं तत् द्वितीयम्।
प्रियं वदेत् व्याहृतं तत् तृतीयं
धर्म्यं वदेत् व्याहृतं तच्चतुर्यम्।।

Silence is said to be better than speech. Speech, if at all, should be truthful. Truthful utterance should also be beneficial. Beneficial utterance of truth should conform to the *dharma*. (Hence silence is better.)

An administrator should seek the wise counsel of the Advisory Committee before taking a decision and communicating it to the general public. The *Mahābhārata* says:

न श्रद्दधाति कल्याणं
परेभ्योऽपि आत्मशङ्कितः।
निराकरोति मित्राणि
यो वै सोऽधमपुरुषः।।

(IV.19)

He is a mean man who does not listen to the good counsel from others, who is suspicious of himself and repudiates his own friends.

But one should be careful about the counsel. The *Mahābhārata* says:

न निह्नवं मन्त्रगतस्य गच्छेत्
संस्पृष्टमन्त्रस्य कुसङ्गतस्य।

न च श्रूयात् नाश्वसिमि त्वयीति
सकारणं व्यपदेशं तु कुर्यात्।।

(V.27)

One should not seek secret counsels of a person who keeps bad company. But he should not drive him away by saying – I do not have faith in you. He should offer some pretext with a plausible reason and withdraw.

One of the channels of communication available for an administrator is through his own subordinates. But he should be choosy about people selected for such an important job. The *Mahābhārata* says:

वाक्यं तु यो नाद्रिमते अनुशिष्टः
प्रत्याहयश्चापि नियुज्यमानः।
प्रज्ञाभिमानी प्रतिकूलवादी
त्याज्यस्स तादृक् त्वयैव भृत्यः।।

(V.26)

There should be an element of suggestion in communication. A censure, for instance, conveyed suggestively will be accepted but not the one hurled at a person directly. Lofty ideas will carry weight only when they are conveyed suggestively. The *Bhagavadgītā* explains the nature of a *yogin* suggestively thus:

या निशा सर्वभूतानां तस्यां जागर्ति संयमी।
यस्यां जाग्रति भूतानि सा निशा पश्यतो मुनेः।।

(II.69)

What is a night for others is the time the *yogin* keeps awake. The time when others keep awake is the night for a 'seeing' *yogin*.

This means that a *yogin* is involved in things beyond this world in which the ordinary men have no interest. The *yogin*, on the other hand, is not interested in the worldly things which attract the attention of the ordinary mortals.

The *Arthaśāstra* also points out certain defects in communication, which have to be avoided: – अकान्तिः व्याघातः पुनरुक्तं अपशब्दः संप्लवः – Absence of charm, contradiction, repetition, incorrect use of a word and confusion. Examples:

Avoid	*Use*
1. Absence of charm: We are in receipt of your order.	We are pleased to receive your order.
2. Contradiction: We are honoured to be dishonoured by you.	We regret to be dishonoured by you.
3. Repetition: The consensus of opinion is that the tax is unfair.	The consensus is that the tax is unfair.
4. Incorrect use of a word: We must take steps to boost the morality of the workers.	We must take steps to boost the morale of the workers.
5. Confusion: Knowing that there would be objection to the price we fixed was the reason we fixed a lower price.	The price was lowered in order to avoid objection on its hike.

Illustrations to these can be found in plenty through the words of *vidūshakas* in Sanskrit drama. The *Dosha prakaraṇa* in the Alaṅkāra works also gives a list of such expressions that are to be avoided. For example:

1. कार्तार्थ्यं लभते कदा?

   'When will he attain the fulfilment of his desires?' Here the word कार्तार्थ्य is harsh to hear, which results in 'absence of charm'.
2. अरण्यमहिषोदग्रविषाणोदरजन्मनाम्।
   महत्यर्घेऽपि मुक्तानां स्त्रियो मुक्ताविभूषणाः।।

   (*Pratāparudrīya*, V. 84)

   'In the forest the womenfolk decorated themselves with pearls that were procured from the horns of the bisons.' Here the possibility of getting pearls from the horns of the bisons is contradictory to nature.
3. जीर्णकाननसंकीर्णे विन्ध्ये काननवृत्तयः। (*Ibid.*, V.29)

   Here the repetition of the word कानन has no significance.
4. कदा भविष्यते वासः ? (*Ibid.*, V.14)

   Here the word भविष्यते is a wrong usage (grammatical mistake).
5. कदा भविष्यते वासः कटकेषु महीभृताम्।

'When will the kings get back to their city (*kaṭaka*) life?' Here the confusion arises due to another meaning of the world *kaṭaka*, that is, 'mountains'.

The *Arthaśāstra* also gives a list of thirty-two devices of preparing a document (like *adhikaraṇa, vidhāna* and *yoga)*. They are selection of topic, statement of contents, employment of technical terms, reasons for establishing something, mention of rules, explanation, caution, reference, application, indication, analogy, implication, doubt, existence of similar situations, corollary, agreement, emphasizing derivation of terms, illustration, exception, the *prima facie* view, the established view, reference to a future proposal, restriction, options available, summary of the proposal and conclusion.

It maybe seen from this list that the approach given by *Arthaśāstra* agrees with the modern concept of Systems Analysis and Systems Approach. Examples to the majority of these items can be found in the *Mahābhārata*.

It is clear, therefore, that the principles of communication were known to the ancient Indians and were put to effective use in the official circles as well as in literary works.

NOTES AND REFERENCES

1. The *Mahābhārata* says:

अभ्यावहति कल्याणं
विविधं वाक् सुभाषिता।
सैव दुर्भाषिता राजन्
अनर्थाय उपपद्यते।।

(Viduraniti, II. 78.)

O King, a speech well-spoken, brings in various kinds of beneficial effects while the same if ill-spoken tends to create troubles.

रोहते सायकैर्विद्धं वनं परशुना हतम् ।
वाचा दुरुक्तं बीभत्सं न संरोहति वाक्क्षतम् ।।

(II.79)

The wound caused by arrows gets healed in due course. Likewise, forest cut down by axe sprouts again but a verbal wound caused by words, ill-uttered and loathsome, will never be healed.

Cf. Many an arrow at random sent
May hit the mark the archer little meant
Many a word at random spoken
May soothe or wound the heart that is broken.

कर्णी नालीकनाराचान् निर्हरन्ति शरीरतः।
वाक्शल्यस्तु न निर्हर्तुं शक्यो हृदिशयो हि सः।।

(II.80)

Arrows of *karṇī* (an arrow with head in the shape of an ear), *nālīka* (an arrow discharged through a tube) and *nārācha* (an arrow made of iron) can be extracted from the body wherein they have pierced, but a wordy dart is impossible for extraction. It remains verily struck in the heart.

वाक्सायका वदनात् निष्पतन्ति दैराहतश्शोचति रात्र्यहानि।
परस्य नामर्मसु ते पतन्ति तान् पण्डितो नावसृजेत् परेभ्यः।। (II. 81)

Wordy arrows issue forth from the mouth and one hit by them grieves both day and night. A wise man should not discharge them at others since they hit the vital part of a man already hurt.

In communication, timeliness plays an important part. Words uttered without the sense of timeliness brings about doom.

अप्राप्तकालं वचनं बृहस्पतिरपि ब्रुवन्।
लभते बुद्धयवज्ञानं अवमानं च भारत।।

(VII.2)

Even Bṛihaspati (guru of gods), if he were to speak untimely words, incurs contempt and disrespect.

2. The receiver is as much important as the sender in communication. The *Mahābhārata* says:

क्षिप्रं विजानाति चिरं श्रृणोति
विज्ञाय चार्थे भजते न कामात्।
नासंस्पृहशे व्यपयुङ्क्त परार्थे
तत् प्रज्ञानं प्रथमं पण्डितस्य

(I.29)

That is the foremost character of a wise man when he understands quickly, bears patiently, grasping the main point quickly, applies it without passion and who spends not his energy in others affairs unasked.

3. Who is a good communicator? The *Mahābhārata* says:

प्रवृत्तवाक् चित्रकथः
अहवान् प्रतिभानवान्।
आशु ग्रन्थस्य वक्ता च
यस्य पण्डित उच्यते।।

(I.35)

One who speaks boldly, who can discourse eloquently on diverse topics in a telling way, who can see the pros and cons of everything, who is endowed with a ready insight into every rising problem, who can quote texts quickly and interpret them intelligently.

4. The *Mahābhārata* says that the following give delight:

समागमश्च सखिभिः महांश्रचैव धनागमः।
पुत्रेण च परिपवङ्त्रः सन्तिपातश्च मैथुने।

समये च प्रियालापः सयूथ्येषु समुन्नतिः।
अभिप्रेतस्य लाभश्च पूजा च धनसंसदि।।

(I. 104)

Union with friends, acquisition of great wealth, embrace of son, conjugal love, sweet conversation at a proper time, elevation among one's own class, acquisition of what is wished for and respect in assemblage.

5. When Dhṛitarāshṭra complains of sleeplessness, Vidura censures him, but in a polite way.

अनियुक्तं बलवता दुर्बलं हीनसाधनम्।
हृतस्वं कामिनं चोरमाविशान्ति प्रजागराः।।

(Udyoga, 33.14)

Sleeplessness overtakes the weak set on by the strong, one bereft of means of livelihood, the man deprived of his wealth, a lover and a thief.

In the next step, Vidura brings out the good nature of Yudhishṭhira.

आनृशंस्यात् अनुक्रोशात्
धर्मात् सत्यात् पराक्रमात्।
गुरुत्वात् त्वयि संप्रेक्ष्य
बदून् क्लेशान् तितिक्षते।।

Mildness, tenderness, righteousness, truthfulness, heroism and consideration for elders endowed with such qualities, Yudhishṭhira is putting up with insults.

Vidura does not want to be very blunt initially but gradually he assumes more authority and censures the king.

6. The *Mahābhārata* has this to say on the role of the president of an assemblage.

अनेना भवति श्रेष्ठो मुच्यन्तोऽपि सभासदः।
कर्तारमेनो गच्छेत् वा निन्द्यो यत्र हि निन्द्यते।।

(III. 41)

When the censurable are condemned, the president becomes sinless as well as the audience and the sin reverts to the sinner himself.

BIBLIOGRAPHY

Arthaśāstra of Kauṭilya, Ed. R.P. Kangle, Motilal Banarsidass, 1973.
Bhāgavadgītā, Edn. Advaita Ashrama, Calcutta, 1956.
Business Communication, Reymond V. Lesikar & John D. Petit, Richard. D. Irwin, Homewood, Illinois, 1966.
Mahābhārata condensed (in the poet's own words), (A.M. Srinivasachariar (Ed.) G.A.Natesan & Co, Madras 1935. (The *Mahābhārata* quotations other than those from *Viduranīti* are from this book only).
Pratāparudrīya, Sanskrit Education Society, Madras, 1970.
Raghuvaṁśa, The Little Flower Company, Madras, 1952.
Śānti – Śāntiparvan of the *Mahābhārata*.
Tarkasaṁgraha, Ramakrishna Math, Madras, 1985
Vākyapadīya, ed. University Manuscript Library, Trivandrum, 1942.
Viduranīti, Ed. P.N. Menon, The Educational Supplies Depot, Palghat, 1962.

20

The *Mahābhārata* in Inscriptions

K.V. Ramesh

In preparing my paper on this topic, I had to necessarily proceed with certain self-imposed restrictions mainly because of the vastness of the two sources I have to deal with, viz., the great epic *Mahābhārata* on the one hand and the available epigraphical wealth on the other. Beginning with the dawn of the Classical Sanskrit age around the commencement of the 4th century AD, as the centuries rolled by, there is a phenomenally progressive increase in the number of inscriptions all over those parts of Asia which had come under the direct influence of the Sanskritic ethos and there is also a proportionate increase in epigraphical references to the two Indian epics in keeping with the growing trend to seek traditional credibility for the glorification of historical personalities. I am confining myself mainly to direct epigraphical references to the *Mahābhārata* and to its main characters. To quote an instance, the charters of the 16th century Āravīḍu dynasty of Vijayanagara trace the origins of the family, no doubt with an eye on earning social credibility, to the Moon, Budha, Purūavas, Āyu, Nahusha, Yayāti, Puru, Bharata, Śāntanu, Vijaya (Arjuna), Abhīmanyu and Parīkshit. Even the Pallavas of Kāñchi claim descent from Bharadvāja, Droṇa and Aśvatthāman (see, e.g., *SII*, II, pt. III, 73 and 74). And these two dynasties are not alone in making such legendary claims. I am ignoring such and similar epigraphical data mainly because the source of such vested legends need not necessarily be the *Mahābhārata*.

Another minor point I would like to mention here, though it may become obvious in the course of reading this paper, is that I am generally, but rather inconsistently, proceeding from the north to the south and am treating this subject, though not very strictly, in three segments, viz., the early period until the end of the 9th century, the medieval period until the end of the 14th century and the post-medieval period. One easily noticeable shortcoming in my paper is that I have helplessly confined myself to the data already familiar to me or which easily caught my attention.

It is only too well known that the two great epics, the *Rāmāyaṇa* and the *Mahābhārata*, have had a degree of influence on the minds of the Indian people, unmatched in depth and extent by any other work anywhere or any time in the world; and, this all encompassing influence can be epigraphically documented for its continual presence at least from the beginnings of the classical age of Indian history, in the beginning of the 4th century AD, if not earlier. The earliest datable reference to the Mahābhārata heroes is to be met with in the Nasik inscription of the nineteenth year of the reign of the Sātavāhana king Vasishṭhīputra Puḷumāvi describing the achievements of his illustrious father Gautamīputra Sātakarṇi who ruled towards the close of the first century AD. It compares Gautamīputra of Rāma (Balarāma), Keśava, Arjuna and Bhīmasena in valour and to, *inter alia*, Janamejaya in lustre. For the text of the inscription, see D.C. Sircar, *Select Inscriptions Bearing on Indian History and Civilization*, I, second revised edn., Calcutta, 1965, pp. 204-05, lines 7-8. And for the period of Gautamīputra Sātakarṇi, vide Ajay Mitra Shastri, *The Sātavāhanas and the Western Kshatrapas: A Historical Framework*, Nagpur, 1998, p. 40. More importantly, this overwhelming influence is easily noticeable not only in the Indian subcontinent but also in those countries of South and South-East Asia where venturesome Indians had settled down and built up kingdoms or spread Indian culture. This paper is concerned only with the influence exerted by the *Mahābhārata* on the people of Indian origin or orientation in the vast area of South and South-East Asia.

The best way to start this subject will be to refer to a far-off South-East Asian Sanskrit inscription from the district town of Champassak in Laos. This undated 64-line inscription, equally distributed on four sides of a pillar, is written in south Indian Brāhmī characters paleographically assignable to the second half of the 5th century AD. It refers itself to the reign of *Mahārājādhirāja* Dēvānīka *née* Maṅgala who, as told in the inscription, was brought hither by the God Liṅgaparvata from a distant land (*dūra-dēśāt*, by which, obviously, an unnamed place in southern India is meant, as implied by the record's palaeography). This Dēvānīka and his followers appear to have been highly nostalgic about the country of their origin and its hoary culture and traditional lores. For, the court poet, who composed this inscription, describes his master as, among other things, *Yudhishṭhira iva saddharmī* (righteous as Yudhishṭhira) and *Dhanañjaya iva ripu-gaṇa-vijayē* (like Arjuna in vanquishing the coterie of the enemies). This comparison of Dēvānīka with the two famous Pāṇḍava brothers illustrates the popularity which the characters of that great epic enjoyed all over the subcontinent as also the fact that this epic ethos had been carried to South-East Asia by the ancient Indian migrants. But the real extent of the popularity and cultural impact of this epic is tellingly brought home by the following facts recorded in that inscription. King Dēvānīka, our inscription says, established a holy centre in his kingdom, nostalgically called Kurukshetra, and also Gaṅgaka; the next then goes on to give, in at least 19 *anushṭubh* verses, a few of which are partly or badly damaged, a vivid description of the extent and sanctity of this holy place. This entire portion has been inspired by the description of holy places occurring in the *Āraṇyakaparvan* of the *Mahābhārata* and at least the three following verses have been lifted from the epic (*The Āraṇyakaparvan, BORI* edn., 1942, pt. 1, *Tīrthayātrāparvan*, p. 285, V.173, 174 and 175; I owe this information to my friend and former colleague, Shri R.S. Bisht, Director, Archaeological Survey of India, New Delhi):

pāṁsavō'pi Kurukshetre Vāyunā samudīritāḥ /
api dushkṛita karmāṇi nayanti paramāṁ gatim
Kurukshetraṁ gamishyāmi Kurukshetre vasāmyahaṁ /
ye vasanti Kurukshetre te vasanti trivishṭape //
pṛithivyāṁ Naimishaṁ puṇyaṁ antarikshesu Pushkaraṁ /
trayāṇāmapi lokānāṁ Kurukshetraṁ viśishyate //

This quotation, more than anything else, should prove even to the skeptics, that at least this part of the great Indian epic is as old as the 5th century AD.

The next epigraphical references of historical significance that occurs to our mind is, of course, the date portion of the text of the well-known Aihoḷe inscription of Chālukya king Polekeśi II. The inscription is dated not only in the usual Śaka era, the year being given as 656, but also in the 3735 which had lapsed after the Bhārata War (*Bhāratād-āhavād-itaḥ).* This would place the end of the great

Bhārata War in AD 3101. Archaeologists and historians would be well warned against treating and summarily dismissing this chronological reckoning as a mere shot in the dark for, dozens of inscriptions from the north as well as the south corroborate this date time and again through the centuries, thus confirming that it is based on an abiding and credible reminiscence.

Apart from these highly significant references, the first of which attests to the abiding influence of the epic on the Indian psyche even across the seas, and the second one gives us a sound and historically positive chronological parameter for the open-minded who would like to avoid western-inspired parachronisms, let us now examine what we can learn from the inscriptions about the nature of the epic in question. Elaborate and painstaking research has been done by modern indologists, Indian as well as Western, to prove that the *Mahābhārata* is not the work of a single author or period and that there have been numerous interpolations from time to time, ordered by royal families from all over the subcontinent who did not want to be left out of that seemingly national event. As per available epigraphical evidence, this is a well-conceded historical fact at least from the beginnings of the classical period. The very fact that, while giving the imprecatory verses, many inscriptions refer to their author as Vedavyāsa-Vyāsa clearly indicates that our ancients believed that the sage had compiled or codified even the Vedic saṁhitās. And in the Khoh grant of Mahārāja Śarvanātha (*CII*, III, No. 31, p. 137), issued in AD 534, the *Mahābhārata* is referred to as the *Śata-sāhasrī-saṁhitā* which is of twofold importance for us. For one thing it shows that even in the first half of the 6th century AD the epic had come to have 100,000 (*śata-sāhasra)* verses, though all of these verses may not have been the same as have come down to us in various recensions. Secondly, the suffix *saṁhitā* (=put together, compiled) shows that even from days of yore, the *Mahābhārata* had been considered as a compilation and not as a composite work. That is obviously the reason why some of the imprecatory verses, stated in many inscriptions as lifted from Vyāsa, are ascribed in many other inscriptions to Manu. This is in keeping with Bühler's discovery (*IA*, XIV, p. 324) that about one-tenth of Manu's verses have found their way into the *Mahābhārata.* Notwithstanding this pardonable confusion, which after all merely conforms to countless such vaguenesses in the history of ancient Indian literature, it is worth pointing out here that as early as in AD 440, the Sultānpur copperplate inscription from Bengal asserts that the imprecatory verses quoted therein were composed by Bhagavān Vyāsa for the *Mahābhārata* (*uktaṁ cha Mahābhārate Bhagavatā Vyāsena)* [*EI*, XXXI, p. 65]. That there was no hard and fast identification of the author of these imprecatory verses, but that they were generally deemed to be epical is brought home to us by an early Kadamba charter (*EC*, IV, p. 49) which introduces the verse in which Vyāsa exhorts Yudhishṭhira to protect grants made to brāhmaṇas as *api ch-ātra Bhīshma-gīta-ślokaḥ!*

It is but natural that the two Indian epics, whatever be their dates of origin, progressively begin to get more and more references from the period of the Guptas and their contemporaries not only in the rest of the subcontinent but also across the seas wherever the Classical Sanskrit age had spread its influence.

The most formal of such references is perhaps to the eldest of the five Pāṇḍava brothers, viz., Yudhishṭhira, who makes an incidental appearance in an oft repeated imprecatory verse, as being advised by Vyāsa to protect gifts given to brāhmaṇas:

pūrva- dattāṁ dvijātibhyō yatnād- raksha Yudhishṭhira /
mahīṁ mahīmatāṁ śreshṭha dānāchchyreyo'nupālanam //

Apart from these references of a formal nature, he and the Kaurava ally, who ultimately turns out, in vain though, to be the eldest of the Pāṇḍavas, viz., Karṇa, happen to be the more frequently, mentioned epigraphical comparisons than any other characters of that epic, though Arjuna and Bhīma are not far behind. To quote only a couple of early instances in his Supia pillar inscription of AD 460-61 (*CII*, III, 1981, No. 32, p. 318), the Gupta emperor Skandagupta is compared with Yudhishṭhira for his truthfulness, good conduct and humility (*dharmma-parataya Yudhishṭhira-tulyasya saty-āchāra-vinayaiḥ*). In an even earlier inscription (*EI*, XXXIV, p. 19) from Nāgārjunakoṇḍa, assignable to the 3rd-4th century AD, the Ikshvāku king Ehavala Chāntamūla is introduced as an equal to many epic heroes, including Yudhishṭhira (*Sagara-Dilīp-Āmbarīsha-Yudhishṭhira-tulya-dharma-vijayasya*). In their genealogical accounts the Vākāṭakas invariably pick up Pṛithvīsheṇa I for being compared with Yudhishṭhira for his good conduct:

Yudhishṭhira-vṛitter-Vākāṭakānām-Mahārāja-Śrī-Pṛithvīsheṇasya

Down in the Deccan, the Vātāpi Chālukya ruler Maṅgalīśa, who tried to deny his nephew, Polekēśi II, the throne which was rightfully his, is eulogized in the Mahākūṭa pillar inscription (*IA*. XIX, pp. 7-20) as being truthful like Yudhishṭhira (*Yudhishṭhira iva satyasandhaḥ)*! Vijayāditya, another successful Chālukya ruler, is praised in his Paṭṭadakal biscriptal inscription (*EI*, III, pp. 1-7) as being munificent like Karṇa and impetuous like Bhīma (*Sūryasutam-iva dānaratas-sadā Vṛikodaram-iva sāhasa-rasikaḥ)*.

The Kāsāre plate of Sendraka Allaśakti, issued in AD 653, has an interesting *Śārdūlavikrīḍitas* verse in double entendre which seeks to compare Allaśakti with Yudhishṭhira:

vipr-ādhishṭhira-sampad-āhita-gurur-dury-āvanaddhas-sadā
śrīmān-Arjuna-karma-bhāvita-manāḥ sad-Bhīmasen-ānviaḥ /
dharmm-ātmā Sahadeva-pūjita-vapus-sāmānya-dānas-sadā
mitakṛin-Nakulo Yudhishṭhira-samo rāj-Āllaśakti kshitau //

In this verse the poet has sought to compare Allaśakti with Yudhishṭhira by playing pun on the names of the remaining four Pāṇḍava brothers. In the case of Yudhishṭhira, who is the *upamāna,* the verse maybe freely rendered as follows: "His fortune is governed by the *brāhmaṇas;* he honours elders; he always leads from the front; his mind is elated by the heroic deeds of Arjuna; he is attended by Bhīmasena: he is (also) called Dharma; his person was worshipped by Sahadeva; he was ever munificent; (the circles of) his friends were strengthened by Nakula (*mitra-kṛit)*". In the case of Allaśakti, who is the *upameya,* my free translation would be: "his fortune is governed by the brāhmaṇas; he honours elders; he always leads from the front; his mind is purified by honest deeds; he is endowed with a fierce army; he is piety incarnate; he is worshipped along with the gods; he is ever munificent; he is the very mongoose in cutting down (the serpents, i.e.) his enemies (*amitra-kṛit)*".

The Mehunabare plates of Sendraka Vairadeva (*EI*, XXXIII, p. 196; AD 702) equates Sendraka Devaśakti's son Daṇḍirāja with gods and mortals when he is praised therein as *tasy-ātmajo Hari-Har-Ārjuna- tulya-vīryaḥ* (i.e. he was equal in valour to Vishṇu, Śiva and Arjuna). Such instances in which the Pāṇḍavas are mentioned alongside the gods in inscriptions are met with more often in the subsequent centuries.

Down south, in their charters the early Kadambas of Banavāsī also make only sparing use of the Bhārata heroes in order to enhance the personalities of their kings. In one of his charters (*EC*, IV, Hs. 18) Kadamba Vijaya Śiva Mṛigeśavarman (*c.* AD 475-90) is eulogized as *Yudhishṭhira iva dharmajña:* , i.e, "as much aware of righteousness as Yudhishṭhira" while in another charter (*Corpus of Kadamba Inscriptions*, Ed. B.R. Gopal, Sirsi 1985, p. 115) Kadamba Harivarman is praised as *sākshād-iva Dharmarāja:*, i.e. he was "verily Yudhishṭhira himself". Again, in a charter of Kṛishṇavarman II (*c.* AD 540-65), his grandfather Vishṇuvarman (*c.* AD 485-95) is described as being equal to Vatsa, Indra and Arjuna respectively in the art of music, in training elephants and in the science of archery:

Vishṇuvarma-dharmamahārājena
Gandharva-hastiśiksā-dhanurvedeshu
Vatsarāj-endr-ārjuna-samena

Further down in the south, the early Gaṅgas (of Taḷakāḍu) also refer to some of the epic characters in a few of their charters, mostly involving comparisons. In two charters (K.V. Ramesh, *Inscriptions of the Western Gaṅgas*, ICHR-Agam Kala Prakashan, Delhi, 1984, [*IWG*] Nos. 12 and 13) Gaṅga Avinīta (*c.* AD 5th century) is eulogized as the "very Yudhishṭhira of his times (*idaṅkāla-Yudhishṭhira:)*. In yet another charter (*IWG*, No.18) Avinīta's son Durvinīta is, in his turn, described as the "very Yudhishṭhira of his times" (*Idaṁyugīna Yudhishṭhiraḥ*).

Gaṅga Śivamāra, who ascended the throne towards the end of the 8th century AD, receives the accolade (*IWG*, Nos. 49 and 90) that though he was Duryodhana, he was still complemented for his qualities as Arjuna meaning thereby, in *double entendre,* that he was invincible (Duryodhana) but was possessed of overtly good qualities like Arjuna (and unlike Duryodhana). In one of the rare epigraphical references to Abhīmanyu, in the Perjjarangi grant (*IWG*, No. 90) of Gaṅga Rājamalla I, he is praised as *Abhīmanyur-iva Subhadr-ābhinandanaḥ*, i.e. he was complemented for his good fortune even as Abhīmanyu was a source of pleasure to (his mother) Subhadrā.

The incomplete Māmbaḷḷi grant (*c.* AD 550, *EC*, IV,YI.167) issued by some Punnata ruler speaks of the sons of King Rashṭravarman in the following words:

Rāshṭravarmmā . . . Prabhāvatyāṁ trīn-putrān-aneka-purusha-guṇa-samanvitān Pāṇḍava-tulya-parākramān-ajītanat l teshu jyeshṭhaḥ Pṛthivīpatiḥ Yudhishṭhira-samaḥ (rest of the text is lost).

It is rather strange that even in a case where only three brothers are born, they are sought to be compared with the Pāṇḍavas.

The late 7th century Kūram grant (*SII*, I, No. 151) of the Pallava dynasty registers grants made for a temple and *brahmadeya* and includes a provision for the recitation of the *Bhārata*.

I have pointed out at the beginning of this paper that the Pallavas of Kāñchi claimed descent from legendary and epic figures such as Bharadvāja, Droṇa and Aśvatthāman. In a bid to further glorify this ancestry, of which Aśvatthāman appears to have been considered as the key personality, Pallava genealogical accounts (see e.g. *SII*, II, Pt. III, p. 347, verse 16) say that the sage Aśvatthāman was "the very incarnation of (Śiva) the enemy of Cupid; he deserved the confidence of the inhabitants of the world; and, at the rise of his anger Kṛishṇa, Arjuna and Bhīma became terrified and threw down their weapons, not daring to give him a fight!"

tasmād-yasmin-krudhyati Kṛishṇ-Arjuna-Bhīmāś-
śastra-tyāgaṁ chakrur-avighnaṁ bhaya-nighnataḥ /
viśvastānāṁ viśvasanīyō munir-āsīd-
Aśvatthāmā Manmatha-śatror-avatāraḥ //

In spite of casting this aspersion on the Pāṇḍavas, the Pallavas had no qualms about comparing themselves in a favourable vein, with the Pāṇḍava heroes. For instance, Pallava Nandivarman (*c.* AD 730) is eulogized as the very Yudhishṭhira in the matter of keeping his subjects happy: *Dharmmaḥ prajā-rañjane* (*Ibid.*, p. 350). He is also compared (*Ibid.*, p. 366) with Nakula in the management of horses (*Nakula iva turaṅgameshu),* with Arjuna in bowmanship (*Arjuna iva kārmukē*) besides being compared with his illustrious, alleged ancestor Droṇa in the science of archery (*Droṇa iva dhanurvede*).

The Taṇḍantōṭṭam plates (*SII*, II, pt. III, p. 527) of the Pallava king Vijaya-Nandivikramavarman (9th century AD) record, in the operative part of the text, which is in Tamil, the grant of 244 measured out shares of land to 213 donees among whom a person (not named) assigned the job of reciting the *Bhārata* is allotted one share (*Bhāratam Vāśippānukkup-paṅg-onrum)*.

From the 10th century onwards, when medieval royal pomposity sets in on a larger scale in epigraphical compositions, we begin to get references more often to the *Mahābhārata* and its episodes and characters, mostly in the context of drawing comparisons.

In a sub-story introduced in the Bilhari stone inscription (*CII*, IV, Pt. I, pp. 204ff., 10th century AD) of the Kalachuri king of Tripurī, Yuvarājadeva II, a new legendary version of the origin of the Chālukya dynasty is given which is worth a narration here if only to illustrate the ways in which Bhārata characters as well as its innumerable narratives were used by poets endowed with fertile imagination. The incident relates to the famous 'lie' uttered by that great votary of 'Truth', Yudhishṭhira, at the behest of Kṛishṇa, that Aśvatthāman had been killed, on hearing which his stunned father Droṇa became an easy target in the great battle. I give below the four verses with V.V. Mirashi's translation:

Bharadvājo nāma chyuta-kalusha-dobshas-samabhavad
ya ekas-sarveshām-upaśama-dhanānām-adhipathiḥ /
tadīyāt-tejastaḥ kṛita-kalaśa-vāsād-yad-abhavat
sa vai Bhāradvājas-tribhuvana-chamatkāra-charitaḥ //

There was (a sage) named Bharadvāja, (who was) free from blemishes of sin, (and) who was the sole lord of those whose wealth is tranquility. What sprang from his male energy deposited in a jar – that verily was Bhāradvāja, i.e., Droṇa whose deeds excited the wonder of the three worlds.

trailōky-āvadhi yasya kīrttilaḍitaṁ lakshmīś-cha vāñchh-āvadhir-
yat-kopah pralay-opapanna-mahima-sāpena chāpēna cha /
varṇyaṁ vā naya-vikram-aika-jaladheḥ kin-tasya yasy-ābhaval-
līlā-kharvita-Śarva-garva-mahimā śishyas-Subhadrāpatiḥ //

His fame gracefully roamed throughout the three worlds; his fortune was limited (only) by his rage, (manifested both) by his curse and his bow, was terrible, such as would be suitable for the destruction of the world. What can we describe of that sole ocean of policy and valour, whose disciple was the husband of Subhadrā (i.e., Arjuna) who with ease humbled the great pride of Śarva. (The reference here is to Arjuna's encounter with Śiva described in the *Mahābhārata*).

Kodaṇda-tāṇḍavana-paṇḍita-bāhudaṇḍam-
uddaṇḍa-kaṇḍa-bhara-khaṇḍita- Pāṇḍu-sainyam /

yaṁ vīkshya vikshata-vipaksha-rājayāgas-
satyād-ṛitasya tapaso'pi sutaś-chachala //

Seeing him whose strong arm was skilful in wielding the bow, and who with his many powerful arrows exterminated the Pāṇḍava army, even that son of Dharma, who was honoured for veracity, swerved (from the truth) when he lost (all) hope of defeating the enemy.

ath-ākshepāt-tena drupada-vipad-artho' ddhata-dhiyā
yad-āttaṁ śāp-āmbhas-taralita- kar-ābaddha-chulukam /
pumānāsīt-tasmin-Vijaya iva sākshad-anu cha taṁ
kulaṁ Chalukyānām-anaṇu-guṇa-sīma pravavṛite //

Now, in the water, of which he in the act of cursing had taken up a handful (*chuluka*) with his trembling hand, in rage to bring calamity on Drupada when insulted (by him), there sprang a man like victory incarnate; from him is descended the family of the Chaulukyas of great merit.

[In a footnote, Mirashi adds that "the allusion here is to an incident in the Bhārata war when Yudhishṭhira was tempted to tell a lie to bring about the death of Droṇa". See *Mahābhārata*, Droṇaparvan, Adhyāya 193, w. 54-59.].

I may now refer to the Pulivarru (Andhra Pradesh) grant of Eastern Chālukya Ammarāja (*EI*, XLI, p.146, 9th century AD) in which the subordinate chief Indaparaja is praised in a passage couched in double entendre. The *Āryāgīti* verse reads:

Nakula-Sahadeva-mūrttiḥ,
Dharmm-ānugatau cha Bhārata-khyātau /
sarvva-dharmma-pravīṇo
nirjta-duryyodhan-āri-sainikamukhyaḥ //

The Kalanda (Orissa; *Ibid.*, XLI, p. 202, 10th century AD) plates of Nayapāladeva say that he was, unto his elder brother Nārāyaṇapāla, what his devoted brother Dhanañjaya (i.e. Arjuna) was to Dharmātmaja (i.e. Yudhishṭhira):

Dharmātmajasy-eva Dhanañjyo'bhūt-tasy-ānujah
Śrī-Nayapāladevaḥ /

The Mahābhārata characters were often exploited by later rulers and commoners to add an aura of grandeur and sanctity to their deeds. In his Khajurāho inscription of AD 1117 (*CII*, VII, Pt. III, p. 389) the Chandella ruler Dhaṅga claims that the emerald *liṅga* installed by him was earlier worshipped by Indra in the heavens, had been presented by him to Kiriṭīn, i.e. Arjuna, who in his turn had brought it down to earth and had been worshipped by Yudhishṭhira himself:

marakatamayaṁ tuṅgaṁ liṅgaṁ yad-architam-aiśvaraṁ
Tridaśapatinā tasmāl-labdhaṁ prasādya Kirīṭinā /
tad-avanitalaṁ ten-anītaṁ Yudhishṭhira-pūjitaṁ jayati
jagati śrī-Dhaṅgena praṇamya niveśitam //

Earlier in the same epigraph (pp. 387-88) the poet has compared the birth of Dhaṅga's father Yaśovarman to his parents, queen Kañchukā and Harsha, with the birth of the great Bhīshma to the River-goddess Gaṅgā and Śāntanu (p. 387, v. 31). Still later, in verse 37 the poet has indulged in a scholastic or laboured *double entendre* in which some of the major Bhārata characters figure:

Gāndhāriṁ bhajatā prahṛishṭa-Śakuni-śvāna-priyāṁ preyasīṁ/
Bhīshma-Droṇa-vachāṁsy-a-Karṇṇa-sukhadāny-ākarṇya sammūchchhatā//
nō Dharmma-prabhavaṁ virodhitavatā prāpy-āpi vaṁsa-kshayaṁ/
na prāptā Dhṛitarāshtrata sasuhṛidā vidveshiṇ-ety-adbhutam//

The import of this rather abstruse composition seems to be:

(1) [In the case of Dhṛitarāshṭra] It is indeed a wonder that he (i.e., Dhṛitarāshṭra), who loved his wife Gāndhāri, who took great pleasure in listening to the voice of (her brother) Śakuni, and who was stupefied by the non-gratifying utterances of Bhīshma, Droṇa and Karṇa, yet did not oppose (his) distinguished (nephew) Dharma (i.e. Yudhishṭhira) even when his own family faced the danger of extinction and (thus) he, in truth, became Dhṛitarāshṭra who was (at once) an adversary and a friend.

(2) [In the case of Yaśovarman] It is indeed a wonder that he (i.e. Yaśovarman), who loved his wife who hailed from Gandhāra and delighted in listening to the (musical) chirping of many birds, and he who was stupefied on hearing the dreadful (*bhīshma)* and deafening (*akarṇṇa*) cries of; the raven (*droṇa)* did not act contrary to established laws even when his family faced the danger of extermination and (thus) did he, in truth, firmly established his royal power *(dhṛita-rāshṭratā),* being surrounded by friends and bereft of enemies.

One point which impresses us when we search for epigraphical references to the *Mahābhārata* is the rather laudable trait in our countrymen, past and present, to judge and treat the characters figuring in that great epic on the basis of individual ethics and not on the basis of the side on which they fought the great battle. This point cannot be better illustrated than by recalling the honour, appreciation and admiration with which Karṇa, who fought on the side of the Kauravas purely for ethical reasons but was, otherwise, a repository of human virtues, is time and again cited for his greatness in contexts of comparison. The fact that he was, after all, one of the Pāṇḍavas, may have been a subconscious influencing factor in this regard. In addition to what I have already cited from epigraphs about this noble character, I may here draw the readers' attention to the Gwalior inscription (*CII*, VII, Pt. III, p. 545, AD 1092) in which, in successive verses (w. 48-51), Dharmasū: (i.e. Yudhishṭhira), Vṛikodara (i.e. Bhīma), Purandaranandana (i.e. Arjuna) and Sūryajanita (i.e. Karna) are cited as *upamanas* for Chandella Mahipals. The verse on Karṇa is worth quoting here for the rather down-to-earth assessment for it contains his successes and failures:

Duryodhan-āri-bala-darpa-hatas-tav-eśa
yatnaḥ par-Ārjuna-yaśaḥ prasaraṁ niroddhum//
tvaṁ ko'si Suryajanita pramad-ārthi-s-ārtha-
daurgatya-kartana-vikartana-sambhavasya//

Here the poet says that on the one hand, Karṇa had destroyed the arrogance of the enemies of Duryodhana and on the other, concedes that he could only attempt at curbing the fame of Arjuna from spreading. Then, there is of course, the usual encomium showered on him for his munificence towards the needy.

In the same inscription, in the context of praising King Mahīpāla's heroic deeds on the battlefields, the composer alludes to the episode narrated in the Virāṭaparvan, wherein sage Vyāsa extols Arjuna for repelling single-handedly the rustlers who had attempted to steal the cows of Uttara:

eken-Ōttara-gograhe vimukhataṁ Pārthena nītāḥ pare
Vyāsena stutir-Arjunasya vihit-ety-ajñayi pūrvaṁ kila

In a hyperbolic verse in praise of a kshatriya chieftain, Argadeva, serving under Chālukya Someśvara (AD 1043-68), the composer of an inscription from Hottal (Maharashtra) gloats that the *Bhārata*, *Rāmāyaṇa*, Purāṇas and the *Ākshyāyikas* has been relegated to the background by the great fame of Argadeva which had permeated in all directions, in all regions, in all towns, along all rivers and atop all mountains:

bhagnā Bhārata-bhāvatā vigalito Rāmāyaṇ-opakrakaḥ
śirṇāi jīrṇa-purāṇa-paddhatir-ito n-ākhyāyikānāṁ gatiḥ /
praty-āśaṁ prati-maṇḍalaṁ prati-puraṁ praty-āpagaṁ praty-agaṁ
tasya kshatriya-puṅgavasya yaśasā trailokyam-āpūritam //

The Masulipatam (Andhra Pradesh) plates (*EI*, XXIV, p. 227; 10th century AD) of the Eastern Chālukya ruler Ammarāja II can be cited as a good illustration to show how the two great epics had gained subcontinental popularity transcending religious barriers. The grant portion of this charter introduces two donor brothers, Bhīma and Naravāhana, as belonging to the Triṇayana-kula and as *jaina-dharma-nirata-charitrau* but eulogizes them as *vikhyātau Rāma-Lakshmaṇāv-iva, yau Bhīm-Ārjuna-sadṛiśau* and *Nakula-Sahadeva- tulyau.*

In an equally hyperbolic praise showered on an Andhra chieftain Annavema of the 14th century, the poet-composer of the Annavarappāḍu plate (*Ibid.*, XXXVI, p.184) claims that Dadhīchi, Karṇa and Śibi, who merely gave away their bones, skin (-mail) and flesh respectively only because they had nothing valuable to give, stood no comparison with the Andhra ruler, who was an adept in driving away poverty and gave away plenty of gifts to supplicants:

arthair-arthijanān kṛitārthayati yo brahmāṇḍadānaṁ mahat
kurwan Vema-suto-'Nnavēma nṛipatir- dāridrya-vidrāvaṇaḥ//
dātrā tena Dadhīchi- Karṇṇa-Śibayas-svarṇṇa-pradān-ākḥamāḥ
sv-āsthi-tvak-piśita-pradās-samatulā bandhā bhaveyuḥ katham//

In medieval Karnataka, too, the *Mahābhārata* and its heroes were often cited as examples by inscriptional composers. A Kannada inscription of Chālukya Jagadekamalla (*Ibid.*, XVI, p. 47), while speaking of a certain Droṇāchārya, a local chieftain of north Karnataka states that true to his name, he was a master of the bow (*Chāpāchāryaṁ)* just like his illustrious namesake, Droṇāchārya the teacher of Gāṇḍīvin (i.e. Arjuna);

Droṇāchāryaṁ Gāṇḍiviy-annan-enipa chāpāchāryaṁ

Besides, there are also straightforward comparisons like *satya-Rādheyaṁ* (i.e. truthful like Rādheya, one of the many aliases of Karṇa) [*Ibid.*, XVI, p. 78, AD 1037]: *para-bala-Pārthaṁ* (i.e. a Pārtha / Arjuna to hostile armies) [*Ibid.*, p. 84, AD 1067]; *Kīchaka-Vṛilodaraṁ* (i.e. destroyer of evil men even as Vṛikodara/Bhīma was the destroyer of the villain Kīchaka) [*Ibid.*, p. 358,11th century]; *bhuja-baḷa- Bhīma*, (i.e., a veritable Bhīma in the strength of his arms) [*SII*, XVIII, Nos. 290, 291, etc.]; *virodhi-Kuru-Kapikētu:* (a veritable Kapiketu, i.e. Arjuna) and so on and so forth.

We have seen earlier in this paper, three sons born to a couple being compared with the Pāṇḍavas. We have an interesting case of a 12th century couple begetting five sons who are very conveniently compared with the *pañcha*-Pāṇḍavas! We learn this from an inscription (*SII*, XVII, No. 117) of Chālukya Vikramāditya VI, dated in AD 1121, hailing from Kāginelli, Dharwar Dist. While giving the genealogy of a donor-family of that township, the poet says about the couple Keta and his wife Kañchikabbe and their issues:

Manneya Ketaṅgaṁ guṇad-unnatiyaṁ taḷeda Kañchikabbegav-ogedar munnina rannar-purushārthatīrthar-aivar-makkaḷu, i.e., "to the chieftain Keta and his wife of noble character, Kañchikabbe, were born, reminiscent of the five gems of yore that were born to Pāṇḍu, five worthy sons." As if not satisfied with that casual comparison, the inscriptional poet further says:

piriyaṁ Bammane Dharmarājan-esedipp-ā Dāsamaṁ Bhīman-ennaroḷaṁ
ballidan-appa Śobhanan-eṁ taṁ mikk-Arjunaṁ siṅganuṁ
purushārthāgraṇiy-Aichanuṁ Nakuḷa-Sādevarkkaḷ-āgalu
vasundhareyoḷu Pāṇḍavar-innuv-irddar-enal-ant-iy-ayvaruṁ rañjiparu

These five sons, viz., Bamma, Dāsa, Śobhana, and Siṅga and Aicha, who were respectively comparable with Dharmarāja, i.e., Yudhishṭhira, Bhīma, Arjuna and Nakula and Sahadeva, led the world around them to believe that the five Pāṇḍavas were still living in their midst!

It is well known that the Hoysaḷas of southern Karnataka constructed very ornately and elaborately sculptured temples many of which featured plastic narratives of events and episodes from popular ancient Indian lores, including the epics. These are there for all to see but we have a rare instance of an inscription actually referring to it. This inscription (*EC*, VII, Md. 29; AD 1234) from a temple in Mandya Dist. says that temple appeared beautiful to the onlookers because it featured in its halls stories from the *Bhārata,* etc. (*Mudadiṁ Bīruva Bhārat-Ādi Katheyiṁ Meyvetta Kūṭaṅgaḷ*).

The abiding love of the Tamils for their ancient language and their keenness in preserving its originality have always prompted them, even from the hoary days of the archaic Tamil Brāhmī inscriptions, to Tamilize non-Tamil names and words when they had to use them. The *Mahābhārata* was no exception to this rule; to cite only one instance out of a legion, the trustee of a temple endowment is named, in a Tamil inscription of AD 1288-89, of the reign of the Pāṇḍya king Vikrama-Pāṇḍya, as Pāṇṭava-tūtan Iyātavan (>Skt. Pāṇḍava-dūtō Yādavaḥ) by which is meant Yādava Kṛishṇa who negotiated with the Kauravas on behalf of the Pāṇḍavas (*SII*, XXVI, No. 522).

Like the 10th century Masulipatam plates to which I have alluded earlier, the Jagannātharāya temple inscriptions (*EI*, XXIV, pp. 66ff.), written in the middle of the 16th century, are a good illustration of the unabated national popularity of the two epics. These inscriptions refer to Abhīmanyu, Suyodhana (i.e. Duryodhana), Karṇa, Rādheya (Karṇa), Rāmānuja (Lakshmaṇa) and others.

Some inscriptions of the rulers of the erstwhile native state of Mysore show that they and their officials attached great value to the *Mahābhārata.* For instance, one of the early rulers of Mysore, viz., Beṭṭada Chāmarāja is praised in a charter (*EC*, III, Nj. 212; AD 1639) issued by his overlord Āravīḍu Veṅkaṭapati of Vijayanagara as *śaurye yas-Savyasāchi, audārye Karṇa-kalpaḥ* (i.e. he who was the equal of Arjuna in valour, and of Karna in generosity). We learn from two inscriptions (*Ibid.*, [Rev.], VI, Kr. 16 and p. 149) that the Mysore king Devarāja-Oḍeya had donated, in AD 1678, the two villages of Birubaḷḷi and Nāṭanahaḷḷi to Aḷagiyaśiṅgar Ayyaṅgār after listening to the donee's recital of the *Mahābhārata* and on the day when he had recited the episode of Yudhishṭhira's coronation:

> *Dēvarājavaḍeyaravaru namma kaiya Mahābhārata keḷi Yudhishṭhir-ābhisheka-śravaṇa-kāladali namage, etc.*

The Tonnūru and Mēlukōṭe plates (*Ibid.*, VI [Rev.], pp. 99 and 215) were composed by the poet Tirumaleyāchārya who was a professional reciter of the two epics, viz., the *Rāmāyaṇa* and the *Mahābhārata*:

Śrī-Rāmāyaṇa-Bhārata-pārāyaṇa-nihita-vṛittinā /
kavinā Tirumaleyāchāryeṇ-edaṁ tāmbraśāsanaṁ likhitam //

The Daḷavāy Agrahāram plates of the Mysore king Kṛishṇarāja Oḍeyar record that his *Daḷapati* Devarāja created an *agrahāra* of 120 vṛittis and granted them to several brāhmaṇas among whom figures Bhārata-Veṅkaṭa Śāstrigaḷu.

I would like to conclude this paper by referring to a couple of 19th century inscriptions (*Ibid.*, 1, Nj. 6, 9 and 11) from Koḍagu (better known as Coorg). Both these inscriptions belong to the local Veerashaiva ruling family, one dated in AD 1817 and belonging to the reign of Liṅgārajendra Oḍeyar II and the other dated in AD 1822 in the reign of Vīrarājendra Oḍeyar. Both the inscriptions describe the rulers as *samasta-praśasta-rājadharm-āvadharaṇa-Yudhishṭhirar* (i.e. one who was the very Yudhishṭhira in the practice of all that is best in (the) realm of polity).

As far as exploitation of epigraphical data on the *Mahābhārata* is concerned, figuratively speaking, I have only touched the tip of the iceberg. I hope this paper will serve as an incentive to upcoming researchers to collect and study all types of direct and indirect information contained in South and South-East Asian inscriptions not only on the *Mahābhārata* but also on the *Rāmāyaṇa*.

21

Jaina Versions of the *Mahābhārata*

Bhagchandra Jain 'Bhaskar'

The *Mahābhārata* legend like the *Rāmāyaṇa* has been a source of inspiration for Indian writers since long. Its main characters are said to be celestial beings. Lord Kṛishṇa, probably a non-Vedic deity, is the prominent character and all the other characters and events revolve around him. The whole folklore then becomes very impressive, supernatural and divine. Jainācharyas used it in their own ways with a somewhat progressive attitude for spreading the Jaina principles. They adopted the versions of the *Mahābhārata* in their literature with some changes according to their needs. They made the whole story rather more logical and practical.

The present paper is confined to Jaina literature written in Sanskrit, Prakrit and Hindi. It will throw a light on certain points which distinguished Jaina versions from that of the *Mahābhārata*.

JAINA LITERATURE ON THE *MAHĀBHĀRATA*

The earliest reference to the Mahābhārata story is found in the *Sṭhāṇāṅga*, *Nāyādhammakahāṅga*, *Antakṛiddaśāṅga*, *Praśnavyākaraṇa*, *Uttarādhyayana*, and *Niryāvalikā*. Amongst non-Āgamic Prakrit texts, the following maybe mentioned: *Vasudevahiṅḍī* of Saṅghadāsagaṇi, *Chauppannamahā-purisachariya* of Śīlāṅka and Amarakavi, *Bhavabhāvanā* and *Upadesamālā* of Hemachandrasūri, *Kumārapāla-paḍiboha* of Sūraprabhasūri, *Kaṇhachariya* of Devendrasūri, and some Kathākośas like *Kathakośaprakaraṇa*, *Kathāratnākośa* and *Ākhyānakamaṇikośa*.

The works in Sanskrit on the story are also found. They include the *Pradyumnacharita* of Mahāsenasūri, *Neminirmāṇakāvya* of Vāgbhaṭa I, *Naranārāyaṇā nanda Mahakāvya* of Vastupāla, *Neminātha*

Mahākāvya of Kirtiratnasūri, *Saptasandhāna Kāvya* of Meghavijaya Upādhyāya, *Dvisandhāna . Mahākāvya* of Dhanañjaya, *Harivaṁśapurāṇa* of Jinasena, *Uttarapurāṇa* of Guṇasena, *Nemidūta* of Vikrama Kavi, *Trishashṭiśalākā Purushacharita* of Hemachandra, *Pāṇḍavapurāṇa* of Vādichandra, *Mahāpurāṇa* of Mallisūri, *Pāṇḍavacharita* of Devaprabhasūri, *Harivaṁśapurāṇa* of Sakalakīrti, *Pāṇḍavapurāṇa* of Śubhachandra and so on.

Some *Apabhraṁśa kāvyas* may also be mentioned as follows:

Rathaṇemichariu of Svayambhū, *Mahāpurāṇa* of Pushpadanta, *Nemināhachariu* of Haribhadra, *Harivaṁśapurāṇa* of Dhaval, *Pajjummachariu* of Simha, *Nemināhachariu* of Lakshamaṇadeva, *Nemināhachariu* of Raidhu, *Pāṇḍavapurāṇa* and *Harivaṁśapurāṇa* of Yaśaḥkīriti, and so forth.

Likewise, so many other Jaina *kāvyas* and other Jaina literature are also found in Hindi, Gujarati, Marathi, Kannada.

The prominent Hindi Jaina literature on *Mahābhārata* maybe mentioned as follows: *Neminātharāsa* of Sumatigaṇi (AD 1238), *Gajasukumālarāsa* of Delhaṇa (13th century AD), *Pradyumnacharita* of Sandhāru (AD 1354), *Nemiphāgu* of Dhanadevagaṇi, *Jayaśekhara-sūri*, etc., *Neminātharāsa* of Puṇyaratana, *Brahmarāyamalla, Kanakakīrti, Keśarasāgara, Nemichandra, Ratanamuni, Vijayadevasūri*, etc., *Harivaṁśapurāṇa* of Brahmajinadāsa, *Śālivāhana, Khuśālachanda Kālā, Nemīśavara kī Veli* of Thākura, *Sāliga*, etc., *Pāṇḍavapurāṇa* of Bulākīdāsa, *Nemināthacharitra* of Jayamala (AD 1757), *Pradyumna-charita* of Munnālāla (AD 1844) and so on. It maybe mentioned here that Hindi Jaina Mahābhārata literature is mostly written in epic poem while non-Jaina literature is mostly in the nature of blank verse.

SOME DIFFERENCES IN JAINA VERSION

We shall point out here only a few main differences which are found in Jaina versions of the *Mahābhārata*. They maybe enumerated as follows:

1. According to Jaina tradition, Lord Kṛishṇa was the ninth Nārāyaṇa Vāsudeva, a brave and valiant king of Dvārakā and southern region (*Ardhachakravartī*) and not the divine personality as found in Mahābhārata tradition. He was, of course, an adherent of seven *ratnas* and a remover of clashes and unrest. He was also a supernatural personality but was not completely detached from

worldly affairs. Lord Kṛishṇa is considered a prominent character in Jaina literature. Vāsudeva maybe an epithet or an ancient title of honour which was used by Vāśudeva Kṛishṇa like Kāśīrāja Poṇḍrika. In a later period, some sorts of amusements (*līlās*) etc., were added to the character of Kṛishṇa, which are also described by Hindi Jaina writers. Jaina traditions, in fact, worshipped him as a warrior.

2. Draupadī is another important character of the *Mahābhārata* who increasingly created problems for Kauravas and Pāṇḍavas. Differences in versions are more pronounced in this character. According to the *Mahābhārata*, Draupadī was Ayonijā and blessed by Lord Śiva for having five husbands as she uttered the sentence "I intend to have a wise husband" five times. As a result, she got five husbands in her next birth as Draupadī.[1] Draupadī is also said to have been the daughter of a ṛishi in her previous birth. The Jaina version of the *Mahābhārata* mentions numerous stories of previous births of Sukumālikā and Nāgaśrī who had five husbands in next birth due to Nidāna Karma and not the blessing of Śiva.

3. Draupadī was born in Pāñchāla,[2] while the Jaina sources name it as Kāmpilyapura,[3] Mākaṇḍa Nagarī[4] and Kākandi Nagarī[5] which can be identified with the present district of Devaria.

4. Drupada was the father in both the traditions. The *Mahābhārata* brings her birth from the Yajñakuṇḍa and describes her as Ayonijā while the Jaina tradition names her mother as Bhogavāti[6] and father as Dṛiḍharatha.[7]

5. Both the versions agree on the Rādhāvedha or Chandrakavedha as the condition of *svayaṁvara* but its way of implementation appears rather difficult. It mentions twenty-two *chakras* in place of one *chakra*. Pāṇḍavas in Jaina version enter into *svayaṁvara* along with Pāṇḍu or Kuntī while it is not so in the *Mahābhārata*. Jaina version does not mention that Dhṛishṭadyumna introduced the kings to Draupadī. She was introduced by priest,[8] maidservant[9] or doorkeeper.[10] After fulfilling the condition, Draupadī garlanded Arjuna and the garlanding was divinely made to all the Pāṇḍavas.[11] According to the *Nāyādhammakahāo*[12] and the *Amama Svāmicharita* of Muniratnasūri,[13] garlanding was made separately to all five brothers. The *Uttarapurāṇa* mentions that the garlanding was made to only Arjuna and not others.[14] On the other hand, the *Jñātādharmakathāṅga* follows the *Mahābhārata*

version.[15]

6. The *Uttarapurāṇa*[16] and the *Pāṇḍavacharita*[17] refer to five sons of Draupadī called as Pāñchāla while the *Jñātādharmakathā*[18] and *Kalpasūtra Kalpalatā*[19] mention Pāṇḍusena as the only son.

7. The temptation for kingdom and jealousy were the main causes behind the *dyūtakṛīḍā* (gambling). But the *Bṛihatkāthakośa*[20] and *Bālabhārata*[21] mention the humiliation of Duryodhana in the assembly of Yudhishṭhira as the main cause. To avenge the humiliation, Duryodhana hatched the conspiracy of gambling and did the *chīraharaṇa* and *keśākarshana* of Draupadī.

8. Jaina tradition mentions mainly the Rāmagiri, Daṇḍakavana, Kāliñjaravana as the forest area[22] where they spent their exile, while the *Mahābhārata* refers to Kāmyakavana, Dvaitavana, Gandhamādana parvata, etc. where Kiramira Rākshasavadha, Bakāsuravadha, Hiḍimbā episode, Draupadīharaṇa, Kṛityā Rākshasī-preshaṇa, Durvāsa-āgamana, etc. took place.

9. Jaina version indicates one hundred and not one hundred and five brothers of Kīchaka who were burnt in funeral pile by Bhīma.[23] The war was held between lord Kṛishṇa and Jarāsandha and not between Kauravas and Pāṇḍavas. Pāṇḍavas and Kauravas were in fact associated with Kṛishṇa and Jarāsandha respectively. Kṛishṇa and his associates defeated Jarāsandha and Kauravas and then Kṛishṇa presented the kingdom of Hastināpura to Pāṇḍavas.[24] Afterwards, Duḥśāsana, Duryodhana and Kṛishṇa were initiated into Jinadīksha and then attained nirvāṇa according to *Harivaṁśapurāṇa*.[25]

10. Draupadī ignored the arrival of Nārada as he is said to be *asaṁyamī, avirata* and *mithyādṛishti* according to the *Jñātādharmakathā*.[26] But the *Harivaṁśapurāṇa*[27] and *Pāṇḍavapurāṇa*[28] are of opinion that as Draupadī was engaged in her own ornamentation, she could not attend the sage Nārada properly. As a result Nārada became furious and went to king Padmanābha, the king of Amarkaṅkā, who kidnapped Draupadī with the assistance of his friend Sāṅgatikadeva.[29] The war was then held between Pāṇḍavas and Padmanābha, and Pāṇḍavas were defeated. Then Kṛishṇa caught him with the help of Susthitadeva and brought him before Draupadī, who forgave him.[30]

11. One day Pāṇḍavas tried to test the power of Kṛishṇa by leaving him alone on the banks of Gaṅgā. Kṛishṇa crossed it and reached to Pāṇḍavas safely. Realizing that Pāṇḍavas tested him,

he became angry and expelled them from his Dvārakā. The Pāṇḍavas went ultimately to south India and established the city of Pāṇḍu-Mathura, where Draupadī gave birth to Pāṇḍusena. Afterwards Pāṇḍavas handed over the kingdom to Pāṇḍusena and got initiated into Jinadīksha along with Draupadī. Pāṇḍavas attained salvation and Draupadī took birth in the Brahmaloka Deva and would attain *mokśa* in the next birth.[31]

12. Kaṁsa was named as he was found in a bell-metal (kaṁsya) box. While he was in womb, his mother Dhāriṇī, wife of Ugrasena, king of Mathura, expressed her desire (*dohada*) to eat her husband's flesh. This was treated as the indication of forthcoming difficulties and hence he was kept in a bell-metal box and thrown away in the sea.[32] Kaṁsa was then brought up by Vāsudeva who married him to Jivāyasā, the daughter of Jarāsandha. His real identity was later on disclosed to Kaṁsa who kept his father Ugrasena in jail and became the king of Mathura.[33] Kaṁsa arranged the marriage of his sister Devakī with Vāsudeva. At the time of marriage celebration, Muni Atimuktaka, younger brother of Kaṁsa, predicted to Jivāyasā, Kaṁsa's wife, that the seventh son of Vāsudeva and Devakī will kill her husband. Then Kaṁsa requested Vāsudeva to hand over all the seven sons of Devakī to him. Vāsudeva and Devakī were then kept in vigilence. In the Mahābhārata tradition, this differs to a certain extent.[34]

13. Due to the mercy of Hariṇagavasi, all the six sons (Anikayaśa, Anantasena, Ajitasena, Nihatāri, Devayaśa and Śatrusena) of Devakī were brought up by Sulaśa and the seventh son was kept with Nanda, the servant of Devakī and Nanda's daughter was handed over to Devakī. Kaṁsa released the daughter under the impression that Devakī delivered a female child. He cut her nose and returned her to Devakī.[35] According to the *Uttarapurāṇa* (pp. 407-11), this daughter (named Alakā) became a Jaina nun who penanced at Vindhyāchala where she was killed by a lion. Subsequently she was worshipped as Vindhyavāsini Devī.

The epic tradition is somewhat different. According to it, Devakī used to visit Nanda's house for having a look at her son under the pretext of cow-worship.[36] Since then cow-worship started.[37]

14. With a view to take revenge with Vāsudeva, Vidyādhara Śūrpaka sent his two daughters Śakunī and Pūtā for killing Kṛishṇa. But Kṛishṇa himself killed both these Vidyādharīs.[38]

According to the *Uttarapurāṇa*, these two were Devīs who came down to rescue Kaṁsa at his instance. In the epic tradition, Pūtā, called Pūtanā, was a *rākshasī* deputed by Kaṁsa for killing Kṛishṇa.[39]

15. The son of Śūrpaka Vidyādhara made efforts to kill Kṛishṇa by pressing him between two Yamala trees, but Kṛishṇa himself destroyed them, and killed the son. Kṛishṇa was then called 'Dāmodara'.[40] Jinasena refers to two Devīs – Yamakā and Arjunā in this connection.[41]

Epic tradition refers to Nalakubera and Manigrīvā Yaksha who took up the form of trees due to the curse of Nārada. They were released from the curse due to the blessings of Kṛishṇa.[42]

16. As soon as Kaṁsa looked at the noseless girl, he remembered the prophecy of Atimuktaka Muni and enquired about his enemy. The astrologer described the enemy and advised that whosoever kills the bull, horse, donkey and ram may be considered as the enemy and that enemy is the seventh son of Devakī, who is called Vāsudeva, the greatest powerful man in the world. Kṛishṇa killed all the four sons of Kaṁsa.[43] The *Uttarapurāṇa* (pp. 427-28) mentions here the name of Arishṭadeva who appeared as a bull. *Śrimad-Bhāgavata* does not refer to donkey but Dhenukāsura takes his place.[44]

17. Kṛishṇa came to know from Baladeva that he was the son of Vāsudeva-Devakī. He then decided to kill Kaṁsa. In the meantime, Kṛishṇa killed Kāliyanāga in the Yamunā river, according to the *Trishashṭi* (8.5.262-65). The *Harivaṁśapurāṇa* and *Uttarapurāṇa* narrate another story in this regard. According to it, Kṛishṇa got the Kamala after killing Kāliyanāga, the protector of the Kamala.[45]

According to *Śrimad-Bhāgavata*, Kṛishṇa purified the Yamunā and saved it from the clutches of Kāliyanāga.[46]

Kaṁsa then arranged the wrestling with Chāṇūra and Mushṭika. At the outset, Kṛishṇa and Balarāma first killed Padmottara and Champaka elephants and then these wrestlers. *Śrimad-Bhāgavata* refers to only one elephant named Kuvalayāpīḍa. The *Trishashṭi* mentions that Kṛishṇa became unconscious during the fighting with Chāṇūra (8.5.284-95), but the *Harivaṁśapurāṇa* does not say so. Kṛishṇa then killed Kaṁsa by keeping a leg on his head.[47] The *Harivaṁśapurāṇa* and *Uttarapurāṇa* differ slightly here. According to the latter, Kaṁsa attacked Kṛishṇa but failed. Samudra-Vijaya and others were overjoyed and freed Ugrasena from jail.

18. Jarāsandha became the enemy of Kṛishṇa and Balarāma. He ordered Samudra-vijaya to handover Kṛishṇa and Balarāma to him. Samudra-vijaya discussed the matter with Chraushṭuki and went towards western coast along with the Yādavas. Kālakumāra, the son of Jarāsandha attacked the Yādavas who were protected by Devas of Kṛishṇa. Kālakumāra died in the fort. Then Kṛishṇa became the king of new Dvārakā near Revataka mountain in Saurashtra.[48]

19. Kṛishṇa married Rukmaṇi and killed Śiśupāla. There were eight *paṭṭamahishīs* of Kṛishṇa (Satyabhāmā, Rukmaṇī, Jāmbavati, Lakshmaṇā, Suśimā, Gaurī, Padmāvatī and Gāndhārī) out of sixteen thousand queens.[49] Atimukataka Muni predicted that Rukmaṇi will deliver a child like Kṛishṇa by the name Pradyumna who will be kidnapped by Kālasamvara Vidyādhara. Kañchaṅamālā will present two vidyās, Prajñapti and Gauri to Pradyumna by which he will never be defeated. Pradyumna had a war with Kṛishṇa and proved himself to be a worthy son.[50] Both, the father and son were acquainted here for the first time. The epic tradition refers to the number of queens of Kṛishṇa to be 16,000 of whom nine were *paṭṭamahishīs*.

20. Satyabhāmā wanted to have a son like Pradyumna. Harinaigamesī gifted a necklace to Kṛishṇa saying that whosoever wears it will get a son like you. Pradyumna got the information through Prajñapti Vidyā and played a mischievious game. He sent Jāmbavatī to Kṛishṇa for sexual intercourse in the form of Satyabhāmā. Finally Jāmbavatī delivered the son Śāmba like Kṛishṇa while Satyabhāmā got the son named Bhīru Kumāra, who appeared fearsome by nature. The *Uttarapurāṇa* names Sambhava Kumāra in place of Śāmba.

21. Pradyumna had good relations with Śāmba. He married Vaidarbhī, the daughter of Rukmi after overpowering an elephant.

22. At the instigation of Jivāyasā, her father Jarāsandha, the king of Rājagṛiha, started war with Kṛishṇa. Kṛishṇa also arrived at Mathura along with Arishṭanemi. Jarāsandha constructed a *chakravyūha* having thousnad ārās or spokes. On the other hand, Yādavas prepared *garuḍavjūhrā*. Finally Kṛishṇa killed Jarāsandha and returned to Dvārakā.[51] According to Vedic tradition, Jarāsandha was killed by Bhīmasena.[52]

23. Bāṇāsura, the Khecharapati of Śrinivāspura, had a daughter named Usha who had a love affair with Aniruddha, the

son of Pradyumna. Aniruddha ultimately married Usha and Kṛishṇa killed Bāṇāsura. Kṛishṇa then became Trīkhaṇḍeśvara.

24. Arishṭanemi, the 22nd Tīrthaṅkara, was the son of Samudra-Vijaya, the cousin of Kṛishṇa. At the time of Kaṁsavadha, he was hardly eight years old. He was brought up at Dvārakā. Kṛishṇa acknowledged his power and ruled over his kingdom. But Arishṭanemi declared that he would accept the Jinadīksha without getting married. Rājimatī, the proposed wife of Arishṭanemi,[53] followed his footsteps. The epic tradition has no such reference.

25. Draupadī is said to be a Sati-śiromaṇi in Jaina tradition due to her penance, though she had a Nidāna Karma in the previous birth of Sādhvī Gopālikā for having five husbands while she looked at the courtesan Devadattā who was busy with her five lovers.[54]

26. Draupadī was kidnapped by Padmanābha, the king of Dhātakīkhaṇḍa who carried her to his capital Amarakaṇkā. Kapila Vāsudeva and Tīrthaṅkara Munisuvrata were there in Dhātakīkhaṇḍa. Two Vāsudevas cannot meet each other according to Jaina tradition. Then Kapila Vāsudeva gave a lesson to Padmanābha and saved Draupadī from his clutches.[55] Pāṇḍavas could not stand before Padmanābha.

27. Gajasukumāla was the eighth son of Devakī. Her first six sons were identical ones who became Jaina monks. Gajasukumāla also renounced the world leaving his wife Somā, the daughter of Somaśarman who kept the firepot on his head and as a result Gajasukumāla died on the spot.[56]

28. According to the *Mahābhārata,* Kuntī did not join the Pāṇḍavas during *vanavāsa* while Jaina tradition says that Kuntī went with them.

29. The *Mahābhārata* says that king Drupada sent his purohita to Duryodhana at the direction of Kṛishṇa while the Jaina tradition mentions that Kṛishṇa sent the message to Duryodhana through Drupada's purohita.[57]

30. According to the *Mahābhārata,* Sañjaya becomes a messenger of Dhṛitarāshṭra and goes to the Pāṇḍavas, whereas the Jaina tradition says that Dhṛitarāshṭra sends the message to Pāṇḍavas for renouncing the idea of a war with Kauravas. Yudhishṭhira replies that to remove the injustice is a justice itself. The *Mahābhārata* mentions that Kṛishṇa went to Dhṛitarāshṭra after having a detailed discussion with Pāṇḍavas, while the Jaina tradition remarks that Kṛishṇa went directly to Dhṛitarāshṭra for creating

peace between the two parties. He insisted that at least five villages be given to the Pāṇḍavas. Duryodhana refused the proposal.[58]

31. Bhīshmapitāmaha advised Kṛishṇa not to indulge in the war. Kṛishṇa honoured the view by saying that he will not use the weapon at all. The *Mahābhārata* on the other hand, says that at the request of Arjuna, Kṛishṇa renounced the idea.[59]

32. Kuntī went herself to Karṇa in epic tradition for informing him that he was her own son while Jaina tradition says that this was disclosed to him by Kṛishṇa.

33. Jaina tradition says that Pāṇḍu was alive during the Mahābhārata War while the epic tradition does not accept it.

34. Jaina texts do not usually mention the Mahābhārata War. However,[60] Jinasena is of the view that war was held between Kṛishṇa and Jarāsandha. Devasūri says that the Kaurava-Pāṇḍava war took place prior to Jarāsandha war.

35. In the absence of the Mahābhārata War, the Jaina texts do not mention any sermon as the *Gītā* does. However, the preachings are inserted here and there.

36. Śiśupālavadha took place during the Jarāsandha war according to Jaina texts, while the *Mahābhārata* does not accept any connection between the two events.

37. Madirā, Dvaipāyana and Agni are proved to be the main reasons behind leaving Dvārakā. Except Kṛishṇa and Balarāma, entire Dvārakā was destroyed in the fire and submerged into the sea. Kṛishṇa and Balarāma went to Jīrṇodyāna. Then Kṛishṇa was killed by Jarākumāra, his own brother, by mistake in the Kauśāmbī forest. It is said in the Jaina texts that Kṛishṇa will be 12th Tīrthaṅkara by the name Amama in future. Balarāma will also achieve salvation during the same time.[61]

38. Jaina texts mention that Kṛishṇa remained in the world for one thousand years while the *Mbh.* says that he was alive for 120 years.

39. Jaina texts say that Balarāma had been roaming with the corpse of Kṛishṇa for six months. Siddhārtha Deva tried to pacify his attachment and finally Balarāma placed him on the fire. Then he kept himself busy in performing the Jaina penance and took the birth in Brahmaloka.

40. Vyāsa was the legitimate son of king Parāśara and Guṇavatī and unlike the *Mahābhārata* had three sons, Dhṛitarāshṭra, Pāṇḍu, and Vidura. Pāṇḍu, became penitent over his killing of a deer,

renounced the world and became a Jaina monk. Dhṛitarāshṭra too after hearing a prophecy about the destruction of his entire family, renounces the world and becomes a Jaina monk.[62]

41. Unlike the *Mahābhārata*, Jaina writers reduce Kṛishṇa to human stature by showing his nature to be scheming and selfish. It is said that at the time of Nemi's marriage, Kṛishṇa had gathered animals to be slaughtered for the marriage feast in order to eliminate Nemi as a rival to the kingdom by provoking him to renunciation.[63]

42. Unlike the *Mahābhārata*, Śāntanu himself is said to have fathered Matsyagandhā.[64]

43. Bhīshma not only took a vow to renounce all rights to his kingdom, but also cut off his own genitals and thus earned his name, Bhīshma, the terrible.[65]

44. Chitrāṅgada and Vichitravīrya, the sons of Śāntanu, defamed Bhīshma, their stepbrother, by linking him in a scandalous relationship with their mother Satyavatī.[66]

45. With a desire to get sons, Gāndhārī copulated with a hundred goats and gave birth to hundred sons, the eldest of whom was Duryodhana.[67]

46. Jainas did not accept the concept of *niyoga* at all as found in the *Mahābhārata*.

47. The story of Ekānaṁsā, the sister of Kṛishna is totally changed in Jaina version. According to it, she was killed by a lion during her penance in the forests of the Vindhya and the people started worshipping her as Durgā Vindhyavāsinī.

48. The life story of Kṛishṇa is also totally changed in the perspective of Jaina principles.

49. Dvaipāyana was a Jaina monk who had great *yogic* powers. If misused, they were capable of burning anything at their will. The sons of Balarāma and Kṛishṇa insulted the *yogī* and as a result the *yogī* destroyed Dvārakā by fire.

50. The Jaina account of the deaths of Balarāma and Kṛishṇa and their passing into heaven and hell respectively are also quite different from the epic tradition.

Thus the Jaina version of the Mahābhārata story is very different from that of the *Mahābhārata* itself. It is, in fact, prone to the tenets of Jainism and the story is altered accordingly. Kṛishṇa in Jaina tradition originally figured as a human hero who followed the righteous path in ruling over his people. But as soon as the epic accepted him as *avatāra* of Vishṇu due to growing devotional movements, the Jainas considered him as *Śalākāpurusha*.

Secondly, the concept of Tīrthaṅkara and Chakravartin would have grown gradually to illustrate the Jaina doctrine of Karma and the path of salvation.

NOTES AND REFERENCES

1. *Mahābhārata Ādi* 6-14; 41-45; 1123-1143.
2. *Bhāratamañjarī, Ādi* 876.
3. *Nāyādhammakahāo*, 16.81; *Uttarapurāṇa*, 72.198.
4. *Ākhyāṇakamṇikośa*, 2.12.89; *Pāṇḍavapurāṇa*, 15.41; *Harivaṁśapurāṇa*, 45.120.
5. *Bṛihatkāthakośa, Kathānaka* 43; *Ārādhanā-prabandha-kośa*, 90.21.7.
6. *Harivaṁśapurāṇa*, 45.121; *Pāṇḍavapurāṇa*, 15.42.302.
7. *Uttarapurāṇa*, 72.198.
8. *Ibid.*, 72,210.
9. *Nāyādhammakahāo*, 16.122.
10. *Pāṇḍavacharita*, 4.56.
11. *Ibid.*, 4,p.57; *Pradyumna-kalikā*, Dvitiya vāchanā, p. 64.
12. *Jñātādharmakathā*, 10.124.434.
13. *Amamasvāmi-charita*, 9,301,365.
14. *Uttarapurāṇa*, 72.211-421; *Harivaṁśapurāṇa*, 45.150-51; *Pāṇḍavapurāṇa*, 15.223-326.
15. *Jñātādharmakathā*, 16.137.437.
16. *Uttarapurāṇa*, 72.224-421.
17. *Pāṇḍavacharita*, *Sarga* 17, p. 279.
18. *Jñātādharmakathā*, 16.216.465.
19. *Kalpasūtra-kalpalatā*, p. 40.
20. *Bṛihatkāthakośa*, 83.54-69.204.
21. *Bālabhārata*, 2.4.84.166.
22. *Harivaṁśapurāṇa*, 47.717; 17.22.551-52; *Bṛihatkāthakośa*, 83.88-207; *Bālabhārata*, 3.1-4; *Pāṇḍavapurāṇa*, 17.145.340.
23. *Bālabhārata*, 2.61; *Pāṇḍavapurāṇa*, 17.315-369
24. *Uttarapurāṇa*, 72.224-422.
25. *Harivaṁśapurāṇa*, 52.88-89.
26. *Jñātādharmakathā*, 16.138.142.
27. *Harivaṁśapurāṇa*, 54.8-609.
28. *Pāṇḍavapurāṇa*, 21.6-8.447.
29. *Jñātādharmakathā*, 16.149.152.
30. *Ibid.*, 16.190.193.
31. *Ibid.*, 16.230. See for these references, Sheela Singh, *Draupadī Kathānaka kā Jaina Śrotoṁ ke Ādhāra para Tulanātmak Adhyayan*, Varanasi.
32. *Trishashṭiśalākāpurushacharita*, 8.2.62.

33. *Ibid.*, 8.2.95-96.
34. *Śrīmad-Bhāgavat* 10.1.55.
35. *Harivaṁśapurāṇa of Jinasena*, 34.32; *Trishashṭi.*, 8.5.115.
36. *Śrīmad-Bhāgavat* 10.4.8-12.
37. *Ibid.*, 10.25.26.
38. *Trishashṭi.*, 8.5.16.
39. *Śrimad-Bhāgavata*, 10.6.4-13.
40. *Trishashṭi.*, 8.5.141; *Bhavabhāvanā*, 2211-15.
41. *Harivaṁśapurāṇa*, 35.45.
42. *Śrīmad-Bhāgavat*, 10.10.1-43.
43. *Trishashṭi*, 8.5.202-7; *Bhavabhāvanā*, 2352-59.
44. *Śrimad-Bhāgavata*, 1.15.20-40.
45. *Harivaṁśapurāṇa*, 36.8-10.
46. *Śrimad-Bhāgavata*, 10.16-17th Chapter.
47. *Trishashṭi*. 8.5.313
48. *Ibid.*, 8.5.344-362; *Harivaṁśapurāṇa* refers to so may wars held between the Yādavas and Jarāsandha.
49. *Antagaḍadasāo*, 1.1; *Vāśudeva Hiṇḍī*, p. 78-79.
50. *Trishashṭi*, 8.6.48-60.
51. *Ibid.*, 8.7.446-457; *Harivaṁśapurāṇa*, 42-67-601.
52. *Mahābhārata*, Sabhā, 19-1522.
53. *Trishashṭi*, Parva 8, Sarga, 51.58; *Harivaṁśapurāṇa*, p. 55.
54. *Trishashṭi*, 8.10; *Pāṇḍavacharitra*, Sarga 4.
55. *Jñātādharmakathā*, 16 etc.
56. *Antagadasūtra*, 171; *Pāṇḍavacharitra*, etc.
57. *Mahābhārata*, Udyoga, 20.
58. *Ibid.*
59. *Pāṇḍavacharitra* of Devaprabhasūri, p. 348.
60. See *Chauppannamahāpurisacharita*, *Trishashṭi*, etc.
61. See *Harivaṁśapurāṇa*, *Pāṇḍavapurāṇa*, etc.
62. *Uttarapurāṇa*, 70.2-3.
63. *Pāṇḍavapurāṇa* of Subhachandra, 22.42-43.
64. Vādiraja's *Pāṇḍavapurāṇa* 1.72-93, P.S. Jaini "*Mahābhārata* Motives in the *Jaina Pāṇḍava Purāṇa*," article published in *Bulletin of the School of Oriental and African Studies*, Vol. XLVII, Pt. 1, pp. 108-115.
65. *Ibid.*, 1.105-106.
66. *Ibid.*, 1.113-118.
67. *Ibid.*, 1.137-45.

22

Tamil Versions of the *Mahābhārata* and Studies on the Tamil Versions

A.A. Manavalan

Literary influences could be classified into two aspects: positive influence and negative influence. Translation, imitation, adaptation and transcreation are considered as forms of positive influence. These influences are found both within a culture and across cultures. Parody, satire, caricature, travesty and counter-design are considered as forms of negative influence. They usually occur within a culture.

This paper tries to trace the influence of the *Mahābhārata* on the literary productions of the Tamils down the centuries from 2nd century BC to 20th century AD. This influence has been found to have occurred in the form of translations, adaptations, transcreations and in the form of references through similes, metaphors and allusions. This is from the point of view of the 'giver'.

This paper also attempts to be a study of literary reception. This is to say, while receiving the Mahābhārata story, the factors such as, what was received as such from the giving culture, what was rejected by the receiving culture and why and how was the material absorbed and integrated, and with what success, will be discussed in this paper.

In keeping with the prescribed space and time for this paper, it is structured into two main sections:

I. Tamil versions of the *Mahābhārata;* and
II. Studies on the Tamil versions.

I

TAMIL VERSIONS OF THE *MAHĀBHĀRATA*

The contacts between the people of the north and the southern parts of India seem to have been flourishing from very early times, say at least from the first millennium BC. We do not, however, have definitive evidences, historical or otherwise, to decide on the dates of such contacts. Scholarly opinions differ. We are, therefore, not in a position to mention the dates of literary migration from the north to the south. This much can, however, be said that there are ample evidences of literary migrations from the north to the south, from as early as the fifth century BC.

The *Tolkāppiyam*, the earliest extant Tamil grammar, prescribes literary translations as one of the four kinds of literary production in Tamil and postulates certain rules for translating northern languages into Tamil (1597, 884, 885). In addition, Tolkāppiyar, the author, prescribes words from northern languages as part of Tamil lexical corpus (880). He does not name the language in all these places but simply refers to them as the language of the north. In view of its probable date of composition (4th century BC), we gather that he may be referring to Pali, Prakrit and Sanskrit, since we have evidences to show that Pali and Prakrit were known to Tamil scholars even before they had contacts with Sanskrit language proper. As far as grammatical theories are concerned, Tolkāppiyar does compare certain items of Tamil grammar with those of Sanskrit (102, 1038). All these references allow us to conclude that northern literary texts were known to Tamil scholarship through translations even before the age of the *Tolkāppiyam*, i.e. prior to 4th century BC.

SANGAM CLASSICS

As far as the *Mahābhārata* is concerned, references are found in the earliest Tamil literary works collectively called Sangam classics, in the form of similes, metaphors and allusions to the characters, episodes and incidents of the story.

1. The second poem in the *Puranānūru*, an anthology of 400 heroic lyrics, hails a Chera king, Perunchōrru utiyan Cheral as the one who provided food for both the parties in the Máhābhārata War.

2. The *Chirupānārruppatai*, (II. 238-41), one of the ten idylls of the Sangam period, refers to a treatise on culinary art authored by Bhīmasena, the elder brother of Arjuna who consigned the Khāṇḍava forest to flames. This has, perhaps, a reference to Bhīmasena being employed as a chef in the palace of the king of Virāṭa during Pāṇḍavas', sojourn incognito in Virāṭadeśa.
3. The *Perumpānārruppatai* (II. 414-20), another longer poem, hails king Tontaimān Ilantirayan for his victory over his enemies, like the Pañcha Pāṇḍavas who won the war after defeating and destroying all the twice fifty (one hundred) warriors (Kauravas).
4. The *Kalittokai*, another anthology of Sangam poems, has several references to the Mahābhārata War and characters.

Poem 25 (1-9) of this anthology depicts a beautiful scene of a male elephant saving its herd from the dangerous fire in a bamboo jungle. The poet compares the saviour elephant to Bhīmasena who, in a similar manner rescued his mother and brothers from the burning palace built by Duryodhana with highly combustible material called lac.

Poem 52 (1-4) describes an elephant that kills its enemy elephant by piercing its tusk into its chest as Bhīmasena, who killed Duryodhana by striking him at his thigh with his mace.

Poem 101 (16-20) presents a similar picture, this time comparing a ferocious bull to Bhīmasena who killed Duḥśasana by ripping open his chest in fulfilment of his vow. There are also references in this anthology to the fateful death of Droṇa and Bhīshma, besides descriptions of the war field in Kurukshetra.

It is to be noted that in all these references, the characters of the *Mahābhārata* are not referred to by their names, but by their specific exploits in the epic. Again, these exploits are not depicted straightaway, but used as similes and always as the vehicle of the simile. It is too obvious to note that only well-known objects, concepts or incidents are employed by poets as vehicles of the simile. It is, therefore, clear that the story of the *Mahābhārata*, its theme and characters were all assimilated into the social psyche of the Tamils long before these poems were composed. As such the resultant impact of the epic on the Tamil society had already become part of its cultural and literary ethos during the period of the Sangam age.

An interesting absence may be noted here. We do not find any reference in these poems to either Kṛishṇa or the *Bhagavadgītā*. Even though Kṛishṇa and Balarāma are repeatedly referred in the *Kalittokai* and the *Paripātal*, their childhood exploits alone are described in these poems, thus drawing their source on the *Bhāgavata*, rather than the *Mahābhārata*.

EARLIEST TAMIL EPICS

References to the Mahābhārata characters, incidents, etc., are found in Tamil epic poetry too from 3rd century AD to 10th century AD.

The *Chilappatikāram*, the first Tamil epic (2nd-3rd century AD), contains the following:

1. With the two feet that scaled all the three worlds, you traversed the distance on foot as an ambassador of the Pāṇḍavas to the Kauravas (17: 34-37).
2. Arjuna burnt down the Khāṇḍava forest (22: 111-112).
3. The Mahābhārata War lasted for 18 days (27: 7-10).
4. The Chera king provided food for both the parties involved in the war (29: 24).
5. The sea-hued (Kṛishṇa) eclipsed the sun with his disc (17: 26).
6. Sing the glory of the sea-hued who served as a charicteer (26: 238-39).

The *Manimēkalai*, (3rd or 4th century AD), the second Tamil epic, refers (3: 146-148) to Arjuna in the form of a eunuch being hounded by the urchins on the street, comparing him to the heroine Manimekalai being thronged by people.

These two epics written centuries after the ancient Sangam classics treat Kannan (Kṛishṇa) as a divine person on the side on the Pāṇḍavas, revealing the fact that certain stories of the *Bhāgavata* and the *Mahābhārata* had, by that time, got amalgamated into a unified entity. The onset of the tide of Bhakti movement cannot be missed at this juncture.

Coming on the heels of these epics, the *Perunkatai* (6th century AD) and the *Chivakachintāmaṇi* (10th century AD) also have made several references to the *Mahābhārata*. Bhīmasena's victory over the Kauravas (3-21: 9-11), Arjuna's scorching down the Khāṇḍava forests (1-46: 90-92), Vyāsa being the head of the Kuru dynasty

(3-15: 25-26), Duryodhana's cutting off Abhimanyu's bowstring from behind (1-56: 56-59) and several other incidents are mentioned in the *Perunkatai*. The *Chivakachintāmaṇi* compares the martial valour of Jīvaka, the hero, with that of Abhimanyu (288); refers to Kṛishṇa's revelation to Karṇa about his birth (456); describes Jīvaka's riding the chariot after the manner of Danañjaya (767) and makes references to Duryodhana's slandering words about the Pāṇḍava's (211), to Droṇa (1646), to Arjuna's mastery over archery (1681), to Bhīma's mastery in the art of cooking (2735) and to certain other incidents.

It may be noted here that these two later epics mention the names of the Pāṇḍavas and the Kauravas as found in the *Mahābhārata*, unlike the earlier Tamil texts which refer to them by their exploits. This change of trend is noteworthy because around this time, say from 6th century AD onwards, the Tamils might have had direct contact with the original Sanskrit texts or with formal translations of the *Mahābhārata* into Tamil.

Another interesting point that emerges from the analysis of the above data is that even though the above Tamil epics or their authors belong to different religions, non-Vedic as it were, they employ stories, incidents and characters drawn from *Mahābhārata* in that, the *Itihāsa* with its import and morals had already attracted the Tamil society which had by that time seamlessly got grafted into its social and literary psyche and therefore these epics made use of them liberally to enunciate their truths among the Tamils.

TAMIL VERSIONS

1. *Bhāratam Padiya Peruntēvanār*

There have been many an attempt from the post-Sangam period at rendering the *Mahābhārata* into Tamil. Two celebrities are known by the name Peruntēvanār as authors of Tamil versions of the epic. The first and the earlier of them is called *Bhāratam Padiya Peruntēvanār* meaning Peruntēvanār who composed the *Bhāratam*. This work is now not available and only some verses from this work are found quoted by commentators of later periods. Scholars assign this author and his work to 5th or 6th century AD. A copperplate inscription of 10th century AD found at Chinnamanur near Madurai says the Pāṇḍiya kings established the Tamil

Academy at Madurai and caused the Tamil translation of the *Mahābhārata*. It is observed that this may be referring to the work of the first Peruntēvanār, which is lost to us. If the available stray poems are any indications as touchstone pieces, the lost work should have been the first full-fledged translation of the *Mahābhārata* into Tamil.

2. *Bhārata Venpā*

The second work ascribed to the second Peruntēvanār is called *Bhārata Venpā* said to have been composed between AD 850-59 under the patronage of Nandivarman III of the Pallava dynasty, better known as the victor of a war at Tellār against the Pāṇḍiya king, Śrīvallabhan.

This *Bhārata Venpā* is the first available *Bhāratam* in Tamil. Even this work is not available in full. The available work contains 830 Venpā verses, beginning with Udyogaparvan and ending with the 13th day battle in Droṇaparvan. Thus, only the middle portion of the work has come down to us. It is in the form of a Champū Kāvya, after the style of the *Takatūr yāttirai,* an earlier work in such a mixed style. The prose pieces are heavily laden with Sanskrit words and phrases while the verses are in clear and chaste Tamil, giving us, as such, a sample of the contemporary prose style.

Additions and Innovations

As a condensed version of the original, it is but natural to expect deletions and condensing to a large extent. Similarly, while receiving a cultural text remote in origin in terms of place and time, the receiver would accommodate the text in keeping with the cultural climate and ethos of his times. When Peruntēvanār came on the socio-literary scene of 9th century Tamil Nadu, the wave of Bhakti cult had swept all over the region with the rise of Vedic religions, revival of ancient literary traditions and the ruling class adjusting itself with the changed social priorities. Consequently, as far as the literary texts related to Vaishṇava following are concerned, Lord Vishṇu, especially Lord Kṛishna, came to be adored as a supreme character both in the rituals of life and letters. It was in such a milieu that the Mahābhārata text was received and Peruntēvanār restructured the action of the epic so as to portray to portray Lord Kṛishṇa as the key character, the *dues ex machina* of the story of the war. Many of the following additions or alterations or innovations as the case may be have been made in the light of the above cultural atmosphere of the 'receiver':

1. Durvāsa gave five *mantras* to Kuntī (poem 220, prose), though according to Vyāsa, Durvāsa gave only one *mantra*.
2. The child Karṇa was laid in a box by Kuntī before being cast into the river (poem 222).
3. It is Kṛishṇa who told Karṇa about the circumstances of his birth (220).
4. Aśvatthāman becomes a suspect in the eyes of Duryodhana due to a trick played by Kṛishṇa and this incident is not mentioned by Vyāsa.
5. Peruntēvanār introduces Śveta episode (14-18) not found in Vyāsa.
6. In Vyāsa, Vidura is known as a minister of high ethical calibre – He is not presented anywhere in Vyāsa as a warrior and a bowman. Peruntēvanār brings in a change in this character who is said to have broken his bow as a protest against Duryodhana's irreverent behaviour towards him (106).
7. The valiant Sahadeva is converted into an evolved man of high wisdom by Peruntēvanār. Kṛishṇa blesses him with his Viśvarūpa (131, 132).
8. Peruntēvanār's Kṛishṇa-Karṇa episode is different from that of Vyāsa.
9. In Vyāsa, Kuntī goes to Karṇa on her own; in Peruntēvanār Kuntī goes to Karṇa as directed by Kṛishṇa.
10. Kṛishṇa commissions Indra to rob Karṇa of his *kavacha* and *kuṇḍala* (276, 283). In Vyāsa, Indra goes to Karṇa on his own accord.
11. Karṇa plays a game of dice with Duryodhana's queen Lakshaṇai (Bhānumatī):

    One day, Karṇa was playing a game of dice with the queen. She lost the game. When she was about to go without paying the stake, Karṇa caught hold of her *sārī*. The girdle (*mekhalā*) of the queen gave way and the precious diamonds in large number fell helter skelter. Just while this happened, Duryodhana entered the chamber. Karṇa was stunned. Duryodhana said smiling, "Shall I pick up the diamonds?" Should Karṇa desert such a friend? No, he would happily die in the service of such a great king—told Karṇa to his mother Kuntī (315, 319, 320).

12. In Peruntēvanār, there is a vivid description of pre-war human sacrifice; Aravan, son of Ulūpī, Arjuna's wife is sacrificed in the battlefield. This entire episode drawn from folklore and designed to celebrate the eminence of Kṛishṇa (Vāsudeva) is an innovation of Peruntēvanār.
13. Peruntēvanār calls Duryodhana, as "aravuyarttōn" meaning 'serpent-bannered'. Vyāsa's work clearly tells us that Duryodhana had an elephant as the emblem of his banner (Droṇaparvan 125-26). Peruntēvanār is the first south Indian author to call Duryodhana as 'serpent-bannered'. Maybe a popular south Indian tradition of legends and folklore has suggested this change. Maybe, this emblem suits the character of Duryodhana admirably well. The fact that almost all the *Mahābhārata* poets of the south (Tamil, Telugu and Kannada and some Sanskrit works like the *Bhārata Champu*) have referred to Duryodhana as 'serpent-bannered' speaks volumes of the force of the popular or legendary tradition of the 'receiver'.

Apart from this change in the emblem of the banner, many of the alterations and innovations discussed above have been incorporated in the later Tamil versions of the *Mahābhārata*, apart from works like Pampa's *Bhāratam* (*Vikramārjunavijaya*), and in portions of Tikkana's version. Thus, Peruntēvanār's *Bhārata Venpā* has been a trend-setter in rendering the *Mahābhārata* in the regional languages of the south.

3. *Māvintam*

This version consisting of 339 Venpā verses narrating the later portion of the Mahābhārata story, namely, Svargārohaṇaparvan. Neither the name of the author nor the date of its composition is mentioned anywhere in the text. Even though the editor of this work published by Saraswathi Mahal Library, Thanjavur (1950), claims that this later work was also composed by Peruntēvanār, the author of the *Bhārata Venpā*, scholars who have made a close study of both these works have concluded that *Māvintam* is a work of a different poet of later age.

4. *Arulnilai Vichākar Bhāratam*

Tiruvālankāttu inscription (13th century AD) records that Arulnilai Vichakan Vatsarājan translated the *Bhāratam* into Tamil. But this work is not available now.

5. *Villiputtūrār Bhāratam*

Villi Bhāratam is the popular name of this work. It is said to have been composed by a very learned poet called Villiputtūrār during the 14th century AD. This is the most popular Tamil version of the Mahābhārata story. Structured into 50 *sargas* and consisting of 4,300 verses in Viruttam metre, this version deals with the first ten Parvans only ending with the victory of Pāṇḍavas and the coronation of Yudhishṭhira. He follows probably the tradition of Kamban whose *Rāmāyaṇa* ends with Śrī Rāma's coronation in Ayodhyā. The Vaishṇava tradition in Tamil Nadu does not, normally, evince any interest in celebrating the final stages of the lives of the great. This applies to the Tamil versions of the *Rāmāyaṇa*, the *Mahābhārata* and the *Bhāgavata*. The Tamil translations of the later portions of these great works, might have been either written by poets of inferior talents or by non-Vaishṇava poets.

It is said that this poet chose to compose his epic poem at the instance of his patron, Varapatiyatkoṇḍan, chieftain of Nadu nāḍu. One of his prefatory verses says, "I consented to write this *Mahābhārata* not because this story had already been sung by great sages and others, but only because this epic involves inevitably the story of Lord Kṛishṇa and I will have the pleasure of singing his glory now and then." This statement of the poet gives us the clue as to the significance attached to the Mahābhārata story by the people in the south.

The poet says that he wrote epic in Tamil on the basis of sage Vyāsa's great work. But Mahābhārata scholars like Ganapathy Iyyer (59), V. Raghavan and others are of the opinion that the *Villi Bhāratam* is based more on *Bāla Bhāratam*, a Sanskrit work by Agastiya Bhaṭṭar, as far as the Ādiparvan and the rest of the story is concerned, it follows the earlier Tamil version *Bhārata Venpā* by Peruntēvanār. They point out several passages from these two works which are literally followed in the *Villi Bhāratam* (60-66). There are also scholars like A. Viswanathan (58-59) who hold that Vyāsa's work is the original source for the *Villi Bhāratam* as far as the basic fabric of the epic is concerned and, of course, Villi has followed the earlier Tamil versions and folk legends in certain aspects of deletions, additions and innovations.

The *Villi Bhāratam* differs from its original in umpteen ways and this aspect alone deserves a separate study. Apart from the additions and innovations made first by Peruntēvanār and later incorporated by Villi, the latter also made several qualitative changes to suit the cultural climate of his times. A noteworthy addition may be mentioned here. While keeping silent over the references in Sangam and post-Sangam works regarding the munificent gesture of a Chera king in providing food for both the armies of the war, the *Villi Bhāratam* introduces all the three Tamil kings as participating in the war in support of the Pāṇḍavas (17th day battle, poem 107-118, 120-134). Again, he describes that the Bhārata warriors used to wear garlands of Vetchi, Vanchi, Tumbai and so on while going on different stages of war, a poetic convention of totemic significance prescribed by Tolkāppiyar in his third book, chapter two. This is an instance of cultural grafting, usually followed by the receiving culture. The *Villi Bhāratam* abounds in such instances.

Another interesting aspect of this Tamil version is its treatment of the message of the *Bhagavadgītā* in a very summarized form. While its earlier version namely, *Bhārata Venpā* spends just three verses (475-477) on it, the *Villi Bhāratam* sums up the message in six verses (29:2-7). Even a yet-to-come later version, *Nallappillai Bhāratam*, an elaborate composition of 14,000 verses, expends just 50 verses on the *Bhagavadgītā*. If such summarized treatment is any indication, we may say that the Tamil versions are more interested in the ethical and aesthetic aspects of the story rather than in the philosophic exposition of the *Gītā*.

Consequent upon the Bhakti cult, and its concomitant emergence of doctrinaire writings, Tamil Nadu entered, during and after the 14th and 15th centuries, an era of Pravachanas or religious discourses catering to the social and quasi-spiritual needs of the Tamil society and by and by the whole of south India. It was at such a juncture that the *Villi Bhāratam* came handy to the Pravachanakartās and even secular scholars to take the Mahābhārata story to the lowest of the low and to the remote villages. One can compare this with the social needs satisfied by Tulsīdasa *Rāmāyaṇa* along the northern states of India, from Bengal to Rajasthan.

6. *Ātiparuvattu Āti Paruvam* by Ampalattatumaiyar

This work composed towards the beginning of the 17th century AD deals with the Ādiparvan of the original. It has 10 sections and 566 verses. It merely narrates the story of the dynasties before and after Śāntanu. Poetically speaking, it is of lesser value and therefore, known only to the specialists and bibliographers.

7. *Aranganāthak Kavirāyar Bhāratam* by Aranganāthak Kavirāyar

Composed in AD 1753 with 45 *sargas* and in 2,477 verses, this work is complementary to *Villi Bhāratam* as it narrates the Mahābhārata story from the 11th Parvan to the end, left out by Villiputtūrār. He just mentions the first ten Parvans dealt in *Villi Bhāratam* and hence, it may be considered as its sequel. Not of much importance as a literary work.

8. *Nallāppillai Bhāratam*

Composed towards the beginning of the 19th century by Nallāppillai, this is the most voluminous of all the Tamil versions. It deals with the *Mahābhārata* in its entirety and runs up to 14,000 verses in length. This augmentation was caused by including almost all the episodes of the *Mahābhārata* and incorporating maximum number of verses from *Villi Bhāratam*. Discourses on *Mahābhāratam* were mostly based on this work and hence it was more popular with Pravachana scholars who took this story to every nook and corner of the northern districts of Tamil Nadu so much so that there is hardly any village in this region where Mahābhārata discourses are not held every year during the summer season, especially in the months of April, May and June. As such, this version has played a major role in familiarizing the people—mostly rural—with the ideals and morals exemplified in the stories of the *Mahābhārata*.

9. *Bhārata Chāra Venpā*

This version by Perumal Swamikal gives in a very summarized form the entire Mahābhārata story in about 748 verses in Venpā metre. Though certain variations have been effected in view of its contemporary climate, none of them is noteworthy; nor has this work any special features worthy of mention. The exact date of this work is not available and it could be, however, said that it is the last of the formal Tamil versions of the *Mahābhārata* and that it might have been composed probably towards the end of the 19th century.

10. Tiraupati Chūl Urai

This is the most modern version of the *Mahābhārata* by R. Srinivasan (1996). Though based on the *Villipāratam*, it narrates the story of the epic in a very summarized form. The medium is a kind of prose-poem of little aesthetic merit. The author exploits the basic fabric of the epic to articulate his own views on contemporary Tamil society. It does not follow the conventional divisions of the epic such as Parvans or Sargas and employs instead seven action headings such as the *Svayaṁvara*, the game of dice, Pāṇḍava's 'exile', etc. Though not of much literary or critical value, this version will certainly help the common man with average education to have an idea of the import of the great epic.

EPISODIC VERSIONS

Apart from the above full versions, there have been through the ages many an attempt at producing episodic versions of the *Mahābhārata* in Tamil. These versions, a kind of *khaṇḍa kāvyas* so to say, were based either on certain incidents of the main story or on certain episodes that occur along the main action of the epic. The following are the most popular episodic versions.

1. *Nalavenpā*

This thirteenth-century work by a poet called Pukalēnti is based upon the Nalopakhyana episode in Vyāsa's epic. Structured into three *khāṇḍas* and consisting of 424 Venpā verses, it deals with the story of Nala, the king of Nishadha, his marriage with Damayantī, the beginnings of his misfortunes and his release therefrom. This is the most widely read and enjoyed work that has been ever composed in Venpā metre. The verses are crisp and sweet, the sentiments are very touching and exhilarating and the imagery very rich and apt, its style simple and flowing and therefore, it is a sheer joy and pleasure to read this little secular epic, scarcely sounding like a translation or an adaptation from an alien culture. No wonder, the Tamil scholarship has praised him as "Venpāvir Pukalēnti", meaning "Venpā, thy name is Pukalēnti".

2. Naidatam

This sixteenth-century work by Ativīrarama Pāṇḍiyan, a royal poet, is not directly based on the *Mahābhārata*, but on *Naishadha*, a *khaṇḍa kāvya* by king Harsha, dealing with the story of Nala. Though it deals elaborately with the story in 28 chapters running to 1,173 verses of Viruttam metre and is planned with carefully designed architectonics proper to an epic poem, this poem does not rise to the level of an aesthetically viable work of any literary merit.

3-5. Purūrava Episode: *Purūrava Charitai,* (17th century) *Purūravach Chakkaravarttikkatai* (19th century) and *Purūrava Nāṭakam*

These are the three works based on the story of king Purūrava in the original epic. Though drawing on the same source, they differ in the portrayal of the character of Purūrava. While in the *Charitai,* the longest of the three with 27 chapters and 920 verses, Purūrava is portrayed as marrying Urvaśi, the *nāṭakam* by an unknown author shows that he redeems Urvaśi from an asura and hands her over to the devas in heaven. And on his way back he marries a princess, Chiraprabhā by name. Though the drama is based on the earlier two works referred to above, it changes the course of action and gives a different story regarding his marriage with Chiraprabhā. This is not found in any Sanskrit work. We are not able to explain this alteration in the drama.

6. Śrīman Naṭarājāṅkita Mahābhārata Śatakam

This modern work (1931) deals with the Mahābhārata story in the form of a Śatakam genre consisting of 101 poems. It is divided into 14 Parvans and the entire work is cast as a book of morals, like *Viveka Chintāmaṇi.* The story of the *Mahābhārata* is made use of for teaching certain general morals. An interesting thing about this short version is that every poem of this Śatakam hails the glory of Lord Naṭarāja as the one who blesses the narration of the story. Except that a novel form is adapted, this work has got nothing important as a piece of literature.

7. *Māri Vāyil* composed by Somasundara Bharathiar (1909)

Māri Vāyil means *megha sandeśam*. This work cast in the genre of *tutu prabandha* sings the pangs of separation of Chitrāṅgadā, the Pāṇḍiya wife of Arjuna* and her request to the north-bound clouds to meet Arjuna in Indraprastha, describe to him her woes of separation and persuade him to return to her. This is the message of this work based on the works of Vyāsa and Villiputtūrār. The *Māri Vāyil* does not contain any deviations from the original but for certain details describing the Pāṇḍiya country, the queen Chitrāṅgada, the landscape from Madurā to Indraprastha and certain references glorifying the Tamil language and its rich heritage. Composed in chaste, beautiful language, the *Māri Vāyil* is one of the best attempts at narrating the ancient classics in Tamil.

8. Pāñchāli Chapatam

The title means "Vow of Pāñchāli" (1912). This Tamil version is by Subramania Bharati, the most famous and representative poet of the 20th century. He was a multifaceted personality—a champion of nationalism and of Indian culture, a pioneer of modern Tamil literature and language, a fearless crusader against any form of suppression or oppression or depression.

According to his own statement, *Pāñchāli Chapatam* has been based on the *Vyāsa Bhāratam*, and it could be said to be almost a translation of the original. As such, he presents Dhṛitarāshṭra in a favourable light, a hater of dice and Duryodhana but as one enslaved by his paternal passion. The style of his narration is racy, spirited and yet most simple and straightforward so that even with an elementary knowledge of Tamil, one could enjoy the poem on his own.

Scholars have found in it an allegory of the contemporary conditions of India and accordingly Pāñchāli is, in their view, Mother India in fetters. K. Meenakshisundaram observes,

> It must be confessed that this song must have been necessitated by India's strenuous struggle against the yoke of an alien rule. One cannot but be conscious of a veiled propaganda in it. In Pāñchāli's strong protest

* According to the *Mahābhārata*, Chitrāṅgadā was the daughter of Chitrarāhana, king of Maṇipura. Ed.

and fearless challenge one may hear the voice of the outraged and insulted India. (27)

Though this poem allows in certain passages, such an allegorical interpretation, it could be read and enjoyed on its own as a piece of brilliant enactment of an old story still relevant to our common human predicaments experienced in our day-to-day life.

9. *Iravicha Marapinar Kātai* (1938)

This is a translation by Marayya Āchārya from the Telugu work *Rāghava Pāṇḍaviyam* by Pingali Suranna. The date of the original is not available in the text. Some scholars ascribe it to the 17th century AD.

The title means 'the story of the kings of the solar and lunar races'. The Telugu title means 'the story of Rāghava and the Pāṇḍavas'. The original and the translation are examples of peculiar poetic exercise in narrating the stories of the *Rāmāyaṇa* and the *Mahābhārata* using the technique of Ślesha *alaṅkāra*, whereby a verse can yield two meanings, one relating to the *Rāmāyaṇa* and the other to the *Mahābhārata*. Laborious both in composition and in comprehension, these works, especially the Tamil version, do not have much literary value. At the most they exhibit the linguistic acrobatics of the authors, perhaps patronized and favourably received by the contemporary readers of old fashion.

FOLK VERSIONS

Reception studies reveal that of the two *itihāsas*, the *Rāmāyaṇa* was adored more by the elite and the educated public, while the *Mahābhārata* was very much loved by the less educated and the rural masses. The fact that more number of people, especially in the rural areas, have been named, till recently, after the names of the Mahābhārata characters and that innumerable villages have established temples for Draupadī and celebrate annual festivals regularly during the months of summer with discourses on the *Mahābhārata* for a month and with street dramas based on the *Mahābhārata* performed for the last ten days during the festival, bears ample evidence to the popular reception of this epic. That is why we have numerous folk versions of the *Mahābhārata*, many times the formal literary versions. This trend of a popular bias towards this story has been there in Tamil Nadu from the 9th century onwards as evidenced from the inscriptions granting lands and revenue for poets and discourse scholars on the *Mahābhārata*.

In view of the limits of this paper in terms of time and space, we cannot deal elaborately with the folk versions which deserve a separate treatment in detail. Apart from those lost in the course of their journey, there are about a hundred versions that have come down to us in folklore forms such as *ammānai, tūtu, mālai, kalavu,* musical plays (*kirtanas*) and folk dramas. Most of them are printed and the rest are alive in palm-leaf manuscripts.

The following are some of the more popular folklore versions:

1. *Bhārata Ammānai* (19th century)

Longest of the ballads; divided into two parts: Balakāṇḍam and Yutta kāṇḍam; first part not available; second part alone runs to 15,000 lines. Based on *Villi Bhāratam,* it is a scholarly writing. Though cast in a folk form, folk elements and refrains characteristic to ballad poetry are absent here

2. *Alli Arachāni Mālai*

This ballad cast as a romantic poem dealing with the affairs of Arjuna with Alli, the princess of the Pāṇḍiya king and with Pavalakkodi, the princess of the coral islands, all deviations from the original except for the names. With the help of Lord Kṛishṇa a trick is played on queen Alli who allows no men into her company and finally, Arjuna marries the humbled lady.

3. *Pavalakkodi Mālai*

This is also a romance ballad. It narrates the love adventure of Arjuna with Pavalakkodi. Alli's son Pulantiran demands a chariot made of coral beads. Arjuna sets out to the coral islands whose queen Pavalakkodi has to be appeased if he is to succeed in his mission. Here again, Kṛishṇa helps him to get his mission fulfilled and to marry the queen Pavalakkodi.

4. Pulantiran Kalavu Mālai

This is a folk song dealing with Pulantiran, the son of Arjuna and Alli. It is a romantic ballad dealing with Pulantiran's adventure in regaining his wife Kalantāri, daughter of Turichatai, sister of Duryodhana.

5. Pulantiran Tūtu

This is a folk song dealing with Pulantiran. *Pulantiran Tūtu* gives a detailed account of his adventures in the court of Duryodhana during his mission as an ambassador from the Pāṇḍavas to demand their share of the kingdom, once their period of exile was over. Pulantiran is angered by the invectives and unrelenting replies of Duryodhana, insults him in turn and returns to Madurai, the kingdom of his mother.

6. Abimannan Sundarī Mālai

This is long ballad in 6,600 lines. It describes the love story of Abhimannan and Sundarī. Arjuna's wife Subhadrā and Kṛishṇa's wife Alarmelu Mankai agree that they would get their children married to each other when they come of age. In course of time Subhadrā gives birth to a male child Abhimannan and Alarmelu Mankai begets a girl child Sundarī. Duryodhana asks Sundarī's hand for his son Lakkunan. Kṛishṇa initially accepts Duryodhana's proposal and buys time by deceit. Meanwhile, Abhimannan with the help of his half-brother Aravan and his cousin Katotkajan wins the hand of Sundarī, of course with the blessings of Kṛishṇa.

7,8. Ēni Ērram and *Pañcha Pāntavar Vanavācham*

These are two other major works in the form of folk ballads. Most of these ballads are ascribed to one poet called Pukalēnti, a different person from the author of the *Nalavenpā*. Most of them belong to the second half of the 18th century; some may have been to the first half of the 19th. They are composed more or less in the same style common to such folk poems during those centuries. The subject matter and the details of narration are all from the native imagination; not to be found in the Sanskrit epic, except for the names of the persons, that too, the major ones.

9. Aravān Ammānai

This ballad composed in the form of Ammānai genre deals with the voluntary sacrifice of Aravān, the son of Arjuna to goddess Kotravai (Durgā). This ballad is still orally sung in honour of Aravān during the eighteen day annual festival called Aravān nōnpu in Vellalur area, near Coimbatore in Tamil Nadu. Closely modelled on the *Villi Bhāratam*, this ballad has gained cultural significance among the people of this area.

10. Karṇa Mahārājan Chantai

This very popular ballad describes the 17th day battle with Karṇa as the Commander of Duryodhana's forces and his death at the hands of Arjuna. It also covers the coronation of Dharmaputra after the destruction of the entire forces of the Kauravas. Ponnuruvi is a new character introduced in the ballad as the wife of Karṇa, with her contempt for him in view of his being the son of a charioteer, until her final reconciliation when he tells her that he was really the eldest son of Kuntī.

11. Kurukshetra Mālai

This ballad composed in Ammānai metre seems to be a sequel to the *Abhimannan Sundarī Mālai* in terms of the hero of this poem and is related to the *Pañcha Pāntavar Vanavācham* as far as the action of the poem is concerned. It deals with the exploits of the hero, Kurukshetran, the son of Sundarī and Abhimannan. His exploits lead to a strange situation wherein Kṛishṇa has to wage a war against the Pāṇḍavas. Stranger still is the action of Duryodhana who joins hands with the Pāṇḍavas to fight against Kṛishṇa. By a sudden miracle in the battlefield, the war is averted. There seems to be no limit to the flights of imagination.

12. Nalachchakkaravartti Ammānai

This ballad composed in Ammānai metre runs up to 2,650 couplets. It deals with the story of king Nala in full, and closely follows the *Naidatam* of Athivirarama Pāṇḍiyan of the 16th century. This ballad by Vennimalāip Pillai was therefore, probably composed during the 18th or 19th century AD.

The *Ponnuruvi Machakkai, Aravalli-Churavalli katai, Arichchantira kummi, Vaikunta Ammānai* and *Pancha Pāntavar Vaikuntak kummi* are some of the other popular works based on the epic of *Mahābhārata*.

Most of the above works are not versions of the *Mahābhārata*. They can be said to have been based on the epic only in the sense that they have been named after certain characters of the epic or certain incidents of the epic action. Thus, the Sanskrit epic just lends its name to these folk poems. The poets of these folk poems have given free vent to their imagination to fashion forth the characters such as Ponnuruvi, Aravalli, Pavalakkoti, Kurukshetran and so on around whom they have woven their own stories in keeping with their social and cultural situations, having their eyes always on their rural audience and taste.

This trend of folk poetry dealing with the story of the *Mahābhārata* continues well up to the first half of the 20th century. The major form of folk poetry during the later period has been the drama. Innumerable music plays called *kirtanas* and street dramas called *terukkuttu* have been written with the themes of the *Mahābhārata* (See the Appendix). Separate surveys have been conducted to collect these folk poems—ballads, cintus dramas, and so on and we are yet to get the final results. These literary works provide rich quarry for not only literary researchers, but also for sociologists.

As far as the folk versions are concerned, no study could be exhaustive. What is given above is only a sample, the tip of an iceberg, of course, the best of it.

II

STUDIES ON THE *MAHĀBHĀRATA* IN TAMIL

As noted under the section, 'Folk versions', scholarly attention to the *Mahābhārata* studies in Tamil was very meagre and unfavourably less than given to the *Rāmāyaṇa* studies. There are about 600 studies in the form of full-fledged booms and research articles on the *Rāmāyaṇa* in Tamil. The Tamil version *Kamba-rāmāyaṇa* has received the greatest attention by the scholars, native and foreign. In addition to its influence on the Indian scene, several translations of this work have appeared in English and Malayalam*

* It has also been translated into Hindi, Ed.

and hardly there is any international conference either on the *Rāmāyaṇa* or on Tamil studies which does not include papers on *Kambarāmāyaṇa*.

We do not see such intense interest bestowed on the Tamil versions of the *Mahābhārata*. Scholarly bias has been always towards the *Rāmāyaṇa*, whereas the less educated and the rural folk were interested in the story of the *Mahābhārata*. But this interest has found no expression in the form of formal studies on it. It was only after Independence when universities and research institutions encouraged formal studies for obtaining research degrees that scholars turned their attention towards *Bhāratam* works in Tamil and that too very few scholars when compared to other works taken for research. Of late, sociologists and folklore scholars have shown much interest in this area and several fieldworks are being undertaken, thanks largely due to the shifting priorities towards social justice.

The following are the important studies available on date on Tamil versions of the *Mahābhārata*:

Chāchanat Tamilkkavi Charitam (1937) and *Arāychchit Tokuti* (1974) by M. Raghavaiyangar. He is the first Tamil scholar to find inscriptional evidences about the *Mahābhāratam* works in Tamil; their dates and details of the poets and patrons were brought to light in these reasonably reliable studies.

An Introduction to the Study of Villi Bhāratam in Tamil (Villi Bhārata Tiravukōl) (1940) by S.K. Ganapathy Iyer. As the title says, it is in the nature of introducing the work to the general audience. This discusses the sources for Villi, the deviations from the original and certain new material added to the source. A useful study to a certain extent.

Pōrkkaviyam (1962) by M. Radhakrishnan. It is a good study of the characters of the *Mahābhāratam*. Differences in the portrayal between the sources and Villi's work are brought out. The ethical aspect of the characters is given more attention.

Bhārati Chapatam (1963) by Mathu. Sa. Vimalanantham is a scholarly work. It deals with the vow of Pāñchāli by Bharati in detail and compares it with the *Villi Bhāratam*, bringing out the modern relevance of the epic as retold by Subramania Bharati.

A Study on the Poetical Works of Subramania Bharati (1965) by K. Meenakshisundaram. This is the first formal study on *Bhāratam* works in Tamil pursued for an M. Litt. degree. It compares the character of Duryodhana, portrayed by Vyāsa, Villi and Subramania Bharati; reliable and resourceful study.

Commentary on the Villi Bhāratam (Tamil) (1957-1966) by V.M. Gopala Krishnamachariar. This is the most exhaustive commentary on the *Villi Bhāratam.* Apart from giving all the variations in the text, it deals with deviations from the original, additions, alterations and innovations by Villi, the aesthetic excellences of the Tamil version, grammatical notes, metric variations and provides choicest quotations from Sanskrit and Tamil texts to illuminate the text and enrich our understanding. This has been the most useful sourcebook for almost all scholars of *Mahābhāratam* literature in Tamil.

A Critical Study of Villi Bhāratam (1978) *Villiputtūrār Bhāratam-oru Tiranayvu* by K. Vellimalāi. This is the first full-fledged formal study of the *Villi Bhāratam*, done for a Ph.D. Thesis, yet to be published. This study discusses the Tamil version in terms of its epic structure, characterization, rhetorical aspects and deviations and deletions from the work of Vyāsa. Packed with accurate data, this unpublished thesis is very useful for a formal understanding of the epic.

Bhārata Nūlkalin Tiranāyvu (1979) by A. Viswanathan. This is the printed version of a Ph.D. Thesis. It is very authentic and elaborate and highly valuable as a sourcebook for any kind of research regarding the Tamil versions of the *Mahābhārata*. It deals with almost all versions in Tamil and analyses them in terms of their structure, metric variations, style and reception among the audience. It gives, for each and every version of the epic, the deviations, additions and innovations in comparison with the Sanskrit original. The various charts appended to the text are highly useful as a databank and shall serve forever as a reliable reference work as far as *Mahābhārata* studies in Tamil are concerned.

Villi Bhāratattil Tamilunarachchi (1981) by M.P. Sivagnanam. This work by a non-formal scholar discusses the *Villi Bhāratam* in terms of Tamil patriotism shown by the author by including non-Vyāsa material, such as singing the glory of the Tamil language, literature,

Tamil landscape and including the Tamil kings as supporters of the Pāṇḍavas' cause.

Villi Bhāratattil Kannan (1989) by S. Valliammal. This is a printed version of a Ph.D. Thesis and as such a formal and data-based study on the *Villi Bhāratam*. It mainly focuses on the role of Kṛishṇa in the story of *Mahābhāratam* as far as the Tamil versions are concerned. It demonstrates that Kṛishṇa plays so prominent a role that he could be considered as the chief protagonist of the epic action. As indicated earlier, the Tamil versions from the very beginning show more interest in the character of Kṛishṇa, a thrust in theme and characterization advanced and advocated by the hymns of Ālwārs and by the expositions of the Āchāryas during the early middle ages.

There have been, besides these studies in book forms, several short articles and papers submitted, and discussed in seminars and conferences, later published in various journals and anthologies. There seems to be nothing special about them except a new trend observed in one or two articles taking the stand that the Pāṇḍavas and Draupadī deserved the treatment they received from the Kauravas and thus show the latter in a favourable light, a kind of negative influence mentioned at the beginning of this paper. Though no full-fledged study on these lines has appeared, this new trend among the younger generation of scholars cannot be missed or ignored. Maybe, Dinakarji's *Kurukshetra* has some critical kinship in this respect.

The author of this paper records hereby his debt of gratitude to the editors of the Tamil versions and to all the authors of the critical works cited and included in the bibliography for the wealth of information offered to him through their works.

BIBLIOGRAPHY

TEXTS DISCUSSED (CHRONOLOGICAL ORDER)

Peruntēvanār Bhāratam – Bhārata Venpā (ed.) A. Gopalaiyan, Madras, 1925.

Māvintam (ed.) Muthurathna Mudaliyar, Thanjavur: Saraswathi Mahal Library, 1950.

Villiputtūrār Bhāratam (ed.) Rajam & Co., Madras, 1959.

Nala Venpā by Pukalēnti. (ed.) Madras: Kazhakam, 1958.

Naitatam by Ativirarama Pandiyan. (ed.) Madras: Kazhakam, 1962.

Āti Paruvattu Āti Paruvam by Ambalattatumaiyar (ed.) T. Chandrasekar, Madras, 1951.

Aranganāthak Kavirāyār Bhāratam (ed.) Govinda Pillai, Madras, 1902.

Purūrava Charitai by Iyamperumal Kavirayar, ed. K.V. Jagannathan, Thanjavur: Saraswathi, Mahal Library, 1950.

Purūrava Nāṭakam, anonymous, (ed.) K.V. Jagannathan, Thanjavur: Saraswati Mahal Library, 1950.

Nallāppillai Bhāratam (ed.) Madras, Atikalanidhi Printers, 1888.

Bhārata Chara Venpā by Perumal Swamikal, (Pub.) 1947.

Bhārata Ammānai, anonymous (ed.) A.M. Parimanam, Thanjavur: Saraswathi Mahal Library, 1990.

Māri Vāyil by Somasundara Bharatiyar, Madurai, 1954.

Pānchāli Chapatam by Subramania Bharatiyar, Madras: Sakti Veliyidu, 1957.

Sriman Naṭarājāṅkita Mahābhārata Chatakam by Krishnamurthy Iyer, Madras, 1931.

Tiraupati Chūl Urai by R. Srinivasan, Chennai: Aniyakam, 1996.

CRITICAL WORKS CONSULTED (ALPHABETICAL ORDER)

Arunachalam, M., *Ballad Poetry*, Thanjavur: Saraswathi Mahal Library, 1976.

Chockkalingam, T.A., "Aravakkotiyon", *Kāppiyach Chintanaikal*, 1961.

Encyclopaedia of Tamil Literature, Vol. I, Madras: Institute of Asian Studies, 1990.

Encyclopaedia of the Folk Culture of Tamil Nadu, Madras: Institute of Asian Studies, 1996.

Ganapathy Aiyar, S.G., *Villi Pāratat Tiravukōl*, Madurai, 1940.

Gopala Krishnamachariar, V.M., *Villiputtūrār Bhāratam*, Madras: 1957-1966.

Hiltebeitel, Alf, *The Ritual of Battle: Kṛishṇa in the Mahābhārata*, New York, Albany: State University of New York Press, 1990.

Jagannathan, K.V., *Tamilk Kāppiyankal*, Chennai: 1940, reprint, 1991.

Kasirajan, R., *Evolution and Evaluation of Epics in Tamil*, Madurai, 1990.

Kirúttinacami, K., "Turōpati Tukilurintatu Chariyē", *Ayvukkovai* – 17 (3), 1985.

Krishnacharya, T.R. (ed.), Preface of *Śrīman Mahābhārata* and an Alphabetical Index. Kumbakonam: Madhva Vilas Book Depot, 1914.

Meenakshisundaram, K., *A Study on the Poetical Works of Subramania Bharati*, Chennai: Pari Nilayam, 1965.

Murukecan, K., "Villi Pāratattil Avala Velippātu", *Ayvukkovai* – 10 (1), 1978.

———, "Taruman Tavaru Ceyyātavanā?", *Ayvukkovai* – 14(1), 1982.

Muttaiya, I., "Mahapāratamum Nāttuppurak Kataippātalkalum" *Ayvukkovai* – 16 (3), 1984.

Palaniyamal, P., *Tamilil Chataka llakkiyankal*, Madurai, 1992.

Perumal, A.N., *Tamil Drama: Origin and Development*, Madras: International Institute of Tamil Studies, 1981.

Pillai, Vaiyapuri, *Kāviya Kālam*, Madras: Tamil Puttakalayam, 1957.

Punkunran, "Pāmara Makkalum Pārata Māntarum" *Ayvukkovai* – 14(3), 1982.

Radhakrishnan, M., *Pōrkkāviyam*, Chennai: Palaniappa Brothers, 1962.

Raghavaiyangar, M., *Chāchanat Tamilk Kavi Charitam*, 1937.

———, *Arāychchit Tokuti*, Chennai: Pari Nilayam, 1974.

Sambasivanar, S., *Navalar Somasundara Bharatiyar*, New Delhi: Sahitya Akademi, 1999.

Savariroyan, D., "Pāṇḍavas and Their Relation to the Tamilian Kings", *Tamilian Antiquary*, Vol. l, No. 1, 1907.

Sivagnanam, M.P., *Villi Pāratattil Tamilunarchchi*, Chennai: Punkoti Patippakam, 1981.

Srinivasa Iyengar, P.T., *History of the Tamils*, New Delhi: Asian Educational Services, reprint 1995.

Subramanian, N., *Tamil Social History*, 2 Vols., Chennai: Institute of Asian Studies, 1997-1998.

Taucker, Kala, K., "Nūrruvaril Oruvan", *Ayvukkovai – 6*, 1974.

Tolkappiyam, Madras: Kazhakam, 1967.

Vaiyapuri Pillai, *Kāviya Kālam*, Madras: Tamil Puttakalayam, 1957.

Valliyammal, S., *Villi pāratattil Kannan*, Chennai, 1989.

Vellimalai, K., "Puranchuvar kōlam cheyvān", *Ayvukkovai – 4*, 1972.

———, "Villi Kanta Vikarnan", *Ayvukkovai – 5*, 1973.

———, "Kuntīyum Kantariyum", *Ayvukkovai – 9*, 1977.

———, "Villiputūrar Pāratam—Oru Tiranāyvu", Ph.D. Thesis, University of Madras, 1978.

Veerasami, V., "Villi Pāratam", *Tamil llakkiyak Kolkai – 3*, Chennai: International Institute of Tamil Studies, 1978.

Venkatesa Acharya, Kambaluru, *Mahābhārata and Variations – Peruntēvanār and Pampa*, Kurnool: Vyāsaraja Publications, 1981.

Vimalanadam, Madhu, Ca., *Pārati Chapatam*, Thanjavur, 1963.

Viswanathan, A., *Parata Nulkalin Tiranayvu*, Karaikkudi, 1979.

APPENDIX A

Formal Literary Genres

Year	*Title*	*Author*
15th c.	Arichchantira Venpā	?
16th c.	Arichchantira Purāṇam	Vīra Kavirāyār
16th c.	Purūrava Charitai	Iyan Perumāḷ
17th c.	Draupatī Kuram	Pukalēnti

APPENDIX B

Musical/Folk Dramas

Year (AD)	*Title*	*Author*
1775	Achōmuki Nāṭakam	Chirkali Aruṇāchala Kavirāyār
1867	Arichchantira Vilācham	Arankapillai Kavirāyār
1870	Mahapārata Vilācham	Rāmānuja Swāmikal
1870	Chutu Tukilurital Nāṭakam	Ramachchantira Kavirāyār
1872	Nala Vilācham	Chapapati Mutaliyār
1873	Arichchantira Vilācham	Parachurāma Kavirāyār
1874	Arichchantira Vilācham	Veṅkaṭarāma Upattiyāyār
1875	Arichchantira Nāṭakam	Varadarājulu Nāiḍu
1876	Mahāpārata Vilācham-Aruchchunan Tapachu	Charavana Pantitār
1877	Tamayantī Nāṭakam	Kirushna Pillai
1880	Mahāpāratam Nachchup Poykai Nāṭakam	Vaiyirakkan Velayutap Pulavar
1881	Abimanyu Yuttam	?
1881	Tukil Urital Nāṭakam	Charavana Pantitar
1882	Śrī Mahāpārata Vilācham	Rāmānuja Swāmikal
1882	Nala Vilācham	Damodara Mutaliyar
1887	Mahāvintam allatu Taruma Nāṭakam	Kalyāṇa Chuppiramaniya Ayyar
1889	Patinettam Por Nāṭakam	Kirushna Pillai
1890	Abimannan Chantai Nāṭakam	?
1890	Kīchaka Chammāra Nāṭakam	Rettinānayakār (ed.)
1890	Arichchantira Vilācham	Muṭṭuchami Pillai

Year (AD)	*Title*	*Author*
1890	Taruma Puttiran Nāṭakam	?
1891	Tiraupati Tulki Urital Nāṭakam	Rattina Chapapati Mutaliyār
1891	Aruchchunan Tapachu Nāṭakam	?
1893	Mahāpārata Vilācham-Nachchuppoykai	?
1893	Arichchantira Nāṭakam	Chivachami
1895	Arichchantira Nāṭakam	Pattirachami Chettiyar
1896	Arichchantira Nāṭakam	Viralinka Bhāratī
1897	Kichaka Vilācham	Kannaiya Naidu
1897	Charāchanta Nāṭakam	Chalai Kirushnachami
1897	Aravān Kalapali Nāṭakam	?
1897	Kirushnan Tūtu Nāṭakam	Murukechan
19th c.	Bhārata Vilācham	Rāmachandra Kavirāyār
19th c.	Mahābhāratak Kirttanam	Muthurāma Mudaliyār
19th c.	Arakku Malikai Nāṭakam	?
19th c.	Mahāpāratak Kummi	Ramasamy Kavirāyār

APPENDIX C

Modern plays based on the Mahābhārata

Year	*Title*	*Author*
1893	Pavalakkoti Nāṭakam	Thiyāgarāja Pillai
1895	Yayāti	P. Sambanda Mutaliyār
1910	Arichchantiran	S. Bavanandam Pillai
1912	Kīchakan Vatam	C.R. Padmanāpa Ayyar
1912	Tamayantī	Piranatārtihara Chivanar
1918	Arichchantiran	P. Sambanda Mutaliyār
1920	Chupattira Kalyanam	Śuddhānanda Bhāratī
1925	Kīchakan	C.R. Namachchivāya Mutaliyār
1929	Chupattira-Arjuna	P. Sambanda Mutaliyār
1929	Chupattira Arjunan Vivakam	K. Pārthasārathy Ayyangār
1930	Pāntavar Agnātavācham	B. Rāmamūrthi Pantulu
1930	Arichchantira Vilācham	Muthusami Pillai
1933	Apimanyu	V. Sāminata Sarmā
1934	Alli Charittiram	Śankaradās Swāmikal

Year	Title	Author
1938	Arichchantiran	Śankaradas Swāmikal
1941	Pavalakkoti Charittiram	Śankaradās Swāmikal
1948	Purūrava Chakkaravarti Nāṭakam	A.K. Rāmachandran
1955	Tamayantī Tirumanam	S. Ilamurukanār
1958	Tērōtti Makan	P.S. Rāmaiyā
1960	Pāratam	C.N. Annādurai
1963	Pānchālī Chapatam	P.S. Rāmaiyā
1963	Katotkajan Tūtu	Suki Subramanian
1965	Kalapali	P.S. Rāmaiyā
1965	Pānchālī Chapatam	A. Vaittiyanatan
1973	Kalappali	K. Vellimalai
1973	Vītuman	K. Vellimalai
1977	Vanna Makal	K. Vellimalai

APPENDIX D

Prose fiction based on the Mahābhārata

Year	Title	Author
1976	Oru tīpam aintu tirikal	Kove. Manisekaran
1978	Yākachalai	Kove. Manisekaran
1994	Kāntari	Kove. Manisekaran

Note: The Appendix is prepared mainly on the basis of A.N. Perumal's *Tamil Drama: Origin and Development*, 1981.

23

Mahābhārata in Early Kannada Literature

Shrinivas Ritti

PREAMBLE

It is well known that no other literary work in India is held in such reverence as the *Mahābhārata* of Vyāsa. It has been a source of inspiration for numerous poets and writers in this country for thousands of years. For believers it is the Fifth Veda and a means of solace for many a troubled mind. It is a source of *dharma*, a perennial guidebook for human behaviour. While it is a rich literature in itself, it has enriched the literature of the country as no other work has ever done to this extent.

WORKS ON MAHĀBHĀRATA THEME IN EARLY KANNADA LITERATURE

It has been well said that the Kannada literature begins with the *Mahābhārata*. The earliest known literary creation is itself on the *Mahābhārata*. It is the famous *Pampa Bhārata* or *Vikramārjuna-vijaya* of the earliest known Kannada poet Pampa (10th cent. AD), which deals with the story of *Mahābhārata*. There could be other earlier works with this theme but "they faded away when Pampa's work appeared" on the literary horizon (*Munnina kabbamam-ellaman-ikki mettidudu*). This mature *kāvya* composed in highly ornate *Champū* style indeed anticipates a long literary tradition behind it. The earliest known Kannada work which was written even earlier than Pampa, viz., *Kavirājamārga* (a work on poetics, 9th century AD), written by the Rāshṭrakūṭa king Amoghavarsha Nṛipatuṅga even mentions quite a few authors and their works which, however, are not available today. Pampa's work, therefore, enjoys the place of pride of being the earliest available *kāvya (Adi-kāvya)* in Kannada and Pampa enjoys the title *Ādi-kavi* till today. Following Pampa another well-known poet Ranna (*Kavi-Ratna,* latter half of 10th century AD) composed *Gadāyuddha* or *Sāhasa-Bhīma-Vijaya,* based on the *Mahābhārata*. Subsequent centuries have also produced many great works based on this great work and the tradition continues even today.

DIFFERENT TRADITIONS OF THE MAHĀBHĀRATA WORKS IN KANNADA

Scholars identify different traditions of Kannada works with the Mahābhārata theme. Foremost among them and the earliest in chronological order is the Jaina tradition or the works written by Jaina writers influenced by Jaina religion and philosophy. Most notable works in this tradition are the above mentioned works of Pampa and Ranna. This tradition is divided into two sections, like the *Jaina-āgama-kāvyas and Laukika-kāvyas*. The former is represented by the Jaina Purāṇas, particularly the *Nēminātha Purāṇa* interwoven with the story of the Tīrthaṇkaras. Laukika-kāvyas are represented by the works on non-religious themes like the works of Pampa and Ranna mentioned above. But even these works are not bereft of the influence of Jaina ideology.

Then there is Vedic or Brāhmaṇical tradition, represented by the works of the Brāhmaṇical writers extolling the glory of God Vishṇu or Kṛishṇa and upholding the Vaidika-dharma. For them, the story is only a vehicle to espouse these causes. One of the most prominent works in this tradition is a very popular work in Kannada, viz., *Karṇāṭa-Bhārata-Kathā-Mañjari* or *Kumarāvyāsa-Bhārata* as it is popularly known, by the poet Nāraṇappa (*c.* 14th century AD). The other one is *Jaimini-Bhārata* of Lakshmīśa (*c.* 16th century AD). Unlike the earlier authors who employed the classical *Champū* form as a means of exhibiting their literary art, Kumāravyāsa and Lakshmīśa employed simpler form of *shaṭpadī* which was easier to understand by the common people. These works have become very popular among the public and their recitation is organized and appreciated even today throughout the length and breadth of Karnataka.

Scholars identify yet another tradition in the Vīraśaiva literature. The Brāhmaṇical themes were not very popular with the Vīraśaivas and there are not many works with these themes in the Viraśaiva literature. Yet the episode of Śiva granting *Pāśupata-astra* to Arjuna has attracted the poet Shaḍaksharadēva of about the 16th century AD who has composed a *kāvya* entitled *Śabara-Śankara-Vilāsa*. The theme has been used to extol the value of devotion to God Śiva which is a cardinal principle in the Vīraśaiva religion.

Now, the fourth tradition is the folk tradition represented by oral narrations like the *Harikathās* and *Kīrtanas* popular among the rural masses and the songs and ballads of unknown authors. Folk theatre also popularized the *Mahābhārata* by staging different episodes in fairs and other religious congregations. Indeed, *Mahābhārata* is also responsible, to an extent, for the growth of folk theatre. Thus there is enormous scope for the study of the *Mahābhārata* theme in early Kannada literature. We, however, intend to restrict our study to the first two traditions only, viz., Jaina and Brāhmaṇical, which have produced outstanding works in Kannada literature.

PAMPA-BHĀRATA

Pampa-Bhārata or *Vikramārjuna-vijaya* has occupied a unique place in the history of Kannada literature, not merely as the earliest known *kāvya*, but as a trendsetter for future writers. The poet composed this work at the behest of his patron Arikēsarin, a ruling chief of Vēmulavāḍa under the Rāshṭrakūṭa king Kṛishṇa III. The patron invited the poet to write a *kāvya* to perpetuate his fame throughout the world. Pampa gladly consented and promised to compose the *kāvya* within a year. He says that he was thorough with the *Mahābhārata* of the great Vyāsamuni and politely submits that he is not so haughty as to claim to be himself Vyāsa. Though he claims to write the whole *Mahābhārata*, he has neither copied nor has he reproduced it. He has imbibed the spirit of the *Mahābhārata* and has recreated it in his own inimitable way, with all the poetical embellishments like *alaṅkāras* and *rasas*. He commences the work with the birth of Arjuna and ends it with his coronation after the Bhārata War, in 14 *āśvāśas*. For him Arjuna is the hero of the *kāvya* who is none other than Arikēsarin himself. His valour, his virtues, his greatness were all before his eyes and throughout the *kāvya*, he sees Arikēsarin alone, in the guise of

Arjuna. He even calls Arjuna a *Sāmanta*, the title was enjoyed by Arikēsarin and says that Arjuna was born of Jakkavve and Narasiṁha who were the parents of Arikēsarin (an anachronism indeed!).

To suit his own taste and creative skill, Pampa has introduced several changes in the narration. He has dropped a few *ākhyānas* and *upākhyānas* in the *Mahābhārata* and has added some of his own. His Jaina affiliation and the contemporary social conditions have obviously played an important role in this process. One glaring example is the role of Kṛishṇa. In the *Vyāsa-Bhārata*, he is the central figure and the pivot around whom all the events and persons revolve. For Pampa this was not necessary, for, after all, he did not believe in his being godhead or *avatāra*. Not that he has undermined the personality or the role of Kṛishṇa, but the prime importance has not been given to him, as has been done by either Vyāsa or the later poet KumaraVyāsa.

It was difficult for Pampa to accept that Draupadī was the wife of five Pāṇḍavas. It looks as though this position was not commonly accepted or appreciated even during the time of Vyāsa. It was perhaps difficult for Pampa to explain this unusual phenomenon in the 10th century, and to a devout Jaina it must have been least convincing. So he tries to ignore the fact and asserts that Draupadī was the wife of Arjuna alone, because he shattered the *Matsya-yantra* and married her. Nevertheless, it was difficult for him to get over the situation, because the fact remained that Bhīma was there as Draupadī's husband to kill Kīchaka to save her from her predicament, and to avenge Duḥśāsana and Duryodhana for the insult perpetrated on her. As though to avoid the anomaly, after the Bhārata War, Pampa performs the *paṭṭabhishēka* of Arjuna instead of Dharmarāja, with Subhadrā as the *paṭṭamahishī.*

This approach of Pampa necessitated him to give a twist to the *tīrthayātrā* of Arjuna for the sin of having seen Dharmarāja and Draupadī in privacy, as stated in *Vyāsa-Bhārata.* He plans a *digvijaya* for Arjuna and utilizes the occasion to extol the valour of his patron. Interestingly, Karnataka becomes a part of his itinerary and Pampa does not hide his bias for the land he loved. He indeed excels in describing its scenic beauty stating that he would like to be born again in this (Banavāsi) land, in any form, even as a cuckoo or a bee.

In Pampa's imagination, the episode of *Yaksha-Praśna* was only a device to save the Pāṇḍavas from being killed through the machinations of Duryodhana whose *purohita* Kanaka sends a demon *Kṛittikā* to kill the Pāṇḍavas. Yamadharma wanted to take away the Pāṇḍavas from their *āśrama* at the time of the arrival of the demon. Yamadharma himself (who was in the guise of Yaksha) explains this to Dharmarāja after he answers all the questions correctly.

In the delineation of the character of Duryodhana, Pampa is in two minds. He is convinced of his wickedness and his contrivances to kill the Pāṇḍavas at any cost. He has depicted him as such. He departs from the *Vyāsa-Bhārata* in many places and accounts for the episodes in his own different way. The episode narrated just now, i.e. *Yaksha-Praśna* is one such example. The *Dyūtaprasaṅga* is yet another example of the cunningness of Duryodhana. In *Vyāsa-Bhārata* the invitation to Dharmarāja for the game of dice is given by Dhṛitarāshṭra (though through the instigation of Duryodhana and Śakuni), and it is sent through Vidura. But in Pampa, the elders are not involved. Śakuni and Duryodhana themselves plan to get the Pāṇḍavas to Hastināvati on an invitation to spend a few days together. On the arrival of the latter, Duryodhana lures Dharmarāja into the game of dice, making it look as though it was a casual pastime and even pretends not to know the game and even loses one or two. Thus, when Dharmarāja becomes engrossed in the game, Śakuni plays his trick and Dharmarāja becomes a victim.

Duryodhana's height of cunningness is shown in his treatment of Karṇa. It is well known that he considered Karṇa as his best friend and honoured him and supported him against all others, who considered him a *sūtaputra*. This friendship is glorified and sublimated. Pampa agrees with all this, but sees a mischievous motive behind this. According to Duryodhana, he knew much earlier the secret of the birth of Karṇa and decided to use him to finish the Pāṇḍavas, to eliminate the thorn with the thorn. The story goes like this – when once Duryodhana and Karṇa were on a hunting expedition, they went to the *āśrama* of a sage called Satyampara. The sage treated both equally. Duryodhana's pride was hurt. He asked the sage in privacy as to how he gave the place of honour to the "fish killer" *(minguliga)* along with him. Thereupon the sage told him about the birth of Karṇa and his position as the senior among the Pāṇḍavas. Duryodhana then decided to use Karṇa to destroy the Pāṇḍavas through him and thus extended his patronage.

However, as the story proceeds, Pampa develops a soft corner for Duryodhana. His noble qualities come to the fore. His respect for elders, his generosity, his remorse for the events, his grief at the death of so many people in the battle, his undaunted pride *(chhala)* are all depicted in a most impressive way.

According to the *Vyāsa-Bhārata*, after the war and the death of all the kith and kin, Duryodhana goes and hides himself in the Vaiśampāyana lake like a coward. Perhaps Pampa did not like it. A hero like Duryodhana would not do so. He could be a villain, but not a coward. A hero as he was, even at such a juncture, he marched through the battlefield studded with dead bodies, with his mace on his shoulder, ready to fight single-handed. Sañjaya stops him. But Duryodhana proceeds further. Sañjaya then persuades him to go to Bhīshma. In the battlefield, Duryodhana sheds tears at the death of so many heroes, his brothers and his best friend Karṇa. He is moved to tears at the sight of Bhīshma lying on the bed of arrows. He says that the latter was put to this plight because of him. Bhīshma consoles him and advises to strike peace with the Pāṇḍavas. But the proud Kaurava refuses and submits that he went to him to bow down to him before proceeding to the battlefield. Bhīshma entreats him saying, 'If you do not give up fighting, at least wait for a day, until the return of Baladēva, Aśvatthāman and Kṛipa'. He initiates him into *jalamantra* by which he can hide under water. But events do not wait. Coaxed by the Pāṇḍavas, he comes out of the lake and the inevitable follows. Thus Pampa revels in his characterization of Duryodhana all admiration he had for him. He was an admixture of good and bad. It was the hand of cruel fate that overpowered the good in him and the noble soul was condemned to be a villain.

Pampa really excels in depicting the character of Karṇa. In the whole of the *Mahābhārata*, his is the sole example of a noble person, an embodiment of all virtues, but a complete victim of fate. All his virtues let him down at the crucial time. Though born of a queen, he had to suffer the ignominy of being a *sūtaputra*. His ardent gurubhakti became detrimental to him. His extreme generosity deprived him of his invincible armour. The fact about his birth incapacitated him from fulfilling his vow. He is the person from whom everybody took something and nobody gave anything. He gave everything to everybody, but took nothing from anybody. Yet he did not swerve from his chosen path. The tragic life of this great and noble soul fills the heart and mind of the poet. He sings the praise of this tragic hero with all his heart, even at the cost of his own hero Arjuna. In an exuberance of ecstacy, he declares that if anybody is to be remembered in the Bhārata, it is Karṇa and Karṇa alone. Says he:

> My dear young man, do not try to remember any body else in Bhārata; if you want to remember any body with single-mindedness, remember Karṇa. Is there any one comparable to Karṇa? The valour of Karṇa, stark truthfulness of Karṇa, greatness of Karṇa, generosity of Karṇa full of these words only Bhārata is indeed the nector of Karṇa (*Karṇa-rasāyana).*

Maybe, Pampa committed a tactical error in glorifying his *pratināyaka*, sidelining his *nāyaka* himself; But he may not only be pardoned but even appreciated for upholding the eternal human values. As he himself has said elsewhere, *Guṇakke machcharam-uṇṭe?* Can virtues be grudged?

Pampa's *Bhārata* is not a mere reproduction of *Vyāsa-Bhārata*, nor is it, its shadow. It is the recreation of the Bhārata story with his ingenious imagination and inimitable style. He was truly the *Ādi-kavi* and his *kāvya*, truly the *Ādi-kāvya.* His patron honoured him not merely with the title *Kavitā-guṇārṇava* but also by granting an *agrahāra* called Dharmapurī. A trilingual inscription of Pampa's brother Jinavallabha not only confirms this fact but also states that he constructed a tank and named it as *Kavitā-guṇārṇava* and laid out a garden named *Madanatilaka*.

GADĀYNDDHA

The *Gadāynddha* or *Sāhasa-Bhīma-vijaya* is another important *kāvya* based on the *Vyāsa-Bhārata* written by another Jaina poet Ranna or Ratna nearly forty years later than Pampa. The latter's work was not only a source of inspiration for him but also provided the source material. Though Ranna tells us that he has written the whole Mahābhārata story in a brief way (*simhāvalokana-karmadim)*, his main theme is the *gadāyuddha*, which forms the subject matter of the 13th *āśvāsa* of Pampa's work. There are indications to show that Ranna is considerably indebted to Pampa.

There are many similarities between the works of Pampa and Ranna. Like Pampa, Ranna also wrote his work to please his patron Irivabeḍaṅga Satyāśraya, one of the early kings of the Kalyāṇa-Chālukya dynasty. He equated the latter with Bhīma of the *Mahābhārata.* Like Pampa, who placed Arjuna on the throne of Hastināvati, Ranna confers that honour on Bhīma. Scholars have shown that Ranna closely followed Pampa and that there are even verbal similarities between the two. Some scholars even call Pampa as the guru of Ranna. It is strange that Ranna does not mention Pampa at all in his work.

Ranna was born in Mudhol, a taluka in the Bijapur district of Karnataka. He belonged to the family of bangle-sellers. He was a devout Jaina and interested in philosophy and literature. He sought the patronage of Chāvuṇḍarāya, the minister of the Ganga kings Mārasiṁha and Rāchamalla. He came back to his native place and secured the patronage of Irivabeḍaṅga Satyāśraya. He was also sponsored by the pious lady Attimabbe, the wife of a chief Nāgadēva. At her behest he wrote *Ajitatīrthankara-Purāṇatilaka,* a *kāvya* on the second Tīrthaṅkara, Ajitanātha. Like Pampa, he also composed two *kāvyas,* one for the glorification of *Jaināgama* and the other on *laukika* theme. He is said to have composed other works also, but they are not available now.

It has been stated above that Ranna heavily drew upon Pampa, but through his own creative genius, he has raised his composition to the status of a great *kāvya.* He claims in one place that he 'broke open the treasure of goddess Sarasvatī' and exploited it best in his compositions. Though most of the characters of the *Mahābhārata* figure in the *kāvya,* Bhīma, of course, is towering among them, being the hero of the *kāvya (kritig-īśan sāhasa-Bhīmam).* But the *pratināyaka* Duryodhana equally shines. Like Pampa who duly recognizes Karṇa, so does Ranna the greatness of Duryodhana. Ranna is best in delineating *vīra* or *raudra-rasa.* Even through words Ranna has been successful in giving the visual effect to his description of the fight between Bhīma and Duryodhana with their mighty maces. *Karuṇa-rasa* also has its own place in the *kāvya.* It flows quietly alongside the roaring waterfall of *vīra-rasa.* If Pampa showed extra sympathy for Karṇa, so did Ranna towards Duryodhana. Ranna is so much enamoured of Duryodhana's virtues that he calls him *Mahānubhāva,* a great soul. The pride of Duryodhana is best exhibited in his answer to Bhīshma, who advises him to strike peace with the Pāṇḍavas. Says he: 'I fight for prestige but not for a piece of land' *(Nelak-irivenendu bagedire chalak-irivem)*. The reader is moved to tears when he reads Duryodhana lamenting on the death of young Abhimanyu. Who will not appreciate his magnanimity when he bows down to the young lad? *(kay mugidam amdu Abhimanyuge Kauravēśvaram)*. Another heartening example of this great hero's magnanimity is shown in his attitude towards Bhīma. When he hit at him with his mace, Bhīma lay unconscious, and he raises his mace up to hit again. But suddenly it occurs to him that it is unethical to hit the one who is lying unconscious and swings the raised mace in the air saying, "I will not hit the one who has fallen" (*iriyen biḷdavanan)*. Thus, like Pampa, Ranna also has preferred to uphold human values to merely extolling valour.

KARṆĀṬA-BHĀRATA-KATHĀ-MANJARI OR KUMĀRAVYĀSA-BHĀRATA

Coming down to the period of Kumāravyāsa and Lakshmīśa from that of Pampa and Ranna, is like entering into the plains after a strenuous, yet enchanting, wandering in the thick woods. The days of the classical *champū* are now replaced by the simpler forms like *Shaṭpadī* and the classical old Kannada makes way for simpler *Naḍu-gannaḍa* or the middle-Kannada, a precursor of modern or *Hosa-gannaḍa*. The literature which was essentially meant for learned paṇḍits now opens itself up for common people with easy diction. Kumāravyāsa's *Karṇāṭa-Bhārata-Kathā-manjari* or *Kumāravyāsa-Bhārata* as it is popularly known, and Lakshmīśa's *Jaiminī-Bhārata* are the two representative works of this period. The two are the most popular works also, whose recitations are enjoyed and appreciated throughout Karnataka to this day.

The *Kumāravyāsa-Bhārata* was composed by Nārāyaṇa or Nāraṇappa, who fondly calls himself Kumāra Vyāsa, or Junior Vyāsa. The work does not give any biographical details of the author. It is only gathered that he belonged to Koḷivāḍa, a village near Gadag, a district headquarters in Karnataka, and that he was a devotee of God Vīranārāyaṇa of that place. Anecdotes go to say that he was not a learned person and that he composed this work with the blessings of Aśvatthāman and in the presence of god Vīranārāyaṇa himself. Even today people show a pillar in the Vīranārāyaṇa temple at Gadag, near which the poet used to sit and write the work.

The work contains ten parvans as against the eighteen of the *Vyāsa-Bhārata.* Here again the anecdote explains that Nāraṇappa was forbidden by Aśvatthāman from mentioning his meeting with him, which promise Nāraṇappa could not keep. In an ecstacy, he mentioned it to somebody and there came the end of his life and he could not complete the work. Apart from the veracity of the story, the fact remains that *Kumāravyāsa-Bhārata* contains only ten parvans. The remaining eight parvans were composed by Timmanna-kavi, reportedly at the behest of the Vijayanagara king Kṛishṇadēvarāya. It is likely that the poet thought that the core of the story ends with the Bhārata War and that it would be sufficient for his narration.

There is no unanimity about his date also. There has been considerable discussion on the point. However, the consensus is that he lived around *c.* AD 1400.

Though the poet has produced one of the best *kāvyas* of the period, he politely submits that the readers should not seek here poetic excellence and that they should look at it as the *mahimā* of the god Padmanābha and *Dharma-vichāra-mantra.* After all, even this was dictated by god Vīranārāyaṇa and he himself was only a scribe! *(Vīra-Nārāyaṇe kavi lipikāra Kumāravyāsa).* Yet, he claims that it caters to the needs of all sections of the people: it is the story of heroism for the heroes; gist of the Vedas for Brāhmaṇas; philosophical discourse for the yogins; lesson on *nīti* for ministers; *śriṅgāra* for the love-lorn and an ornament for learned. Thus it is indeed the guru of the *kāvyas.*

For Nāraṇappa, there was no problem of the motive for the work nor was there a problem of source. He was prompted by the urge to narrate *Kṛishṇa-kathā* which Kṛishṇa himself would appreciate *(Kṛishṇa mechchalike).* For this purpose there could be no better source than the 'Fifth Veda' (*paṁchama-śruti*), the *Vyāsa-Bhārata,* by reading which the people would get the *phala* of *Vēda-pārayāṇa.*

Essentially, Nāraṇappa has faithfully rendered the *Vyāsa-Bhārata* in Kannada verse in *Bhāminī-shaṭpadī,* a metre which lends itself to musical recitation and this has made the work so popular. Though he has almost closely followed Vyāsa, he has introduced his own changes and innovations to suit his own ideology, his own attitude towards life and contemporary social conditions. He had other models before him like the works of Pampa and Ranna and even earlier, works like those of Bhāsa and Bhaṭṭanārāyaṇa. We may notice here some of the changes he has introduced in his narration.

When Kṛishṇa arrives at the camp of Duryodhana as *dūta* of the Pāṇḍavas, the *Vyāsa-Bhārata* tells us that Duryodhana got up from his seat and honoured him. But Nāraṇappa's Duryodhana acts in a different way. He even did not move from his seat. Thereupon Kṛishṇa presses the ground with his toe and down comes Duryodhana to his feet along with his seat! It has been suggested that Nāraṇappa might have borrowed this idea from the *Dūtavākya* of Bhāsa.

The Dūrvāsa episode also gets a new touch at the hands of Nāraṇappa. This sage is sent by Duryodhana to the camp of the Pāṇḍavas to placate them. Dūrvāsa pays an untimely visit to them and demands food. Embarrassed Draupadī implores Kṛishṇa who comes to her rescue. According to the *Vyāsa-Bhārata*, Dūrvāsa flees the scene on hearing the arrival of Kṛishṇa, whereas in Nāraṇappa, he goes and meets Kṛishṇa, praises him and blesses the Pāṇḍavas. Nāraṇappa has made the best use of the occasion to exhibit his bhakti to God. In fact, he never misses a single occasion, or rather he creates as many as possible, to sing the glory of his God.

In the episode of killing Duḥśāsana also, Nāraṇappa departs from the usual story and makes the *raudra* situation more *raudra* as though to exhibit his skill in delineating this *rasa*. Bhīma's anger knows no bounds and for him no amount of atrocity is enough to avenge the wrong done. He tears open the heart of Duḥśāsana, gets Draupadī to the battlefield, smears the enemy's blood to her hair and combs it with his teeth and decorates her hair with a garland of intestines! Pampa narrates the incident briefly. It is suggested that possibly Nāraṇappa might have been influenced by Pampa or even Bhaṭṭanārāyaṇa, the author of *Vēṇī-saṁhāra*, in this respect.

Nāraṇappa is at his best in delineating *hāsya-rasa*, in the episode of Uttarakumāra. He has transformed the whole episode into a humorous drama. Uttara's *paurasha* or the vain boast of his valour before women in the harem, the latter coaxing him to go to the battle, his boast that he would destroy the Kauravas in a moment and establish a camp at Hastināpura, his assuring Bṛihannaḷe that he would defeat Bhīshma – all produce ripples of laughter. But what a turn of events! It is now his turn to be the *sārathi* of Arjuna. There is final victory and Uttara claims it for himself! Who does not laugh and yet sympathize with this *śabda-śūra?* Only Nāraṇappa could handle this story so deftly.

With all this, for Nāraṇappa, Kṛishṇa is the central figure, a friend, a brother, a saviour and an upholder of Dharma. Let alone the Pāṇḍavas, who were his very heart *(mama hṛidayā hi Pāṇḍavāḥ)* even Duryodhana acknowledges his *devatva* before departing from this world!

JAIMINI-BHĀRATA

Lakshmīśa also derives his material from the *Mahābhārata,* but not directly. He borrows the theme from the Sanskrit *Jaimini-Bhārata* supposed to have been written in about the 13th century AD. It is said that the work which covered the whole of Bhārata is lost except the Aśvamedhikaparvan. Lakshmīśa has fully utilized it for his *kāvya.*

Lakshmīśa claims to have belonged to Devanūr or Surapura, but the place is not identified with accuracy. Some scholars identify it with Surpur in the Gulbarga district, while others place it near Kadur in Chikkamagalur district. It has also been held that he might have written this work between AD 1510-1515, during the period of the Vijayanagara king Kṛishṇadevarāya. It is even suggested that Lakshmīśa had in mind this king when he described Kṛishṇa, the real *nāyaka* of his *kāvya.* The description of Bhadrāvati in the *kāvya* is supposed to tally with the description of Vijayanagara.

Lakshmīśa's *Jaimini-Bhārata* is more or less a faithful rendering of Sanskrit *Jaimini-Bhārata* in Kannada verse, in *Vārdhika shaṭpadī.* Like *Kumāravyāsa-Bhārata,* this work also has been very popular and is recited and listened to with devotion throughout Karnataka.

The Sanskrit work in Purāṇic style has been given a golden touch of poetry by Lakshmīśa through his skill in delineating different *rasas* and the use of *alaṅkāras.* The dramatic element introduced in many of the episodes has enhanced the literary value of the work. The whole *kāvya,* in fact, is the storehouse of episodes and stories. Prominent among such episodes are, obtaining the sacrifical horse from Yauvānāśva, the story of Marutta, the marriage of Pramīṁā, the fight between Arjuna and Babhruvāhana, Saṅgraha Rāmāyaṇa, the story of Chandrahāsa and so on. Lakshmīśa has utilized these stories to exhibit his poetic skill even elaborating some of them from the brief accounts in the original. For example in Sanskrit *Jaimini-Bhārata,* the story of *Rāmāyaṇa* commences with the killing of Rāvaṇa while Lakshmīśa starts with Daśaratha's desire to have a son. Likewise, different events are elaborated creating an opportunity for the description of nature, seasons, sunrise, sunset and the like, and thus exhibit his poetic skill.

Finally, like Nāraṇappa, Lakshmīśa also is an ardent Kṛishṇa bhakta. If the former's work is *Kṛishṇa-kathā,* that of the latter is *Kṛishṇa-charitāmṛita (Puṇyamidu Kṛishṇa-charitāmṛitaṁ).* The popularity of the *Jaimini-Bhārata* is vouchsafed by an unusually large number of manuscripts on palm-leaf and paper discovered in different parts of Karnataka.

Thus it can be said that the *Mahābhārata* has enriched Kannada literature, through everlasting and most popular *kāvyas* which continue to be reckoned as great works even today. As a corollary, Kannada literature has popularized the *Mahābhārata,* preaching to the people of the remotest corners its eternal message *yatō dharmah tatō jayah.*

[The paper seeks to introduce the Kannada works with Mahābhārata theme to the wider academic community. Intricate discussions of the controversies on the life, date and works of the poet and detailed comparative studies, are beyond the scope of this paper.]

BIBLIOGRAPHY
(All the books are in Kannada)

Pampa-Bhāratam (Vikramārjuna-Vijayam) of Pampa, ed. N. Anantar-angachar, Kannada Sahitya Parishad, Bangalore, 1977.

Pamap Mahakavi, ed. R.S. Mugali, Karnataka Vidyavardhak Sangha, Dharwad, 1951.

Mahakavi Pampa and his Works (3rd edn.), Karnataka University, Dharwad, 1976.

Sāhasa-Bhīma-Vijayam (Gadāyuddham) of Ranna, (2nd edn.), ed. K.V. Krishna Bhat, Gita Book House, Mysore, 1973.

B.M. Srikanthaih, *Rannakavi-Prasasti;* (2nd edn.), Kannada Sahitya Parishad, Bangalore, 1978.

Mahākavi Ranna and his Works, (2nd edn.), Karnataka University, Dharwad, 1969.

M.S. Latthe, *Chaladanka Malla,* Kartikeya Prakashana, Kalaburgi, 1975.

Karnāṭa-Bhārata-Kathā-Manjarī of Kumāravyāsa, ed. Kuvempu and Masti Venkatesh Ayyanger, Mysore University, 1974.

KumaraVyāsa-Prasasti, (2nd edn.), ed. B.M. Shrikanthaiah, Kannada Sahitya Parishad, Bangalore. 1978.

Jaimini-Bhārata of Lakshmīśa, ed. Devudu Narasimha Sastri, Government of Karnataka, 1985.

Jaimini-Bhārata of Lakshmīśa: A Study; Vaman, Bendre, Gita Book House, Mysore, 1979.

Shaṭpadī Literature in Kannada, Karnataka University, Dharwad, 1975.

Karnāṭaka-Kavicharite (Rev. edn.) Kannada Sahitya Parishad, Bangalore, 1961.

Inscriptions of Andhra Pradesh, (Karimnagar District), ed. P.V. Parabrahma Sastri, Government of Andhra Pradesh, Hyderabad, 1974.

Prabuddha Karnāṭaka, Journal of the Mysore University, Vols. 15, 23 and 32.

24

Mahābhārata and Marathi Vernacular Writers

M.R. Joshi

I. MARATHI VERSIONS OF *MAHĀBHĀRATA*

The aim and purpose of my paper is to show the impact of the *Mahābhārata* on Marathi literature. Marathi is a well-known vernacular language of Maharashtra. In course of time, Marathi developed into a powerful instrument of literary expression. There are a number of philosophical works like the *Vivekasindhu* and the *Jñāneśvarī*. All these works are the main repositories of Śaṅkara's philosophy.

There is also the Mahānubhāva literature but it is poetic and religious. Among the celebrated writers and literary luminaries, Jñānadeva is the first and foremost. He has composed many works. Among them the *Jñāneśvarī* is the magnum opus of his brilliant literary career. It is a well-known Marathi commentry on the *Bhagavadgītā* in *ovī* metre. In this great work, after saluting Lord Gaṇeśa, Śārada and his spiritual preceptor Śrī Nivṛttināth, Jñānadeva has acknowledged the supremacy of the *Mahābhārata* in all the fields of life. According to Jñānadeva, the *Mahābhārata* is history and there are a number of historical events. Moreover, it is a measuring rod of all the literary ideas. Jñānadeva emphatically says that all the literary forms like *Akhyāyana* are to be found in the *Mahābhārata*. In short, the *Mahābhārata* is the standard measurement of all the cultural, religious, historical and literary events. Moreover, it is a storehouse of *navarasas* and the predominant *rasa* of the *Mahābhārata* is *śānta*. It is the torch-bearer so far as poetry and poetics are concerned. In the annals of Marathi literary tradition, Jñānadeva is the first and foremost who has emphasized the various aspects of this Great Epic. Later writers on the *Mahābhārata* have tried their best to step in the footsteps of Jñānadeva. Mukteśvara and Moropant are two great writers on the *Mahābhārata* belonging to the classical tradition, who tried their best to model their works on Jñānadeva's appreciation of the *Mahābhārata*.

Jñānadeva (AD 1275-1296) in his epoch-making work has for the first time shown the correlation between the *Bhagavadgītā* and the *Mahābhārata*. To him the *Gītā* is the very soul and essence of the *Mahābhārata* and furnishes interesting information regarding the total number of the *Mahābhārata* ślokas also. According to Jñānadeva's computation *Mahābhārata* contains one lakh twenty-five thousand ślokas whereas the popular tradition, mentions one lakh ślokas. Most probably instead of clubbing *Harivaṁśa* with the *Mahābhārata*, Jñānadeva has included the *Bhāgavata Purāṇa* in the *Mahābhārata*. Among academic circles and scholarly world, the *Harivaṁśa* is presumed to be an appendix to the *Mahābhārata*. But on the other hand, there are reputed writers who used to link the *Bhāgavata* with the *Mahābhārata*. Jñānadeva and Kṛishṇa Dayārṇava, the well-known commentator of *Bhāgavata*, are the two famous literary personalities who have linked the *Bhāgavata* with the *Mahābhārata*. This theory of clubbing the *Bhāgavata* and the *Mahābhārata* has bearing upon the relative position of both the works. In this regard it is interesting to know that Kṛishṇa Dayārṇava's spiritual lineage is related to the house of Nilakaṇṭha Chaudharī, the well-known commentator of the Great Epic. His spiritual preceptor was Govinda Swāmi who was the son of Nilakaṇṭha Chaudharī. So being close to Nilakaṇṭha Chaudharī's house, he had an access to the original text of the *Mahābhārata* commentary. It is to be noted that Kṛishṇa Dayārṇava's commentry on the Xth canto of the *Bhāgavata* is under the influence of *Bhārata bhāva dīpa*. So reading the *Bhāgavata* in the light of the *Mahābhārata* text is one of the striking features of the study of the Great Epic in Maharashtra. Of course, credit goes to Jñānadeva, who was the pioneer of this trend. There are nineteen chapters in the first canto of the *Bhāgavata*. Out of these, thirteen chapters are directly related to the epic. A minute study of these chapters shows ample similarity. All these chapters clearly show that they have common source material. So while giving proper and considerate treatment of the text of the *Mahābhārata*, Jñānadeva gave equal importance to the relative text appearing in *Bhāgavata* also.

While Jñānadeva was writing his great commentary on the *Bhagavadgītā*, his junior contemporary Vishṇudāsa Nāmadeva (AD 1378-1438) was busy in writing *Mahābhārata*. It is to be noted that there is a controversy amongst Marathi schclars regarding the original name and place of this author. However, I have in my literary history shown that Vishṇudāsa Nāmadeva and the great saint Nāmadeva, are two different personalities. Vishṇudāsa Nāmadeva was the pupil-student of Parasābhāgavata who was the disciple of Nāmadeva, the great saint of Maharashtra. So we get the relative chronological order of these three great saint poets as follows:- Nāmadeva, Parasabhāgavata and Vishṇudāsa Nāmadeva. For the first time in Marathi literary history, we find a complete rendering of the *Mahābhārata*. He composed the Great Epic in *ovī* metre. I have in my private collection a manuscript copy of his work with the total no. of ovīs 20,000. So it is one of the greatest works in Marathi literature. It is to be noted that there are scholars who have studied and submitted their Ph.D. Theses on Vishṇudāsa Nāma's stupendous work. However, the original work is still unpublished. Vishṇudāsa's *Nāma Mahābhārata* was very popular and a large number of its manuscript copies are available in various places and MSS collections in Maharashtra.

Vishṇudāsa Nāmadeva composed his work on the line of Vyāsadeva; we find 18 parvans and 20,000 ovīs. Even though at the very beginning he has saluted and shown highest regard for Vyāsadeva, he never imitates him blindly. It seems that he had before him the *Jaimini Bhārata* together with an oral version of *Mahābhārata* containing various stories.

So *Jaimini Bhārata* was the major source of his epic work. Later writers like Nāma Pāṭhaka, Kṛishṇadāsa Nama, Kṛishṇadāsa Mahānubhāva, Navarasa Nārāyaṇa and others composed their works on the source material of *Jaimini Bhārata*. Here, we come across two independent traditions: one headed by Jñānadeva, the great intellectual leader of classical literature and the other under the leadership of Vishṇudāsa Nāma belonging to the folk tradition. These two traditions working independently of each other, seem to have led the literary as well as cultural movement throughout the annals of Maharashtra. It is worthwhile to see and note that writers and composers belong to folk traditions. They come from the traditional stock of discourser class who were never serious regarding the literary aspect of their works. These were story-tellers.

However, these story-tellers have for the first time eked out successfully all sort of material from Purāṇa literature and presented it through their works, thereby building and formulating a parallel folk tradition in Marathi literature. These writers have profusely availed the rich folk literature and mingled it with the popular stories of the *Mahābhārata*. Vishṇudāsa Nāma was the first writer who formulated folk stories with the texture of the Great Epic. His work contains 20,000 ovīs and is divided into sixteen parvans. The order and sequence of the parvans is as follows:-

Ādi – Sabhā – Udyoga – Araṇya – Virāṭ – Bhīshma – Droṇa – Karṇa – Śalya – Gadā – Śānti – Strī – Sauptika – Anuśāsana – Svargārohaṇa. So far as the content is concerned, he follows *Jaimini Bhārata* but in the order of parvans he is the follower of Vyāsa. It is to be noted that in the colophon of his work he has clearly mentioned the work as *śata-sāhasrī*. Moreover, his treatment in the work is according to the prevalent text of the epic.

Mukteśvara (AD 1574-1650), the grandson of saint Ekanātha was the contemporary of Shahaji, the father of great Shivaji. He composed the Great Epic; but only five cantos are available. His style is poetic, pleasant and lucid. His treatment of the subject bears the stamp of originality. His ideas are indeed effective and are testimony of his poetic genius. In the introductory portion, he expresses highest regard for Vyāsa and praises Jñānadeva and Ekanātha. Even though he shows great respect to the composer of the Great Epic, his work is not imitative in nature. He calls his composition *Mahārāshṭra-bhāshā-bandha*. Mukteśvara belongs to classical tradition and is proud of the treatment of the subject. He says that earlier poets like Vishṇudāsa Nāma and others have poorly treated the subject, have vitiated the *Mahābhārata* text and are not faithful to the original. Throughout, he exhibits a rare combination of creative genius and outstanding scholarship.

The Saraswati Mahal Library, Thanjavur, is rich in the literary works of Marathi writers, the most noteworthy being those of Raghunātha Paṇḍita, Ānandatanaya and Mādhavasvāmī. All these poets are the ardent followers of Rāmadāsa Svāmī, the great saint poet of Maharashtra. Mādhavasvamī's (AD 1628-1714) spiritual order is as follows:- Rāmadāsa-Rāghavasvāmī, Mādhavasvāmī. He was a resident of Tiruvelundura which is situated on the bank of the Kaveri in the very vicinity of Thanjavur. Mādhavasvāmī was a voluminous writer and there are a number of works to be found written under his name. All these works are in manuscript form. He composed two Great Epics, i.e. *Rāmāyaṇa* and *Mahābhārata*. Mādhava's *Mahābhārata* is a great work, both in content and size. He started writing his *Mahābhārata* on the bank of the Kaveri in the year AD 1703 and completed it in AD 1707. Even though he has composed all the parvans and complete text in Marathi, still he could not give it a proper shape. However, the sequence of his composition is slightly different and hence unusual. In the beginning of every parvan, he mentions the commencing date and time of his work. The order of parvans is as follows:-

Ādi – Sabhā – Udyoga – Araṇya – Virāṭ – Bhīshma – Droṇa – Karṇa – Śalya – Sauptika – Strī – Śānti – Anuśāsana – Aśvamedha – Āśrama – Mausala – Mahāprāsthānika – Svargārohaṇa. This author clearly shows that he has rendered the complete work of Vyāsa in Marathi. His work is in ovī metre and there are 1,10, 170 ovīs in his huge work. However, the total number of ovīs varies from text to text. There are six manuscript copies deposited in the famous Saraswati Mahal Library at Thanjavur, giving different numbers of ovīs. This huge work is still in unpublished form and the work is available only in manuscripts. It is to be noted that Mādhavasvāmī's work is an exhaustive and detailed exposition of all the contents of the original epic work. In this work, we find the very interesting references which afford material for textual criticism of the *Mahābhārata*. Both Mādhavasvāmī and his great predecessor Mukteśvara have clearly mentioned that there are 8,800 kūṭa ślokas in the *Mahābhārata*. These kūṭa ślokas referred to those verses which are puzzles and hence obscure. Moreover, they are related to Vyāsa Gaṇeśa episode in the *Mahābhārata*.

Śrīdhara (AD 1678-1729), the great saint poet of Paṇḍharpur, was a prolific writer and composed a number of works in Marathi. Originally he was a bonafide resident of Nazare, a small village situated in Solāpur District. After some time he shifted along with his family members from Nazare to Paṇḍharpur, the great pilgrim centre of Maharashtra. Afterwards he became a permanent resident of Paṇḍharpur. While residing there, he wrote his major works – *Harivijaya, Rāmavijaya* and *Pāṇḍavapratāpa*. Of these, *Harivijaya* is first and foremost and was completed on 10-11-1702. Then follows *Rāmavijaya* and the completion date given by the author is 8-3-1703. The third work *Pāṇḍavapratāpa* was also completed at Paṇḍharpur on 13-1-1714. This work is based on the *Mahābhārata* and reminds us of many contemporary incidents in Maratha history. Here, we find for the first time an echo of some contemporary historical events.

These incidents are indicative of the Mughal-Maratha War. Emperor Aurangzeb invaded and started war against the Marathas. With the object of defeating them, he established his military camp at Brahampurī on the banks of river Bhīma. He was there for four years. From Brahmapurī he deputed his military general to vanquish and destroy the image of Śrī Viṭṭhal. The emperor was bent upon destroying the holy shrine and pilgrim centre. But fortunately the image of Śrī Viṭṭhal was saved as it was removed and taken in safe custody. Afterwards the image was again ceremoniously reinstalled in the shrine. In order to commemorate this incident, Śrīdhara composed the *Harivijaya* as a mark of victory. Śrīdhara gives a vivid description of the incident in both the works, i.e. *Harivijaya* and *Pāṇḍavapratāpa* which preserve reminiscences of historical events. These works give a graphic account of the valour of brave Maratha soldiers. The *Pāṇḍavapratāpa* deserves our special attention as it has a definite importance. Here the writer has propounded the theory of Mahārāshṭra Dharma. The Maratha-Mughal War has multifarious dimensions. It was a symbolic war also. Kṛishṇa, Rama and Pāṇḍavas were liberators. They destroyed demons and vanquished the evil elements. Aurangzeb was not only ambitious and expansionist but also *mlechchhadiya*, i.e. a demon in the disguise of *mlechchha*. Here Śrīdhara imitates and follows the great saint Rāmadāsa Swāmī who propagates the regeneration of the nation on the basis of Mahārāshṭra Dharma. The propagator of this theory firmly believes that the life-mission of Lord Rāma and Kṛishṇa together with the Pāṇḍavas was to protect religion and culture from the clutches of tyrants. Therefore, a number of Marathi saint-poets writing on the *Rāmāyaṇa* and the *Mahābhārata* invoke the blessing of their respective deities and infuse the spirit of religion and culture.

Moropant (AD 1713-1794) was a great exponent of the Vyāsa Bhārata in Marathi. Being a prolific writer, he composed a number of literary works. All these works are popular as they are of rich literary merits. Moropant was a contemporary of Bājirāo II, the great Peshwā. During his tenure, Moropant rendered the whole of the *Mahābhārata* which is known as *Āryabhārata* in Marathi. He surpasses all earlier writers and their works in point of classical treatment of the subject-matter. He presents lively characters and shows originality as he visualizes them. His treatment and rearrangement of the original epic with appropriate changes is noteworthy. As a matter of fact, he has reconstructed the whole text taking into consideration the text commentary on the *Mahābhārata*. This commentary on the *Mahābhārata* is known as *Bhārata-bhava-dīpa* and its writer is Nilkaṇṭha Chaudharī. Moropant's style is lucid and poetic.

Moropant is a towering literary personality, he gathered around him a number of poets who tried their best to follow his footsteps. In Marathi literary circle, there was lively discussion among the critics and scholars regarding the literary features of Moropant's work and his influence on the mode of poetry.

However, in modern times, we do find a number of books on the *Mahābhārata*; but the writers of the books are more interested only in literary criticism and the study of the characters of the Great Epic.

II. MAHĀBHĀRATA-BASED MODERN STUDIES AND LITERATURE

C.V. Vaidya is a great name in the world of orientalists and indologists. He wrote on history, language and literature and devoted himself to the studies of the *Rāmāyaṇa* and the *Mahābhārata*, the two Great Epics of this ancient land. He brought out two separate treatises on the *Mahābhārata*. In the year 1904, he published his findings on *Mahābhārata* under the title *Mahābhārata: A Criticism*. He followed it up because the *Mahābhārata* is not only a piece of poetry but also a traditional cultural history which, being encyclopaedic, opens new frontiers of knowledge. So C.V. Vaidya carried on a searching investigation of all the relevant problems confronting various scholars since long. In 1918, he again published his findings as an appendix to the version of the *Mahābhārata* in 18 chapters. It is in Marathi and captioned *Mahābhāratācha Upasaṁhāra* (*Mahābhārata: Epilogue*). This work is the first Marathi treatise on the *Mahābhārata* and discusses almost all the relevant topics and subjects. For his study he has chosen three versions of the epic, which were available in vulgate form then. He based his findings on the printed text and did not take into consideration the various manuscripts as they were scattered and beyond his reach. On the basis of available source material he discussed the original title and came to the conclusion that the present work is a composite one. Vyāsa was the original writer and in the course of time the work was enlarged by his disciples. Hence Sauti is responsible for recasting the whole text. The inflated text was accepted by all. Then he switched over to the date of Mahābhārata War and came to the conclusion that it was fought in the year 3101 BC.

The *Mahābhārata* is the first available text, which provides ample historical information dealing with almost all the branches of state and government. The epic furnishes us the lists and names of different royal dynasties and their kingdoms. All these reveal precious geographical details of that time. The war fought between the Kauravas and the Pāṇḍavas was a major historical event which threw light on the role of various dynastical royal families. Vaidya elaborated the political events of that age systematically into authentic history together with all the allied topics. In addition to it, he presented an account of all the cultural movements and religious life. The writer of the *Mahābhārata* was also the author of *Bhāgavata Purāṇa* and composer of *Vedāntasūtra*. These two works are fountain of various Vedāntic doctrines like Vedānta Sāṅkhya and Pāñcharātra, the two ancient systems of philosophy. Vaidya has carefully pointed out the outstanding features of these two principal doctrines of ancient India. He also took into consideration various social customs, the nature of Niyoga and the status of Sūta class and discussed at length various problems that are related to the original work of Vyāsadeva. However, recent research has shown the limitations of his stupendous work. But that he is the pioneer of the *Mahābhārata* studies and laid the foundation stone of that branch of knowledge, is an acknowledged fact.

In the month of March and April 1951, Balshastri Haridas, a well-known scholar, delivered a lecture series on the *Mahābhārata*, which has been compiled and edited in a book-form. There are twenty-six articles all bearing a stamp of profound scholarship and erudition. According to him, the Great Epic is encyclopaedic, representing the cultural history, literature and values of the Hindu ethos and civilization. It is a historical account of Hindu way of life and is in conformity with rules and regulations of Vedic past. Therefore, the story of the epic is not only confined to the traditional chronicle of the Kuru dynasty but is a treasure-house of religio-cultural events which furnishes ample material enlightening about the norms and functions of the government. It gives a vivid account of social system and relations of the period. In addition to it, the *Mahābhārata* gives a reliable information of the origin and development of kingship and the state. No doubt the king emperor was supreme and absolute but he was not totalitarian. He had to carry certain functions and was bound to ethical norms. The king and his councillors were subject to the traditional rules and regulations. Both were answerable to the group of religious persons of highest order. These were the sages who invoked a profound respect and regard from the king as well as his council of ministers. The ascetics, the sages and the seers were the product of Vedic culture and were absolutely free from worldly pursuits and pleasures. Whenever required, they guided and addressed the monarchs also. So both the state and society were at a highly developed stage but the ideal state and society began to show cracks and the signs of decadence. We find Jarāsəndha, and Kaṁsa as imperial rulers who were engaged in consolidating their imperial kingdom into a totalitarian state. Duryodhana was an ambitious imperialist. The kings and the monarchies, propelled by unbridled ambition, joined the imperialists, while the spiritual masters lost all their cultural heritage. They began to serve the rulers. So Droṇāchārya began his career as a tutor. Droṇāchārya, Bhīshma, Karṇa, Yudhishṭhira, Arjuna, Vidura, Bhīma, Dhṛitarāshṭra, Duryodhana, Gāndhārī, Kuntī and Draupadī are the principal characters of the epic. The author has given a spell-bound description and a graphic sketch of their life, which is very lively and illustrative. But Devakīnandana Kṛishṇa is superb. He is the God incarnate. His emergence in the epic is divine and celestial. He enthralls everyone. Kṛishṇa is the embodiment of perfection and is the solution to all the problems.

The Great Epic *Mahābhārata* is a perennial source of inspiration and attraction to the poets, critics as well as scholars. It has the capacity to invoke the students and scholars of all disciplines.

Eiravati Karve, the anthropologist, has tried to present the epic in her own perspective. Her *Yugānta* is a new addition to the literature on the *Mahābhārata*. The book contains the biographical sketch of principal characters of the *Mahābhārata* which include Gandhārī, Kuntī, Draupadī. Besides these, she has dealt with Kṛishṇa Vāsudeva and other incidents of the epic which involve various problems as well. Her approach to the epic is very different from traditional and is based on the critical edition prepared by Bhandarkar Oriental Research Institute, Pune. She goes on examining and evaluating various facets of the social order and civilization of the *Mahābhārata* age. She belongs to the school which believes in Aryan invasion theory and treats the text in that perspective. She is destructive in her approach and her ignorance of the original story is crystal clear. Moreover, she is weak in Sanskrit and poor in textual problems of the epic. Many a time her interpretation of the text is far away from the original text. It is painful to note that occasionally she takes liberty to twist the facts, ignoring the date and period of the epic story. Her materialistic interpretation of epic history is a fine example of author's confused state of mind. In the process she has tarnished and belittled everything. She surpasses even her fellow travellers in depicting the characters in altruism.

Her comments spread all over only show her inclination and prove the hollowness of her arguments. One is pained to see that the author is not acclimatized with the style of Vyāsa and her conclusions are often erroneous as she has heavily relied upon the so-called critical text of the Institute. The text prepared is open to critical evaluation as it explicitly states that it has three variations and the original was *Jaya*. V.S. Sukthankar and his followers have yet to produce the *Jaya* text.

Karve's appreciation of the epic heroes suffers from her unsympathetic understanding and lacks the appreciation of Hindu ethos. Her whims and prejudices are most active when she deals with traditional study of the plot. Karve has neither philosophy nor the Indian mind. She has discussed the Mahābhārata characters in a strange manner.

Durga Bhagwat's *Vyāsaparva* is a collection of critical essays on the *Mahābhārata* with an aesthetic approach to the topic. She is a reputed literary figure of modern Marathi literature. She has examined and tried to evaluate the whole story by presenting the principal characters of the *Mahābhārata*. The book contains ten literary essays, presented in chaste elegant poetic diction endowed with splendid ideas and flashes of imagination. Out of the vast material available, she has chosen and concentrated upon those which help in portraying the principal characters of the epic including Kṛishṇa, Droṇāchārya, Aśvatthāman, Duryodhana, Karṇa, Arjuna, Yudhishṭhira, Bhīshma, Viduṛa, and of course,

Draupadī. Interestingly, she has practically connived at the traditional Rasadhvani theory and built up the whole edifice of her presentation on Aristotelian line. The poetic theory expounded by the great philosopher Aristotle, has been applied to Great Epics and the author has tried to give a new perspective. In addition, Durga Bhagwat takes up the tragedy concept and reproduces the treatment of Shakespearean tragedy norms to the *Mahābhārata*. On the line of the studies in Shakespearean tragedies, the author has tried to theorize the various elements found in the *Mahābhārata*. She built them with the assumption that the *Mahābhārata* is a dramatic version of epic story. So she went on portraying the main individual characters of the epic as dramatic personae. Obviously allured by the Shakespearean scholars' work on tragedies, Durga Bhagwat also tried to picturize the *Mahābhārata* as a work of the art of poetry. The role of destiny, the active participant coming from folklore stock, the changes in human life, the Karma theory, the principle of life divine, manifestation of the present with its historic past, forceful dialogues, dramatic elements and beautiful rhythmic poetry and spiritual discourses are at their height. The *Mahābhārata* is the very soul of Hindu ethos, but unfortunately, Durga Bhagwat did not take it into consideration and confined herself to pointing out the literary values of the Great Epic. She has devoted herself to applying the western literary concept of tragedy to Vyāsa's work. As a matter of fact, the *Mahābhārata* is perfection of literary composition and is not a modification of any literary form or a drama retold with narrative description. So her assumption that the *Mahābhārata* is a work of super dramatic skill is itself untenable and far from truth. The *Mahābhārata* being the magnum opus, evokes the feeling of those readers who are acclimatized and are conversant with Hindu ethos. There is a wide difference in literary taste and judgement as nations have their own characters and have special appeal. As there is a difference of literary judgement, one is at pains to sympathize with her.

The idea that the so-called literary work *Jaya hā Narācha Itihāsa āhe* by Anand Sadhale is tailored to suit one's ideological designs, is not something new for the students of the *Mahābhārata*. The book is a piece of literary scam and swindle in the Marathi critical history. Sadhale was eager to attain an honourable position in modern Marathi literary history and he resorted simply to degrading the characters of the Great Epic who have commanded respect and affection of the masses. To defame the Great Epic was his principal task in which he has miserably failed. He presumes himself to be a critic and research scholar of high order but his book is full proof of his poor scholarship. His treatment of the subject is the acknowledgement of his inability to understand the text and non-conversance with the Hindu ethos. He takes pleasure in distorting the story with inappropriate comments. He also wants to boast that he is the only one who could interpret the text of the revised version that has been prepared by Bhandarkar Institute. He wants to retell the original corpus of the epic. So he thinks that *Jaya* was the original version of the vulgate text of the *Mahābhārata*. But unfortunately the editors of the revised text are of the opinion that *Jaya* was not the original work of Vyāsa.

The *Mṛituñjaya*, a literary fiction on the life and achievement of Karṇa by Shivaja Savant is a recent addition to the *Mahābhārata* literature. He tries to portray the achievements of Karṇa by giving a new orientation to his deeds as well as character. The writer belongs to the stock of those who are under the impression that Karṇa was deliberately relegated not only from the contemporaries but also from the writer of the epic. So Savant glorifies this epic character whom he treated as the real hero. He praised Karṇa for his splendid deeds and the role played by him in the *Mahābhārata*, thereby denying the due share to others. As the author has an inclination towards Karṇa's role, he takes liberty to twist the plot of the epic to his convenience, thereby reproducing the text of the *Mahābhārata* at his free will.

Modern Marathi literary circle's sudden spate of evaluating and presenting the story of *Mahābhārata* with different approaches, once again proves the importance of the *Mahābhārata* among the masses. One such attempt is seen in a book by Daji Panshihar with the title *Mahābhārata-Eka Sūḍāchā Parvāsa*. The theme and title indicate the literary approach of the writer to the Great Epic. The author tries to show that the whole story of the epic revolves around the central idea of vengeance. Almost all the major characters of the epic are repulsive by nature and engaged in settling accounts with each other. The book is a collection of articles serialized and published in 1977.

However, the *Mahābhārata* continues to invite attention of scholars and serious students. Vijay Deshmukh is one of them.

He is particularly fascinated by Karṇa. So he has treated this topic with a new perspective and held the view that ultimately Karṇa surrendered himself and met a heroic death in the battlefield. This is the conclusion which he put forth before all the persons interested in the role of Karṇa. To prove his contention, Deshmukh presented his findings in a book entitled *Sūryaputra Karṇa.* The work is divided into forty chapters and is written in a lucid style. His findings are interesting and compel the reader to peruse the original work.

The characters rather than the plot have attracted number of writers to the Great Epic. One of them is Prema Kantak whose work bears the title *Mahābhārata Eka Mukta Chintana* (Stray Thoughts on the *Mahābhārata*). However, we come across certain serious attempts by well-known authors who have tried their best to present a graphic account of the Great Epic. R.S. Walmbe, the well-known literary critic of Marathi, writes one such work. His *Rādheya Karṇa* is a fine piece of literary craft which gives a living sketch of Karṇa and Bhīshma, the two principal characters of the *Mahābhārata*. Next to Walmbe we find a beautiful literary life-sketch of Karṇa by G.N. Dandekar in his *Karṇāyana.*

It is a strange coincidence in history of the *Mahābhārata* studies that a treatise by Anantarao Athavale's *Mahābhārata*: *Vāstava Darśana* should come up on the lines of Vaidya's work to refute the unwarranted conclusions, arrived at under the pretext of literary criticism. Athavale, now a monk of Śaṅkarāchārya monistic philosophical school, has in his *Mahābhāratāchī Mārekarī* examined and evaluated all the theories based on various arguments and approaches to the epic and emerge successfully in setting up the whole story in a proper perspective. For this he critically examined the mischievous conclusions based on faulty readings of the epic text. An erudite scholar as he is, he has pointed out the wrong readings and irrelevant referential quotations made by the committed individual writers who presumed themselves to be authorities on the *Mahābhārata*. So the author took up the gauntlet and gave a smashing reply to all these self-styled writers who camouflaged themselves as authority to pass any remark in form of final verdict. So he took them to the task and pointed out their mistakes. He had a dig at those who tried to propound wrong theories on whimsical grounds. He is best at polemics and superb in dialectics. He is consistent in his approach and sound in treatment. His arguments are thought-provoking and potent with meanings. His work presents great erudition and critical insight. He has answered all the relevant objections and wound up all the controversies on the *Mahābhārata* to everyone's satisfaction. The sub-title *Mahābhāratāchī Mārekarī* may bewilder a layman who is not accustomed with the syntactical structure of Marathi language. The author intends to bracket those writers who systematically want to demolish the influence of the *Mahābhārata*. The book contains forty chapters which are elaborate in presentation and subject.

25

Mahābhārata and its Study in Gujarati

Bharati Shelat

The *Mahābhārata* despite being a storehouse of legends and stories, is an *itihāsa* or history, since it records as its core the story of Kuru-Pāṇḍavas, the Pāñchālas and a host of other contemporary *janas*, as faithfully as the real story of a fraternal feud leading to a devastating war could be, but all put in a literary form by an imaginatively effective poet. The people of India have been singing and reciting it through the ages and allowing the characters, events and situations presented in it to affect their lives very deeply and widely. They have been believing this core story at any rate as a true interpretation of what had actually happened at a given time and place. In other words, the Bhāratayuddhakathā has been through the centuries, woven into the very texture of India's life and culture, and is thus, an important and inalienable part of the lives of countless millions of people of this land.

The *Mahābhārata* and its stories have been rendered and composed in old and medieval Gujarati language since early 15th century AD. Prior to great Gujarati poet Premānanda, great Gujarati writers like Nākara (AD 1516-68), Vishṇudāsa (V.S. 1634-81 – AD 1578-1625), Haridāsa (V.S. 1644 – AD 1587-88 AD), Śivadāsa (V.S. 1673 – AD 1616-17), Avichaladāssa (V.S. 1695 – AD 1639), Bhāu (V.S. 1676-79 – AD 1620-23), Vaikuṇṭha (V.S. 1707-16 – AD 1651-60), Surabhaṭa (V.S. 1648 – AD 1592), Mukunda (V.S. 1652 – AD 1595-96), Ratneśvara (V.S. 1748 – AD 1691-92), Rāmakṛishṇa (V.S. 1758 – AD 1701-02), Jaso, Kuberadās, Potho and Tulasī composed various parvans of the *Mahābhārata* in Deśī[1] (Gujarati) *padabandha*. Manuscripts of all the 18 parvans except Śānti, Anuśāsana and Āśramavāsika have been found preserved in various institutions and libraries like Gujarat Vernacular Society, Ahmedabad; Forbes Gujarati Sabha, Mumbai; Dahilakshmi Library, Nadiad; Oriental Institute, Vadodara; Deccan College Library, Pune and private collection of Ichchharam Suryaram Desai, Mumbai. Padmashri K.K. Shastree edited various parvans composed by Gujarati poets in *padabandha*. Some well-known Gujarati poets composed several parvans of the *Mahābhārata*. They are as follows:

1. *Ādiparvan* of Nākara, Haridāsa, Vishṇudāsa, Manohardāsa and Sundaradāsa.
2. *Sabhāparvan* of Nākara, Kāśīsuta Śedhajī, Vishṇudāsa and Śivadāsa.
3. *Āraṇyakaparvan* of Nākara, Vishṇudāsa and Avichaladāsa.
4. *Virāṭaparvan* of Nākara, Kāśīsuta Śedhajī and Vishṇudāsa.
5. *Udyogaparvan* of Vishṇudāsa, Bhāu, Bhāiyāsuta and Vaikuṇṭha.
6. *Bhīshmaparvan* of Vishṇudāsa, Jaso and Vaikuṇṭha.
7. *Droṇaparvan* of Vishṇudāsa and Bhāu.
8. *Karṇaparvan* of Nākara, Vishṇudāsa, Bhāu and Vaikuṇṭha.
9. *Śalyaparvan* of Nākara, Vishṇudāsa and Vaikuṇṭha.
10. *Sauptikaparvan* of Nākara and Vishṇudāsa.
11. *Strīparvan* of Nākara and Vishṇudāsa.
12. *Śāntiparvan*, Only 21st *adhyāya* of *Śāntiparvan* and *Rājadharma* in *Śāntiparvan* have been composed. Poets' names are not found.
13. *Anuśāsanaparvan*, No manuscript found so far.
14. *Aśvamedhaparvan*, Some scattered *ākhyānas* from this parvan have been found composed by Kānadāsa, Nākara, Vishṇudāsa, Mukunda, Kuberadāsa, Potho, Tulasī, Dhīro, Bhāu and Ratneśvara.
15. *Āśramavāsikaparvan*, No manuscript found so far.
16. *Mausalaparvan* of Vishṇudāsa and Śivadāsa.
17. *Mahāprasthānaparvan* of Vishṇudāsa.
18. *Svargārohaṇīparvan* of Vishṇudāsa, Ratneśvara, Rāmakṛishṇa and Surabhaṭa.

K.K. Shastree edited *Ādiparvan* of poet Haridāsa Raikva of Bareja (Ahmedabad) on the basis of 5 manuscripts preserved in Dalapatram MSS collection of Gujarat Vernacular Society, Ahmedabad.[2] It was completed in V.S. 1644, Āshaḍha, su. di. 12 (Vaishṇavī Nandā Ekādaśī), Bhṛiguvāra, Siddhi yoga (7 July 1587).

संव्वत षट्दश वेद उदधि वर्षागमि आषाढ़ मास;
उत्तम पक्ष शशाङ्क-कराङ्कित हरिदिन व्रतविश्वास . . .२०

नन्दातिथि भृगुवार उत्तम, सिद्धियोग अपार;
वृश्चिक-शशिदिन, मध्य दिवाकर पूर्णग्रन्थ विस्तार . . .२१

Kaḍavuṅ 88

The *Ādiparvan* composed by the poet Nākara[3] (V.S. 1572-1624 – AD 1515-16 to 1568), Vishṇudāsa[4] (V.S. 1624-1668 – AD 1568-1612), Manoharadāsa[5] (V.S. 1660 – AD 1603-04), and Mādhavadāsa[6] (V.S. 1675-1705 – AD 1618-1699) are still unpublished.

The *Sabhāparvan* composed by Vishṇudāsa has been edited by K.K. Shastree on the basis of one MSS (V.S. 1908 – AD 1852) from the private collection of Natvarlal Desai.[7] The name of the poet has been mentioned in the beginning, at the end of the 19th kaḍavāṅ and in the end of the work. The date of the composition of this work is given in kaḍavāṅ 36.14:

संव्वत सोल चोपन-मधि, उत्तम दिवस अपार;
अश्विन मास, कृष्ण पक्ष पावन, तृतीया नि रविवार . . .१४

V.S. 1654, Aśvina, Kṛishṇapaksha tṛitīyā, Ravivāra (13 Sept. 1597).

The poet Vishṇudāsa followed the episodes from Sanskrit *Sabhāparvan* and represented them briefly but vividly, for example:

भीमार्जुनावुभौ नेत्रे मनो मन्ये जनार्दनम् ।
मनश्चक्षुविहीनस्य कीद्दशं जीवितं भवेत् ।। (संस्कृत सभा., १६.२)

पणि जरासन्ध महाबलिउ राय, भीम अर्जुन त्व्हां नवि मोकलाय;
ए मुझ दृष्टि उभय, परिब्रह्म! नेत्र विना कहु, जीवूं किम्म?
(विष्णुदास, सभ., ७.४६)

The *Āraṇyakaparvan* composed by the Vaiśya poet Nākara has also been edited by K.K. Shastree on the basis of one MSS (no. 25) preserved in the Gujarat Vernacular Society, dated V.S. 1923, Bhādarvā su. di.2 (31 Aug. 1867).[8] Besides. Nākara, Vishṇudāsa and Avichaladāsa also composed *Āraṇyakaparvan* in V.S. 1646[9] (AD 1590-91) and V.S. 1695[10] (AD 1638-39) respectively. At the end of *Āraṇyakaparvan*, the date of the composition in mentioned as V.S. 1646, Jyeshṭhā, ba.di. 5, Guruvāra (14 May 1590).

संवत सोळ सड चालीश वरखे जेठ मासे पूर्ण कीधुं हरखे
तिथि पंचमी ने गुरुवार तव पूर्ण कीधुं में सार

(K.K. Shastree, '*Kavicharita*', part 1 & 2, Ahmedabad, 1952, pp. 333 f.)

From the date of the composition of his works, it is known that Nākara was famous as an Ākhyānakāra since V.S. 1572:

संवत पंदर बोतेर अभ्यास बुधाष्टमी भादरवो मास

(Nākara's *Hariśchandrākhyāna* published in *Bṛihadkāvya-dohana*, Vol. VI , p. 706).

(Nākara was unable to follow the original Sanskrit. He did not follow the original *Mahābhārata* kathā. But he composed *Mahābhārata* parvans in Gujarati independently. In this *Virāṭaparvan* (kaḍavāṅ 65-22), he mentioned that he composed the poems for the maintenance of one Nāgara brāhmaṇa (Nāhna), son of Madana:

करि ग्रंथ वाडव-करि सूंप्युं, विश्वि पुण्यविस्तार रे
वृद्धनागर कुलि नाह्म मदनसुत गाइ थाइ भवनिस्तार रे

Nākara has not composed *Ādi* and *Sabhāparvans* independently. He included these two parvans in his *Āraṇyakaparvan*. He composed *Bhīma* and *Gadā* extensively, though these two are sub-parvans of the *Mahābhārata*. He included *Udyogaparvan* briefly in the *Gadāparvan*. Here he adopted the method of *Pūrva-Kathānusandhāna* in which he represents the story in brief from the former section. We get an idea of poet's *prauḍhi* from his compositions of *Mahābhārata* parvans in Gujarati. The earliest parvans of the *Mahābhārata* ever composed in Deśī (Gujarati) are those of poet Nākara, a voluminous writer of Baroda. He received the honour of composing the *Mahābhārata* in Deśī *padabandha* for the first time. Among the Mahābhārata *ākhyānas*, this poet also composed *Virāṭaparvan* in Deśī in V.S. 1601 (AD 1544-45) for the first time.[11] Śālisūri's *Virāṭaparvan* composed in *vṛittabandha* belongs to 15th century AD.[12]

Nākara composed an independent Nalākhyāna in V.S. 1581 (AD 1524-25) on the basis of *Āraṇyakaparvāntargata Nalopākhyāna* in the *Mahābhārata*, and contributed many parvans from *Mahābhārata* like *Ādi, Sabha, Āraṇyaka, Virāṭa, Karṇa* (unpublished), *Śalya* (unpub.), *Bhīma* (unpub.), *Gadā* (pub.), *Sauptika* and

Strī to Gujarati literature till V.S. 1624 (AD 1567-68) or 1627 (AD 1570-71).[13] The best specimen of poetry as well as *Ḍhāḷas* we find, is in Nākara's *Virāṭaparvan*. He gave a new shape to the original episode of the *Mahābhārata* and represented with various sentiments like *vīra, karuṇa, raudra, bhayānaka, hāsya* and *adbhuta* (*Kavicharita*, p. 212).

Nakara's *Virāṭaparvan* was edited in 1936 by K.K. Shastree[14] on the basis of 13 MSS[15] preserved in various collections like Gujarat Vernacular Society, Forbes Gujarati Sabha and private collection of Natvarlal I. Desai. Kāśīsuta Shedhajī composed *Virāṭaparvan* in V.S. 1648 (AD 1591-92). Five MSS of his *Virāṭaparvan* have been found in different collections.[16]

A Sārasvata brāhmaṇa, Vaikuṇṭha of Kutiyana (Saurashtra) composed *Nalakathā* (V.S. 1702 – AD 1645-46), *Śalyaparvan* (V.S. 1707 – AD 1650-51) and *Bhīshma-Karṇaparvan* (V.S. 1716 – AD 1659-60).

Vishṇudāsa, a Nāgara brāhmaṇa of Cambay contributed many compositions to the Gujarati *ākhyāna* literature. He composed many parvans of the *Mahābhārata* in addition to writing several *ākhyānas*. He composed *Virāṭa, Āraṇyaka* (V.S. 1646 – AD 1589-90), *Sabhā* (V.S. 1654 – AD 1597-98), *Ādi, Udyoga, Karṇa* (V.S. 1655 – AD 1598-99), *Droṇa* (V.S. 1657 – AD 1600-01), *Bhīshma* (V.S. 1663 – AD 1606-07) *Śalyaparvan, Gadā, Sauptika, Strī* and *Mausala, Prasthāna* and *Svargārohaṇī*.

Poet Bhāu, an Audichya brāhmaṇa of Sūrat wrote *Aśvamedha-parvan* (V.S. 1679 – AD 1622-23), *Droṇaparvan* and *Udyogaparvān-targata Pāṇḍava Vishṭi* (V.S. 1676 – AD 1619-20).

The *Bhīshmaparvan* of Vaikuṇṭha, *Droṇa* of Bhāu and *Karṇa* of Vishṇudāsa have been edited by K.K. Shastree in the *Mahābhārata*, Vol. IV, Forbes Gujarati Sabha, Mumbai, 1941. In editing *Bhīshmaparvan*, three MSS were collated.[17] For *Droṇaparvan*, one MSS[18] and for *Karṇaparvan* three MSS[19] have been used. Other MSS of *Bhīshmaparvan* so far found are 7[20], of *Droṇaparvan* 3[21] and of *Karṇaparvan* 2.[22]

The MS of Nakāra's *Śalya, Sauptikaparvans* in Devanāgari script (V.S. 1923 – AD 1866-67) has been preserved in Gujarati Vidyasabha collection. The MSS of Vishṇudāsa's *Gadāparvan* and *Strīparvan* are found in Forbes Gujarati Sabha collection (no. 360 क dated V.S. 1820, Bhādaravā, su.di. 2, Budha and no. 103 ङ dated V.S. 1797). These five parvans were edited by K.K. Shastree in 1950.

Vishṇudāsa and Vaikuṇṭha also have composed *Śalyaparvan*. Two MSS dated V.S. 1797 and V.S. 1820[23] and one MS dated V.S. 1928[24] of Vaikuṇṭha's *Śalyaparvan* have been found.

The *Mausalaparvan* of the poet Śivadāsa, *Prasthānaparvan* of Vishṇudāsa and *Svargārohaṇaparvan* of Rāmakṛishṇa and Ratneśvara have been edited by K.K. Shastree (*Mahābhārata*, Vol. VII, Forbes Gujarati Sabha, Bombay, 1949). For editing *Mausalaparvan* of Śivadāsa, three MSS have been used. They are: (1) MS dated V.S. 1797 written in Gujarati script from Forbes Gujarati Sabha (no. 103 ख) (2) MS dated V.S. 1820, of Devanāgari script from Forbes Gujarati Sabha (no. 360 घ) and (3) MS (of 8 kaḍavāṅs) in Gujarati script from Gujarati Press, Bombay, private collection (no. 332 क).

Poet Vishṇudāsa has also composed *Mausalaparvan*, the MS of which is found in Forbes Gujarati Sabha (no. 360 घ). Vishṇudāsa's *Svargārohaṇaparvan* remains unpublished. Two MSS of this parvan have been preserved in Forbes Gujarati Sabha (no. 103 घ dated *circa* V.S. 1797 and Ambalal Jani private collection (no. 25 dated V.S. *circa* 1830). The poet has mentioned at the end of this parvan that he finished the whole *Mahābhārata* within three years.

Poet Surabhaṭa (V.S. 1704 – AD 1647-48) composed *Svargārohaṇī* in simple deśī-*bandha* in 22 kadavāṅs. He was a Purāṇika Raikva brāhmaṇa of Kaloli (Gujarat). In the colophon of this parvan he writes:[25]

संवत् १७०४ चारोतर शार।। जेष्ट माश बारेश गुरुवार।
श्वर्गारोहेणी कीधी ग्रंथ।। जेहेमां शकल धरमनो पंथ।।
गाम कलोली रहेवुं वास। रचीक (रइक्य) भ्रंमग्नान वेद आचार।
रूडी स्तुति नारायणनी करे।। सुरभट सुत तेहेनो मंन धरे।। १

(Kaḍavan 22)

24 MSS of this parvan by Surabhaṭa have been found so far; 7[26] in Dalapatram Coll., 2[27] in Forbes Gujarati Sabha coll., 4[28] in Dahilakshmi Library Nadiad coll., 5[29] in Oriental Institute, Vadodara coll., 5[30] in Purushottam Mavaji coll. and 2[31] in M.T.B. College, Surat coll.

No MSS of *Śāntiparvan, Anuśāsanaparvan* and *Āśramavāsika-parvan* have been found so far.

From the beginning of the 15th century AD, poets worked through the medium of old Gujarati. In many cases, the works were handed down from generation to generation by professional reciters of the Purāṇas or Purāṇikas; and every reciter went on making such changes in their form, language and substance as the occasion and the taste of his audience required.

Among the poets who composed short *ākhyānas* on the episodes from the *Mahābhārata*, Bhālaṇa (a Moḍha brāhmaṇa of Pāṭan, *circa* V.S. 1550), the father of the Ākhyāha, was the foremost. He gave the name Gurjara Bhāsha for the first time to medieval Gujarati language. He contributed several *prauḍha* ākhyāhas to medieval Gujarati literature. He appears to have supplied a growing need and on his own admission, evoked considerable antagonism from those who found his method undignified for a Purāṇika of learning. His *Nalākhyāna* produced a short *ākhyāna* on the episode of Nala and Damayantī from the *Mahābhārata*. He also wrote *Durvāsākhyāna* from the *Mahābhārata*.[32] Bhālaṇa (*c.* AD 1426-1500) deserves a high place in Gujarati literature as the pioneer of the new tradition, through the *ākhyānas* which gave Gujarat a new literature.

During Narasimha Mehta age, poet Dehala (V.S. 1540-50) composed in *khaṇḍakāvya, Abhinav-Uzaṇuṅ,* describing Abhimanyu story. Poet Janatāpidāsa of Bandhārā caste and a resident of Hariyad (S.Guj.) used some portion of Dehala's *Abhinav-Uzaṇuṅ* story in his *Abhimanyuakhyāna* (completed in V.S. 1708).[33] Ahilochan-pañjara episode in this *khaṇḍakāvya* was narrated interestingly.

Bhālaṇa's knowledge of Sanskrit and Vraja-bhāshā was good. Bhālaṇa has contributed 16 independent poetries – all *ākhyānas*. Among these 16 *ākhyānas*, *Nalākhyāna* and *Kādambarī* are his best *ākhyānas*. Prior to Bhālaṇa, no *ākhyānas* arranged in kaḍavāṅs have been found so far.

Bhālaṇa's early works were mere renderings of the *ākhyāyikās*. But later, he borrowed the episodes from several sources, pruned or altered them, and added fresh materials to produce a new work. In his works, presumably composed during his last days, the *ākhyāna* reached an advanced stage of evolution. It was a Gujarati *ākhyāyikā*. With contemporary sentiments and the Purāṇika plot and characters altered to suit them, it became a new and distinct literary form. His *Nalākhyāna* was the original of many subsequent copies. Besides many *Mahābhārata* parvans, Nākara wrote *Abhimaṇyuakhyāna, Karṇacharita* (both unpub.), *Chandrahāsākhyāna, Nalākhyāna,* etc.

Bhālaṇa created his poetry in both pada and kaḍavāṅ method. Nākara developed both short and long kaḍavāṅs style. In his *Virāṭaparvan* he mentioned that he used 15 *rāgas* and number of Kaḍavāṅs is 65.

वैराटपर्व कीधूं परिपूरण पद अष्टादशशिं पचाश रे
रागे पन्नर नि कडवां पांसठि, ओत्तम कथा अविनाशी रे. . . .१८

Kaḍavāṅ 65.18

In his *Nalākhyāna,* Nākara describes the beauty of Damayantī through the speech of Haṁsa to king Nala very lucidly:

ब्रह्मा बेठो भांजे घडे अंदूना (इन्दुना) तनने नितनित नडे . . .७६
प्रतिब्यंब नीपाइ जोय! दमंती मुख समतूल्य न होए,
तोहरे मुख तां छि कलंकं! दमंतीनुं मुख छे नीकलंक . . . ७७
लजा पांमी इन्दु जाय . . . दलनि उलवे खोसाय . . .

Nākara composed some *ākhyānas* like *Chandrahāsākhyāna* and *Sudhanvākhyāna* from the *upākhyānas* of the Sanskrit *Aśvamedhaparvan* of Jaiminī. He also wrote *Abhimanyuākhyāna, Karṇacharita* and *Nalākhyāna* from the small episodes of *Mahābhārata*. His compositions of *Mahābhārata* parvans in Gujarati *padabandha* are the best representaticns of his *prauḍhi.* His description of Draupadī by Yudhishṭhira with tears in his eyes before going to Virāṭanagara is the best example of Karuṇa *rasa.*

द्रुपदसुता निहाली भूपति आण्या अश्रुपातः
ए घडा जेवडुं माणिक मानिनी, किम रहिशि परहाथि ? ९
पुरुष तणी तां वात पाधरी, जिम तिम करीनइ, रहिशि,
परभूपति-वशिं पडी प्रेमदा, केही परि दिन लेशि ? १०
अम्यो तां अछता थइनि रहिवूं , कांइ न थाइ प्राण;
कन्दर्प कोटि कामिनी कोमल, मुख सोल कला शशि जाणि ११
नयन चंचल तीक्ष्ण शरशरखां, भ्रमइ कोदण्डत्रटि धरिआं;
मन्मथ-मेगल हाथि वशि नित्य; कयम जाइ वशि करिआं ? १२

Virāṭaparvan, Kaḍavāṅ 25.9-12

Nākara used line-ending *Dohābandha* parallelism or double refrain like 'सुणि सुंदरी' and 'गिहिली कुणि करि' in kaḍavāṅs 49-50 of the *Virāṭaparvan* in a dialogue form. For example:

राइ युधिष्ठिर उचरइ, 'सुणि सुन्दरी!
तूं माणेश दुःख लगार; गहिली कुणि करी? १
पछर ए आपुणि मारीशि, सुखि सुन्दरी?
आंहांथी चालीशि तेणी वार; गहिली कुणि करो? २

Kaḍavāṅ 49

One poet Vishṇudāsa Māṅgu (*circa* V.S. 1600) wrote *Aśvamedhakathā* (translation of the *Jaiminīya Aśvamedha*).[34] In the MS (Guj. Vidya. MSS coll., no. 426) at the end of each *varga*, the poet says:

जैमुनि जनमेजय संवाद! अश्वमेघ कथा-अनुवाद,
विष्णुदास मांगु कहि सरग! एटलि तरणि पुहुता वरग.

The poet Rājadharadāsa (V.S. 1621 – AD 1564-65) composed the *Chandrahāsākhyāna* in 27 kaḍavāṅs from the *Chandrahāsakathā* of the *Jaiminīya Aśvamedha*.[35]

The poet Vishṇudāsa, a Nāgara brāhmaṇa of Cambay (AD 1578-1657) contributed about twenty-seven works to Gujarati *ākhyāna* literature. He has versified many parvans of the *Mahābhārata* and almost all the khāṇḍas of the *Rāmāyaṇa* in addition to writing several *ākhyānas*. The poet has composed 15 parvans of the *Mahābhārata*. They are *Virāṭa, Āraṇyaka* (V.S. 1646), *Sabhā* (V.S. 1654), *Ādi, Udyoga, Karṇa* (V.S. 1655), *Droṇa* (V.S. 1657), *Bhīshma* (V.S. 1663), *Śalya,Gadā, Sauptika, Strī* (V.S. 1665), *Mauśala, Prasthāna* (V.S. 1668) and *Svargārohaṇī*. He also composed works like *Yuvanāśva Kathā, Bhīmahāsya Kathā, Anuśālva Ākhyāna, Chaṇḍi-Ākhyāna Aśvaprayāṇa, Niladhvajākhyāna, Sudhanvākhyāna* (V.S. 1632), *Babhruvāhanākhyāna, Lavakusākhyāna, Moradhvajākhyāna* and *Chandrahāsākhyāna* (V.S. 1634).

Vishṇudāsa's poems, though very simple, at times had shown that he was able to infuse force and feeling, whenever occasions required it, in the narration of incidents.

Cambay was the well-known centre for Ākhyānkāras during Haridāsa's time[36] (V.S. 1637). They composed their poetry after hearing the recitals of Sanskrit knowing Purāṇikas like Haribhaṭa, Bhudhara Vyāsa, Viśvanātha Vyāsa and Balkṛishṇa Bhaṭṭa.[37]

The poet Lakshmīdāsa (V.S. 1639-72) of Mahemdavad (Guj.) wrote his *Chandrahāsākhyāna* in 45 kaḍavāṅs on the basis of the *Jaiminīya Aśvamedhaparvan*. There is one big poem *Karṇaparvan*, which may be ascribed to Lakshmīdāsa. The MS is incomplete in the beginning and at the end.[38] In 73rd kaḍavāṅ, the name of the poet is mentioned.

एक कथा तां वैशंपायन जन्मेजिनि किहिसि
लष्यमीदास किहि कर्ण–संघाति अर्जन यूधि–जसि २५

Kāśīsuta Shedhijī (V.S. 1647-48) of Cambay composed his *Draupadīvastrāharaṇa* (a portion of *Sabhāparvan*) in V.S. 1648. His *Virāṭaparvan* was composed in V.S. 1648, whereas his *Sabhāparvan* is undated. The poet himself gives his name as Kāshīsuta. From his *Hanumāncharitra* his first name seems to be Shedhajī. All his poems are still unpublished.[39] One Devadāsa (*c.* V.S. 17th century) composed *Aśvamedhaparvan* (incomplete) on the basis of the *Jaiminīya Aśvamedha*.

Among the Purāṇika poets, who composed the *Mahābhārata* parvans in Gujarati *padabandha*, Manohardāsa's contribution is also notable. He has faithfully followed the *Mahābhārata kathā*. One Māṇabhaṭṭa named Mohandāsa wrote a *Saṅkīrṇa Kāvya* on the basis of Haridāsa's *Ādiparvan* (V.S. 1644) and Manohardāsa's *Ādiparvan* (V.S. 1660).[40] Manohardāsa started his poem with the sacrifice performed by Janamejaya and had given the description of Kaliyuga in the form of a dialogue between Kṛishṇa and Arjuna.

The poet Śivadāsa (V.S. 1667-77) wrote his *Draupadī-Svayaṁvara* in V.S. 1673 at Bijapur (Deccan). He also wrote *Mausalaparvan*. The date of the composition is not mentioned in the colophon. His *Sabhāparvan* is dated V.S. 1670. There is nothing striking in his poems. Kṛishṇadāsa wrote the *Chandrahāsākhyāna* in V.S. 1684 on the basis of two MSS from Dahilakshmi Library, Nadiad (V.S. 1866) and Gujarati Press, Bombay (*Gujarati Hātha Pratonī Saṅkalita Yādī*, p. 21). Bhāu (V.S. 1676-79), an Audīchya brahmin of Surat, has contributed *Aśvamedhaparvan, Droṇa, Udyoga* and *Udyogaparvāntargata Pāṇḍavavishṭi* to old Gujarati literature. His *Droṇaparvan* and *Pāṇḍavavishṭi* are published (*Kavicharira*, Vols. 1-2, p. 457). The colophon of the *Pāṇḍavavishṭi* mentions the date of composition as follows:

संवत दश शत (?षट्) छोतरो आनंद शुं रे,
शाके पंदर बेताल मन गोविंद शुं रे,
चैत्र मास सोहामणो आनंद शुं रे,
मुने देवे करी संभाल मन गोविंद शुं रे . . .१६
छंद पदबंध जाणुं नहि आनंद शुं रे,
न जाणु गुरु लघुनो ठाम मन गोविंदशुं रे,
करी जोडी विप्र भाऊ कहे आ० हवे मुक्ति आपो
श्रीराम, मन० ...१७

Bhāu wrote the *Udyogaparvan* of 1765 Kaḍīs in V.S. 1676 (AD 1619-20). His *Droṇaparvan* is of 35 kaḍavāṅs and 1487 kaḍīs. At the end of the poem, the essence of *Karṇaparvan* has been given. He wrote his *Aśvamedhaparvan* in V.S. 1679, Śaka 1544 (AD 1622).

संवत १६ ओगणाशीए।। शाके १५४४ पंनरशे चौआल।।
आक्षांन जमलां बे हतां।। मल माश देव वीशाल।।
अधी(धि)क माश आखाड मधे।। सुंक्ल पक्ष ते शार।।
त्रीजी तीथी सुभदाईनी।। नखेत्र पूस्य रवीवार।।

After hearing the recitals from his guru Nārāyaṇa Bhaṭṭa, he wrote these *ākhyānas*.

Avichaladāsa, a Sāṭhodarā of Nadiad, composed the *Āraṇyakaparvan* of 75 kaḍavāṅs - 7,070 kaḍīs.

गुजर खंडे नटपद्र निवास। नागर नारायणना दास।
संवत १६ पंचाणुओ धन्य। श्रावण वदि एकादशी दिन।।
विष्णुदाससुत अविचल वाणे। सकल सभाने दे कल्याण।।

(Āraṇyaka Kaḍavāṅ 75)

It is known from the colophon of the *Āraṇyakaparvan* that Avichaladāsa wrote the MS for his guru, in his own handwriting and gave it to him. It is unpublished.

Harjīsuta Rāvajī (V.S. 1689 – AD 1632-33) composed the *Udyogaparvan*, (Guj. Vidya Sabha, MS no. 1694 ख) in 53 kaḍavāṅs and 28 rāgas. Vaikuṇṭha (V.S. 1694-1724), son of Tulasī, wrote *Udyogaparvan*, *Bhīshmaparvan*, *Karṇaparvan*, *Śalya* and *Nalakathā*. He started writing *Nalakathā* in 2,681 kaḍīs in V.S. 1702, Āśvina, su.di. 15, Guruvāra (25 Sept. AD 1645) and completed in V.S. 1709 (Āśvina), Ekādaśī (AD 1652-53).

He wrote the *Karṇaparvan* in V.S. 1716 (AD 1659-60), *Śalyaparvan* in V.S. 1707 (AD 1650-51). Rāmakṛishṇa wrote his *Svargārohaṇī* in V.S. 1750 (AD 1693-94).[41]

Potho (*c.* later half of the 17th century) composed the *Moradhvajākhyāna and Sudhanvākhyāna* on the basis of the *Jaiminīya Aśvamedha*. He has given Sanskrit quotations in Gujarati *ākhyāna*. Both these are devotional poems.

In the beginning, in 9 kaḍavāṅs the poet has given the description of Kaliyuga. In the MSS of the *Svargārohaṇīparvan*, Surabhaṭa's name is given. The episode of Kṛishṇalīlā sung by Draupadī after Kṛishṇa had gone to Svadhāma is poetic.[42]

Morāsuta Govinda (V.S. 1705 – AD 1648-49) wrote his *Sudhanvākhyāna*. He was a native of Surat and Kansārā by caste.

संवत सत्तर सत पांच वरषे ।। व्रखा रत अखाड।।
शुक्ल पक्ष द्वी(द्वि)तीआ रवी(वि)।। पालवुं प्रभूजी लाड।। ४८
कथा ए आरंभ कीधो।। सुभ नक्षत्र वेला सार।।
श्रावण सुध बुधवार द्वी(द्वि)तीआ।। पुरंण टाइ नीरधार।। ४८

Mādhavadāsa, a Vālmīka Kāyastha poet of Surat composed his *Ādiparvan* in Gujarati *padabandha* in V.S. 1675, Āśvina, su. di. 14*, *Ravivāra* (13 Sept. 1619).

संवत सोल पंचोतेर पुरण उत्तम अस्वन मास,
शुक्लपक्ष ने चतुरदशी रवीवारे पोहोती छे आश...१७

(Ādi, Kaḍavāṅ 128)

The *Abhimanyuākhyāna* of Janatāpīdāsa (V.S. 1708 – AD 1651-52) is an independent poem. The poet has made some changes in the *Mahābhārata* episodes to make the poem lucid and interesting. The poem depicts Adbhuta *rasa*. His *Babhrūvahanākhyāna* was composed in V.S. 1768 (or V.S. 1708). Its MS is preserved in Dahilakshmi Library, Nadiad.

The three poets of the brilliant group dominating the 17th century are Akhā Bhagat (AD 1615-1674), Premānanda (AD 1636-1734) and Śāmal (AD 1640-1730). Akhā revelled in philosophy, Premānanda in delineation and description of human and physical nature and Śamal in story-telling. The verse literature of Gujarat thus made an entirely new and welcome departure, beginning with Akhā.

The laurel crown is ungrudgingly placed on the brow of Premānanda who followed Akhā. If any single individual has uplifted the language and literature of Gujarat from the mere obscurity, if any single poet has brought it in line with the much-renowned and cultured literatures of Sanskrit and Prakrit, it is Premānanda. He was the greatest literary figure of the age.

The *Nalākhyāna* (of 64 kaḍavāṅs) is perhaps the most popular

*In the given date, the *tīthi* does not tally with the weekday according to either *Chaitrādi* or the *Kārttikādi* system of years. The given date then would correspond to Sunday, 13 Sept., AD. 1618 according to the *Chaitradi* system of years.

of Premānanda's *ākhyānas*. This poem is characterized by an ornate style, elaborate descriptions and intense emotions. It is evidently an attempt to produce a masterpiece on the conventional model. The description of Damayantī is in the approved hyperbolic style of the period.

दमयंतीनो चोटलो, देखी अति सोहाग।
अभिमान मूकी लज्जा आणी, पाताळ पेठो नाग।।
भीमक सुतानुं वदन सुधाकर, देखीने शोभाय।
चंद्रमा तो क्षीण पामी, आभमां संताय।।
सृष्टि करतां ब्रह्माजीए, भर्युं तेजनुं पात्र।
ते तेजनुं प्रजापतिये घड्युं, दमयंतीनुं गात्र।।
तेमांथी कांई शेष वाध्युं, घडतां खेरो पडियो।
ब्रह्माए एकठुं करीने, तेनो चंद्रमा घडियो।।

The serpent saw the lovely braid of Damayantī, and humbled and ashamed, crawled in the nether regions. The moon saw the sweet face of Bhīmaka's daughter, waned, and hid behind the cloud. At creation, Brahmā collected light in a pot, and made the limbs of Damayantī out of it. Part of it lay unused; parts lay scattered about; Brahmā put them together and created the moon.

This *ākhyāna*, though largely based on a predecessor's work, is an independent work of art, every line of which testifies to the touch of a skilled artist. Premānanda was a profound observer, no detail escaped him. He depicted passion, situation and the character in a vivid style. Among the literary artists of the period, he was truly a creative artist and could give a glimpse of actual life.

Premānanda composed with incredible facility, *ākhyānas* from the *Mahābhārata*; like *Chandrahāsākhyāna* (AD 1671), *Ṛishyaśṛigākhyāna* (AD 1673), *Abhimanyu-ākhyāna* (AD 1676) *Draupadīsvayaṁvara*, *Nalākhyāna* (AD 1685), *Draupadīharaṇa* (AD 1689) *Subhadrāharaṇa* (AD 1702) and *Ashṭāvakrākhyāna* (AD 1710). His first average work was *Svarganisaraṇī*. He confessed in this work:

काव्यकविता कंई नव जाणूं, पहेली कविता कीधी रे राम।
उदर निमित्ते निसरणी गाई।।

Premānanda's *Abhimanyuākhyāna* describes the exploits of Abhimanyu, the son of Arjuna and Subhadrā, Kṛishṇa's sister.

The poet took the old *rāsā* form of the *ākhyāna* as he found it, a long, poetic composition divided into kaḍavāṅs in Deśī and rounded by two lines of *valaṇ*. But he used it with freedom and vigour. In his best works, the story was rapid and gripping narrative; but he broke it up at frequent intervals to make room for long descriptions with real life. He used his art so skilfully that the *ākhyāna* became, like modern novel, an elastic medium for all literary purposes.

Premānanda has been credited with writing eleven plays, three of which were published some sixty years ago. They are named *Roshadarśikā-Satyabhāmākhyāna, Pāñchāli-prasannākhyāna* and *Tapatyākhyāna,* the first two of which are concerned with popular subjects in connection with Kṛishṇa and the Pāṇḍavas. From a literary and artistic point of view they are inferior to the poet's other works. Both stage and dramatic literature were unknown to Gujarat in the whole period of five centuries. Old Gujarati had no drama, and to the literary men of Gujarat, from Somasundara to Dayārāma, the dramatic presentation of character, incident and dialogue was an unknown art.[43]

With a humorous twinkle in his eye and a joyous note in his voice, Premānanda passes on to his world-weary generation the inspiration of Vyāsa. Premānanda's son Vallabha is said to have composed, among other works, *Duḥśāsana-rudhirapānākhyāna* (AD 1724), *Kuntīprasannākhyāna* (AD 1781) and *Yudhishṭhiravṛikodar-ākhyāna.*

Ākhyānakāra Harjīsuta Kāhān (V.S. 1693-95 – AD 1636-39) composed his *Aśvamedhaparvan* in V.S. 1693, Mārgaśirsa, śu. di. 2, Ravivāra (20 Nov. AD 1636) from *Jaiminīya Mahābhāratāntargata Aśvamedhaparvan.*[44] The colophon of his first *Ākhyāna Yauvanāśva* mentions:

हरजी-सुत काहानउ केहे रसिक ए पदबंध।
अश्वमेधना आरंभ क्येरी कथा तणो समंध।। २८
संवत सोळसे त्राणुवो मार्गशीर्ष जे मास।
दिवस द्वितीया शुक्ल क्येरी कर्यूं गाम अभ्यास।। २९
रविवारने दिन सबल शुभ कह्या गुण-गोविंद।

काहानजी केहे हरिकृपाथी सदा शुभ आनंद... ।। ३०

He completed 14th *Chandrahāsākhyāna* in V.S. 1693, Śrāvaṇa, su. di. 4, Ravi (16 July AD 1637) and rest of the portion on V.S. 1695, Pausha, Makara Saṅkrānti (12 Jan. 1639). His guru was Damodara. In the beginning of many *ākhyānas* he has prayed to his guru. He has composed his poems in general deśī bandhas and rāgas. Rarely he used the combination of Rāga Mevāḍa-Āsāvarī, Mevāḍakedāro, etc. He used the names of sections like *Zamak, Alaṅkāra, Chhanda* and *Sūtra* instead of Kaḍavāṅs.[45]

Śāmaḷa Bhaṭṭa was, after Premānanda, the most notable poet of the period. He was a Śrīgoḍa Mālvī brāhmaṇa of Vengaṇapur (modern Gomatipur, a suburb of Ahmedabad) and knew Sanskrit, Braja and Persian. He left behind him no followers, and no school of poetry.

The work on the *Mahābhārata* attributed to him is *Draupadīvastrāharaṇa*. He attempted Puraṇika subjects, but could only produce ordinary *ākhyānas*. His greatness lies in his matchless style and wonderful power of story-telling, in presenting didactic and worldly maxims in striking parallelisms; and in preserving the romantic atmosphere of early fiction and thereby providing a valuable literature of escape from the morbid influences of his times.

From the beginning of the 15th century AD, poets worked through the medium of old Gujarati. But their language has been transformed out of recognition. Manuscripts of some of their works, recovered so far, have been written years after the author's death. In many cases, the works were handed down from generation to generation by professional reciters of the Purāṇas, or Purāṇikas and every reciter went on making such changes in their form, language and substance as the occasion and the taste of his audience required. The *gāgariā bhaṭ* preserved most of these works in the form of *ākhyānas*.

The *gāgariā bhaṭ* or *māṇ bhaṭ* is peculiar to Gujarat and has played a great part in the evolution and preservation of this class of literature. He is the popular counterpart of the Puraṇika, who, generally well-read in Sanskrit, recites the Purāṇas from the original to select audience at his own house. But the *gāgariā bhaṭ* is rarely acquainted with Sanskrit; he knows only the *ākhyānas*, or the episodes from *Mahābhārata*, *Rāmāyaṇa* and the Purāṇas in Gujarati verse which he has learnt from the apprenticeship. He goes from place to place with a couple of disciples. His stock-in-trade is his *ākhyānas*, his tact and his *māṇ* or *gāgar*, a large copper pot with a narrow neck from which he gets his name. With his nimble fingers loaded with brass rings, he starts playing upon the *gāgar* as on a hand-drum, and makes the pot resound with his skilful raps. The bhaṭ recites an *ākhyāna*, explains many parts of it; adds a flourish here, a touch there to move or tickle the audience; improvizes new stories and introduces lively anecdotes. These bhaṭs flourished in Gujarat for more than five hundred years. They provided free entertainment and education, religious and secular and helped to preserve Purāṇic literature. But these reciters were scarcely qualified to reproduce the spirit, the art or the idealism of the original Purāṇas; and were mostly content with mechanical repetition of narrative verses handed down from teacher to disciple. Their range of emotion, sentiment and thought was limited; their language suited to illiterate audience, lacked refinement and expressiveness. But the service which the *gāgariā bhaṭ* rendered to our culture was immense.[46]

Thus many medieval poets composed *Mahābhārata* parvans in Gujarati *padabandha* and wrote various *ākhyānas* in Gujarati based on *Mahābhārata* episodes.

NOTES AND REFERENCES

1. According to the *Saṅgīta Ratnākara* (13th century AD), Deśī is the music, singing and dancing which is pleasing to the tastes of people in different countries. Deśī metres could be sung to melodies which are also known as Deśī. Old Gujarati *rāsās* and *ākhyānas* are made up in kaḍavāṅs, *garabīs* and *padas* in Deśī frequently interspersed with other kinds of metres. Among the popular Deśī metres in Gujarati are *Prabhātiāṅs, Pada, Gīta, Garabo, Garabī, Māsā, Āratī,* etc. (K.M. Munshi, *Gujarat and its Literature*, Bharatiya Vidya Bhavan, Bombay, 3rd Ed., 1967, Appendix, p. 382).
2. Nos. 255 (copying year V.S. 1903), 266, 338, (copying year V.S. 1727), 345-345 अ (copying year V.S. 1761). *Gujarati Hāthapratonī Saṅkalita Yādī* (up to AD 1937) prepared by K.K. Shastree, Gujarat Vernacular Society, Ahmedabad, 1939, p. 243; *Śrī Mahābhārata* (Gujarati *Padabandha*), Vol. I, (*Ādiparvan* by Raikva poet Haridāsa and *Sabhāparvan* by poet Vishṇudāsa), ed. K.K. Shastree, Forbes Gujarati Sabha, Bombay, 1933, Intro., pp. 16 f.
3. K.K. Shastree, *Guj. Hāth. Saṅ. Yādī*, p. 92.2 (Vadodara, Ori. Insti.

MSS Coll., no. 662).

4. *Ibid.*, p. 199.4 (Dalapataram Coll., no. 127 क).
5. *Ibid.*, p. 149.1 (Dahilakshmi library, Nadiad Coll., no. 8.2).
6. *Ibid.*, p. 155.1 (Dalapataram Coll., no. 30).
7. *Ibid.*, p. 204.34; *The Mahābhārata: Sabhāparvan* (ed. K.K. Shastree, Vol. I, p. 23).
8. *Ibid.*, p. 92; *The Mahābhārata* (Guj. *Padabandha*), Vol. II, ed. K.K. Shastree, p. 41.
9. Only the portion of *Nalākhyāna* from this parvan has been published by B.N. Mehta with his *Sabhāparvan*. One MS of Vishṇudāsa's *Āraṇyakaparvan* dated V. S. 1887 – AD 1830-31 has been preserved in Forbes Gujarati Sabha MSS Collection (no. 342 ग).
10. This parvan under the title *Vanaparvan* has been published by Baladevarām Krishṇarām master with some changes.
    The MS of Avichaladāsa's *Āraṇyakaparvan* is preserved in Dalapatram MSS Collection, Guj. Verna. So. (no. 477 क).
11. *The Mahābhārata* (Guj. *Padabandha*), ed. K.K. Shastree, Vol. II, Bombay, 1934, p. 43.
12. *Ibid.*, p. 40, f.n. 1; K.K. Shastree, *Kavicharita*, Guj. Vidyasabha, Ahmedabad, 1952, p. 203, f.n. 1.
13. *Ibid.*, Intro., pp. 47 ff.
14. *The Mahābhārata* (Guj. *Padabandha*), Vol. III, ed. K.K. Shastree, (*Virāṭaparvan* of Nākara), Forbes Gujarati Sabha, Bombay, 1936.
15. MSS in Gujarati Vernacular So. Coll. nos. 294 अ , 326, 353, 443 and 26.
    Forbes Gujarati Sabha Coll. nos. 64 क, 85 क, and 59 क.
    Natvarlal I. Desai Private Coll. 4 MSS. One MS edited by Chhaganlal V. Raval and published by Forbes Guj. Sabha.
16. A MS dated V.S. 1874 (AD 1817-18) from Dalapatram Collection (Guj. Ver. So. no. 18); MS. no. 655 जी dated V.S. 1756 (AD 1699-1700) from the same collection; two MSS nos. 178 ख -179 dated V.S. 1761 (AD 1704-05) and no. 229 ठ (V.S. 1763 – AD 1706-07) incomplete from Forbes Gujarati Sabha, Bombay; one MS no. 641a from Oriental Institute, Baroda, dated V.S. 1712 (AD 1655-56).
    Three MSS of the anonymous writer:
    1. MS dated V.S. 1575 (AD 1518-19) from Dalpatram Coll., no. 552 क.
    2. MS dated 1839 (AD 1782-83) from Oriental Insti., Baroda, no. 666a.
    3. MS from Purushottam Visram Mavaji's private coll., no. 195.
    Guj. Hāth. Saṁ. Yādī, pp. 265, 282, 290.
17. Karshanji Bambhaniya's copy dated V.S. 1927 (AD 1870-71); MS from Guj. Ver. Society, dated V.S. 1864 (AD 1807-08), no. 601 and MS from Gujarati Printing Press, Bombay, dated V.S. 1926 (AD 1869-

70).

18. Only one MS from Guj. Ver. Society dated 1864, no. 277 अ.
19. Three MSS – a MS from Forbes Guj. Sabha dated V.S. 1713 (AD 1656-57); one MS from Guj. Ver. So, dated V.S. 1868 (1811-12), no. 277. The work was composed in V.S. 1684 (AD 1627-28); One MS from Forbes Guj. Sabha, no. 66, copied in V.S. 1869 (AD 1812-13), (*Mahābhārata*, Vol. 4, ed. K.K. Shastree, Forbes Gujarati Sabha Mumbai, p. 6).
20. *Bhīshmaparvan* of Vishṇudāsa—MS no. 8 ब dated V.S. 1890 from Guj. Ver. Society, MS no. 66 न— (dated *c.* V.S. 1819) and no. 356 (incom.) from Forbes Guj. Sabha, MS no. 331 क (dated V.S. 1783) and no. 332 ख of Guj. Press private coll., MS no. 220 from Purushottam Mavaji's private coll., MS. no. 56 from M.T.B. College Surat coll.,
21. Unpublished *Droṇaparvan* of Vishṇudāsa—MS no. 24 dated V.S. 1907 *c.* and no. 902 dated *c.* 1800 of Guj. Ver. So. Coll., MS no. 331 ख (dated V.S. 1783) of Gujarati Press private coll.
22. Unpublished *Karṇaparvan* of Vishṇudāsa—MS no. 335 (dated V.S. 1889) and no. 336 (dated V.S. 1800) from Gujarati Press private coll.
23. MSS nos. 103 च and 360 ख from Forbes Gujarati Sabha, Bombay Collection.
24. MS no. 337 from Gujarati Press private coll.
25. MS from Forbes Gujarati Sabha Coll., no. 82; K.K. Shastree, *Kavicharita*,Vols. 1-2, p. 585.
26. MS dated V.S. 1890 (no. 212), no. 242 (dated 1879), no. 425 and 473 (V.S. 1906), no. 554 क (V.S. 1906, no. 600 क (*c.* V.S. 1905), no. 899 (incom.) and no. 1039 ड (incom.).
27. MS no. 82 क (V.S. 1824) and no. 319 ञ (V.S. 1860).
28. MSS nos. 1-1, 1-2 (incom.), nos. 8-9 (16 kaḍavāṅs) and nos. 8-12 (V.S. 1887).
29. MS no. 665c (V.S. 1900), no. 1013 (V.S. 1865), no. 873b (V.S. 1895), no. 1020, 7550d (V.S. 1799).
30. MS no. 2, 43 (incom.), 106, 116, 127.
31. MS no. 13 (V.S. 1910), 23 (*c.* V.S. 1942).
32. K.M. Munshi, *op.cit.*, p. 171.
33. *Kavicharita*, p. 120; Some Jān Bhagat also followed the story from Dehala's poem in his detailed *Abhimanyu-ākhyāna* (*Ibid.*, p. 122).
34. *Ibid.*, p. 281.
35. *Ibid.*, pp. 310 f.
36. K.M. Jhaveri, *Milestones in Gujarati Literature*, 1914, pp. 119 f.
37. *Kavicharita*, p. 374.
38. Guj. Vidya Sabha MSS Coll., Ahmedabad, no. 336 ब; *Kavicharita*, p. 384.
39. *Ibid.*, pp. 393 ff.

40. MS no. 225 (Guj. Vidya Sabha MSS Coll.); *Kavicharita*, p. 427, f.n. 2.
41. *Ibid.*, p. 497.
42. *Ibid.*, p. 587.
43. K.M. Munshi, *op.cit.*, p. 251.
44. Oriental Insti., Baroda Coll., no. 1015.
45. *The Mahābhārata* (Guj. *Padabandha*), Vol. VI, ed. K.K. Shastree, Forbes Gujarati Sabha, Bombay, 1951, Intro.
46. K.M. Munshi, *op.cit.*, pp. 166 f.

26

महाभारत के प्रमुख पात्रों की आयु
एक विवेचन

योगेश्वरी शास्त्री

महाभारत युद्ध भारतीय इतिहास की एक अभूतपूर्व घटना है और अनेक दृष्टियों से उसका विशिष्ट महत्त्व है। इस युद्ध में *महाभारत* के अनुसार, भारत के अधिकांश प्रदेशों की राजसत्ताओं ने कौरवों अथवा पाण्डवों की ओर से सक्रिय भूमिका अदा की। इस युद्ध के साथ ही द्वापर की समाप्ति होकर कलियुग का आरम्भ हुआ। इससे स्पष्ट है कि महाभारत युद्ध प्राचीन भारतीयों की दृष्टि में कितना महत्त्वपूर्ण था। किसी भी युद्ध में योद्धाओं की सफलता के लिए उनका स्वस्थ और बलवान होना अपेक्षित है और इस दृष्टि से उनकी आयु का अत्यधिक महत्त्व है। *महाभारत* में कुछ ऐसे उल्लेख हैं जिनसे भीष्म, द्रोण, युधिष्ठिर, भीमसेन, अर्जुन, नकुल, सहदेव, दुर्योधन, घटोत्कच, अभिमन्यु इत्यादि प्रमुख पात्रों की आयु पर महत्त्वपूर्ण प्रकाश पड़ता है। प्रस्तुत लेख का उद्देश्य *महाभारत* के वर्णन के आधार पर इन पात्रों की आयु का निर्धारण है। यद्यपि उनकी आयु के कुछ स्पष्ट उल्लेख भी मिलते हैं तथापि मुख्यतः उनके जीवन की घटनाओं और उनके बीच के अन्तराल को ध्यान में रखकर उनकी सामान्य आयु निकालने का प्रयत्न किया गया है।

भीष्म पितामह

भीष्म पितामह की आयु के निर्धारण के लिए इस लेख में उनकी माँ गंगा द्वारा अपने पति शान्तनु के हाथों भीष्म (देवव्रत) को सौंपने का वर्णन है। जिस समय उनको सौंपा गया, *महाभारत* के वर्णन के अनुसार वह शस्त्र और शास्त्र में पारंगत हो चुके थे। इसके लिए कम से कम बीस वर्ष की आयु अपेक्षित है।[1] *महाभारत* में यह स्पष्ट उल्लेख है कि राजा शान्तनु ने राजकाज में सहयोग के लिए देवव्रत को समस्त पौरवों के बीच युवराज पद पर अभिषिक्त किया गया और इस अमित पराक्रमी राजा

शान्तनु ने अपने गुणवान् पुत्र के साथ आनंदपूर्वक रहते हुए चार वर्ष व्यतीत किये[2]। भीष्म (देवव्रत) के जीवन की दूसरी महत्त्वपूर्ण घटना राजा शान्तनु का सत्यवती से विवाह है, जिसके कारण भीषण प्रतिज्ञा करके देवव्रत भीष्म कहलाये। इस समय तक भीष्म की आयु चौबीस वर्ष की हो चुकी थी। कुछ समय पश्चात् सत्यवती के गर्भ से चित्राङ्गद एवं विचित्रवीर्य पैदा हुए[3]। *महाभारत* में इनके समय का उल्लेख नहीं किया गया है। केवल "ततः" एवं "अथापरं" इन दो शब्दों का उल्लेख है। साधारण रूप से इन बालकों में दो वर्ष का अन्तराल तो रखना अपेक्षित ही होगा। अतः विचित्रवीर्य के पैदा होने के समय तक भीष्म की आयु सत्ताईस वर्ष की हो चुकी थी। शान्तनु के देहान्त के पश्चात् चित्राङ्गद को राजगद्दी पर आसीन करने का उल्लेख *महाभारत* में आता अवश्य है किन्तु उसकी उम्र का उल्लेख नहीं किया गया है। साधारणतः उस समय उसकी उम्र सोलह वर्ष की अपेक्षित की जा सकती है। *महाभारत* के अनुसार तीन वर्ष तक गन्धर्वराज के साथ भयंकर युद्ध करते हुए चित्राङ्गद मारा जाता है[4]। अर्थात् उस समय चित्राङ्गद की उम्र उन्नीस वर्ष रही होगी। राजगद्दी पुनः रिक्त हो जाती है। उस समय विचित्रवीर्य युवावस्था को प्राप्त नहीं हुआ था[5]। विचित्रवीर्य को चित्राङ्गद से दो वर्ष छोटा माने तो उनकी आयु शान्तनु की मृत्यु के समय सतरह वर्ष होनी चाहिए। भीष्म इस समय तक चवालीस वर्ष के हो चुके थे। *महाभारत* के अनुसार उन्होंने विचित्रवीर्य के युवावस्था तक पहुँचने तक राज्य संभाला[6]। यदि यह काल हम पाँच वर्ष का मानें तो भीष्म की आयु उनंचास वर्ष एवं विचित्रवीर्य की आयु बाईस वर्ष होनी अपेक्षित है। इसी अवस्था में काशीराज की पुत्रियों – अम्बिका और अम्बालिका – के साथ विचित्रवीर्य का विवाह होता है। विवाह के पश्चात् सात वर्ष तक निरन्तर विहार के कारण राजयक्ष्मा से उनकी मृत्यु का स्पष्ट उल्लेख *महाभारत* में आता है[7]। अतः उनतीस वर्ष की अवस्था में विचित्रवीर्य का देहान्त होता है। उस समय भीष्म की उम्र छप्पन वर्ष की हो चुकी थी। पुनः राजगद्दी पर संकट उपस्थित होता है। अतः माता सत्यवती ने भीष्म के परामर्श से कृष्ण द्वैपायन व्यास द्वारा नियोग की व्यवस्था की। इस व्यवस्था में एक वर्ष लगना स्वाभाविक ही है। अतः अम्बिका के गर्भ से व्यासपुत्र धृतराष्ट्र के पैदा होते समय भीष्म की उम्र अट्ठावन वर्ष तथा अम्बालिका के गर्भ से व्यासपुत्र पाण्डु के पैदा होते समय भीष्म की उम्र उनसठ वर्ष रही होगी। भीष्म की देखरेख में राजकुमार तथा हस्तिनापुर विकसित हो रहे थे। उन्होंने राजकुमारों का यज्ञोपवीत संस्कार करवाया[8]। यद्यपि *महाभारत* में तीनों कुमारों का यज्ञोपवीत एक साथ कराने का उल्लेख आता है, किन्तु क्षत्रियों का यज्ञोपवीत ग्यारह वर्ष की अवस्था में होने के कारण कुमारों की अवस्था में एक-एक वर्ष का अन्तर होना स्वाभाविक है। अतः धृतराष्ट्र के यज्ञोपवीत के समय भीष्म की उम्र सत्तर वर्ष तथा पाण्डु के समय इकत्तर वर्ष रही होगी। विद्याध्ययन में पारंगत होने के पश्चात् धृतराष्ट्र के जन्मान्ध होने के कारण पाण्डु

को राजगद्दी देने का *महाभारत* में उल्लेख आता है[9]। शस्त्र-शास्त्र के इस अध्ययन के समय को यदि दस वर्ष माना जाये तो पाण्डु की उम्र राजगद्दी के समय इक्कीस वर्ष रही होगी और भीष्म की इक्यासी वर्ष। सुबल की पुत्री गांधारी का विवाह धृतराष्ट्र के साथ, पाण्डु का विवाह कुन्ती के साथ और फिर कुछ समय पश्चात् माद्री के साथ होता है। एक माह तक राजभवन में रानियों के साथ विहार करने के पश्चात् राजा पाण्डु समूची पृथ्वी पर विजय प्राप्त करने की इच्छा से राजधानी से बाहर निकलते हैं। वे दशार्ण, मगध, विदेह, काशी, सुह्म, पुण्ड्र आदि पर विजय प्राप्त कर कुरूकुल का यश बढ़ाते हैं। इसके पश्चात् वे पत्नियों के साथ वन-विहार को चले जाते हैं। इन सभी घटनाओं को घटित होने में कम से कम सात वर्ष का समय तो व्यतीत हुआ ही होगा, अर्थात् उस समय पाण्डु की उम्र अठ्ठाईस वर्ष तथा भीष्म की अठ्ठासी वर्ष अपेक्षित की जा सकती है।

वन में पाण्डु द्वारा मृगरूपधारी मुनि का मृगरूपधारिणी पत्नी के साथ समागम के समय वध करना तथा उनसे शाप प्राप्त करना[10], पाण्डु का सन्यास ग्रहण करना तथा पत्नियों के अनुरोध पर वानप्रस्थ आश्रम में प्रवेश करना तथा पितृऋण से उर्ऋण होने के लिए कुन्ती से नियोग द्वारा सन्तान प्राप्ति की इच्छा प्रकट करना, इन सब घटनाओं का समय कम से कम दो वर्ष तो माना ही जा सकता है। अर्थात् उस समय पाण्डु की उम्र तीस वर्ष और भीष्म की नब्बे वर्ष रही होगी। *महाभारत* के अनुसार जब गांधारी को गर्भधारण किये एक वर्ष बीत गया उस समय कुन्ती ने विधिपूर्वक मंत्र का जाप किया तथा धर्म का आवाहन किया[11]। तदनन्तर उचित समय पर युधिष्ठिर का जन्म हुआ। पाण्डु के आग्रह पर वायु का आवाहन करके कुन्ती ने भीम को उत्पन्न किया। इसी प्रकार कुछ काल पश्चात् इन्द्र का आवाहन कर अर्जुन को जन्म दिया। पाण्डु की इच्छा से कुन्ती द्वारा माद्री को मन्त्र देना और अश्विनी कुमारों के आवाहन पर नकुल-सहदेव का जन्म होने का उल्लेख भी *महाभारत* में आता है। इसी प्रकार *महाभारत* के अनुसार जिस दिन दुर्योधन का जन्म हुआ उसी दिन परम पराक्रमी महाबाहु भीमसेन भी उत्पन्न हुए[12]। इस उल्लेख से यह स्पष्ट हो जाता है कि युधिष्ठिर दुर्योधन से ज्येष्ठ थे तथा भीम और दुर्योधन की उम्र समान थी। पाण्डवों के जन्म के बीच यदि हम दो-दो[13] वर्षों का अन्तराल रखें तो पाण्डु की उम्र सहदेव तक आते आते अड़तीस वर्ष की, तथा भीष्म की अठ्ठानवे वर्ष की हो जाती है। *महाभारत* में पाण्डुपुत्रों के गर्भाधान, चूडाकरण तथा उपनयन आदि संस्कारों के साथ-साथ वेदाध्ययन में पारंगत होने का भी उल्लेख आता है[14]। तत्पश्चात् अर्जुन के चौदह वर्ष का हो जाने पर एक दिन माद्री के प्रति पाण्डु का काम-मोहित होना एवं शापवश मृत्युमुखी हो जाने का वर्णन भी *महाभारत* में मिलता है[15]। अर्जुन की चौदह वर्ष की उम्र के इस उल्लेख से यह स्पष्ट हो जाता है कि पाण्डु निधन के समय बावन वर्ष के रहे होंगे तथा इस समय तक भीष्म की आयु

एक सौ बारह वर्ष, युधिष्ठिर की अठारह वर्ष, भीम की सोलह वर्ष, दुर्योधन की सोलह वर्ष, अर्जुन की चौदह वर्ष तथा नकुल-सहदेव की बारह वर्ष अपेक्षित की जा सकती है। पाण्डु के निधन के पश्चात् माद्री का उनके साथ सती होना, पाँचों पाण्डवों सहित कुन्ती का हस्तिनापुर आना, वहाँ पाण्डु और माद्री की अस्थियों का दाह-संस्कार कराना, भाई-बन्धुओं द्वारा जलांजलि देना, पाण्डवों और धृतराष्ट्रपुत्रों की बालक्रीड़ा, दुर्योधन का भीम को विष खिलाकर गंगा में ढकेल देना, सत्यवती, अम्बिका एवं अम्बालिका का वन-गमन, द्रोण का आगमन, कौरवों और पाण्डवों की अस्त्र-शस्त्र शिक्षा का आचार्य द्वारा परीक्षण, इन सभी घटनाओं के घटित होने के लिए पाँच वर्ष का समय आसानी से दिया जा सकता है। अर्थात् शस्त्र परीक्षा के समय भीष्म की उम्र एक सौ सतरह वर्ष, युधिष्ठिर की तेईस, भीम की इक्कीस, दुर्योधन की इक्कीस, अर्जुन की उन्नीस तथा नकुल-सहदेव की सतरह वर्ष रही होगी। शस्त्र परीक्षा के पश्चात् गुरु-दक्षिणा के रूप में आचार्य द्रोण का शिष्यों द्वारा द्रुपद पर आक्रमण करवाना, दुर्योधन का द्रुपद से पराजित होना, अर्जुन का द्रुपद को बन्दी बनाना, द्रोण द्वारा द्रुपद को आधा राज्य दे देना तथा एक वर्ष पश्चात् युधिष्ठिर का युवराज पद पर अभिषेक[16] आदि घटनाओं का वर्णन *महाभारत* में मिलता है। अर्थात् युवराज बनते समय युधिष्ठिर की उम्र चौबीस वर्ष, भीम की बाईस वर्ष, दुर्योधन की बाईस वर्ष, अर्जुन की बीस वर्ष, नकुल-सहदेव की अठारह वर्ष और भीष्म की एक सौ अठारह वर्ष रही होगी। युधिष्ठिर के युवराज बनने के पश्चात् शौर्य-प्रदर्शन के लिए अर्जुन का भीमसेन की सहायता से पूर्व दिशा के सम्पूर्ण योद्धाओं तथा दस हजार रथियों को जीतना, अर्जुन की दक्षिण दिशा पर विजय, तत्पश्चात् दुर्योधन की सलाह से धृतराष्ट्र द्वारा पाण्डवों को वारणावत भेजना, खनिक का सुरंग खोदना तथा पाण्डवों का वारणावत में एक वर्ष[17] तक रहना आदि का वर्णन *महाभारत* में प्राप्य है। इस घटना के पश्चात् भीष्म की आयु एक सौ उन्नीस वर्ष, अर्जुन की इक्कीस वर्ष, नकुल-सहदेव की उन्नीस वर्ष तथा दुर्योधन की तेईस वर्ष हो जाती है। इसके पश्चात् पाण्डवों का लाक्षागृह से बचकर नाव से गंगा पार करना, दक्षिण दिशा की ओर जाना, भीम द्वारा हिडिम्ब का वध, हिडिम्बा से मिलन और घटोत्कच की उत्पत्ति, एकचक्रा नगरी में पाण्डवों का प्रवेश, ब्राह्मण के घर पर निवास, भीम द्वारा बकासुर-वध, पाण्डवों का पांचाल देश जाना, अंगारपर्ण गन्धर्व को पराजित करना, द्रुपद की राजधानी में जाकर कुम्हार के घर रुकना, द्रौपदी-स्वयंवर में जाना, अर्जुन का लक्ष्य वेधना तथा द्रौपदी का विवाह पाण्डवों से होना, पाण्डवों के प्रति धृतराष्ट्र का प्रेम दिखाना,दुर्योधन की चिन्ता, भीष्म की दुर्योधन को पाण्डवों को आधा राज्य देने की सलाह, द्रोणाचार्य की पाण्डवों को उपहार भेजने और बुलाने की सलाह, धृतराष्ट्र की आज्ञा से विदुर का द्रुपद के यहाँ जाना, पाण्डवों को हस्तिनापुर बुलाना, आधा राज्य देना, इन्द्रप्रस्थ नगर का निर्माण करना, पाण्डवों में द्रौपदी को लेकर फूट न

पड़े अतः नारद का समझाना तथा कुछ नियम निर्धारित करना, अर्जुन का गोधन की रक्षा के लिए नियम भंग करना, भाई की आज्ञा लेकर अर्जुन का बारह वर्ष के वनवास के लिए प्रस्थान करना[18] तथा बारह वर्ष पूर्ण होने पर खाण्डवप्रस्थ लौटना[19] एवं कुछ काल पश्चात् (लगभग एक वर्ष) अभिमन्यु का पैदा होना[20] आदि *महाभारत* में वर्णित इन सब घटनाओं के आधार पर भीष्म की अभी तक की उम्र रेखा एक सौ इकतीस होती है। अर्जुन के खाण्डवप्रस्थ लौटने के पश्चात् की घटनाओं में खाण्डवप्रस्थ का जलाना, देवताओं की पराजय, मयासुर की रक्षा, मयासुर से सभाभवन बनवाना, कृष्ण का द्वारका जाना, सभाभवन का चौदह महीनों[21] में बनकर तैयार होना, युधिष्ठिर का सभाभवन में प्रवेश करना आदि सब मिलाकर इन घटनाओं का समय दो वर्ष तो हो ही सकता है। अर्थात् इस समय तक भीष्म की उम्र एक सौ तैंतीस वर्ष की हो चुकी थी। तत्पश्चात् युधिष्ठिर द्वारा राजसूय यज्ञ का संकल्प करना, कृष्ण, अर्जुन एवं भीम की मगध-यात्रा, भीम द्वारा जरासंध-वध, कृष्ण आदि का इन्द्रप्रस्थ आना और वहाँ से द्वारका जाना, चारों पाण्डवों का दिग्विजय के लिए निकलना, अर्जुन का उत्तर दिशा, भीम का पूर्व दिशा, सहदेव का दक्षिण दिशा तथा नकुल का पश्चिम दिशा पर विजय प्राप्त करना और इन्द्रप्रस्थ लौटना, कृष्ण की आज्ञा से राजसूय यज्ञ के लिए युधिष्ठिर का ब्राह्मणों, राजाओं, सगे-सम्बन्धियों को निमंत्रण भेजना, कृष्ण का अग्रपूजा में शिशुपाल का विरोध तथा कृष्ण द्वारा उसका वध, यज्ञ की समाप्ति, दुर्योधन का सभाभवन देखना, भ्रमवश पानी में गिरना, दीवार से टकराना आदि घटनाओं को हम कम से कम पाँच वर्ष का समय तो दे ही सकते हैं। अर्थात उस समय तक भीष्म की उम्र एक सौ अड़तीस वर्ष हो चुकी थी। तत्पश्चात् पाण्डवों की समृद्धि से जलने के कारण धृतराष्ट्र की आज्ञा से विदुर को भेजकर पाण्डवों को द्यूतक्रीड़ा के लिए हस्तिनापुर बुलाना, द्यूतक्रीड़ा में युधिष्ठिर का धन, राज्य, भाइयों तथा द्रौपदी सहित हारना, दुःशासन का एकवस्त्रा, रजःस्वला द्रौपदी को केश पकड़कर भरी सभा में घसीटकर लाना, चीरहरण करना, भीमसेन का क्रोधित होना तथा युद्ध में दुःशासन की छाती फाड़कर लहू पीने की प्रतिज्ञा करना, धृतराष्ट्र का युधिष्ठिर को सब कुछ लौटा देना और इन्द्रप्रस्थ भेजना, दुर्योधन का धृतराष्ट्र को अर्जुन की वीरता से भय बतलाकर पुनः द्यूतक्रीड़ा के लिए पाण्डवों को बुलाना, गांधारी का धृतराष्ट्र को चेतावनी देना और धृतराष्ट्र द्वारा अस्वीकृत किया जाना, सबके मना करने पर भी धृतराष्ट्र की आज्ञा से युधिष्ठिर का द्यूत खेलना और हारना, शर्त हारने पर बारह वर्ष का वनवास और एक वर्ष का अज्ञातवास मिलना, वन जाते समय अर्जुन का भीम से कहना कि "साधु पुरुष वाणी द्वारा सूचित नहीं करते, आज से चौहदवें वर्ष में जो घटना घटित होगी, उसे स्वयं ही देख लेंगे",[22] तत्पश्चात् कुन्ती का विदुर के घर रहना, पाण्डवों का धृतराष्ट्र आदि से विदा लेना, *महाभारत* में उल्लिखित इन घटनाओं के आधार पर वनवास-समाप्ति तक भीष्म की आयु एक सौ इक्यावन वर्ष हो चुकी थी।

अभिमन्यु के विवाह के पश्चात् की सारी घटनाएँ – पाण्डवों द्वारा पुरोहित को हस्तिनापुर भेजना, उसका कौरव-सभा में भाषण, कर्ण का आक्षेप, कृष्ण का दुर्योधन और अर्जुन दोनों को युद्ध में सहायता देना, शल्य का दुर्योधन के साथ आना, धृतराष्ट्र का संजय को पाण्डवों के पास भेजना तथा शान्ति की प्रार्थना करना, इन्द्रप्रस्थ देने पर शान्ति हो सकती है ऐसा युधिष्ठिर का कहना, संजय को प्रत्युत्तर देते हुए धृतराष्ट्र को कृष्ण की चेतावनी देना, संजय की विदाई, विदुर का धृतराष्ट्र को समझाना, कौरव-सभा में संजय द्वारा अर्जुन-संवाद सुनाना, भीष्म का दुर्योधन को सन्धि के लिए समझाना, कृष्ण का कौरव-सभा में शान्तिदूत बनकर जाना, सन्धि का प्रयत्न करना, धृतराष्ट्र के अनुरोध पर कृष्ण का दुर्योधन का समझाना, भीष्म, द्रोण, विदुर एवं धृतराष्ट्र का दुर्योधन को समझाना, कृष्ण को दुर्योधन का राज्य न देने का निश्चय सुनाना, दुर्योधन का कृष्ण को पकड़ने का षडयंत्र करना, सात्यकि द्वारा भंडाफोड़ करना, कृष्ण द्वारा सिंह-गर्जना, विराटरूप दर्शन कराकर कौरवों की सभा से प्रस्थान करना, कृष्ण का कर्ण को पाण्डव-पक्ष में आने के लिए समझाना, कुन्ती का कर्ण को समझाना, धृतराष्ट्र का दुर्योधन को पाण्डवों को आधा राज्य देने का आदेश, सबकुछ प्रयत्न असफल होना, दोनों पक्षों का अपने-अपने सेनापति बनाना, युद्ध के नियम निर्धारण करना, कुरूक्षेत्र में प्रवेश करना, शिविर का निर्माण करना, बलराम का पाण्डवों से विदा लेकर तीर्थ जाना, रुक्मी का युद्ध में सहायता के लिए आना, किन्तु दोनों पक्षों के द्वारा कोरा उत्तर देने पर निकल जाना, दुर्योधन द्वारा उलूक को दूत बनाकर भेजना, पाण्डव-सभा में उसका संदेश सुनाना, पाण्डव-पक्ष की ओर से दुर्योधन को उत्तर, उत्तर सुनकर सेना को तैयार होने का आदेश, युद्ध का आरम्भ, आरम्भ होते ही अर्जुन का मोहग्रसित होकर हथियार डालना, कृष्ण का (गीता) उपदेश देना, इन सभी घटानाओं को हम कम से कम दो वर्ष तो दे ही सकते हैं, अतः युद्ध के समय तक भीष्म की आयु एक सौ तिरपन वर्ष की थी।

अतः एक सौ तिरपन वर्ष की आयु में भीष्म ने महाभारत युद्ध में कौरव-सेना का सेनापतित्व दस दिन के लिए संभाला। पाण्डवों के लिए उनको मारना बहुत ही कठीन कार्य था। अंतिम दो दिनों के युद्ध में तो उन्होंने भंयकर तबाही मचा दी थी। अतः उनको मारने के लिए पाण्डवों को शिखंडी का आश्रय लेना पड़ा। यह भीष्म की अकाट्य वीरता का प्रमाण है और एक सौ तिरपन वर्ष के योद्धा के सम्बन्ध में निश्चय ही विचारणीय प्रश्न है। उनके नेतृत्व का काल कौरव-सेना के लिए सबसे अधिक सफलता का रहा यद्यपि इस अवधि में भी कई महान् कौरव सेनानायक मारे गये। किन्तु बाद के समय को देखते हुए यह एक अद्भुत प्रदर्शन था यह मानना पड़ेगा।

द्रोणाचार्यः

भीष्म पितामह के बाद द्रोणाचार्य कौरव-सेना के सेनापति बने और उनके नेतृत्व में कौरव-सेना ने पाँच दिन तक युद्ध किया। यह देखना उपादेय होगा कि युद्ध के

समय द्रोणाचार्य का वय क्या था, इस सम्बन्ध में *महाभारत* में केवल एक ही उल्लेख मिलता है, जैसा कि निम्नलिखित विवेचन से स्पष्ट होता है।

महाभारत में द्रोण का आगमन पितृविहीन पाण्डुपुत्रों के वन से लौटने के बाद होता है। वे कौरवों और पाण्डवों दोनों के ही गुरु थे। वह शिष्यों का उपयोग द्रुपद से अपना प्रतिशोध लेने के लिए करते हैं, यह गुरु-दक्षिणा के समय स्पष्ट हो जाता है। उस समय अर्जुन द्रुपद को बंदी बनाकर द्रोण को सौंपता है और द्रोण आधा राज्य रखकर आधा द्रुपद को लौटाते हैं। कौरव-सभा में उनका स्थान महत्त्वपूर्ण है। कौरवों द्वारा सम्मानित होकर, यश और वैभवपूर्ण जिन्दगी व्यतीत करते हुए वे अन्त में युद्ध में उन्हीं के पक्ष का समर्थन करते हैं। उनकी उम्र का उल्लेख सम्पूर्ण *महाभारत* में एक ही स्थान पर आता है। द्रोणवधपर्व में संजय द्वारा धृतराष्ट्र से कहा गया है कि "आचार्य के शरीर का रंग सांवला था, उनकी अवस्था पिच्यासी वर्ष की हो चुकी थी और उनके ऊपर से लेकर कान तक के बाल सफेद हो गये थे। फिर भी आपके हित के लिए वे संग्राम में सोलह वर्ष की उम्र के तरुण के समान विचरते थे"[23]।

पिच्यासी वर्ष के द्रोणचार्य ने पाँच दिन के युद्ध में भयंकर मारकाट की। वे दुर्योधन की इच्छा पूरी करने के लिए युधिष्ठिर को जीवित पकड़ने की प्रतिज्ञा करते हैं तथा पाण्डव-पक्ष के अनेक वीरों का वध करते हैं। गरुडव्यूह का निर्माण कर गजसेना का भारी संहार करते हैं। पांचालकुमार सत्यजित् का, विराट के छोटे भाई शतानीक का, दृढसेन, क्षेम तथा वसुदान नामक राजाओं का वध करते हैं। इसी प्रकार युद्ध में सात्यकि, चेकितान कुमार, सेनाबिन्दु तथा सुवर्चा इन सभी राजाओं को पराजित करते हैं। दुर्योधन के उपालम्भ से दुखित होकर चक्रव्यूह की रचना करते हैं, अर्जुन को त्रिगर्तों से युद्ध के लिए दूर भेजकर अभिमन्यु-वध करवाते हैं। तेरहवें दिन (द्रोण के नेतृत्व का तीसरा दिन) का युद्ध महाभयंकर होता है। वे अर्जुन, धृष्टद्युम्न तथा युधिष्ठिर के साथ भयंकर युद्ध करते हैं तथा उन्हें पराजित भी करते हैं। वीरकेतु आदि पांचालों को बृहतक्षेत्र, धृष्टकेतु, जरासंघ-पुत्र सहदेव, धृष्टद्युम्नकुमार, क्षालधर्मा एवं शिबि का वध करते हैं। वीर घटोत्कच का वध भी इन्हीं के नेतृत्व में कर्ण द्वारा होता है। ये द्रुपद के पौत्रों, द्रुपद एवं विराट् का वध भी स्वयं ही करते हैं। इनकी भयंकर वीरता को सहन न कर पाने के कारण ही युधिष्ठिर अश्वत्थामा की मृत्यु का समाचार देकर गुरु द्रोण को अस्त्र-शस्त्र त्याग करने को मजबूर कर देते हैं और अन्त में धृष्टद्युम्न द्वारा इसी अवस्था में मार दिये जाते हैं। इस प्रकार पाँच दिन रण में भयंकर तबाही मचाकर, प्रसिद्ध सेनानायकों का वध करके, कौरवों के प्रति अपना कर्त्तव्य निभाकर यह महान् सेनानायक पिच्यासी वर्ष की अवस्था में शरीर त्याग देता है।

पिच्यासी वर्ष का वृद्ध इतने महान् वीर योद्धाओं का वध कर सकेगा, जिसकी

वीरता को देखकर युवावर्ग भी भयभीत होगा, बार-बार सेना पलायन करेगी और अन्त में उस अबध्य महान् सेनानायक को धोखे से मारना भी इस बात का प्रमाण है कि वह महान् वीर था। उसका सामना करना सबके लिए कठिन हो रहा था। *महाभारत* का यह एक विचारणीय प्रश्न है।

अभिमन्यु

भीष्म के सेनापतित्व तक तो युद्ध के निर्धारित नियमों का थोड़े बहुत अपवादों के साथ पालन किया जाता रहा। परन्तु उसके बाद तो ये नियम जैसे रह ही नहीं गये और इसका सबसे बड़ा उदाहरण है अभिमन्यु के साथ कौरवों का युद्ध। इस युद्ध के समय अभिमन्यु की आयु बहुत कम थी, जैसा कि अधोलिखित विवेचन से स्पष्ट है।

पाण्डुपुत्रों के गर्भाधान से लेकर चूडाकरण और उपनयन तक सभी संस्कार तथा वेदाध्ययन एवं तपस्या के लिए आए हुए महात्मा राजा शुक द्वारा शतश्रृंग पर्वत पर पाण्डवों को धनुर्वेद में पारंगत करने का वर्णन *महाभारत* में आता है[24]। पाण्डु के निधन के समय अर्जुन की उम्र चौदह वर्ष की थी इसका उल्लेख भी *महाभारत* में किया गया है,[25] पाण्डवों के कुन्ती के साथ हस्तिनापुर आने के पश्चात् अनेक घटनाएँ घटती हैं, जैसे – पाण्डु और माद्री की अस्थियों का दाह-संस्कार, भाई-बन्धुओं द्वारा जलांजलि, पाण्डवों तथा धृतराष्ट्र-पुत्रों की बालक्रीड़ा, दुर्योधन का भीम को विष खिलाकर गंगा में ढकेलना, सत्यवती, अम्बिका तथा अम्बालिका का वन-गमन, द्रोण का आगमन और कौरव-पाण्डवों की शिक्षा, इन सभी घटनाओं के लिए पाँच वर्ष का समय दिया जा सकता है, अतः आचार्य द्रोण द्वारा राजकुमारों की शस्त्र-परिक्षा के समय अर्जुन की उम्र उन्नीस वर्ष अपेक्षित की जा सकती है। उसके बाद की घटनाओं में गुरु-दक्षिणा हेतु प्रथम दुर्योधन और द्रुपद का युद्ध, दुर्योधन की पराजय, अर्जुन द्वारा द्रुपद को बन्दी बनाया जाना तथा एक वर्ष पश्चात् धृतराष्ट्र द्वारा पाण्डु-पुत्र युधिष्ठिर को युवराज पद पर अभिषिक्त करना,[26] राष्ट्र की वृद्धि तथा शौर्य दिखाने हेतु अर्जुन और भीम का पूर्व तथा दक्षिण दिशा को विजित करना,[27] दुर्योधन की सलाह से धृतराष्ट्र द्वारा पाण्डवों को वारणावत भेजा जाना, वहाँ एक वर्ष तक निवास करना[28], लाक्षागृह का जलना तथा बाद की सभी घटनाओं को यदि हम छोड़ भी दें तो द्रौपदी-विवाह के समय अर्जुन की उम्र इक्कीस वर्ष अपेक्षित की जा सकती है। इसके पश्चात् पाण्डवों का हस्तिनापुर आना तथा आधा राज्य प्राप्त करना, द्रौपदी को लेकर फूट न हो अतः नारदजी द्वारा समझाना, एक नियम निर्धारण करना, गोधन की रक्षा के लिए अर्जुन का नियम भंग करना और बारह वर्ष के लिए वनवास जाना,[29] गंगाद्वार में ऐरावत कुलोत्पन्न कौरव्य नामक नागराज की कन्या उलूपी से विवाह करना, पुत्र इरावान् का उत्पन्न होना, मणिपूर-नरेश चित्रवाहन की पुत्री चित्राङ्गदा से विवाह करना, तीन वर्ष तक उसके साथ नगर में निवास करना[30],

पुत्र बभ्रुवाहन का जन्म होना, प्रभास तीर्थ में कृष्ण का मिलना, रैवतक पर्वत पर सुभद्रा के प्रति आसक्त होना, द्वारकापुरी जाना, कृष्ण की सलाह तथा युधिष्ठिर की सहमति से सुभद्रा-हरण एवं विवाह करना तथा एक वर्ष से[31] अधिक समय तक द्वारका में सुभद्रा के साथ निवास करना, वहाँ से पुष्कर तीर्थ जाना, वनवास की शेष अवधि वहीं पूर्ण करके[32] इन्द्रप्रस्थ लौटना, लगभग एक वर्ष पश्चात् अभिमन्यु का जन्म होना[33]। उपर्युक्त तथ्यों के आधार पर इस समय तक अर्जुन की उम्र चौंतीस वर्ष की होती है। अर्जुन के खाण्डवप्रस्थ लौटने के बाद की घटनाएँ इस प्रकार हैं – अर्जुन का कृष्ण के साथ खाण्डववन जाना, ब्राह्मणवेशधारी अग्नि से मिलना, खाण्डववन को जलाना, देवताओं को पराजित करना तथा मयासुर की रक्षा करना, मयासुर से कृष्ण द्वारा अद्वितीय सभाभवन का चौदह महीनों में पूर्ण होना।[34] इन घटनाओं और चौदह महीनों की अवधि सब मिलाकर दो वर्ष तो माना ही जा सकता है, अर्थात् अर्जुन की उम्र इस समय छत्तीस वर्ष की रही होगी। तत्पश्चात् युधिष्ठिर का सभाभवन में प्रवेश करना, उनका राजसूय यज्ञ करने का संकल्प करना, श्रीकृष्ण, अर्जुन और भीम का मगध की ओर प्रस्थान, जरासंध-वध, बंदी राजाओं की मुक्ति, जरासंध-पुत्र सहदेव को राजगद्दी पर बैठाना, कृष्ण आदि का इन्द्रप्रस्थ आना, वहाँ से द्वारका जाना, चारों पाण्डवों की दिग्वियज-यात्रा, अर्जुन का उत्तर दिशा, भीम का पूर्व दिशा, सहदेव का दक्षिण दिशा तथा नकुल का पश्चिम दिशा की ओर प्रस्थान करना तथा सभी दिशाओं को जीतकर इन्द्रप्रस्थ लौटना, कृष्ण की आज्ञा से युधिष्ठिर का राजसूय यज्ञ की दीक्षा लेना, राजाओं, ब्राह्मणों और सगे-सम्बन्धियों को निमंत्रण भेजना, कृष्ण की अग्रपूजा करना, शिशुपाल का अग्रपूजा का विरोध तथा कृष्ण द्वारा उसका वध, यज्ञ की समाप्ति, राजाओं का स्वदेश लौटना, दुर्योधन एवं शकुनि का मयसभा देखना, दुर्योधन का भ्रमवश पानी में गिरना, दीवार से टकराना, उसका क्रोधित होकर हस्तिनापुर जाना, इन सभी घटनाओं को घटित होने में कम से कम पाँच वर्ष तो लगे ही होंगे। अतः इस समय अर्जुन की अवस्था इकतालीस वर्ष की अपेक्षित की जा सकती है तथा अभिमन्यु की सात वर्ष। तत्पश्चात् धृतराष्ट्र द्वारा विदुर को भेजकर पाण्डवों को द्यूत के लिए हस्तिनापुर आमंत्रित करना, द्यूतक्रीड़ा में युधिष्ठिर का राज्य, धन, भाइयों तथा द्रौपदी हार जाना, दुःशासन का द्रौपदी को केश पकड़कर सभा में लाया जाना, भीम का क्रोधित होकर युद्ध में दुःशासन की छाती का लहू पीने की प्रतिज्ञा करना, धृतराष्ट्र का युधिष्ठिर को सब कुछ लौटाकर इन्द्रप्रस्थ भेजना, दुर्योधन का धृतराष्ट्र से अर्जुन की वीरता का भय बतलाकर पुनः द्यूतक्रीड़ा के लिए पाण्डवों को आमंत्रित करवाना, सबके मना करने पर भी धृतराष्ट्र की आज्ञा से युधिष्ठिर का द्यूत खेलना और हारना तथा शर्त के अनुसार बारह वर्ष वनवास और एक वर्ष अज्ञातवास के लिए निकल पड़ना, *महाभारत* में बारह वर्ष बीतने तथा तेरहवें वर्ष के प्रारम्भ होने का वर्णन विराट्पर्व में आता है[35] जहाँ पाण्डव

गुप्तरूप से एक वर्ष व्यतीत करने की योजना बनाते हैं तथा युधिष्ठिर कङ्क, भीम वल्लभ, अर्जुन बृहन्नला, नकुल ग्रान्धिपाल, सहदेव तन्तिपाल और द्रौपदी सैरन्ध्री बनकर राजा विराट् के यहाँ अपना समय बिताते हैं। तत्पश्चात् दुर्योधन को गुप्तचरों द्वारा कीचकवध की घटना सुनाना, दुर्योधन का शक करना और भीष्म आदि की सम्मति लेकर मत्स्य देश पर धावा बोलना, पाण्डवों के साथ विराट् द्वारा युद्ध का सामना करना और पाण्डवों का जीतना, कौरवों का विराट् की गायों का उत्तर दिशा की ओर से आकर अपहरण करना, उत्तर को युद्ध के लिए प्रेरित करना, अर्जुन का उत्तर का सारथी बनना, उत्तर का भयभीत होकर रणभूमि से भागना, अर्जुन द्वारा उत्तर से शमीवृक्ष से अपने हथियार उतारना, कौरव-सेना को पराजित करना, विराट् की गायों को छुड़ाना, इस समय तक पाण्डवों के तेरह वर्ष बीत जाना, चान्द्र वर्ष और सौर वर्ष दोनों ही गणनाओं से समय का पूर्ण होना[36], पाण्डवों का प्रकट होना, राजा विराट् का प्रसन्न होकर उत्तरा के साथ अर्जुन-पुत्र अभिमन्यु का विवाह निश्चित करना तथा राजा विराट् के उपप्लव्य नामक नगर में पाण्डवों द्वारा अपने सगे-सम्बन्धियों को बुलाकर अभिमन्यु-उत्तरा का विवाह रचाना, कृष्ण का द्वारका लौट जाने का वर्णन है। विवाह के समय अभिमन्यु की उम्र बीस वर्ष तथा अर्जुन की चव्वन वर्ष अपेक्षित की जा सकती है।

अभिमन्यु-विवाह के पश्चात् की सारी घटनाएँ युद्ध का रोकने से सम्बन्धित है। इनमें सर्वप्रथम पुरोहित का हस्तिनापुर में कौरव-सभा में भाषण, कर्ण का आक्षेप, कृष्ण का दुर्योधन और अर्जुन दोनों को युद्ध में सहायता देना, शल्य का दुर्योधन से प्रसन्न होकर युद्ध में उसका साथ देना, धृतराष्ट्र का संजय को पाण्डवों के पास भेजना, संजय द्वारा धृतराष्ट्र को संदेश देना और शान्ति की प्रार्थना करना, इन्द्रप्रस्थ देने पर ही शान्ति होगी ऐसा युधिष्ठिर का कहना, संजय को प्रत्युत्तर देते हुए कृष्ण का संजय को धृतराष्ट्र के लिए चेतावनी देना, संजय की विदाई, युधिष्ठिर का संदेश, विदुर द्वारा धृतराष्ट्र को समझाना, कौरव-सभा में संजय द्वारा अर्जुन संवाद सुनाना, भीष्म का दुर्योधन को सन्धि के लिए समझाना, धृतराष्ट्र का दुर्योधन को समझाना, दुर्योधन द्वारा युद्ध का निश्चय, कृष्ण का कौरव-सभा में शान्तिदूत बनकर जाना, सन्धि का प्रयत्न करना, सभा में भाषण देना, धृतराष्ट्र के अनुरोध पर कृष्ण का दुर्योधन को समझाना, भीष्म, द्रोण, विदुर तथा धृतराष्ट्र का दुर्योधन को समझाना, कृष्ण को दुर्योधन का उत्तर राज्य न देने का निश्चय, कृष्ण का दुर्योधन को फटकारना, दुर्योधन का कृष्ण को पकड़ने का षड्यंत्र करना, सात्यकि द्वारा भंडाफोड़, कृष्ण की सिंह-गर्जना, धृतराष्ट्र एवं गांधारी का पुनः दुर्योधन को समझाना, कृष्ण का विश्वरूप दर्शन कराना तथा कौरव-सभा से प्रस्थान करना, कृष्ण का कर्ण को पाण्डव-पक्ष में आने के लिए समझाना, कुन्ती का कर्ण को समझाना, धृतराष्ट्र का दुर्योधन को पाण्डवों को आधा राज्य देने का आदेश, सब प्रयत्नों का असफल होना,

दोनों पक्षों का अपने-अपने सेनापति निर्धारित करना, कुरूक्षेत्र-प्रवेश, शिविर का निर्माण करना, दुर्योधन द्वारा भीष्म को प्रधान सेनापति बनाना तथा पाण्डवों द्वारा धृष्टद्युम्न को सेनापति बनाना, बलराम का आना और पाण्डवों से विदा लेकर तीर्थ को निकल जाना, रुक्मी का युद्ध में सहायता के लिए आना किन्तु दोनों पक्षों के द्वारा कोरा उत्तर देने पर निकल जाना, दुर्योधन द्वारा उलूक को दूत बनाकर भेजना, पाण्डव-सभा में उसका संदेश सुनाना, पाण्डव पक्ष की ओर से दुर्योधन को उत्तर, उत्तर सुनकर सेना तैयार होने का आदेश देना, युद्ध का आरम्भ, इन सभी घटनाओं को हम कम से कम दो वर्ष का समय दे सकते हैं। अतः युद्ध के समय तक अर्जुन की उम्र छप्पन वर्ष तथा अभिमन्यु की बाईस वर्ष तो अपेक्षित की जा सकती है।

बाईस वर्ष के योद्धा अभिमन्यु का भीष्म के सेनापतित्व के समय से ही *महाभारत* में वर्णन प्रारम्भ हो जाता है। उसकी वीरता और शूरता भीष्म, द्रोण तथा अन्य कौरवों द्वारा स्थान-स्थान पर सराही गई है। वह भीष्म के साथ युद्ध करता है तथा उसे रोकने के लिए भीष्म को दिव्यास्त्रों का प्रयोग भी करना पड़ता है। अभिमन्यु का भीष्म द्वारा बनाये गये व्यूह का भंग करना, भीष्म-अर्जुन युद्ध के समय ढाल बनकर खड़ा होना, भीष्म, कृप, द्रोण, अश्वत्थामा जैसे महारथियों के साथ युद्ध करना और उन्हें पराजित करना। अनेकदा कौरव-पक्ष के महारथियों से घिरने के पश्चात् भी सकुशल बच निकलना, समस्त महारथियों पर अभिमन्यु का आक्रमण असह्य हो जाना आदि अभिमन्यु की वीरता के वर्णनों से भीष्म-नेतृत्व के दस दिन भरे पड़े हैं। द्रोणाचार्य का सेनापतित्व-काल, जो पाँच दिन चलता है उसमे प्रथम दिन से ही अभिमन्यु की वीरता की चर्चा प्रारम्भ हो जाती है। वह कौरवों पर आक्रमण कर उनके ध्वज, छत्र, धनुष काटकर उन्हें तथा उनके सारथि को क्षत-विक्षत कर देता है। जयद्रथ के सामना करने पर उसे भी घायल करता है। अन्य राजाओं द्वारा घिर जाने पर वह उत्साहपूर्वक सबको घायल कर घेरे से मुक्त हो जाता है। महाभारत युद्ध के तेरहवें दिन (द्रोण के सेनापतित्व के तीसरे दिन) के युद्ध में अर्जुन को दूर संसप्तकगणों से लड़ने निकल जाने पर द्रोण द्वारा चक्रव्यूह रचना, अभिमन्यु द्वारा चक्रव्यूह भेदना, जयद्रथ द्वारा व्यूह के अन्दर किसी भी पाण्डव वीर को प्रवेश न करने के कारण अभिमन्यु का कौरवों में एकाकी पड़ जाना किन्तु हमेशा की भाँति शत्रुओं द्वारा घेर लिए जाने पर भी न घबराने वाला यह निडर योद्धा युद्धभूमि में योद्धाओं का, रथों का, गजों का संहार पतंगों की भाँति प्रारम्भ कर देता है। वह भगवान विष्णु के समान युद्ध में सुशोभित होता है। शत्रु उससे भयभीत होकर दिशाओं को देखने लगते हैं तथा उनके मुख सूखने लगते हैं। इसी अवस्था में वह वीर योद्धा अश्मकपुत्र को मार डालता है तथा शल्य को घायल कर देता है। कौरव-पक्ष के अन्य योद्धाओं में कर्ण के भाई का तथा वसातीय आदि योद्धाओं का वध करता है। उससे भयाक्रान्त होकर द्रोण की सेना के पांव उखड़ जातें हैं। इसी समय कृपाचार्य उसकी वीरता की सराहना करते हुए कहतें हैं कि 'उन्होनें आज तक अभिमन्यु के समान दूसरा

वीर नहीं देखा'। इतना ही नहीं सत्यश्रवा, रुक्मरथ तथा उसके मित्रगणों और सैकड़ों राजकुमारों का उसके द्वारा वध किये जाने का वर्णन *महाभारत* के द्रोणपर्व के तेरहवें दिन (द्रोण के सेनापतित्व का तीसरा दिन) आता है। इसी दिन उसके द्वारा दुर्योधन को पराजित करना, लक्ष्मण तथा क्रथ-पुत्र का वध करना, वृन्दारक तथा दस हजार अन्य राजाओं सहित कोसल-नरेश बृहद्बल का वध करना, अश्वकेतु, भोज और कर्ण के मन्त्री का वध करना भी शामिल है। ऐसी ही कठिन परिस्थिति में युद्ध करता हुआ वह धनुष, रथ, ढाल और तलवार से रहित होकर रणभूमि में रथ के पहिये को ढाल बनाकर काल के समान विचरण करते हुए कालिकेय, वसति तथा कैकय रथियों का वध करता है और इसी समय वह कौरव-पक्ष के छह महारथियों द्वारा क्रूरतापूर्वक मारा जाता है।

इस अद्भुत वीर के लिए धृतराष्ट्र संयज से कहते हैं कि वह तरुण कुमार अभी बालक था, युद्ध की कला में पूरा प्रवीण नहीं हुआ था। फिर गहन वन में फसें हुए सुन्दर अश्व की भाँति वह उस विषम संग्राम में कैसे सकुशल रह सकता था[37]। इस श्लोक से भी अभिमन्यु की आयु बाईस वर्ष से अधिक नहीं थी यह प्रमाणित होता है। उसने अभी-अभी युवावस्था में पदार्पण ही किया था कि वह वीर स्वर्गलोक सिधार गया।

बाईस वर्ष का तरुण, निपट एकाकी अवस्था में शत्रु-पक्ष से घिरकर भी अनेक योद्धाओं का वध कर सकेगा, जिसकी वीरता को देखकर शत्रु-पक्ष भयभीत हो उठेगा, बार-बार शत्रु-पक्ष के योद्धा मिलकर उसको मारने का प्रयास करेंगे और अन्त में उस महान वीर तरुण बालक को नियम भंग करते हुए सबका एक साथ घेरकर मारना भी इस बात का प्रमाण है कि वह अकेला ही सब पर भारी पड़ रहा था। उसका सामना करना सबके लिए असह्य हो उठा था। *महाभारत* का यह भी एक विचारणीय प्रश्न है।

ऊपर हमने *महाभारत* में उल्लिखित घटनाओं और स्पष्ट आयु-संकेतों के आधार पर भीष्म, द्रोण, दुर्योधन, पाण्डवों तथा अभिमन्यु की आयु निश्चित करने का प्रयत्न किया है। यह लेख से संलग्न चार्ट में भी प्रदर्शित किया गया है। जैसा कि इस विवेचन से स्पष्ट है। इनमें से भीष्म और द्रोण की आयु तो युद्ध के सनय बहुत अधिक थी, इतनी अधिक कि हम उनके युद्ध में भाग लेने की कल्पना भी नहीं कर सकते। इस लेख में हमने घटनाओं को न्यूनतम समय दिया है और यदि इन घटनाओं के घटने में कुछ कम समय भी लगा हो तो वह आठ-दस वर्ष कम हो सकती है, पर इतना होने पर भी उनकी आयु युद्ध के समय अकल्पनीय है। इसमें कहां तक सच्चाई है यह निर्णय करना कठिन है। सबसे कम आयु थी अभिमन्यु की और उसके द्वारा युद्ध में इतनी वीरता प्रदर्शित करना और अनेक विख्यात महारथियों के साथ इतना भयानक युद्ध करना भी आश्चर्य की बात है।

महाभारत के पात्रों की युद्ध के समय की आयु

कृष्ण
56

कृष्ण-द्वैपायन व्यास
128

भीष्म पितामह 153

कौरव

पाण्डव

धृतराष्ट्र
95

गांधारी
90

निधन के समय
पाण्डु
52

माद्री
33

दुर्योधन
58

दुःशासन
56

युद्ध के समय कुन्ती
90

कर्ण
62

युधिष्ठिर
60

भीम
58

अर्जुन
56

नकुल
54

सहदेव
54

घटोत्कच
35

अभिमन्यु
22

युद्ध के समय **द्रोणाचार्य**
85

कृपाचार्य
लगभग 85

द्रुपद (पांचालनरेश और द्रोणाचार्य के सहपाठी)
85

शिखंडी
54

धृष्टद्युम्न
52

द्रौपदी
50

वनगमन के समय

1. सत्यवती (शान्तनु की पत्नी)
   98
2. अम्बिका (विचित्रवीर्य की पत्नी)
   69
3. अम्बालिका (विचित्रवीर्य की पत्नी)
   69

NOTES AND REFERENCES

1. महाभारत, गीताप्रेस, गोरखपुर, आदिपर्व 100/33-37

यं पुत्रमष्टमं राजंस्त्वं पुरा मय्यविन्दथाः ।
स चायं पुरुषव्याघ्र सर्वास्त्रविदनुत्तमः ।। 33 ।।

वेदानधिजगे साङ्गान् वसिष्ठादेष वीर्यवान्।
कृतास्त्रः परमेष्वासो देवराजसमो युधि ।। 35 ।।

2. वही, 100/44-45,

राष्ट्रं च रञ्जयामास वृत्तेन भरतर्षभ ।
स तथा सह पुत्रेण रममाणो महीमतिः ।। 44 ।।

वर्तयामास वर्षाणि चत्वार्यमितविक्रमः ।
स कदाचिद् वनं यातो यमुनामभितो नदीम् ।। 45 ।।

3. वही, 101/2-3

ततः शान्तनवो धीमान् सत्यवत्यामजायत।
वीरश्चित्राङ्गदो नाम वीर्यवान् पुरुषेश्रवरः ।। 2 ।।

अथापरं महेष्वासं सत्यवत्यां सुतं प्रभुः ।
विचित्रवीर्यं राजानं जनयामास वीर्यवान् ।। 3 ।।

4. वही, 101/8

तेनास्य सुमहद् युद्धं कुरूक्षेत्रे बभूव ह ।
तयोर्बलवतोस्तत्र गन्धर्वकुरुमुख्ययोः।
नद्यास्तीरे सरस्वत्याः समास्तिस्त्रोऽभवद् रणः।। 8 ।।

5. वही, 101/4

अप्राप्तवति तस्मिंस्तु यौवनं पुरुषर्षभ।
स राजा शान्तनुर्धीमान् कालधर्ममुपेयिवान्।। 4 ।।

6. वही, 102/1

हते चित्राङ्गदे भीष्मो बाले भ्रातरि कौरव।
पालयामास तद् राज्यं सत्यवत्या मते स्थितः।। 1 ।।

7. वही, 102/70

ताभ्यां सह समाः सप्त विहरन् पृथिवीपतिः।
विचित्रवीर्यस्तरुणो यक्ष्मणा समगृह्यत।। 70 ।।

8. वही, 108/18

संस्कारैः संस्कृतास्ते तु व्रताध्ययनसंयुताः।
श्रमव्यायामकुशलाः समपद्यन्त यौवनम्।। 18 ।।

9. वही, 108/19-25 तक

धृतराष्ट्रस्त्वचक्षुष्ट्वाद् राज्यं न प्रत्यपधत।
पारशवत्वाद् विदुरो राजा पाण्डुर्बभूवह।। 25 ।।

10. तुम्हें भी ऐसी ही मृत्यु प्राप्त हो।
11. वही, 122/1
संवत्सरधृते गर्भे गान्धार्या जनमेजय।
आह्वयामास वै कुन्ती गर्भार्थं धर्ममच्युतम्।।1।।
12. वही, 114/27
तस्मिन्नेव महाबाहुर्जज्ञे भीमोऽपि वीर्यवान्।
स जातमात्र एवाथ धृतराष्ट्रसुतो नृप।।27।।
13. वही, 123/22
अनुसंवत्सरं जाता अपि ते कुरुसत्तमाः।
पाण्डुपुत्रा व्यराजन्त पञ्च संवत्सरा इव।।22।।
[प्रतिवर्ष एक-एक करके उत्पन्न होने का उल्लेख है जो असम्भव है]
14. वही, 123/32
ततः पाण्डुः क्रियाः सर्वाः पाण्डवानामकारयत्।
गर्भधानादिकृत्यानि चौलोपनयनानि च।।
काश्यपः कृतवान् सर्वमुपाकर्म च भारत।
चौलोपनयानादूर्ध्वपमृषभाक्षा यशस्विनः।।
वैदिकाध्ययने सर्वे समपद्यन्त पारगाः ।।32।।
15. वही, 124/2, 12
पुर्णे चतुर्दशे वर्ष फाल्गुनस्य च धीमतः।
× × × ×
तस्मिन् काले समाहूय माद्रीं मदनमोहितः।।2।।
स तया सह संगभ्य भार्यया कुरुनन्दनः।
पाण्डुः परमधर्मात्मा युयुजे कालधर्मणा।।12।।
16. वही, 138/1
ततः संवत्सरस्यान्ते यौवराज्याय पार्थिव।
स्थापितो धृतराष्ट्रेण पाण्डुपुत्रो युद्धिष्ठिरः ।।1।।
17. वही, 147/1
तांस्तु दृष्ट्वा सुमनसः परिसंवत्सरोषितान्।
विश्वस्तानिव संलक्ष्य हर्षं चक्रे पुरोचनः ।।1।।
18. वही, 213/35
सोऽभ्यनुज्ञाय राजानं वनचर्याय दीक्षितः।
वने द्वादश वर्षाणि वासायानुजगाम ह।।35।।
19. वही, 220/15
पुर्णे तु द्वादशे वर्षे खाण्डवप्रस्थमागतः ।।15।।
20. वही, 220/65
ततः सुभद्रा सौभद्रं केशवस्य प्रिया स्वसा।
जयन्तमिव पौलोमी ख्यातिमन्तमजीजनत।।65।।

21. सभापर्व, 3/37
ईदृशीं तां सभां कृत्वा मासैः परिचतुर्दशैः।
निष्ठितां धर्मराजाय मयो राजन् न्यवेदयत्।।37।।
22. वही, 77/30
नैवं वाचा व्यवसितं भीम विज्ञायते सताम्।
इतश्चतुर्दशे वर्षे द्रष्टारो यद् भविष्यति।।30।।
23. वही, 192/64
आकर्णपलितः श्यामो वयसाशीतिपञ्चकः ।।64।।
त्वत्कृते व्यचरत् संख्ये स तु षोडशवर्षवत्।
24. आदिपर्व, 123/32
ततः पाण्डुः क्रियाः सर्वाः पाण्डवानामकारयत्।
गर्भाधानादिकृत्यानि चौलोपनयनानि ।।
× × × ×
शर्यातिः पृषतः पुत्रः शुको नाम परंतपः।।
× × × ×
शतश्रृङ्गे तपस्तेपे शाकमूलफलाशनः ।।
तेनोपकरणश्रेष्ठैः शिक्षया चोपबृंहिताः।
तत्प्रसादाद् धनुर्वेदे समपद्यन्त पारगाः।।
25. वही, 124/1, 2, 12
पुर्णे चतुर्दशे वर्षे फाल्गुनस्य च धीमतः।
तदा उत्तरफल्गुन्यां प्रवृत्ते स्वस्तिवाचने।।
26. वही, 138/21
ततः संवत्सरस्यान्ते यौवराज्याय पार्थिव।
स्थापितो धृतराष्ट्रेण पाण्डुपुत्रो युधिष्ठिरः ।।1।।
27. वही, 138/24-25
28. वही, 147/1
तांस्तु दृष्ट्व सुमनसः परिसंवत्सरोषितान्।
विश्वस्तानिव संलक्ष्य हर्षं चक्रे पुरोचनः।।1।।
29. वही, 213/35
सोऽभ्यनुज्ञाय राजानं वनचर्याय दीक्षितः।
वने द्वादश वर्षाणि वासायानुजगाम ह।।35।।
30. वही, 214/26
स तथेति प्रतिज्ञाय तां कन्यां प्रतिगृह्य च।
उवास नगर तस्मिंस्तिस्त्रः कुन्तीसुतः समाः।।26।।
31. वही, 220/13
निवृत्तश्चार्जुनस्तत्र विवाहं कृतवान प्रभुः।
उषित्वा तत्र कौन्तेयः संवत्सरपराः क्षपाः।।13।।

32. वही, 220/14
विह्लत्य च यथाकामं पूजितो वृष्णिनन्दनै।
पुष्करे तु ततः शेषं काले वर्तितवान् प्रभुः।।14।।
33. वही, 220/65
ततः सुभद्रा सौभद्रं केशवस्य प्रिया स्वसा।
जयन्तमिव पीलोमी ख्यातिमन्तमजीजनत्।।65।।
34. सभापर्व, 3/37
ईदृशीं तां सभां कृत्वा मासैः परिचतुर्दशैः।
निष्ठितां धर्मराजाय मयो राजन् न्यवेदयत्।।37।।
35. विराटपर्व, 1/8
द्वादशेमानि वर्षाणि राज्यविप्रोषिता वयम्।
त्रयोदशोऽयं सम्प्राप्तः कृच्छात् परमदुर्वसः।।8।।
36. वही, 52/4
एषामभ्यधिका मासाः पञ्च च द्वादश क्षपाः।
त्रयोदशानां वर्षाणाभिती में वर्तते मतिः।।4।।
37. द्रोणपर्व, 51/13
कथं हि बालस्तरुणो द्धेनाम विशारदः
सदश्व डव सम्बाधे विषमे क्षेममर्हति ।।13।।